(ex•ploring)

1. To investigate in a systematic way: examine. 2. To search into or range over for the purpose of discovery.

(ex•ploring)

SERIES

1. To investigate in a systematic way: examine. 2. To search into or range over for the purpose of discovery.

Microsoft® Office

Excel 2007

COMPREHENSIVE

SECOND EDITION

Robert T. Grauer

Keith Mulbery | Judy Scheeren

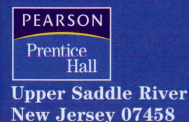

PEARSON

Prentice Hall

Upper Saddle River
New Jersey 07458

Library of Congress Cataloging-in-Publication Data
Information is available.

VP/Publisher: Natalie E. Anderson
Senior Acquisitions Editor: Melissa Sabella
Director, Product Development: Pamela Hersperger
Product Development Manager: Eileen Bien Calabro
Editorial Project Manager: Meghan Bisi
Freelance Editorial Project Manager: Claire Hunter
Editorial Assistant: Melissa Arlio
AVP/Executive Editor, Media: Richard Keaveny
AVP/Executive Producer: Lisa Strite
Editorial Media Project Manager: Ashley Lulling
Production Media Project Manager: Lorena Cerisano
Marketing Manager: Maggie Moylan
Marketing Assistant: Angela Frey
Senior Managing Editor: Cynthia Zonneveld
Associate Managing Editor: Camille Trentacoste
Production Project Manager: Ruth Ferrera-Kargov
Senior Operations Director: Nick Sklitsis
Senior Art Director: Jonathan Boylan
Art Director: Anthony Gemmellaro
Cover Design: Anthony Gemmellaro
Cover Illustration/Photo: Courtesy of Getty Images/Laurent Hamels
Composition: GGS Book Services
Full-Service Project Management: GGS Book Services
Printer/Binder: Banta/Menasha
Typeface: 10/12 Palatino

Microsoft, Windows, Vista, Word, PowerPoint, Outlook, FrontPage, Visual Basic, MSN, The Microsoft Network, and/or other Microsoft products referenced herein are either trademarks or registered trademarks of Microsoft Corporation in the U.S.A. and other countries. Screen shots and icons reprinted with permission from the Microsoft Corporation. This book is not sponsored or endorsed by or affiliated with Microsoft Corporation.

Credits and acknowledgments borrowed from other sources and reproduced, with permission, in this textbook appear on appropriate page within text.

Excel Data for Hospitality Capstone Exercises: David "Tug Boat" Mack, Brent "Goat Cheese" Hystead, and John "Lance" Burandt.

Pearson Prentice Hall™ is a trademark of Pearson Education, Inc.
Pearson® is a registered trademark of Pearson plc
Prentice Hall® is a registered trademark of Pearson Education, Inc.

Pearson Education LTD., London
Pearson Education Singapore, Pte. Ltd
Pearson Education, Canada, Inc.
Pearson Education–Japan
Pearson Education Australia PTY, Limited

Pearson Education North Asia Ltd., Hong Kong
Pearson Educación de Mexico, S.A. de C.V.
Pearson Education Malaysia, Pte. Ltd.
Pearson Education, Upper Saddle River, New Jersey

10 9 8 7 6 5 4
ISBN-13: 978-0-13-503227-5
ISBN-10: 0-13-503227-X

Dedications

To Marion—my wife, my lover, and my best friend.
Robert Grauer

I would like to dedicate this book to my family and close friends who provided a
strong community of emotional support and patience as I completed my doctorate program and worked
on this edition of the Exploring series.
Keith Mulbery

Thanks for my husband, Bill, for all the support and energy that has helped
me to put ideas on paper. His encouragement made it all possible.

Thanks also to my parents who believe in learning at any age.
And, a special thanks to the following people for their contributions: Frank Lucente, colleague,
friend, and mentor for sharing his tips and unique teaching style; and the students at Westmoreland County
Community College who make it all worthwhile.
Judy Scheeren

About the Authors

Dr. Robert T. Grauer

Dr. Robert T. Grauer is an Associate Professor in the Department of Computer Information Systems at the University of Miami, where he has been honored with the Outstanding Teacher Award in the School of Business. He is the vision behind the Exploring Series, which is about to sell its 3 millionth copy.

Dr. Grauer has written more than 50 books on programming and information systems. His work has been translated into three foreign languages and is used in all aspects of higher education at both national and international levels.

Dr. Grauer also has been a consultant to several major corporations including IBM and American Express. He received his Ph.D. in operations research in 1972 from the Polytechnic Institute of Brooklyn.

Dr. Keith Mulbery

Dr. Keith Mulbery is an Associate Professor in the Information Systems and Technology Department at Utah Valley State College, where he teaches computer applications, programming, and MIS classes. He has written more than 15 software textbooks and business communication test banks. In January 2001, he received the Utah Valley State College Board of Trustees Award of Excellence for authoring *MOUS Essentials Word 2000*. In addition to his series editor and authoring experience, he also served as a developmental editor on two word processing textbooks. In 2007, he received the UVSC School of Technology and Computing Scholar Award.

He received his B.S. and M.Ed. (majoring in Business Education) from Southwestern Oklahoma State University and earned his Ph.D. in Education with an emphasis in Business Information Systems at Utah State University in 2006. His dissertation topic was computer-assisted instruction using TAIT to supplement traditional instruction in basic computer proficiency courses.

Judith Scheeren

Judith Scheeren is a professor of computer technology at Westmoreland County Community College in Youngwood, Pennsylvania where she received the Outstanding Teacher award. She holds an M.S.I.S. She holds an M.S. from the University of Pittsburgh and an advanced certificate in online teaching and learning from the University of California at Hayward. She has several years of experience in the computer industry with Fortune 500 companies. She has developed and written training materials for custom applications in both the public and private sectors. She also has written books on desktop publishing.

Contributing Authors

Linda Ericksen, Office Fundamentals Chapter

Linda Ericksen is Associate Professor of Software Engineering at the University of Advancing Technology in Tempe, Arizona. She is the author of over 20 college-level computer text books on topics ranging from the Internet through many software applications, writing for major publishers such as Que, Addison-Wesley, and Course Technology. She was also the author of her own popular series for Prentice Hall, the Quick Simple Series, which featured Microsoft Office 2000.

Jean Kotsiovos, Health Care, Legal, Arts, and Hospitality Exercises

Jean Kotsiovos is the Assistant Dean of Curriculum for the School of Information Systems and Technology at Kaplan University. She received her B.S. degree in

Information and Decision Sciences from the University of Illinois at Chicago and her M.A. in Education with an emphasis in Computer Education from Governors State University. She started her career in the IT industry as a programmer/analyst.

She has worked in various positions in higher education as an instructor, program coordinator, department chair, and assistant dean. She has developed numerous courses and programs in information technology for both online and traditional institutions. She has created training materials and presented a variety of workshops on computer applications. She resides in Illinois with her husband and two children. She enjoys traveling and spending time with her family.

LindaLee Massoud, Legal Exercises

LindaLee Massoud has been a professor at Mott Community College in Flint, Michigan for almost 29 years. She currently teaches a variety of computer software and programming classes in the Computer Information Systems program (Technology Division). She is also an attorney in private practice and a pilot.

Margo Mills, Arts and Hospitality Exercises

Margo Mills has been teaching students to use computer software in the Twin Cities for over 14 years. Very quickly she discovered that she was put on this earth to be paid to talk. After eight years in the corporate training arena, she was hired as a business instructor at Minneapolis Business College where she has worked happily for the last year and has fallen completely in love with her students.

Brief Contents

Contents

CHAPTER TWO | Formulas and Functions: Math Basics for Spreadsheet Use 137

CHAPTER THREE | Charts: Delivering a Message 187

CHAPTER FOUR | Working with Large Worksheets and Tables: Manipulating Worksheets and Table Management 243

CHAPTER FIVE | Data to Information: Data Tables, Conditional Formatting, PivotTables, and PivotCharts   303

CHAPTER SIX | Data Tables and Amortization Tables: Revisiting Data Tables and Amortizing   377

CHAPTER SEVEN | Data Consolidation, Links, and Formula Auditing: Worksheet References, File Linking, and Auditing Formulas   443

CHAPTER EIGHT | What-If Analysis: Using Spreadsheets for Decision Making 505

CHAPTER NINE | Collaboration and Workbook Distribution: Sharing, Distributing, and Working with Excel Options 559

CHAPTER TEN | Templates, Styles, the Web, and Macros: Automating Workbooks 617

CAPSTONE EXERCISES | Using Excel in the Legal Profession, Health Care, the Arts, and Hospitality 689

Acknowledgments

The success of the Exploring series is attributed to contributions from numerous individuals. First and foremost, our heartfelt appreciation to Melissa Sabella, senior acquisitions editor, for providing new leadership and direction to capitalize on the strength and tradition of the Exploring series while implementing innovative ideas into the Exploring Office 2007 edition. Scott Davidson, senior marketing manager, was an invaluable addition to the team who believes in the mission of this series passionately and did an amazing job communicating its message.

During the first few months of the project, Eileen Clark, senior editorial project manager, kept the team focused on the vision, pedagogy, and voice that has been the driving force behind the success of the Exploring series. Claire Hunter, market development editor, facilitated communication between the editorial team and the reviewers to ensure that this edition meets the changing needs of computer professors and students at the collegiate level. Keith Mulbery gave up many nights and weekends (including Thanksgiving) to jump in and help out with anything that was asked of him, including assisting with topical organization, reviewing and revising content, capturing screenshots, and ensuring chapter manuscripts adhered to series guidelines.

Meghan Bisi, editorial project manager, professionally and patiently managed the flow of reviews and manuscript files among the team to ensure timely publication of this book. Laura Town, developmental editor, provided an objective perspective in reviewing the content and organization of selected chapters. Eileen Calabro, product development manager, facilitated communication among the editorial team, authors, and production during a transitional stage. The team at GGS worked through software delays, style changes and anything else we threw at them to bring the whole thing together. Art director Blair Brown's conversations with students and professors across the country yielded a design that addressed the realities of today's students with function and style.

A special thanks to the following for the use of their work in the PowerPoint section of the text: Cameron Martin, Ph.D., Assistant to the President, Utah Valley State College, for the use of the Institutional Policies and Procedures Approval Process flowchart; Nick Finner, Paralegal Studies, Utah Valley State College, for the use of his research relating to the elderly population residing in the prisons of Utah; Ryan Phillips, Xeric Landscape and Design (XericUtah.com), for sharing Xeric's concepts for creating beautiful, drought-tolerant landscapes and for the photographs illustrating these concepts; Jo Porter, Photographer, Mapleton, Utah, for allowing the use of her beautiful engagement and wedding photographs; and David and Ali Valeti for the photographs of their baby and their family.

The following organizations and individuals generously provided data and structure from their organizational databases: Replacements, Ltd., Shweta Ponnappa, JC Raulston Arboretum at North Carolina State University, and Valerie Tyson. We deeply appreciate the ability to give students a feel for "real" data.

The new members of the Exploring author team would like to especially thank Bob Grauer for his vision in developing Exploring and his leadership in creating this highly successful series.

Maryann Barber would like to thank Bob Grauer for a wonderful collaboration and providing the opportunities through which so much of her life has changed.

The Exploring team would like to especially thank the following instructors who drew on their experience in the classroom and their software expertise to give us daily advice on how to improve this book. Their impact can be seen on every page:

Barbara Stover, Marion Technical College

Bob McCloud, Sacred Heart University

Cassie Georgetti, Florida Technical College

Dana Johnson, North Dakota State University

Jim Pepe, Bentley College

Judy Brown, The University of Memphis

Lancie Anthony Affonso, College of Charleston

Mimi Duncan, University of Missouri – St. Louis

Minnie Proctor, Indian River Community College

Richard Albright, Goldey-Beacom College

We also want to acknowledge all the reviewers of the Exploring 2007 series. Their valuable comments and constructive criticism greatly improved this edition:

Aaron Schorr
Fashion Institute of Technology

Alicia Stonesifer
La Salle University

Allen Alexander, Delaware
Tech & Community College

Amy Williams, Abraham
Baldwin Agriculture College

Annie Brown
Hawaii Community College

Barbara Cierny
Harper College

Barbara Hearn
Community College of Philadelphia

Barbara Meguro
University of Hawaii at Hilo

Bette Pitts
South Plains College

Beverly Fite
Amarillo College

Bill Wagner
Villanova

Brandi N. Guidry
University of Louisiana at Lafayette

Brian Powell
West Virginia University – Morgantown
Campus

Carl Farrell
Hawaii Pacific University

Carl Penzuil
Ithaca College

Carole Bagley;
University of St. Thomas

Catherine Hain
Central New Mexico CC

Charles Edwards
University of Texas of the Permian Basin

Christine L. Moore
College of Charleston

David Barnes
Penn State Altoona

David Childress;
Ashland Community College

David Law, Alfred
State College

Dennis Chalupa
Houston Baptist

Diane Stark
Phoenix College

Dianna Patterson
Texarkana College

Dianne Ross
University of Louisiana at Lafayette

Dr. Behrooz Saghafi
Chicago State University

Dr. Gladys Swindler
Fort Hays State University

Dr. Joe Teng
Barry University

Dr. Karen Nantz
Eastern Illinois University.

Duane D. Lintner
Amarillo College

Elizabeth Edmiston
North Carolina Central University

Erhan Uskup
Houston Community College

Fred Hills, McClellan
Community College

Gary R. Armstrong
Shippensburg University of Pennsylvania

Glenna Vanderhoof
Missouri State

Gregg Asher
Minnesota State University, Mankato

Hong K. Sung
University of Central Oklahoma

Hyekyung Clark
Central New Mexico CC

J Patrick Fenton
West Valley College

Jana Carver
Amarillo College

Jane Cheng
Bloomfield College

Janos T. Fustos
Metropolitan State College of Denver

Jeffrey A Hassett
University of Utah

Jennifer Pickle
Amarillo College

Jerry Kolata
New England Institute of Technology

Jesse Day
South Plains College

John Arehart
Longwood University

John Lee Reardon
University of Hawaii, Manoa

Joshua Mindel
San Francisco State University

Karen Wisniewski
County College of Morris

Karl Smart
Central Michigan University

Kathryn L. Hatch
University of Arizona

Krista Terry
Radford University

Laura McManamon
University of Dayton

Laura Reid
University of Western Ontario

Linda Johnsonius
Murray State University

Lori Kelley
Madison Area Technical College

Lucy Parker,
California State University, Northridge

Lynda Henrie
LDS Business College

Malia Young
Utah State University

Margie Martyn
Baldwin Wallace

Marianne Trudgeon
Fanshawe College

Marilyn Hibbert
Salt Lake Community College

Marjean Lake
LDS Business College

Mark Olaveson
Brigham Young University

Nancy Sardone
Seton Hall University

Patricia Joseph
Slippery Rock University.

Patrick Hogan
Cape Fear Community College

Paula F. Bell
Lock Haven University of Pennsylvania

Paulette Comet
Community College of Baltimore County,
Catonsville

Pratap Kotala
North Dakota State University

Richard Blamer
John Carroll University

Richard Herschel
St. Joseph's University

Richard Hewer
Ferris State University

Robert Gordon
Hofstra University

Robert Marmelstein
East Stroudsburg University

Robert Stumbur
Northern Alberta Institute of Technology

Roberta I. Hollen
University of Central Oklahoma

Roland Moreira
South Plains College

Ron Murch
University of Calgary

Rory J. de Simone
University of Florida

Ruth Neal
Navarro College

Sandra M. Brown
Finger Lakes Community College

Sharon Mulroney
Mount Royal College

Stephen E. Lunce
Midwestern State University

Steve Schwarz
Raritan Valley Community College

Steven Choy
University of Calgary

Susan Byrne
St. Clair College

Thomas Setaro
Brookdale Community College

Todd McLeod
Fresno City College

Vickie Pickett
Midland College

Vipul Gupta
St Joseph's University

Vivek Shah
Texas State University - San Marcos

Wei-Lun Chuang
Utah State University

William Dorin
Indiana University Northwest

Finally, we wish to acknowledge reviewers of previous editions of the Exploring series—we wouldn't have made it to the 7th edition without you:

Alan Moltz
Naugatuck Valley Technical Community
College

Alok Charturvedi
Purdue University

Antonio Vargas
El Paso Community College

Barbara Sherman
Buffalo State College

Bill Daley
University of Oregon

Bill Morse
DeVry Institute of Technology

Bonnie Homan
San Francisco State University

Carl M. Briggs
Indiana University School of Business

Carlotta Eaton
Radford University

Carolyn DiLeo
Westchester Community College

Cody Copeland
Johnson County Community College

Connie Wells
Georgia State University

Daniela Marghitu
Auburn University

David B. Meinert
Southwest Missouri State University

David Douglas
University of Arkansas

David Langley
University of Oregon

David Rinehard
Lansing Community College

David Weiner
University of San Francisco

Dean Combellick
Scottsdale Community College

Delores Pusins
Hillsborough Community College

Don Belle
Central Piedmont Community College

Douglas Cross
Clackamas Community College

Ernie Ivey
Polk Community College

Gale E. Rand
College Misericordia

Helen Stoloff
Hudson Valley Community College

Herach Safarian
College of the Canyons

Jack Zeller
Kirkwood Community College

James Franck
College of St. Scholastica

James Gips
Boston College

Jane King
Everett Community College

Janis Cox
Tri-County Technical College

Jerry Chin
Southwest Missouri State University

Jill Chapnick
Florida International University

Jim Pruitt
Central Washington University

John Lesson
University of Central Florida

John Shepherd
Duquesne University

Judith M. Fitspatrick
Gulf Coast Community College

Judith Rice
Santa Fe Community College

Judy Dolan
Palomar College

Karen Tracey
Central Connecticut State University

Kevin Pauli
University of Nebraska

Kim Montney
Kellogg Community College

Kimberly Chambers
Scottsdale Community College

Larry S. Corman
Fort Lewis College

Lynn Band
Middlesex Community College

Margaret Thomas
Ohio University

Marguerite Nedreberg
Youngstown State University

Marilyn Salas
Scottsdale Community College

Martin Crossland
Southwest Missouri State University

Mary McKenry Percival
University of Miami

Michael Hassett
Fort Hayes State University

Michael Stewardson
San Jacinto College – North

Midge Gerber
Southwestern Oklahoma State University

Mike Hearn
Community College of Philadelphia

Mike Kelly
Community College of Rhode Island

Mike Thomas
Indiana University School of Business

Paul E. Daurelle
Western Piedmont Community College

Ranette Halverson
Midwestern State University

Raymond Frost
Central Connecticut State University

Robert Spear, Prince
George's Community College

Rose M. Laird
Northern Virginia Community College

Sally Visci
Lorain County Community College

Shawna DePlonty
Sault College of Applied Arts and Technology

Stuart P. Brian
Holy Family College

Susan Fry
Boise State Universtiy

Suzanne Tomlinson
Iowa State University

Vernon Griffin
Austin Community College

Wallace John Whistance-Smith
Ryerson Polytechnic University

Walter Johnson
Community College of Philadelphia

Wanda D. Heller
Seminole Community College

We very much appreciate the following individuals for painstakingly checking every step and every explanation for technical accuracy, while dealing with an entirely new software application:

Barbara Waxer

Bill Daley

Beverly Fite

Dawn Wood

Denise Askew

Elizabeth Lockley

James Reidel

Janet Pickard

Janice Snyder

Jean Kotsiovos

Jeremy Harris

John Griffin

Joyce Neilsen

Julie Boyles

LeeAnn Bates

Lynn Bowen

Mara Zebest

Mary E. Pascarella

Michael Meyers

Sue McCrory

Tom McKenzie

Preface

The Exploring Series

Exploring has been Prentice Hall's most successful Office Application series of the past 15 years. For Office 2007 Exploring has undergone the most extensive changes in its history, so that it can truly move today's student "beyond the point and click."

The goal of Exploring has always been to teach more than just the steps to accomplish a task – the series provides the theoretical foundation necessary for a student to understand when and why to apply a skill. This way, students achieve a broader understanding of Office.

Today's students are changing and Exploring has evolved with them. Prentice Hall traveled to college campuses across the country and spoke directly to students to determine how they study and prepare for class. We also spoke with hundreds of professors about the best ways to administer materials to such a diverse body of students.

Here is what we learned

Students go to college now with a different set of skills than they did 5 years ago. The new edition of Exploring moves students beyond the basics of the software at a faster pace, without sacrificing coverage of the fundamental skills that everybody needs to know. This ensures that students will be engaged from Chapter 1 to the end of the book.

Students have diverse career goals. With this in mind, we broadened the examples in the text (and the accompanying Instructor Resources) to include the health sciences, hospitality, urban planning, business and more. Exploring will be relevant to every student in the course.

Students read, prepare and study differently than they used to. Rather than reading a book cover to cover students want to easily identify what they need to know, and then learn it efficiently. We have added key features that will bring students into the content and make the text easy to use such as objective mapping, pull quotes, and key terms in the margins.

Moving students beyond the point and click

All of these additions mean students will be more engaged, achieve a higher level of understanding, and successfully complete this course. In addition to the experience and expertise of the series creator and author Robert T. Grauer we have assembled a tremendously talented team of supporting authors to assist with this critical revision. Each of them is equally dedicated to the Exploring mission of **moving students beyond the point and click.**

Key Features of the Office 2007 revision include

- **New** **Office Fundamentals Chapter** efficiently covers skills common among all applications like save, print, and bold to avoid repetition in each Office application's first chapter, along with coverage of problem solving skills to prepare students to apply what they learn in any situation.

- **New** **Moving Beyond the Basics** introduces advanced skills earlier because students are learning basic skills faster.

- **White Pages/Yellow Pages clearly** distinguish the theory (white pages) from the skills covered in the Hands-On exercises (yellow pages) so students always know what they are supposed to be doing.

- **New** **Objective Mapping** enables students to skip the skills and concepts they know, and quickly find those they don't, by scanning the chapter opener page for the page numbers of the material they need.

- **New** **Pull Quotes** entice students into the theory by highlighting the most interesting points.

- **New** **Conceptual Animations** connect the theory with the skills, by illustrating tough to understand concepts with interactive multimedia.

- **New** **More End of Chapter Exercises** offer instructors more options for assessment. Each chapter has approximately 12–15 exercises ranging from Multiple Choice questions to open-ended projects.

- **New** **More Levels of End of Chapter Exercises,** including new Mid-Level Exercises tell students what to do, but not how to do it, and Capstone Exercises cover all of the skills within each chapter.

- **New** **Mini Cases with Rubrics** are open ended exercises that guide both instructors and students to a solution with a specific rubric for each mini case.

- **New** **Cumulative Capstone Exercises** for each application tie application use to real-life professional situations in the arts, hospitality, legal, and health care industries.

Instructor and Student Resources

Instructor Chapter Reference Cards

A four page color card for every chapter that includes a:

- *Concept Summary* that outlines the KEY objectives to cover in class with tips on where students get stuck as well as how to get them un-stuck. It helps bridge the gap between the instructor and student when discussing more difficult topics.

- *Case Study Lecture Demonstration Document* which provides instructors with a lecture sample based on the chapter opening case that will guide students to critically use the skills covered in the chapter, with examples of other ways the skills can be applied.

The Enhanced Instructor's Resource Center on CD-ROM includes:

- **Additional Capstone Production Tests** allow instructors to assess all the skills in a chapter with a single project.

- **Mini Case Rubrics** in Microsoft® Word format enable instructors to customize the assignment for their class.

- **PowerPoint® Presentations** for each chapter with notes included for online students.

- **Lesson Plans** that provide a detailed blueprint for an instructor to achieve chapter learning objectives and outcomes.

- **Student Data Files**

- **Annotated Solution Files**

- **Complete Test Bank**

- **Test Gen Software with QuizMaster**

TestGen is a test generator program that lets you view and easily edit testbank questions, transfer them to tests, and print in a variety of formats suitable to your teaching situation. The program also offers many options for organizing and displaying testbanks and tests. A random number test generator enables you to create multiple versions of an exam.

QuizMaster, also included in this package, allows students to take tests created with TestGen on a local area network. The QuizMaster Utility built into TestGen lets instructors view student records and print a variety of reports. Building tests is easy with Test-Gen, and exams can be easily uploaded into WebCT, BlackBoard, and CourseCompass.

Prentice Hall's Companion Web Site

www.prenhall.com/exploring offers expanded IT resources and downloadable supplements. This site also includes an online study guide for student self-study.

Online Course Cartridges

Flexible, robust and customizable content is available for all major online course platforms that include everything instructors need in one place.
www.prenhall.com/webct
www.prenhall.com/blackboard
www.coursecompass.com

myitlab for Microsoft Office 2007, is a solution designed by professors that allows you to easily deliver Office courses with defensible assessment and outcomes-based training.

The new *Exploring Office 2007* System will seamlessly integrate online assessment and training with the new myitlab for Microsoft Office 2007!

Integrated Assessment and Training

To fully integrate the new myitlab into the *Exploring Office 2007* System we built myitlab assessment and training directly from the *Exploring* instructional content. No longer is the technology just mapped to your textbook.

This 1:1 content relationship between the *Exploring* text and myitlab means that your online assessment and training will work with your textbook to move your students beyond the point and click.

Advanced Reporting

With myitlab you will get advanced reporting capabilities including a detailed student click stream. This ability to see exactly what actions your students took on a test, click-by-click, provides you with true defensible grading.

In addition, myitlab for Office 2007 will feature. . .

Project-based assessment: Test students on Exploring projects, or break down assignments into individual Office application skills.

Outcomes-based training: Students train on what they don't know without having to relearn skills they already know.

Optimal performance and uptime: Provided by a world-class hosting environment.

Dedicated student and instructor support: Professional tech support is available by phone and email when you need it.

No installation required! myitlab runs entirely from the Web.

And much more!

www.prenhall.com/myitlab

Office Fundamentals Chapter

efficiently covers skills common among all applications like save, print, and bold to avoid repetition in each 1st application chapter.

chapter 1 | Office Fundamentals

Using Word, Excel, Access, and PowerPoint

bjectives

After you read this chapter you will be able to:

1. Identify common interface components **(page 4)**.
2. Use Office 2007 Help **(page 10)**.
3. Open a file **(page 18)**.
4. Save a file **(page 21)**.
5. Print a document **(page 24)**.
6. Select text to edit **(page 31)**.
7. Insert text and change to the Overtype mode **(page 32)**.
8. Move and copy text **(page 34)**.
9. Find, replace, and go to text **(page 36)**.
10. Use the Undo and Redo commands **(page 39)**.
11. Use language tools **(page 39)**.
12. Apply font attributes **(page 43)**.
13. Copy formats with the Format Painter **(page 47)**.

Hands-On Exercises

Exercises	Skills Covered
1. IDENTIFYING PROGRAM INTERFACE COMPONENTS AND USING HELP (page 12)	• Use PowerPoint's Office Button, Get Help in a Dialog Box, and Use the Zoom Slider • Use Excel's Ribbon, Get Help from an Enhanced ScreenTip, and Use the Zoom Dialog Box • Search Help in Access • Use Word's Status Bar • Search Help and Print a Help Topic
2. PERFORMING UNIVERSAL TASKS (page 28) **Open:** chap1_ho2_sample.docx **Save as:** chap1_ho2_solution.docx	• Open a File and Save it with a Different Name • Use Print Preview and Select Options • Print a Document
3. PERFORMING BASIC TASKS (page 48) **Open:** chap1_ho3_internet_docx **Save as:** chap_ho3_internet_solution.docx	• Cut, Copy, Paste, and Undo • Find and Replace Text • Check Spelling • Choose Synonyms and Use Thesaurus • Use the Research Tool • Apply Font Attributes • Use Format Painter

Microsoft Office 2007 Software Office Fundamentals

1

chapter 3 | **Access**

Customize, Analyze, and Summarize Query Data

Creating and Using Queries to Make Decisions

bjectives

After you read this chapter you will be able to:

1. Understand the order of precedence (**page 679**).
2. Create a calculated field in a query (**page 679**).
3. Create expressions with the Expression Builder (**page 679**).
4. Create and edit Access functions (**page 690**).
5. Perform date arithmetic (**page 694**).
6. Create and work with data aggregates (**page 704**).

Hands-On Exercises

Exercises	Skills Covered
1. CALCULATED QUERY FIELDS (PAGE 683) **Open:** chap3_ho1-3_realestate.accdb **Save:** chap3_ho1-3_realestate_solution.accdb **Back up as:** chap3_ho1_realestate_solution.accdb	• Copy a Database and Start the Query • Select the Fields, Save, and Open the Query • Create a Calculated Field and Run the Query • Verify the Calculated Results • Recover from a Common Error
2. EXPRESSION BUILDER, FUNCTIONS, AND DATE ARITHMETIC (page 695) **Open:** chap3_ho1-3_realestate.accdb (from Exercise 1) **Save:** chap3_ho1-3_realestate_solution.accdb (additional modifications) **Back up as:** chap3_ho2_realestate_solution.accdb	• Create a Select Query • Use the Expression Builder • Create Calculations Using Input Stored in a Different Query or Table • Edit Expressions Using the Expression Builder • Use Functions • Work with Date Arithmetic
3. DATA AGGREGATES (page 707) **Open:** chap3_ho1-3_realestate.accdb (from Exercise 2) **Save:** chap3_ho1-3_realestate_solution.accdb (additional modifications)	• Add a Total Row • Create a Totals Query Based on a Select Query • Add Fields to the Design Grid • Add Grouping Options and Specify Summary Statistics

Access 2007 | 677

Objective Mapping

allows students to skip the skills and concepts they know and quickly find those they don't by scanning the chapter opening page for the page numbers of the material they need.

Case Study

begins each chapter to provide an effective overview of what students can accomplish by completing the chapter.

CASE STUDY

West Transylvania College Athletic Department

The athletic department of West Transylvania College has reached a fork in the road. A significant alumni contingent insists that the college upgrade its athletic program from NCAA Division II to Division I. This process will involve adding sports, funding athletic scholarships, expanding staff, and coordinating a variety of fundraising activities.

Tom Hunt, the athletic director, wants to determine if the funding support is available both inside and outside the college to accomplish this goal. You are helping Tom prepare the five-year projected budget based on current budget figures. The plan is to increase revenues at a rate of 10% per year for five years while handling an estimated 8% increase in expenses over the same five-year period. Tom feels that a 10% increase in revenue versus an 8% increase in expenses should make the upgrade viable. Tom wants to examine how increased alumni giving, increases in college fees, and grant monies will increase the revenue flow. The Transylvania College's Athletic Committee and its Alumni Association Board of Directors want Tom to present an analysis of funding and expenses to determine if the move to NCAA Division I is feasible. As Tom's student assistant this year, it is your responsibility to help him with special projects. Tom prepared the basic projected budget spreadsheet and has asked you to finish it for him.

Case Study

Your Assignment

- Read the chapter carefully and pay close attention to mathematical operations, formulas, and functions.
- Open *chap2_case_athletics*, which contains the partially completed, projected budget spreadsheet.
- Study the structure of the worksheet to determine what type of formulas you need to complete the financial calculations. Identify how you would perform calculations if you were using a calculator and make a list of formulas using regular language to determine if the financial goals will be met. As you read the chapter, identify formulas and functions that will help you complete the financial analysis. You will insert formulas in the revenue and expenditures sections for column C. Use appropriate cell references in formulas. Do not enter constant values within a formula; instead enter the 10% and 8% increases in an input area. Use appropriate functions for column totals in both the revenue and expenditures sections. Insert formulas for the Net Operating Margin and Net Margin rows. Copy the formulas.
- Review the spreadsheet and identify weaknesses in the formatting. Use your knowledge of good formatting design to improve the appearance of the spreadsheet so that it will be attractive to the Athletic Committee and the alumni board. You will format cells as currency with 0 decimals and widen columns as needed. Merge and center the title and use an attractive fill color. Emphasize the totals and margin rows with borders. Enter your name and current date. Create a custom footer that includes a page number and your instructor's name. Print the worksheet as displayed and again with cell formulas displayed. Save the workbook as **chap2_case_athletics_solution**.

Key Terms

are called out in the margins of the chapter so students can more effectively study definitions.

Pull Quotes

entice students into the theory by highlighting the most interesting points.

A **table** is a series of rows and columns that organize data.

A **cell** is the intersection of a row and column in a table.

> The table feature is one of the most powerful in Word and is the basis for an almost limitless variety of documents. It is very easy to create once you understand how a table works.

Tables

A **table** is a series of rows and columns that organize data effectively. The rows and columns in a table intersect to form **cells**. The table feature is one of the most powerful in Word and is an easy way to organize a series of data in a columnar list format such as employee names, inventory lists, and e-mail addresses. The Vacation Planner in Figure 3.1, for example, is actually a 4x9 table (4 columns and 9 rows). The completed table looks impressive, but it is very easy to create once you understand how a table works. In addition to the organizational benefits, tables make an excellent alignment tool. For example, you can create tables to organize data such as employee lists with phone numbers and e-mail addresses. The Exploring series uses tables to provide descriptions for various software commands. Although you can align text with tabs, you have more format control when you create a table. (See the Practice Exercises at the end of the chapter for other examples.)

Vacation Planner			
Item	Number of Days	Amount per Day (est)	Total Amount
Airline Ticket			449.00
Amusement Park Tickets	4	50.00	200.00
Hotel	5	120.00	600.00
Meals	6	50.00	300.00
Rental Car	5	30.00	150.00
Souvenirs	5	20.00	100.00
TOTAL EXPECTED EXPENSES			$1799.00

Figure 3.1 The Vacation Planner

In this section, you insert a table in a document. After inserting the table, you can insert or delete columns and rows if you need to change the structure. Furthermore, you learn how to merge and split cells within the table. Finally, you change the row height and column width to accommodate data in the table.

Inserting a Table

You can create a table from the Insert tab. Click Table in the Tables group on the Insert tab to see a gallery of cells from which you select the number of columns and rows you require in the table, or you can choose the Insert Table command below the gallery to display the Insert Table dialog box and enter the table composition you prefer. When you select the table dimension from the gallery or from the Insert Table dialog box, Word creates a table structure with the number of columns and rows you specify. After you define a table, you can enter text, numbers, or graphics in individual cells. Text

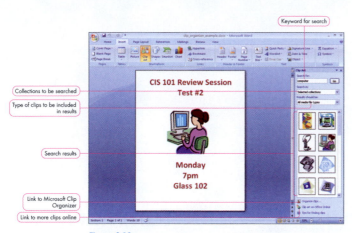

Keyword for search

Collections to be searched

Type of clips to be included in results

Search results

Link to Microsoft Clip Organizer

Link to more clips online

Figure 3.18 The Clip Art Task Pane

White Pages/ Yellow Pages

clearly distinguishes the theory (white pages) from the skills covered in the Hands-On exercises (yellow pages) so students always know what they are supposed to be doing.

You can access the Microsoft Clip Organizer (to view the various collections) by clicking Organize clips at the bottom of the Clip Art task pane. You also can access the Clip Organizer when you are not using Word; click the Start button on the taskbar, click All Programs, Micros... Clip Organizer. Once in the Organiz... ous collections, reorganize the exis... add new clips (with their associated... the bottom of the task pane in Figur... and tips for finding more relevant cl...

Insert a Picture

In addition to the collection of clip ... you also can insert your own picture... ital camera attached to your comput... Word. After you save the picture to ... on the Insert tab to locate and inser... opens so that you can navigate to th... insert the picture, there are many c... mands are discussed in the next sect...

Formatting a Grap...

When you inse...
fined size. For ...
very large and ...
resized. Most ti...
within the do...

(Remember that graphical elements should enhance a document, not overpower it.)

Refer to Figure 3.24 as you complete Step 2.

a. Click once on the clip art object to select it. Click **Text Wrapping** in the Arrange group on the Picture Tools Format tab to display the text wrapping options, and then select **Square**, as shown in Figure 3.24.

You must change the layout in order to move and size the object.

b. Click **Position** in the Arrange group, and then click **More Layout Options.** Click the **Picture Position tab** in the Advanced Layout dialog box, if necessary, then click **Alignment** in the *Horizontal* section. Click the **Alignment drop-down arrow** and select **Right**. Deselect the **Allow overlap check box** in the *Options* section. Click **OK**.

c. Click **Crop** in the Size group, then hold your mouse over the sizing handles and notice how the pointer changes to angular shapes. Click the **bottom center handle** and drag it up. Drag the side handles inward to remove excess space surrounding the graphical object.

d. Click the Shape **Height box** in the Size group and type **2.77**.

Notice the width is changed automatically to retain the proportion.

e. Save the document.

Click to select Square Text Wrapping style

Point to sizing handles

Figure 3.24 Formatting Clip Art

Step 3
Create a WordArt
Object

Refer to Figure 3.25 as you complete Step 3.

a. Press **Ctrl+End** to move to the end of the document. Click the **Insert tab**, and then click **WordArt** in the Text group to display the WordArt gallery.

b. Click **WordArt Style 28** on the bottom row of the gallery.

The Edit WordArt Text dialog box displays, as shown in Figure 3.25.

Summary

1. **Create a presentation using a template.** Using a template saves you a great deal of time and enables you to create a more professional presentation. Templates incorporate a theme, a layout, and content that can be modified. You can use templates that are installed when Microsoft Office is installed, or you can download templates from Microsoft Office Online. Microsoft is constantly adding templates to the online site for your use.

2. **Modify a template.** In addition to changing the content of a template, you can modify the structure and design. The structure is modified by changing the layout of a slide. To change the layout, drag placeholders to new locations or resize placeholders. You can even add placeholders so that elements such as logos can be included.

3. **Create a presentation in Outline view.** When you use a storyboard to determine your content, you create a basic outline. Then you can enter your presentation in Outline view, which enables you to concentrate on the content of the presentation. Using Outline view keeps you from getting buried in design issues at the cost of your content. It also saves you time because you can enter the information without having to move from placeholder to placeholder.

4. **Modify an outline structure.** Because the Outline view gives you a global view of the presentation, it helps you see the underlying structure of the presentation. You are able to see where content needs to be strengthened, or where the flow of information needs to be revised. If you find a slide with content that would be presented better in another location in the slide show, you can use the Collapse and Expand features to easily move it. By collapsing the slide content, you can drag it to a new location and then expand it. To move individual bullet points, cut and paste the bullet point or drag-and-drop it.

5. **Print an outline.** When you present, using the outline version of your slide show as a reference is a boon. No matter how well you know your information, it is easy to forget to present some information when facing an audience. While you would print speaker's notes if you have many details, you can print the outline as a quick reference. The outline can be printed in either the collapsed or the expanded form, giving you far fewer pages to shuffle in front of an audience than printing speaker's notes would.

6. **Import an outline.** You do not need to re-enter information from an outline created in Microsoft Word or another word processor. You can use the Open feature to import any outline that has been saved in a format that PowerPoint can read. In addition to a Word outline, you can use the common generic formats Rich Text Format and Plain Text Format.

7. **Add existing content to a presentation.** After you spend time creating the slides in a slide show, you may find that slides in the slide show would be appropriate in another show at a later date. Any slide you create can be reused in another presentation, thereby saving you considerable time and effort. You simply open the Reuse Slides pane, locate the slide show with the slide you need, and then click on the thumbnail of the slide to insert a copy of it in the new slide show.

8. **Examine slide show design principles.** With a basic understanding of slide show design principles you can create presentations that reflect your personality in a professional way. The goal of applying these principles is to create a slide show that focuses the audience on the message of the slide without being distracted by clutter or unreadable text.

9. **Apply and modify a design theme.** PowerPoint provides you with themes to help you create a clean, professional look for your presentation. Once a theme is applied you can modify the theme by changing the color scheme, the font scheme, the effects scheme, or the background style.

10. **Insert a header or footer.** Identifying information can be included in a header or footer. You may, for example, wish to include the group to whom you are presenting, or the location of the presentation, or a copyright notation for original work. You can apply footers to slides, handouts, and Notes pages. Headers may be applied to handouts and Notes pages.

Summary

links directly back to the objectives so students can more effectively study and locate the concepts that they need to focus on.

More End-of-Chapter Exercises with New Levels of Assessment

offer instructors more options for assessment. Each chapter has approximately 12-15 projects per chapter ranging from multiple choice to open-ended projects.

Practice Exercises

reinforce skills learned in the chapter with specific directions on what to do and how to do it.

New Mid-Level Exercises

assess the skills learned in the chapter by directing the students on what to do but not how to do it.

New Capstone Exercises

cover all of the skills with in each chapter without telling students how to perform the skills.

Mini Cases with Rubrics

are open ended exercises that guide both instructors and students to a solution with a specific rubric for each Mini Case.

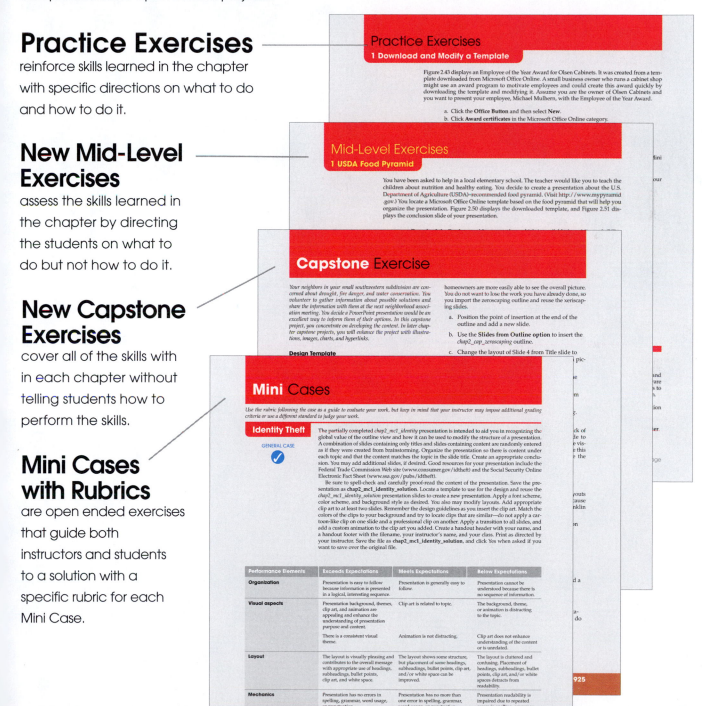

Using Word, Excel, Access, and PowerPoint

bjectives

After you read this chapter, you will be able to:

1. Identify common interface components **(page 4).**

2. Use Office 2007 Help **(page 10).**

3. Open a file **(page 18).**

4. Save a file **(page 21).**

5. Print a document **(page 24).**

6. Select text to edit **(page 31).**

7. Insert text and change to the Overtype mode **(page 32).**

8. Move and copy text **(page 34).**

9. Find, replace, and go to text **(page 36).**

10. Use the Undo and Redo commands **(page 39).**

11. Use language tools **(page 39).**

12. Apply font attributes **(page 43).**

13. Copy formats with the Format Painter **(page 47).**

Hands-On Exercises

Exercises	Skills Covered
1. IDENTIFYING PROGRAM INTERFACE COMPONENTS AND USING HELP (page 12)	• Use PowerPoint's Office Button, Get Help in a Dialog Box, and Use the Zoom Slider • Use Excel's Ribbon, Get Help from an Enhanced ScreenTip, and Use the Zoom Dialog Box • Search Help in Access • Use Word's Status Bar • Search Help and Print a Help Topic
2. PERFORMING UNIVERSAL TASKS (page 28) **Open:** chap1_ho2_sample.docx **Save as:** chap1_ho2_solution.docx	• Open a File and Save It with a Different Name • Use Print Preview and Select Options • Print a Document
3. PERFORMING BASIC TASKS (page 48) **Open:** chap1_ho3_internet_docx **Save as:** chap_ho3_internet_solution.docx	• Cut, Copy, Paste, and Undo • Find and Replace Text • Check Spelling • Choose Synonyms and Use Thesaurus • Use the Research Tool • Apply Font Attributes • Use Format Painter

CASE STUDY

Color Theory Design

Natalie Trevino's first job after finishing her interior design degree is with Color Theory Design of San Diego. Her new supervisor has asked her to review a letter written to an important client and to make any changes or corrections she thinks will improve it. Even though Natalie has used word processing software in the past, she is unfamiliar with Microsoft Office 2007. She needs to get up to speed with Word 2007 so that she can open the letter, edit the content, format the appearance, re-save the file, and print the client letter. Natalie wants to successfully complete this important first task, plus she wants to become familiar with all of Office 2007 because she realizes that her new employer, CTD, makes extensive use of all the Office products.

Case Study

In addition, Natalie needs to improve the appearance of an Excel workbook by applying font attributes, correcting spelling errors, changing the zoom magnification, and printing the worksheet. Finally, Natalie needs to modify a short PowerPoint presentation that features supplemental design information for CTD's important client.

Your Assignment

- Read the chapter and open the existing client letter, *chap1_case_design*.
- Edit the letter by inserting and overtyping text and moving existing text to improve the letter's readability.
- Find and replace text that you want to update.
- Check the spelling and improve the vocabulary by using the thesaurus.
- Modify the letter's appearance by applying font attributes.
- Save the file as **chap1_case_design_solution**, print preview, and print a copy of the letter.
- Open the *chap1_case_bid* workbook in Excel, apply bold and blue font color to the column headings, spell-check the worksheet, change the zoom to 125%, print preview, and print the workbook. Save the workbook as **chap1_case_bid_solution**.
- Open the *chap1_case_design* presentation in PowerPoint, spell-check the presentation, format text, and save it as **chap1_case_design_solution**.

Microsoft Office 2007 Software

Which software application should you choose? You have to start with an analysis of the output required.

Microsoft Office 2007 is composed of several software applications, of which the primary components are Word, Excel, PowerPoint, and Access. These programs are powerful tools that can be used to increase productivity in creating, editing, saving, and printing files. Each program is a specialized and sophisticated program, so it is necessary to use the correct one to successfully complete a task, much like using the correct tool in the physical world. For example, you use a hammer, not a screwdriver, to pound a nail into the wall. Using the correct tool gets the job done correctly and efficiently the first time; using the wrong tool may require redoing the task, thus wasting time. Likewise, you should use the most appropriate software application to create and work with computer data.

Choosing the appropriate application to use in a situation seems easy to the beginner. If you need to create a letter, you type the letter in Word. However, as situations increase in complexity, so does the need to think through using each application. For example, you can create an address book of names and addresses in Word to create form letters; you can create an address list in Excel and then use spreadsheet commands to manipulate the data; further, you can store addresses in an Access database table and then use database capabilities to manipulate the data. Which software application should you choose? You have to start with an analysis of the output required. If you only want a form letter as the final product, then you might use Word; however, if you want to spot customer trends with the data and provide detailed reports, you would use Access. Table 1.1 describes the main characteristics of the four primary programs in Microsoft Office 2007 to help you decide which program to use for particular tasks.

Table 1.1 Office Products

Office 2007 Product	Application Characteristics
Word 2007	***Word processing software*** is used with text to create, edit, and format documents such as letters, memos, reports, brochures, resumes, and flyers.
Excel 2007	***Spreadsheet software*** is used to store quantitative data and to perform accurate and rapid calculations with results ranging from simple budgets to financial analyses and statistical analyses.
PowerPoint 2007	***Presentation graphics software*** is used to create slide shows for presentation by a speaker, to be published as part of a Web site, or to run as a stand-alone application on a computer kiosk.
Access 2007	***Relational database software*** is used to store data and convert it into information. Database software is used primarily for decision-making by businesses that compile data from multiple records stored in tables to produce informative reports.

Word processing software is used primarily with text to create, edit, and format documents.

Spreadsheet software is used primarily with numbers to create worksheets.

Presentation graphics software is used primarily to create electronic slide shows.

Relational database software is used to store data and convert it into information.

In this section, you explore the common interface among the programs. You learn the names of the interface elements. In addition, you learn how to use Help to get assistance in using the software.

Identifying Common Interface Components

A **user interface** is the meeting point between computer software and the person using it and provides the means for a person to communicate with a software program. Word, Excel, PowerPoint, and Access share the overall Microsoft Office 2007 interface. This interface is made up of three main sections of the screen display shown in Figure 1.1.

Office button, Quick Access Toolbar, and title bar

Ribbon

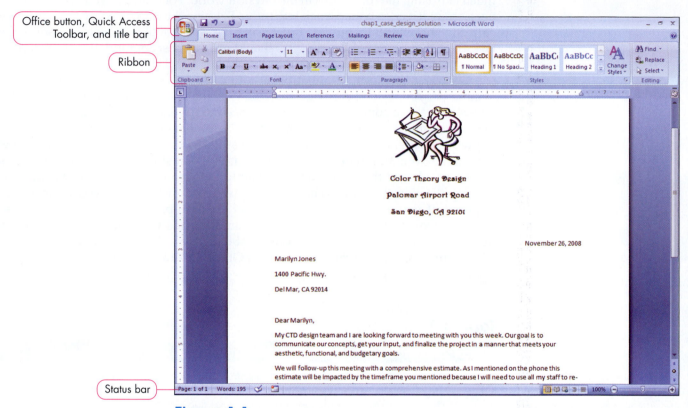

Color Theory Design

Palomar Airport Road

San Diego, CA 92101

November 26, 2008

Marilyn Jones

1400 Pacific Hwy.

Del Mar, CA 92014

Dear Marilyn,

My CTD design team and I are looking forward to meeting with you this week. Our goal is to communicate our concepts, get your input, and finalize the project in a manner that meets your aesthetic, functional, and budgetary goals.

We will follow-up this meeting with a comprehensive estimate. As I mentioned on the phone this estimate will be impacted by the timeframe you mentioned because I will need to use all my staff to re-

Status bar

Figure 1.1 Office 2007 Interface

Use the Office Button and Quick Access Toolbar

The first section of the Office 2007 interface contains three distinct items: the Microsoft Office Button (referred to as Office Button in the Exploring series), Quick Access Toolbar, and the title bar. These three items are located at the top of the interface for quick access and reference. The following paragraphs explain each item.

The **Office Button** is an icon that, when clicked, displays the **Office menu**, a list of commands that you can perform on the entire file or for the specific Office program. For example, when you want to perform a task that involves the entire document, such as saving, printing, or sharing a file with others, you use the commands on the Office menu. You also use the Office menu commands to work with the entire program, such as customizing program settings or exiting from the program. Some commands on the Office menu perform a default action when you click them, such as Save—the file open in the active window is saved. However, other commands open a submenu when you point to or click the command. Figure 1.2 displays the Office menu in Access 2007.

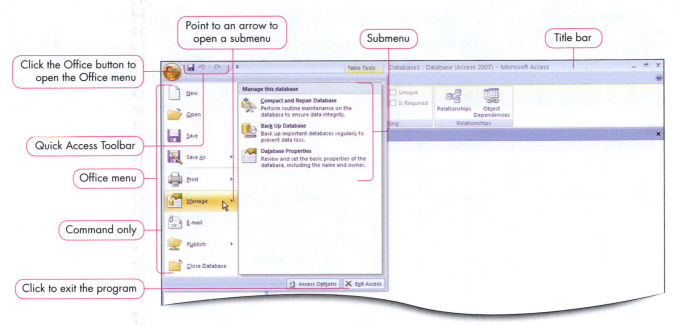

Point to an arrow to open a submenu

Submenu

Title bar

Click the Office button to open the Office menu

Quick Access Toolbar

Office menu

Command only

Click to exit the program

Figure 1.2 Access Office Menu

TIP Displaying the Office Menu from the Keyboard

If you prefer to use a keyboard shortcut to display the Office menu instead of clicking the Office Button, press Alt+F.

The **Quick Access Toolbar** contains buttons for frequently used commands.

The second item at the top of the window is the **Quick Access Toolbar**, which contains buttons for frequently used commands, such as saving a file or undoing an action. This toolbar keeps buttons for common tasks on the screen at all times, enabling you to be more productive in using these frequently used commands.

TIP Customizing the Quick Access Toolbar

As you become more familiar with Microsoft Office 2007, you might find that you need quick access to additional commands, such as Print Preview or Spelling & Grammar. You can easily customize the Quick Access Toolbar by clicking the Customize Quick Access Toolbar drop-down arrow on the right end of the toolbar and adding command buttons from the list that displays. You also can customize the toolbar by changing where it displays. If you want it closer to the document window, you can move the toolbar below the Ribbon.

A **title bar** displays the program name and file name at the top of a window.

The third item at the top of the screen is the **title bar**, which displays the name of the open program and the file name at the top of a window. For example, in Figure 1.1, *chap1_case_design_solution* is the name of a document, and *Microsoft Word* is the name of the program. In Figure 1.2, *Database1* is the name of the file, and *Microsoft Access* is the name of the program.

The **Ribbon** is a large strip of visual commands that enables you to perform tasks.

(The Ribbon is the command center of the Microsoft Office 2007 interface, providing access to the functionality of the programs.)

Familiarize Yourself with the Ribbon

The second section of the Office 2007 interface is the **Ribbon**, a large strip of visual commands that displays across the screen below the Office Button, Quick Access Toolbar, and the title bar. The Ribbon is the most important section of the interface: It is the command center of the Microsoft Office 2007 interface, providing access to the functionality of the programs (see Figure 1.3).

Figure 1.3 The Ribbon

The Ribbon has three main components: tabs, groups, and commands. The following list describes each component.

Tabs, which look like folder tabs, divide the Ribbon into task-oriented categories.

- **Tabs**, which look like folder tabs, divide the Ribbon into task-oriented sections. For example, the Ribbon in Word contains these tabs: Home, Insert, Page Layout, Reference, Mailings, Review, and View. When you click the Home tab, you see a set of core commands for that program. When you click the Insert tab, you see a set of commands that enable you to insert objects, such as tables, clip art, headers, page numbers, etc.

Groups organize similar commands together within each tab.

- **Groups** organize related commands together on each tab. For example, the Home tab in Word contains these groups: Clipboard, Font, Paragraph, Styles, and Editing. These groups help organize related commands together so that you can find them easily. For example, the Font group contains font-related commands, such as Font, Font Size, Bold, Italic, Underline, Highlighter, and Font Color.

A **command** is a visual icon in each group that you click to perform a task.

- **Commands** are specific tasks performed. Commands appear as visual icons or buttons within the groups on the Ribbon. The icons are designed to provide a visual clue of the purpose of the command. For example, the Bold command looks like a bolded B in the Font group on the Home tab. You simply click the desired command to perform the respective task.

The Ribbon has the same basic design—tabs, groups, and commands—across all Microsoft Office 2007 applications. When you first start using an Office 2007 application, you use the Home tab most often. The groups of commands on the Home tab are designed to get you started using the software. For example, the Home tab contains commands to help you create, edit, and format a document in Word, a worksheet in Excel, and a presentation in PowerPoint. In Access, the Home tab contains groups of commands to insert, delete, and edit records in a database table. While three of the four applications contain an Insert tab, the specific groups and commands differ by application. Regardless of the application, however, the Insert tab contains commands to *insert something*, whether it is a page number in Word, a column chart in Excel, or a shape in PowerPoint. One of the best ways to develop an understanding of the Ribbon is to study its structure in each application. As you explore each program, you will notice the similarities in how commands are grouped on tabs, and you will notice the differences specific to each application.

The Ribbon provides an extensive sets of commands that you use when creating and editing documents, worksheets, slides, tables, or other items. Figure 1.4 points out other important components of the Ribbon.

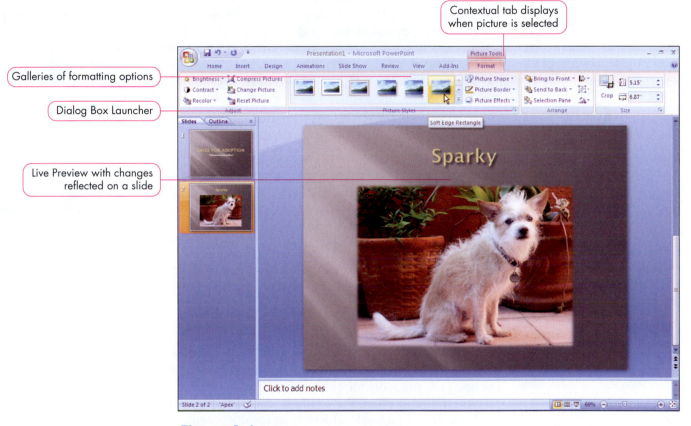

Figure 1.4 PowerPoint with Ribbon

A **dialog box** is a window that provides options related to a group of commands.

A **Dialog Box Launcher** is a small icon that, when clicked, opens a related dialog box.

A **gallery** is a set of options that appears as thumbnail graphics.

Live Preview provides a preview of the results for gallery options.

Figure 1.4 shows examples of four other components of the Ribbon. These components include a Dialog Box Launcher, a gallery, Live Preview, and a contextual tab. The following list describes each component:

- A **Dialog Box Launcher** is a small icon located on the right side of some group names that you click to open a related **dialog box**, which is a window that provides options related to a group of commands.

- A **gallery** is a set of options that appear as thumbnail graphics that visually represent the option results. For example, if you create a chart in Excel, a gallery of chart formatting options provides numerous choices for formatting the chart.

- **Live Preview** works with the galleries, providing a preview of the results of formatting in the document. As you move your mouse pointer over the gallery thumbnails, you see how each formatting option affects the selected item in your document, worksheet, or presentation. This feature increases productivity because you see the results immediately. If you do not like the results, keep moving the mouse pointer over other gallery options until you find a result you like.

A *contextual tab* is a tab that provides specialized commands that display only when the object they affect is selected.

- A *contextual tab* provides specialized commands that display only when the object they affect is selected. For example, if you insert a picture on a slide, PowerPoint displays a contextual tab on the Ribbon with commands specifically related to the selected image. When you click outside the picture to deselect it, the contextual tab disappears.

TIP   Using Keyboard Shortcuts

Many people who have used previous Office products like to use the keyboard to initiate commands. Microsoft Office 2007 makes it possible for you to continue to use keyboard shortcuts for commands on the Ribbon. Simply press Alt on the keyboard to display the Ribbon and Quick Access Toolbar with shortcuts called Key Tips. A *Key Tip* is the letter or number that displays over each feature on the Ribbon or Quick Access Toolbar and is the keyboard equivalent that you press. Notice the Key Tips that display in Figure 1.5 as a result of pressing Alt on the keyboard. Other keyboard shortcuts, such as Ctrl+C to copy text, remain the same from previous versions of Microsoft Office.

A *Key Tip* is the letter or number that displays over each feature on the Ribbon and Quick Access Toolbar and is the keyboard equivalent that you press.

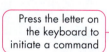

Press the letter on the keyboard to initiate a command

Figure 1.5   Key Tips Displayed for Ribbon and Quick Access Toolbar

---

Use the Status Bar

The *status bar* displays below the document and provides information about the open file and buttons for quick access.

The third major section of the Office 2007 user interface is the status bar. The *status bar* displays at the bottom of the program window and contains information about the open file and tools for quick access. The status bar contains details for the file in the specific application. For example, the Word status bar shows the current page, total number of pages, total words in the document, and proofreading status. The PowerPoint status bar shows the slide number, total slides in the presentation, and the applied theme. The Excel status bar provides general instructions and displays the average, count, and sum of values for selected cells. In each program, the status bar also includes View commands from the View tab for quick access. You can use the View commands to change the way the document, worksheet, or presentation displays onscreen. Table 1.2 describes the main characteristics of each Word 2007 view.

Table 1.2 Word Document Views

View Option	Characteristics
Print Layout	Displays the document as it will appear when printed.
Full Screen Reading	Displays the document on the entire screen to make reading long documents easier. To remove Full Screen Reading, press the Esc key on the keyboard.
Web Page	Displays the document as it would look as a Web page.
Outline	Displays the document as an outline.
Draft	Displays the document for quick editing without additional elements such as headers or footers.

The **_Zoom slider_** enables you to increase or decrease the magnification of the file onscreen.

The **_Zoom slider_**, located on the right edge of the status bar, enables you to drag the slide control to change the magnification of the current document, worksheet, or presentation. You can change the display to zoom in on the file to get a close up view, or you can zoom out to get an overview of the file. To use the Zoom slider, click and drag the slider control to the right to increase the zoom or to the left to decrease the zoom. If you want to set a specific zoom, such as 78%, you can type the precise value in the Zoom dialog box when you click Zoom on the View tab. Figure 1.6 shows the Zoom dialog box and the elements on Word's status bar. The Zoom dialog box in Excel and PowerPoint looks similar to the Word Zoom dialog box, but it contains fewer options in the other programs.

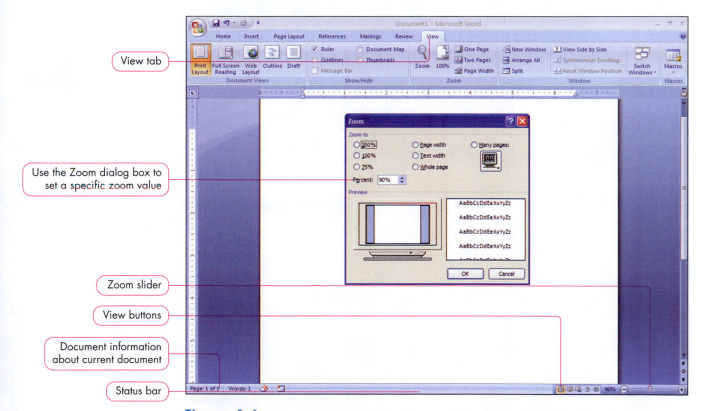

Figure 1.6 View Tab, Zoom Dialog Box, and the Status Bar in Word

Using Office 2007 Help

Help is always available when you use any Office 2007 program.

Have you ever started a project such as assembling an entertainment center and had to abandon it because you had no way to get help when you got stuck? Microsoft Office includes features that keep this type of scenario from happening when you use Word, Excel, Access, or PowerPoint. In fact, several methods are available to locate help when you need assistance performing tasks. Help is always available when you use any Office 2007 program. Help files reside on your computer when you install Microsoft Office, and Microsoft provides additional help files on its Web site. If you link to Microsoft Office Online, you not only have access to help files for all applications, you also have access to up-to-date products, files, and graphics to help you complete projects.

Use Office 2007 Help

To access Help, press F1 on the keyboard or click the Help button on the right edge of the Ribbon shown in Figure 1.7. If you know the topic you want help with, such as printing, you can type the key term in the Search box to display help files on that topic. Help also displays general topics in the lower part of the Help window that are links to further information. To display a table of contents for the Help files, click the Show Table of Contents button, and after locating the desired help topic, you can print the information for future reference by clicking the Print button. Figure 1.7 shows these elements in Excel Help.

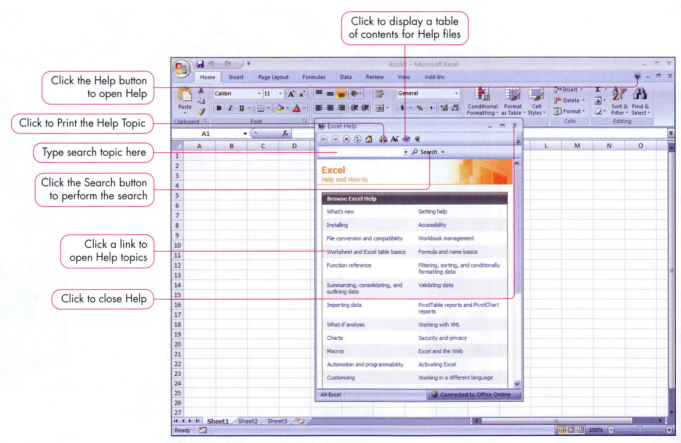

Figure 1.7 Excel Help

Use Enhanced ScreenTips

An ***Enhanced ScreenTip*** displays the name and brief description of a command when you rest the pointer on a command.

Another method for getting help is to use the Office 2007 Enhanced ScreenTips. An ***Enhanced ScreenTip*** displays when you rest the mouse pointer on a command. Notice in Figure 1.8 that the Enhanced ScreenTip provides the command name, a brief description of the command, and a link for additional help. To get help on the specific command, keep the pointer resting on the command and press F1 if the Enhanced ScreenTip displays a Help icon. The advantage of this method is that you do not have to find the correct information yourself because the Enhanced ScreenTip help is context sensitive.

Figure 1.8 Enhanced ScreenTip

Get Help with Dialog Boxes

As you work within a dialog box, you might need help with some of the numerous options contained in that dialog box, but you do not want to close the dialog box to get assistance. For example, if you open the Insert Picture dialog box and want help with inserting files, click the Help button located on the title bar of the dialog box to display help for the dialog box. Figure 1.9 shows the Insert Picture dialog box with Help displayed.

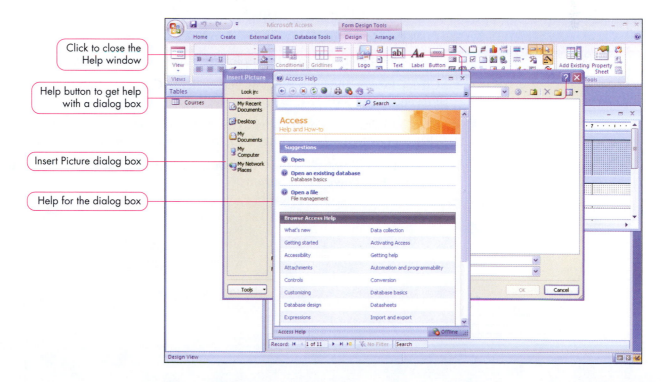

Figure 1.9 Help with Dialog Boxes

Hands-On Exercises

1 | Identifying Program Interface Components and Using Help

Skills covered: 1. Use PowerPoint's Office Button, Get Help in a Dialog Box, and Use the Zoom Slider **2.** Use Excel's Ribbon, Get Help from an Enhanced ScreenTip, and Use the Zoom Dialog Box **3.** Search Help in Access **4.** Use Word's Status Bar **5.** Search Help and Print a Help Topic

---

Step 1
Use PowerPoint's Office Button, Get Help in a Dialog Box, and Use the Zoom Slider

Refer to Figure 1.10 as you complete Step 1.

a. Click **Start** to display the Start menu. Click (or point to) **All Programs**, click **Microsoft Office**, then click **Microsoft Office PowerPoint 2007** to start the program.

b. Point to and rest the mouse on the Office Button, and then do the same to the Quick Access Toolbar.

As you rest the mouse pointer on each object, you see an Enhanced ScreenTip for that object.

TROUBLESHOOTING: If you do not see the Enhanced ScreenTip, keep the mouse pointer on the object a little longer.

c. Click the **Office Button** and slowly move your mouse down the list of menu options, pointing to the arrow after any command name that has one.

The Office menu displays, and as you move the mouse down the list, submenus display for menu options that have an arrow.

d. Select **New**.

The New Presentation dialog box displays. Depending on how Microsoft Office 2007 was installed, your screen may vary. If Microsoft Office 2007 was fully installed, you should see a thumbnail to create a Blank Presentation, and you may see additional thumbnails in the *Recently Used Templates* section of the dialog box.

e. Click the **Help button** on the title bar of the New Presentation dialog box.

PowerPoint Help displays the topic *Create a new file from a template*.

f. Click **Close** on the Help Window and click the **Cancel** button in the New Presentation dialog box.

g. Click and drag the **Zoom slider** to the right to increase the magnification. Then click and drag the **Zoom slider** back to the center point for a 100% zoom.

h. To exit PowerPoint, click the **Office Button** to display the Office menu, and then click the **Exit PowerPoint button**.

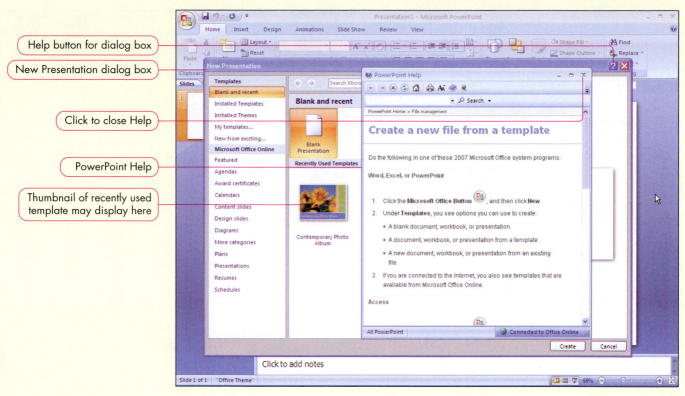

Figure 1.10 PowerPoint Help for New Presentations Dialog Box

Labels on figure:
- Help button for dialog box
- New Presentation dialog box
- Click to close Help
- PowerPoint Help
- Thumbnail of recently used template may display here

Step 2

Use Excel's Ribbon, Get Help from an Enhanced ScreenTip, and Use the Zoom Dialog Box

Refer to Figure 1.11 as you complete Step 2.

a. Click **Start** to display the Start menu. Click (or point to) **All Programs**, click **Microsoft Office**, then click **Microsoft Office Excel 2007** to open the program.

b. Click the **Insert tab** on the Ribbon.

   The Insert tab contains groups of commands for inserting objects, such as tables, illustrations, charts, links, and text.

c. Rest the mouse on **Hyperlink** in the Links group on the Insert tab.

   The Enhanced ScreenTip for Hyperlinks displays. Notice the Enhanced ScreenTip contains a Help icon.

d. Press **F1** on the keyboard.

   Excel Help displays the *Create or remove a hyperlink* Help topic.

   TROUBLESHOOTING: If you are not connected to the Internet, you might not see the context-sensitive help.

e. Click the **Close button** on the Help window.

f. Click the **View tab** on the Ribbon and click **Zoom** in the Zoom group.

   The Zoom dialog box appears so that you can change the zoom percentage.

g. Click the **200%** option and click **OK**.

   The worksheet is now magnified to 200% of its regular size.

h. Click **Zoom** in the Zoom group on the View tab, click the **100%** option, and click **OK**.

   The worksheet is now restored to 100%.

i. To exit Excel, click the **Office Button** to display the Office menu, and then click the **Exit Excel button**.

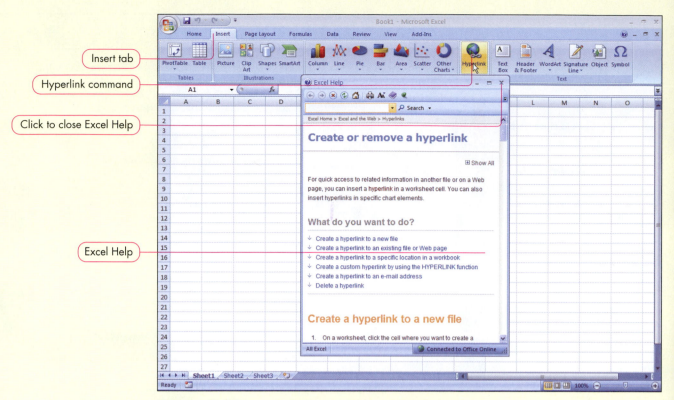

Insert tab

Hyperlink command

Click to close Excel Help

Excel Help

Figure 1.11 Excel Ribbon with Help

Refer to Figure 1.12 as you complete Step 3.

a. Click **Start** to display the Start menu. Click (or point to) **All Programs**, click **Microsoft Office**, then click **Microsoft Office Access 2007** to start the program.

Access opens and displays the Getting Started with Microsoft Access screen.

TROUBLESHOOTING: If you are not familiar with Access, just use the opening screen that displays and continue with the exercise.

b. Press **F1** on the keyboard.

Access Help displays.

c. Type **table** in the Search box in the Access Help window.

d. Click the **Search** button.

Access displays help topics.

e. Click the topic **Create a table in a database**.

The help topic displays.

f. Click the **Close** button on the Access Help window.

Access Help closes.

g. To exit Access, click the **Office Button** to display the Office menu, and then click the **Exit Access button**.

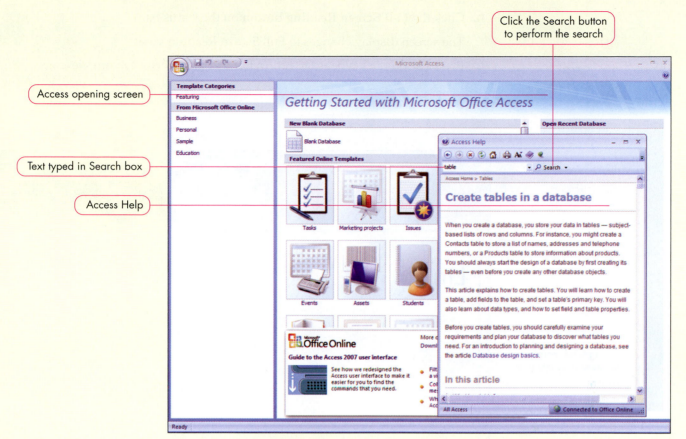

Figure 1.12 Access Help

Refer to Figure 1.13 as you complete Step 4.

a. Click **Start** to display the Start menu. Click (or point to) **All Programs**, click **Microsoft Office**, then click **Microsoft Office Word 2007** to start the program.

Word opens with a blank document ready for you to start typing.

b. Type your first name.

Your first name displays in the document window.

c. Point your mouse to the **Zoom slider** on the status bar.

d. Click and drag the **Zoom slider** to the right to increase the magnification.

The document with your first name increases in size onscreen.

e. Click and drag the slider control to the left to decrease the magnification.

The document with your first name decreases in size.

f. Click and drag the **Zoom slider** back to the center.

The document returns to 100% magnification.

g. Slowly point the mouse to the buttons on the status bar.

A ScreenTip displays the names of the buttons.

h. Click the **Full Screen Reading button** on the status bar.

The screen display changes to Full Screen Reading view.

i. Press **Esc** on the keyboard to return the display to Print Layout view.

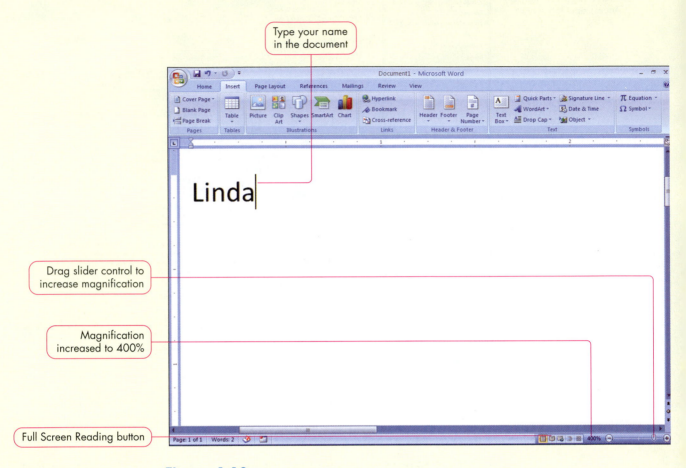

Figure 1.13 The Word Status Bar

Refer to Figure 1.14 as you complete Step 5.

a. With Word open on the screen, press **F1** on the keyboard.

Word Help displays.

b. Type **zoom** in the Search box in the Word Help window.

c. Click the **Search** button.

Word Help displays related topics.

d. Click the topic **Zoom in or out of a document, presentation, or worksheet**.

The help topic displays.

TROUBLESHOOTING: If you do not have a printer that is ready to print, skip Step 5e and continue with the exercise.

e. Turn on the attached printer, be sure it has paper, and then click the Word Help **Print** button.

The Help topic prints on the attached printer.

f. Click the **Show Table of Contents** button on the Word Help toolbar.

The Table of Contents pane displays on the left side of the Word Help dialog box so that you can click popular Help topics, such as *What's new*. You can click a closed book icon to see specific topics to click for additional information, and you can click an open book icon to close the main Help topic.

g. Click the **Close** button on Word Help.

Word Help closes.

h. To exit Word, click the **Office Button** to display the Office menu, and then click the **Exit Word button**.

A warning appears stating that you have not saved changes to your document.

i. Click **No** in the Word warning box.

You exit Word without saving the document.

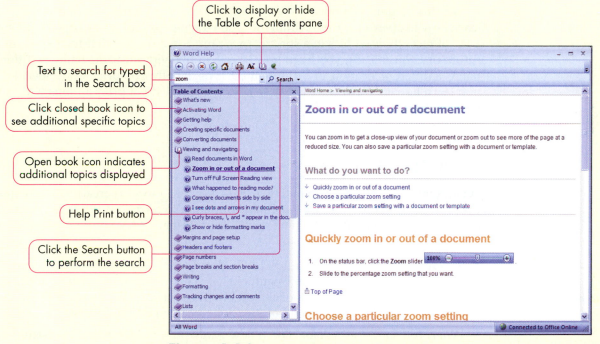

Figure 1.14 Word Help

Universal Tasks

Today, storing large amounts of information on a computer is taken for granted, but in reality, computers would not have become very important if you could not save and re-use the files you create.

One of the most useful and important aspects of using computers is the ability to save and re-use information. For example, you can store letters, reports, budgets, presentations, and databases as files to reopen and use at some time in the future. Today, storing large amounts of information on a computer is taken for granted, but in reality, computers would not have become very important if you could not save and re-use the files you create.

Three fundamental tasks are so important for productivity that they are considered universal to most every computer program, including Office 2007:

- opening files that have been saved
- saving files you create
- printing files

In this section, you open a file within an Office 2007 program. Specifically, you learn how to open a file from within the Open dialog box and how to open a file from a list of recently used files in a specific program. You also save files to keep them for future use. Specifically, you learn how to save a file with the same name, a different name, a different location, or a different file type. Finally, you print a file. Specifically, you learn how to preview a file before printing it and select print options within the Print dialog box.

Opening a File

When you start any program in Office 2007, you need to start creating a new file or open an existing one. You use the Open command to retrieve a file saved on a storage device and place it in the random access memory (RAM) of your computer so you can work on it. For example:

The *insertion point* is the blinking vertical line in the document, cell, slide show, or database table designating the current location where text you type displays.

- When you start Word 2007, a new blank document named Document1 opens. You can either start typing in Document1, or you can open an existing document. The *insertion point*, which looks like a blinking vertical line, displays in the document designating the current location where text you type displays.

- When you start PowerPoint 2007, a new blank presentation named Presentation1 opens. You can either start creating a new slide for the blank presentation, or you can open an existing presentation.

- When you start Excel 2007, a new blank workbook named Book1 opens. You can either start inputting labels and values into Book1, or you can open an existing workbook.

- When you start Access 2007—unlike Word, PowerPoint, and Excel—a new blank database is not created automatically for you. In order to get started using Access, you must create and name a database first or open an existing database.

Open a File Using the Open Dialog Box

Opening a file in any of the Office 2007 applications is an easy process: Use the Open command from the Office menu and specify the file to open. However, locating the file to open can be difficult at times because you might not know where the file you want to use is located. You can open files stored on your computer or on a remote computer that you have access to. Further, files are saved in folders, and you might need to look for files located within folders or subfolders. The Open dialog box, shown in Figure 1.15, contains many features designed for file management; however, two features are designed specifically to help you locate files.

- **Look in**—provides a hierarchical view of the structure of folders and subfolders on your computer or on any computer network you are attached to. Move up or down in the structure to find a specific location or folder and then click the desired location to select it. The file list in the center of the dialog box displays the subfolders and files saved in the location you select. Table 1.3 lists and describes the toolbar buttons.
- **My Places bar**—provides a list of shortcut links to specific folders on your computer and locations on a computer network that you are attached to. Click a link to select it, and the file list changes to display subfolders and files in that location.

Table 1.3 Toolbar Buttons

Buttons	Characteristics
Previous Folder	Returns to the previous folder you viewed.
Up One Level	Moves up one level in the folder structure from the current folder.
Delete	Deletes the selected file or selected folder.
Create New Folder	Creates a new folder within the current folder.
Views	Changes the way the list of folders and files displays in the File list.

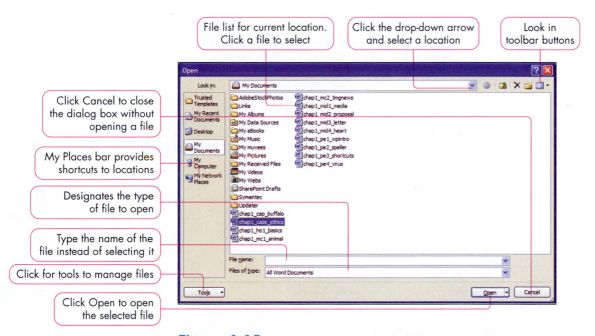

Figure 1.15 Open Dialog Box in Word

After you locate and select the file, click the Open button in the dialog box to display the file on the screen. However, if, for example, you work as part of a workgroup that shares files with each other, you might find the need to open files in a more specialized way. Microsoft Office programs provide several options for opening files when you click the drop-down arrow on the Open button. For example, if you want to keep the original file intact, you might open the file as a copy of the original. Table 1.4 describes the Open options.

Table 1.4 Open Options

Open Options	Characteristics
Open	Opens the selected file with the ability to read and write (edit).
Open Read-Only	Opens the selected file with the ability to read the contents but prevents you from changing or editing it.
Open as Copy	Opens the selected file as a copy of the original so that if you edit the file, the original remains unchanged.
Open in Browser	Opens the selected file in a Web browser.
Open with Transform	Opens a file and provides the ability to transform it into another type of document, such as an HTML document.
Open and Repair	Opens the selected file and attempts to repair any damage. If you have difficulty opening a file, try to open it by selecting Open and Repair.

Open Files Using the Recent Documents List

Office 2007 provides a quick method for accessing files you used recently. The Recent Documents list displays when the Office menu opens and provides a list of links to the last few files you used. The list changes as you work in the application to reflect only the most recent files. Figure 1.16 shows the Office menu with the Recent Documents list.

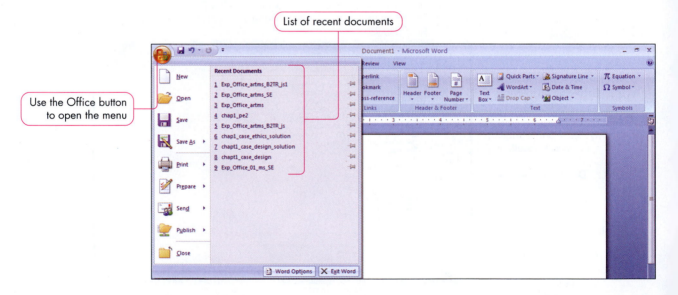

Figure 1.16 The Recent Documents List

As you use the Office application and open several files, the list of Recent Documents changes; however, you can designate files to keep displayed on the Recent Documents list at all times. Notice the icon of the pushpin that displays immediately following each file name on the Recent Documents list. Just as you use pushpins to post an important notice in the real world, you use pushpins here to designate important files that you want easy access to. To pin a specific file to the Recent Documents list, click the icon of a gray pushpin. The shape of the pin changes as if pushed in, and the color of the pin changes to green designating that the file is pinned permanently on the list. However, if later you decide to remove the file from the list, you can unpin it by simply clicking the green pushpin, changing the icon back to gray, and the file will disappear from the list over time. Notice the Recent Documents list with both gray and green pushpins in Figure 1.17.

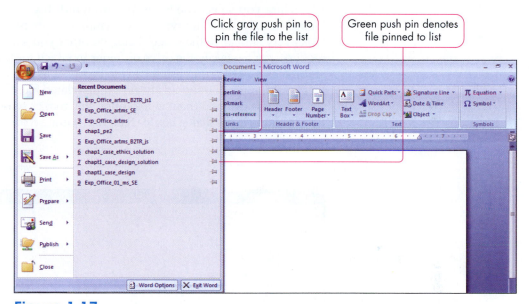

Click gray push pin to pin the file to the list

Green push pin denotes file pinned to list

Figure 1.17 The Recent Documents List

Saving a File

As you work with any Office 2007 application and create files, you will need to save them for future use. While you are working on a file, it is stored in the temporary memory or RAM of your computer. When you save a file, the contents of the file stored in RAM are saved to the hard drive of your computer or to a storage device such as a flash drive. As you create, edit, and format a complex file such as a report, slide show, or budget, you should consider saving several versions of it as you work. For example, you might number versions or use the date in the file name to designate each version. Using this method enables you to revert to a previous version of the document if necessary. To save a file you create in Word, PowerPoint, or Excel, click the Office Button to display the Office menu. Office provides two commands that work similarly: Save and Save As. Table 1.5 describes the characteristics of these two commands.

> As you create, edit, and format a complex file such as a report, slide show, or budget, you should consider saving several versions of it as you work.

Table 1.5 Save Options

Command	Characteristics
Save	Saves the open document: • If this is the first time the document is being saved, Office 2007 opens the Save As dialog box so that you can name the file. • If this document was saved previously, the document is automatically saved using the original file name.
Save As	Opens the Save As dialog box: • If this is the first time the document is being saved, use the Save As dialog box to name the file. • If this document was saved previously, use this option to save the file with a new name, in a new location, or as a new file type preserving the original file with its original name.

When you select the Save As command, the Save As dialog box appears (see Figure 1.18). Notice that saving and opening files are related, that the Save As dialog box looks very similar to the Open dialog box that you saw in Figure 1.15. The dialog box requires you to specify the drive or folder in which to store the file, the name of the file, and the type of file you wish the file to be saved as. Additionally, because finding saved files is important, you should always group related files together in folders, so that you or someone else can find them in a location that makes sense. You can use the Create New Folder button in the dialog box to create and name a folder, and then save related files to it.

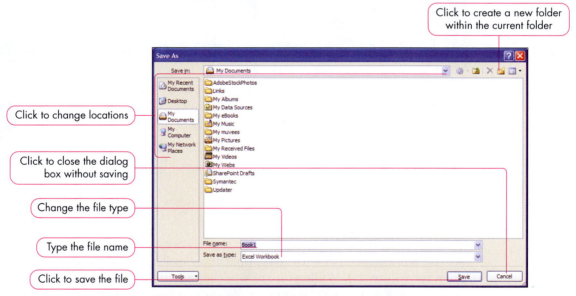

Figure 1.18 Save As Dialog Box in Excel

All subsequent executions of the Save command save the file under the assigned name, replacing the previously saved version with the new version. Pressing Ctrl+S is another way to activate the Save command. If you want to change the name of the file, use the Save As command. Word, PowerPoint, and Excel use the same basic process for saving files, which include the following options:

• naming and saving a previously unsaved file

• saving an updated file with the same name and replacing the original file with the updated one

• saving an updated file with a different name or in a different location to keep the original intact

• saving the file in a different file format

Office 2007 saves files in a different format from previous versions of the software. Office now makes use of XML formats for files created in Word, PowerPoint, and Excel. For example, in previous versions of Word, all documents were saved with the three-letter extension .doc. Now Word saves default documents with the four-letter extension .docx. The new XML format makes use of file compression to save storage space for the user. The files are compressed automatically when saved and uncompressed when opened. Another important feature is that the XML format makes using the files you create in Office 2007 easier to open in other software. This increased portability of files is a major benefit in any workplace that might have numerous applications to deal with. The new file format also differentiates between files that contain *macros*, which are small programs that automate tasks in a file, and those that do not. This specification of files that contain macros enables a virus checker to rigorously check for damaging programs hidden in files. A *virus checker* is software that scans files for a hidden program that can damage your computer. Table 1.6 lists the file formats with the four-letter extension for Word, PowerPoint, and Excel, and a five-letter extension for Access.

A *macro* is a small program that automates tasks in a file.

A *virus checker* is software that scans files for a hidden program that can damage your computer.

A *template* is a file that contains formatting and design elements.

Table 1.6 Word, PowerPoint, Excel, and Access File Extensions

File Format	Characteristics
Word	.docx—default document format .docm—a document that contains macros .dotx—a template without macros (a **template** is a file that contains formatting and design elements) .dotm—a template with macros
PowerPoint	.pptx—default presentation format .pptm—a presentation that contains macros .potx—a template .potm—a template with macros .ppam—an add-in that contains macros .ppsx—a slide show .ppsm—a slide show with macros .sldx—a slide saved independently of a presentation .sldm—a slide saved independently of a presentation that contains a macro .thmx—a theme used to format a slide
Excel	.xlsx—default workbook .xlsm—a workbook with macros .xltx—a template .xltm—a template with a macro .xlsb—non-XML binary workbook—for previous versions of the software .xlam—an add-in that contains macros
Access	.accdb—default database

Access 2007 saves data differently from Word, PowerPoint, and Excel. When you start Access, which is a relational database, you must create a database and define at least one table for your data. Then as you work, your data is stored automatically. This powerful software enables multiple users access to up-to-date data. The concepts of saving, opening, and printing remain the same, but the process of how data is saved is unique to this powerful environment.

A **shortcut menu** displays when you right-click the mouse on an object and provides a list of commands pertaining to the object you clicked.

TIP Changing the Display of the My Places Bar

Sometimes finding saved files can be a time-consuming chore. To help you quickly locate files, Office 2007 provides options for changing the display of the My Places bar. In Word, PowerPoint, Excel, and Access, you can create shortcuts to folders where you store commonly used files and add them to the My Places bar. From the Open or Save As dialog box, select the location in the Look in list you want to add to the bar. With the desired location selected, point to an empty space below the existing shortcuts on the My Places bar. Right-click the mouse to display a **shortcut menu**, which displays when you right-click the mouse on an object and provides a list of commands pertaining to the object you clicked. From the shortcut menu, choose Add (folder name)—the folder name is the name of the location you selected in the Look in box. The new shortcut is added to the bottom of the My Places bar. Notice the shortcut menu in Figure 1.19, which also provides options to change the order of added shortcuts or remove an unwanted shortcut. However, you can only remove the shortcuts that you add to the bar; the default shortcuts cannot be removed.

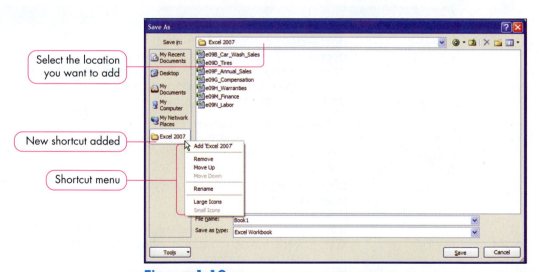

Select the location you want to add

New shortcut added

Shortcut menu

Figure 1.19 Save As Dialog Box with New Shortcut Added to My Places Bar

Printing a Document

As you work with Office 2007 applications, you will need to print hard copies of documents, such as letters to mail, presentation notes to distribute to accompany a slide show, budget spreadsheets to distribute at a staff meeting, or database summary reports to submit. Office provides flexibility so that you can preview the document before you send it to the printer; you also can select from numerous print options, such as changing the number of copies printed; or you can simply and quickly print the current document on the default printer.

Preview Before You Print

It is highly recommended that you preview your document before you print because Print Preview displays all the document elements, such as graphics and formatting, as they will appear when printed on paper. Previewing the document first enables you to make any changes that you need to make without wasting paper. Previewing documents uses the same method in all Office 2007 applications, that is, point to the arrow next to the Print command on the Office menu and select Print Preview to display the current document, worksheet, presentation, or database table in the Print Preview window. Figure 1.20 shows the Print Preview window in Word 2007.

> It is highly recommended that you preview your document before you print because Print Preview displays all the document elements, such as graphics and formatting, as they will appear when printed on paper.

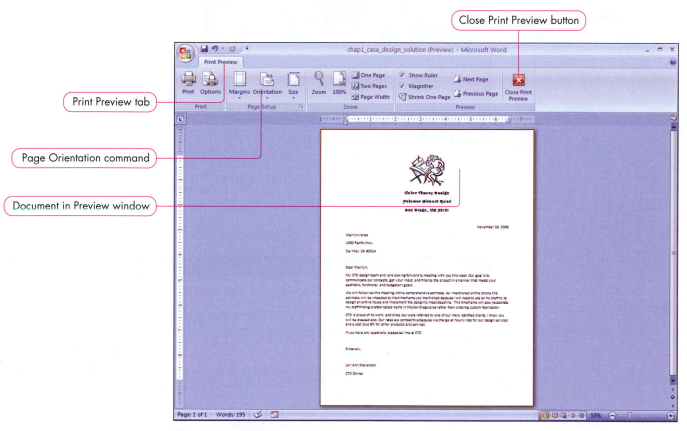

Figure 1.20 Print Preview Window

As you preview the document, you can get a closer look at the results by changing the zoom. Notice that the mouse pointer displays in the Preview window as a magnifying glass with a plus sign, so that you can simply click in the document to increase the zoom. Once clicked, the plus sign changes to a minus sign, enabling you to click in the document again to decrease the zoom. You also can use the Zoom group on the Print Preview tab or the Zoom slider on the status bar to change the view of the document.

Other options on the Print Preview tab change depending on the application that you are using. For example, you might want to change the orientation to switch from portrait to landscape. Refer to Figure 1.20. *Portrait orientation* is longer than it is wide, like the portrait of a person; whereas, *landscape orientation* is wider than it is long, resembling a landscape scene. You also can change the size of the paper or other options from the Print Preview tab.

Portrait orientation is longer than it is wide—like the portrait of a person.

Landscape orientation is wider than it is long, resembling a landscape scene.

If you need to edit the document before printing, close the Print Preview window and return to the document. However, if you are satisfied with the document and want to print, click Print in the Print group on the Print Preview tab. The Print dialog box displays. Figure 1.21 shows Word's Print dialog box.

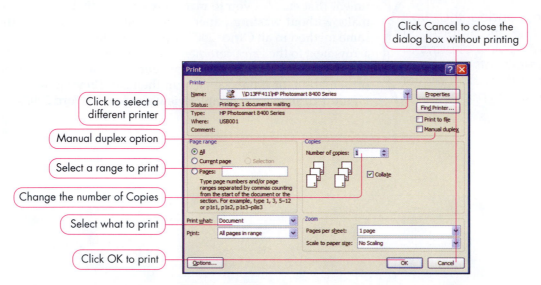

Figure 1.21 Print Dialog Box

The Print dialog box provides numerous options for selecting the correct printer, selecting what to print, and selecting how to print. Table 1.7 describes several important and often-used features of the Print dialog box.

Table 1.7 Print Dialog Box

Print Option	Characteristics
All	Select to print all the pages in the file.
Current page/slide	Select to print only the page or slide with the insertion point. This is a handy feature when you notice an error in a file, and you only want to reprint the corrected page.
Pages	Select to print only specific pages in a document. You must specify page numbers in the text box.
Number of Copies	Change the number of copies printed from the default 1 to the number desired.
Collate	Click if you are printing multiple copies of a multi-page file, and you want to print an entire first copy before printing an entire second copy, and so forth.
Print what	Select from options on what to print, varying with each application.
Selection	Select to print only selected text or objects in an Excel worksheet.
Active sheet(s)	Select to print only the active worksheet(s) in Excel.
Entire workbook	Select to print all worksheets in the Excel workbook.

As you work with other Office 2007 applications, you will notice that the main print options remain unchanged; however, the details vary based on the specific task of the application. For example, the *Print what* option in PowerPoint includes options such as printing the slide, printing handouts, printing notes, or printing an outline of the presentation.

A **duplex printer** prints on both sides of the page.

A **manual duplex** operation allows you to print on both sides of the paper by printing first on one side and then on the other.

Print Without Previewing the File

If you want to print a file without previewing the results, select Print from the Office menu, and the Print dialog box displays. You can still make changes in the Print dialog box, or just immediately send the print job to the printer. However, if you just want to print quickly, Office 2007 provides a quick print option that enables you to send the current file to the default printer without opening the Print dialog box. This is a handy feature to use if you have only one printer attached and you want to print the current file without changing any print options. You have two ways to quick print:

- Select Quick Print from the Office menu.
- Customize the Quick Access toolbar to add the Print icon. Click the icon to print the current file without opening the Print dialog box.

Hands-On Exercises

2 | Performing Universal Tasks

Skills covered: 1. Open a File and Save It with a Different Name **2.** Use Print Preview and Select Options **3.** Print a Document

Step 1

Open a File and Save It with a Different Name

Refer to Figure 1.22 as you complete Step 1.

a. Start Word, click the **Office Button** to display the Office menu, and then select **Open**.

The Open dialog box displays.

b. If necessary, click the **File Type List** button to locate the files for this textbook to find *chap1_ho2_sample*.

TROUBLESHOOTING: If you have trouble finding the files that accompany this text, you may want to ask your instructor where they are located.

c. Select the file and click **Open**.

The document displays on the screen.

d. Click the **Office Button**, and then select **Save As** on the Office menu.

The Save As dialog box displays.

e. In the *File name* box, type **chap1_ho2_solution**.

f. Check the location listed in the **Save in** box. If you need to change locations to save your files, use the **Save in drop-down arrow** to select the correct location.

g. Make sure that the *Save as type* option is Word Document.

TROUBLESHOOTING: Be sure that you click the **Save As** command rather than pointing to the arrow after the command, and be sure that Word Document is specified in the Save as type box.

h. Click the **Save button** in the dialog box to save the file under the new name.

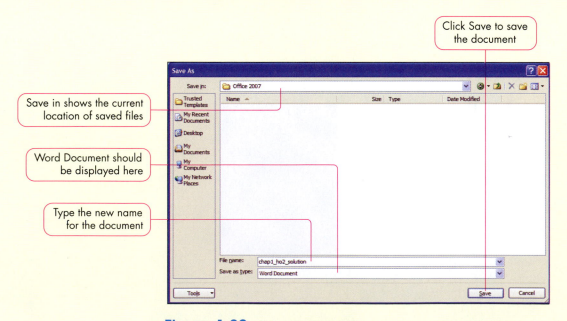

Click Save to save the document

Save in shows the current location of saved files

Word Document should be displayed here

Type the new name for the document

Figure 1.22 Save As Dialog Box

Refer to Figure 1.23 as you complete Step 2.

a. With the document displayed on the screen, click the **Office Button** and point to the arrow following **Print** on the Office menu.

The Print submenu displays.

b. Select **Print Preview**.

The document displays in the Print Preview window.

c. Point the magnifying glass mouse pointer in the document and click the mouse once.

TROUBLESHOOTING: If you do not see the magnifying glass pointer, point the mouse in the document and keep it still for a moment.

The document magnification increases.

d. Point the magnifying glass mouse pointer in the document and click the mouse again.

The document magnification decreases.

e. Click **Orientation** in the Page Setup group on the Print Preview tab.

The orientation options display.

f. Click **Landscape**.

The document orientation changes to landscape.

g. Click **Orientation** a second time, and then choose **Portrait**.

The document returns to portrait orientation.

h. Click the **Close Print Preview** button on the Print Preview tab.

i. The Print Preview window closes.

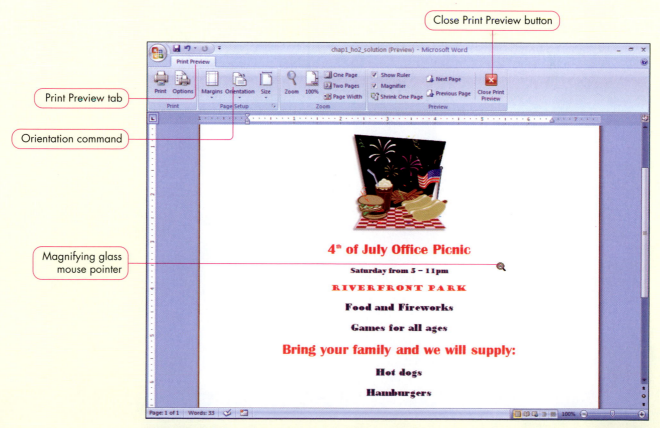

Figure 1.23 Print Preview

Step 3
Print a Document

Refer to Figure 1.24 as you complete Step 3.

a. Click the **Office Button**, and then point to the arrow next to **Print** on the Office menu.

The print options display.

b. Select **Print**.

The Print dialog box displays.

TROUBLESHOOTING: Be sure that your printer is turned on and has paper loaded.

c. If necessary, select the correct printer in the **Name box** by clicking the drop-down arrow and selecting from the resulting list.

d. Click **OK**.

The Word document prints on the selected printer.

e. To exit Word, click the **Office Button**, and then click the **Exit Word button**.

f. If prompted to save the file, choose **No**.

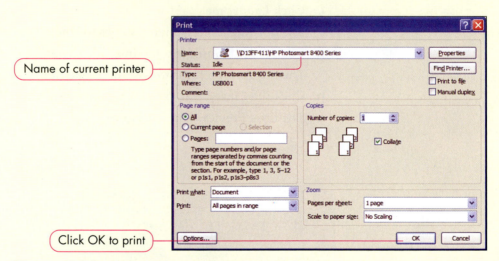

Name of current printer

Click OK to print

Figure 1.24 The Print Dialog Box

Basic Tasks

Many of the operations you perform in one Office program are the same or similar in all Office applications. These tasks are referred to as basic tasks and include such operations as inserting and typing over, copying and moving items, finding and replacing text, undoing and redoing commands, checking spelling and grammar, using the thesaurus, and using formatting tools. Once you learn the underlying concepts of these operations, you can apply them in different applications.

Most basic tasks in Word fall into two categories:

- editing a document
- formatting a document

Most successful writers use many word processing features to revise and edit documents, and most would agree that the revision process takes more time than the initial writing process. Errors such as spelling and grammar need to be eliminated to produce error-free writing. However, to turn a rough draft into a finished document, such as a report for a class or for a business, requires writers to revise and edit several times by adding text, removing text, replacing text, and moving text around to make the meaning clearer. Writers also improve their writing using tools to conduct research to make the information accurate and to find the most appropriate word using the thesaurus. Modern word processing applications such as Word 2007 provide these tools and more to aid the writer.

> Most successful writers use many word processing features to revise and edit documents, and most would agree that the revision process takes more time than the initial writing process.

The second category of basic tasks is formatting text in a document. Formatting text includes changing the type, the size, and appearance of text. You might want to apply formatting to simply improve the look of a document, or you might want to emphasize particular aspects of your message. Remember that a poorly formatted document or workbook probably will not be read. So whether you are creating your résumé or the income statement for a corporation's annual report, how the output looks is important. Office 2007 provides many tools for formatting documents, but in this section, you will start by learning to apply font attributes and copy those to other locations in the document.

In this section, you learn to perform basic tasks in Office 2007, using Word 2007 as the model. As you progress in learning other Office programs such as PowerPoint, Excel, and Access, you will apply the same principles in other applications.

Selecting Text to Edit

Most editing processes involve identifying the text that the writer wants to work with. For example, to specify which text to edit, you must select it. The most common method used to select text is to use the mouse. Point to one end of the text you want to select (either the beginning or end) and click-and-drag over the text. The selected text displays highlighted with a light blue background so that it stands out from other text and is ready for you to work with. The *Mini toolbar* displays when you select text in Word, Excel, and PowerPoint. It displays above the selected text as semitransparent and remains semitransparent until you point to it. Often-used commands from the Clipboard, Font, and Paragraph groups on the Home tab are repeated on the Mini toolbar for quick access. Figure 1.25 shows selected text with the Mini toolbar fully displayed in the document.

The *Mini toolbar* displays above the selected text as semitransparent and repeats often-used commands.

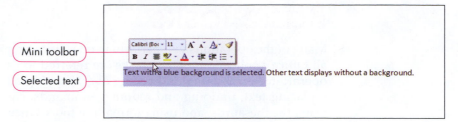

Mini toolbar

Selected text

Figure 1.25 Selected Text

Sometimes you want to select only one word or character, and trying to drag over it to select it can be frustrating. Table 1.8 describes other methods used to select text.

Table 1.8 Easy Text Selection in Word

Outcome Desired	Method
Select a word	Double-click the word.
One line of text	Point the mouse to the left of the line, and when the mouse pointer changes to a right-pointing arrow, click the mouse.
A sentence	Hold down Ctrl and click in the sentence to select.
A paragraph	Triple-click the mouse in the paragraph.
One character to the left of the insertion point	Hold down Shift and press the left arrow key.
One character to the right of the insertion point	Hold down Shift and press the right arrow key.

TIP   Selecting Large Amounts of Text

As you edit documents, you might need to select a large portion of a document. However, as you click-and-drag over the text, you might have trouble stopping the selection at the desired location because the document scrolls by too quickly. This is actually a handy feature in Word 2007 that scrolls through the document when you drag the mouse pointer at the edge of the document window.

To select a large portion of a document, click the insertion point at the beginning of the desired selection. Then move the display to the end of the selection using the scroll bar at the right edge of the window. Scrolling leaves the insertion point where you placed it. When you reach the end of the text you want to select, hold down Shift and click the mouse. The entire body of text is selected.

Inserting Text and Changing to the Overtype Mode

Insert is adding text in a document.

As you create and edit documents using Word, you will need to *insert* text, which is adding text in a document. To insert or add text, point and click the mouse in the location where the text should display. With the insertion point in the location to insert the text, simply start typing. Any existing text moves to the right, making room for the new inserted text. At times, you might need to add a large amount of text in a document, and you might want to replace or type over existing text instead of inserting text. This task can be accomplished two ways:

- Select the text to replace and start typing. The new text replaces the selected text.

Overtype mode replaces the existing text with text you type character by character.

- Switch to *Overtype mode*, which replaces the existing text with text you type character by character. To change to Overtype mode, select the Word Options button on the Office menu. Select the option Use Overtype Mode in the Editing Options section of the Advanced tab. Later, if you want to return to Insert mode, repeat these steps to deselect the overtype mode option. Figure 1.26 shows the Word Options dialog box.

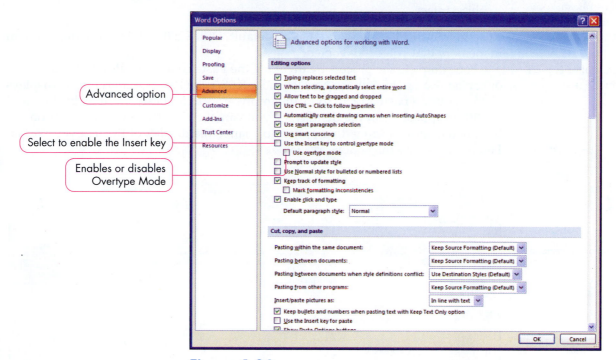

Figure 1.26 The Word Options Dialog Box

TIP   Using the Insert Key on the Keyboard

If you find that you need to switch between Insert and Overtype mode often, you can enable Insert on the keyboard by clicking the Word Options button on the Office menu. Select the option Use the Insert Key to Control Overtype Mode in the Editing Options section on the Advanced tab. Refer to Figure 1.26. You can now use Insert on the keyboard to switch between the two modes, and this option stays in effect until you go back to the Word Options dialog box and deselect it.

Moving and Copying Text

As you revise a document, you might find that you need to move text from one location to another to improve the readability of the content. To move text, you must cut the selected text from its original location and then place it in the new location by pasting it there. To duplicate text, you must copy the selected text in its original location and then paste the duplicate in the desired location. To decide whether you should use the Cut or Copy command in the Clipboard group on the Home tab to perform the task, you must notice the difference in the results of each command:

Cut removes the original text or object from its current location.

Copy makes a duplicate copy of the text or object, leaving the original intact.

Paste places the cut or copied text or object in the new location.

- *Cut* removes the selected original text or object from its current location.
- *Copy* makes a duplicate copy of the text or object, leaving the original text or object intact.

Keep in mind while you work, that by default, Office 2007 retains only the last item in memory that you cut or copied.

You complete the process by invoking the Paste command. *Paste* places the cut or copied text or object in the new location. Notice the Paste Options button displays along with the pasted text. You can simply ignore the Paste Options button, and it will disappear from the display, or you can click the drop-down arrow on the button and select a formatting option to change the display of the text you pasted. Figure 1.27 shows the options available.

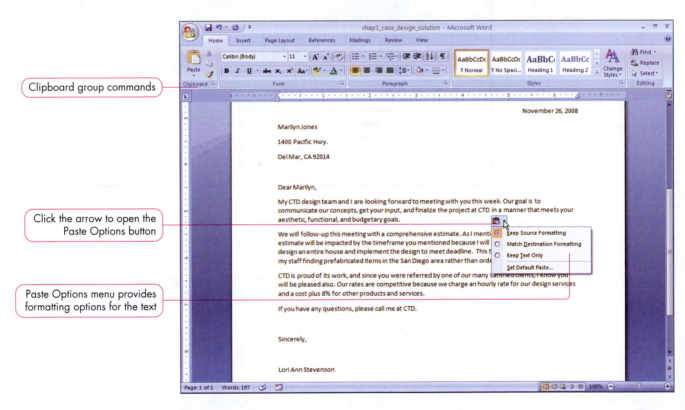

Clipboard group commands

Click the arrow to open the Paste Options button

Paste Options menu provides formatting options for the text

Figure 1.27 Text Pasted in the Document

TIP | Moving and Copying Using Shortcuts

You can use alternative methods instead of using the commands located on the Home tab to cut, copy, and paste text. Office 2007 provides the following shortcuts:

- After selecting text, point back to the selected text and right-click the mouse. The shortcut menu displays, allowing you to choose Cut or Copy. Move the insertion point to the desired location, right-click the mouse again, and choose Paste from the shortcut menu.

- After selecting text, use the keyboard shortcut combinations Ctrl+C to copy or Ctrl+X to cut text. Move the insertion point to the new location and press Ctrl+V to paste. These keyboard shortcuts work in most Windows applications, so they can be very useful.

- After selecting text, you can move it a short distance in the document by dragging to the new location. Point to the selected text, hold down the left mouse button, and then drag to the desired location. While you are dragging the mouse, the pointer changes to a left-pointing arrow with a box attached to it. Release the mouse button when you have placed the insertion point in the desired location, and the text displays in the new location.

Use the Office Clipboard

The **Clipboard** is a memory location that holds up to 24 items for you to paste into the current document, another file, or another application.

Office 2007 provides an option that enables you to cut or copy multiple items to the **Clipboard**, which is a memory location that holds up to 24 items for you to paste into the current file, another file, or another application. The Clipboard stays active only while you are using one of the Office 2007 applications. When you exit from all Office 2007 applications, all items on the Clipboard are deleted. To accumulate items on the Clipboard, you must first display it by clicking the Dialog Box Launcher in the Clipboard group on the Home tab. When the Clipboard pane is open on the screen, its memory location is active, and the Clipboard accumulates all items you cut or copy up to the maximum 24. To paste an item from the Clipboard, point to it, click the resulting drop-down arrow, and choose Paste. To change how the Clipboard functions, use the Options button shown in Figure 1.28. One of the most important options allows the Clipboard to accumulate items even when it is not open on the screen. To activate the Clipboard so that it works in the background, click the Options button in the Clipboard, and then select Collect without Showing Office Clipboard.

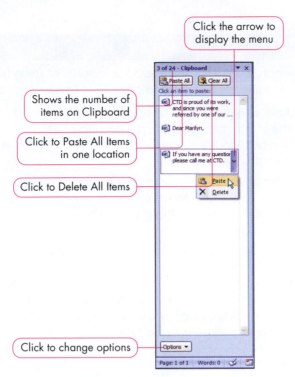

Figure 1.28 Clipboard

Finding, Replacing, and Going to Text

You can waste a great deal of time slowly scrolling through a document trying to locate text or other items. Office 2007 provides features that speed up editing by automatically finding text and objects in a document, thus making you more productive. Office 2007 provides the following three related operations that all use the Find and Replace dialog box:

- The *Find* command enables you to locate a word or group of words in a document quickly.

- The *Replace* command not only finds text quickly, it replaces a word or group of words with other text.

- The *Go To* command moves the insertion point to a specific location in the document.

Find locates a word or group of words in a document.

Replace not only finds text, it replaces a word or group of words with other text.

Go To moves the insertion point to a specific location in the document.

Find Text

To locate text in an Office file, choose the Find command in the Editing group on the Home tab and type the text you want to locate in the resulting dialog box, as shown in Figure 1.29. After you type the text to locate, you can find the next instance after the insertion point and work through the file until you find the instance of the text you were looking for. Alternatively, you can find all instances of the text in the file at one time. If you decide to find every instance at once, the Office application temporarily highlights each one, and the text stays highlighted until you perform another operation in the file.

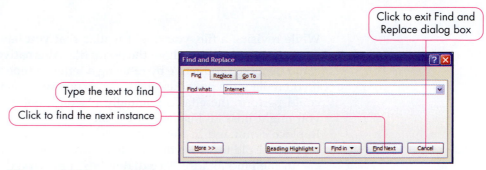

Click to exit Find and Replace dialog box

Type the text to find

Click to find the next instance

Figure 1.29 Find Tab of the Find and Replace Dialog Box

TIP Finding and Highlighting Text in Word

Sometimes, temporarily highlighting all instances of text is not sufficient to help you edit the text you find. If you want Word to find all instances of specific text in a document and keep the highlighting from disappearing until you want it to, you can use the Reading Highlight option in the Find dialog box. One nice feature of this option is that even though the text remains highlighted on the screen, the document prints normally without highlighting. Figure 1.30 shows the Find and Replace dialog box with the Reading Highlight options that you use to highlight or remove the highlight from a document.

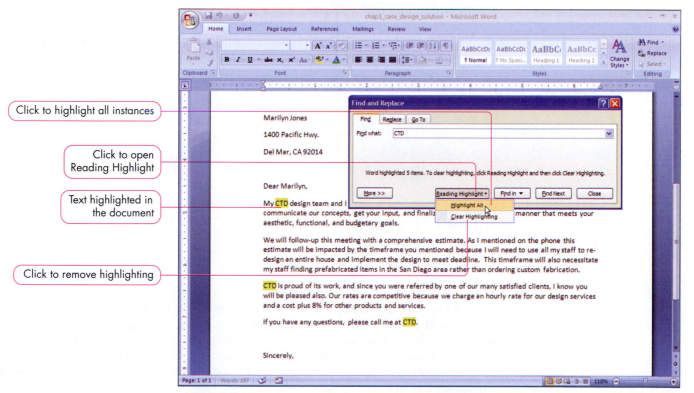

Click to highlight all instances

Click to open Reading Highlight

Text highlighted in the document

Click to remove highlighting

Figure 1.30 Find and Replace Dialog Box with Highlighting Options

Replace Text

While revising a file, you might realize that you have used an incorrect term and need to replace it throughout the entire file. Alternatively, you might realize that you could be more productive by re-using a letter or report that you polished and saved if you replace the previous client's or corporation's name with a new one. While you could perform these tasks manually, it would not be worth the time involved, and you might miss an instance of the old text, which could prove embarrassing. The Replace command in the Editing group on the Home tab can quickly and easily replace the old text with the new text throughout an entire file.

In the Find and Replace dialog box, first type the text to find, using the same process you used with the Find command. Second, type the text to replace the existing text with. Third, specify how you want Word to perform the operation. You can either replace each instance of the text individually, which can be time-consuming but allows you to decide whether to replace each instance one at a time, or you can replace every instance of the text in the document all at once. Word (but not the other Office applications) also provides options in the dialog box that help you replace only the correct text in the document. Click the More button to display these options. The most important one is the Find whole words only option. This option forces the application to find only complete words, not text that is part of other words. For instance, if you are searching for the word *off* to replace with other text, you would not want Word to replace the *off* in *office* with other text. Figure 1.31 shows these options along with the options for replacing text.

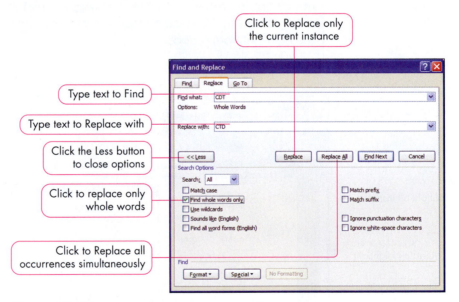

Figure 1.31 Find and Replace Dialog Box

Go Directly to a Location in a File

If you are editing a long document and want to move within it quickly, you can use the Go To command by clicking the down arrow on the Find command in the Editing group on the Home tab rather than slowly scrolling through an entire document or workbook. For example, if you want to move the insertion point to page 40 in a 200-page document, choose the Go To command and type 40 in the *Enter page number* text box. Notice the list of objects you can choose from in the Go to what section of the dialog box in Figure 1.32.

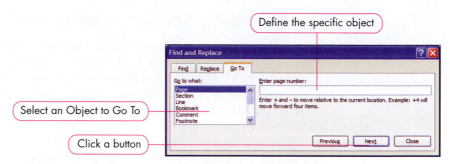

Figure 1.32 Go To Tab of the Find and Replace Dialog Box

Using the Undo and Redo Commands

The ***Undo*** command cancels your last one or more operations.

The ***Redo*** command reinstates or reverses an action performed by the Undo command.

As you create and edit files, you may perform an operation by mistake or simply change your mind about an edit you make. Office applications provide the ***Undo*** command, which can cancel your previous operation or even your last few operations. After using Undo to reverse an action or operation, you might decide that you want to use the ***Redo*** command to reinstate or reverse the action taken by the Undo command.

To undo the last action you performed, click Undo on the Quick Access Toolbar. For example, if you deleted text by mistake, immediately click Undo to restore it. If, however, you deleted some text and then performed several other operations, you can find the correct action to undo, with the understanding that all actions after that one will also be undone. To review a list of the last few actions you performed, click the Undo drop-down arrow and select the desired one from the list—Undo highlights all actions in the list down to that item and will undo all of the highlighted actions. Figure 1.33 shows a list of recent actions in PowerPoint. To reinstate or reverse an action as a result of using the Undo command, click Redo on the Quick Access Toolbar.

The ***Repeat*** command repeats only the last action you performed.

The ***Repeat*** command provides limited use because it repeats only the last action you performed. To repeat the last action, click Repeat on the Quick Access Toolbar. If the Office application is able to repeat your last action, the results will display in the document. Note that the Repeat command is replaced with the Redo command after you use the Undo command. For example, Figure 1.33 shows the Redo command after the Undo command has been used, and Figure 1.34 shows the Repeat command when Undo has not been used.

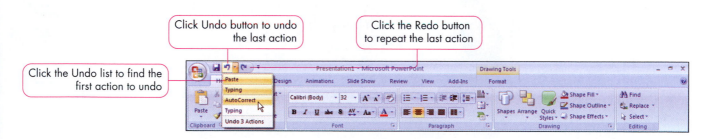

Figure 1.33 Undo and Redo Buttons

Using Language Tools

Documents, spreadsheets, and presentations represent the author, so remember that errors in writing can keep people from getting a desired job, or once on the job, can keep them from getting a desired promotion. To avoid holding yourself back, you should polish your final documents before submitting them electronically or as a hard copy. Office 2007 provides built-in proofing tools to help you fix spelling and grammar errors and help you locate the correct word or information.

Check Spelling and Grammar Automatically

By default, Office applications check spelling as you type and flag potential spelling errors by underlining them with a red wavy line. Word also flags potential grammar errors by underlining them with a green wavy line. You can fix these errors as you enter text, or you can ignore the errors and fix them all at once.

To fix spelling errors as you type, simply move the insertion point to a red wavy underlined word and correct the spelling yourself. If you spell the word correctly, the red wavy underline disappears. However, if you need help figuring out the correct spelling for the flagged word, then point to the error and right-click the mouse. The shortcut menu displays with possible corrections for the error. If you find the correction on the shortcut menu, click it to replace the word in the document. To fix grammar errors, follow the same process, but when the shortcut menu displays, you can choose to view more information to see rules that apply to the potential error. Notice the errors flagged in Figure 1.34. Note that the Mini toolbar also displays automatically.

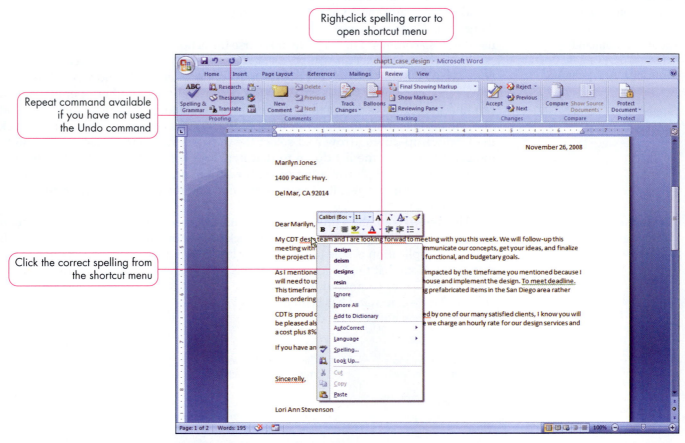

Figure 1.34 Automatic Spell and Grammar Check

Check Spelling and Grammar at Once

Some people prefer to wait until they complete typing the entire document and then check spelling and grammar at once. To check for errors, click Spelling & Grammar in Word (Spelling in Excel or PowerPoint) in the Proofing group on the Review tab. As the checking proceeds through the file and detects any spelling or grammar errors, it displays the Spelling dialog box if you are using Excel or PowerPoint, or the Spelling and Grammar dialog box in Word. You can either correct or ignore the changes that the Spelling checker proposes to your document. For example, Figure 1.35 shows the Spelling and Grammar dialog box with a misspelled word in the top section and Word's suggestions in the bottom section. Select the correction from the list and change the current instance, or you can change all instances of the error throughout the document. However, sometimes the flagged word might be a specialized term or a person's name, so if the flagged word is not a spelling error, you can ignore it once in the current document or throughout the entire document; further, you could add the word to the spell-check list so that it never flags that spelling again.

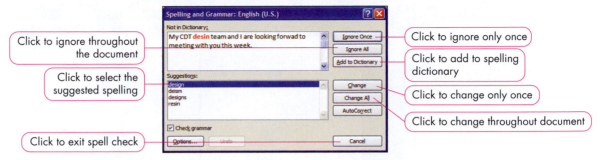

Click to ignore throughout the document

Click to select the suggested spelling

Click to exit spell check

Click to ignore only once

Click to add to spelling dictionary

Click to change only once

Click to change throughout document

Figure 1.35 Spelling and Grammar Dialog Box

TIP   Proofreading Your Document

The spelling and grammar checks available in Word provide great help improving your documents. However, you should not forget that you still have to proofread your document to ensure that the writing is clear, appropriate for the intended audience, and makes sense.

Use the Thesaurus

As you edit a document, spreadsheet, or presentation, you might want to improve your writing by finding a better or different word for a particular situation. For example, say you are stuck and cannot think of a better word for *big*, and you would like to find an alternative word that means the same. Word, Excel, and PowerPoint provide a built-in thesaurus, which is an electronic version of a book of synonyms. Synonyms are different words with the same or similar meaning, and antonyms are words with the opposite meaning.

The easiest method for accessing the Thesaurus is to point to the word in the file that you want to find an alternative for and right-click the mouse. When the shortcut menu displays, point to Synonyms, and the program displays a list of alternatives. Notice the shortcut menu and list of synonyms in Figure 1.36. To select one of the alternative words on the list, click it, and the word you select replaces the original word. If you do not see an alternative on the list that you want to use and you want to investigate further, click Thesaurus on the shortcut menu to open the full Thesaurus.

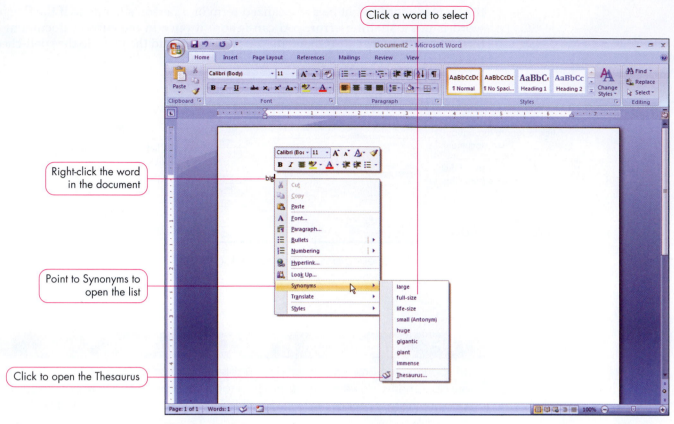

Click a word to select

Right-click the word in the document

Point to Synonyms to open the list

Click to open the Thesaurus

Figure 1.36   Shortcut Menu with Synonyms

An alternative method for opening the full Thesaurus is to place the insertion point in the word you want to look up, and then click the Thesaurus command in the Proofing group on the Review tab. The Thesaurus opens with alternatives for the selected word. You can use one of the words presented in the pane, or you can look up additional words. If you do not find the word you want, use the Search option to find more alternatives. Figure 1.37 shows the Thesaurus.

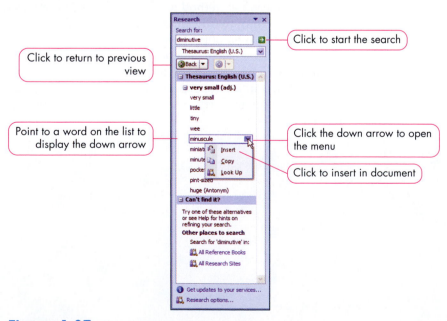

Click to start the search

Click to return to previous view

Point to a word on the list to display the down arrow

Click the down arrow to open the menu

Click to insert in document

Figure 1.37   The Thesaurus

Conduct Research

As you work in Word, Excel, or PowerPoint, you might need to find the definition of a word or look up an item in the encyclopedia to include accurate information. Office 2007 provides quick access to research tools. To access research tools, click the Research button in the Proofing group on the Review tab. Notice in Figure 1.38 that you can specify what you want to research and specify where to Search. Using this feature, you can choose from reference books, research sites, and business and financial sites.

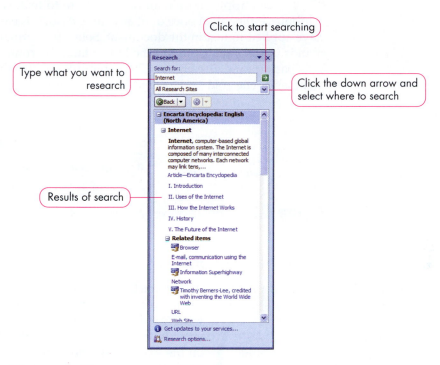

Figure 1.38 Research Task Pane

> ### TIP Avoiding Plagiarism
>
> If you use the research feature in Office to find information in an encyclopedia or in other locations to help you create your document, then you need to credit the source of that information. Avoid the problem of plagiarism, which is borrowing other people's words or ideas, by citing all sources that you use. You might want to check with your instructor for the exact format for citing sources.

Applying Font Attributes

Taking the time to format text helps the reader find important information in the document by making it stand out and helps the reader understand the message by emphasizing key items.

After you have edited a document, you might want to improve its visual appeal by formatting the text. *Formatting text* changes an individual letter, a word, or a body of selected text. Taking the time to format text helps the reader find important information in the document by making it stand out and helps the reader understand the message by emphasizing key items. You can format the text in the document by changing the following font attributes:

Formatting text changes an individual letter, a word, or a body of selected text.

- font face or size
- font attributes such as bold, underline, or italic
- font color

The Font group on the Home tab—available in Word, Excel, PowerPoint, and Access—provides many formatting options, and Office provides two methods for applying these font attributes:

- Choose the font attributes first, and then type the text. The text displays in the document with the formatting.
- Type the text, select the text to format, and choose the font attributes. The selected text displays with the formatting.

You can apply more than one attribute to text, so you can select one or more attributes either all at once or at any time. Also, it is easy to see which attributes you have applied to text in the document. Select the formatted text and look at the commands in the Font group on the Home tab. The commands in effect display with a gold background. See Figure 1.39. To remove an effect from text, select it and click the command. The gold background disappears for attributes that are no longer in effect.

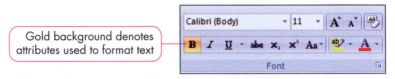

Gold background denotes attributes used to format text

Figure 1.39 Font Group of the Home tab

Change the Font

A *font* is a named set of characters with the same design.

A *font* is a named set of characters with the same design, and Office 2007 provides many built-in fonts for you to choose from. Remember that more is not always better when applied to fonts, so limit the number of font changes in your document. Additionally, the choice of a font should depend on the intent of the document and should never overpower the message. For example, using a fancy or highly stylized font that may be difficult to read for a client letter might seem odd to the person receiving it and overpower the intended message.

> Remember that more is not always better when applied to fonts, so limit the number of font changes in your document.

One powerful feature of Office 2007 that can help you decide how a font will look in your document is Live Preview. First, select the existing text, and then click the drop-down arrow on the Font list in the Font group on the Home tab. As you point to a font name in the list, Live Preview changes the selected text in the document to that font. Figure 1.40 shows the selected text displaying in a different font as a result of Live Preview.

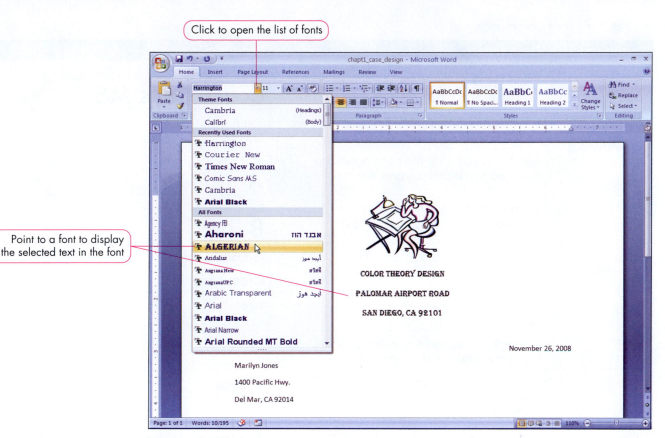

Figure 1.40 Font List

Change the Font Size, Color, and Attributes

Besides changing the font, you also can change the size, color, and other attributes of text in a document. Because these formatting operations are used so frequently, Office places many of these commands in several places for easy access:

- in the Font group on the Home tab
- on the Mini toolbar
- in the Font dialog box

Table 1.9 describes the commands that display in the Font group of the Home tab and in the Font dialog box.

Table 1.9 Font Commands

Command	Description	Example
Font	Enables you to designate the font.	Arial Comic Sans MS
Font Size	Enables you to designate an exact font size.	Size 8 Size 18
Grow Font	Each time you click the command, the selected text increases one size.	A A
Shrink Font	Each time you click the command, the selected text decreases one size.	B B
Clear Formatting	Removes all formatting from the selected text.	*Formatted* Cleared
Bold	Makes the text darker than the surrounding text.	**Bold**
Italic	Places the selected text in italic, that is, slants the letters to the right.	*Italic*
Underline	Places a line under the text. Click the drop-down arrow to change the underline style.	Underline
Strikethrough	Draws a line through the middle of the text.	~~Strikethrough~~
Subscript	Places selected text below the baseline.	Sub$_{script}$
Superscript	Places selected text above the line of letters.	Super^{script}
Change Case	Changes the case of the selected text. Click the drop-down arrow to select the desired case.	lowercase UPPERCASE
Text Highlight Color	Makes selected text look like it was highlighted with a marker pen. Click the drop-down arrow to change color and other options.	Highlighted
Font Color	Changes the color of selected text. Click the drop-down arrow to change colors.	Font Color

If you have several formatting changes to make, click the Dialog Box Launcher in the Font group on the Home tab to display the Font dialog box. The Font dialog box is handy because all the formatting features display in one location, and it provides additional options such as changing the underline color. Figure 1.41 shows the Font dialog box in Word.

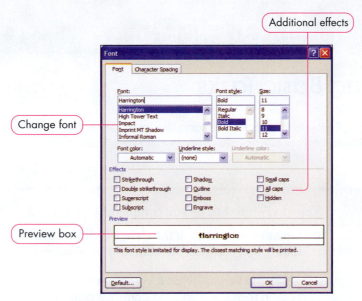

Figure 1.41 Font Dialog Box

Copying Formats with the Format Painter

After formatting text in one part of a document, you might want to apply that same formatting to other text in a different location in the document. You could try to remember all the formatting options you selected, but that process would be time-consuming and could produce inconsistent results. Office 2007 provides a shortcut method called the *Format Painter*, which copies the formatting of text from one location to another.

The ***Format Painter*** copies the formatting of text from one location to another.

Select the formatted text you want to copy and click the Format Painter in the Clipboard group on the Home tab to copy the format. Single-click the command to turn it on to copy formatting to one location—the option turns off automatically after one copy—or double-click the command to turn it on for unlimited format copying—you must press Esc on the keyboard to turn it off.

Hands-On Exercises

3 | Performing Basic Tasks

Skills covered: 1. Cut, Copy, Paste, and Undo **2.** Find and Replace Text **3.** Check Spelling **4.** Choose Synonyms and Use Thesaurus **5.** Use the Research Tool **6.** Apply Font Attributes **7.** Use Format Painter

Step 1 **Cut, Copy, Paste, and Undo**	Refer to Figure 1.42 as you complete Steps 1 and 2. **a.** Open Word and click the **Office Button**, click **Open**, and then using the Open dialog box features, navigate to your classroom file location. **TROUBLESHOOTING:** If you have trouble finding the file, remember to use the Look in feature to find the correct location. **b.** Select the file *chap1_ho3_internet* and click the **Open** button. The Word document displays on the screen. **c.** Click the **Office Button** and select **Save As**. If necessary, use the **Look in** feature to change to the location where you save files. The Save As dialog box displays. **d.** Type the new file name, **chap1_ho3_internet_solution**, be sure that *Word Document* displays in the *Save as type* box, and click **Save**. The file is saved with the new name. **e.** Click to place the insertion point at the beginning of the second sentence in the first paragraph. Type **These developments brought together**, and then press **Spacebar**. The text moves to the right, making room for the new inserted text. **f.** Press and hold down **Ctrl** as you click this sentence below the heading The World Wide Web: *The Netscape browser led in user share until Microsoft Internet Explorer took the lead in 1999.* **g.** Click **Cut** in the Clipboard group on the Home tab. The text disappears from the document. **h.** Move the insertion point to the end of the last paragraph and click **Paste** in the Clipboard group on the Home tab. The text displays in the new location. **i.** Reselect the sentence you just moved and click **Copy** in the Clipboard group on the Home tab. **j.** Move the insertion point to the end of the first paragraph beginning *The idea* and click the right mouse button. The shortcut menu displays. **k.** Select **Paste** from the shortcut menu. The text remains in the original position and is copied to the second location. **l.** Click **Undo** on the Quick Access Toolbar to undo the last paste.

Refer to Figure 1.42 to complete Step 2.

a. Press **Ctrl + Home** to move the insertion point to the beginning of the document. Click **Replace** in the Editing group on the Home tab.

The Find and Replace dialog box displays.

b. Type **Internet** in the *Find what* box and type **World Wide Web** in the *Replace with* box.

c. Click the **Replace All** button. Click **OK** to close the information box that informs you that Word has made seven replacements. Click **Close** to close the Find and Replace dialog box.

All instances of Internet have been replaced with World Wide Web in the document.

d. Click **Undo** on the Quick Access Toolbar.

All instances of *World Wide Web* have changed back to *Internet* in the document.

e. Click **Replace** in the Editing group on the Home tab.

The Find and Replace dialog box displays with the text you typed still in the boxes.

f. Click the **Find Next** button.

The first instance of the text *Internet* is highlighted.

g. Click the **Replace** button.

The first instance of Internet is replaced with World Wide Web, and the next instance of Internet is highlighted.

h. Click the **Find Next** button.

The highlight moves to the next instance of Internet without changing the previous one.

i. Click the **Close** button to close the Find and Replace dialog box.

The Find and Replace dialog box closes.

The World Wide Web

By Linda Ericksen

The idea of a big computer network that would allow communicatin among users of various computers developed over time. These developments brought together the network of networks known as the Internet, which included both technological developments and the merging together of existing network infrastructure and telecommunication systems. This network provides users with email, chat, file transfer, Web pages and other files.

History of Internet

In 1957, the Soviet Union lanched the first satellite, Sputnik I, triggering President Dwight Eisenhower to create the ARPA agency to regain the technological lead in the arms race. Practical implementations of a large computer network began during the late 1960's and 1970's. By the 1980's, technologies we now recognise as the basis of the modern Internet began to spread over the globe.

In 1990, ARPANET was replaced by NSFNET which connected universities in North America, and later research facilities in Europe

were added. Use of the Internet exploded after 1990, causing the US Government to transfer management to independent orginizations.

The World Wide Web

The World Wide Web was developed in the 1980's in Europe and then rapidly spread around the world. The World Wide Web is a set of linked documents on computers connected by the Internet. These documents make use of hyperliks to link documents together. To use hyperlinks, browser software was developed. The Netscape browser led in user share until Microsoft Internet Explorer took the lead in 1999

Browsers

The first widely used web browser was Mosaic, and the programming team went on to develop the first commercial web browser called Netscape Navigator.

Figure 1.42 Edited Document (Shown in Full Screen Reading View)

13. Word flags misspelled words by marking them with which one of the following?

    (a) A green wavy underline

    (b) Boldfacing them

    (c) A red wavy underline

    (d) A double-underline in black

14. Which of the following displays when you select text in a document?

    (a) The Mini toolbar

    (b) The Quick Access Toolbar

    (c) A shortcut menu

    (d) The Ribbon

15. Formatting text allows you to change which of the following text attributes?

    (a) The font

    (b) The font size

    (c) The font type

    (d) All of the above

Practice Exercises

1 Using Help and Print Preview in Access 2007

a. Open Access. Click the **Office Button**, and then select **Open**. Use the Look in feature to find the *chap1_pe1* database, and then click **Open**.

b. At the right side of the Ribbon, click the **Help** button. In the Help window, type **table** in the **Type words to search for** box. Click the **Search** button.

c. Click the topic *Create a Table*. Browse the content of the Help window, and then click the **Close** button in the Help window.

d. Double-click the **Courses table** in the left pane. The table opens in Datasheet view.

e. Click the **Office Button**, point to the arrow after the **Print** command, and select **Print Preview** to open the Print Preview window with the Courses table displayed.

f. Point the mouse pointer on the table and click to magnify the display. Compare your screen to Figure 1.45.

g. Click the **Close Print Preview** button on the Print Preview tab.

h. Click the **Office Button**, and then click the **Exit Access button**.

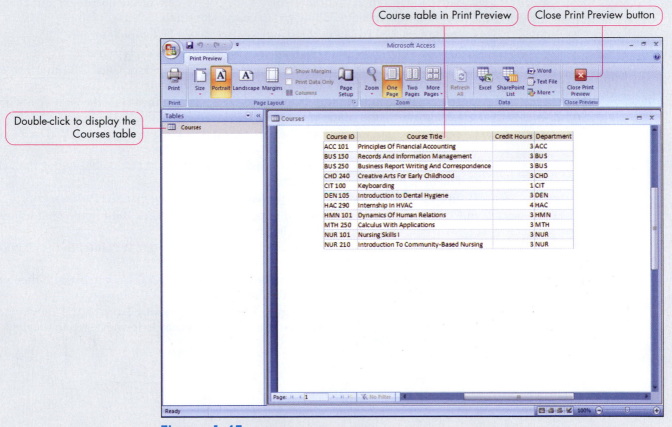

Figure 1.45 Access Print Preview

...continued on Next Page

2 Avoiding Fraud Report

As part of your Introduction to Computers course, you have prepared an oral report on phishing. You want to provide class members with a handout that summarizes the main points of your report. This handout is in the rough stages, so you need to edit it, and you also realize that you can format some of the text to emphasize the main points.

a. Start Word. Click the **Office Button**, and then select **Open**. Use the *Look in* feature to find the *chap1_pe2* document, and then click **Open**.

b. Click the **Office Button**, and then select **Save As**. In the *File name* box, type the document name, **chap1_pe2_solution**, be sure that Word document displays in the *Save as type* box, and use the *Look in* option to move to the location where you save your class files. Click **Save**.

c. In the document, click after the word Name and type **your name**.

d. Select your name, and then click **Bold** and **Italic** on the Mini toolbar—remember to point to the Mini toolbar to make it display fully. Your name displays in bold and italic.

e. Move the insertion point immediately before the title of the document and click the **Replace** button in the Editing group on the Home tab.

f. In the *Find what* box of the Find and Replace dialog box, type **internet**.

g. In the *Replace with* box of the Find and Replace dialog box, type **email**.

h. Click the **Replace All** button to have Word replace the text. Click **OK**, and then click **Close** to close the dialog boxes.

i. To format the title of the document, first select it, and then click the **Font arrow** in the Font group on the Home tab to display the available fonts.

j. Scroll down and choose the **Impact** font if you have it; otherwise, use one that is available.

k. Place the insertion point in the word *Phishng*. Right-click the word, and then click **Phishing** from the shortcut menu.

l. To emphasize important text in the list, double-click the first **NOT** to select it.

m. Click the **Font Color** arrow and select Red, and then click **Bold** in the Font group on the Home tab to apply bold to the text.

n. With the first instance of NOT selected, double-click **Format Painter** in the Clipboard group on the Home tab.

o. Double-click the second and then the third instance of **NOT** in the list, and then press **Esc** on the keyboard to turn off the Format Painter.

p. Compare your document to Figure 1.46. Save by clicking **Save** on the Quick Access Toolbar. Close the document and exit Word or proceed to the next step to preview and print the document.

...continued on Next Page

Email Scams

Name: *Student name*

Phishing is fraudulent activity that uses email to scam unsuspecting victims into providing personal information. This information includes credit card numbers, social security numbers, and other sensitive information that allows criminals to defraud people.

If you receive an email asking you to verify an account number, update information, confirm your identity to avoid fraud, or provide other information, close the email immediately. The email may even contain a link to what appears at first glance to be your actual banking institution or credit card institution. However, many of these fraudsters are so adept that they create look-alike Web sites to gather information for criminal activity. Follow these steps:

Do **NOT** click any links.

Do **NOT** open any attachments.

Do **NOT** reply to the email.

Close the email immediately.

Call your bank or credit card institution immediately to report the scam.

Delete the email.

Remember, never provide any information without checking the source of the request.

Figure 1.46 Phishing Document

3 Previewing and Printing a Document

You created a handout to accompany your oral presentation in the previous exercise. Now you want to print it out so that you can distribute it.

    a. If necessary, open the *chap1_pe2_solution* document that you saved in the previous exercise.
    b. Click the **Office Button**, point to the arrow after the Print command, and select **Print Preview** to open the Print Preview window with the document displayed.

...continued on Next Page

c. Point the mouse pointer in the document and click to magnify the display. Click the mouse pointer a second time to reduce the display.

d. To change the orientation of the document, click **Orientation** in the Page Setup group and choose **Landscape**.

e. Click **Undo** on the Quick Access Toolbar to undo the last command, which returns the document to portrait orientation. Compare your results to the zoomed document in Figure 1.47.

f. Click **Print** on the Print Preview tab to display the Print dialog box.

g. Click **OK** to print the document.

h. Close the document without saving it.

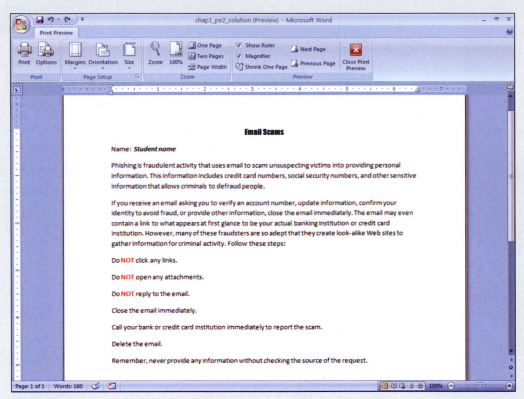

Figure 1.47 Document in Print Preview Window

4 Editing a Promotion Flyer

You work for Business Express, formerly known as Print Express, a regional company specializing in business centers that design and produce documents for local businesses and individuals. Business Express has just undergone a major transition along with a name change. Your job is to edit and refine an existing flyer to inform customers of the new changes. Proceed as follows:

a. Open Word. Click the **Office Button**, and then select **Open**. Use the *Look in* feature to find the *chap1_pe4* document.

b. Click the **Office Button** again and select **Save As**. Type the document name, **chap1_pe4_solution**, be sure that Word document displays in the *Save as type* box, and use the *Look in* option to move to the location where you save your class files.

c. Place the insertion point at the beginning of the document, and then click **Spelling & Grammar** in the Proofing group on the Review tab to open the Spelling and Grammar dialog box.

d. Click the **Change** button three times to correct the spelling errors. Click **OK** to close the completion box.

...continued on Next Page

e. Place the insertion point at the end of the first sentence of the document—just before the period. To insert the following text, press **Spacebar** and type **that offers complete business solutions**.

f. Place the insertion point in *good* in the first sentence of the third paragraph and right-click the mouse.

g. Point to **Synonyms**, and then click **first-rate** to replace the word in the document.

h. Place the insertion point in *bigger* in the last sentence of the third paragraph and click **Thesaurus** in the Proofing group on the Review tab. Point to **superior** and click the drop-down arrow that displays. Click **Insert** from the menu to replace the word in the document, and then click the **Close** button on the Thesaurus.

i. Select the last full paragraph of the document and click **Cut** in the Clipboard group on the Home tab to remove the paragraph from the document.

j. Place the insertion point at the beginning of the new last paragraph and click **Paste** in the Clipboard group on the Home tab to display the text.

k. Click **Undo** on the Quick Access Toolbar twice to undo the paste operation and to undo the cut operation—placing the text back in its original location.

l. Place the insertion point after the colon at the bottom of the document and type **your name**.

m. Compare your results to Figure 1.48, and then save and close the document.

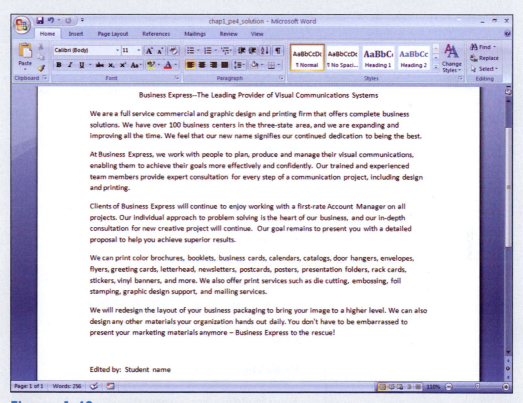

Figure 1.48 Business Flyer

Mid-Level Exercises

1 Updating a Training Document

Your position as trainer for a large building supply company involves training all new employees. It is your job to familiarize new employees with the services provided by Castle Home Building Supply. You distribute a list at the training session and you realize that it needs updating before the next session, so you decide to edit and format it.

a. Start Word. Open the *chap1_mid1* file and save it as **chap1_mid1_solution**.

b. Change the title font to Arial Rounded MT Bold size 16 and change the font color to dark brown.

c. Make the subtitle Arial Unicode MS and italic.

d. Cut the item *Help with permits* and make it the second item on the list.

e. In the first list item, insert **and** after the word *fair*.

f. Change the word *help* in the last list item to **Assistance**.

g. Select the list of items excluding the heading, Services Provided.

h. Bold the list and change the font size to 16.

i. Save the document and compare it to Figure 1.49.

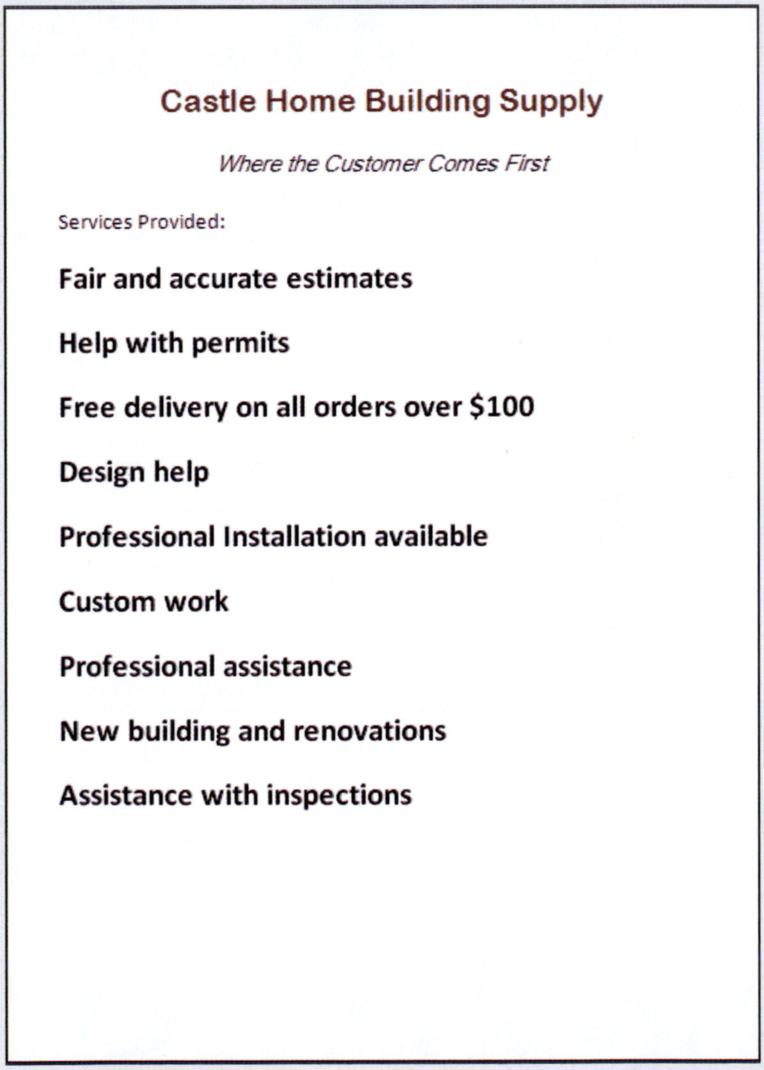

Castle Home Building Supply

Where the Customer Comes First

Services Provided:

Fair and accurate estimates

Help with permits

Free delivery on all orders over $100

Design help

Professional Installation available

Custom work

Professional assistance

New building and renovations

Assistance with inspections

Figure 1.49 Training Document

...continued on Next Page

The owner of the Bayside Restaurant wants your help formatting his menu so that it is more pleasing to customers; follow the steps below:

a. Open the *chap1_mid2* document and save it as **chap1_mid2_solution**.

b. Format the menu title as Broadway size 16.

c. Format the three headings: Appetizers, Soups and Salads, and Lunch or Dinner Anytime! as Bodoni MT Black, size 12, and change the font color to Dark Red. Remember to format the first one and use the Format Painter for the second two headings.

d. Format all the dish names, such as Nachos, using the Outline Font Effects.

e. Bold all the prices in the document.

f. Preview the document, compare to Figure 1.50, and then print it.

g. Save and close the document.

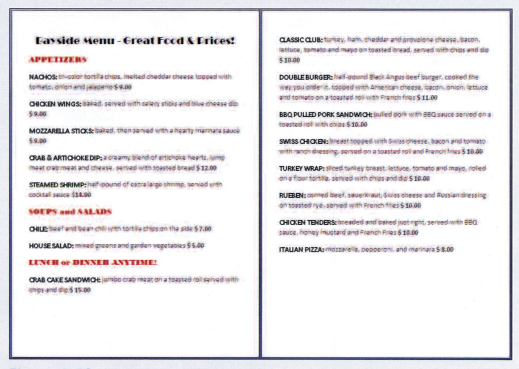

Figure 1.50 The Formatted Menu

...continued on Next Page

Your job duties at Health First Insurance, Inc., involve maintaining the correspondence. You need to update the welcome letter you send to clients to reflect the company's new name, new address, and other important elements, and then address it to a new client. Proceed as follows.

a. Open the *chap1_mid3* document and save it as **chap1_mid3_solution**.

b. Run the Spelling check to eliminate the errors.

c. Use Replace to change **University Insurance, Inc.** to **Health First Insurance, Inc**. throughout the letter.

d. Change the Address from **123 Main St**. to **1717 N. Zapata Way**.

e. Change the inside address that now has **Client name, Client Address, Client City, State and Zip Code** to **your name and complete address**. Also change the salutation to your name.

f. Move the first paragraph so that it becomes the last paragraph in the body of the letter.

g. Preview the letter to be sure that it fits on one page, compare it with Figure 1.51, and then print it.

h. Save and close the document.

Health First Insurance, Inc.

1717 N. Zapata Way

Laredo, TX 78043

Student name

Student Address

Student City, State, and Zip Code

Dear Student name:

Welcome to the Health First Insurance, Inc. We have received and accepted your application and premium for health insurance. Please detach and the ID cards attached to this letter and keep with you at all times for identification, reference and access to emergency phone assistance and Pre Notification numbers in the event of a claim.

Enclosed you will find a Certificate of Coverage detailing the benefits, limits, exclusions and provisions of the Health First Insurance, Inc. Medical Plan. Please review the Certificate of Coverage thoroughly and contact us if you have any questions regarding the terms and provisions.

In order for you and your dependents to receive adequate medical treatment and for your assistance, the Health First Insurance, Inc. Medical Plan requires any insured (or someone on their behalf) to Pre-notify Health First Insurance, Inc., for any hospital admission prior to admittance (or within 36 hours after an emergency admission). Additionally, the Health First Insurance, Inc. Medical Plan requires all insured to utilize the provider network.

We appreciate your confidence in our organization and look forward to serving your insurance needs.

Sincerely,

Maria Fernandez

Agent

Health First Insurance, Inc.

Figure 1.51 The Updated Letter

Capstone Exercise

In this project, you work with a business plan for Far East Trading Company that will be submitted to funding sources in order to secure loans. The document requires editing to polish the final product and formatting to enhance readability and emphasize important information.

Editing the Document

This document is ready for editing, so proceed as follows:

a. Open the *chap1_cap* document. Save the document as **chap1_cap_solution**.

b. Run the Spelling and Grammar check to eliminate all spelling and grammar errors in the document.

c. Use the Thesaurus to find a synonym for the word **unique** in the second paragraph of the document.

d. Use the Go To command to move to page 3 and change the $175,000 to $250,000.

e. Move the entire second section of the document (notice the numbers preceding it) now located at the end of the document to its correct location after the first section.

f. Insert the street **1879 Columbia Ave.** before Portland in the first paragraph.

g. Copy the inserted street address to section 2.3 and place it in front of Portland there also.

h. Replace the initials **FET** with **FETC** for every instance in the document.

i. Type over 1998 in the third paragraph so that it says 2008.

Formatting the Document

Next, you will apply formatting techniques to the document. These format options will further increase the readability and attractiveness of your document.

a. Select the two-line title and change the font to Engravers MT, size 14, and change the color to Dark Red.

b. Select the first heading in the document: 1.0 Executive Summary, then change the font to Gautami, bold, and change the color to Dark Blue.

c. Use the Format Painter to make all the main numbered headings the same formatting, that is 2.0, 3.0, 4.0, and 5.0.

d. The first three numbered sections have subsections such as 1.1, 1.2. Select the heading 1.1 and format it for bold, italic, and change the color to a lighter blue—Aqua, Accents, Darker 25%.

e. Use the Format Painter to make all the numbered subsections the same formatting.

Printing the Document

To finish the job, you need to print the business plan.

a. Preview the document to check your results.

b. Print the document.

c. Save your changes and close the document.

Mini Cases

Use the rubric following the case as a guide to evaluate our work, but keep in mind that your instructor may impose additional grading criteria or use a different standard to judge your work.

A Thank-You Letter

GENERAL CASE

As the new volunteer coordinator for Special Olympics in your area, you need to send out information for prospective volunteers, and the letter you were given needs editing and formatting. Open the *chap1_mc1* document and make necessary changes to improve the appearance. You should use Replace to change the text (insert your state name), use the current date and your name and address information, format to make the letter more appealing, and eliminate all errors. Your finished document should be saved as **chap1_mc1_solution**.

Performance Elements	Exceeds Expectations	Meets Expectations	Below Expectations
Corrected all errors	Document contains no errors.	Document contains minimal errors.	Document contains several errors.
Use of character formatting features such as font, font size, font color, or other attributes	Used character formatting options throughout entire document.	Used character formatting options in most sections of document.	Used character formatting options on a small portion of document.
Inserted text where instructed	The letter is complete with all required information inserted.	The letter is mostly complete.	Letter is incomplete. .

The Information Request Letter

RESEARCH CASE

Search the Internet for opportunities to teach abroad or for internships available in your major. Have fun finding a dream opportunity. Use the address information you find on the Web site that interests you, and compose a letter asking for additional information. For example, you might want to teach English in China, so search for that information. Your finished document should be saved as **chap1_mc2_solution**.

Performance Elements	Exceeds Expectations	Meets Expectations	Below Expectations
Use of character formatting	Three or more character formats applied to text.	One or two character formats applied to text.	Does not apply character formats to text.
Language tools	No spelling or grammar errors.	One spelling or grammar error.	More than one spelling or grammar error.
Presentation	Information is easy to read and understand.	Information is somewhat unclear.	Letter is unclear.

Movie Memorabilia

DISASTER RECOVERY

Use the following rubrics to guide your evaluation of your work, but keep in mind that your instructor may impose additional grading criteria.

Open the *chap1_mc3* document that can be found in the Exploring folder. The advertising document is over-formatted, and it contains several errors and problems. For example, the text has been formatted in many fonts that are difficult to read. The light color of the text also has made the document difficult to read. You should improve the formatting so that it is consistent, helps the audience read the document, and is pleasing to look at. Your finished document should be saved as **chap1_mc3_solution**.

Performance Elements	Exceeds Expectations	Meets Expectations	Below Expectations
Type of font chosen to format document	Number and style of fonts appropriate for short document.	Number or style of fonts appropriate for short document.	Overused number of fonts or chose inappropriate font.
Color of font chosen to format document	Appropriate font colors for document.	Most font colors appropriate.	Overuse of font colors.
Overall document appeal	Document looks appealing.	Document mostly looks appealing.	Did not improve document much.

Introduction to Excel

What Can I Do with a Spreadsheet?

 **bjectives**

After you read this chapter, you will be able to:

1. Define worksheets and workbooks (**page 72**).
2. Use spreadsheets across disciplines (**page 72**).
3. Plan for good workbook and worksheet design (**page 73**).
4. Identify Excel window components (**page 75**).
5. Enter and edit data in cells (**page 80**).
6. Describe and use symbols and the order of precedence (**page 86**).
7. Display cell formulas (**page 88**).
8. Insert and delete rows and columns (**page 89**).
9. Use cell ranges; Excel move; copy, paste, paste special; and AutoFill (**page 90**).
10. Manage worksheets (**page 98**).
11. Format worksheets (**page 99**).
12. Select page setup options for printing (**page 111**).
13. Manage cell comments (**page 114**).

Hands-On Exercises

Exercises	Skills Covered
1. INTRODUCTION TO MICROSOFT EXCEL (page 82) **Open:** none **Save as:** chap1_ho1_jake_solution.xlsx	• Plan Your Workbook • Start Microsoft Office Excel 2007 • Enter and Edit Data in Cells • Use the Save As Command and Explore the Worksheet
2. JAKE'S GYM CONTINUED (page 93) **Open:** chap1_ho2_jake.xlsx **Save as:** chap1_ho2_jake_solution.xlsx	• Open an Existing Workbook • Use Save As to Save an Existing Workbook • Insert a Row and Compute Totals • Copy the Formulas • Continue the Calculations • Insert a Column
3. FORMATTING JAKE'S GYM WORKSHEET (page 105) **Open:** chap1_ho2_jake_solution.xlsx (from Exercise 2) **Save as:** chap1_ho3_jake_solution (additional modifications)	• Manage the Workbook • Apply Number Formats • Apply Font Attributes and Borders • Change Alignment Attributes • Insert an Image
4. PRINTING JAKE'S GYM WORKSHEET (page 115) **Open:** chap1_ho3_jake_solution (from Exercise 3) **Save as:** chap1_ho4_jake_solution (additional modifications)	• Insert a Comment • Insert Custom Header and Footer • Format to Print the Worksheet

CASE STUDY

Weddings by Grace

Grace Galia is a wedding consultant who specializes in all aspects of wedding planning for her clients. Although more and more couples are striving to cut costs by handling most of the planning on their own, Grace is successfully growing her business based on a proven history of superbly run events resulting in many happy newlyweds. She offers her clients a complete wedding package that includes the cocktail hour, dinner, and beverage (including alcohol). The client chooses the type of dinner (e.g., chicken, salmon, filet mignon, or some combination), which determines the cost per guest, and specifies the number of guests, and then the cost of the reception is obtained by simple multiplication.

Case Study

Grace provides a detailed budget to all of her clients that divides the cost of a wedding into three major categories—the ceremony, the reception (based on the package selected), and other items such as music and photography. She asks each client for their total budget, and then works closely with the client to allocate that amount over the myriad items that will be necessary. Grace promises to take the stress out of planning, and she advertises a turnkey operation, from invitations to thank-you notes. She assures her clients that their needs will be met without the clients overextending themselves financially. Grace has asked you, her manager trainee, to complete her worksheet comparing the two wedding plans she offers her clients.

Your Assignment

- Read the chapter carefully, focusing on spreadsheet formulas and basic spreadsheet commands.
- Open *chap1_case_wedding*, which contains the partially completed worksheet, and save it as **chap1_case_wedding_solution**.
- Insert formulas to calculate the cost of the reception in both options.
- Use appropriate formulas to calculate the difference in cost for each item in the two options.
- Copy the total formula to the difference column.
- Format cells as currency with no decimals. Widen or narrow columns as necessary to conform to good design principles.
- Emphasize totals with borders and separate the categories with a complimentary fill color.
- Merge and center rows 1 and 2 so the headings are centered over the worksheet. Change the font, font color, and font size to match your design.
- Insert an appropriate image in the space indicated. You may have to resize to fit.
- Emphasize the category headings.
- Add your name and today's date to the worksheet.
- Choose the options you need to set from the Page Setup dialog box.

Introduction to Spreadsheets

After word processing, a spreadsheet program is the second most common software application in use. The most popular spreadsheet program used in businesses and organizations around the world is Microsoft Excel. A **spreadsheet** is the computerized equivalent of a ledger. It is a grid of rows and columns enabling users to organize data, recalculate results for cells containing formulas when any data in input cells change, and make decisions based on quantitative data. A **spreadsheet program** is a computer application, such as Microsoft Excel, that you use to build and manipulate electronic spreadsheets. The spreadsheet has become a much more powerful tool since the first spreadsheet program, VisiCalc, was introduced in 1979.

Before the introduction of spreadsheet software, people used ledgers to track expenses and other quantitative data. Ledgers have been the basis of accounting for hundreds of years, but the accountant was always faced with the issue of making changes to correct errors or update values. The major issue, however, was the time and work involved in changing the ledger and manually calculating the results again. Figure 1.1 shows an edited ledger page that had to be recalculated. A spreadsheet makes these changes in a significantly shorter period of time and, if the data and formulas are correct, does not make errors. Any area that has numeric data is a potential area of application for a spreadsheet. Herein lies the advantage of the electronic spreadsheet: quicker, more accurate changes than were possible with a manual ledger. Further, the use of formulas and functions in Excel, along with the ability to easily copy these formulas, adds to the program's functionality and power. Figure 1.2 shows an electronic spreadsheet, and Figure 1.3 shows that the results are automatically recalculated after changing the unit price.

> A spreadsheet makes these changes in a significantly shorter period of time and, if the data and formulas are correct, does not make errors.

Changes made manually

		1	2	3	4	5	6	
1	UNIT PRICE		22 / 20					1
2	UNIT SALES		1,200					2
3	GROSS PROFIT		24,000 / 264					3
4								4
5	EXPENSES							5
6	PRODUCTION		10,000					6
7	DISTRIBUTION		1,200					7
8	MARKETING		5,000					8
9	OVERHEAD		3,000					9
10	TOTAL EXPENSES		19,200					10
11			72					11
12	NET PROFIT		4,800					12

Figure 1.1 Ledger

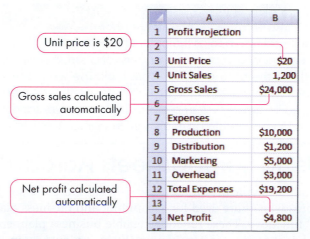

Unit price is $20

Gross sales calculated automatically

Net profit calculated automatically

	A	B
1	Profit Projection	
2		
3	Unit Price	$20
4	Unit Sales	1,200
5	Gross Sales	$24,000
6		
7	Expenses	
8	Production	$10,000
9	Distribution	$1,200
10	Marketing	$5,000
11	Overhead	$3,000
12	Total Expenses	$19,200
13		
14	Net Profit	$4,800

Figure 1.2 Original Spreadsheet

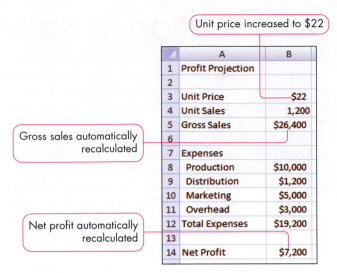

Unit price increased to $22

Gross sales automatically recalculated

Net profit automatically recalculated

	A	B
1	Profit Projection	
2		
3	Unit Price	$22
4	Unit Sales	1,200
5	Gross Sales	$26,400
6		
7	Expenses	
8	Production	$10,000
9	Distribution	$1,200
10	Marketing	$5,000
11	Overhead	$3,000
12	Total Expenses	$19,200
13		
14	Net Profit	$7,200

Figure 1.3 Modified Spreadsheet

In this section, you learn about workbooks and worksheets and how spreadsheets are used in various disciplines. You plan good workbook and worksheet design and identify Excel window components prior to creating a spreadsheet.

Defining Worksheets and Workbooks

A *worksheet* is a spreadsheet that may contain formulas, functions, values, text, and graphics.

A *workbook* is a file containing related worksheets.

A *worksheet* is a single spreadsheet consisting of a grid of columns and rows that often contain descriptive labels, numeric values, formulas, functions, and graphics. The terms worksheet and spreadsheet are often used interchangeably. A *workbook* is a collection of related worksheets contained within a single file. Storing multiple worksheets within one workbook helps organize related data in one file. In addition, it enables you to perform calculations among the worksheets within the workbook.

Managers often create workbooks to store an organization's annual budget. The workbook may consist of five worksheets, one for each quarter, with the fifth spreadsheet showing summary figures. Alternatively, individuals and families often create a budget workbook of 12 worksheets, one for each month, to store personal income and expenses. Instructors often create a workbook to store a grade book with individual worksheets for each class. On a personal level, you might want to list your DVD collection in one workbook in which you have a worksheet for each category, such as action, comedy, drama, etc. Within each worksheet, you list the DVD title, release date, purchase price, and so on. Regardless of the situation, you can use one workbook to contain many related worksheets.

TIP | The Workbook

An Excel workbook is the electronic equivalent of the three-ring binder. A workbook contains one or more worksheets (or chart sheets), each of which is identified by a tab at the bottom of the workbook. The worksheets in a workbook are normally related to one another; for example, each worksheet may contain the sales for a specific division within a company. The advantage of a workbook is that all of its worksheets are stored in a single file, which is accessed as a unit.

Using Spreadsheets Across Disciplines

Students typically think spreadsheets are used solely for business applications. Spreadsheets are used for accounting and business planning using powerful "what-if" functions. These functions enable business planners to project different amounts of profit as other factors change. Even students can use basic "what if" analysis with a budget to determine if they can afford a particular payment or determine if they have sufficient income to buy a new car.

Spreadsheets are, however, used in many other areas. Because of the powerful graphing or charting feature of Excel, geologists and physical scientists use spreadsheets to store data about earthquakes or other physical phenomena, chart the data with a scatter chart, and then plot it on maps to predict where these phenomena might occur. Historians and social scientists have long used spreadsheets for predicting voting behavior or supporting or refuting theses such as Beard's Economic Interpretation of the Constitution. Figure 1.4 shows another use for spreadsheets—a summary of temperatures over time for several cities.

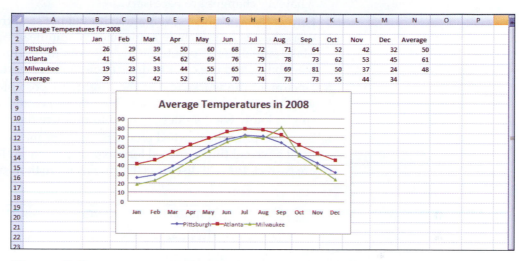

	A	B	C	D	E	F	G	H	I	J	K	L	M	N
1	Average Temperatures for 2008													
2		Jan	Feb	Mar	Apr	May	Jun	Jul	Aug	Sep	Oct	Nov	Dec	Average
3	Pittsburgh	26	29	39	50	60	68	72	71	64	52	42	32	50
4	Atlanta	41	45	54	62	69	76	79	78	73	62	53	45	61
5	Milwaukee	19	23	33	44	55	65	71	69	81	50	37	24	48
6	Average	29	32	42	52	61	70	74	73	73	55	44	34	

Figure 1.4 Temperatures over Time by City Example Spreadsheet

Educators at all levels—elementary school teachers through university professors—are increasing their use of electronic spreadsheets. Many Web sites now show literally thousands of examples of how educators are using spreadsheets in their classrooms. Once both students and teachers understand the basics of Excel, the possibilities are endless. As noted, spreadsheets are widely used in education. The most common use of Excel is in creating grade book spreadsheets.

Planning for Good Workbook and Worksheet Design

Figures 1.5, 1.6, and 1.7 show three views of a teacher's grade book. The first figure shows a grade book as a teacher might keep it with paper and pencil. The second figure shows the grade book in a spreadsheet program, and the third figure shows the grade book after some changes are made. The handwritten version of the grade book has the teacher writing in grades and calculating averages with a calculator or on paper. If changes are necessary, out comes the eraser and correction fluid. The second and third examples using the electronic spreadsheet show its simplicity. The teacher can easily enter grades, change grades, use weighted items, and recalculate—that is the power of the spreadsheet. For many teachers the spreadsheet grade book is such an integral part of their work that they have never seen or cannot remember a paper grade book.

You should plan the structure of the spreadsheet before you start entering data into a new worksheet. At times, it may be necessary for you to sit with paper and pencil and create the spreadsheet design on paper. See Figure 1.5 for an example of a handwritten grade book. The steps that are necessary for the design of a workbook and a worksheet include the following:

1. Figure out the purpose of the spreadsheet and how it will be constructed. For example, a professor's purpose is to create an electronic grade book to store student names and scores and to calculate student grades.

2. Make it obvious where data are to be entered. The teacher needs to store student first names, last names, and three test scores for all students in the class. See Figure 1.6 for a sample worksheet.

3. Enter data and set up formulas wherever possible. Avoid constants (raw numbers) in formulas; use cell references to cells containing numbers instead. Never do manually what Excel can do automatically. You could, for example, calculate each student's class average. Furthermore, you can calculate the class average for each test to see if the tests are too easy or too difficult.

4. Test, test, and test again to make sure the results are what you expect. It is easy to make mistakes when entering data and when constructing formulas. Make whatever changes are necessary.

5. Format the worksheet so it is attractive but not so obtrusive that the purpose of the worksheet is lost. Include a title and column headings, and center the headings. Make sure decimal points align. Add bold to headings, increase the font size for readability, and use color to draw attention to important values or to trends.

6. Document the worksheet as thoroughly as possible. Include the current date, your name, class, and semester. Include cell comments describing the formulas so you know what values are used to produce the results.

7. Save and print the finished product. Auditors and teachers may require you to print a second time with cell formulas displayed so they can verify the formulas are correct. We will discuss cell formulas more thoroughly later in the chapter.

Student	Test 1	Test 2	Final	Average
Adams	100	90	81	90.3
Baker	90	76	87	84.3
Glassman	90	78	78	82.0
Moldof	60	60	40	53.3
Walker	80	80	90	83.3
Class Average	84.0	76.8	75.2	

Walker's average grade is 83.3

Walker's final exam grade is 90

Figure 1.5 The Professor's Grade Book

	A	B	C	D	E	F
1	Student	Test 1	Test 2	Final	Average	
2						
3	Adams	100	90	81	90.3	
4	Baker	90	76	87	84.3	
5	Glassman	90	78	78	82.0	
6	Moldof	60	60	40	53.3	
7	Walker	80	80	90	83.3	
8						
9	Class Average	84.0	76.8	75.2		
10						

Walker's final exam grade is 90

Figure 1.6 Original Grades

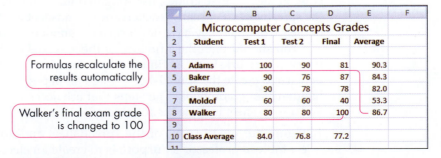

	A	B	C	D	E	F
1	Microcomputer Concepts Grades					
2	Student	Test 1	Test 2	Final	Average	
3						
4	Adams	100	90	81	90.3	
5	Baker	90	76	87	84.3	
6	Glassman	90	78	78	82.0	
7	Moldof	60	60	40	53.3	
8	Walker	80	80	100	86.7	
9						
10	Class Average	84.0	76.8	77.2		
11						

Formulas recalculate the results automatically

Walker's final exam grade is changed to 100

Figure 1.7 Modified Spreadsheet

Identifying Excel Window Components

Each window in Excel has its own Minimize, Maximize, and Close buttons. The title bar contains the name of the application (Excel) and the name of the workbook you are using. At the bottom and right of the document window are the vertical and horizontal scroll bars. The *active cell* is the cell you are working in, the cell where information or data will be input. Its cell reference appears in the name box, its contents in the formula bar, and it is surrounded by a dark black box. The active cell can be changed by clicking in a different cell or using the arrow keys to move to another cell.

The active cell is the cell you are working in, the cell where information or data will be input.

The Excel window includes items that are similar to other Office applications and items that are unique to the Excel application. See Figure 1.8, the Excel window, with the parts of the window identified. The following paragraphs name and describe items in the Excel window.

- **Ribbon**: The Ribbon is made of tabs, groups, and commands.
- **Tab**: Each tab is made up of several groups so that you can see all of its functions without opening menus. The contents of each tab are shown on the reference page. This defines the tabs, the groups they contain, and their general function. You will refer to this page frequently.
- **Office Menu**: The Office menu displays when you click the Office Button in the upper left of the Excel window and contains the following commands, all of which open dialog boxes: New, Open, Save, Save As, Finish, Share, Print, and Close. A list of recently used workbooks and an extensive Excel Options section displays. See Figure 1.9 for the contents of the Office menu.
- **Formula Bar**: The formula bar appears below the Ribbon and above the workbook screen and shows the active cell's contents. The *formula bar* displays the contents of cells; you can enter or edit cell contents here or directly in the active cell.
- **Name Box**: The *name box* is another name for the cell reference of the cell currently used in the worksheet. The name box appears to the left of the formula bar and displays the active cell's address (D4) or a name it has been assigned.
- **Sheet Tabs**: *Sheet tabs* are located at the bottom left of the Excel window and tell the user what sheets of a workbook are available. Three sheet tabs, initially named Sheet1, Sheet2, and Sheet3, are included when you open a new workbook in Excel. To move between sheets, click on the sheet you want to work with. You can even rename sheets with more meaningful names. If you create more sheets than can be displayed, you can use the sheet tab scroll buttons to scroll through all sheet tabs.
- **Status Bar**: The status bar is located at the bottom of the Excel window. It is below the sheet tabs and above the Windows taskbar and displays information about a selected command or operation in progress. For example, it displays CAPS when Caps Lock is active and the default setting is On.
- **Select All Button**: The *Select All button* is the square at the intersection of the rows and column headings, and you can use it to select all elements of the worksheet.

The *formula bar* is used to enter or edit cell contents.

The *name box* indicates the location or name for the active cell.

Sheet tabs tell the user what sheets of a workbook are available.

The *Select All button* is clicked to select all elements of the worksheet.

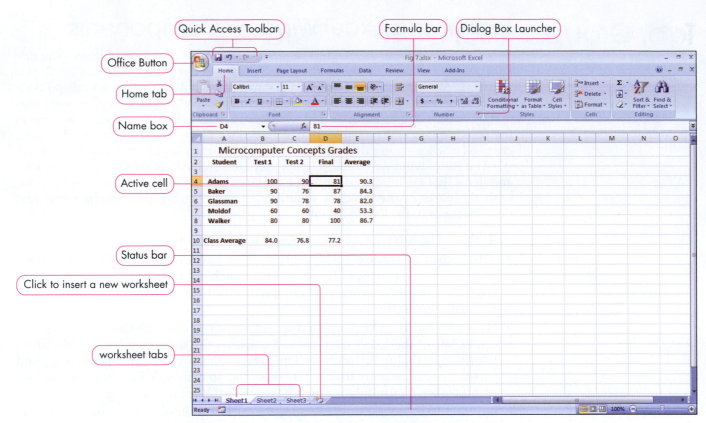

Figure 1.8 The Excel Window

Figure 1.9 The Office Menu

Tab, Group, Description | Reference

Tab and Group	Description
Home	
Clipboard Font Alignment Number Style Cells Editing	The basic Excel tab. Contains basic editing functions such as cut and paste along with most formatting actions. As with all groups, pull-down areas are available and do increase functionality. Your Tabs may display differently depending on your screen resolution.

Insert	
Tables Illustrations Charts Links Text	Brings together all insert functions in one area. Includes ability to create charts and add tables. Contains powerful picture functions. Headers and footers are inserted here.

Page Layout	
Themes Page Setup Scale to Fit Sheet Options Arrange	Contains all functions associated with page appearance, setup, and printing. Also controls the display of sheet options, such as gridlines and headings.

Formulas	
Function Library Defined Names Formula Auditing Calculation	The area that contains the mathematical backbone of Excel. Includes basic areas (Function Library) as well as more advanced (Formula Auditing).

Data

Get External Data
Connections
Sort & Filter
Data Tools
Outline

The heart of the database portions of Excel. While not a true relational database, it has much power and includes Goal Seek and Scenario Manager.

Review

Proofing
Comments
Changes

Contains all reviewing tools in Excel, including such things as spelling, the use of comments, and sharing and protection.

View

Workbook Views
Show/Hide
Zoom
Window
Macros

Contains basic and advanced view settings. Some of these options also appear below the horizontal and vertical scroll bars.

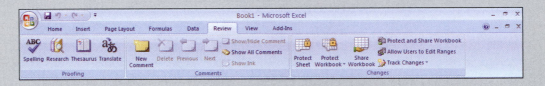

Navigate in Worksheets

Selecting cells to make them active and navigating from cell to cell are basic navigational skills in Excel. Using the mouse is probably the most convenient way to select a cell and navigate. To make a cell active, click on the desired cell. Making another cell active simply involves clicking on another cell. If the cell to be made active is not visible, use the vertical or horizontal scroll bars or the arrow keys to move so the desired cell is visible.

The other way is to use different keys to navigate through the worksheet. Table 1.1 shows keys that can be used to move in a worksheet.

Table 1.1 Keystrokes and Actions

Keystroke	Action
↑	Moves up one cell.
↓	Moves down one cell.
←	Moves left one cell.
→	Moves right one cell.
PgUp	Moves active cell up one screen.
PgDn	Moves active cell down one screen.
Home	Moves active cell to column A of current row.
Ctrl+Home	Moves active cell to cell A1.
Ctrl+End	Moves to the rightmost, lowermost active corner of the worksheet.
F5	Displays the GoTo dialog box to enter any cell address.

Identify Columns, Rows, and Cells

A spreadsheet is divided into columns and rows, with each column and row assigned a heading. Columns are assigned alphabetic headings from column A to Z, continue from AA to AZ, and then from BA to BZ until the last of the 18,278 columns is reached. Rows have numeric headings ranging from 1 to 1,048,576 (the maximum number of rows allowed).

A *cell* is the intersection of a column and row.

A *cell reference* is designated by a column letter and a row number.

The intersection of a column and row forms a *cell*, with the number of cells in a spreadsheet equal to the number of columns times the number of rows. Each cell has a unique *cell reference*, which is the intersection of a column and row designated by a column letter and a row number. For example, the cell at the intersection of column A and row 9 is known as cell A9. The column heading always precedes the row heading in the cell reference.

Start Excel and Create a New Worksheet

The first thing you should do is open Excel. You can do this by taking the following steps:

1. Click the Start button to display the Start menu. Position the mouse pointer over All Programs, select Microsoft Office, and then select Microsoft Office Excel 2007 from its location on the Programs menu.
2. Maximize the Excel program if necessary.

This opens a new Excel workbook with the default three-sheet worksheet tabs. When Excel is already open and you want to open a new workbook, complete the following steps:

1. Click the Office Button.
2. Select New and then select Blank Workbook.

A new workbook is now open.

Entering and Editing Data in Cells

The three types of data that can be entered in a cell in an Excel worksheet are text, values, and formulas, which also include functions. You can create very sophisticated workbooks and simple worksheets with any combination of text, values, and formulas.

Enter Text

Text includes letters, numbers, symbols, and spaces.

Text is any combination of entries from the keyboard and includes letters, numbers, symbols, and spaces. Even though text entries may be used as data, they are most often used to identify and document the spreadsheet. Text is used to indicate the title of the spreadsheet. Typically text is used for row and column labels. When you need to enter text, click in the cell where the text is to appear, type the text, and either press Enter or click the ✓ on the formula bar.

Sometimes, you may have a long label that does not fit well in the cell. You can insert a line break to display the label on multiple lines within the cell. To insert a line break, press Alt+Enter where you want to start the next line of text within the cell.

Enter Values

A **value** is a number that represent a quantity, an amount, a date, or time.

Values are numbers entered in a cell that represent a quantity, an amount, a date, or time. As a general rule, Excel can recognize if you are entering text or values by what is typed. The biggest difference between text and value entries is that value entries can be the basis of calculation while text cannot.

Enter Formulas

A **formula** is a combination of numbers, cell references, operators, and/or functions.

Formulas (and their shorthand form, functions) are the combination of constants, cell references, arithmetic operations, and/or functions displayed in a calculation. For Excel to recognize a formula, it must always start with an equal sign (=). You learn about basic formulas in this chapter. Chapter 2 provides a detailed discussion of formulas and functions. At this point, it is sufficient to say that =A2+B2 is an example of a formula to perform addition.

TIP   AutoComplete

As soon as you begin typing a label into a cell, Excel searches for and automatically displays any other label in that column that matches the letters you typed. AutoComplete is helpful if you want to repeat a label, but it can be distracting if you want to enter a different label that begins with the same letter. To turn the feature on (or off), click the Office Button, click Excel Options, and click Advanced. Check (clear) the Enable AutoComplete for cell values check box to enable (disable) the AutoComplete feature.

Edit and Clear Cell Contents

You have several ways to edit the contents of a cell. You will probably select and stay with one technique that you find most convenient. The first method is to select the cell you want to edit, click in the formula bar, make changes, and then press Enter. The second method requires that you double-click in the cell to be edited, make the edits, and then press Enter. The third method is similar except that you select the cell, press the F2 key, and then make the edit.

You have two options to clear the contents of a cell. First, just click on a cell and press Delete. The second option involves clicking the Clear arrow in the Editing group on the Home tab. This gives you several options as to what will be cleared from the cell (see Figure 1.10).

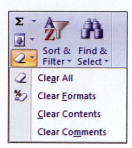

Figure 1.10 Clear Pull-down List

Use Save and Save As

It is basic computer practice that files, including workbooks, should be saved often. If you are using a workbook and you do not want to change its name, the easiest way to save it is to click the Office Button and select Save. If you prefer keyboard shortcuts, press Ctrl+S. You also can click Save on the Quick Access Toolbar.

The first time you save a workbook, you can use the Save command or the Save As command that is located on the Office menu. For an unnamed file, either command displays the Save As dialog box. You can then assign a file name that is descriptive of the workbook (gradebook08, for example), determine the file location, and choose the file type. After selecting the appropriate options, click Save. When you use the Save command after initially saving a workbook, the subsequent changes are saved under the same workbook name and in the same location. If you want to assign a different name to a modified workbook so that you can preserve the original workbook, use the Save As command.

TIP File Management with Excel

Use the Office Button in the Open or Save As dialog box to perform basic file management within any Office application. You can select any existing file or folder, and delete it or rename it. You can also create a new folder, which is very useful when you begin to work with a large number of documents. You can also use the Views button to change the way the files are listed within the dialog box.

Hands-On Exercises

1 | Introduction to Microsoft Excel

Skills covered: 1. Plan Your Workbook **2.** Start Microsoft Office Excel 2007 **3.** Enter and Edit Data in Cells **4.** Use the Save As Command and Explore the Worksheet

Step 1	Refer to Figure 1.11 as you complete Step 1.
Plan Your Workbook	

a. Prepare notes before beginning Excel.

Specify or define the problem. What statistics will be produced by your spreadsheet? Do you already have the statistics, or do you need to collect them from another source? Brainstorm about what formulas and functions will be required. Experiment with paper and pencil and a calculator. The first spreadsheet you create will be a sample showing membership sales in a gym. This sample worksheet includes monthly sales by region for both first and second quarters. Also included are the calculations to determine total monthly sales, average monthly sales, total and average sales by region, and increase or decrease in sales between the first and second quarters.

b. Simplify your Excel spreadsheet for those who will enter data.

You should treat your Excel workbook like a Microsoft Word document by doing such things as adding cell comments, giving instructions, and using attractive formatting.

c. Consider these layout suggestions when designing your Excel spreadsheets:

- Reserve the first row for a spreadsheet title.

- Reserve a row for column headings.

- Reserve a column at the left for row headings.

- Do not leave blank rows and columns for white space within the spreadsheet layout.

- Widen the columns and rows and use alignment instead of leaving blank rows or columns.

- Save your work often.

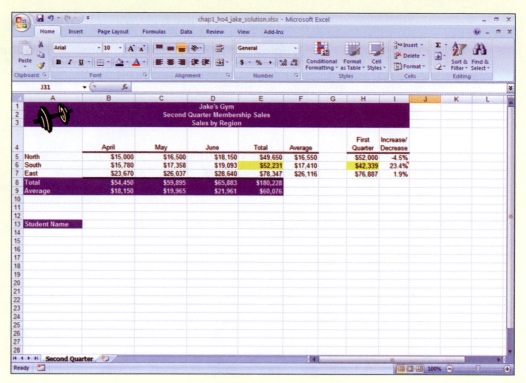

Figure 1.11 Well-Designed Spreadsheet

a. Click the **Start button** to display the Start menu. Click (or point to) **All Programs**, click **Microsoft Office**, and then click **Microsoft Office Excel 2007** to start the program.

You should be familiar with basic file management and very comfortable moving and copying files from one folder to another. If not, you may want to review the Help material for basic file management.

b. If necessary, click the **Maximize** button in the application window so that Excel takes the entire desktop, as shown in Figure 1.11. Click the **Maximize** button in the document window (if necessary) so that the workbook window is as large as possible.

Refer to Figure 1.12 as you complete Step 3.

a. Click **cell A1**, type **Jake's Gym**, and press **Enter**.

b. In **cell A2**, type **Second Quarter Membership Sales**.

c. Click **cell B3**, type the label **April**, and press the **right arrow**.

d. Type the label **May**, and press the **right arrow**. Complete the typing for **cells D3** through **H3** as shown. Do not be concerned if the entire column label is not visible.

D3	June
E3	Total
F3	Average
G3	First Quarter
H3	Increase/Decrease

e. Enter the data for three regions as shown below:

Region	April	May	June	First Quarter
North	15000	16500	18150	31000
South	15780	17358	19093	42339
East	23670	26037	28640	76887

TROUBLESHOOTING: Data entry is important for good spreadsheet use. Verify values as you finish typing them. To change an entry, click on the cell and retype the value. To delete an entry, click on the cell and press Delete.

f. Type **Total** in **cell A7** and type **Average** in **cell A8**.

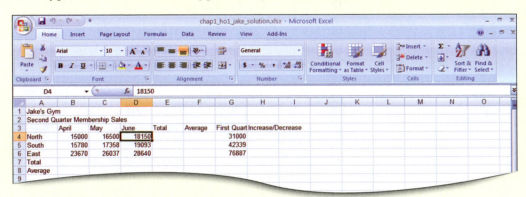

Figure 1.12 Jake's Gym Data

Step 4

Use the Save As Command and Explore the Worksheet

Refer to Figures 1.12 and 1.13 as you complete Step 4. Your ribbon may not display exactly as shown because of different screen resolutions.

a. Click the **Office Button** and click **Save As** to display the Save As dialog box shown in Figure 1.13.

b. Type **chap1_ho1_jake_solution** as the name of the new workbook.

A file name may contain up to 255 characters. Spaces, underscores, and commas are allowed in the filename.

c. Navigate to the location of your data files and click the **Save button**.

You should see the workbook in Figure 1.12.

d. Click in **cell D4**, the cell containing 18150 or the North June sales.

Cell D4 is now the active cell and is surrounded by a heavy border. The name box indicates that cell D4 is the active cell, and its contents are displayed in the formula bar.

e. Click in **cell D5** (or press the down arrow key) to make it the active cell.

The name box indicates cell D5.

f. Refer to Table 1.1 as you move around the worksheet.

g. Close the *chap1_ho1_jake_solution* workbook.

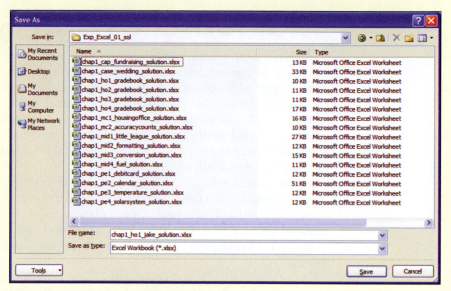

Figure 1.13 Save As Dialog Box

TIP   Keyboard Shortcuts—The Dialog Box

Press Tab or Shift+Tab to move forward or backward between fields in a dialog box, or press Alt plus the underlined letter to move directly to an option. You will see underlined letters in words in dialog boxes. These are the letters you use in conjunction with the Alt key. Use the spacebar to toggle check boxes on or off and the up (or down) arrow keys to move between options in a list box. Press Enter to activate the highlighted command and Esc to exit the dialog box without accepting the changes. These are universal shortcuts and apply to any Windows application.

Mathematics and Formulas

You have used calculators where numbers are entered, the correct arithmetic function key is pressed, and the correct answer appears. What is missing though is the knowledge of the process, or how to arrive at the correct answer. These mathematical processes are the key to understanding and using Excel. Without knowing the process and how to apply it in Excel, you are left with just numbers, not answers. Arithmetic and mathematics produce answers by calculating numbers using Excel. You might want to think of Excel as a gigantic calculating program on the most powerful calculator of all, a computer.

With Excel, when any change is made, the entire worksheet is updated based on this new value. This fact brings us back to an important question: Why use Excel when one could just as easily perform calculations on a calculator or on paper? What happens if profit is 4% rather than 5%? In the pre-Excel days, answering these questions required rewriting and retyping the whole business plan using pencil, paper, and typewriter.

> Formulas can be as simple or as complex as necessary, but always begin with an = sign and contain mathematical operators.

In this section, you learn about the mathematical operations that are the backbone of Excel. You also will see that the order these mathematical operations are performed in can have a significant impact on the results. We touch briefly on the construction of mathematical expressions, called *formulas*, that direct Excel to perform mathematical operations and arrive at a calculated result. Whenever you want Excel to perform a calculation, you must enter an equal sign (=) in the cell where the answer is to appear. For example, if you wanted to calculate the sum of cells C2 and C3 in cell C4, you would do the following:

1. Click in cell C4 and type an = sign.
2. Click in cell C2 and type a + sign.
3. Click in cell C3 and press Enter.

This is an extremely simplified example but the principle holds true in all formulas. See Table 1.2 for examples of formulas. Formulas can be as simple or as complex as necessary, but always begin with an = sign and often contain mathematical operators.

Table 1.2 Formula Examples

Operation	Formula
Addition	=C1+C2
Subtraction	=C2-C1
Multiplication	=C1*C2
Division	=C1/C2

Describing and Using Symbols and the Order of Precedence

The four mathematical functions—addition, subtraction, multiplication, and division—are the basis of all mathematical operations. Table 1.3 lists the arithmetic operators and their purposes.

Table 1.3 Arithmetic Operators and Symbols

Operation	Common Symbol	Symbol in Excel
Addition	+	+
Subtraction	−	−
Multiplication	X	*
Division	÷	/
Exponentiation	^	^

Enter Cell References in Formulas

If this were all there was to it, Excel would be effortless for all of us, but two other things need to be done if Excel is to perform mathematical functions as it was designed to do. First, rather than entering the numbers that are contained in the cells, Excel works at its full potential if cell references (C5, B2, etc.) are used rather than the numbers themselves. See Figure 1.14 for an example.

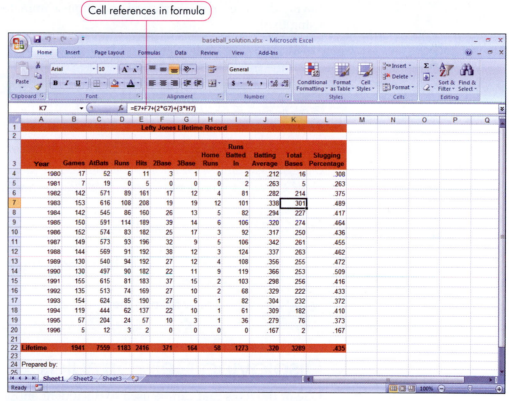

Figure 1.14 Baseball Statistics with Cell References

The first thing to consider is how Excel (or the computer) recognizes that you want to perform a mathematical operation. For example, you decide that you need to add the contents of cells C1 and C2 and place the sum in cell C3. In C1 you have the number 5, and in C2 you have the number 3. If you enter 5+3 and press Enter, the result you see will be "5+3." This is not the answer, however, that you are looking for. You want the result of 8. Anytime you want Excel to perform a mathematical calculation, you must begin by typing =. The equal sign tells Excel "get ready to do some math." One way to get the answer of 8 is by typing =5+3 and pressing Enter to see the sum, 8, in cell C3.

If you then change the number in cell C1 from 5 to 7, you must now change the 5 to a 7 in the formula in cell C3 to calculate the new result. Excel gives you an easier and much more efficient way to update results of calculations so you do not have to change the content of cell C3 every time the values in cells C1 or C2 change. This operation is done by using cell references. Rather than using the expression =5+3 in cell C3 to get a sum, you should enter the expression =C1+C2 in cell C3. This way, even if you change the values of cell C1 or C2, the value in cell C3 remains the sum of cells C1 and C2 because you are using cell references rather than the value in the cells.

Control the Results with the Order of Precedence

The **order of precedence** controls the sequence in which arithmetic operations are performed, which affects the result.

Before moving on to formulas, the final mathematics concept you need to know is order of precedence. The *order of precedence* are rules that control the order or sequence in which arithmetic operations are performed, which in turn, will change the result reported in Excel. Excel performs mathematical calculations left to right in this order: parentheses, exponentiation, multiplication or division, and finally addition or subtraction.

Review the expressions in Table 1.4 and notice how the parentheses change the value of the expression. In the second expression, the addition inside the parentheses is performed before the multiplication, changing the order of operations. Strictly following the order of mathematical operations eliminates many puzzling results when using Excel.

Table 1.4 Examples of Order of Precedence

Expression	Order to Perform Calculations	Output
= 6 + 6 * 2	Multiply first **and then** add.	18
= (6 + 6) * 2	Add the values inside the parentheses first **and then** multiply.	24
= 6 + 6 ^ 2	Simplify the exponent first: 36=6*6, **and then** add.	42
= 10/2 + 3	Divide first **and then** add.	8
= 10/(2+3)	Add first to simplify the parenthetical expression **and then** divide.	2
= 10 * 2 - 3 * 2	Multiply first **and then** subtract.	14

Displaying Cell Formulas

One of the tools that can be used to document an Excel worksheet is the ability to display cell formulas. When you display formulas, they will appear in the cells instead of the results of the calculation. See Figures 1.15 and 1.16. The quickest way to display cell formulas is to press Ctrl+~. The tilde (~) key is in the upper-left corner of the keyboard, under Esc. Note: you do not press the Shift key with the tilde key to make cell formulas visible in your worksheet.

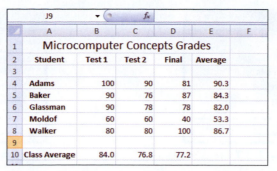

	A	B	C	D	E	F
1	Microcomputer Concepts Grades					
2	**Student**	**Test 1**	**Test 2**	**Final**	**Average**	
3						
4	**Adams**	100	90	81	90.3	
5	**Baker**	90	76	87	84.3	
6	**Glassman**	90	78	78	82.0	
7	**Moldof**	60	60	40	53.3	
8	**Walker**	80	80	100	86.7	
9						
10	**Class Average**	84.0	76.8	77.2		

Figure 1.15 Spreadsheet with Values Displayed

	A	B	C	D	E
1	Microcomputer Concepts Grades				
2	**Student**	**Test 1**	**Test 2**	**Final**	**Average**
3					
4	**Adams**	100	90	81	=AVERAGE(B4:D4)
5	**Baker**	90	76	87	=AVERAGE(B5:D5)
6	**Glassman**	90	78	78	=AVERAGE(B6:D6)
7	**Moldof**	60	60	40	=AVERAGE(B7:D7)
8	**Walker**	80	80	100	=AVERAGE(B8:D8)
9					
10	**Class Average**	=AVERAGE(B4:B9)	=AVERAGE(C4:C9)	=AVERAGE(D4:D9)	
11					

Figure 1.16 Spreadsheet with Formulas Displayed

Inserting and Deleting Rows and Columns

After you construct a worksheet, it is often necessary to add or delete columns or rows of information. For example, in a grade book kept by a professor, names are constantly added or deleted. This process typically involves the use of the Insert command that adds cells, rows, or columns or the Delete command that deletes cells, rows, or columns. When you use either command, the cell references in existing cells are adjusted automatically to reflect the insertion or deletion. These commands also allow sheets to be added or deleted from the workbook.

To insert a row, click in the row below where you want a row inserted (rows are always inserted above, and columns are always inserted to the left of, the selected cell), and then click the Insert down arrow in the Cells group on the Home tab. You would then select Insert Sheet Rows. To insert a column, the user would select Insert Sheet Columns. For example, if the active cell is E4, row 4 is the current row. The row added is inserted above. If a column is inserted, it is inserted to the left of E4. The process is similar for deleting rows and columns, except you begin by choosing the Delete pull-down arrow in the Cells group. The row above the row selected is deleted, and the column to the left of the selected column is deleted.

TIP   Inserting and Deleting Individual Cells

In some situations, you may need to insert and delete individual cells instead of inserting or deleting an entire row or column. To insert a cell, click in the cell where you want the new cell, click the Insert pull-down arrow in the Cells group on the Home tab, and then click Insert Cells to display the Insert dialog box. Click the appropriate option to shift cells right or down and click OK (see Figure 1.17). To delete a cell or cells, select the cell(s), click the Delete arrow in the Cells group on the Cells tab, and then click Delete Cells to display the Delete dialog box. Click the appropriate option to shift cells right or down and click OK (see Figure 1.18).

Figure 1.17 Insert Dialog Box

Figure 1.18 Delete Dialog Box

Using Cell Ranges; Excel Move; Copy, Paste, Paste Special; and AutoFill

Each of these topics is a basic editing function in Excel. They will be discussed in detail here, and you will be able to show your proficiency with them in Hands-On Exercise 2.

Select a Range

A *range* is a rectangular group of cells.

Every command in Excel applies to a rectangular group of cells known as a *range*. A range may be as small as a single cell or as large as the entire worksheet. It may consist of a row or part of a row, a column or part of a column, or multiple rows or columns. The cells within a range are specified by indicating the diagonally opposite corners, typically the upper-left and lower-right corners of the rectangle. Many different ranges could be selected in conjunction with the worksheet shown in Figure 1.19. For example, the 1980 Player data is contained in the range B4:I4. The Lifetime Totals are found in the range B22:L22. The Batting Averages are found in the range J4:J20.

> A range may be as small as a single cell or as large as the entire worksheet.

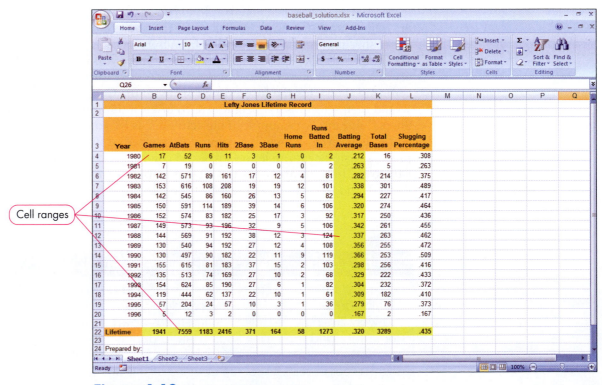

Figure 1.19 Defined Ranges

The easiest way to select a range is to click and drag—click at the beginning of the range and then press and hold the left mouse button as you drag the mouse to the end of the range, where you release the mouse. To select an entire column, click the column letter. To select an entire row, click the row number. Once selected, the range is highlighted, and its cells will be affected by any subsequent command. The range remains selected until another range is defined or until you click another cell anywhere on the worksheet.

Move a Cell's Contents

The ***move operation*** transfers the content of a cell or cell range from one location to another, with the cells where the move originated becoming empty.

The ***move operation*** transfers the content of a cell or cell range from one location in the worksheet to another, with the cells where the move originated becoming empty. The use of the move command can be confusing when you copy a cell containing a formula. Cell references in formulas are adjusted relative to the new location within the spreadsheet. You can use the drag-and-drop technique to move a range of cells or the cut and paste method. To use the cut and paste method:

1. Select the range of cells to be moved.
2. Pick Cut in the Clipboard group on the Home tab.
3. Select the range the cells will be moved to.
4. Click Paste in the Clipboard group on the Home tab.

The ***delete operation*** removes all content from a cell or from a selected cell range.

The ***delete operation*** removes all content from a cell or from a selected cell range. While there are several ways to execute the delete operation, the most simple is to select a cell or range of cells and press Delete to remove the information from the cell(s).

Copy, Paste, Paste Special

The Copy, Paste, and Paste Special operations are essential editing operations in any Microsoft Office 2007 application. The Copy command enables you to begin to duplicate information in a cell or range of cells into another cell or range of cells. In order to copy material, you select the cell(s) to be copied and click Copy in the Clipboard group on the Home tab. The Paste operation enables you to duplicate cell contents that you have copied to a new location. Once the contents of a cell or range of cells have been copied, select the location on the worksheet where the material is to be copied to and click Paste in the Clipboard group on the Home tab. The Paste Special operation provides several different options when pasting material (see Figure 1.20). The power of the Copy and Paste operation is enhanced with the use of Paste Special in Excel.

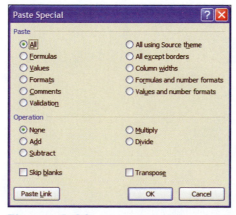

Figure 1.20 Paste Special Dialog Box

Use AutoFill

AutoFill enables you to copy the content of a cell or a range of cells by dragging the fill handle over an adjacent cell or range of cells.

The *fill handle* is a small black square appearing in the bottom-right corner of a cell.

AutoFill is an Excel operation that enables you to copy the content of a cell or a range of cells by dragging the *fill handle* (a small black square appearing in the bottom-right corner of a cell) over an adjacent cell or range of cells. AutoFill can be used in two different ways. First, you can use it to repetitively copy the contents of one cell. To do this, click the cell and use the fill handle to repeat the content. This operation is valuable for copying formulas, because the cell references are updated automatically during the AutoFill process. AutoFill also can be used to complete a sequence. For example, if you enter January in a cell, you can use AutoFill to enter the rest of the months of the year.

You can complete the quarters of a year by typing Qtr 1 in a cell and using AutoFill to fill in Qtr 2, Qtr 3, and Qtr 4 in sequence. Other sequences you can complete are weekdays and weekday abbreviations by typing the first item and using AutoFill to complete the other entries. For numeric values, however, you must specify the first two values in sequence. For example, if you want to fill in 5, 10, 15, and so on, you must enter the first two values in two cells, select the two cells, and then use AutoFill so that Excel knows to increment by 5.

TIP   Two Different Clipboards

The Office Clipboard holds a total of up to 24 objects from multiple applications, as opposed to the Windows Clipboard, which stores only the results of the last Cut or Copy command. Thus, each time you execute a Cut or Copy command, the contents of the Windows Clipboard are replaced, whereas the copied object is added to the objects already in the Office Clipboard. To display the Office Clipboard, click the Home tab and click the arrow to the right of the word Clipboard. Leave the Clipboard open as you execute multiple cut and copy operations to observe what happens.

Hands-On Exercises

2 | Jake's Gym Continued

Skills covered: 1. Open an Existing Workbook **2.** Use Save As to Save an Existing Workbook **3.** Insert a Row and Compute Totals **4.** Copy the Formulas **5.** Continue the Calculations **6.** Insert a Column

---

<table>
<tr>
<td>

Step 1

Open an Existing Workbook

</td>
<td>

Refer to Figures 1.21 and 1.22 as you complete Step 1.

a. Click the **Office Button** and select **Open**.

You should see the Open dialog box, similar to Figure 1.21.

b. Click the **Views drop-down arrow**, and then select **Details**.

You changed the file list to a detailed list view, which shows more information.

c. Click the arrow on the **Look In** list box and click the appropriate drive depending on the location of your data.

You are navigating to the file you want to open.

d. Click the scroll arrow if necessary in order to select *chap1_ho2_jake*. Click **Open** to open the workbook shown in Figure 1.22.

</td>
</tr>
</table>

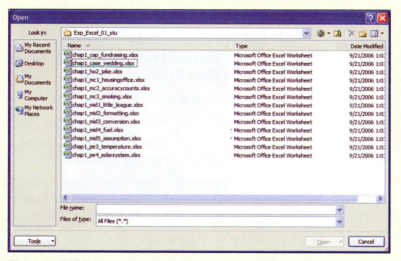

Figure 1.21   Open Dialog Box

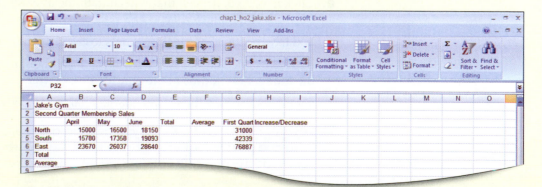

Figure 1.22   Original Jake's Gym Spreadsheet

Step 2
Use Save As to Save an Existing Workbook

a. Click the **Office Button** and select **Save As** to display the Save As dialog box.

b. Type **chap1_ho2_jake_solution** as the name of the new workbook.

A file name may contain up to 255 characters. Spaces, underscores, and commas are allowed in the file name.

c. Click the **Save** button.

Two identical copies of the file exist on disk, *chap1_ho2_jake* and *chap1_ho2_jake_ solution*, which you just created. The title bar shows the latter name, which is the workbook currently in memory. You will work with *chap1_ho2_jake_solution* workbook but can always return to the original *chap1_ho2_jake* workbook if necessary.

TIP · Create a New Folder

Do you work with a large number of different workbooks? If so, it may be useful to store those workbooks in different folders, perhaps one folder for each subject you are taking. Click the Office Button, select Save As to display the Save As dialog box, and then click the Create New Folder button to display the associated dialog box. Enter the name of the folder, and then click OK. After you create the folder, use the *Look in* box to change to that folder the next time you open that workbook.

Step 3
Insert a Row and Compute Totals

Refer to Figure 1.23 as you complete Step 3.

a. Select **row 3**, click the **Insert arrow** in the Cells group on the Home tab, and select **Insert Sheet Rows**.

You have inserted a new row between rows 2 and 3.

b. Click in **cell A3**. Type **Sales by Region** and press **Enter**.

c. Click in **cell E5**, the cell that will contain the quarterly sales total for the North region. Type **=B5+C5+D5** and press **Enter**.

The border appearing around cells B5, C5, and D5 indicates they are part of the formula you are creating. You entered the formula to compute a total.

d. Click in **cell E5**, check to make sure the formula matches the formula in the formula bar in Figure 1.23.

If necessary, click in the formula box in the formula bar and make the appropriate changes so that you have the correct formula in cell E5.

e. Click in **cell F5**, the cell that will contain the average sales for the North region for the second quarter. Type **=E5**.

You have begun to create the formula to calculate the average for the second quarter.

f. Type **/3** to calculate the average for the second quarter by dividing the total by 3, the number of months in the quarter. Press **Enter**.

Total sales, 49650, is the second quarter total, and 16550 is the average quarterly sales.

TROUBLESHOOTING: If you type an extra arithmetic symbol at the end of a formula and press Enter, Excel will display an error message box suggesting a correction. Read the message carefully before selecting Yes or No.

g. Click in **cell F5** and verify that the formula **=E5/3** is correct.

h. Type your name in **cell A13** and click **Save** on the Quick Access Toolbar to save the workbook.

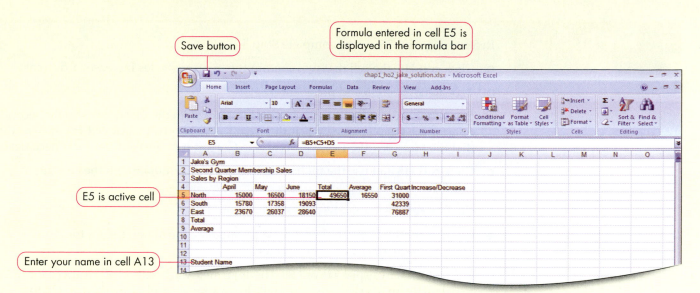

Figure 1.23 Insert Name and Compute Totals

Step 4
Copy the Formulas

Refer to Figure 1.24 as you complete Step 4.

a. Click **cell E5**.

Point to the fill handle in the lower-right corner of cell E5. The mouse pointer changes to a thin crosshair.

b. Drag the fill handle to **cell E7** (the last cell in the region total column).

A light gray color appears as you drag the fill handle, as shown in Figure 1.24.

c. Release the mouse to complete the copy operation.

The formulas for region totals have been copied to the corresponding rows for the other regions. When you click in cell E7, the cell displaying the total for the East region, you should see the formula: =B7+C7+D7.

d. Click **cell F5** and drag the fill handle to **cell F7** to copy the average sales formula down the column.

e. Save the workbook.

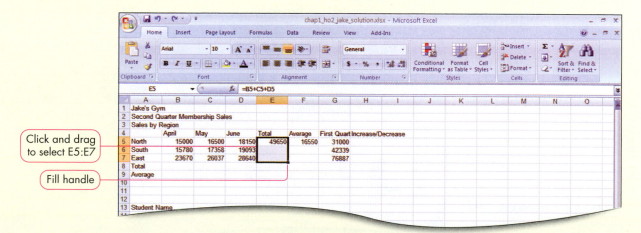

Figure 1.24 Copy the Formulas

<table>
<tr><td>Step 5
Continue the
Calculations</td><td></td></tr>
</table>

Refer to Figure 1.25 as you complete Step 5.

a. Click **cell H5**, the cell that will contain the quarterly sales increase or decrease.

b. Type **=(E5–G5)/G5** and press **Enter**.

You should see 0.601613 as the increase in sales from the first quarter to the second quarter for the North region. If this result is not correct, click cell H5 and verify that the formula =(E5-G5)/G5 is correct. Correct it in the formula bar if necessary.

c. Click **cell H5** and use the fill handle to copy the formula down the column to **cell H7**.

d. Click in **cell B8**. Type **=B5+B6+B7** and press **Enter**.

e. Click in **cell B9** to begin the formula to calculate the average sales for April. Type **=(B5+B6+B7)/3** and press Enter.

The result 18150 displays in cell B9. This is an awkward method of creating a formula to calculate an average, and you will learn to use another method in Chapter 2. However, this formula illustrates the use of parentheses to control the order of precedence. Furthermore, while you typically avoid constant values such as 3 in a formula, it is sometimes acceptable if that value will never change, such as we will always have three months in a quarter.

TROUBLESHOOTING: The parentheses used in the formula force the addition before the division and must be used to calculate the correct value.

f. Click **cell B8** and drag through **cell B9** to select both cells. Drag the fill handle in the lower-right corner of cell B9 across through **cell E9** to copy the formulas.

You copied the formulas to calculate both the monthly sales totals and averages for columns B through E.

g. Click in **cell G5** and type **52000**, then press **Enter**. See Figure 1.25.

Updated information shows that the first-quarter earnings in the North region were misreported. The new number, 52000, represents a decrease in sales between the first and second quarters in the North region.

h. Save the workbook.

You entered the formulas to calculate the appropriate totals and averages for all regions for the second quarter. You also entered the formula to determine the increase or decrease in sales from the first quarter to the second quarter.

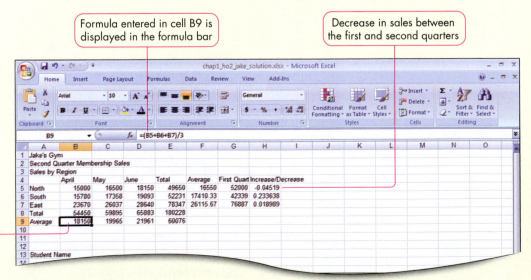

Figure 1.25 Continue the Calculations

Step 6
Insert a Column

Refer to Figure 1.26 as you complete Step 6.

a. Click the **column letter G**, the column to the left of where you want to insert a column.

When you insert a column, it appears to the left of your initial selection, and the columns are moved to the right.

b. Click on the **Insert down arrow** in the Cells group on the Home tab.

Figure 1.26 shows the Insert options in the Cells group.

c. Select **Insert Sheet Columns**.

You inserted a blank column to the left of the First Quarter column or column G.

d. Save the *chap1_ho2_jake_solution* workbook and keep it onscreen if you plan to continue to the next hands-on exercise. Close the workbook and exit Excel if you do not want to continue with the next exercise at this time.

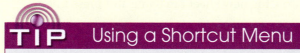

Figure 1.26 Insert a Column

TIP Using a Shortcut Menu

Another method to insert a row or column is to right-click anywhere on a row or column to show a shortcut menu. Click Insert to insert a row or a column and then select the appropriate option from the dialog box. Rows are inserted above the active cell, and columns are inserted to the left of the active cell.

Workbook and Worksheet Enhancements

At the beginning of this chapter, you learned that a worksheet or spreadsheet is a grid containing columns and rows to store numerical data. Further, you learned that a workbook is a single file that contains one or more related worksheets. So far, you have created one worksheet within a workbook. However, as you continue using Excel to develop workbooks for personal and professional use, you need to learn how to manage multiple worksheets.

In this section, you learn how to manage worksheets. Specifically, you rename worksheets and change worksheet tab colors. Furthermore, you learn how to insert, delete, add, and move worksheets.

Managing Worksheets

When you start a new blank workbook in Excel, the workbook contains three worksheets by default. These worksheets are called Sheet1, Sheet2, and Sheet3. You can insert additional worksheets if you need to store related worksheet data in the same workbook, or you can delete worksheets that you do not need. Furthermore, you can rename worksheets, rearrange the sequence of worksheets, or change the color of the worksheet tabs.

Rename Worksheets

As you have learned, it is a simple matter to move among sheets in a workbook by clicking on the appropriate sheet tab at the bottom of the worksheet window. You also learned that the default names of sheets in a new workbook are Sheet1, Sheet2, etc. To give workbook sheets more meaningful names, you will want to rename them. For example, if your budget workbook contains worksheets for each month, you should name the worksheets by month, such as *January* and *February*. A teacher who uses a workbook to store a grade book for several classes should name each sheet by class name or number, such as *MIS 1000* and *MIS 2450*. Follow these steps to rename a worksheet tab:

1. Right-click a sheet tab to show a shortcut menu.
2. Select Rename and the sheet tab name is highlighted.
3. Type the new sheet tab name and press Enter.

Change Worksheet Tab Color

The sheet tabs are blue in color by default. The active worksheet tab is white. When you use multiple worksheets, you might find it helpful to add a color to sheet tabs in order to make the tab stand out or to emphasize the difference between sheets. For example, you might want the January tab to be blue, the February tab to be red, and the March tab to be green in a workbook containing monthly worksheets. Changing the color of the tabs in workbooks when sheets have similar names helps to identify the tab you want to work with. Follow these steps to change the worksheet tab color:

1. Right-click the Sheet1 tab.
2. Select Tab Color.
3. You select Theme Colors, Standard Colors, No Color, or More Colors.

Move, Delete, Copy, and Add Worksheets

The fastest way to move a worksheet is to click and drag the worksheet tab. To delete a worksheet in a workbook, right-click on the sheet tab and select Delete from the shortcut menu. You can copy a worksheet in similar fashion by pressing and holding

Ctrl as you drag the worksheet tab. Move, Copy, and Delete worksheet operations also are accomplished by right-clicking the desired sheet tab and selecting the needed option from the shortcut menu.

To add a new blank worksheet, click Insert Worksheet to the right of the last worksheet tab or right-click any sheet tab, and select Worksheet from the Insert dialog box, and click OK.

You might want to move a worksheet to reorder existing sheets. For example, January is the first budget sheet, but at the end of January you move it after December so February is the sheet that opens first. If a professor is no longer teaching a course, she might delete a grade book sheet. Once a grade book sheet is created, it can be copied, modified, and used for another course.

TIP Moving, Copying, and Renaming Worksheets

The fastest way to move a worksheet is to click and drag the worksheet tab. You can copy a worksheet in similar fashion by pressing and holding Ctrl as you drag the worksheet tab. To rename a worksheet, double-click its tab to select the current name, type the new name, and press Enter.

Formatting Worksheets

. . . formatting procedures allow you to prepare a more eye-appealing worksheet.

Formatting worksheets allows you to change or alter the way numbers and text are presented. You can change alignment, fonts, the style of text, and the format of values, and apply borders and shading to cells, for example. These formatting procedures allow you to prepare a more eye-appealing worksheet. You format to draw attention to important areas of the worksheet, and you can emphasize totals or summary area values.

Merge and Center Labels

The **merge and center cells** option centers an entry across a range of selected cells.

You may want to place a title at the top of a worksheet and center it over the material contained in the worksheet. Centering helps to unify the information on the worksheet. The best way to do this is to **merge and center cells** into one cell across the top of the worksheet and center the content of the merged cell. See Figure 1.27, the before, and Figure 1.28, the after. The merged cells are treated as one single cell. This is a toggle command and can be undone by clicking Merge & Center a second time. To merge cells and center a title across columns A through L you would:

1. Enter the title in cell A1.
2. Select cells A1:L1.
3. Click Merge & Center in the Alignment group on the Home tab.

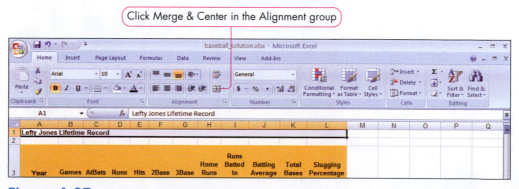

Figure 1.27 Merge and Center Title

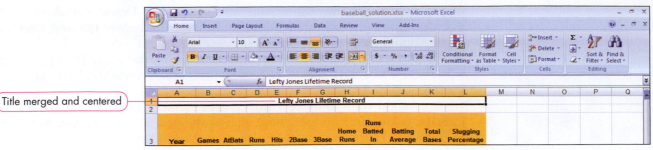

Figure 1.28 Merged and Centered Title

Adjust Cell Height and Width

It often is necessary to change the height and/or width of a cell so all of its contents are visible. When labels are longer than the cell width, they are displayed in the next cell if it is empty. If the adjacent cell is not empty, the label is truncated. Numbers appear as a series of pound signs (######) when the cell is not wide enough to display the complete number. To widen a column, drag the border between column headings to change the column width.

For example, to increase or decrease the width of column A, point to the border, and you will see a two-headed arrow. Drag the border between column headings A and B to the right or left. You also can double-click the right boundary of a column heading to change the column width to accommodate the widest entry in that column.

To increase or decrease the width of row 1, drag the border between row headings 1 and 2 up or down. You can also double-click the bottom boundary of a row heading to change the row height to accommodate entries in their entirety. Alternatively, right-click on the row number to show a shortcut menu and select Row Height. Enter an integer and click OK.

AutoFit automatically adjusts the height and width of cells.

AutoFit is an important command used when formatting a spreadsheet to automatically adjust the height and width of cells. You can choose from two types of AutoFit commands available in Format in the Cells group on the Home tab (see Figure 1.29). The AutoFit Column Width changes the column width of the selected columns to fit the contents of the column. AutoFit Row Height changes the row height of the selected row to fit the contents of the row.

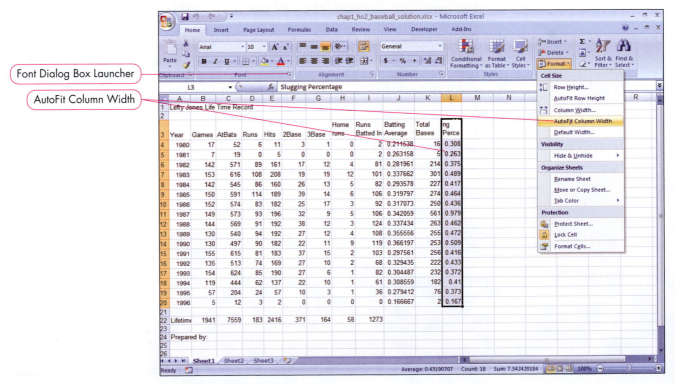

Figure 1.29 AutoFit

TIP   Multiple Row Height/Column Width

To change the row height of many rows at one time, select the multiple rows and right-click to show the shortcut menu. Select Row Height and enter a number in the Row Height dialog box as shown in Figure 1.30. Click OK. To change the column width of many columns at one time, select the multiple columns and right-click to show the shortcut menu. Select Column Width and enter a number in the Column Width dialog box. Click OK.

Figure 1.30   Row Height Dialog Box

Apply Borders and Shading

You have several options to choose from when adding borders to cells or applying a shade to cells. You can select a cell border from Borders in the Font group on the Home tab or you can use the Border tab in the Format Cells dialog box. Either way, you can create a border around a cell (or cells) for additional emphasis. Click the Font Dialog Box Launcher in the Font group on the Home tab (see Figure 1.29), and then click the Border tab. Figure 1.31 shows the Border tab in the Format Cells dialog box. Select (click) the line style at the left of the dialog box, and then click the left, right, top, and/or bottom border. It is possible to outline the entire cell or selected cells, or choose the specific side or sides; for example, thicker lines on the bottom and right sides produce a drop shadow, which can be very effective. Also, you can specify a different line style and/or a different color for the border, but a color printer is needed to see the effect on the printed output.

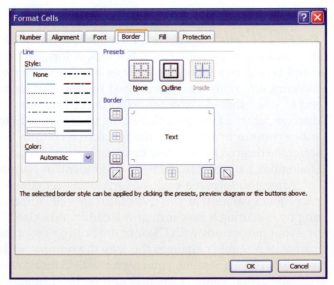

Figure 1.31   Border Tab on the Format Cells Dialog Box

You can add a shade to a cell from Fill Color in the Font group on the Home tab or you can use the Fill tab in the Format Cells dialog box. The Fill tab and Fill Color enable you to choose a different color in which to shade the cell and further emphasize its contents. The Pattern Style drop-down list lets you select an alternate pattern, such as dots or slanted lines. Click OK to accept the settings and close the dialog box. Figure 1.32 shows the Fill tab of the Format Cells dialog box.

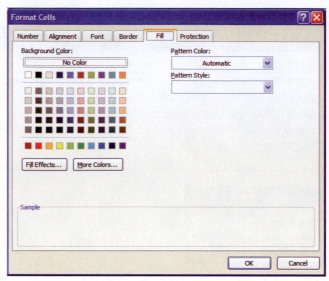

Figure 1.32 Fill Tab on the Format Cells Dialog Box

Insert Clip Art

A good way to enhance the appearance of a spreadsheet is to insert a clip art image. These images can represent the subject of the spreadsheet, the company preparing the spreadsheet, or even the personal interests of the person preparing the spreadsheet. You should use caution when inserting clip art because they can be distracting to the user of the spreadsheet or can take large amounts of disk space and slow operations on the spreadsheet. If you want to insert clip art, click Clip Art in the Illustrations group on the Insert tab to open the Clip Art task pane. Type a keyword in the Search for text box and click Go to begin the search for images matching your keyword. When you find an appropriate image, double-click it to place it in your spreadsheet. You can now move and resize the image as desired.

Format Cells

The **Format Cells** operation controls formatting for numbers, alignment, fonts, borders, colors, and patterns.

The *Format Cells* dialog box and commands on the Home tab control the formatting for numbers, alignment, fonts, borders, colors, and patterns. Execution of the command produces a tabbed dialog box in which you choose the particular formatting category, and then enter the desired options. All formatting is done within the context of select-then-do. You can select the cells to which the formatting is to apply and then execute the Format Cells command. If you want to apply the same formats to an entire column or row, click the respective column letter or row number, and then select the desired format. You can display the Format Cells dialog box by clicking the Dialog Box Launcher in the Font, Alignment, or Number group.

After you format a cell, the formatting remains in the cell and is applied to all subsequent values that you enter into that cell. You can, however, change the formatting by executing a new formatting command. Also, you can remove the formatting by using the options with Clear in the Editing group on the Home tab. Changing the format of a number changes the way the number is displayed, but does not change its value. If, for example, you entered 1.2345 into a cell, but displayed the number as 1.23, the actual value (1.2345) would be used in all calculations involving that cell. The numeric formats are shown and described in Table 1.5. They are accessed by clicking the Number Format down arrow in the Number group on the Home tab. The tabbed Format Cells dialog box is displayed by selecting More.

Table 1.5 Formatting Definitions

Format Style	Definition
General	The default format for numeric entries and displays a number according to the way it was originally entered. Numbers are shown as integers (e.g., 123), decimal fractions (e.g., 1.23), or in scientific notation (e.g., 1.23E+10) if the number exceeds 11 digits.
Number	Displays a number with or without the 1000 separator (e.g., a comma) and with any number of decimal places. Negative numbers can be displayed with parentheses and/or can be shown in red.
Currency	Displays a number with the 1000 separator and an optional dollar sign (which is placed immediately to the left of the number). Negative values can be preceded by a minus sign or displayed with parentheses, and/or can be shown in red.
Accounting	Displays a number with the 1000 separator, an optional dollar sign (at the left border of the cell, vertically aligned within a column), negative values in parentheses, and zero values as hyphens.
Date	Displays the date in different ways, such as March 14, 2009, 3/14/09, or 14-Mar-09.
Time	Displays the time in different formats, such as 10:50 PM or the equivalent 22:50 (24-hour time).
Percentage	Shows when the number is multiplied by 100 for display purposes only, a percent sign is included, and any number of decimal places can be specified.
Fraction	Displays a number as a fraction, and is appropriate when there is no exact decimal equivalent. A fraction is entered into a cell by preceding the fraction with an equal sign—for example, =1/3. If the cell is not formatted as a fraction, you will see the results of the formula.
Scientific	Displays a number as a decimal fraction followed by a whole number exponent of 10; for example, the number 12345 would appear as 1.2345E+04. The exponent, +04 in the example, is the number of places the decimal point is moved to the left (or right if the exponent is negative). Very small numbers have negative exponents.
Text	Left aligns the entry and is useful for numerical values that have leading zeros and should be treated as text, such as ZIP codes.
Special	Displays a number with editing characters, such as hyphens in a Social Security number.
Custom	Enables you to select a predefined customized number format or use special symbols to create your own customized number format.

Use Fonts

You can use the same fonts in Excel as you can in any other Windows application. All fonts are WYSIWYG (What You See Is What You Get), meaning that the worksheet you see on the monitor will match the printed worksheet.

Any entry in a worksheet may be displayed in any font, style, or point size, as indicated in the Font group on the Home tab, as shown in Figure 1.33. The example shows Arial, Bold, Italic, and 14 points. Special effects, such as subscripts or superscripts, are also possible. You can even select a different color, but you will need a color printer to see the effect on the printed page.

Figure 1.33 Font Group on the Home Tab

Alignment of Cell Contents

The Alignment tab in the Format Cells dialog box and the Alignment group on the Home tab together give you a wealth of options to choose from. Changing the orientation of cell contents is useful when labels are too long and widening columns is not an option. Wrapping text in a cell also reduces the need to widen a column when space is at a premium. Centering, right aligning, or left aligning text can be done for emphasis or to best display cell contents in columns. When the height of rows is changed, it is necessary to vertically adjust alignment for ease of reading. Figure 1.34 shows both the Alignment group and the Format Cells dialog box with the Alignment tab visible.

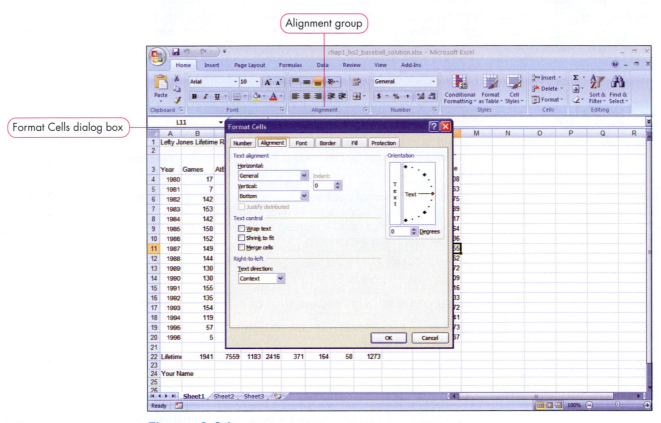

Figure 1.34 Alignment Group and Alignment Tab

TIP   Use Restraint

More is not better, especially in the case of too many typefaces and styles, which produce cluttered worksheets that impress no one. Limit yourself to a maximum of two typefaces per worksheet, but choose multiple sizes or styles within those typefaces. Use boldface or italics for emphasis, but do so in moderation, because if you emphasize too many elements, the effect is lost. Figure 1.37 shows locations of number format commands.

Hands-On Exercises

3 | Formatting Jake's Gym Worksheet

Skills covered: 1. Manage the Workbook **2.** Apply Number Formats **3.** Apply Font Attributes and Borders **4.** Change Alignment Attributes **5.** Insert an Image

---

Step 1
Manage the Workbook

Refer to Figure 1.35 as you complete Step 1.

a. If necessary, open the *chap1_ho2_jake_solution* workbook and save it as **chap1_ho3_jake_solution**.

b. Right-click **Sheet1 tab** at the bottom of the worksheet and select **Rename** from the shortcut menu.

> You selected the generic Sheet1 tab so you can give it a more meaningful name.

c. Type **Second Quarter** and press **Enter**.

d. Right-click on the **Second Quarter** sheet tab and select **Tab Color**.

e. Select **Aqua, Accent 5** color from the Theme Colors gallery.

> You applied a color to the Second Quarter sheet tab to make it more distinctive.

f. Right-click the **Sheet2 tab** and click **Delete**.

g. Right-click the **Sheet3 tab** and click **Delete**.

> You have deleted the unused worksheets from the workbook.

h. Save the workbook.

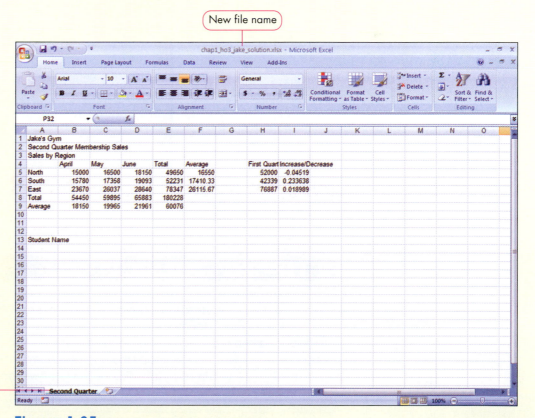

Figure 1.35 Workbook Management

Refer to Figure 1.36 as you complete Step 2.

a. Click and drag to select the **range I5:I7**.

   You selected the range of cells to be formatted.

b. Click the **Home tab** and click the **Number Dialog Box Launcher** in the Number group.

   The Format Cells dialog box shown in Figure 1.36 is now displayed on your screen.

c. Click the **Number tab** and select **Percentage** from the *Category* list.

d. Type **1** in the Decimal places box. Click **OK** to close the dialog box.

   You formatted the increase or decrease in sales as a percentage with 1 decimal place.

e. Click and drag to select the **range B5:H9**.

f. Click the **Number Dialog Box Launcher** in the Number group.

g. Click the **Number tab** and select **Currency** from the *Category* list.

h. Type **0** for the Decimal places box. Click **OK** to close the dialog box.

   You formatted the remaining values as currency with 0 decimal places.

i. Save the workbook.

Use the Format Cells dialog box to format the increase or decrease in sales

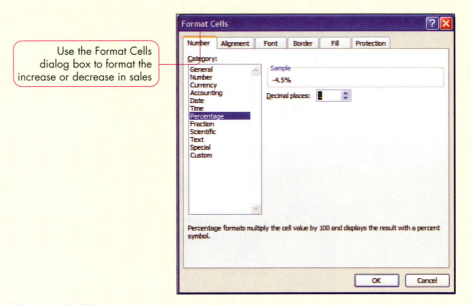

Figure 1.36 Apply Number Format

 TIP   Number Formats

You can change some number formats in the Number group on the Home tab. For example, you can click Accounting Number Format to display dollar signs and align decimal points for monetary amounts. You can click the Number down arrow to select various number formats, such as Number, Accounting, Date, Percentage, and Fraction. The Number group also contains commands to increase or decrease the number of decimal points. Figure 1.37 shows locations of number format commands.

Refer to Figure 1.37 as you complete Step 3. Your screen display may be different depending on your screen resolution.

a. Click and drag to select the **range A1:I3**.

b. Press and hold **Ctrl** while selecting the **range A8:E9**. Continue to press and hold Ctrl while clicking **cell A13** to select it.

You selected several ranges of noncontiguous cells and you can now apply multiple formats to these ranges.

c. Click the **Fill Color** arrow in the Font group and select the color **Purple**.

d. Click the **Font Color** arrow in the Font group and select **White, Background 1**.

> **TROUBLESHOOTING:** If you apply a format and change your mind, just apply another format or clear the formatting using Clear in the Editing group on the Home tab.

e. Click **Bold** in the Font group to make the text stand out.

You formatted parts of the worksheet by using a color fill, a font color, and a font enhancement. You want to draw attention to these areas of the worksheet.

f. Select the **range B4:F4**, then press and hold **Ctrl** while selecting the **ranges H4:I4** and **B7:E7**.

g. Click **More Borders arrow** in Font group and click **Bottom Double Border**.

You again selected noncontiguous ranges of cells and then applied a double border to the bottom of the cells.

h. Select **cell E6**, press and hold **Ctrl** while selecting **cell H6,** and select **Yellow** from **Fill Color** in the Font group.

This highlights the large increase in sales in the South region between the first and second quarter.

i. Save the workbook.

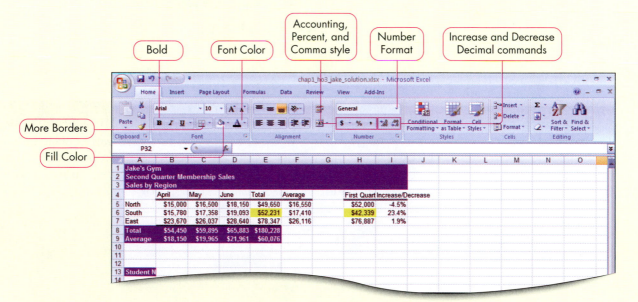

Figure 1.37 Continue Formatting Attributes and Borders

Refer to Figure 1.38 as you complete Step 4.

a. Click on the **Home tab** if it is not already active.

b. Click and drag to select the **range A1:I1**.

c. Click **Merge & Center** in the Alignment group on the Home tab.

d. Click and drag to select the **range A2:I2**.

e. Click **Merge & Center** in the Alignment group on the Home tab.

f. Click and drag to select the **range A3:I3**.

g. Click **Merge & Center** in the Alignment group on the Home tab.

You have now merged cells and centered the title and two subtitles in single cells. You cannot select more than one row and merge into a single cell.

h. Click and drag to select the **range A4:I4**.

i. Right-click on the selected cell range to display a shortcut menu, then select **Format Cells** to display the dialog box.

j. Click the **Alignment tab**, and then click the **Wrap text check box** in the *Text control* section.

k. Click the **Horizontal drop-down arrow** in the *Text alignment* section, select **Center**, and click **OK** to accept the settings and close the dialog box.

You used the shortcut menu to open the dialog box and made two enhancements to the selected text. It is more efficient to make multiple changes using a dialog box.

TROUBLESHOOTING: If your monitor is set for a high resolution or if you have a wide screen monitor, you may see text by some of the command icons. For example, you might see the words *Wrap Text* by the Wrap Text command in the Alignment group. If you want your screen to have the same resolution as the figures shown in this textbook, change your resolution to 1024 × 768.

l. Widen **column A** so all text is visible.

TIP   Split a Cell

If you merge too many cells or decide you no longer want cells to be merged, you can split the merged cell into individual cells again. To do this, select the merged cell and click Merge & Center in the Alignment group or deselect Merge cells on the Alignment tab in the Format Cells dialog box.

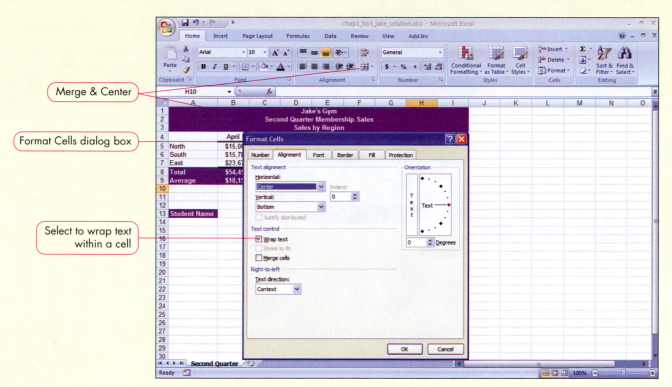

Figure 1.38 Change Alignment Attributes

Step 5
Insert an Image

Refer to Figure 1.39 as you complete Step 5.

a. Click in **cell A1**, click the **Insert tab**, and click **Clip Art** in the Illustrations group. A Clip Art task pane opens. Type **barbell** in the **Search for** box and click **Go**.

You are going to insert a clip art image in the worksheet but must first search for an appropriate image.

b. Click to insert the image shown in Figure 1.39. Click the image to select it and drag the lower-right sizing handle to resize the image to fit the worksheet.

When working with images, it is necessary to resize the images and widen columns or change row height.

c. Save the *chap1_ho3_jake_solution* workbook and keep it onscreen if you plan to continue to the next hands-on exercise. Close the workbook and exit Excel if you do not want to continue with the next exercise at this time.

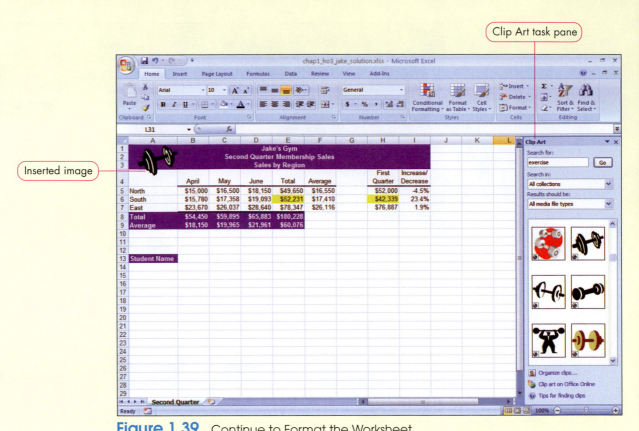

Figure 1.39 Continue to Format the Worksheet

Page Setup and Printing

The Page Setup command gives you complete control of the printed worksheet. Many of the options may not appear significant now, but you will appreciate them as

> The Page Setup command gives you complete control of the printed worksheet.

you develop larger and more complicated worksheets later in the text. Workbooks and worksheets become part of auditor's reports in organizations' annual reports and quarterly reports. Spreadsheets are part of dissertations and grade books, and are the basis for budgeting both for personal use and corporate use. As you can see, printing workbooks and worksheets is an important function.

In this section, you select options in the Page Setup dialog box that will help make your printouts look more professional.

Selecting Page Setup Options for Printing

The key to selecting correct settings to print lies within the Page Setup dialog box. This dialog box contains four tabs. You will make selections from each to indicate the printing settings for the worksheet you want to print. The Page Setup dialog box also contains the Print Preview button. This appears on each tab, and you will use the preview feature to view your selections from each tab. Print preview is a handy and efficient way to see how the printed output will appear without wasting paper. To launch the Print Dialog box, you click the Page Setup Dialog Box Launcher from the Page Setup group on the Page Layout tab. This dialog box is shown in Figure 1.40.

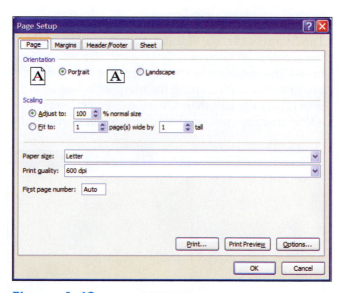

Figure 1.40 Page Setup Dialog Box

Specify Page Options with the Page Tab

The first tab that is open in the Page Setup dialog box is the Page tab, as shown in Figure 1.41. Note that you can use the Print Preview button from any of the Page Setup dialog box tabs and that the Options button takes the user to settings for the particular printer he or she is using. The Print Preview command shows you how the worksheet will appear when printed and saves you from having to rely on trial and error.

The Page orientation options determine the orientation and scaling of the printed page. *Portrait orientation* (8.5 × 11) prints vertically down the page. *Landscape orientation* (11 × 8.5) prints horizontally across the page and is used when the worksheet is too wide to fit on a portrait page. Changing the page orientation to landscape is often an acceptable solution to fit a worksheet on one page. The other option, scaling, can produce uneven results when you print a workbook consisting of multiple worksheets.

Portrait orientation prints vertically down the page.

Landscape orientation prints horizontally across the page.

Scaling option buttons are used to choose the scaling factor. You can reduce or enlarge the output by a designated scaling factor, or you can force the output to fit on a specified number of pages. The latter option is typically used to force a worksheet to fit on a single page. The Paper size and Print quality lists present several options for the size paper your printer is using and the dpi (Dots Per Inch) quality of the printer.

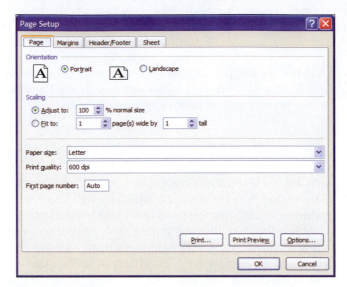

Figure 1.41   Page Tab

Use the Margins Tab to Set Margins

The Margins tab (see Figure 1.42) not only controls the margins, but is used to center the worksheet horizontally or vertically on the page. The Margins tab also determines the distance of the header and footer from the edge of the page. You must exercise caution in setting the margins as not all printers can accept very small margins (generally less than .25 inches). Worksheets appear more professional when you adjust margins and center the worksheet horizontally and vertically on a page.

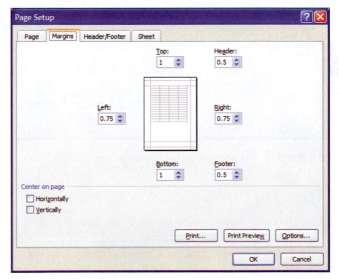

Figure 1.42   Margins

Create Headers and Footers with Header/Footer Tab

The Header/Footer tab, shown in Figure 1.43, lets you create a header and/or footer that appears at the top and/or bottom of every page. The pull-down list boxes let you choose from several preformatted entries, or alternatively, you can click the Custom Header or Custom Footer button, and then click the appropriate formatting button to customize either entry. Table 1.6 below shows a summary of the formatting buttons for headers and footers. You can use headers and footers to provide additional information about the worksheet. You can include your name, the date the worksheet was prepared, and page numbers, for example.

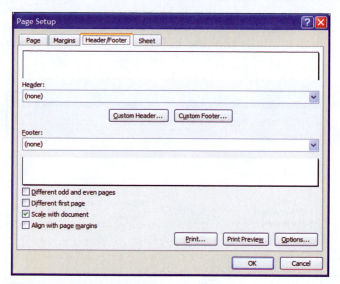

Figure 1.43 Headers and Footers

Table 1.6 Header/Footer Button Summary

Button	Name	Code Entered	Result
A	Format Text	None	Sets font, size, and text style.
#	Insert Page Number	&(Page)	Inserts page number.
	Insert Number of Pages	&(Pages)	Indicates total number of pages.
	Insert Date	&(Date)	Inserts the current date.
	Insert Time	&(Time)	Inserts the current time.
	Insert File Path	&(Path)&(File)	Indicates path and file name.
	Insert File Name	&(File)	Indicates the file name.
	Insert Sheet Name	&(Tab)	Shows the name of the active worksheet.
	Insert Picture	&(Picture)	Inserts an image file.
	Format Picture	None	Opens the Format Picture dialog box.

Select Sheet Options from the Sheet Tab

The Sheet tab contains several additional options, as shown in Figure 1.44. The Gridlines option prints lines to separate the cells within the worksheet. The Row and Column Headings option displays the column letters and row numbers. Both options should be selected for most worksheets. Just because you see gridlines on the screen does not mean they print. You must intentionally select the options to print both gridlines and row and column headings if you want them to print.

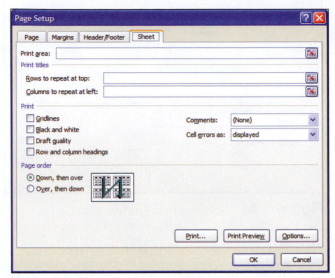

Figure 1.44 Sheet Tab

TIP   Print Preview

The Print Preview button is on all tabs of the Page Setup dialog box. This button is used to verify options as you make your page setup choices. Print Preview is a paper-saving feature because you can preview before printing. The Print button is located on all tabs of the Page Setup dialog box.

Managing Cell Comments

A **comment** adds documentation to a cell.

The use of cell *comments* in Excel is an important yet simple way to provide documentation to others who may view the file. Comments add documentation to a cell and are inserted in a cell to explain the preparer's thoughts to or define formulas for those using the workbook. Often, the creator of a file will want to provide information about a cell or cells in a worksheet without them always being visible. Inserting comments will accomplish this result. A red triangle appears in the cell containing the comment, and the comment is visible when you point at the cell. See Figure 1.45. To create a cell comment:

1. Click the cell requiring a comment.
2. On the Review tab, in the Comments group, click New Comment.
3. Enter the comment.
4. Click any other cell to complete the process.
5. Or right-click on the cell requiring a comment and select Insert Comment from the shortcut menu.

4 | Printing Jake's Gym Worksheet

Skills covered: 1. Insert a Comment **2.** Insert Custom Header and Footer **3.** Format to Print the Worksheet

---

Step 1
Insert a Comment

Refer to Figure 1.45 as you complete Step 1.

a. Open the *chap1_ho3_jake_solution* workbook and save it as **chap1_ho4_jake_ solution**.

b. Click in **cell I6**.

You will type a descriptive comment in the selected cell.

c. Click the **Review tab** and click **New Comment** in the Comments group.

The name in the comment box will be different depending on how the application was registered.

d. Type **The largest percent of increase**.

e. Click any other cell to complete the process.

You can also right-click the cell requiring a comment and select Insert Comment from the shortcut menu.

TROUBLESHOOTING: You can print your comments by first clicking in the cell containing a comment, and then clicking Show All Comments in the Comments group of the Review tab. Then select As displayed on sheet from the Comments list in the Sheet tab of the Page Setup dialog box.

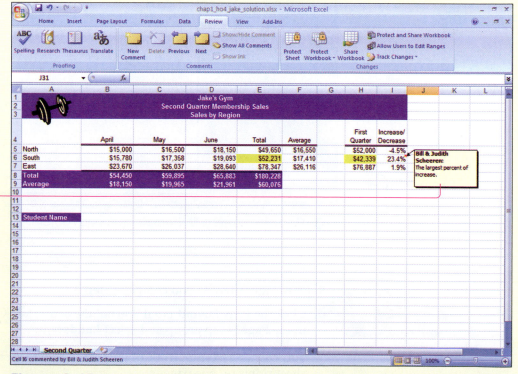

Figure 1.45 Insert a Comment

Step 2

Insert Custom Header and Footer

Refer to Figure 1.46 as you complete Step 2.

a. Click the **Page Layout tab** and click the **Page Setup Dialog Box Launcher** in the Page Setup group.

You opened the Page Setup box so you can make several selections at one time.

b. Click the **Header/Footer tab**.

c. Click **Custom Header** and type your name in the left section.

d. Click in the right section and click **Insert Page Number**. Click **OK**.

You created a header so your name and page number will display at the top of the spreadsheet page.

e. Click **Custom Footer** and click in the center section. Type your instructor's name.

f. Click in the right section, click **Insert Date**, and click **OK**.

You created a footer so your instructor's name and the date will print at the bottom of the spreadsheet page.

g. Click **Print Preview**.

You use the preview feature to verify the accuracy and placement of your header and footer information. You can also determine how much of the worksheet will print on a page. Close Print Preview when you are finished.

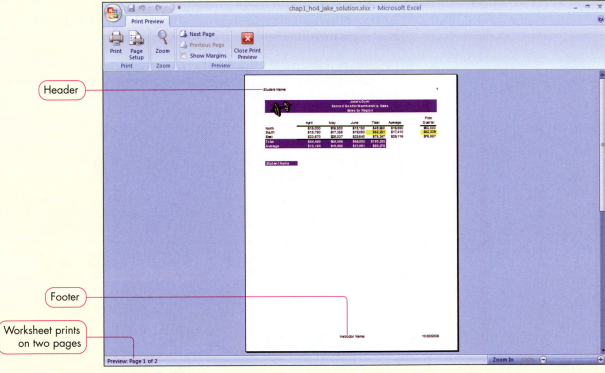

Figure 1.46 Insert a Custom Header and Footer

Step 3

Format to Print the Worksheet

Refer to Figure 1.47 as you complete Step 3.

a. Click the **Page Layout tab** if it is not the active tab. Click the **Orientation** arrow in the Page Setup group and select **Landscape**.

You changed from portrait to landscape as one method to make sure the worksheet prints on one page.

b. Click the **Size** arrow in the Page Setup group, select **More Paper Sizes**, and click the **Fit to: 1 page option** in the *Scaling* section.

You opened the Page Setup dialog box and selected *Fit to 1 page* to force the worksheet to print on a single page, another method to print the worksheet on one page. You will continue to make selections from the Page Setup dialog box.

c. Click the **Margins tab** in the Page Setup dialog box and click the **Horizontally** and **Vertically check boxes** in the *Center on page* section.

Printing a worksheet that is centered both horizontally and vertically results in a Professional-appearing document.

d. Click the **Sheet tab** in the Page Setup dialog box and click the **Row and column headings** and **Gridlines check boxes** in the *Print* section. Click the **Print Preview button** and click **OK**.

Row and column headings and gridlines facilitate reading the data in a worksheet.

e. Click **Print** to print the worksheet and click **OK** to close the dialog box.

f. Save the workbook and press **Ctrl+~** to show the cell formulas rather than the displayed values. See Figure 1.47. Adjust the column widths as necessary to print on one page and then print the worksheet a second time.

Displaying and printing cell formulas is one of the more important tasks associated with worksheet creation. Formulas are the basis of many values, and it is necessary to verify the accuracy of the values. Analyzing the formulas and perhaps manually calculating the formulas is one way to verify accuracy. Printing with formulas displayed is part of worksheet documentation. (Submit assignment electronically or print as directed by your instructor.)

g. Close the workbook. Do not save the changes unless your instructor tells you to save the worksheet.

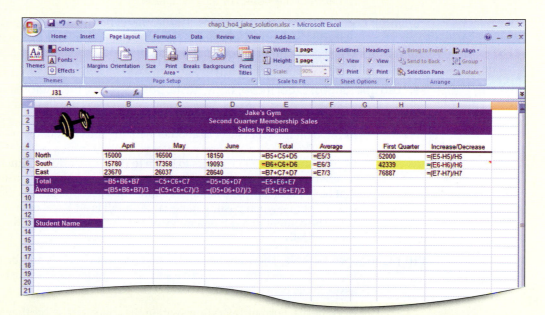

Figure 1.47 Displayed Cell Formulas

TIP   Quit Without Saving

At times, you may not want to save the changes to a workbook—for example, when you have edited it beyond recognition and wish you had never started. Click the Office Button, click the Close command, and then click No in response to the message asking whether to save the changes. Click the Office Button, click the file's name at the right of the menu to reopen the file, and then begin all over.

Summary

1. **Define worksheets and workbooks.** A spreadsheet is the computerized equivalent of an accountant's ledger. It is divided into rows and columns, with each row and column assigned a heading. The intersection of a row and column forms a cell. Spreadsheet is a generic term. Workbook and worksheet are Excel specific. An Excel workbook contains one or more worksheets.

2. **Use spreadsheets across disciplines.** Spreadsheets are used in many areas other than business. Because of the powerful graphing or charting feature of Excel, geologists and physical scientists use spreadsheets to store data about earthquakes or other physical phenomena and then graph it. Historians and social scientists have long used the power of spreadsheets for such uses as predicting voting behavior.

3. **Plan for good workbook and worksheet design.** Planning a spreadsheet before entering data into it is a necessary activity. The more prior planning that is done, the better the spreadsheet will appear, and it also will ensure that the spreadsheet shows what it is supposed to.

4. **Identify Excel window components.** The elements of the Excel window include the ribbon, tabs, and groups. There are also quick buttons above the tabs to simplify some functions. The formula bar, sheet tabs, the status bar, and the Select All button are parts of the Excel window.

5. **Enter and edit data in cells.** You can enter three types of data in an Excel worksheet. They are text, values, and formulas. Each of these types of data has different uses in Excel.

6. **Describe and use symbols and the order of precedence.** Mathematical symbols are the base of all calculations in Excel. Understanding the order of precedence also helps clarify how mathematical calculations occur in Excel.

7. **Display cell formulas.** One of the tools that can be used to document an Excel worksheet is the ability to display cell formulas. When this tool is used, the formulas that appear in cells are shown rather than the results of the calculation.

8. **Insert and delete rows and columns.** This feature typically involves the use of the Insert command that adds cells, rows, or columns or the Delete command that deletes cells, rows, or columns. When either of these commands is used, the cell references in existing cells are automatically adjusted to reflect the insertion or deletion.

9. **Use cell ranges; Excel move; copy, paste, paste special; and AutoFill.** Each of these topics is a basic editing function in Excel. Every command in Excel applies to a rectangular group of cells known as a *range*. The Move operation transfers the content of a cell or cell range from one location on the worksheet to another with the cells where the move originated becoming empty. The Delete operation removes all content from a cell or from a selected cell range. The Copy command enables users to begin to duplicate information in a cell or range of cells into another cell or range of cells. The Paste operation enables the user to duplicate cell contents that have been copied to a new location. The Paste Special operation enables users several different options when pasting material. AutoFill is an Excel operation that enables users to copy the content of a cell or a range of cells by dragging the fill handle over another cell or range of cells.

10. **Manage worksheets.** These are operations that users of Excel should be familiar with in order to make worksheets more attractive and also to understand some basic operations that can assist in the construction of worksheets.

11. **Format worksheets.** Formatting is done within the context of select-then-do; that is, select the cell or range of cells, then execute the appropriate command. The Format Cells command controls the formatting for numbers, alignment, fonts, borders, and patterns (colors). The Formatting toolbar simplifies the formatting process. As you format a worksheet to improve its appearance, you might want to insert clip art as well.

12. **Select page setup options for printing.** The Page Setup command provides complete control over the printed page, enabling you to print a worksheet with or without gridlines or row and column headings. The Page Setup command also controls margins, headers and footers, centering the worksheet on a page, and orientation. The Print Preview command shows the worksheet as it will print and should be used prior to printing.

13. **Manage cell comments.** The use of comments in Excel is an important, yet simple, way to provide documentation to others who may view the file. Often the creator of a file will want to provide information about a cell or cells in a worksheet without them always being visible.

Key Terms

Multiple Choice

1. Which of the following is true?

   (a) A worksheet contains one or more workbooks.

   (b) A workbook contains one or more worksheets.

   (c) A spreadsheet contains one or more worksheets.

   (d) A worksheet contains one or more spreadsheets.

2. The cell at the intersection of the second column and third row is cell:

   (a) B3

   (b) 3B

   (c) C2

   (d) 2C

3. Which options are mutually exclusive in the Page Setup menu?

   (a) Portrait and landscape orientation

   (b) Cell gridlines and row and column headings

   (c) Left and right margins

   (d) Fit to page and Adjust to normal size

4. Which of the following is not a symbol for a mathematical operation in Excel?

   (a) +

   (b) −

   (c) C

   (d) *

5. Which command enables you to change the margins for a printed worksheet?

   (a) View

   (b) Edit

   (c) Page Setup

   (d) Options

6. What is the effect of typing F5+F6 into a cell without a beginning equal sign?

   (a) The entry is equivalent to the formula =F5+F6.

   (b) The cell will display the contents of cell F5 plus cell F6.

   (c) The entry will be treated as a text entry and display F5+F6 in the cell.

   (d) The entry will be rejected by Excel, which will signal an error message.

7. The Save command:

   (a) Brings a workbook from disk into memory.

   (b) Brings a workbook from disk into memory and then erases the workbook on disk.

   (c) Stores the workbook in memory on disk.

   (d) Stores the workbook in memory on disk and then erases the workbook from memory.

8. Which of the following is not a basic mathematical operation?

   (a) Parentheses

   (b) Division

   (c) Multiplication

   (d) Subtraction

9. Given the formula =B5*B6+C3/D4^2, which expression would be evaluated first?

   (a) B5*B6

   (b) D4^2

   (c) C3/D4

   (d) It is impossible to determine.

10. If you see the term "C3" used in relation to Excel, this refers to what?

    (a) Absolute reference

    (b) Cell reference

    (c) Worksheet reference

    (d) Mixed reference

11. Which of the following is the correct order of mathematical operations?

    (a) Parentheses, multiplication or division, addition or subtraction

    (b) Parentheses, exponents, multiplication or division, addition or subtraction

    (c) Parentheses, exponents, addition or subtraction, multiplication or division

    (d) Multiplication or division, addition or subtraction, parentheses, exponents

12. What is the answer to =10+4*3?

    (a) 42

    (b) 22

    (c) 34

    (d) 17

...continued on Next Page

13. What is the answer to =(6*5)+4?

(a) 34
(b) 44
(c) 26
(d) 54

14. The fill handle is used to:

(a) Copy
(b) Paste
(c) Cut
(d) Select

15. The small black square in the bottom-right corner of a cell is called what?

(a) Pointer
(b) Fill handle
(c) Cross hair
(d) Select box

16. A red triangle in a cell indicates which of the following:

(a) A cell is locked.
(b) The cell contains an absolute reference.
(c) The cell contains a comment.
(d) The cell contains numeric data.

17. Which of the following is entered first when creating a formula?

(a) The equal sign
(b) A mathematical operator
(c) A function
(d) A value

18. What is the end result of clicking in a cell and then clicking Italic on the Home tab twice in a row?

(a) The cell contents are displayed in italic.
(b) The cell contents are not displayed in ordinary (non-italicized) type.
(c) The cell contents are unchanged and appear exactly as they did prior to clicking the Italic button twice in a row.
(d) Impossible to determine.

19. Which option is not available when creating a custom header or custom footer?

(a) Format Text
(b) Insert Formula
(c) Insert Number of Pages
(d) Format Picture

1 Verifying a Debit Card

One of the more common challenges beginning college students face is keeping track of their finances. The worksheet in this problem is one that you could use to verify your weekly debit card expenditures. Failure to track your debit card correctly could lead to financial disaster, as you are charged for overdrafts and could get a bad credit rating. You will use the data shown in the table below to create the worksheet. Refer to Figure 1.48 as you complete this exercise.

a. Start Excel and select **New** to display a blank workbook. Save the workbook as **chap1_pe1_debitcard_solution**.

b. Click in **cell A1** and type **Your Name Debit Card**. Do not worry about formatting at this time. Enter the labels as shown in the table below:

Cell Address	Label
A2	Item #
B2	Date
C2	Description
D2	Amount
E2	Deposit
F2	Balance

c. Click in **cell F3** and type the initial balance of **1000**. You will format the values later. Use the table below to enter the data for the first item:

Cell Reference	Data
A4	100
B4	6/2
C4	Rent
D4	575

d. Click in **cell F4** and type the formula **=F3-D4+E4** to compute the balance. The formula is entered so that the balance is computed correctly. It does not matter if an amount or deposit is entered as the transaction because Excel treats the blank cells as zeros.

e. Enter data in rows 5 through 7, as shown in Figure 1.48. Type **Weekly Verification** in cell C8. Click in **cell F4** and use the fill handle to copy the formula to **cells F5:F7**.

f. Insert a new row above row 8 by right-clicking in row 8, selecting **Insert** from the shortcut menu, clicking **Entire row** in the Insert dialog box, and then clicking **OK**.

g. Click in **cell D9** to enter the formula to total your weekly expenditure amount. Type **=D4+D6+D7** and press **Enter**. If the formula is entered correctly, you will see 670.43 in cell D9.

h. Click in **cell E9** and type **=E5** to enter the formula to total your weekly deposit. If the formula is entered correctly, you will see 250 as the total first week deposit.

i. To verify your balance, click in **cell F9,** and type **=F3-D9+E9,** and press **Enter**. If you entered the formula correctly, you will see 579.57 as the balance.

j. Right-click **cell F9** and select **Insert Comment**. Type the following comment: **Balance is equal to the initial balance minus the amounts and ATM withdrawals plus the deposits.**

k. Format the completed worksheet, as shown in Figure 1.48. Click in **cell D3**, and then click and drag to select the **range D3:F9**. Click the **Home tab** and click the **Number Format down arrow** in the Number group. Click **Currency** from the Number Format gallery.

l. Click and drag to select the **range B4:B7**. Click the **Number Format down arrow** in the Number group. Click **Short Date** from the Number Format gallery. Select the **range**

...continued on Next Page

A4:A7; press and hold **Ctrl** while dragging to select the **range A2:F2**. Click **Center** in the Alignment group on the Home tab.

m. Click and drag to select the **range A1:F2**. Click the **Fill Color arrow** in the Font group and select the color **Orange**. Click the **Font Color arrow** in the Font group and select **Blue**. Click **Bold** in the Font group and **select 16** from **Font Size** list to make the text stand out. Click **More Borders** in the Font group and click **Top and Thick Bottom Border**.

n. Widen columns A through F so all text is visible by dragging the right border of each column to the right.

o. Click and drag to select the **range A1:F1**. Click **Merge & Center** in the Alignment group on the Home tab.

p. Click the **Page Layout tab** and click the **Page Setup Dialog Box Launcher** in the Page Setup group. Click the **Header/Footer tab**, click **Custom Header**, and type **Your Name** in the *Left section*. Click in the *Right section* and click **Insert Page Number**. Click **OK**.

q. Click **Custom Footer** and click in the *Center section*. Type **Your Instructor's Name**. Click in the *Right section*, click **Insert Date**, and click **OK**. Click **Print Preview**. Click **Page Setup** on the Print Preview tab.

r. Click the **Margins tab** in the Page Setup dialog box and click the **Horizontally** and **Vertically check boxes** in the *Center on page* section. Click the **Sheet tab** and click the **Row and column headings** and **Gridlines check boxes** in the *Print* section. Click **OK**. Click **Close Print Preview** on the Print Preview tab.

s. Click **Save** on the Quick Access Toolbar to save the workbook. Click the **Office Button**, select **Print**, and select **Quick Print** to print the worksheet.

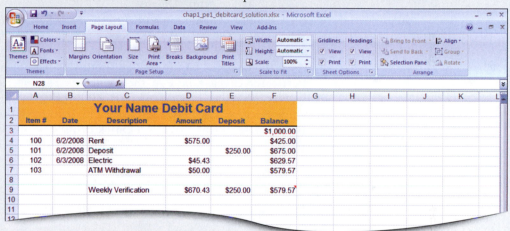

Figure 1.48 Verify Your Debit Card

2 Formatting—Create a Calendar

Excel is a spreadsheet application that gives you a row column table to work with. In this exercise, you will use the row column table to create a calendar worksheet that also demonstrates the formatting capabilities available in Excel. You will insert images representing a variety of activities in a particular month. Review Figure 1.49 to see a sample calendar page.

a. Start Excel to display a blank workbook and save it as **chap1_pe2_calendar_solution**.

b. In **cell D1**, enter the month and year for which you will create the calendar—July, for example. Click and drag to select **cells D1:F1**, then click **Merge & Center** in the Alignment group on the Home tab. Use the Font group to select **Comic Sans MS** font and **26** for the font size. Type **Your Name** in **cell D2** and press **Enter**. Click and drag to select **cells D2:F2** and merge and center as described above. Use the Font group to select **Comic Sans MS** font and **14** for the font size.

c. Right-click **row 1**, select **Row Height** from the shortcut menu, and type **39** in the Row Height dialog box to increase the row height. In similar fashion, right-click **row 2** and verify the row height is **21**.

d. Select **columns B** through **H**, right-click, select **Column Width** from the shortcut menu, and type **16** to change the width of the selected columns.

...continued on Next Page

e. Press and hold **Ctrl** while selecting the **ranges B1:H3, B4:B8,** and **H4:H8.** Click the **Fill Color** arrow in the Font group and select the color **Blue.** Click the **Font Color** arrow in the Font group and select **White, Background 1.** Click **Bold** in the Font group to make the text stand out.

f. Click in **cell B3,** type **Sunday,** and press **Enter.** Click **cell B3** to make it the active cell. Click and drag the fill handle from **cell B3** to **H3** to automatically enter the remaining days of the week.

g. Keeping cells B3:H3 selected, click **Center** in the Alignment group on the Home tab. Increase the row height by right-clicking **row 3,** selecting **Row Height** and typing **23.25** in the Row Height dialog box, and then clicking **OK.**

h. Click **cell D4** and type **1** for the first day of the month. Type numbers for the remaining 30 days of the month in rows **4** through **8.** Increase the row height in rows 4 through 8 to **65.** Select rows **4** through **8,** and click **Top Align,** and click **Align Text Left** in the Alignment group on the Home tab. Click and drag to select **cells B4:H8,** then select **Arial, 14 point,** and **Bold** in the Font group on the Home tab. Click and drag to select **cells B3:H8,** right-click the selected cells, select **Format Cells** to open the Format cells dialog box. Click **Border,** and then click both **Outline** and **Inside** in the *Presets section.* Click **OK.**

i. Click **Clip Art** in the Illustrations group on the Insert tab and type **Fourth of July** in the **Search for** text box. Insert and resize the images, as shown in Figure 1.49. Search for **Cardinal,** insert, and resize the image shown in Figure 1.49.

j. Right-click on the **Sheet1 tab,** select **Rename,** and type **July.** Right-click the July tab, select **Tab Color,** and select **Red.** Delete the remaining sheets by right-clicking the sheet tab and selecting **Delete.**

k. Click the **Page Layout tab** and click the **Page Setup Dialog Box Launcher** in the Page Setup group. Click the **Header/Footer tab.** Click **Custom Footer** and type **Your Name** in the *Left section.* Click in the *Right section* and type your instructor's name. Click **OK.**

l. Click the **Margins tab** in the Page Setup dialog box and click the **Horizontally** and **Vertically check boxes** in the *Center on page* section. Click the **Page tab,** click **Landscape** in the *Orientation section,* **Fit to 1 Page(s)** under *Scaling* and click **OK.**

m. Click **Save** on the Quick Access Toolbar to save the workbook. Click the **Office Button,** select **Print,** and select **Quick Print** to print the worksheet.

Figure 1.49 Create a Calendar

...continued on Next Page

Your hobby is collecting, recording, and monitoring metrological data to track trends in temperature. Figure 1.50 displays the average temperature for summer in three American cities. Working with the partially completed workbook, you will create formulas, copy and paste a portion of a spreadsheet, and format both worksheets in an attractive and readable manner.

a. Open the *chap1_pe3_temperature* workbook and save it as **chap1_pe3_temperature_solution** so that you can return to the original workbook if necessary.

b. Click in **cell E3**, type =(B3+C3+D3)/3, and press **Enter**. You entered the formula to calculate the average summer temperature for Pittsburgh. Click in **cell E3** and use the fill handle to copy the formula to **cells E4:E5**.

c. Click in **cell A6** and type **Monthly Averages**. Enter the formula to calculate the average temperature for June by clicking in **cell B6** and typing =(B3+B4+B5)/3, then pressing **Enter**. Click in **cell B6** and use the fill handle to copy the formula to **cells C6:D6**.

d. Click in **cell E9** and type =(B9+C9+D9)/3, then press **Enter** to calculate the average temperature by city for the winter months. Click in **cell E9** and use the fill handle to copy the formula to **cells E10:E11**.

e. Click in **cell A12** and type **Monthly Averages**. Click in **cell B12** and type =(B9+B10+B11)/3, then pressing **Enter** to calculate the average temperature for December. Click in **cell B12** and use the fill handle to copy the formula to **cells C12:D12**.

f. Format numbers in column E and rows 6 and 12 with 2 decimals by pressing and holding **Ctrl** while selecting **cells E3:E5, E9:E11, B6:D6, and B12:D12**. Click the **Number Format arrow** in the Number group on the Home tab and select **Number**. Widen **column A** to **18**, and **columns B** through **E** to **11**.

g. Insert a blank row above row 1 by right-clicking the row number and selecting **Insert** from the shortcut menu. Type the title **Temperature Comparison** in **cell A1**.

h. Select **cells A1:E1** and click **Merge & Center** in the Alignment group. Repeat for cells **A2:E2** and cells **A8:E8**. Press and hold **Ctrl** while selecting **A1:E2** and **A8:E8**, and then select **Light Blue** from **Fill Color** and **White, Background 1** from **Font Color** in the Font group. Change the title font and size by selecting **cells A1:E1** and then selecting **Comic Sans MS** from the **Font** drop-down list and **18** from the **Font Size** drop-down list in the Font group.

i. Press and hold **Ctrl** while selecting **cells B3:E3** and **B9:E9** and clicking **Center** in the Alignment group.

j. Press and hold **Ctrl** while selecting **cells A1:E3, A7:E9**, and **A13:E13** and click **Bold** in the Font group.

k. Press and hold **Ctrl** while selecting **A4:A6** and **A10:A12** and clicking **Increase Indent** in the Alignment group.

l. Type **Your Name** in **cell G1** to identify the worksheet as yours.

m. You will move your winter temperature data, as well as the title to a new sheet, and then rename and change the color of both sheet tabs and delete Sheet3. Select **cell A1** and click **Copy** in the Clipboard group on the Home tab.

n. Click the **Sheet2 tab**, make sure cell A1 is the active cell, and click the **Paste down arrow** in the Clipboard group, and select **Paste Special**. Select **All** from the *Paste* section of the Paste Special dialog box, and then click **OK** to paste the formatted title in cell A1. Immediately open the Paste Special dialog box again and select **Column widths** from the *Paste* section. When you click **OK** to close, you will see the correct column widths.

o. Click the **Sheet1 tab**, press **Esc** to cancel the previous selected range, select **cells A8:E13**, and click **Copy** in the Clipboard group. Click the **Sheet2 tab**, make sure **cell A2** is the active cell, click the **Paste down arrow** in the Clipboard group, and select **Paste Special**. Select **All** from the *Paste* section of the Paste Special dialog box, and then click **OK** to paste the formatted portion of the worksheet in cell A2. Click **Sheet1** and delete the winter portion of the worksheet by right-clicking and selecting **Delete** from the shortcut menu. Select **Shift cells up** and click **OK**. Right-click the **Sheet1 tab**, select **Rename**, and type **Summer**. Right-click the **Sheet2 tab**, select **Rename**, and type **Winter**. Right-click the **Sheet3 tab**, and select **Delete**. Right-click the **Summer tab** and select **Red** from the **Tab color palette**. Repeat but choose **Blue** for the **Winter tab**.

...continued on Next Page

p. Click the **Page Layout tab** and click the **Page Setup Dialog Box Launcher** in the Page Setup group. Click the **Header/Footer tab**. Click **Custom Header** and type **Your Name** in the *Left section*. Click in the *Right section* and type your course name. Click **OK**.

q. Click the **Margins tab** in the Page Setup dialog box, click **Horizontally** and **Vertically check boxes** in the *Center on page* section, and click **OK**.

r. Print the worksheet two ways, to show both displayed values and cell formula. Save the workbook.

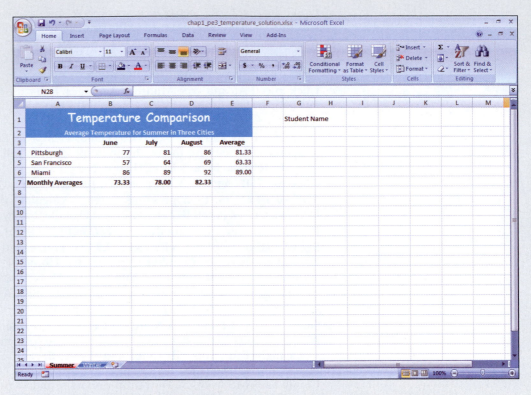

Figure 1.50 Temperature Data

4 Astronomy Lab

The potential uses of a spreadsheet are limited only by your imagination, as shown by Figure 1.51, which displays a spreadsheet with information about our solar system. Your astronomy professor asked you to complete the worksheet as part of your lab assignment. You will open the partially completed version of the workbook and complete the worksheet by developing the formulas for the first planet, copying those formulas to the remaining rows in the worksheet, and then formatting the worksheet for your professor.

a. Open the *chap1_pe4_solarsystem* workbook and save it as **chap1_pe4_solarsystem_solution** so that you can return to the original workbook if necessary.

b. Click in **cell C14** and enter 150 as a weight in pounds on Earth. Click in cell **C15** and enter **=3.141597**, which is the value of Pi for this worksheet.

c. Click in **cell D4** and enter the formula to compute the diameter of the first planet (Mercury). The diameter of a planet is equal to twice its radius. Type **=2*B4** and press **Enter**.

d. Click in **cell E4** and enter the formula to compute the circumference of a planet. The circumference is equal to the diameter times Pi. Type **=3.141597*D4** and press enter.

e. Click in **cell F4** and enter the formula to compute the surface area, which is equal to four times Pi times the radius squared. This is the formula to compute the surface area of a sphere, which is different from the formula to compute the area of a circle. Type **=4*3.141597*B4^2** and press **Enter**.

...continued on Next Page

f. Click in **cell G4** and enter the formula to compute your weight on Mercury, which is your weight on Earth times the relative gravity of Mercury compared to that of Earth. Type **=150*C4** and press **Enter**. The weight in the example is 150, but you will enter your weight and the result will be different.

g. To copy the formulas, select **cells D4:G4** and use the **fill handle** to copy the formula to **cells D4:G11**.

h. Click in **cell E14** and type **Your Name**. Format the worksheet appropriately making sure to do the following:

- Merge and center the cells in **row 1**.

- Format numbers in columns **B, D, E,** and **F** as Number with 0 decimal places. Check the box to use 1000 separator (,).

- Widen columns as necessary.

- Bold rows **1, 3,** and **13**.

- Use **Dark Blue, Text 2** fill and **White, Background 1** font color for cell ranges **A1:G3, A13:C13,** and **E13:F13**.

i. Use the Page Setup dialog box to specify:

- **Landscape** orientation and appropriate **scaling** so that the entire worksheet fits on a single page.

- Create a custom header that includes the name of your institution and the current date.

- Display gridlines and row and column headings.

- **Center** the worksheet **horizontally** on the page.

j. Print the worksheet two ways in order to show both displayed values and cell formulas.

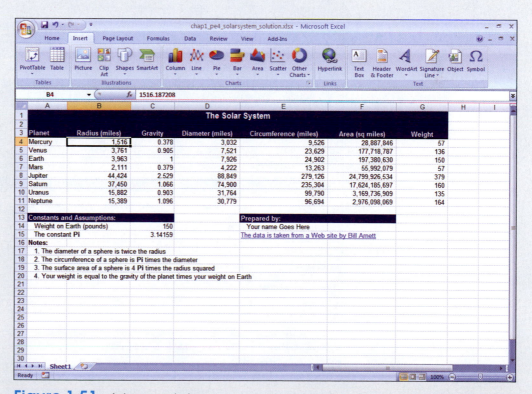

Figure 1.51 Astronomy Lab

Your mother has appointed you the family statistician for your siblings throughout their Little League career. Figure 1.52 displays the completed worksheet showing the statistical data from the last two seasons. Your task is to enter the formulas, format, and print the worksheet for your mother. You will calculate batting averages, totals for statistical data, and family totals.

a. Open the *chap1_mid1_little_league* workbook and save it as **chap1_mid1_little_ league_solution** so that you can return to the original workbook if necessary.

b. Click in **cell B16** and type **Your Name**. Enter the formula to compute totals in cells **C7:I7** and **C14:I14**. Click in **cell J4** and enter a formula to compute batting average, Hits/At Bats.

c. Click and drag to select the formula in **cell J4** and copy the formula to **cells J5:J7**. Enter the formula to determine the Batting Average and copy it for the 2007 season.

d. Click in **cell A18** and type **Family Batting Average**. Enter a formula in **cell B18** to calculate the family batting average. Hint: Parentheses are important here.

e. Format the worksheet exactly as shown in Figure 1.52.

f. Print the worksheet twice, once to show displayed values and once to show the cell formulas. Use **landscape** orientation and be sure that the worksheet fits on one sheet of paper.

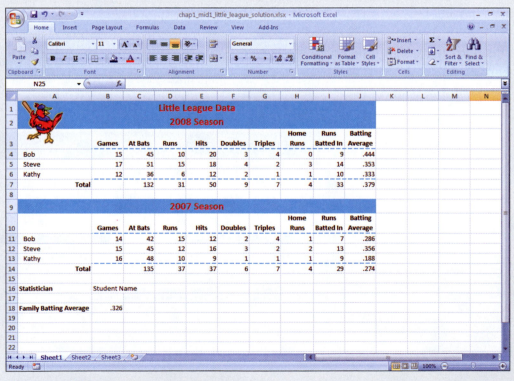

Figure 1.52 Little League Statistician

...continued on Next Page

Your computer professor has determined that you need more practice with basic formatting and cell operations in Excel. The workbook in Figure 1.53 offers this practice for you. Remember to start in cell A1 and work your way down the worksheet, using the instructions in each cell.

a. Open the *chap1_mid2_formatting* workbook and save it as **chap1_mid2_formatting_ solution** so that you can return to the original workbook if necessary. Click in **cell A1** and type your name, then change the formatting as indicated. Merge and center **cells A1** and **B1** into a single cell.

b. Change the width of column A to **53**.

c. Move to **cell A3** and format the text as indicated in the cell. Move to **cell B3** and double underline the text in Green.

d. Format **cells A4:B7** according to the instructions in the respective cells.

e. Follow the instructions in cells A8 to A14 to format the contents of cells **B8 to B14**. Click in **cell B4**, click the Format Painter tool, and then click and drag **cells A8:A14** to apply the formatting from **cell B4**.

f. Click in **cell A15**, then deselect the Merge & Center command to split the merged cell into two cells. Follow the instructions in the cell to wrap and center the text. Cell B15 should be blank when you are finished.

g. Right-click in **cell A16**, select Insert from the shortcut menu, click to shift cells down, and then click **OK**. You have inserted a new cell A16, but the contents in cell B16 should remain the same. Format **cell B16**.

h. Merge cells **A17** and **B17**, and then complete the indicated formatting.

i. Use the Page Setup command to display gridlines and row and column headings. Change to landscape orientation and center the worksheet horizontally on the page. Add a custom footer that contains your name and the date and time you completed the assignment. Print the completed workbook.

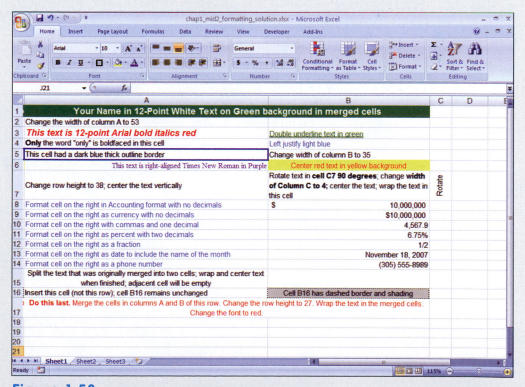

Figure 1.53 Exploring Formatting Options

...continued on Next Page

3 Measurement Conversions

You work in a testing lab for a major industrial company, and your supervisor has asked you to prepare a table of conversion factors and a table of equivalencies. You will use this as a "crib sheet" during your work and in the preparation of reports, so you want to make it as complete and as accurate as possible. The workbook in Figure 1.54 provides practice with formulas, formatting, and basic cell operations. You do have to match the formatting exactly and you must enter the identical values into column G.

a. Open the *chap1_mid3_conversion* workbook and save it as **chap1_mid3_conversion_ solution** so that you can return to the original workbook if necessary. Click in **cell E8** and type the formula **=1/E7**. Cell E7 contains the value to convert inches to centimeters; the reciprocal of that value will convert centimeters to inches. Enter the appropriate formula into **cell E19** to convert kilograms to pounds.

b. A kilobyte is mistakenly thought of as 1,000 bytes, whereas it is actually 1,024 (2^{10}) bytes. In similar fashion, a megabyte and a gigabyte are 2^{20} and 2^{30} bytes. Use this information to enter the appropriate formulas to display the conversion factors in cells **E21**, **E22**, and **E23**.

c. Enter the formulas for the first conversion into row 7. Click in **cell H7** and type **=C7**. Click in **cell J7** and type **=E7*G7**. Click in **cell K7** and type **=D7**. Copy the formulas in row 7 to the remaining rows in the worksheet. The use of formulas for columns H through K builds flexibility into the worksheet; that is, you can change any of the conversion factors on the left side of the worksheet and the right side will be updated automatically.

d. Enter a set of values in column G for conversion; for example, type 12 in **cell G7** to convert 12 inches to centimeters. The result should appear automatically in **cell J7**.

e. Type your name in **cell G3**. Use Aqua as the fill color in cells **G7:G23** and other ranges of cells, as shown in Figure 1.54.

f. Use the Merge & Center command as necessary throughout the worksheet to approximate the formatting in Figure 1.54. Change the orientation in column B so that the various labels are displayed as indicated.

g. Display the border around the groups of cells, as shown in Figure 1.54.

h. Print the displayed values and the cell formulas. Be sure to show the row and column headings as well as the gridlines. Use landscape orientation to be sure the worksheet fits on a single sheet of paper.

...continued on Next Page

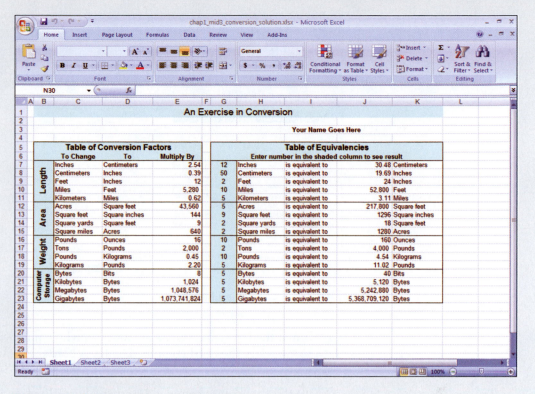

Figure 1.54 Measurement Conversions

4 Fuel Efficiency

Your summer vacation involved traveling through several states to visit relatives and to view the scenic attractions. While traveling, you kept a travel log of mileage and gasoline purchases. Now that the vacation is over, you want to determine the fuel efficiency of your automobile. The partially completed worksheet in Figure 1.55 includes the beginning mileage for the vacation trips and the amount of fuel purchased. This exercise provides practice with formulas, formatting, copying, and basic cell operations.

a. Open the *chap1_mid4_fuel* workbook and save it as **chap1_mid4_fuel_solution** so that you can return to the original workbook if necessary. Click in **cell C12** and change the gallons to **9.2** because you are correcting a typing error.

b. Insert a new column between columns B and C and type **Miles Driven** in **cell C3**.

c. Select **cells A5:A12**, copy the selected range, and paste it in **cells B4:B11**. This ensures that the ending mileage for one trip is the same as the beginning mileage for the next trip. Click **cell B12** and type **34525**, the mileage at the end of the last trip.

d. Use cell references and create the formula to calculate the miles driven for each trip. Use cell references and create the formula to calculate the miles per gallon for each trip.

e. Select **cells A1:E1** and apply the Dark Blue fill color. Apply the following formats to **cell A1**: Times New Roman, 16 point, Bold, White font color. Merge and center the title over columns A through E.

f. Word-wrap the contents of **cells C3** and **E3**. Bold and center horizontally the headings in row 3. Apply the following number formats to the values in columns A and B: whole numbers, no decimals, comma format.

...continued on Next Page

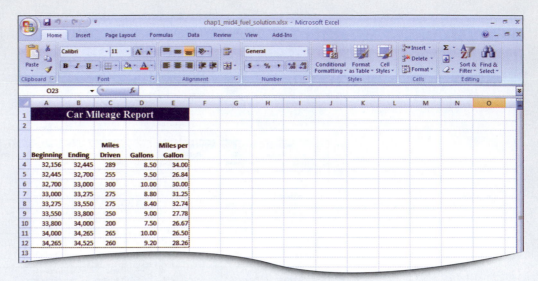

Figure 1.55 Fuel Efficiency

g. Format the last two columns of values as whole numbers with two decimals. Center the values in the third column. Display a border around **cells A4:E12**, as shown in Figure 1.55.

h. Use the Page Setup command to display gridlines and row and column headings. Change to landscape orientation and center the worksheet horizontally on the page. Add a custom footer that contains your name and the date and time you completed the assignment. Print the completed workbook.

5 Freshman Seminar Grade Book

Figure 1.56 displays your instructor's sample grade book complete with a grading scheme. Students take three exams worth 100 points each, submit a term paper and various homework assignments worth 50 points each, and then receive a grade for the semester based on their total points. The maximum number of points is 400. Your semester average is computed by dividing your total points by the maximum total points. You will complete the Freshman Seminar Grade Book worksheet so the displayed values match Figure 1.56.

a. Open the *chap1_mid5_assumption* workbook and save it as **chap1_mid5_assumption_ solution** so that you can return to the original workbook if necessary.

b. Click in **cell A6** and type **Your Name**. Enter your test scores: **98, 87, and 99**. The term paper is worth **46** and the homework **24**. Insert a column between columns D and E. Type **Exam Total** in **cell E3**. Click in **cell E4** and enter a formula to compute Smith's exam total points. Click in **cell H4** and enter a formula that will compute Smith's total points for the semester. Click in **cell I4** and enter a formula to compute Smith's semester average.

c. Click and drag to select the formula in **cell E4**. Copy this formula through **E6**. Click and drag to select the formulas in **cells H4:I4** and copy the formulas through **I6**.

d. Click in **cell B7** and enter a formula that will compute the class average on the first exam. Copy this formula to cells **C7:H7**.

e. Insert a column between columns C and D and type **Percent Change in Exams** in **cell D3**. Click in **cell D4** and enter the formula to calculate the change in exam scores between the first and second exam.

f. Format the worksheet appropriately, as shown in Figure 1.56.

...continued on Next Page

g. Add your name as the grading assistant, then print the worksheet twice, once to show displayed values and once to show the cell formulas. Use landscape orientation and be sure that the worksheet fits on one sheet of paper.

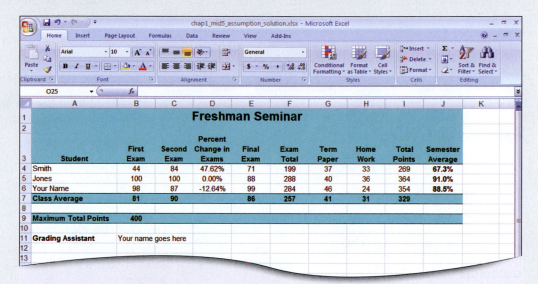

Figure 1.56 Freshman Seminar Grade Book

Capstone Exercise

You are the new assistant to the band director for the Upper Saddle River Marching Band and you must prepare a report showing the status of the marching band fund-raising event for the board of trustees. The report will summarize sales of all items and include the total profit to date with the amount remaining to reach the profit goal. You will open the partially completed workbook, create formulas, and format for presentation to the board of trustees.

Open and Save Worksheet

You must open a worksheet that has the fundraising sales information in it and complete the worksheet.

a. Open the *chap1_cap_fundraising* workbook.

b. Save it as **chap1_cap_fundraising_solution**.

c. Type your name in **cell A20**.

Calculate Values

You are to create the formulas used to calculate profit per item and profit based on the number of items sold. You create a formula to calculate total profit to date and the remaining profit needed to reach the goal.

a. Enter the profit per item formula in **column C**. The profit per item is 50% of the sales price.

b. Enter the profit formula in **column E**. The profit is the profit per item multiplied by the number of items sold.

c. Copy all appropriate formulas.

d. Enter a formula to calculate the total profit to date in **cell E15**.

e. The formula for calculating the remaining profit to reach the goal is the goal minus the total profit to date. Enter the formula in **cell E16**.

Format the Worksheet

Now that you have finished the calculations, you must format the worksheet in a professional manner and suitable for presentation to the board of trustees of the college.

a. Insert a comment in **cell E16** and explain the formula in **cell E16**.

b. Format all money figures as currency with two decimals.

c. Center and merge rows 1 and 2. Center row 4.

d. Change the font to Arial and increase font size in rows 1, 2, and 3, increasing row height and column width as needed.

e. Change font color and bold in rows 1, 2, 3, and 4.

f. Place borders at the top and bottom of **cells A4:E4**. Place a border at the bottom of **cells A14:E14**.

g. Change the fill color for **cells E4:E14**.

h. Search for the keyword **marching band** in the Clip Art task pane. Insert the bass drums image in **cell E2**, resizing as necessary.

Lay Out the Worksheet

Now that you have finished the major formatting, you must lay out the worksheet to further separate and define areas of the worksheet. This step makes the worksheet more aesthetically pleasing and easier to read.

a. Insert new rows above **row 4** and the new **row 16**.

b. Delete sheet tabs 2 and 3.

c. Change the color of the Sheet1 tab to **purple**.

d. Rename Sheet1 as **Fundraising**.

Print the Report

Before printing the report, you see it is missing the standard headers and should be printed in landscape orientation to fit on one page. You also want to show and print the cell formulas.

a. Create a custom footer with your name on the left and today's date on the right.

b. Change the page orientation to landscape.

c. Print the worksheet with displayed values.

d. Print the worksheet again with cell formulas but make sure to fit the worksheet on one page.

e. Save your changes and exit Excel.

Mini Cases

Use the rubric following the case as a guide to evaluate your work, but keep in mind that your instructor may impose additional grading criteria or use a different standard to judge your work.

Housing Office

GENERAL CASE

Your supervisor in the student housing office has asked for your help in preparing a workbook for her annual budget. Open the partially completed *chap1_mc1_housingoffice* workbook and save it as **chap1_mc1_housingoffice_solution**. This workbook is intended to compute the revenue for the dorms on campus. The revenue includes the income from single rooms, double rooms, and the associated meal plans. Your assignment is to complete the workbook. If you do the assignment correctly, the total revenue for Douglass Hall should be $5,325,000. Note that each double room has two students, each of whom is required to pay for the meal plan. Format the completed worksheet as appropriate. Place your name somewhere in the worksheet and print the worksheet two ways in order to show both displayed values and cell formulas. Be sure to use the Page Setup command to specify landscape orientation and appropriate scaling so that the entire worksheet fits on a single page.

Performance Elements	Exceeds Expectations	Meets Expectations	Below Expectations
Create formulas	All formulas work and most efficiently stated.	Formulas are correct.	No formulas, numbers entered.
Attractive, appropriate format	Well formatted and easy to read.	Adequately formatted, difficult to read.	No formatting.
Print formulas and values	Prints both formulas and values.	Prints either formulas or values.	No printout.

The Cost of Smoking

RESEARCH CASE

Smoking is hazardous to your health as well as your pocketbook. A one-pack-a-day habit, at $4.50/pack, will cost you more than $1,600 per year. Use the Web to find the current price for the items listed in the worksheet that you could purchase in one year. Open the partially completed *chap1_mc2_smoking* workbook, save it as **chap1_mc2_smoking_solution**, and compute the number of various items that you could buy over the course of a year in lieu of cigarettes. The approximate prices have been entered already, but you need not use these numbers and/or you can substitute additional items of your own. Place your name somewhere in the worksheet and print the worksheet two ways to show both displayed values and cell. Be sure to use the Page Setup command to specify landscape orientation and appropriate scaling so that the entire worksheet fits on a single page.

Performance Elements	Exceeds Expectations	Meets Expectations	Below Expectations
Research current prices	Prices current within 30 days.	Prices current within 3 months.	Prices more than 3 months old.
Create formulas	All formulas work and most efficiently stated.	Formulas are correct.	No formulas, numbers entered.
Format for one sheet	Formatted correctly and easy to read.	Adequately formatted, difficult to read.	Not formatted for one sheet.
Print values and cell formulas	Values and formulas both printed.	Values or formulas printed.	No print.

Accuracy Counts

DISASTER RECOVERY

The *chap1_mc3_accuracycounts* workbook was the last assignment completed by your predecessor prior to his unfortunate dismissal. The worksheet contains a significant error, which caused your company to underbid a contract and assume a subsequent loss of $200,000. As you look for the error, do not be distracted by the attractive formatting. The shading, lines, and other touches are nice, but accuracy is more important than anything else. Write a memo to your instructor describing the nature of the error. Include suggestions in the memo on how to avoid mistakes of this nature in the future. Open the *chap1_mc3_accuracycounts* workbook and save it as **chap1_mc3_accuracycounts_solution**.

Performance Elements	Exceeds Expectations	Meets Expectations	Below Expectations
Identify and correct the error	Error correctly identified within 10 minutes.	Error correctly identified within 20 minutes.	Error not identified.
Explain the error	Complete and correct explanation of the error.	Explanation is too brief to fully explain the error.	No explanation.
Describe how to prevent the error	Prevention description correct.	Prevention description too brief to be of any value.	No prevention description.

Formulas and Functions

Math Basics for Spreadsheet Use

bjectives

After you read this chapter, you will be able to:

1. Create and copy formulas **(page 139)**.
2. Use relative and absolute cell addresses **(page 140)**.
3. Use AutoSum **(page 147)**.
4. Insert basic statistical functions **(page 148)**.
5. Use date functions **(page 150)**.
6. Use the IF function **(page 157)**.
7. Use the VLOOKUP function **(page 158)**.
8. Use the PMT function **(page 166)**.
9. Use the FV function **(page 167)**.

Hands-On Exercises

Exercises	Skills Covered
1. SMITHTOWN HOSPITAL RADIOLOGY DEPARTMENT PAYROLL (PAGE 142) **Open:** chap2_ho1_payroll.xlsx **Save as:** chap2_ho1_payroll_solution.xlsx	• Compute the Gross Pay • Complete the Calculations • Copy the Formulas with the Fill Handle
2. COMPLETING THE SMITHTOWN HOSPITAL RADIOLOGY DEPARTMENT PAYROLL (PAGE 152) **Open:** chap2_ho1_payroll_solution.xlsx (from Exercise 1) **Save as:** chap2_ho2_payroll_solution.xlsx (additional modifications)	• Compute the Totals • Using Other General Functions • Apply Number Formatting • Apply Font and Alignment Formatting • Insert a Comment to Complete the Worksheet
3. ATHLETIC DEPARTMENT ELIGIBILITY GRADEBOOK (PAGE 161) **Open:** chap2_ho3_gradebook.xlsx **Save as:** chap2_ho3_gradebook_solution.xlsx	• Use the IF Function • Use the VLOOKUP Function • Copy the IF and VLOOKUP Functions • Apply Page Setup Options and Print the Worksheet
4. PURCHASING A VAN FOR THE SCHOOL FOR EXCEPTIONAL CHILDREN (PAGE 168) **Open:** New workbook **Save as:** chap2_ho4_van_solution.xlsx	• Create the Worksheet • Insert the PMT Function • Format the Worksheet • Complete the Worksheet

CASE STUDY

West Transylvania College Athletic Department

The athletic department of West Transylvania College has reached a fork in the road. A significant alumni contingent insists that the college upgrade its athletic program from NCAA Division II to Division I. This process will involve adding sports, funding athletic scholarships, expanding staff, and coordinating a variety of fundraising activities.

Tom Hunt, the athletic director, wants to determine if the funding support is available both inside and outside the college to accomplish this goal. You are helping Tom prepare the five-year projected budget based on current budget figures. The plan is to increase revenues at a rate of 10% per year for five years while handling an estimated 8% increase in expenses over the same five-year period. Tom feels that a 10% increase in revenue versus an 8% increase in expenses should make the upgrade viable. Tom wants to examine how increased alumni giving, increases in college fees, and grant monies will increase the revenue flow. The Transylvania College's Athletic Committee and its Alumni Association Board of Directors want Tom to present an analysis of funding and expenses to determine if the move to NCAA Division I is feasible. As Tom's student assistant this year, it is your responsibility to help him with special projects. Tom prepared the basic projected budget spreadsheet and has asked you to finish it for him.

Case Study

Your Assignment

- Read the chapter carefully and pay close attention to mathematical operations, formulas, and functions.

- Open *chap2_case_athletics*, which contains the partially completed, projected budget spreadsheet.

- Study the structure of the worksheet to determine what type of formulas you need to complete the financial calculations. Identify how you would perform calculations if you were using a calculator and make a list of formulas using regular language to determine if the financial goals will be met. As you read the chapter, identify formulas and functions that will help you complete the financial analysis. You will insert formulas in the revenue and expenditures sections for column C. Use appropriate cell references in formulas. Do not enter constant values within a formula; instead enter the 10% and 8% increases in an input area. Use appropriate functions for column totals in both the revenue and expenditures sections. Insert formulas for the Net Operating Margin and Net Margin rows. Copy the formulas.

- Review the spreadsheet and identify weaknesses in the formatting. Use your knowledge of good formatting design to improve the appearance of the spreadsheet so that it will be attractive to the Athletic Committee and the alumni board. You will format cells as currency with 0 decimals and widen columns as needed. Merge and center the title and use an attractive fill color. Emphasize the totals and margin rows with borders. Enter your name and current date. Create a custom footer that includes a page number and your instructor's name. Print the worksheet as displayed and again with cell formulas displayed. Save the workbook as **chap2_case_athletics_solution**.

Formula Basics

Mathematical operations are the backbone of Excel. The order in which these mathematical operations are performed has a significant impact on the answers that are arrived at. We touched briefly on the construction of mathematical expressions or *formulas* that direct Excel to perform mathematical operations and arrive at a calculated result. A formula also may be defined as the combination of constants, cell references, and arithmetic operations displayed in a calculation. Formulas can be as simple or as complex as necessary, but they always begin with an = sign and contain mathematical operators. In this section, you learn how to use the pointing method to create formulas and the fill handle to copy formulas. Finally, you learn how to prevent a cell reference from changing when you copy a formula to other cells.

A *formula* performs mathematical operations that produce a calculated result.

> Formulas can be as simple or as complex as necessary, but they always begin with an = sign and contain mathematical operators.

Creating and Copying Formulas

As you recall, whenever you want Excel to perform a calculation, you must enter an equal sign (=) in the cell where the answer is to appear. The equal sign indicates within Excel that a mathematical calculation is about to begin. Previously, you created formulas by typing in the cell references. Here in Chapter 2, you enter cell references to create a formula in a more efficient, straightforward way.

Point to Create a Formula

> Rather than typing a cell address . . . as you construct a formula, you can use an alternative method that involves *minimal* typing.

Pointing uses the mouse or arrow keys to select the cell directly when creating a formula.

As previously discussed, the creation of formulas in Excel is the mathematical basis for the program and the use of cell references is integral in the creation of formulas. However, rather than typing a cell address, such as C2, as you construct a formula, you can use an alternative method that involves *minimal* typing. *Pointing* uses the mouse or arrow keys to select the cell directly when creating a formula. To use the pointing technique to create a formula:

1. Click on the cell where the formula will be entered.
2. Type an equal sign (=) to start a formula.
3. Click on the cell with the value to be entered in the formula.
4. Type a mathematical operator.
5. Continue clicking on cells and typing operators to finish the formula.
6. Press Enter to complete the formula.

While the formulas may be more complex than indicated in this example, the steps are the same.

Copy Formulas with the Fill Handle

The *fill handle* is a small black square in the bottom-right corner of a selected cell.

Another powerful copying tool in Excel is the *fill handle*, which is a small black solid square in the bottom-right corner of a selected cell. Using the fill handle provides another, clear-cut alternative method for copying the contents of a cell. You can use the fill handle to duplicate formulas. To copy and paste using the fill handle:

1. Click on the cell (or drag through the cells) to be copied.
2. Position the mouse pointer directly over the fill handle on the cell or cells to be copied. The pointer changes to a thin crosshair.
3. Click and hold down the left mouse button while dragging over the destination cells. Note that using the fill handle only works with contiguous or adjacent cells.

4. Release the mouse button. If the cell to be copied contained a formula, the formula is copied, the cell references are changed appropriately, and Excel performs the calculations.

TIP   Contiguous Cells

In addition to using the fill handle to copy formulas, you can also use the fill handle to finish a text series. For example, you can use the fill handle to complete the days of the week, the four quarters of a year, and the month names to simplify the data-entry process. Type January in a cell, select the cell, click on the fill handle, drag to cover a total of 12 cells. Figure 2.1 shows before and after using the fill handle to complete the January through December series.

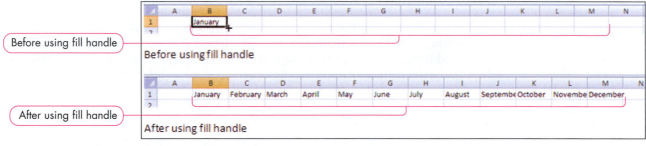

Before using fill handle

After using fill handle

Figure 2.1 Fill Handle

Using Relative and Absolute Cell Addresses

Excel uses three different ways to express a reference to a cell in a formula. These references are relative, absolute, and mixed, and each affects copying cell references in different ways.

A *relative cell reference* is a typical cell reference that changes when copied.

A ***relative cell reference*** within a formula is a cell reference that changes *relative to* the direction in which the formula is being copied. It is expressed in the form C13 (column letter, row number) and is adjusted or changed according to the direction and relative distance it is copied. When you copy a formula containing a relative cell reference over multiple columns, the column letter changes. When you copy a formula containing a relative cell reference down multiple rows, the row number changes. For example, if you copy the contents of cell C5, =C3+C4, to cell E5, the formula becomes =E3+E4. If you copy the contents of cell C5, =C3+C4, to cell E6, the formula becomes =E4+E5.

An *absolute cell reference*, indicated by dollar signs before the column letter and row number, stays the same regardless of where a formula is copied.

An ***absolute cell reference*** in a formula, on the other hand, is one that stays the same no matter where you copy a formula. An absolute cell reference appears with dollar signs before both the column letter and row number ($C$13). Absolute cell references are used when the value in the cell seldom changes but the formula containing the absolute cell reference is copied. An example would be in a payroll spreadsheet that includes a calculation for state income tax using a constant tax rate. The reference to the cell that contains the state income rate (C13)

> A benefit of an absolute cell reference is that if an input value changes, . . . you type the new input value in only one cell and Excel recalculates . . . all the formulas. You do not have to individually edit cells containing formulas. . . .

would therefore be expressed as an absolute cell reference when used in a formula (=$C$13*D26). The absolute address prevents the cell reference from changing when you copy the formula to calculate the amount of state income tax for the other employees. A benefit of an absolute cell reference is that if an input value changes, for example if the state income tax rate changes from 14% to 15.5% in this example, you type the new input value in only one cell and Excel recalculates the amount of state tax for all the formulas. You do not have to individually edit cells containing formulas to change the tax rate value because the formulas contain an absolute cell reference to the cell containing the state tax rate.

The third type of cell reference, the ***mixed cell reference***, occurs when you create a formula that combines an absolute reference with a relative reference ($C13 or C$13). As a result, either the row number or column letter does not change when the cell is copied. Using the relative cell reference C13, it would be expressed as a mixed reference either as $C13 or C$13. In the first case, the column C is absolute and the row number is relative; in the second case, the row 13 is absolute and the column C is relative.

The ***mixed cell reference*** combines an absolute reference with a relative reference.

TIP   The F4 Key

The F4 key toggles through relative, absolute, and mixed references. Click on any cell reference within a formula on the formula bar; for example, click on B4 in the formula =B4+B5. Press F4, and B4 changes to an absolute reference, $B$4. Press F4 a second time, and $B$4 becomes a mixed reference, B$4; press F4 again, and it is a different mixed reference, $B4. Press F4 a fourth time, and the cell reference returns to the original relative reference, B4.

In the first hands-on exercise, you calculate the gross pay for employees in the Smithtown Radiology Department using the pointing method. You perform other payroll calculations, and then use the fill handle to copy the formulas for the remaining employees.

Hands-On Exercises

1 | Smithtown Hospital Radiology Department Payroll

Skills covered: 1. Compute the Gross Pay **2.** Complete the Calculations **3.** Copy the Formulas with the Fill Handle

---

Step 1
Compute the Gross Pay

Refer to Figure 2.2 as you complete Step 1.

a. Start Excel. Open the *chap2_ho1_payroll* workbook to display the worksheet shown in Figure 2.2.

b. Save the workbook as **chap2_ho1_payroll_solution** so that you can return to the original workbook if necessary.

c. Click in **cell F4**, the cell that will contain gross pay for Dwyer. Press = on the keyboard to begin pointing, click **cell C4** (producing a moving border around the cell), press the **asterisk key** (*), and then click **cell D4**.

You have entered the first part of the formula to compute the gross pay.

d. Press the **plus sign** (+), click **cell E4**, press *, click **cell C4**, press *, click **cell D20**, press **F4** to change the cell reference to **$D$20**, and then press **Enter**.

The formula, =C4*D4+E4*C4*$D$20, calculates the gross pay for employee Dwyer by multiplying the $8 hourly wage by 40 regular hours. This amount is added to the 8 overtime hours, multiplied by the $8 hourly wage, multiplied by the 1.5 overtime rate. Note the use of the absolute address ($D$20) in the formula. You should see 416 as the displayed value in cell F4.

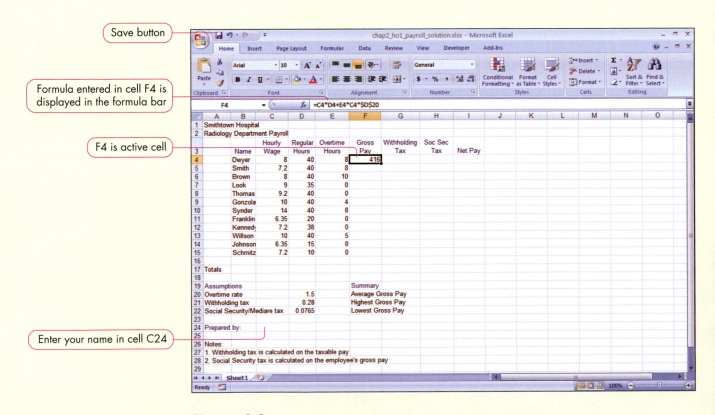

Figure 2.2 Compute the Gross Pay with Absolute Reference

e. Click in **cell F4** to be sure that the formula you entered matches the formula shown in the formula bar in Figure 2.2. If necessary, click in the formula bar and make the appropriate changes so the formula is correct in cell F4.

f. Enter your name in **cell C24** and save the workbook.

Step 2
Complete the Calculations

a. Click in **cell G4**, the cell that will contain the withholding tax for Dwyer. Press = to begin pointing, and then click **cell F4**, the cell containing the gross pay cell. Press the * and click **cell D21**, the withholding tax.

Cell G4 now contains the formula =F4*D21 that calculates Dwyer's withholding tax. However, if you were to copy the formula now, the copied formula would be =F5*D22, which is not quite correct. If a cell address is not made explicitly absolute, Excel's default relative address mode will automatically change a cell address when a formula is copied.

b. Verify that the insertion point is within or immediately behind cell reference D21 and press **F4**.

Pressing F4 changes the cell reference to $D$21 and explicitly makes the cell address an absolute reference. The formula can be copied and will calculate the desired result.

c. Press **Enter**.

The value in cell G4 should be 116.48. This amount is Dwyer's withholding tax.

d. Use the pointing method to enter the remaining formulas for Dwyer. Click in **cell H4** and enter the formula **=F4*$D$22**.

The formula calculates the employee's Social Security tax, which is 7.65% of the gross pay. The formula uses an absolute reference ($D$22) so the cell reference will not change when you copy the formula for the other employees. The value in cell H4 should be 31.824, and this is Dwyer's Social Security tax.

e. Click in **cell I4**, and enter the formula **=F4–(G4+H4)**. Press **Enter** when you finish.

The formula adds the withholding tax and Social Security tax, and then subtracts the total tax from the gross pay. The formula uses only relative cell addresses because you want the copied formulas to refer to the appropriate gross pay and tax cells for each respective employee. The value in cell I4 should be 267.696, and this amount is Dwyer's net pay.

f. Save the workbook.

Step 3
Copy the Formulas with the Fill Handle

Refer to Figure 2.3 as you complete Step 3.

a. Click and drag to select **cells F4:I4**, as shown in Figure 2.3. Point to the fill handle in the lower-right corner of **cell I4**. The mouse pointer changes to a thin crosshair.

You have selected the range containing formulas that you want to copy. Pointing to the fill handle triggers the display of the thin crosshair.

b. Drag the fill handle to **cell I15**, the lower-right cell in the range of employee calculations, and release the mouse to complete the copy operation.

The formulas for Dwyer have been copied to the corresponding rows. You can use Excel to calculate the gross pay, withholding tax, Social Security tax, and net pay for each employee.

c. Click in **cell F5**, the cell containing the gross pay for Smith.

You should see the formula =C5*D5+E5*C5*$D$20.

d. Click in **cell G5**, the cell containing the withholding tax for Smith.

You should see the formula =F5*$D$21, which contains a relative reference (F5) that is adjusted from one row to the next, and an absolute reference ($D$21) that remains constant from one employee to the next.

e. Save the *chap2_ho1_payroll_solution* workbook and keep it onscreen if you plan to continue to the next hands-on exercise. Save the workbook. Close the workbook and exit Excel if you do not want to continue with the next exercise at this time.

TROUBLESHOOTING: If you double-click a cell that contains a formula, Excel will display the formula, highlight the components, and allow for editing in the cell. If you double-click a cell that contains values or text, you can edit the data directly in the cell.

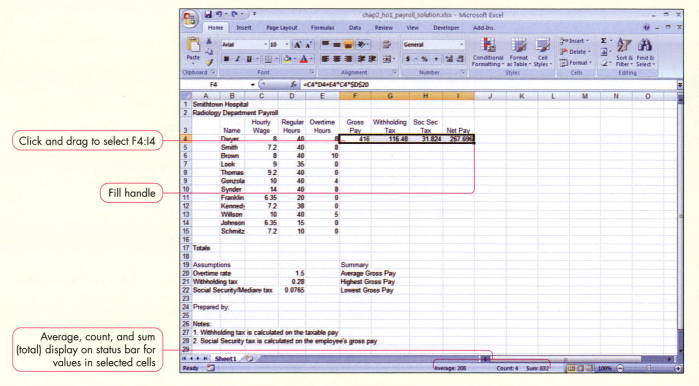

Figure 2.3 Copy the Formulas

TIP Isolate Assumptions

The formulas in a worksheet should always be based on cell references rather than specific values—for example, C25 or $C$25 rather than .07. The cells containing the values are clearly labeled and set apart from the rest of the worksheet. You can vary the inputs (or assumptions on which the worksheet is based) to see the effect within the worksheet. The chance for error is minimized because you are changing the contents of just a single cell instead of multiple formulas that reference those values. Excel automatically recalculates formulas when values change.

Function Basics

SUM Function | Reference

SUM(number1,number2,. . .)

A *function* is a preconstructed formula that makes difficult computations less complicated.

The **SUM function**, represented by Σ or sigma, adds up or sums the numeric entries within a range of cells.

You also can construct formulas by using a *function*, a preconstructed formula that makes difficult computations less complicated. But keep in mind that functions CANNOT replace all formulas. Functions take a value or values, perform an operation, and return a value or values. The most often used function in Excel is the *SUM function*, represented by Σ or sigma. It adds or sums numeric entries within a range of cells, and then displays the result in the cell containing the function. This function is so useful that the SUM function has its own command in the Function Library group on the Formulas tab. In all, Excel contains more than 325 functions, which are broken down into categories, as shown in Table 2.1.

When you want to use a function, keep two things in mind. The first is the *syntax* of the function or, more simply put, the rules for constructing the function. The second is the function's *arguments*, which are values as input that perform an indicated calculation, and then return another value as output or the data to be used in the function. While users often type functions such as =SUM(C7:C14), it also is possible to click Insert Function in the Function Library group on the Formulas tab to display the Insert Function dialog box. Using the Insert Function dialog box enables you to select the function to be used (such as MAX, SUM, etc.) from the complete list

Syntax refers to the rules for constructing the function.

Arguments are values as input that perform an indicated calculation, and then return another value as output.

> Using Insert Function greatly simplifies the construction of functions. . . .

of functions and specify the arguments to be used in the function. Using Insert Function greatly simplifies the construction of functions by making it easier to select and construct functions. Clicking Insert Function in the Function Library group on the Formulas tab (see Figure 2.4) displays the Insert Function dialog box shown in Figure 2.5. Use the Insert Function dialog box to do the following:

Table 2.1 Function Category and Descriptions

Category Group	Description
Cube	Works with multi-dimensional data stored on an SQL server.
Database	Analyzes data stored in Excel.
Date & Time	Works with dates and time.
Financial	Works with financial-related data.
Information	Determines what type of data is in a cell.
Logical	Calculates yes/no answers.
Lookup & Reference	Provides answers after searching a table.
Math & Trig	Performs standard math and trig functions.
Statistical	Calculates standard statistical functions.
Text	Analyzes labels.

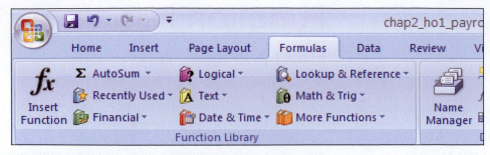

Figure 2.4 Function Library

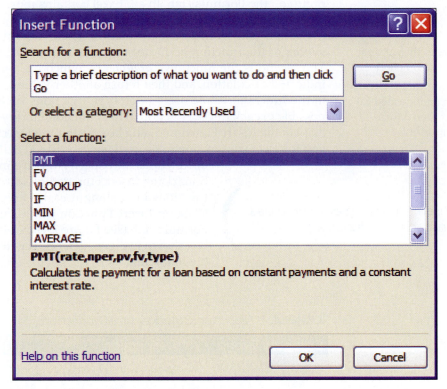

Figure 2.5 Insert Function Dialog Box

1. Search for a function by typing a brief description of what you want the function to do.
2. Select a function from the *Most Recently Used* list, by function category displayed in alphabetical order, or from an alphabetical list of *All* functions.
3. Click the function name to see the syntax and description or double-click the function name to see the function and the Function Arguments dialog box for help with adding the correct arguments. Figure 2.6 shows the Function Arguments dialog box for the SUM function.

If you know the category of the function you want to use, you can click the appropriate command in the Function Library group on the Formulas tab. Select the function and use the Function Arguments dialog box to add the arguments. See Figure 2.4 for the Function Library group.

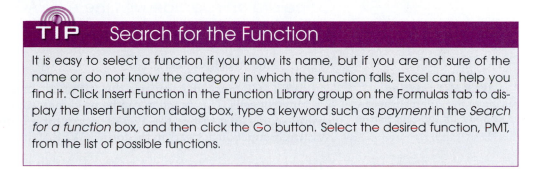

Figure 2.6 Function Arguments Box

In this section, you insert a variety of commonly used functions, such as the SUM function.

Using AutoSum

In this chapter, you will examine several different commonly used functions, beginning with the SUM function. You can create formulas in different ways. For example, if you want to add the contents of cells C4 through C10, the formula would be written =C4+C5+C6+C7+C8+C9+C10. However, creating this type of formula manually is time-consuming and increases the probability of entering an inaccurate cell address. This process would be especially problematic if you had to add values stored in several hundred cells. Using the SUM function simplifies this operation and improves the accuracy of the addition. To create the same formula using the SUM function, you can type **=SUM(C4:C10)**. The C4:C10 represents the cell range containing the values to be summed. Rather than typing this entire formula, you can also type **=SUM(**, and then click and drag to select the range of cells containing values to be summed, then type the closing parenthesis. Alternatively, you can click Σ (AutoSum) in the Function Library group on the Formulas tab. To use the AutoSum, click the cell where you want to see the results, and then click AutoSum. Drag to select the cell range or values to be summed and press Enter to see the total.

Inserting Basic Statistical Functions

The use of the SUM function, the most basic statistical function, already has been discussed. Now you will learn several other commonly used statistical functions. These functions perform a variety of calculations to identify key values to help people make decisions. For example, you can use functions to calculate how much you spend on average per month on DVD rentals, what your highest electric bill is to control spending, and what your lowest test score is so you know what you have to study for the final exam. You can use the statistical functions to create or monitor your budget. Climatologists use statistical functions to compare rainfall averages over time in specific geographic areas.

Calculate an Average with the AVERAGE Function

AVERAGE Function | Reference

AVERAGE(number1,number2,. . .)

The ***AVERAGE function*** calculates the arithmetic mean, or average, for the values in an argument list.

The *AVERAGE function* calculates the arithmetic mean, or average, for the values in a range of cells. This function can be used for such calculations as the average of several scores on a test or the average score for a number of rounds of golf. The AVERAGE function appears in the form =AVERAGE(C6:C24).

Identify the Lowest Value with the MIN Function

MIN Function | Reference

MIN(number1,number2,. . .)

The ***MIN function*** determines the smallest value of all cells in a list of arguments.

The *MIN function* determines the smallest value of all cells in a list of arguments. An application of the MIN might be to determine the lowest score on a test. The function typically appears as =MIN(C6:C24). Although you could manually inspect a range of values to identify the lowest value, doing so is inefficient, especially in large spreadsheets. The MIN function increases your efficiency by always identifying the lowest value in the range. If you change values in the range, the MIN function will identify the new lowest value and display this value in the cell containing the MIN function.

Identify the Highest Value with the MAX Function

MAX Function | Reference

MAX(number1,number2,. . .)

The ***MAX function*** determines the highest value of all cells in a list of arguments.

The *MAX function* is the opposite of the MIN function in that it analyzes an argument list to determine the highest value, as in the highest score on a test or the highest points a basketball player scored in a game in a season. This function appears as =MAX(C6:C24). Like the MIN function, when the values in the range change, the MAX function will display the new highest value within the range of cells. Generally the MIN and MAX statistical functions are discussed in concert with the AVERAGE function. These three functions are typically beginning statistical functions and are used together as a start point for more sophisticated analysis. They also are commonly used educational statistics in gradebooks and in analysis of test scores.

Identify the Total Number with the COUNT and COUNTA Functions

COUNT Function | Reference

COUNT(value1,value2,. . .)

COUNTA Function | Reference

COUNTA(value1,value2,. . .)

The **COUNT function** counts the number of cells in a range that contain numerical data.

The **COUNTA function** counts the number of cells in a range that are not blank.

The two basic count functions, COUNT and COUNTA, enable a user to count the cells in a range that meet a particular criterion. The **COUNT function** counts the number of cells in a range that contain numerical data. This function is expressed as =COUNT(C6:C24). The **COUNTA function** counts the number of cells in a range that are not blank. This function is expressed as =COUNTA(C6:C24). These functions might be used to verify data entry; for example, you may need to verify that the correct type of data has been entered into the appropriate number of cells. The COUNT function is used to verify that cells have numbers in them and the COUNTA function is used to make sure data are in every cell.

Determine the Midpoint Value with the MEDIAN Function

MEDIAN Function | Reference

MEDIAN(number1,number2,. . .)

The **MEDIAN function** finds the midpoint value in a set of values.

Another easy basic statistical function often overlooked is the **MEDIAN function** that finds the midpoint value in a set of values. It is helpful to identify at what value ½ of the population is above or below. The median shows that half of the sample data are above a particular value and half are below that value. The median is particularly useful because the AVERAGE function often is influenced by extreme numbers. For example, if 10 grades are between 90 and 100 and the eleventh grade is 0, the extreme value of 0 distorts the overall average as an indicator of the set of grades. See Table 2.2 for this example. Note that 86 is the average and 95 is the median.

Table 2.2   Compare Average and Median

Scores	
99	
98	
97	
96	
95	
95	Midpoint Score (half the scores above and half the scores below this score)
93	
92	
91	
90	
0	
86	Average Score (Equal to the sum of the values divided by the number of values)
95	Median (midpoint) Score

Using Date Functions

Before electronic spreadsheets, you could spend hours trying to figure out pay dates for the next year or when a new employee's probation period was up. Excel enables you to increase your productivity by using date and time functions. These functions help in two ways: by efficiently handling time-consuming procedures and by helping you analyze data related to the passing of time. For example, you can use the date and time functions to calculate when employees are eligible for certain benefits or how many days it takes to complete a project. You also can use the date functions to help you calculate if an account is 30, 60, or more days past due. Excel converts and stores dates as numbers. Using date functions allows you to calculate the difference between dates, add or subtract days from a given date, and so on.

TODAY Function | Reference

TODAY( )

The ***TODAY function*** displays the current date in a cell.

The ***TODAY function*** is a date-related function that places the current date in a cell. The function is expressed as =TODAY(). This function is updated when the worksheet is calculated or the file is opened. Unlike the statistical functions you just learned about, some date functions like TODAY() do not require cell references or data as arguments. However, you must still include the parentheses for the function to work.

NOW Function | Reference

NOW( )

The ***NOW function*** uses the computer's clock to display the current date and time side by side in a cell.

The ***NOW function*** uses the computer's clock to display the current date and time side by side in a cell. It returns the time the workbook was last opened, so the value will change every time the workbook is opened. The Now function does the same thing as the Today function, except the result is formatted to display the current time as well as the current date. Both of these functions will display the current date/time when the spreadsheet file is opened. Thus, date/time is always current; it is not the date/time when the function was first entered in the cell. The NOW function is expressed as =NOW(). Note that failure to insert the parentheses will cause Excel to return an error message.

Functions Used | Reference

Name	Syntax	Definition
SUM	SUM(number1,number2, . . .)	The **SUM function**, represented by Σ or sigma, adds up or sums the numeric entries within a range of cells.
AVERAGE	AVERAGE(number1,number2, . . .)	The **AVERAGE function** calculates the arithmetic mean, or average, for the values in an argument list.
MIN	MIN(number1,number2, . . .)	The **MIN function** determines the smallest value of all cells in a list of arguments.
MAX	MAX(number1,number2, . . .)	The **MAX function** determines the highest value of all cells in a list of arguments.
COUNT	COUNT(value1,value2, . . .)	The **COUNT function** counts the number of cells in a range that contain numerical data.
COUNTA	COUNTA(value1,value2, . . .)	The **COUNTA function** counts the number of cells in a range that are not blank.
MEDIAN	MEDIAN(number1,number2, . . .)	The **MEDIAN function** finds the midpoint value in a set of values.
NOW	NOW( )	The **NOW function** uses the computer's clock to display the current date and time side by side in a cell.
TODAY	TODAY( )	The **TODAY function** displays the current date in a cell.
IF	IF(logical_test,value_if_true,value_if_false)	The **IF function** is the most basic logical function in that it returns one value when a condition is met and returns another value when the condition is not met.
VLOOKUP	VLOOKUP(lookup_value,table_array, col_index_num,range_lookup)	The **VLOOKUP function** allows the Excel user to look up an answer from a table of possible answers.
PMT	PMT(rate,nper,pv,fv,type)	The **PMT function** calculates the payment on a loan.
FV	FV(rate,nper,pmt,pv,type)	The **FV function** returns the future value of an investment

Table 2.3 Comparison Operators

Operator	Description
=	Equal to
<>	Not equal to
<	Less than
>	Greater than
<=	Less than or equal to
>=	Greater than or equal to

The small sample worksheet, Figure 2.10, shows the data the IF function uses to create the examples in Table 2.4. Arguments may be numeric, cell references to display cells' contents, a formula, a function, or a text entry. Review Table 2.4 to see how Excel evaluates conditions and the results.

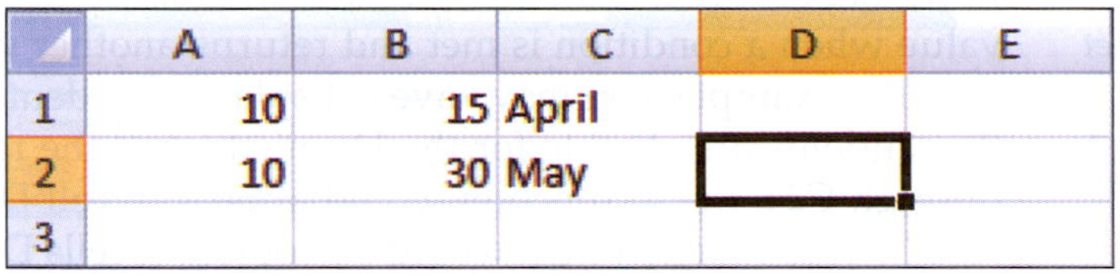

	A	B	C	D	E
1	10	15	April		
2	10	30	May		
3					

Figure 2.10 IF Data

Table 2.4 IF Function, Evaluation, and Result

IF Function	Evaluation	Result
=IF(A1=A2,1000,2000)	10 is equal to 10, TRUE	1000
=IF(A1<>A2,1000,2000)	10 is not equal to 10, FALSE	2000
=If(A1<>A2,B1,B2)	10 is not equal to10, FALSE	30
=IF(A1<B2,MAX(B1:B2),MIN(B1:B2))	10 is less than 30, TRUE	30
=IF(A1<A2,B1+10,B1-10)	10 is less than 10, FALSE	5
=IF(A1=A2,C1,C2)	10 is equal to 10, TRUE	April

Using the VLOOKUP Function

VLOOKUP Function | Reference

VLOOKUP(lookup_value,table_array,col_index_num,range_lookup)

When you order something on the Web or by catalog, you look up the shipping costs for your order. You find the information you want because you look up a specific piece of information (the total amount of your order) to find the associated information (the shipping cost). The VLOOKUP function works the same way. You can use the VLOOKUP function to find a company's specific tax rate from a table or look up your own tax rate. The *VLOOKUP function* evaluates a value and looks up this value in a vertical table to return a value, text, or formula. Use VLOOKUP to search for exact matches or for the nearest value that is less than or equal to the search value (such as assigning a shipping cost of $15.25 to an order of $300.87). Or use the VLOOKUP function to assign a B grade for an 87% class average.

The **VLOOKUP function** looks up an answer from a vertical table of possible answers.

Understand the VLOOKUP Function Syntax

The VLOOKUP function has three arguments:

1. a lookup value stored in a cell,
2. a range of cells containing a lookup table, and
3. the number of the column within the lookup table that contains the value to return.

One use of a VLOOKUP function is the assignment of letter grades in a gradebook based on numeric values. Figure 2.11 shows a portion of a worksheet with a Grading Criteria Table that associates letter grades with the numerical value earned by a student. The first student's overall class average is 76.3. You can use the VLOOKUP function to identify the cell containing the student's numerical average and use that value to look up the equivalent letter grade in a table. To determine the letter grade in cell J4 based on a numeric value in cell I4, you would use the following:

=VLOOKUP(I4,$I$20:$J$24,2)

Column number with the grade

Range of the table

Value to lookup (semester average)

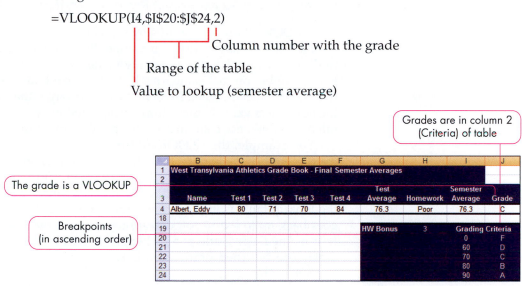

Figure 2.11 VLOOKUP Table Data

The **lookup value** is the value to look up in a reference table.

The **lookup table** is a range of cells containing the reference table.

The **column index number** is the column number in the lookup table that contains return values.

Cell I4 is the *lookup value* that represents the cell containing the value to look up in a table. In this example, the lookup value is 76.3. The table that Excel searches using a lookup function is called a *lookup table*. In this example, the lookup table is stored in the range $I$20:$J$24. Note that an absolute reference is used so the address is not changed when the formula is copied to other cells. Furthermore, the table lookup range should *not* include the table column headings. The *column index number*, indicated by col_index_num in the function, refers to the number of the column in the lookup table that contains the return values. In the example, the col_index_num of 2 returns the value in the second column in the lookup table that corresponds to the value being looked up.

Structure the Lookup Table

The VLOOKUP function searches the left column of a table for a specific value and returns a corresponding value from the same row but a different column. You set up the table to include unique values in the left column (for example, ranges of total amounts or numeric ranges to assign letter grades), and then Excel retrieves the associated information (for example, shipping cost or letter grade) from another column. In Figure 2.11, the lookup table extends over two columns, I and J, and five rows, 20 through 24. The table is located in the range I20:J24.

You should set up the lookup table before using the VLOOKUP function. The left column, known as the lookup column, of the table includes the reference data used to look up information in the table, such as customer number, income, grade points, or the total amount range of the order. The other columns include information related to the first column, such as customer credit limit, tax rate, letter grades, or shipping cost. The values in the left or lookup column must be sorted in ascending order, from lowest to highest value. However, instead of typing an entire range, such as 80–89, for the range of B grades, you enter breakpoints only. The *breakpoint* is the lowest numeric value for a specific category or in a series of a lookup table to produce a corresponding result to return for a lookup function. Breakpoints are listed in ascending order in the first column of the lookup table. For example, the breakpoints in the gradebook lookup table represent the lowest numerical score to earn a particular letter grade. The breakpoints are listed in column I, and the corresponding letter grades are found in column J.

A **breakpoint** is the lowest numeric value for a category or series in a lookup table to produce a corresponding result for a lookup function.

Understand How Excel Processes the Lookup

The VLOOKUP function works by searching in the left column of the lookup table until it finds an exact match or a number that is larger than the lookup value. If Excel finds an exact match, it returns the value stored in the column designated by the index number on that same row. If the table contains breakpoints for ranges rather than exact matches, when Excel finds a value larger than the lookup value, it returns the next lower value in the column designated by the col_index_num. To work accurately, the reference column must be in ascending order.

For example, the VLOOKUP function to assign letter grades works like this: Excel identifies the lookup value (76.3 stored in I4) and compares it to the values in the lookup table (stored in I20:J24). It tries to find an exact match; however, the table contains breakpoints rather than every conceivable numeric average. Because the lookup table is in ascending order, it notices that 76.3 is not equal to 80, so it goes back up to the 70 row. Excel then looks at the column index number of 2 and returns the letter grade of C, which is located in the second column of the lookup table. The returned grade of C is then stored in the cell J4, which contains the VLOOKUP function.

Instead of looking up values in a range, you might need to look up a value for an *exact* match. When this is the case, you must use the optional range_lookup argument in the VLOOKUP function. By default, the range_lookup is implicitly set to TRUE, which is appropriate to look up values in a range. However, to look up an exact match, you must specify FALSE in the range_lookup argument. The VLOOKUP function returns a value for the first lookup_value that matches the first column of the table_array. If no exact match is found, the function returns #N/A.

TIP	HLOOKUP Function

The VLOOKUP function is arranged vertically in a table, while its counterpart, the HLOOKUP function, is arranged horizontally. Use the HLOOKUP function when your comparison values are located in a row across the top of a table of data and you want to look down a specified number of rows.

3 | Athletic Department Eligibility Gradebook

Skills covered: 1. Use the IF Function **2.** Use the VLOOKUP Function **3.** Copy the IF and VLOOKUP Functions **4.** Apply Page Setup Options and Print the Worksheet

---

Step 1 **Use the IF Function**	Refer to Figure 2.12 as you complete Step 1.

a. Open the *chap2_ho3_gradebook* workbook and save it as **chap2_ho3_gradebook_solution** so that you can return to the original workbook if necessary.

The partially completed gradebook contains student test scores and their respective test averages. You need to create an IF function to determine if students have completed their homework. If they did, they receive a 3-point bonus added to their semester average. Those students who did not complete homework receive no bonus, so their semester average is the same as their test average.

b. Click in **cell I4**. Click the **Formulas tab** and click **Insert Function** in the Function Library group. Select the **IF** function from the *Select a function* list. Click **OK** to close the Insert Function dialog box and display the Function Argument dialog box.

You will use the Function Arguments dialog box to build the IF function.

c. Click in the **Logical_test** box, keep the Function Arguments dialog box open but drag it down to see cell H4, click **cell H4** in the worksheet, and type **="OK"** to complete the logical test.

d. Click in the **Value_if_true** box, keep the Function Arguments dialog box open, click **cell G4** in the worksheet, type **+**, and click **cell H19**. Press **F4** to change H19 to an absolute cell reference.

e. Click in the **Value_if_false** box, keep the Function Arguments dialog box open, and click **cell G4** in the worksheet.

TROUBLESHOOTING: Text values used in arguments must be enclosed in quotes.

f. Click **OK** to insert the function into the worksheet. Save the workbook.

Because Eddy's homework was "Poor," he did not earn the 3-point bonus. His semester average is the same as his test average.

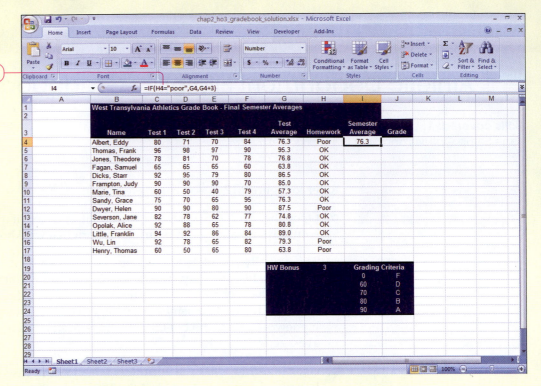

Figure 2.12 Athletics Gradebook

<table>
<tr><td rowspan="2" style="background:gold; color:white; padding:20px; font-size:2em;">Step 2
Use the VLOOKUP Function</td></tr>
</table>

Refer to Figure 2.11 as you complete Step 2.

a. Click in **cell J4** and click the **Lookup & Reference arrow** in the Function Library group on the Formulas tab. Select **VLOOKUP**.

You will create a VLOOKUP function using the semester average stored in column I to determine the letter grade for each student.

b. Click in the **Lookup_value** box and click **cell I4** in the worksheet.

The first student's semester average, which is stored in cell I4, is the value to look up.

c. Click in the **Table_array** box. Click **cell I20** and drag to **cell J24**, and then press **F4** to convert the entire range reference to absolute ($I$20:$J$24).

The table containing the letter grade equivalents is stored in I20:J24. You made the reference absolute so that the cell addresses do not change when you copy the function for the remaining student athletes.

d. Click in the **Col_index_num** box and type **2**.

e. Click **OK** to insert the function into the worksheet and save the workbook.

The first student's letter grade is C because his semester average of 76.3 is over 70 but less than 80.

TROUBLESHOOTING: Make sure to use an absolute reference with the table in the VLOOKUP function. You will see inaccurate results if you forget to use absolute references.

Step 3
Copy the IF and VLOOKUP Functions

Refer to Figure 2.13 as you complete Step 3.

a. Copy the IF and VLOOKUP Functions by selecting **cells I4:J4**, point to the fill handle in the lower-right corner of **cell J4**, and drag the fill handle over cells **I17:J17**.

You just copied the original IF and VLOOKUP functions for the rest of the students.

b. Check that the semester averages are formatted to one decimal place.

c. Click **cell A19** and enter your name. Click **cell A1** and type **=TODAY()** to enter today's date.

d. Click **cell A1** and hold **Ctrl** as you click **cell A19**. Click the **Home tab** and click **Bold** in the Font group. Save the workbook.

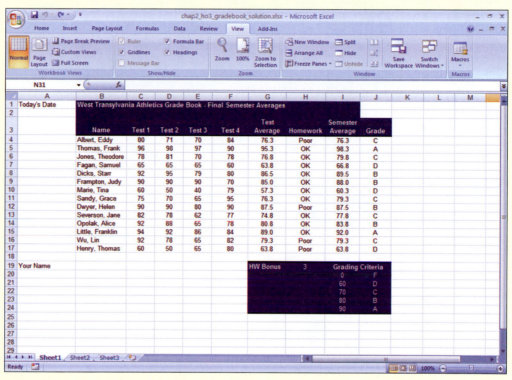

Figure 2.13 Athletics Gradebook

Step 4
Apply Page Setup Options and Print the Worksheet

a. Click the **Page Layout tab** and click **Margins** in the Page Setup group. Click **Custom Margins** to display the Margins tab in the Page Setup dialog box.

b. Click the **Horizontally check box** in the *Center on page* section to center the worksheet between the left and right margins.

c. Click the **Sheet tab**. Click the **Gridlines check box** and click the **Row and column headings check box** in the *Print* section.

d. Click **OK**. Save the workbook.

e. Click the **Office Button** and select **Print**. Click the **Preview button** to see how the workbook will print.

TROUBLESHOOTING: If the worksheet previews as two pages in the Print Preview window, close the Print Preview window, display the Page Setup dialog box, and decrease the scaling. Display the worksheet in Print Preview again to make sure the worksheet fits on one page.

f. Click the **Print button**, and then click **OK** to print the worksheet.

g. Press **Ctrl + ~** to show the cell formulas rather than the values. Adjust the column width as necessary and print the worksheet a second time. Close the workbook without saving.

Financial Functions

A spreadsheet is a tool used for decision-making. Many decisions typically involve financial situations: payments, investments, interest rates, and so on. Excel contains several financial functions to help you perform calculations with monetary values.

Review Figures 2.14, 2.15, 2.16, and 2.17 to see how a worksheet might be applied to the purchase of a car. You need to know the monthly payment, which depends on the price of the car, the down payment, and the terms of the loan. In other words:

(
Can you afford the monthly payment on the car of your choice?
)

- Can you afford the monthly payment on the car of your choice?
- What if you settle for a less expensive car and receive a manufacturer's rebate?
- What if you work next summer to earn money for a down payment?
- What if you extend the life of the loan and receive a better interest rate?
- Have you accounted for additional items such as insurance, gas, and maintenance?

The answers to these and other questions determine whether you can afford a car, and if so, which car, and how you will pay for it. The decision is made easier by developing the worksheet in Figure 2.14, and then by changing the various input values as indicated.

The availability of the worksheet lets you consider several alternatives. You realize that the purchase of a $14,999 car, as shown in Figure 2.15, is prohibitive because the monthly payment is almost $476.96. Settling for a less expensive car, coming up with a substantial down payment, and obtaining a manufacturer's rebate in Figure 2.16 help, but the $317.97 monthly payment is still too high. Extending the loan to a fourth year

	A	B
1	Purchase Price	
2	Manufacturer's Rebate	
3	Down Payment	
4	Amount to Finance	=B1-B2-B3
5	Interest Rate	
6	Term (years)	
7	Monthly Payment	=PMT(B5/12,B6*12,-B4)
8		

No specific data has been entered

Figure 2.14 Spreadsheets for Decision-Making

	A	B	C	D
1	Purchase Price	$14,999		
2	Manufacturer's Rebate			
3	Down Payment			
4	Amount to Finance	$14,999		
5	Interest Rate	9%		
6	Term (years)	3		
7	Monthly Payment	$476.96		
8				

Data entered

Figure 2.15 Spreadsheets for Decision-Making

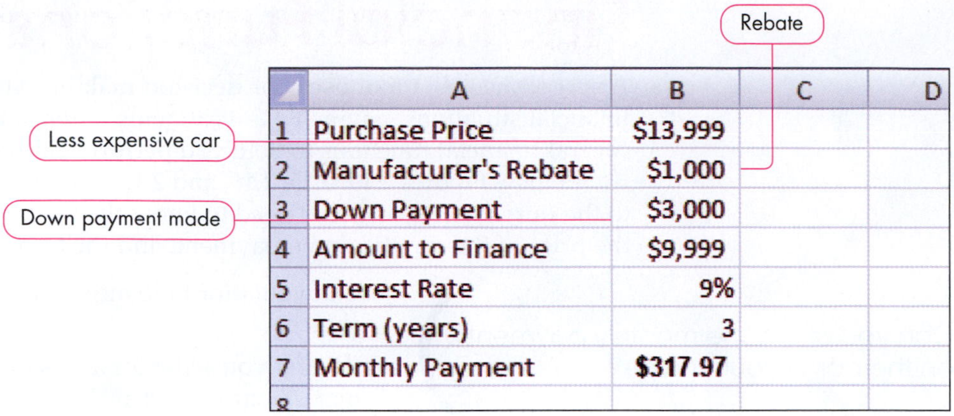

Figure 2.16 Spreadsheets for Decision-Making

	A	B	C	D
1	Purchase Price	$13,999		
2	Manufacturer's Rebate	$1,000		
3	Down Payment	$3,000		
4	Amount to Finance	$9,999		
5	Interest Rate	9%		
6	Term (years)	3		
7	Monthly Payment	$317.97		

Rebate → B2
Less expensive car → A1
Down payment made → A3

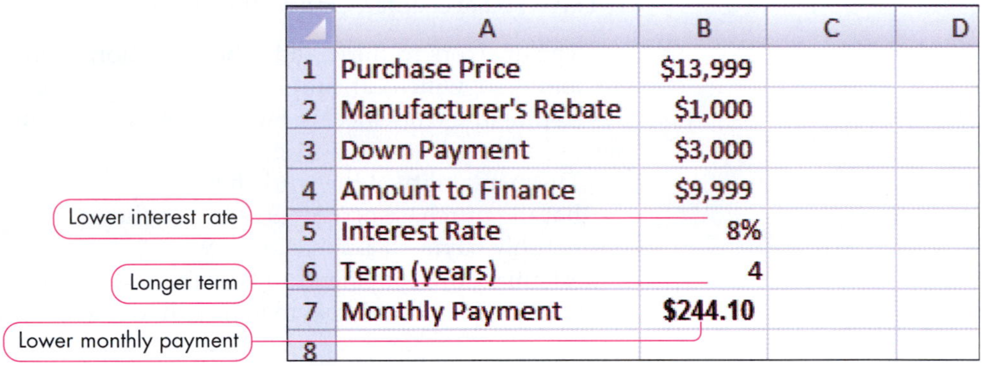

Figure 2.17 Spreadsheets for Decision-Making

	A	B	C	D
1	Purchase Price	$13,999		
2	Manufacturer's Rebate	$1,000		
3	Down Payment	$3,000		
4	Amount to Finance	$9,999		
5	Interest Rate	8%		
6	Term (years)	4		
7	Monthly Payment	$244.10		

Lower interest rate → A5
Longer term → A6
Lower monthly payment → A7

at a lower interest rate, as in Figure 2.17, reduces the monthly payment to $244.10, which is closer to your budgeted amount.

Using the PMT Function

PMT Function | Reference

PMT(rate,nper,pv,fv,type)

The **PMT function** calculates the payment on a loan.

The **PMT function** calculates payments for a loan that is paid off at a fixed amount at a periodic rate. The PMT function requires three arguments: the interest rate per period, the number of periods, and the amount of the loan, from which it computes the associated payment on a loan. The arguments are placed in parentheses and are separated by commas. Consider the PMT function as it might apply to Figure 2.15:

=PMT(.09/12,36,–14999)

Amount of loan (as a *negative* amount)

Number of periods (3 years × 12 months/year)

Interest rate per period (annual rate divided by 12)

Instead of using specific values, however, you should use cell references in the PMT function arguments, so that you can easily change the input values in the individual cells instead of editing the values in the function itself. The PMT function is entered as =PMT(B5/12,B6*12,–B4) to reflect the terms of a specific loan whose arguments are in cells B4, B5, and B6. You must divide the 9% annual percentage rate (APR) by 12 months to obtain the monthly *periodic* rate. Next, you must multiply the

3-year term by the number of payments per year. Because you will make monthly payments, you multiply 3 by 12 months to calculate the total number of months in the term, which is 36. The amount of the loan is a minus figure because it is a debt. The loan is considered a negative because it is an outflow of cash or an expense. The amount of the loan is entered as a negative amount so the worksheet will display a positive value after calculations.

Using the FV Function

FV Function | Reference

FV(rate,nper,pmt,pv,type)

The **FV function** returns the future value of an investment.

The **FV function** returns the future value of an investment if you know the interest rate, the term, and the periodic payment. You can use the FV function to determine how much an IRA would be worth in a particular period of time. This function would be expressed as =FV(rate,nper,payment).

Assume that you plan to contribute $3,000 a year to an IRA, that you expect to earn 7% annually, and that you will be contributing for 40 years. The future value of that investment—the amount you will have at age 65—would be $598,905! You would have contributed $120,000 ($3,000 a year for 40 years). The difference, more than $470,000, results from compound interest you will earn over the life of your investment of $120,000!

(. . . more than $470,000, results from compound interest you will earn over the life of your investment of $120,000!)

The FV function has three arguments—the interest rate (also called the rate of return), the number of periods (how long you will pay into the IRA), and the periodic investment (how much you will invest into the IRA per year). The FV function corresponding to the earlier example would be:

Amount at retirement =FV(Rate of return, Term, Periodic payment)

$3,000

40 years

7%

Computed value becomes $598,905

It is more practical, however, to enter the values into a worksheet and then use cell references within the FV function. If, for example, cells A1, A2, and A3 contained the rate of return, term, and annual contribution, respectively, the resulting FV function would be =FV(A1,A2,–A3). The periodic payment is preceded by a minus sign, just as the principal in the PMT function.

These financial functions as well as the other examples of functions provide you with the tools to perform sophisticated mathematical, statistical, and financial calculations.

TIP | Financial Functions

Excel contains over 50 financial functions. To learn about these functions, display the Insert Function dialog box, click the Or select a category drop-down arrow, and select Financial. You can scroll through the alphabetical list of financial functions to see the syntax and purpose for each function.

Peer Tutoring

DISASTER RECOVERY

As part of your service-learning project, you volunteered to tutor students in Excel. Open the spreadsheet *chap2_mc3_tutoring*, save it as **chap2_mc3_tutoring_solution**, and find five errors. Correct the errors and explain how the errors might have occurred and how they can be prevented. Include your explanation in the cells below the spreadsheet.

Performance Elements	Exceeds Expectations	Meets Expectations	Below Expectations
Identify five errors	Identified all five errors.	Identified four errors.	Identified three or fewer errors.
Correct five errors	Corrected all five errors.	Corrected four errors.	Corrected three or fewer errors.
Explain the error	Complete and correct explanation of each error.	Explanation is too brief to fully explain errors.	No explanations.
Prevention description	Prevention description correct and practical.	Prevention description but obtuse.	No prevention description.

Charts

Delivering a Message

Objectives

After you read this chapter, you will be able to:

1. Choose a chart type **(page 189)**.
2. Create a chart **(page 196)**.
3. Modify a chart **(page 208)**.
4. Enhance charts with graphic shapes **(page 211)**.
5. Embed charts **(page 217)**.
6. Print charts **(page 218)**.

Hands-On Exercises

Exercises	Skills Covered
1. THE FIRST CHART (page 201) **Open:** chap3_ho1_sales.xlsx **Save as:** chap3_ho1_sales_solution.xlsx	• Use AutoSum • Create the Chart • Complete the Chart • Move and Size the Chart • Change the Worksheet • Change the Chart Type • Create a Second Chart
2. MULTIPLE DATA SERIES (page 212) **Open:** chap3_ho1_sales_solution.xlsx (from Exercise 1) **Save as:** chap3_ho2_sales_solution.xlsx (additional modifications)	• Rename the Worksheet • Create Chart with Multiple Data Series • Copy the Chart • Change the Source Data • Change the Chart Type • Insert a Graphic Shape and Add a Text Box
3. EMBEDDING, PRINTING, AND SAVING A CHART AS A WEB PAGE (page 220) **Open:** chap3_ho2_sales_solution.xlsx (from Exercise 2), chap3_ho3_memo.docx **Save as:** chap3_ho3_sales_solution.xlsx (additional modifications), chap_ho3_memo_solution.docx	• Embed a Chart in Microsoft Word • Copy the Worksheet • Embed the Data • Copy the Chart • Embed the Chart • Modify the Worksheet • Update the Links • Print Worksheet and Chart • Save and View Chart as Web Page

CASE STUDY

The Changing Student Population

Congratulations! You have just been hired as a student intern in the Admissions Office. Helen Dwyer, the dean of admissions, has asked you to start tomorrow morning to help her prepare for an upcoming presentation with the Board of Trustees in which she will report on enrollment trends over the past four years. Daytime enrollments have been steady, whereas enrollments in evening and distance (online) learning are increasing significantly. Dean Dwyer has asked for a chart(s) to summarize the data. She also would like your thoughts on what impact (if any) the Internet and the trend toward lifelong learning have had on the college population. The dean has asked you to present the infor-

Case Study

mation in the form of a memo addressed to the Board of Trustees with the data and graph embedded onto that page.

Dean Dwyer will be presenting her findings on "The Changing Student Population" to the Board of Trustees in two weeks. She will speak briefly and then open the floor for questions and discussion among the group. She has invited you to the meeting to answer specific questions pertaining to these trends from a student's perspective. This is an outstanding opportunity for you to participate with a key group of individuals who support the university. Be prepared to present yourself appropriately!

Your Assignment

- Read the chapter carefully and pay close attention to sections that demonstrate chart creation, chart formatting, and chart printing.
- Open the workbook *chap3_case_enrollment*, which has the enrollment statistics partially completed. You will save your workbook as **chap3_case_enrollment_solution**.
- When you review the workbook, think about the mathematical operations, formulas, and functions you would use to complete the worksheet. You will create formulas and functions to calculate annual totals and type of course totals. You also will format cells appropriately: use numbers with commas, merge and center the title, use an attractive fill color, and increase font sizes for improved readability.
- As you read the chapter, pay particular attention to the types of charts that are discussed. Some are more appropriate for presenting enrollment data than others. You will use your understanding of chart methods to determine the most appropriate charts used with the enrollment data. You will create charts to emphasize enrollment data on separate sheets. Remember to format the charts for a professional presentation that includes titles, legends, and data labels.
- As part of your presentation, you also must consider the preparation of a memo describing the enrollment information presented both in the worksheet and in the chart. The worksheet and the charts will be embedded in the final memo. The memo in Microsoft Word will summarize your enrollment data findings and include the embedded worksheet and charts.
- Remember that you will present the information to the university Board of Trustees, and the trustees will expect a professional, polished report. Save the memo as **chap3_case_enrollment_solution** after creating custom footers that include the page number, your name, and your instructor's name. Print the memo, the worksheet, and the charts.

A Picture Is the Message

A *chart* is a graphic representation of data.

A picture really is worth a thousand words. Excel makes it easy to create a *chart*, which is a graphic or visual representation of data. Once data is displayed in a chart, the options to enhance the information for more visual appeal and ease of analysis are almost unlimited. Because large amounts of data are available, using graphical analysis is valuable to discover what messages are hidden in the data.

In this chapter, you learn the importance of determining the message to be conveyed by a chart. You select the type of chart that best presents your message. You create and modify a chart, enhance a chart with a shape, plot multiple sets of data, embed a chart in a worksheet, and create a chart in a separate chart sheet. You enhance a chart by creating lines, objects, and 3-D shapes. The second half of the chapter explains how to create a compound document, in which a chart and its associated worksheet are dynamically linked to a memo created in Word.

Choosing a Chart Type

Managers know that a graphic representation of data is an attractive, clear way to convey information. Business graphics are one of the most exciting Windows applications, where charts (graphs) are created in a straightforward manner from a worksheet with just a few keystrokes or mouse clicks.

In this section, you learn chart terminology and how to choose a chart type based on your needs. For example, you learn when to use a column chart and when to use a pie chart. You select the range of cells containing the numerical values and labels from which to create the chart, choose the chart type, insert the chart, and designate the chart's location.

A *data point* is a numeric value that describes a single item on a chart.

A *data series* is a group of related data points.

A *category label* describes a group of data points in a chart.

A chart is based on numeric values in the cells called *data points*. For example, a data point might be the database sales for Milwaukee. A group of related data points that appear in row(s) or column(s) in the worksheet create a *data series*. For example, a data series might be a collection of database data points for four different cities. In every data series, exactly one data point is connected to a numerical value contained in a cell. Textual information, such as column and row headings (cities, months, years, product names, etc.), are used for descriptive entries called *category labels*.

The worksheet in Figure 3.1 is used throughout the chapter as the basis for the charts you create. As you can see from the worksheet, the company sells different types of software programs, and it has sales in four cities. You believe that the sales numbers are more easily grasped when they are presented graphically instead of only relying on the numbers. You need to develop a series of charts to convey the sales numbers.

	Transylvania Software Sales				
	Milwaukee	Buffalo	Harrisburg	Pittsburgh	Total
Word Processing	$50,000	$67,500	$200,000	$141,000	$458,500
Spreadsheets	$44,000	$18,000	$11,500	$105,000	$178,500
Database	$12,000	$7,500	$6,000	$30,000	$55,500
Total	$106,000	$93,000	$217,500	$276,000	

Figure 3.1 Worksheet for Charts

The sales data in the worksheet can be presented several ways—for example, by city, by product, or by a combination of the two. Determine which type of chart is best suited to answer the following questions:

- What percentage of the total revenue comes from each city? What percentage comes from each product?

- How much revenue is produced by each city? What is the revenue for each product?

- What is the rank of each city with respect to sales?
- How much revenue does each product produce in each city?

In every instance, realize that a chart exists only to deliver a message and that *you cannot create an effective chart unless you are sure of what that message is*. The next several pages discuss various types of charts, each of which is best suited to a particular type of message. After you understand how charts are used conceptually, you will create various charts in Excel.

> (... you cannot create an effective chart unless you are sure of what that message is.)

Create Column Charts

A *column chart* displays data comparisons vertically in columns.

The *X or horizontal axis* depicts categorical labels.

The *Y or vertical axis* depicts numerical values.

The *plot area* contains graphical representation of values in data series.

The *chart area* contains the entire chart and all of its elements.

A *column chart* displays data vertically in a column formation and is used to compare values across different categories. Figure 3.2 shows total revenue by geographic area based on the worksheet data from Figure 3.1. The category labels represented by cities stored in cells B3:E3 are shown along the *X or horizontal axis*, whereas the data points representing total monthly sales stored in cells B7:E7 are shown along the *Y or vertical axis*. The height of each column represents the value of the individual data points. The *plot area* of a chart is the area containing the graphical representation of the values in a data series. The *chart area* contains the entire chart and all of its elements.

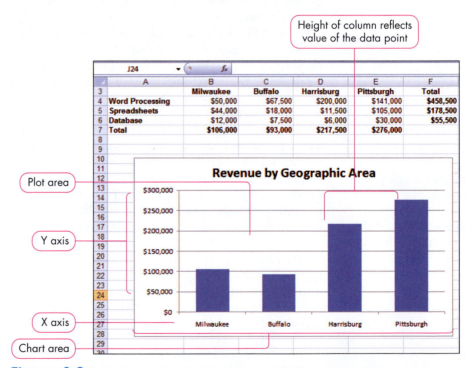

Figure 3.2 Column Chart Depicting Revenue by Geographic Area

Different types of column charts can be created to add interest or clarify the data representation. Figure 3.3 is an example of a three-dimensional (3-D) column chart. The 3-D charts present a more dynamic representation of data, as this chart demonstrates. However, the 3-D column chart is sometimes misleading. Professors often discourage students from using 3-D charts because the charts do not clearly communicate the data—the third dimension distorts data. In 3-D column charts, some columns appear taller or smaller than they really are because they are either somewhat behind or at an angle to other columns. See Figure 3.3 for an example of this. For example, the Milwaukee total is $106,000, but the 3-D column chart makes it appear less than $100,000.

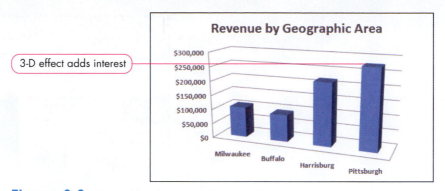

Figure 3.3 Three-Dimensional Column Chart

A *multiple data series* compares two or more sets of data in one chart.

Another example of the use of column charts is to compare *multiple data series*—two or more data series—on the same chart. The concept of charting multiple data series will be discussed at some length later in the chapter, but this concept involves the use of clustered column charts.

The choice of clustered versus stacked column charts depends on the intended message. If you want the audience to see the individual sales in each city or product category, the clustered column chart in Figure 3.4 is more appropriate. If, on the other hand, you want to emphasize the total sales for each city or product category, the stacked columns are preferable. The advantage of the stacked column is that the totals are shown clearly and can be compared easily. The disadvantage is that the segments within each column do not start at the same point, making it difficult to determine the actual sales for the individual categories. *Clustered column charts* group similar data together in columns making visual comparison of the data easier to determine. *Stacked column charts* place similar data in one column with each data series a different color. The effect emphasizes the total of the data series.

A *clustered column chart* groups similar data in columns, making visual comparison easier to determine.

A *stacked column chart* places (stacks) data in one column with each data series a different color for each category.

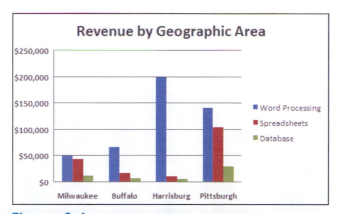

Figure 3.4 Clustered Column Chart

The scale on the Y axis is different for charts with clustered columns versus charts with stacked columns. The clustered columns in Figure 3.4 show the sales of each product category and so the Y axis goes to $250,000. The stacked columns in Figure 3.5 reflect the total sales for all products in each city, and thus the scale goes to $300,000. For a stacked column chart to make sense, its numbers must be additive. You would not convert a column chart that plots units and dollar sales side by side to a stacked column chart, because units and dollars are not additive, that is, you cannot add products and revenue. The chart in Figure 3.5 also displays a legend on the right side of the chart. A *legend* identifies the format or color of the data used for each series in a chart.

A *legend* identifies the format or color of each data series.

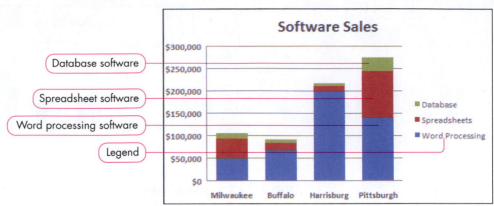

Figure 3.5 Stacked Columns

Column charts are most effective when they are limited to small numbers of categories—generally seven or fewer. If more categories exist, they end up being plotted so close together that reading and labeling become difficult or impossible.

Create a Bar Chart

A ***bar chart*** is a column chart that has been given a horizontal orientation.

A ***bar chart*** is basically a column chart that has a horizontal orientation, as shown in Figure 3.6. Many people prefer this representation because it emphasizes the difference between items. Further, long descriptive labels are easier to read in a bar chart than in a column chart. Sorting the data points either from lowest to highest or highest to lowest makes a bar chart even more effective. The most basic bar chart is a clustered bar chart.

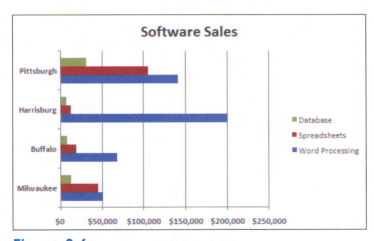

Figure 3.6 Clustered Bar Chart

Create a Pie Chart

A ***pie chart*** displays proportional relationships.

A ***pie chart*** is the most effective way to display proportional relationships. It is the type of chart to select whenever words like *percentage* or *market share* appear in the message to be delivered. The pie, or complete circle, denotes the total amount. Each slice of the pie corresponds to its respective percentage of the total.

The pie chart in Figure 3.7 divides the pie representing total sales into four slices, one for each city. The size of each slice is proportional to the percentage of total sales in that city. The chart depicts a single data series, which appears in cells B7:E7 on the associated worksheet. The data series has four data points corresponding to the total sales in each city. The data labels are placed in the wedges if they fit. If they do not fit, they are placed outside the wedge with a line pointing to the appropriate wedge.

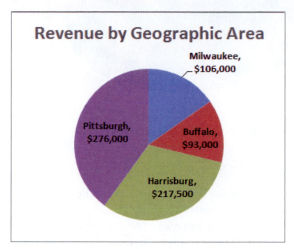

Figure 3.7 Pie Chart Showing Values

To create the pie chart, Excel computes the total sales ($692,000 in our example), calculates the percentage contributed by each city, and draws each slice of the pie in proportion to its computed percentage. Pittsburgh's sales of $276,000 account for 40% of the total, so this slice of the pie is allotted 40% of the area of the circle.

An *exploded pie chart* separates one or more slices of the pie chart for emphasis.

An *exploded pie chart*, shown in Figure 3.8, separates one or more slices of the pie for emphasis. Another way to achieve emphasis in a chart is to choose a title that reflects the message you are trying to deliver. The title in Figure 3.7, *Revenue by Geographic Area*, is neutral and leaves the reader to develop his or her own conclusion about the relative contribution of each area. In contrast, the title in Figure 3.8, *Buffalo Accounts for Only 13% of the Revenue*, is more suggestive and emphasizes the problems in this office. The title could be changed to *Pittsburgh Exceeds 40% of Total Revenue* if the intent were to emphasize the contribution of Pittsburgh.

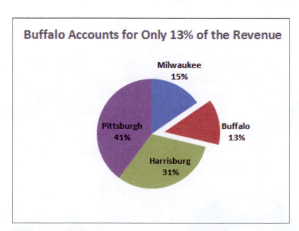

Figure 3.8 Pie Chart Showing Percentages

A *three-dimensional pie chart* is a pie chart that contains a three-dimensional view.

Three-dimensional pie charts may be created in exploded or unexploded format. See Figure 3.9 for an example of an unexploded pie chart. The 3-D chart is misleading because it appears as though the Harrisburg slice is larger than the Pittsburgh slice. This difference is why 3-D charts are seldom used. A pie chart is easiest to read when the number of slices is small (for example, not more than six or seven), and when small categories (percentages less than five) are grouped into a single category called *Other*.

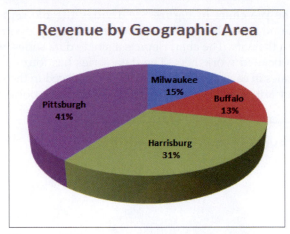

Figure 3.9 Three-Dimensional Pie Chart

Create a Line Chart

A line chart uses a line to connect data points in order to show trends over a long period of time.

A *line chart* shows trends over a period of time. A line connects data points. A line chart is used frequently to show stock market or economic trends. The X axis represents time, such as ten-year increments, whereas the vertical axis represents the value of a stock or quantity. The line chart enables a user to easily spot trends in the data. Figure 3.10 shows a line chart with yearly increments for four years.

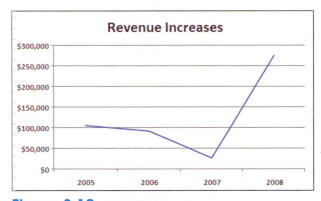

Figure 3.10 Line Chart

Create Other Chart Types

A doughnut chart displays values as percentages of the whole.

The *doughnut chart* is similar to a pie chart in that it shows relationship of parts to a whole, but the doughnut chart can display more than one series of data, and it has a hole in the middle (see Figure 3.11). Chart designers sometimes use the doughnut hole for titles. Each ring represents a data series. Note, however, the display of the data series in a doughnut chart can be confusing.

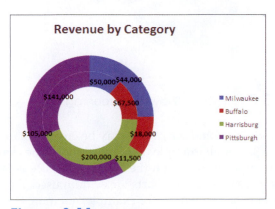

Figure 3.11 Doughnut Chart

A *scatter (XY) chart* shows a relationship between two variables. Scatter charts are
used to represent the data from scientific or educational experiments that demonstrate
relationships. A scatter chart is essentially the plotted dots without any connecting line.
A scatter chart is used to determine if a relationship exists between two different sets of
numerical data. If you plot people's wages and educational levels, you can see if a relationship between wages and education levels exists. Figure 3.12 shows a comparison of
temperature over time. As the month of April passes, the temperatures rise. However,
higher- and lower-than-normal temperatures affect the trend.

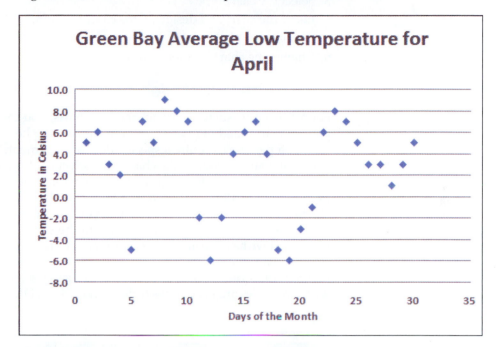

Figure 3.12   Scatter Chart

Stock charts have only one major purpose: to show the high, low, and close
prices for individual stocks over a period of time. While stock charts may have some
other uses, such as showing a range of temperatures over a period of time, they usually are used to show stock prices. Figure 3.13 shows a stock chart that displays opening stock price, high stock price, low stock price, and closing stock price over time.

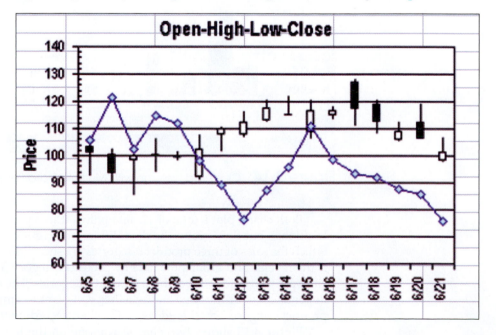

Figure 3.13   Stock Chart

Creating a Chart

Creating a chart in Excel is quick. Excel provides a variety of chart types that you can use when you create a chart. The main types of charts are described above. The six main steps to create a chart are the following:

1. Specify the data series.
2. Select the range of cells to chart.
3. Select the chart type.
4. Insert the chart and designate the chart location.
5. Choose chart options.
6. Change the chart location and size.

Specify the Data Series

For most charts, such as column and bar charts, you can plot the data in a chart that you have arranged in rows or columns on a worksheet. Some chart types, however, such as a pie chart, require a specific data arrangement. On the worksheet, select the data you want to plot as a pie chart, then select pie from the types of charts available.

The charts presented so far in the chapter displayed only a single data series, such as the total sales by location or the total sales by product category. Although such charts are useful, it is often more informative to view multiple data series, which are ranges of data values plotted as a unit in the same chart. Figure 3.14 displays the worksheet we have been using throughout the chapter. Figure 3.4 displays a clustered column chart that plots multiple data series that exist as rows (cells B4:E4, B5:E5, and B6:E6) within the worksheet. Figure 3.14 displays a chart based on the same data when the series are in columns (cells B4:B6, C4:C6, D4:D6, and E4:E6).

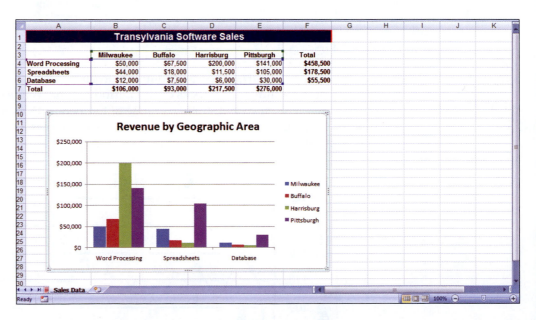

Figure 3.14 Clustered Column with Multiple Data Series as Columns

Both charts plot a total of 12 data points (three product categories for each of four locations), but they group the data differently. Figure 3.4 displays the data by city in which the sales of three product categories are shown for each of four cities. Figure 3.14 is the reverse and groups the data by product category. This time, the sales in the four cities are shown for each of three product categories. The choice between the two charts depends on your message and whether you want to emphasize revenue by city or by product category. You should create the chart according to your intended purpose.

Figure 3.15 shows two charts. The one on the left plots data series in the cells B4:E4, B5:E5, and B6:E6, whereas the chart on the right plots the same data series but

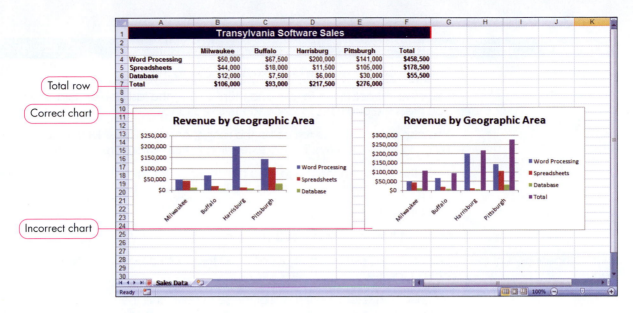

Figure 3.15

includes B7:E7, which is the total for all products. Including the total row figures (or column total figures) dramatically skews the chart, presents a misleading picture, and indicates you have selected an incorrect range for your chart. Do NOT include totals and individual data points on the same chart.

Select the Range to Chart

Too often Excel users do not put any thought into the data they select for a chart. Selecting the correct data goes hand-in-hand with having a plan for what a chart should display. For example, a user would not want to show totals in column totals that represent only several months. Even though it is a simple process to deselect cells once they have been selected, users should have a plan before selecting cells for a chart. Table 3.1 describes different techniques for selecting cells.

Select the Chart Type

After you select the range of cells that you want to chart, your next step is to select the type of chart you want to create. Each type of chart is designed to visually illustrate a particular type of data. Table 3.2 lists the different types of charts and their purposes. Use this table as a guide for selecting the type of chart you want to use for the worksheet data.

In the Charts group on the Insert tab, do one of the following:

1. Click the chart type, and then click a chart subtype that you want to use.
2. To see all available chart types, click a chart type, and then click All Chart Types to display the Create Chart dialog box.
3. Click the arrows to scroll through all available chart types and chart subtypes, and then click the one that you want to use.

Insert the Chart and Designate the Chart Location

Excel places the chart as an embedded object on the current worksheet. You can leave the chart on the same worksheet as the worksheet data used to create the chart, or you can place the chart in a separate chart sheet. If you leave the chart in the same worksheet, you can print the worksheet and chart on the same page. If you want to print a full-sized chart, you can move the chart to its own chart sheet.

Table 3.1 Cell Selection Techniques

To Select	Do This
A single cell	Click the cell or press the arrow keys to move to the cell.
A range of cells	Click the first cell in the range, and then drag to the last cell, or hold down Shift while you press the arrow keys to extend the selection.
	You also can select the first cell in the range, and then press F8 to extend the selection by using the arrow keys. To stop extending the selection, press F8 again.
A large range of cells	Click the first cell in the range, and then hold down Shift while you click the last cell in the range. You can scroll to make the last cell visible.
All cells on a worksheet	Click the Select All button.
	To select the entire worksheet, you also can press Ctrl+A.
Nonadjacent cells or cell ranges	Select the first cell or range of cells, and then hold down Ctrl while you select the other cells or ranges.
	You also can select the first cell or range of cells, and then press Shift+F8 to add another nonadjacent cell or range to the selection. To stop adding cells or ranges to the selection, press Shift+F8 again.
An entire row or column	Click the row or column heading.
	You also can select cells in a row or column by selecting the first cell and then pressing Ctrl+Shift+Arrow key (Right Arrow or Left Arrow for rows, Up Arrow or Down Arrow for columns).
Adjacent rows or columns	Drag across the row or column headings. Or select the first row or column, then hold down Shift while you select the last row or column.
Noncontiguous rows or columns	Click the column or row heading of the first row or column in your selection, then hold down Ctrl while you click the column or row headings of other rows or columns that you want to add to the selection.

Table 3.2 Chart Types and Purposes

Chart Type	Purpose
Column	Compares categories, shows changes over time.
Bar	Shows comparison between independent variables. Not used for time or dates.
Pie	Shows percentages of a whole. Exploded pie emphasizes a popular category.
Line	Shows change in a series over categories or time.
Doughnut	Compares how two or more series contribute to the whole.
Scatter	Shows correlation between two sets of values.
Stock	Shows high-low stock prices.

To change the location of a chart to another sheet or a new sheet:

1. Click the embedded chart or the chart sheet to select it and to display the chart tools.
2. Click Move Chart in the Location group on the Design tab.
3. In the *Choose where you want the chart to be placed* section, do one of the following:
   - Click *New sheet* to display the chart in its own chart sheet.
   - Click *Object in*, click the drop-down arrow, and select a worksheet to move the chart to another worksheet.

Choose Chart Options

When you create a chart, the Chart Tools contextual tab is available. The Design, Layout, and Format tabs are displayed in Chart Tools. You can use the commands on these tabs to modify the chart. For example, use the Design tab to display the data series by row or by column, make changes to the source data of the chart, change the location of the chart, change the chart type, save a chart as a template, or select predefined layout and formatting options. Use the Layout tab to change the display of chart elements such as chart titles and data labels, use drawing tools, or add text boxes and pictures to the chart. Use the Format tab to add fill colors, change line styles, or apply special effects. Review the Reference Page for examples of the contextual chart tools tab with the Design, Layout, and Design tabs depicted.

Chart Tools | Reference

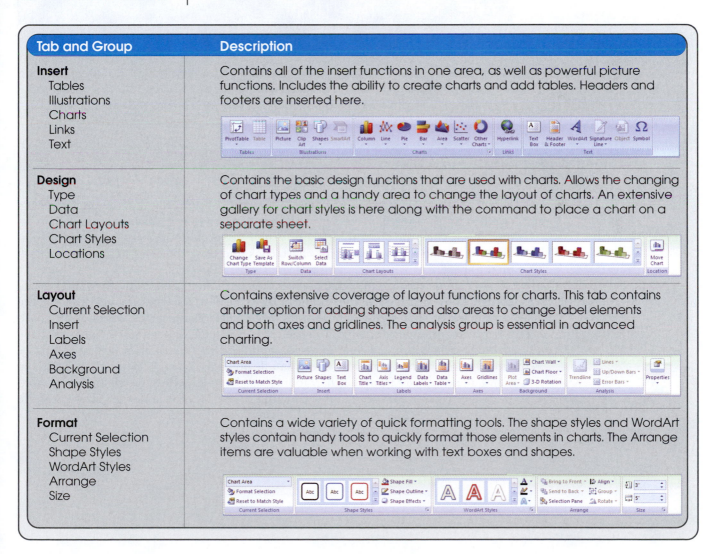

Tab and Group	Description
Insert Tables Illustrations Charts Links Text	Contains all of the insert functions in one area, as well as powerful picture functions. Includes the ability to create charts and add tables. Headers and footers are inserted here.
Design Type Data Chart Layouts Chart Styles Locations	Contains the basic design functions that are used with charts. Allows the changing of chart types and a handy area to change the layout of charts. An extensive gallery for chart styles is here along with the command to place a chart on a separate sheet.
Layout Current Selection Insert Labels Axes Background Analysis	Contains extensive coverage of layout functions for charts. This tab contains another option for adding shapes and also areas to change label elements and both axes and gridlines. The analysis group is essential in advanced charting.
Format Current Selection Shape Styles WordArt Styles Arrange Size	Contains a wide variety of quick formatting tools. The shape styles and WordArt styles contain handy tools to quickly format those elements in charts. The Arrange items are valuable when working with text boxes and shapes.

Add Graphics in Charts

You may want to add graphics, such as company logos or representative clip art, to charts to personalize the charts or make them more distinctive. In either case, the procedure is simple. Again, this is a case where less is sometimes more. Be sparing in the use of graphics that can change the message being conveyed.

To add a graphic to a chart:

1. In the Illustrations section on the Insert tab, select the medium where the graphic will come from (Picture, Clip Art, or Smart Art).
2. Search for and insert the graphic.
3. Size and move the graphic on the chart as desired.

TIP   Set a Time Limit

You can customize virtually every aspect of every object within a chart. That is the good news. It is also bad news because you can spend inordinate amounts of time for little or no gain. It is fun to experiment, but set a time limit and stop when you reach the allocated time. The default settings are often adequate to convey your message, and further experimentation might prove counterproductive.

Change the Chart Location and Size

Whether the chart is embedded on the worksheet with the data or on a separate sheet, at times you will need to move a chart or to change its size. To move a chart on any sheet, click the chart to select it. When the pointer appears as a four-headed arrow while on the margin of the chart, click and drag the chart to another location on the sheet.

To change the size of a chart, select the chart. Sizing handles are located in the corners of the chart and at the middle of the edge borders. Clicking and dragging the middle left or right sizing handle of the edge borders adjusts the width of the chart. Drag the sizing handle away from the chart to stretch or widen the chart; drag the sizing handle within the chart to decrease the width of the chart. Clicking and dragging the top or bottom middle sizing handle adjusts the height of the chart. Drag the sizing handle away from the chart to increase its height; drag the sizing handle into the chart to decrease its height. Clicking and dragging a corner sizing handle increases or decreases the height and width of the chart proportionately.

Hands-On Exercises

1 | The First Chart

Skills covered: 1. Use AutoSum **2.** Create the Chart **3.** Complete the Chart **4.** Move and Size the Chart **5.** Change the Worksheet **6.** Change the Chart Type **7.** Create a Second Chart

---

Step 1
Use AutoSum

Use Figure 3.16 as a guide as you work through the steps in the exercise.

a. Start Excel. Open the *chap3_ho1_sales* workbook and save it as **chap3_ho1_sales_ solution**.

b. Click and drag to select **cells B7:E7** (the cells that will contain the total sales for each location). Click **AutoSum** in the Editing group on the Home tab to compute the total for each city.

c. Click and drag to select **cells F4:F6**, and then click **AutoSum**.

 The SUM function is entered automatically into these cells to total the entries to the left of the selected cells.

d. Click and drag to select **cells B4:F7** and format these cells with the currency symbol and no decimal places.

e. Bold the row and column headings and the totals. Center the entries in **cells B3:F3**.

f. Save the workbook.

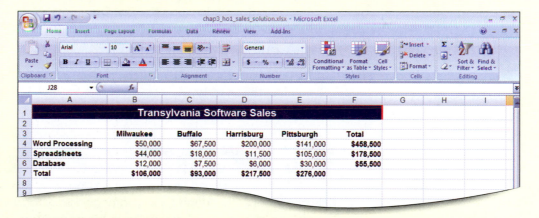

Figure 3.16 Formatted Worksheet with Totals

Step 2
Create the Chart

Refer to Figure 3.17 as you complete Step 2. Note that the colors displayed in figures may not match your screen display.

a. Select **cells B3:E3** to select the category labels (the names of the cities). Press and hold **Ctrl** as you drag the mouse over **cells B7:E7** to select the data series (the cells containing the total sales for the individual cities).

 You have selected the cities that will become the X axis in your chart. You selected B7 through E7 as the values that will become the data series.

b. Check that **cells B3:E3** and **cells B7:E7** are selected. Click the **Insert tab** and click **Column** in the Charts group.

 You should see the Column Chart palette, as shown in Figure 3.17. When the Column chart type and Clustered column subtype are selected, the chart appears on Sheet1. Note that your default colors may differ from those displayed in your textbook.

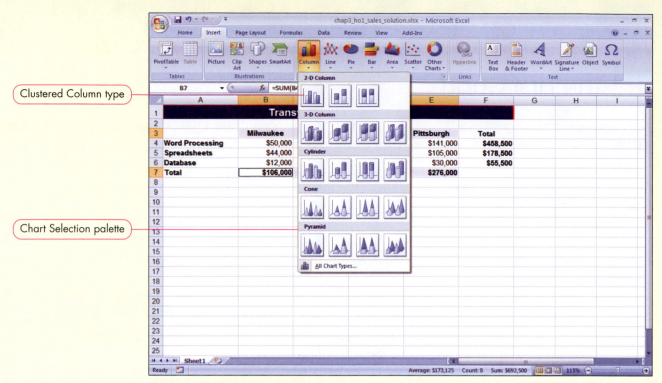

Clustered Column type

Chart Selection palette

Figure 3.17 Gallery of Chart Types

TROUBLESHOOTING: If you select too little or too much data for charting purposes, you can change your data ranges. Make the Design tab active, then click Edit Data Source to open the Edit Data Source dialog box. Click Edit and select the correct data range.

c. Click **Clustered Column** in the *2-D Column* section to insert a chart.

As you move the mouse over the palette, a ScreenTip appears that indicates the name of the chart type.

TIP The F11 Key

The F11 key is the fastest way to create a chart in its own sheet. Select the worksheet data, including the legends and category labels, and then press F11 to create the chart. The chart displays according to the default format built into the Excel column chart. After you create the chart, you can use the Chart Tools tabs, Mini toolbars, or shortcut menus to choose a different chart type and customize the formatting.

Step 3
Complete the Chart

Refer to Figure 3.18 as you complete Step 3.

a. Click the chart object to make the chart active. Click the **Layout tab**, click **Chart Title** in the Labels group, and then click **Above Chart** to create a title for the chart.

You selected the chart, and then selected the placement of the chart title using the Chart Tools tabs.

b. Type **Revenue by Geographic Area** for the title and press **Enter**.

c. Click **Legend** in the Labels group of the Layout tab and select **None** to delete the legend.

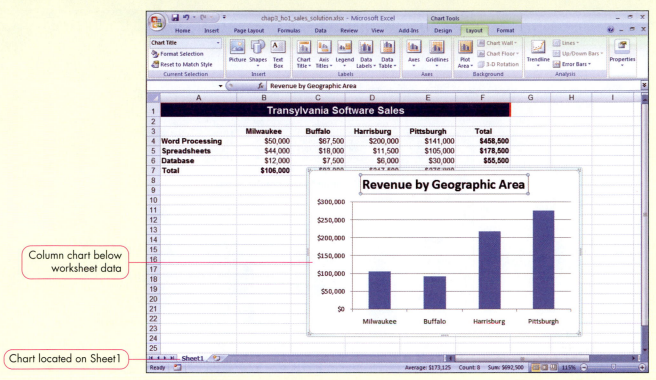

Column chart below worksheet data

Chart located on Sheet1

Figure 3.18 Column Chart with Title

<table>
<tr><td></td><td></td><td>Milwaukee</td><td>Buffalo</td><td>Harrisburg</td><td>Pittsburgh</td><td>Total</td></tr>
<tr><td></td><td>Word Processing</td><td>$50,000</td><td>$67,500</td><td>$200,000</td><td>$141,000</td><td>$458,500</td></tr>
<tr><td></td><td>Spreadsheets</td><td>$44,000</td><td>$18,000</td><td>$11,500</td><td>$105,000</td><td>$178,500</td></tr>
<tr><td></td><td>Database</td><td>$12,000</td><td>$7,500</td><td>$6,000</td><td>$30,000</td><td>$55,500</td></tr>
<tr><td></td><td>Total</td><td>$106,000</td><td></td><td></td><td></td><td></td></tr>
</table>

Step 4
Move and Size the Chart

Refer to Figure 3.19 as you complete Step 4.

a. Move and size the chart just as you would any other Windows object.

You should see the completed chart in Figure 3.19. When you click the chart, the sizing handles indicate the chart is selected and will be affected by subsequent commands.

1. Click the chart border to select the chart, then click on the highlighted outline of the chart and drag (the mouse pointer changes to a four-sided arrow) to move the chart so that the top left side of the chart starts in **cell A9**.

2. Drag a corner handle (the mouse pointer changes to a double arrow) to change the length and width of the chart simultaneously so that the chart covers the **range A9:G29**.

b. Click outside the chart to deselect it. The sizing handles are no longer visible.

When working with any graphic object in Excel, you can resize it by making it active and dragging sizing handles that appear at the corners and on the perimeter of the object.

c. Save the workbook.

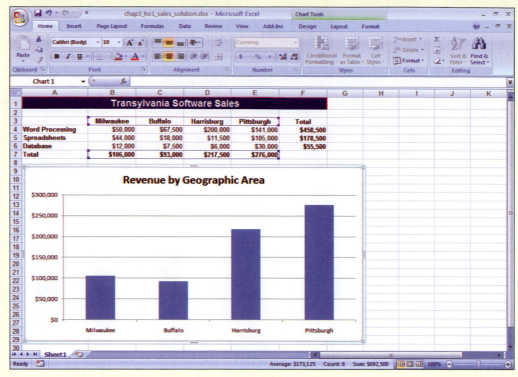

Figure 3.19 Chart Size and Location Changed

TIP   Embedded Charts

An embedded chart is treated as an object that can be moved, sized, copied, or deleted just as any other Windows object. To move an embedded chart, click the border of the chart to select the chart and drag it to a new location in the worksheet. To size the chart, select it and then drag any of the eight sizing handles in the desired direction. To delete the chart, select it and press Delete. To copy the chart, select it, click Copy in the Clipboard group on the Home tab to copy the chart to the clipboard, click elsewhere in the workbook where you want the copied chart to go, and click Paste.

Step 5
Change the Worksheet

Refer to Figure 3.20 as you complete Step 5.

a. Click in **cell B4**. Change the entry to **$225,000** and press **Enter**.

Any changes in a worksheet are automatically reflected in the associated chart. The total sales for Milwaukee in cell B7 change automatically to reflect the increased sales for word processing. The column for Milwaukee also changes in the chart and is now larger than the column for Pittsburgh.

b. Click in **cell B3**. Change the entry to **Chicago** and press **Enter**.

The category label on the X axis changes automatically to reflect the new city name (see Figure 3.20).

c. Click **Undo** twice on the Quick Access Toolbar.

You changed the worksheet and chart back to Milwaukee and $50,000 by clicking Undo twice. The worksheet and chart are restored to their earlier values.

d. Save the workbook.

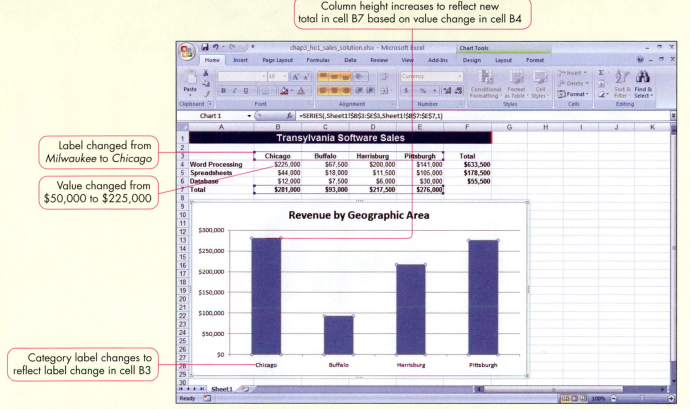

Column height increases to reflect new total in cell B7 based on value change in cell B4

Label changed from *Milwaukee* to *Chicago*

Value changed from $50,000 to $225,000

Category label changes to reflect label change in cell B3

Figure 3.20 Temporary Data Changes Affect Chart

Step 6
Change the Chart Type

Refer to Figure 3.21 as you complete Step 6.

a. Click the chart border area to select the chart, click **Change Chart Type** in the Type group on the Design tab, click the **Pie** type, and then click **Pie** (the first button in the Pie row). Click **OK**, and the chart changes to a pie chart.

You used the Design tab to change the type of chart. The following steps will guide you through adding data labels to the chart area, and formatting those data labels as percentages.

b. Point to any pie wedge, click the right mouse button to display a shortcut menu, and click **Add Data Labels**.

c. Right-click the mouse button on any pie wedge to display a shortcut menu and select **Format Data Labels** to display the Format Data Labels dialog box. Make sure **Label Options** in the left column is selected, and then click the **Category Name** and **Percentage** check boxes to format the data labels. Remove the checks from the **Value** and **Show Leader Lines** check boxes.

d. Change the values in the data labels to percentages by clicking **Number** below *Label Options* on the left side of the dialog box, click **Percentage** in *Category* list, type **0** in the **Decimal places** box, and click **Close** to accept the settings and close the dialog box.

The pie chart now displays data labels as percentages. The Number format is the default when initially inserting data labels.

e. Modify each component as necessary:

1. Click the plot area to select the chart. Click and drag the sizing handles to increase the size of the plot area within the embedded chart.

2. Click a label to select all data labels. Click the **Home tab**, click the **Font Size down arrow** in the Font group, and select **12**.

f. Save the workbook.

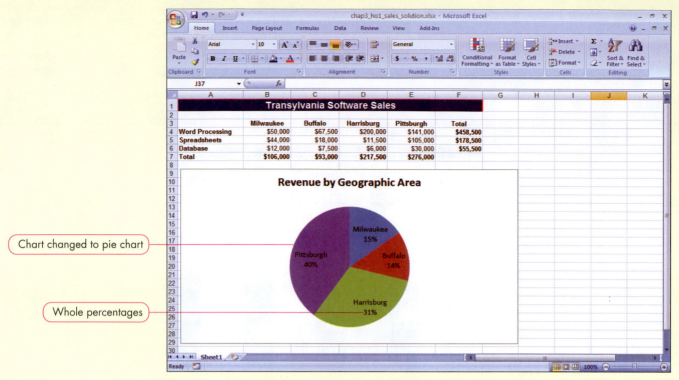

Chart changed to pie chart

Whole percentages

Figure 3.21 Chart Changed to Pie Chart

Step 7
Create a Second Chart

Refer to Figure 3.22 as you complete Step 7.

a. Click and drag to select **cells A4:A6** in the worksheet. Press and hold **Ctrl** as you drag the mouse to select **cells F4:F6**.

b. Click the **Insert tab**, click **Column** in the Charts group, and select **3-D Clustered Column**.

When the Column chart type and 3-D Clustered Column subtype are selected, the chart appears on Sheet1. The values (the data being plotted) are in cells F4:F6. The category labels for the X axis are in cells A4:A6.

c. Click **Chart Title** in the Labels group on the Layout tab and select **Centered Overlay Title**.

d. Type **Revenue by Product Category** for the title. Click **Legend** in the Labels group on the Layout tab and select **None** to delete the legend.

You have created a title for your 3-D clustered column chart. You deleted the legend because you have only one data series.

e. Click the **Design tab** and click **Move Chart** in the Location group. Click **New sheet**, and then click **OK** to display the chart on a new sheet and close the Move Chart dialog box.

The 3-D column chart has been created in the chart sheet labeled Chart1, as shown in Figure 3.22.

f. Save the workbook. Exit Excel if you do not want to continue with the next exercise at this time.

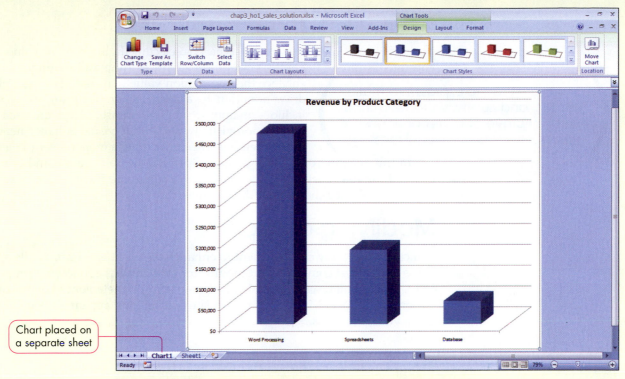

Chart placed on a separate sheet

Figure 3.22 Chart Moved to Chart1 Sheet

Chart Enhancements

Now that you already have created a chart by selecting the appropriate values and labels, you must improve the appearance of the chart. Adding and editing chart elements enhance the information value of a chart. For example, you can draw attention to a specific bar using an arrow shape that includes an appropriate text phrase. Charts are used to express information visually, and subtle visual enhancements improve comprehension while presenting a more powerful message.

> Charts are used to express information visually, and subtle visual enhancements improve comprehension while presenting a more powerful message.

In this section you modify a chart. Specifically, you change and edit chart elements, format a chart, add data labels, and change the fill color for chart elements. Then you enhance charts by adding shapes.

Modifying a Chart

You can modify any chart element to enhance the chart and improve its appearance. Some of the most common chart modifications include the following properties: size, color, font, format, scale, or style just by selecting the element and choosing from a variety of options. Mini toolbars and shortcut menus appear as needed for you to make your selections.

TIP   Anatomy of a Chart

A chart is composed of multiple components (objects), each of which can be selected and changed separately. Point to any part of a chart to display a ScreenTip indicating the name of the component, then click the mouse to select that component and display the sizing handles. You can then click and drag the object within the chart and/or right-click the mouse to display a Mini toolbar and shortcut menu with commands pertaining to the selected object.

Change and Edit Chart Elements

It is often necessary to change chart elements such as titles and axes. For example, you might need to change the title of the chart or adjust the font size of the title to balance the title text and the chart size. You can change these elements to reflect different words or edit the elements to reflect formatting changes.

On a chart, do one of the following:

- To edit the contents of a title, click the chart or axis title that you want to change.
- To edit the contents of a data label, click twice on the data label that you want to change.
- Click again to place the title or data label in editing mode, drag to select the text that you want to change, type the new text or value, and then press Enter.

To format the text, select it, and then click the formatting options that you want on the Mini toolbar. You can also use the formatting buttons in the Font group on the Home tab. To format the entire title or data label, right-click the selected text, select Format Chart Title, Format Axis Title, or Format Data Labels on the shortcut menu, and then select the formatting options that you want.

Format a Chart

The options for formatting a chart may be approached in two ways, either by using the tabs or by selecting the chart and then right-clicking and using the various format commands on the shortcut menu. Table 3.3 shows the different tabs and the formatting capabilities available with each. Figures 3.23 through 3.26 show these tabs as defined in Table 3.3.

Table 3.3 Tab and Format Features

Tab	Format Features
Insert	Insert shapes, insert illustrations, create and edit WordArt and textboxes, insert symbols.
Design	Change chart type, edit the data sources, change the chart style and layout, and change the location of the chart.
Layout	Again allows the insertion of shapes, graphics, and text boxes. Add or change chart title, axis title, legend, data labels, and data table. Format axis and change the background.
Format	Deals with more sophisticated control of WordArt, shapes, and arrangement.

Figure 3.23 Insert Tab

Figure 3.24 Design Tab

Figure 3.25 Layout Tab

Figure 3.26 Format Tab

Add Data Labels

A ***data label*** is the value or name of a data point.

One of the features of Excel charting that does much to enhance charts is the use of ***data labels***, which are the value or name of a data point. The exact values of data shown by charts are not always clear, particularly in 3-D charts, as well as scatter charts and some line charts. It assists the readers of your charts if you label the data points with text and their values. These labels amplify the data represented in the chart by providing their numerical values on the chart. To add data labels to a chart:

1. Select the chart that will have data labels added.

2. Click on the Data Labels list in the Labels group on the Layout tab.

3. Select the location for the data labels on the chart.

Change the Fill Color for Chart Elements

Another component you can change is the color or fill pattern of any element in the chart. Colors are used to accentuate data presented in chart form. Colors also are used to underplay data presented in chart form. Charts often are used in Microsoft PowerPoint for presentation, so you must pay attention to contrast and use appropriate colors for large screen display. Remember also that color blindness and other visual impairments can change how charts are viewed. To change the color of a data series in a column chart:

1. Right-click on any column to open the shortcut menu.
2. Select Format Data Series.
3. Select Fill from the Series Options and select a color from the Color list.
4. Click Close.

To change the color of the plot area, right-click on the plot area to open the shortcut menu and select Format Plot area. Repeat Steps 3 and 4 above.

Another unique feature you can use to enhance a chart and make the data more meaningful is to use an image in the data series. See Figure 3.27 for an example of a chart using an image of an apple to represent bushels of apples. To use an image as a data series, select the data series, click the Shape Fill down arrow in the Shape Styles group on the Format tab, and select Picture. From the Insert Picture dialog box, select the image and click Insert.

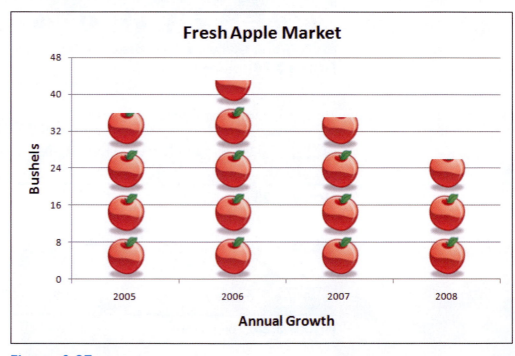

Figure 3.27 Images in Charts

TIP   Quick Layout

Excel enables you to instantly change the look of a chart. After creating a chart, quickly apply a predefined layout to the chart. Choose from a variety of useful predefined layouts and then manually customize the layout of individual chart elements if desired. Select the chart before formatting. This action displays Chart Tools tab, adding the Design, Layout, and Format tabs. On the Design tab, in the Chart Layouts group, click the chart layout that you want to use. To see all available layouts, click More.

TIP   Shape Fill

As an alternative to right-clicking a chart element to change a fill color, you can select the specific chart element, such as one data series and click the Shape Fill down arrow in the Shape Styles group on the Format tab. You can choose specific colors, such as **Red, Accent 2, Lighter 60%** in the *Theme Colors* section, or you can select a regular color from the *Standard Colors* section.

Enhancing Charts with Graphic Shapes

Using shapes is a technique that lets you add pre-made graphics to a chart to emphasize the content of a part of a chart. Ready-made shapes come in forms such as rectangles, circles, arrows, lines, flowchart symbols, and callouts. Words also can be placed in shapes using text boxes.

Shapes can be inserted either from the Insert tab or from the Layout tab. You want to experiment with both techniques and decide which you prefer. To insert a shape using the Layout tab:

1. Click the Shapes pull-down menu on the Layout tab.

2. Click on the shape you want to insert.

3. Place the crosshair pointer over the location on the chart where the graphic is to be located and drag the pointer to place the shape. To constrain the drawing element to the proportion illustrated in the shapes palette, hold Shift while you drag the pointer to place the shape.

4. Release the mouse button.

5. To resize a shape, select the shape and use one of the nine selection handles to change its size.

6. Rotate the graphic by clicking the green rotation handle and dragging to rotate the shape.

7. Change the shape of the graphic by clicking the yellow diamond tool and dragging.

Hands-On Exercises

2 | Multiple Data Series

Skills covered: 1. Rename the Worksheet **2.** Create Chart with Multiple Data Series **3.** Copy the Chart **4.** Change the Source Data **5.** Change the Chart Type **6.** Insert a Graphic Shape and Add a Text Box

---

Step 1
Rename the Worksheet

Refer to Figure 3.28 as you complete Step 1.

a. Open the *chap3_ho1_sales_solution* workbook if you closed it at the end of the previous exercise. Save the workbook as **chap3_ho2_sales_solution**.

b. Point to the workbook tab labeled Sheet1, right-click the mouse to display a shortcut menu, and then click **Rename**.

The name of the worksheet (Sheet1) is selected.

c. Type **Sales Data** to change the name of the worksheet to the more descriptive name. Press **Enter**. Right-click the worksheet tab a second time, select **Tab Color**, then change the color to the **Blue, Accent 1** theme shade.

You renamed the worksheet and will have changed the color of the sheet tab.

d. Change the name of the Chart1 sheet to **Column Chart**. Change the tab color to the **Red, Accent 2** theme shade. Save the workbook.

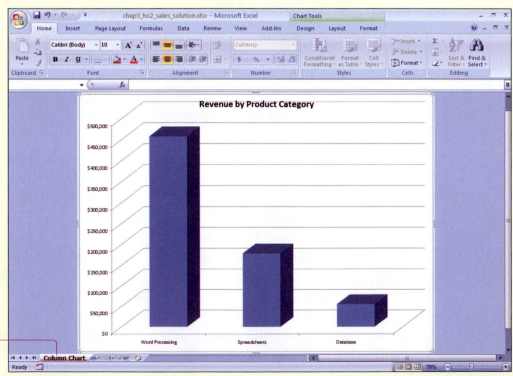

Figure 3.28 Renamed Worksheet

<table>
<tr><td>

Step 2

Create Chart with Multiple Data Series

</td><td>

Refer to Figure 3.29 as you complete Step 2.

a. Click the **Sales Data tab**, then click and drag to select **cells A3:E6**.

b. Click the **Insert tab**, click the **Column** list in the Chart group, and select **Clustered Column** as the subtype from the gallery of column chart types.

This type of chart is best for displaying multiple data series.

c. Click **Chart Title** in the Labels group on the Layout tab and select **Above Chart** to create a title for the chart.

d. Type **Revenue by City** for the chart title and press **Enter**.

Using appropriate chart titles is essential as no chart should appear without a title. Viewers of your chart need to be able to quickly identify the subject of the chart.

e. Click **Move Chart** in the Location group on the Design tab. Click **New sheet**, and then click **OK**.

You have moved the chart from the Sales Data sheet to a new chart sheet.

f. Change the name of the Chart2 sheet to **Revenue by City**. Your sheet name for the chart may differ. Change the tab color to theme shade **Orange, Accent 6**. Save the workbook.

After changing both the tab name and tab color, your chart should be similar to Figure 3.29.

</td></tr>
</table>

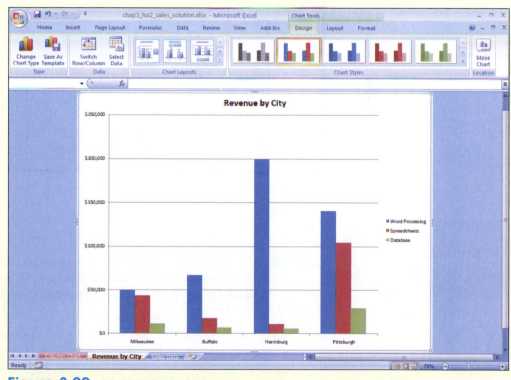

Figure 3.29 Multiple Data Series

<table>
<tr><td>

Step 3

Copy the Chart

</td><td>

Refer to Figure 3.30 as you complete Step 3.

a. Click anywhere in the chart title to select the title. Click the **Font Size** list box on the Home tab and change to **24-point** type to enlarge the title.

You changed the font size of the title to make it easier to read.

</td></tr>
</table>

b. Point to the worksheet tab named **Revenue by City** and click to select it if it is not already selected. Then click **Format** in the Cells group of the Home tab. Click **Move or Copy sheet** to display the dialog box shown in Figure 3.30.

c. Click **Sales Data** in the Before Sheet list box. Check the box to **Create a copy**. Click **OK**.

d. A duplicate worksheet called Chart (4) (your sheet tab name may vary) is created and appears before or to the left of the Sales Data worksheet.

You have now created a copy of the original chart and can enhance it without having to replot the data.

TROUBLESHOOTING: The appearance of the Chart Tools tabs will change depending on the type of chart created and the location of the chart.

e. Double-click the newly created worksheet tab to select the name. Type **Revenue by Product** as the new name and save the workbook.

Figure 3.30 Move or Copy Dialog Box

Step 4	
Change the Source Data	Refer to Figure 3.31 as you complete Step 4.

a. Click the **Revenue by Product tab** to make it the active sheet if it is not already active. Click anywhere in the title of the chart, select the word *City*, and then type **Product Category** to replace the selected text. Click outside the title to deselect it.

You edited the title of the chart to reflect the new data source.

b. Click the **Design tab** and click **Select Data** in the Data group to display the Select Data Source dialog box, as shown in Figure 3.31.

c. Click the **Switch Row/Column button**. Click **OK** to close the Select Data Source dialog box.

Your original chart plotted the data in rows. The chart originally contained three data series, one series for each product. Your new chart plots the data in columns. The chart contains four data series, one for each city.

d. Save the workbook.

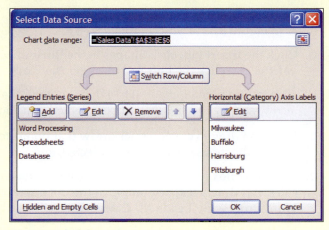

Figure 3.31 Edit Data Source Dialog Box

Refer to Figure 3.32 as you complete Step 5.

a. Click the chart border area to select the chart, click **Change Chart Type** in the Type group on the Design tab, and click the **Stacked Column** (the second from the left in the top row of the column chart gallery). Click **OK**.

The chart changes to a stacked column chart.

b. Right-click the legend and select 14 points font size from the Mini toolbar.

You increased the font size of the legend to make it more readable. Your chart should be similar to Figure 3.32.

c. Save the workbook.

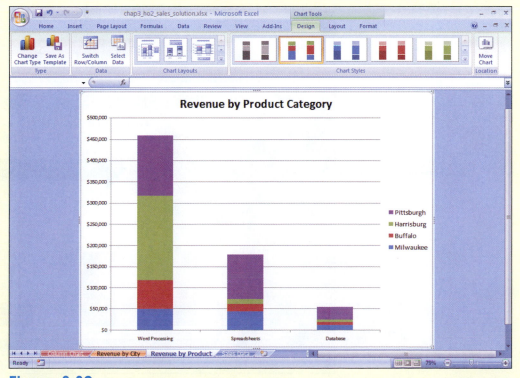

Figure 3.32 Stacked Column Chart

Refer to Figure 3.33 as you complete Step 6.

a. Click the **Insert tab**, click **Shapes** in the Illustrations group to view the Shapes palette, and click the **Left Arrow** under the Block Arrow category.

The mouse pointer changes to a thin crosshair that you will drag to "draw" the arrow shape. The crosshair appears when you click in the chart.

b. Click and drag to create a thick arrow that points to the Word Processing column. Release the mouse. The arrow is selected, and you are viewing the **Format** tab.

c. Click **Text Box** in the Insert Shapes group on the Format tab to insert a text box. Click and drag a text box on top of the thick arrow. Release the mouse. Type **Word Processing Leads All Categories.**

You can use shapes to draw attention to significant trends or changes in date. The text in the shape describes the trend or change.

d. Select the text you just typed, then right-click to display a shortcut menu and Mini toolbar. Use the Mini toolbar to change the font to **12-point** bold white.

TROUBLESHOOTING: Should you have difficulty selecting the text box, right-click on the text itself to reshow the shortcut menu and Mini toolbar.

e. Click the title of the chart and you will see sizing handles around the title to indicate it has been selected. Click the **Font Size down arrow** on the Home tab. Click **28** to increase the size of the title. Your chart will be similar to Figure 3.33.

Increasing the size of the title enables your viewers to quickly see the subject of the chart.

f. Save the workbook, but do not print it. Exit Excel if you do not want to continue with the next exercise at this time.

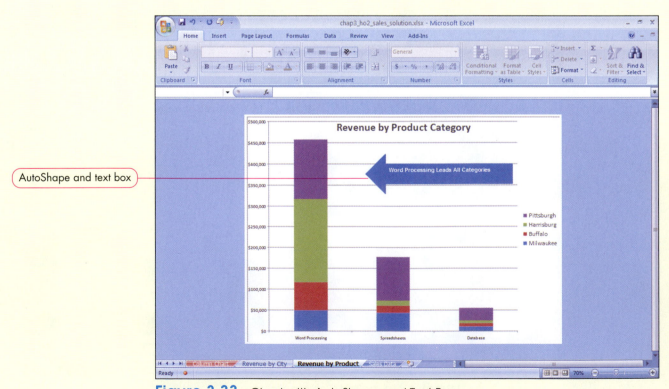

Figure 3.33 Chart with AutoShape and Text Box

Chart Distribution

You can create visual information masterpieces that could be shared with others.

You can create visual information masterpieces that could be shared with others. Charts are used as documentation in Web pages, memos, reports, research papers, books, and a variety of other types of documents. Therefore, it is important to experience how charts are transferred to these documents.

In this section, you embed Excel charts in other Microsoft Office applications. Then you learn how to print the chart within a worksheet or by itself. Finally, you learn how to save a chart as a Web file.

Embedding Charts

Microsoft Excel 2007 is just one application in the Microsoft Office 2007 suite. The applications are integrated and enable for data sharing. It is straightforward to copy worksheets and charts and paste in Word and PowerPoint. You can then format the objects in Word or PowerPoint.

Export to Other Applications

Microsoft Office 2007 enables you to create a file in one application that contains data (objects) from another application. The memo in Figure 3.34, for example, was created in Word, and it contains an **object** (a chart) that was developed in Excel. The Excel object is linked to the Word document, so that any changes to the Excel workbook data are automatically reflected in the Word document. Formatting of the object

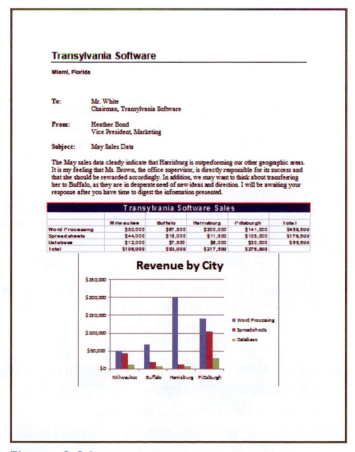

Figure 3.34 Memo in Microsoft Office Word

in Excel after it is placed in the Word document will not be seen in the Word document. The steps to embed a chart in a Word (or PowerPoint) document are:

1. Click on the chart in Excel to select it.
2. Click Copy in the Clipboard group on the Home tab.
3. Open the appropriate Word or PowerPoint document.
4. Click Paste in the Clipboard group on the Home tab.

Remember that changes to the worksheet data made in Excel will automatically update the chart in Excel and the other application, but changes in formatting will not be updated in the other application.

TIP   Hiding and Unhiding a Worksheet

A chart delivers a message more effectively than the corresponding numeric data, and thus it may be convenient to hide the associated worksheet on which the chart is based. Click the Home tab. Then click Format in the Cells group, click Hide & Unhide, and then Hide Sheet the worksheet you want to hide. Repeat the selecting Unhide Sheet to make the worksheet visible again.

Printing Charts

Printing charts is a straightforward operation but requires that you closely observe the Print Preview window in the Print group on the Office menu. You have to see what will print to make sure this is what you want to print. Printing is an output that many Excel users prefer because the chart is often part of a report, research paper, or some other paper document.

Print an Object in a Worksheet

If the chart is contained on the same worksheet page as the data, you have two options, either to print only the chart or only the data table, or to print both. To print only the chart, click on the chart to ensure it is selected. You then select Print Preview from the Print group on the Office menu. Verify that only the chart is selected for printing. Then select the Page Setup options that best show the printed chart, and then print the chart.

If you want to print both the chart and the data table, the above steps are followed except you must ensure that the chart is deselected. This is a case where the use of the Print Preview command is essential to ensure the correct items are being printed.

Print a Full-Page Chart

The options above can be difficult to use if a full-page printing of a chart is desired. The easier option is to place the chart on a separate sheet in the workbook and print it from there.

1. Click to select the chart.
2. Click Move Chart in the Location group on the Design tab.
3. Click the New Sheet option.
4. Move to the sheet added in Step 3.
5. Use Print Preview to ensure the chart will be displayed properly when printed.
6. Select the appropriate Page Setup options and print the chart.

Save as a Web Page

Excel users can place an Excel chart (and sometimes entire workbooks) on the World Wide Web. The first step to placement on the Web is to save the worksheet as a Web page. To do this:

1. Click the Office Button and select Save As.
2. Select Web Page (*.htm; *.html) from the *Save as Type* menu.
3. Title the file appropriately and save it to the desired location.
4. You can preview the chart or workbook by opening your browser, navigating to the location of the Web page, and opening it.

Hands-On Exercises

3 | Embedding, Printing, and Saving a Chart as a Web Page

Skills covered: 1. Embed a Chart in Microsoft Word **2.** Copy the Worksheet **3.** Embed the Data **4.** Copy the Chart **5.** Embed the Chart **6.** Modify the Worksheet **7.** Update the Links **8.** Print Worksheet and Chart **9.** Save and View Chart as Web Page

---

Step 1

Embed a Chart in Microsoft Word

Refer to Figure 3.35 as you complete Step 1.

a. Start Word and if necessary, click the **Maximize** button in the application window so that Word takes up the entire screen.

b. Click the **Office Button** and select **Open**.

　1. Open the *chap3_ho3_memo* document.

　2. Save the document as **chap3_ho3_memo_solution**.

c. Click **Print Layout** on the status bar to change to the Print Layout view, and then set the **Zoom slider** to **100**% if necessary.

　The software memo is open on your desktop.

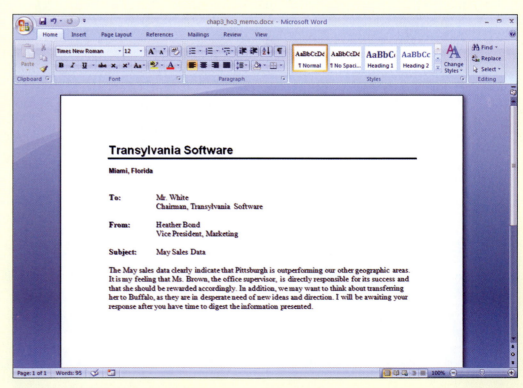

Figure 3.35 Memo in Word

Step 2
Copy the Worksheet

Refer to Figure 3.36 as you complete Step 2.

a. Open the *chap3_ho2_sales_solution* workbook from the previous exercise.

- If you did not close Microsoft Excel at the end of the previous exercise, you will see its button on the taskbar. Click the **Microsoft Excel button** to return to the *chap3_ho2_sales_solution* workbook.

- If you closed Microsoft Excel, start Excel again, and then open the *chap3_ho2_sales_solution* workbook.

b. Save the workbook as **chap3_ho3_sales_solution**.

The taskbar contains a button for both Microsoft Word and Microsoft Excel. You can click either button to move back and forth between the open applications. End by clicking the Microsoft Excel button to make it the active application.

c. Click the **Sales Data tab**. Click and drag to select **cells A1:F7** to select the entire worksheet, as shown in Figure 3.36.

d. Right-click the selected area and select **Copy** from the shortcut menu.

A moving border appears around the entire worksheet, indicating that it has been copied to the clipboard.

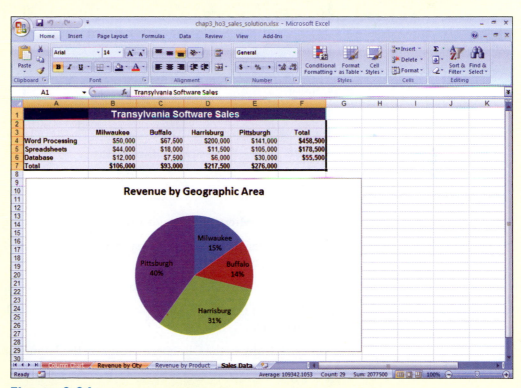

Figure 3.36 Worksheet Data to Copy

Step 3
Embed the Data

Refer to Figure 3.37 as you complete Step 3.

a. Click the **Microsoft Word button** on the taskbar to display the *chap3_ho3_memo_solution* document. Press **Ctrl+End** to move to the end of the memo and press **Enter** to insert a blank line, which is where you will insert the Excel worksheet.

Microsoft Word is the active window, and the insertion point is at the end of the Memo document.

b. Open the **Paste** list in the Clipboard group on the Home tab and select **Paste Special** to display the dialog box shown in Figure 3.37.

c. Click **Microsoft Office Excel Worksheet Object** in the As list. Click **Paste link**. Click **OK** to insert the worksheet into the document.

Using the Paste Special option gives you the opportunity to paste the object and establish the link for later data editing in Excel.

d. Right-click the worksheet, select **Format Object** on the shortcut menu to display the associated dialog box, and click the **Layout tab**.

TROUBLESHOOTING: If you paste the spreadsheet only, it becomes a table in Word, not an object. You cannot format it because it is not an object with a link to Excel. You must use the Paste Special option to make sure the worksheet link is created.

e. Choose **Square** in the *Wrapping Style* section and click **Center**. Click **OK** to accept the settings and close the dialog box. Click anywhere outside the table to deselect it. Save the *chap3_ho3_memo_solution* document.

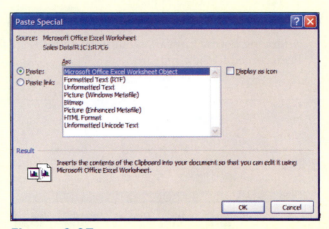

Figure 3.37 Paste Special Dialog Box

Step 4
Copy the Chart

a. Click the **Microsoft Excel button** on the taskbar to return to the worksheet.

b. Click outside the selected area to deselect the cells. Press **Esc** to remove the moving border.

c. Click the **Revenue by City tab** and click the chart area to select the chart.

The chart is selected when you see the sizing handles on the border of the chart area.

d. Click **Copy** in the Clipboard group on the Home tab.

Step 5
Embed the Chart

Refer to Figure 3.38 as you complete Step 5.

a. Switch to **Word** and click **Paste** in the Clipboard group on the Home tab.

b. Click the **Smart Tag** down arrow and verify that Chart (link to Excel data) is selected.

You pasted the chart object into your Memo. As an object, it will be updated when the spreadsheet data is updated. The object permits chart formatting within the Word document.

TROUBLESHOOTING: If the object moves to another page, use the resize handles to shrink the object until it fits on the previous page.

c. Click on the chart, and then click **Center** in the Paragraph group on the Home tab to center the chart.

d. Click the **Office Button**, select **Print**, and then select **Print Preview**.

Your document should be similar to Figure 3.38. You use Print Preview to view your document to verify that the elements fit on one page.

e. Close Print Preview. Save the document.

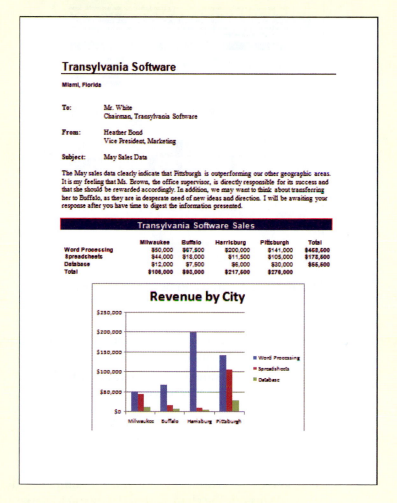

Figure 3.38 Chart Embedded in Memo

Step 6
Modify the Worksheet

Refer to Figure 3.39 as you complete Step 6.

a. Working in the Word document, click anywhere in the worksheet to select the worksheet and display the sizing handles.

The status bar indicates that you can double-click to edit the worksheet.

b. Double-click the worksheet to start Excel so you can change the data.

Excel starts and reopens the *chap3_ho3_sales_solution* workbook.

c. Click **Maximize** to maximize the Excel window, if needed.

d. Click the **Sales Data tab** within the workbook, if needed. Click in **cell B4**. Type **$150,000** and press **Enter**.

The wedge for Milwaukee shows the increase in the chart.

e. Click the **Revenue by City tab** to select the chart sheet. Save the workbook.

The chart reflects the increased sales for Milwaukee.

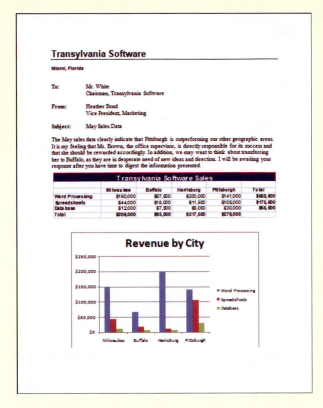

Figure 3.39 Modified Worksheet Changes Reflected in Word Document

---

a. Click the **Microsoft Word button** on the taskbar to display the *chap3_ho3_ solution* document.

The worksheet and chart update automatically to reflect $150,000 for word processing sales in Milwaukee.

> **TROUBLESHOOTING:** If the worksheet and chart do not automatically update, then point to the sheet object and click the right mouse button. Select Update Link from the shortcut menu.

b. Zoom to the **Whole Page** to view the completed document. Click and drag the worksheet or the chart within the memo to make any last-minute changes.

c. Save the memo again and close Word.

Refer to Figure 3.40 as you complete Step 8.

a. Click on the **Sales Data tab** to make the Sales Data sheet active. Click the chart area to select it. Click **Move Chart** on the Design tab to display the dialog box. Click **New Sheet** and click **OK** to close the dialog box.

The chart has been moved from below the spreadsheet to a new page and is displayed as full-screen view.

b. Click the **Office Button** and select **Print Preview** from the Print menu. Click **Show Margins** on the **Preview** group to toggle the display of the margins on and off. Click **Close Print Preview** to return to the chart.

You used Print Preview and the Show Margins option to verify that the chart displays properly before printing.

c. Click **Page Setup** dialog box launcher on the Page Layout tab. Click the **Page tab** in the Page Setup dialog box. Verify that **Landscape** is selected.

Changing the print option to Landscape enables you to see more of the chart.

d. Click the **Header/Footer tab** in the Page Setup dialog box, and then click **Custom Footer** to display the Footer dialog box.

e. Click the text box for the left section and enter your name. Click the text box for the center section and enter your instructor's name.

Headers and footers provide documentation on each page for any worksheet and chart.

f. Click the text box for the right section. Click the **Insert Date** button, press **Spacebar**, and then click the **Insert Time** button. Click **OK** to accept these settings and close the Footer dialog box. Click **OK** to close the Page Setup dialog box.

You used the Page Setup options to change to landscape mode and create a custom header and footer on the page with the chart.

g. Print the workbook. Close the workbook without saving.

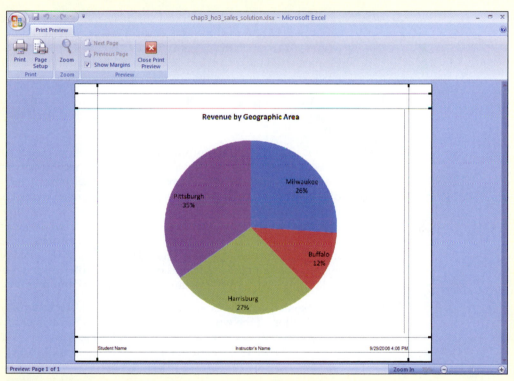

Figure 3.40 Print Preview of Chart with Custom Footers and Margin

---

Step 9
Save and View Chart as Web Page

a. Start Excel and open the *chap3_ho3_sales_solution* workbook.

b. Click on the **Revenue by Product tab** to make it the active sheet. Click the **Office Button** and select **Save As**.

c. Select **Web Page** from the *Save as type* list. Click **Selection: Chart**. Title the file appropriately and save it to the desired location.

d. You can preview the chart or workbook by opening your browser, navigating to the location of the Web page, and opening it.

Summary

1. **Choose a chart type.** A chart is a graphic representation of data in a worksheet. The type of chart chosen depends on the message to be conveyed. A pie chart is best for proportional relationships. A column or bar chart is used to show actual numbers rather than percentages. A line chart is preferable for time-related data. The choice between a clustered and a stacked column chart depends on the intended message. A clustered chart shows the contribution of each data point, but the total for each series is not as clear as with a stacked column chart. The stacked column chart, on the other hand, shows the totals clearly, but the contribution of the individual data points is obscured because the segments do not start at zero. It is important that charts are created accurately and that they do not mislead the reader. Stacked column charts should not add dissimilar quantities such as units and dollars.

2. **Create a chart.** Using the Insert tab is an effortless way to create charts. The title of a chart can help to convey the message. A neutral title such as "Revenue by City" leaves the reader to draw his or her own conclusion. Using a different title such as "Boston Leads All Cities" or "New York Is Trailing Badly" sends a very different message.

3. **Modify a chart.** Once created, a chart can be enhanced with arrows and text boxes. Multiple data series may be specified in either rows or columns. If the data are in rows, the first row is assumed to contain the category labels, and the first column is assumed to contain the legend. Conversely, if the data are in columns, the first column is assumed to contain the category labels, and the first row the legend.

4. **Enhance charts with graphic shapes.** These objects can be moved or sized and/or modified with respect to their color and other properties. The chart itself can also be modified using various tabs.

5. **Embed charts.** A chart may be embedded in a worksheet or created in a separate chart sheet. An embedded chart may be moved within a worksheet by selecting it and dragging it to its new location. An embedded chart may be sized by selecting it and dragging any of the sizing handles in the desired direction. Object embedding enables the creation of a compound document containing data from multiple applications. The essential difference between linking and embedding is whether the object is stored within the compound document (embedding) or in its own file (linking). An embedded object is stored in the compound document, which in turn becomes the only user (client) of that object. A linked object is stored in its own file, and the compound document is one of many potential users of that object. The same chart can be linked to a Word document and a PowerPoint presentation.

6. **Print charts.** Several options exist for printing charts. Users can print one chart, several charts, or a combination of the worksheet and the charts. Placing a chart on a separate sheet enables the user to print the chart in full-page format. Charts and worksheets can be saved as Web pages in HTML format and then be published to the World Wide Web (WWW).

Key Terms

Multiple Choice

1. Which type of chart is best to portray proportion or market share?

   (a) Pie chart

   (b) Line chart

   (c) Column chart

   (d) Combination chart

2. Which of the following chart types is *not* suitable to display multiple data series?

   (a) Pie chart

   (b) Horizontal bar chart

   (c) Column chart

   (d) All of the above are equally suitable.

3. Which of the following is best to display additive information from multiple data series?

   (a) A column chart with the data series stacked one on top of another

   (b) A column chart with the data series side by side

   (c) A scatter chart with two data series

   (d) A pie chart with five to ten wedges

4. A workbook can contain:

   (a) A separate chart sheet for every workbook

   (b) A separate workbook for every chart sheet

   (c) A sheet with both a workbook and chart

   (d) A separate chart sheet for every worksheet

5. Which of the following is true regarding an embedded chart?

   (a) It can be moved elsewhere within the worksheet.

   (b) It can be made larger or smaller.

   (c) Both (a) and (b).

   (d) Neither (a) nor (b).

6. Which of the following will produce a shortcut menu?

   (a) Pointing to a workbook tab and clicking the right mouse button

   (b) Pointing to an embedded chart and clicking the right mouse button

   (c) Pointing to a selected cell range and clicking the right mouse button

   (d) All of the above

7. Which of the following is done *prior* to beginning to create a chart?

   (a) The data series are selected.

   (b) The location of the embedded chart within the worksheet is specified.

   (c) The workbook is saved.

   (d) The worksheet is formatted.

8. Which of the following will display sizing handles when selected?

   (a) An embedded chart

   (b) The title of a chart

   (c) A text box or arrow

   (d) All of the above

9. How do you switch between open applications?

   (a) Click the appropriate button on the taskbar.

   (b) Click the Start button in the taskbar.

   (c) Use Shift+Tab to cycle through the applications.

   (d) Use Crtl+~ to cycle through the applications.

10. To represent multiple data series on the same chart:

    (a) The data series must be in rows, and the rows must be adjacent to one another on the worksheet.

    (b) The data series must be in columns, and the columns must be adjacent to one another on the worksheet.

    (c) The data series may be in rows or columns so long as they are adjacent to one another.

    (d) The data series may be in rows or columns with no requirement to be next to one another.

11. If multiple data series are selected and rows are specified:

    (a) The first row will be used for the category labels.

    (b) The first row will be used for the legend.

    (c) The first column will be used for the legend.

    (d) The first column will be used for the category labels.

...continued on Next Page

12. If multiple data series are selected and columns are specified:

    (a) The first column will be used for the category (X axis) labels.

    (b) The first row will be used for the legend.

    (c) Both (a) and (b).

    (d) Neither (a) nor (b).

13. Which of the following is true about the scale on the Y axis in a column chart that plots multiple data series clustered versus one that stacks the values one on top of another?

    (a) The scale for the stacked columns chart contains larger values than the clustered chart.

    (b) The scale for the clustered columns contains larger values than the stacked columns.

    (c) The values on the scale will be the same for both charts.

    (d) The values will be different, but it is not possible to tell which chart has higher values.

14. A workbook includes a revenue worksheet with two embedded charts. The workbook also includes one chart in its own worksheet. How many files does it take to store this workbook?

    (a) 1

    (b) 2

    (c) 3

    (d) 4

15. You have created a Word document and embedded an Excel worksheet in that document. You make a change to the worksheet. What happens to the worksheet in the Word document?

    (a) It will be updated when you select the Refresh Data command.

    (b) It is unchanged.

    (c) It is automatically updated to reflect the changes.

    (d) You cannot change the worksheet because you have embedded it in a Word document.

16. You have selected cells B5:B10 as the data series for a chart and specified the data series are in columns. Which of the following is the legend text?

    (a) Cells B5 through F5

    (b) Cells C6 through F10

    (c) Cells B5 through B10

    (d) It is impossible to determine from the information given.

17. The same data range is used as the basis for an embedded pie chart, as well as a column chart in a chart sheet. Which chart(s) will change if you change the values in the data range?

    (a) The column chart

    (b) The pie chart

    (c) Both the pie chart and the column chart

    (d) Neither the pie chart nor the column chart

Your summer job is with the professional organization representing theme parks across the country. You have gathered data on theme park admissions in four areas of the country. In this exercise, you will finish the worksheet and create charts. The completed version of the worksheet is shown in Figure 3.41.

a. Open the *chap3_pe1_vacation* workbook and save it as **chap3_pe1_vacation_solution**.

b. Select **cells B8:E8**. Click **AutoSum** in the Editing group on the Home tab to compute the total for each quarter. Select **cells F4:F8**, and then click **AutoSum**.

c. Select **cells B4:F8** and format these cells as **Number with Commas** and no decimals. Bold the row and column headings and the totals. Center the entries in **cells B3:F3**. Select **cells A1:F1**, then click **Merge & Center** in the Alignment group on the Home tab to center the title. With the same cells selected, choose the **Blue, Accent 1** theme color from the **Fill Color** list. Increase the title font size to **14 points** and change the Font color to **White, Background 1**. Select **cells B3:F3** and change the fill and font color to the same as used in row 1. Similarly, change **cell A8**. Save the workbook.

d. Complete the substeps to create a column chart that shows the number of admissions for each region and for each quarter within each region and insert the graphic, as shown in Figure 3.41:

- Select **cells A3:E7**. Click the **Insert tab** and click **Column** in the Chart group. When the Column chart type and Clustered Column subtype are selected, the chart appears on Admissions Data worksheet.

- Click the outline of the chart to select it. Using the four-headed arrow, drag the chart into position under the worksheet.

- Right-click the legend and select **Bold** and **Italic** to format the legend.

- Click the **Insert tab** and click the Left Arrow in the Shapes group. Click and drag to create a thick arrow that points to the **1st Quarter South** column. Release the mouse. The arrow is selected, and you are viewing the Format tab.

- Click **Text Box** in the Insert Shapes group on the Format tab to insert a text box. Click and drag a text box on top of the thick arrow. Release the mouse. Enter text by typing **South First-Quarter Admissions High**. Select the text you just typed and use the Mini toolbar to change the font to **9-point** bold white.

e. Complete the substeps to create a pie chart, in its own sheet, that shows the percentage of the total number of admissions in each region:

- Select **cells A4:A7**, then press and hold **Ctrl** while selecting **cells F4:F7**.

- Click the **Insert tab** to make it active. Click **Pie** in the Charts group and the pie chart appears on the Admissions Data sheet. Click **Move Chart** on the Design tab, click the **New Sheet** option, and click **OK**. Right-click the **Chart 1 tab** just created and select **Rename** from the shortcut menu. Type **Pie Chart** and press **Enter**.

- Right-click any pie wedge and select **Add Data Labels** to add data labels to the chart area. Right-click any pie wedge and select **Format Data Labels** to display the Format Data Labels dialog box. Click **Label Options**, and then click the **Category Name** and **Percentage check boxes** to format the data labels. Remove the check from the **Value** check box.

- Change the values in the data labels to percentages by clicking **Number** in Label options, click **Percentage** in **Category** options and click **Close** to accept the settings and close the dialog box. Right-click any data label and increase the font size to **14-point** italic.

...continued on Next Page

- Click **Legend** in the Labels group on the Layout tab and select **None** to delete the legend.

- Click **Chart Title** in the Labels group on the Layout tab and select **Centered Overlay Title**. Type **Vacation Park Admissions by Region**.

f. Complete the substeps to create a stacked column chart, in its own sheet, showing the number of admissions for each quarter and for each region within each quarter:

- Select **cells A3:E7**. Click the **Insert tab** and click **Column** in the Charts group. When the Column chart type and Stacked Column in 3-D subtype are selected, the chart appears on Sheet1.

- Click **Move Chart** on the Design tab, click the **New sheet** option, and click **OK**. Right-click the **Chart 2 tab** just created and select **Rename**. Type **Stacked Column** and press **Enter**.

- Click in the outline of the chart to select the entire chart. Click the **Data Labels** list in the Labels group on the Layout tab and select **Show**. Click **Chart Title** in the **Labels** group on the **Layout** tab and select **Centered Overlay Title**. Type **Admissions by Quarter and Region Within Quarter**. Change the color of each worksheet tab to **Blue, Accent 1**.

g. Click the **Stacked Column tab** to make it the active sheet. Click the **Office Button** and select **Save As**. Select **Web Page** from the *Save as type* list. Click **Selection: Chart**. Click **Change Title** and type **Vacation Web Page**, then click **OK** and save it. You can preview the chart by opening your Internet browser, navigating to the location of the Web page, and opening it.

h. Create a custom header for the worksheet that includes your name, your course, and your instructor's name. Create a custom footer for the worksheet that includes the name of the worksheet. Print the entire workbook, consisting of the worksheet in Figure 3.41, plus the additional sheets you created. Use portrait orientation for the **Admissions Data** worksheet and landscape orientation for the other worksheets. Save and close the workbook.

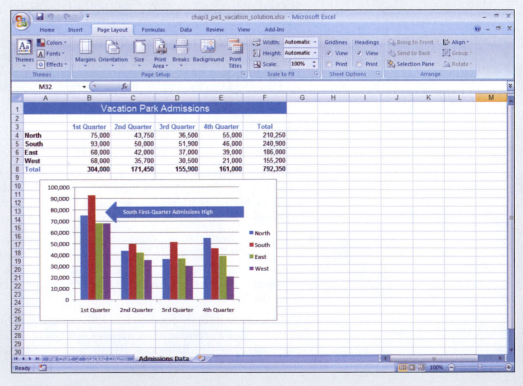

Figure 3.41 Vacation Park Charts

...continued on Next Page

The worksheet shown in Figure 3.42 shows third-quarter revenues for each salesperson at AnytimeTalk, Inc., the cellular company where you will do your internship this summer. One of your assigned duties is to complete the Fourth-Quarter Revenue worksheet and create a column chart showing a comparison of each salesperson's total sales for the fourth quarter. The chart is to be formatted for a professional presentation.

a. Open the *chap3_pe2_talk* workbook and save it as **chap3_pe2_talk_solution**.

b. Click and drag to select **cells E3:E7**. Click **AutoSum** in the Editing group on the Home tab to compute the total for each salesperson. Click and drag to select **cells B8:E8**, and then click **AutoSum** to compute the totals for each month and the total for the quarter.

c. Click and drag to select **cells B3:E8** and format these cells as **Currency with no decimals**. Bold the row and column headings and the totals. Center the entries in **cells B2:E2**.

d. Select **cells A1:E1**, then click **Merge & Center** in the Alignment group on the Home tab to center the title. With the same cells selected, choose **Orange, Accent 6** from the theme colors in the **Fill Color** list. Increase the title font size to **18 points** and change the Font color to **Orange, Accent 6, Darker 50%**.

e. Increase the height of row 1 as necessary to display the title. Select **cells A2:E2** and change the Font color to the same theme color used in row 1.

f. Select **cells A4:E4** and use Fill Color in the Font group on the Home tab to highlight the cells with a theme shade. Similarly, change **cell A8**. Save the workbook.

g. Select **cells A3:A7**, and while holding **Ctrl**, select **cells E3:E7**. Click the **Insert tab** and click **Column** in the Chart group. When the Column chart type and Clustered Cylinder column subtype are selected, the chart appears on the Sales Data sheet.

h. Click the white background of the chart to select it and using the four-headed arrow, drag the chart into position below the worksheet data. Right-click the legend and select **Delete** to delete the legend.

i. Right-click any cylinder and select **Add Data Labels** to add data labels to the chart area. Right-click any cylinder and select **Format Data Labels** to display the Format Data Labels dialog box.

j. Triple-click the second column to select just this column. Right-click the selected column, select **Format Data Point**, click the **Fill** option in the associated dialog box, click **Gradient Fill**, and then change the color of this column to the coordinating theme shade. Select **Close** to close the dialog box.

k. Click in **cell A4** and enter your name. The value on the X axis changes automatically to reflect the entry in cell A4. Open the **Chart Title** menu in the Labels group on the Layout tab. Click **Above Chart** and type **Fourth-Quarter Revenues** as the title of the chart.

l. Click the **Insert tab**. Click **Line Callout 1** in the Shapes group. Click and drag to create a callout that points to your cylinder. Release the mouse. The callout is selected, and you are viewing the Format tab. Change the Shape Fill color and the Shape Outline color by selecting appropriate theme colors from the **Shape Fill** list and the **Shape Outline** list in the Shape Styles group on the Format tab.

m. Click **Text Box** in the Insert group on the Layout tab to insert a text box. Click and drag a text box on top of the callout. Release the mouse. Type the words **This Cylinder Represents My Data**. Select the text you just typed, right-click the selected text, and change the font to **10 point** from the Mini toolbar.

n. Right-click the border of the chart, select **Format Chart Area**, then change the border to include rounded corners with a shadow effect. Use the Border Styles and Shadow options to make the changes to match Figure 3.42.

o. Save the workbook and print the completed worksheet. Close the workbook.

...continued on Next Page

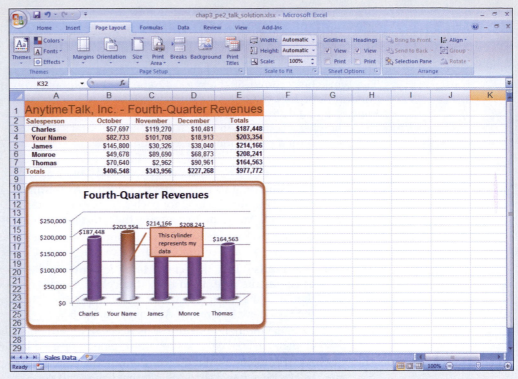

Figure 3.42 AnytimeTalk, Inc.

3 Printing Charts

Your sister asked you to chart weekly sales from her chain of mystery bookstores. As shown in Figure 3.43, stores are in four cities, and you must plot four product lines. You will create the charts as embedded objects on the worksheet. Do not be concerned about the placement of each chart until you have completed all four charts. The first chart is a clustered column and emphasizes the sales in each city (the data are in rows). The second chart is a stacked column version of the first chart. The third chart (that begins in column H of the worksheet) is a clustered column chart that emphasizes the sales in each product line (the data are in columns). The fourth chart is a stacked column version of the third chart. Figure 3.43 shows a reduced screen view of the four charts.

a. Open the *chap3_pe3_print* workbook and save it as **chap3_pe3_print_solution**.

b. Select **cells A2:E6** and click the **2-D Column** area of **Column** in the Charts group on the Insert tab to embed a clustered column chart. With the chart selected, click **Style 16** in the Chart Styles group on the Design tab. To add a chart title, click **Layout 1** in the Chart Layouts group on the Design tab. To change the default title, select the words *Chart Title* and type **Weekly Sales by Location and Product Line**. Select the title, right-click and change the font size to 14 points. Drag the chart into position below the workbook. Save the workbook.

c. Select the chart, click the **Home tab**, click **Copy** in the Clipboard group to copy the chart, click in **cell A27**, and click **Paste** in the Clipboard group on the Home tab. With the chart selected, click the **Design tab** and click **Change Chart Type** in the Type group. Click **Stacked Column** in the Column area of the Change Chart Type dialog box and click **OK**. Save the workbook.

d. Select the **first** chart, click the **Home tab**, click in **cell H2**, and click **Paste**. With the chart selected, click the **Design tab** and click **Switch Row/Column** in the Data group. Save the workbook.

e. Select the chart, click the **Home tab**, click **Copy** to copy the chart, click in **cell H19**, and click **Paste** on the Home tab. With the chart selected, click the **Design tab** and click **Change Chart Type** in the Type group. Click the **Stacked Column** in the Column area of the Change Chart Type dialog box and click **OK**. Save the workbook.

...continued on Next Page

f. Click **Page Break Preview** in the Workbook Views group on the View tab. Your screen should be similar to Figure 3.43. You will see one or more dotted lines that show where the page breaks will occur. You will also see a message indicating that you can change the location of the page breaks. Click **OK** after you have read the message.

g. Remove any existing page breaks by clicking and dragging the solid blue line that indicates the break. (You can insert horizontal or vertical page breaks by clicking the appropriate cell, clicking **Breaks** in the Page Setup group on the Page Layout **tab**, and selecting **Page Break**.) To return to Normal view, click **Normal** in the Workbook Views group on the View tab.

h. Print the worksheet and four embedded charts on one page. Change to landscape orientation for a more attractive layout. Open the **Orientation** list in the Page Setup group on the Page Layout tab and select **Landscape**. Click the **Page Layout tab** and use the Page Setup dialog box to create a custom header with your name, your course, and your instructor's name. Create a custom footer that contains today's date, the name of the workbook, and the current time. Click **OK** to close the dialog box. Print the worksheet. Save and close the workbook.

i. Write a short note to your instructor that describes the differences between the charts. Suggest a different title for one or more charts that helps to convey a specific message.

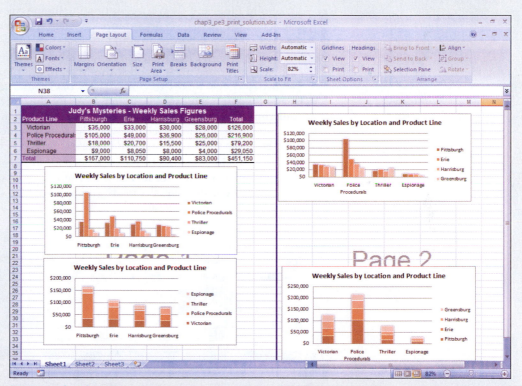

Figure 3.43 Printing Charts

4 Stock Price Comparisons

Figure 3.44 contains a combination chart to display different kinds of information on different scales for multiple data series. You start by creating a clustered column chart for the revenue and profits, and then you create a second data series to chart the stock prices as a line. Two different scales are necessary because the magnitudes of the numbers differ significantly. Your investment club asked you to make a recommendation about the purchase of the stock based on your analysis.

a. Open the *chap3_pe4_stock* workbook and save it as **chap3_pe4_stock_solution**.

b. Select **cells A1:F4**. Click the **Insert tab** and click **Column** in the Charts group. Then select **Clustered Column** from the 2-D Column row. Select **Style 7** from the Design tab.

...continued on Next Page

c. Click chart outline to select the chart and using the four-headed arrow, drag the chart into position under the worksheet. Right-click the legend and select **Format Legend**. In the *Legend Options* section, click **Bottom** as the legend position and click **Close**.

You are now going to add a secondary vertical axis to display Stock Price because the size of the numbers differs significantly from Revenue and Profit.

d. Click the chart to make it active. Click the **Format tab**. Click the **Chart Elements down arrow** in the Current Selection group and select **Series "Stock Price"** as the data series to plot on the secondary axis.

e. Click **Format Selection** in the Current Selection group and click **Secondary Axis** in *Series Options* in the Format Data Series dialog box. Click **Close** to close the dialog box. Click the **Layout tab**, click **Axes** in the Axes group, select **Secondary Vertical Axis**, and select **Show Default Axis**.

f. Change the data series to a line chart to distinguish the secondary axis. Click the **Format tab**, click the **Chart Elements down arrow** in the Current Selection group, and select **Series "Stock Price."** Click the **Design tab**, click **Change Chart Type** in the Type group, select **Line** as the chart type, and then click the first example of a line chart. Click **OK** to view the combination chart.

g. Right-click on the chart but above the plot area, select **Format Chart Area**, click **Border Styles**, check **Rounded Corners** and increase the width to 1.5 pts, click **Border Color**, click **Solid Line**, and choose a coordinating theme color from the color selection menu. Click **Shadow** and select an appropriate shadow from the **Presets** list. Click **Close** to see the customized border around the chart.

h. Deselect the chart. Click the **Page Layout tab** and open the *Page Setup* dialog box. Click **Landscape** for orientation, click the **Margins tab**, and click the **Horizontally** and **Vertically check boxes** to center the worksheet and chart on the page. Click the **Header/Footer tab** create a custom header for the worksheet that includes **your name**, **your course name**, and **your instructor's name**. Create a custom footer that contains the name of the **file** in which the worksheet is contained, **today's date**, and the **current time**. Save the workbook and print your worksheet. Close the workbook.

i. What do you think should be the more important factor influencing a company's stock price, its revenue (sales) or its profit (net income)? Could the situation depicted in the worksheet occur in the real world? Summarize your thoughts in a brief note to your instructor. Print the document.

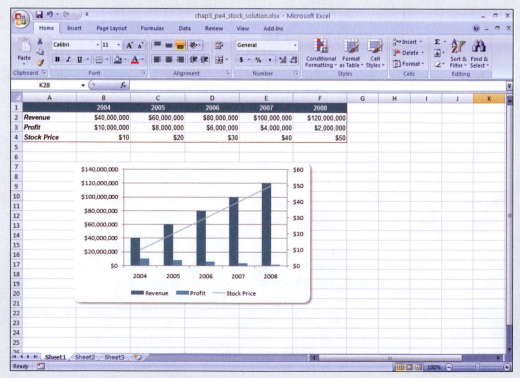

Figure 3.44 Stock Price Comparison

The Word document in Figure 3.45 displays descriptive information about a car you are interested in purchasing, a picture of the car, and a hyperlink to the Web site where the information was obtained. In addition, the document is linked to an Excel workbook that computes the car payment for you, based on the loan parameters that you provide. Your assignment is to create a similar document based on any car you choose.

a. Open the *chap3_mid1_auto* document and save it as **chap3_mid1_auto_solution**.

b. Locate a Web site that contains information about the car you are interested in. You can go to the Web site of the manufacturer, or you can go to a general site such as carpoint.msn.com, which contains information about all makes and models. Select the car you want and obtain the retail price of the car.

c. Enter the price of the car, a hypothetical down payment, the interest rate of the car loan, and the term of the loan in the indicated cells. The monthly payment will be determined automatically by the PMT function that is stored in the workbook. Use Help if needed to review the PMT function. Save the workbook.

d. Select **cells A3:B9** (the cells that contain the information you want to insert into the Word document) and copy the selected range to the Clipboard.

e. Open the partially completed *chap3_mid1_auto* Word document. Use the Paste Special option to paste the worksheet data. Press **Ctrl+End** to position the insertion point at the end of the document. Save the Word document as **chap3_mid1_auto solution**.

f. Use the taskbar to return to the Excel workbook. Change the amount of the down payment to **$6,500** and the interest rate for your loan to **4%**. Save the workbook. Close Excel. Return to the Word document, which should reflect the updated loan information.

g. Return to the Web page that contains the information about your car. Right-click the picture of the car that appears within the Web page and select **Save As** to save the picture of the car to your computer. Use the **Insert** command to insert the picture that you just obtained.

h. Complete the Word document by inserting some descriptive information about your car. Print the completed document. Save and close the document.

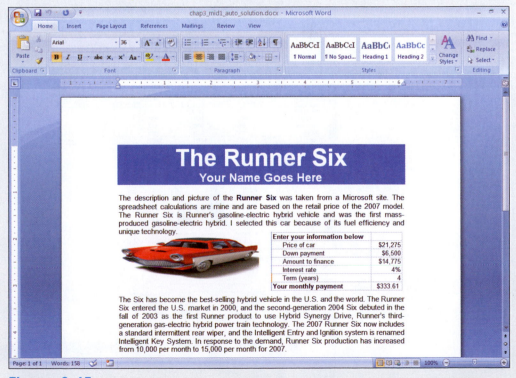

Figure 3.45 The Next Car You Purchase

...continued on Next Page

2 Comparison of Rows and Columns

Figure 3.46 displays a worksheet with two similar charts detailing annual visits to different exhibits at the local Petting Zoo, one that plots data by rows and the other by columns. The distinction depends on the message you want to deliver. Both charts are correct. You collected the data at your summer job at the Petting Zoo and must now plot it for your intern supervisor as part of the analysis of the most popular animals at the zoo. You will create both charts shown and for comparison purposes create two more charts on a new sheet to determine the best presentation of data.

a. Open the *chap3_mid2_zoo* workbook and save it as **chap3_mid2_zoo_solution**.

b. Use **AutoSum** to compute the total number of visits for each animal category and each quarter. Rename the Sheet1 tab as **Side by Side Columns**. Format the worksheet in an attractive manner by matching the formatting shown in Figure 3.46.

c. Create each of the charts as embedded charts on the current worksheet. The first chart specifies that the data series are in columns. The second chart specifies the data series are in rows.

d. Change to landscape orientation when the chart is printed. Create a custom header that includes your name, your course, and your instructor's name. Create a custom footer with the name of the worksheet, today's date, and the current time. Specify that the worksheet will be printed at 110% to create a more attractive printed page. Be sure, however, that the worksheet and associated charts fit on a single page.

e. Copy the worksheet and name the duplicate worksheet as **Stacked Columns**.

f. Select the first chart in the newly created Stacked Columns worksheet. Change the chart type to Stacked Columns. Change the chart type of the second chart to Stacked Columns as well. Repeat step d for the Stacked Columns worksheet.

g. Print the completed workbook (both worksheets). Add a short note that summarizes the difference between plotting data in rows versus columns and between clustered column charts and stacked column charts. Save and close the workbook.

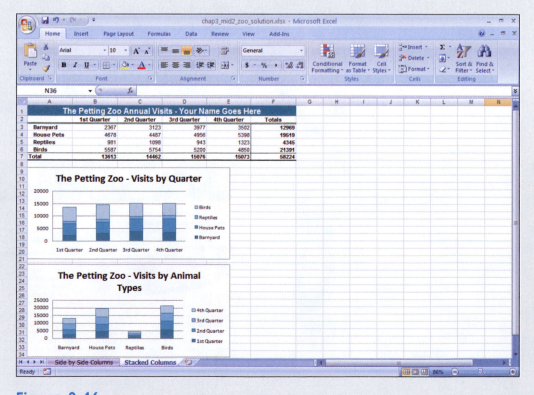

Figure 3.46 Comparison of Rows and Columns

...continued on Next Page

Your first job is as a management trainee at the Needlework Nook, a store specializing in home arts. The store manager has asked you to examine sales for the four quarters of the current year in five categories. She also has asked you to chart the sales figures. Complete the partially completed version of the spreadsheet in Figure 3.47 and create a chart that highlights quarterly product sales for the current year.

a. Open the *chap3_mid3_homearts* workbook and save it as **chap3_mid3_homearts_solution**.

b. Use the **AutoSum** command to compute the totals for the quarters and categories of products. Format the completed worksheet in an attractive manner duplicating the formatting exactly as shown. Rename sheet 1 as **Current Year**.

c. Create a stacked column chart based on the data in **cells A2:E7**. Specify that the data series are in rows so that each column represents total sales for each quarter. Display the legend on the right side of the chart. Save the chart in its own sheet called **Graphical Analysis**.

d. Experiment with variations of the chart created. Change the chart type from a stacked column to a clustered column and change the orientation of the data series from rows to columns. Choose the chart most appropriate to show the sales by quarter and category. Also experiment with the placement of the legend by moving to the bottom and the top. After experimenting with the placement of the legend, place it to the right of the chart.

e. Add data labels to the stacks on the Graphical Analysis sheet. Change the color of the worksheet tabs to **Aqua Accent 5** for the Current Year tab and **Aqua, Accent 5, Darker 50%** for the Graphical Analysis tab.

f. Use the Page Setup dialog box to display gridlines and row and column headings. Create a custom header that includes your name, your course, and your instructor's name. Create a custom footer with the name of the worksheet, today's date, and the current time.

g. Print the completed workbook consisting of two worksheets. Save and close the workbook.

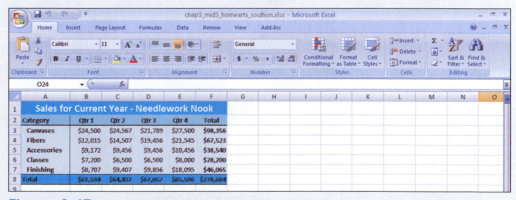

Figure 3.47 Home Arts

Your sociology professor wants to know the correlation between time spent studying for quizzes and quiz scores, if any. You recorded the time spent studying for 10 quizzes and asked two friends to do the same thing. Now you must plot the data in a scatter chart and complete the analysis. Use the worksheet shown in Figure 3.48 and chart your data.

a. Open the *chap3_mid4_scatter* workbook and save it as **chap3_mid4_scatter_solution**.

b. Insert a row above the worksheet and type the title **Test Analysis**. Center the title above the worksheet. Format the completed worksheet in an attractive manner. You do not have to duplicate our formatting exactly.

c. Create a scatter chart based on the data in **cells A2:E12**. Display the legend to the right of the chart.

d. Insert a chart title **Study Time and Quiz Scores.** Add an X-axis title **Time in Hours** and a Y-axis title **Test Score**.

e. Change the chart type to **Scatter with Smooth Lines and Markers**. Change the chart style so the colors are more vibrant.

f. Remember to add your analysis of the correlation between study time and quiz scores below the chart.

g. Delete the Sheet2 and Sheet3 tabs and rename Sheet1 as **Test Scores**. Add a tab color, Red, to the Test Scores tab.

h. Use the Page Setup dialog box to display gridlines and row and column headings. Create a custom header that includes your name, your course, and your instructor's name. Create a custom footer with the name of the worksheet, today's date, and the current time.

i. Print the completed workbook making sure the worksheet, chart, and analysis fit on one page. Save and close the workbook.

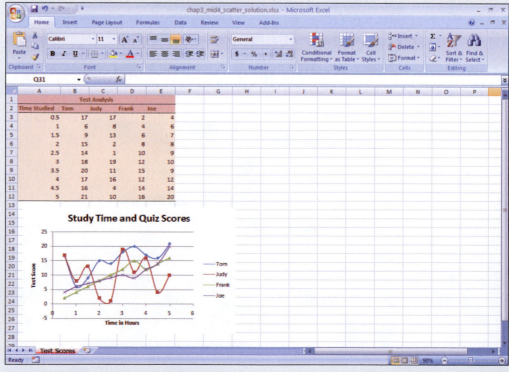

Figure 3.48 Study Analysis

Your computer professor has asked you to provide a comparison of computer sales across the country. Complete the worksheet as shown in Figure 3.49 but include three charts to show the sales in a variety of ways. Include a summary indicating the most effective chart and why you consider it the most effective for comparing sales data.

a. Open the *chap3_mid5_computer* workbook and save it as **chap3_mid5_computer_solution**.

b. Use **AutoSum** to compute the totals for the corporation in column F and row 6.

c. Format **cells B3:F6** as currency, zero decimal. Center the title above the worksheet. Format the completed worksheet in an attractive manner. You do not have to duplicate our formatting exactly.

d. Use the completed worksheet as the basis for a stacked column chart with the data plotted in rows.

e. Create a pie chart showing total sales by city, placing it on a separate sheet. Rename the sheet as **Sales by City**.

f. Make a cluster column chart, placing it on a separate sheet and renaming the sheet **Sales by Product**. Include a legend below the chart, a chart title, axes titles, and a shape to draw attention to the city with the highest notebook sales. Include an appropriate text message on the shape.

g. Use the Page Setup dialog box to display gridlines and row and column headings. Create a custom footer that contains your name, the name of the worksheet, and today's date. Print the entire workbook. Save and close the workbook.

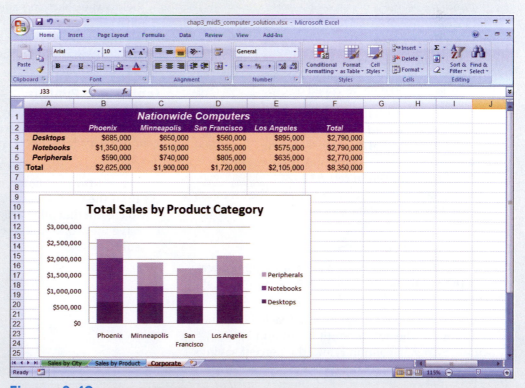

Figure 3.49 Computer Sales Analysis

Capstone Exercise

What if people split a dinner check using the principles of the progressive income tax that is central to our tax code? Five lifelong friends of various means meet once a week for dinner and split the $100 check according to their ability to pay. Tom, Dick, and Harry are of relatively modest means and pay $1, $4, and $9, respectively. Ben and Ken are far more prosperous and pay $18 and $68, respectively.

The friends were quite satisfied with the arrangement until the owner offered a rebate. "You are excellent customers, and I will reduce the cost of your meal by $15." The question became how to divide the $15 windfall to give everyone his fair share? The proprietor suggested that they allocate the savings according to the amount each contributed to the original check. He made a quick calculation, and then rounded each person's share to an integer, using the Integer function. For example, Tom's new bill should have been 85 cents, but it was decided he would eat for free. In similar fashion, Dick now owes $3, Harry $7, Ben $15, and Ken $60. (Ken, the most prosperous individual, made up the difference with respect to the cents that were dropped.) The new total is $85, and everyone saves money.

Once outside the restaurant, the friends began to compare their savings. Tom and Dick each complained that they saved only $1. Harry grumbled that he saved only $2. Ben thought it unfair that Ken saved more than the other four friends combined. Everyone continued to pick on Ken. The next week, Ken felt so uncomfortable that he did not show up, so his former friends ate without him. But when the bill came, they were $60 short.

Create the Worksheet

You will create the worksheet that is the basis for the charts. The first sheet, which you will name Numerical Analysis, contains the labels and data described below.

a. Enter a title in row 1. In row 3, enter the following labels: **Person**, **% Paid**, **Amount**, **Projected Saving**, **New Amount**, **Actual Saving**, **% Saving**. Type **Total** in **cell A9** and type **The Original Total** in **cell A11** and **Reduction in Bill** in **cell A12**.

b. Type the names, the percent paid, and the amounts in **cells A4:C8**. This data is in the description of the problem.

Calculations and Formatting

The analysis includes calculations and formatting necessary for presentation. You will create the formulas and select appropriate formatting options.

a. Calculate the projected savings for each individual in column D, the new amount in column E, the actual savings in column F, and the percent savings in column G.

b. Calculate appropriate totals in **cells B9:G9**.

c. Calculate the original total in **cell C11** and the reduction in bill in **cell C12**.

d. Format columns B through G as appropriate for the values displayed.

e. Format the remainder of the worksheet with appropriate colors, borders, fonts, and font size.

Create the Charts

You will create the charts based on the worksheet values. The charts provide information visually and help you to analyze that information. You will create three charts: a pie chart, a clustered column chart, and a combination chart.

a. Create a pie chart on a separate sheet that shows the percentage of the bill each individual pays before the refund. Include descriptive titles and labels.

b. Create a column chart on a separate sheet showing the amount each individual saves. Include data labels below the chart and an overlay showing the percentage of savings.

c. Add a shape with text box describing the results depicted on the chart. Include descriptive titles.

d. Create a clustered column chart on a separate sheet showing the new amount of the bill and the actual savings for each individual. Include data labels below the chart and a legend to the right of the chart.

e. Include a shape with a text box describing the data depicted in the chart. Include descriptive titles and labels.

Footers and Printing

Your instructor requires documentation for assignments. You will print the data sheet and the three chart sheets with your name, page numbers, and your instructor's name.

a. Create a custom footer that includes the page number, instructor's name, and your name.

b. Print the worksheet and charts in landscape format to ensure that all charts print on separate pages.

c. Save the workbook as **chap3_cap_dinner_solution**.

Mini Cases

Use the rubric following the case as a guide to evaluate your work, but keep in mind that your instructor may impose additional grading criteria or use a different standard to judge your work.

Designer Clothing

GENERAL CASE

This assignment asks you to complete a worksheet and create an associated chart for a designer clothing boutique, and then link these Excel objects to an appropriate memo. Open the partially completed *chap3_mc1_design* workbook; compute the sales totals for each individual salesperson as well as the totals for each quarter, then format the resulting worksheet in an attractive fashion. Include your name in the title of the worksheet (cell A1). We have started the memo for you and have saved the text in the *chap3_mc1_design* Word document. Open the Word document, and then link the Excel worksheet to the Word document. Repeat the process to link the Excel chart to the Word document. Print the completed document for your instructor. Save as **chap3_mc1_design_solution.**

Performance Elements	Exceeds Expectations	Meets Expectations	Below Expectations
Compute totals	Totals all correct.	Inconsistent use of SUM function.	Typed in the number.
Attractive, appropriate format	Very attractive.	Adequate.	Ugly.
Embed sheet	Sheet embedded correctly.	Sheet embedded but not in correct location.	No embedded sheet.
Embed chart	Chart embedded correctly.	Sheet embedded but not in correct location.	No embedded sheet.

The Convention Planner

RESEARCH CASE

Your first task as a convention planner is to evaluate the hotel capacity for the host city in order to make recommendations as to which hotels should host the convention. The data form can be found in the *chap3_mc2_convention* workbook, which contains a single worksheet. You are to select a city for the convention and research six different hotels in that city. For each hotel, determine the number of standard and deluxe rooms and the rate for each. Insert this information into the worksheet. Complete the worksheet by computing the total number of rooms in each category. Format the worksheet in an attractive way. Create a stacked column chart that shows the total capacity for each hotel. Create a second chart that shows the percentage of total capacity for each hotel. Store each chart in its own worksheet, and then print the entire workbook for your instructor. Save the workbook as **chap3_mc2_convention_solution.**

Performance Elements	Exceeds Expectations	Meets Expectations	Below Expectations
Research hotel information	Found six hotels and data.	Found six hotels but incomplete data.	Found fewer than six hotels with incomplete data.
Create totals	Totals all correct.	Inconsistent use of SUM function.	Typed in the number.
Format attractive	Very attractive.	Adequate.	Ugly.
Create stacked column chart	Chart created correctly.	Incorrect data used for chart.	No chart.
Create second chart	Chart created correctly.	Incorrect data used for chart.	No chart.
Charts on separate sheets	Both charts on separate sheets.	One chart on separate sheet.	No chart.
Printing	Three printed sheets.	Two printed sheets.	No printed output.

Peer Tutoring

DISASTER RECOVERY

As part of your service learning project you volunteer tutoring students in Excel, you will identify and correct six separate errors in the chart. Your biggest task will be selecting the correct type of chart to show the data most clearly. Open the spreadsheet *chap3_mc3_peer* and find six errors. Correct the errors and explain how the errors might have occurred and how they can be prevented. Include your explanation in the cells below the embedded chart. Save as **chap3_mc3_peer_solution**.

Performance Elements	Exceeds Expectations	Meets Expectations	Below Expectations
Identify six errors	Finds all six errors.	Finds four errors.	Finds three or fewer errors.
Explain the error	Complete and correct explanation of each error.	Explanation is too brief to fully explain error.	No explanations.
Prevention description	Prevention description correct and practical.	Prevention description but obtuse.	No prevention description.

Working with Large Worksheets and Tables

Manipulating Worksheets and Table Management

 **bjectives**

After you read this chapter, you will be able to:

1. Freeze rows and columns **(page 246)**.

2. Hide and unhide rows, columns, and worksheets **(page 247)**.

3. Protect a cell, a worksheet, and a workbook **(page 248)**.

4. Control calculation **(page 251)**.

5. Print large worksheets **(page 251)**.

6. Explore basic table management **(page 263)**.

7. Sort data **(page 268)**.

8. Filter and total data **(page 272)**.

Hands-On Exercises

Exercises	Skills Covered
1. **MARCHING BAND ROSTER (page 255)** **Open:** chap4_ho1_band.xlsx **Save as:** chap4_ho1_band_solution.xlsx	• Freeze and Unfreeze Rows and Columns • Hide and Unhide Rows, Columns, and Worksheets • Protect a Worksheet and a Workbook and Control Calculations • Print a Large Worksheet
2. **MARCHING BAND ROSTER REVISITED (page 277)** **Open:** chap4_ho1_band_solution.xlsx (from Exercise 1) **Save as:** chap4_ho2_band_solution.xlsx (additional modifications)	• Create a Table • Add, Edit, or Delete Records, and Use Find and Replace • Format a Table • Sort a Table • Filter a Table • Create Column Totals and a Summary Report • Print the Completed Worksheet

CASE STUDY

The Spa Experts

You and Tim like to relax and went into business shortly after graduation selling spas and hot tubs. Business has been good, and your expansive showroom and wide selection appeal to a variety of customers. You and your business partner maintain a large inventory to attract the impulse buyer and currently have agreements with three manufacturers: Serenity Spas, The Original Hot Tub, and Port-a-Spa. Each manufacturer offers spas and hot tubs that appeal to different segments of the market with prices ranging from affordable to exorbitant.

The business has grown rapidly, and you need to analyze the sales data in order to increase future profits—for example, which vendor generates the most sales? Who is the leading salesperson? Do most customers purchase their spa or finance it? Are sales promotions necessary to promote business, or will customers pay the full price? You have created a simple worksheet that has sales data for the current month. Each transaction appears on a separate row and contains the name of the salesperson, the manufacturer, and the amount of the sale. You will see an indication of whether the spa was purchased or financed, and whether a promotion was in effect. You are preparing a worksheet for Tim to keep him updated on sales for the current month.

Case Study

Your Assignment

- Read the chapter carefully and pay close attention to sections that demonstrate working with data tables, sorting information, filtering data, preparing summary reports, charting summary data, and printing large worksheets.

- Open the *chap4_case_spa* workbook, which contains the partially completed financial worksheet, and save it as **chap4_case_spa_solution**.

- Study the structure of the worksheet to determine what sorts will be required, perform the appropriate sort, and create a summary report showing total sales by salesperson.

- Identify how you would prepare a summary report and how you would then chart the data. Determine how you can format the worksheet to best print it and the chart. Convert the range to a data table and prepare a chart illustrating total sales by salesperson. Substitute your name for Jessica Benjamin throughout the worksheet.

- Create a custom footer, include gridlines and row and column headings, landscape the worksheet, and center it horizontally and vertically on the page. Repeat the first three rows on each sheet when printing. Print the worksheet and the chart. Adjust the page break so all sales for a salesperson appear on the same page.

- Filter the data table so you only see the spas that are financed. Change the page print area by adjusting the margins to print just the financed spas, not the totals. Print the filtered report.

Large Worksheet Preparation

Working with large worksheets, those that are too big to display within one monitor screen, can confuse users because they are not able to view the entire worksheet at one time. When this occurs, it is necessary for you to know how to view parts of the worksheet not visible, how to keep some parts of the worksheet always in view, and how to hide selected rows and columns. These ideas are illustrated in Figure 4.1, which shows a large worksheet with cell A1 as the active cell. It shows columns A through H and rows 1 through 30. Items that begin in column I or row 31 are not visible in this view.

> Working with large worksheets . . . can confuse users because they are not able to view the entire worksheet at one time.

In order to view other columns, you can click the horizontal scroll bar to view one or more columns to the right. When the active cell is in the rightmost visible column (H1 for example), pressing the right arrow key does the same thing. Clicking the down arrow in the vertical scroll bar or pressing the down arrow key when the active cell is in the bottom visible row moves the screen down one row. This is known as scrolling, but it does not address the issue of rows and columns formerly visible becoming invisible as the scrolling occurs.

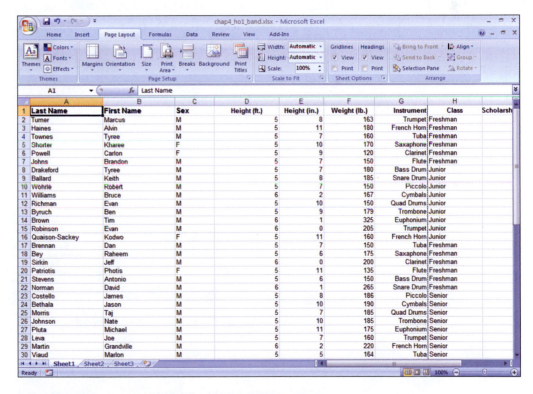

Figure 4.1 Large Worksheet

TIP   Go to a Specific Cell

Pressing Ctrl+Home and Ctrl+End takes you to the upper-left and bottom-right cells within a worksheet, respectively. But how do you get to a specific cell? One way is to click the Find & Select down arrow in the Editing group on the Home tab and select the Go To command (or press F5 or press Ctrl+G) to display the Go To dialog box, enter the address of the cell in the Reference text box, then press Enter to go directly to the cell.

Freezing Rows and Columns

Freezing is the process of keeping headings on the screen at all times.

When you scroll to parts of a worksheet not initially visible, some rows and columns disappear from view. It is sometimes valuable to be able to view row and column headings no matter where you scroll. This is done by *freezing*, which is the process that enables you to keep headings on the screen as you work with large worksheets, rows, and columns, as shown in Figure 4.2. Rows and columns that were not previously visible now are visible and so are the row and column headings. Figure 4.2 also shows a horizontal line and a vertical line after particular rows and columns, indicating they are frozen.

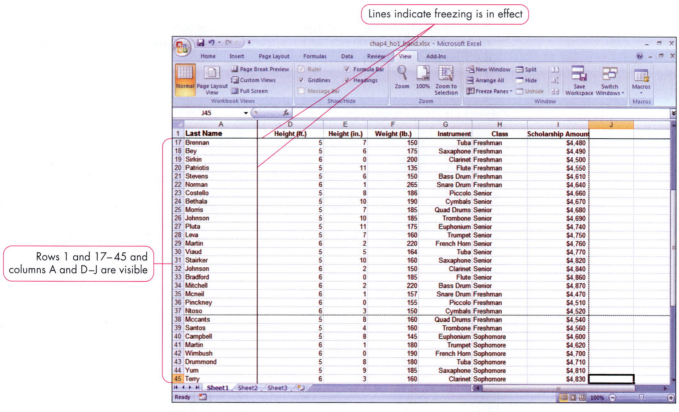

Figure 4.2 Visible Rows and Column Headings

To freeze columns and rows:

1. Select the cell below the row(s) and to the right of the column(s) you want to freeze.
2. Click the View tab and click Freeze Panes in the Window group. You can freeze both rows and columns or just the top row or the first column. After making your selection, you can unfreeze rows and columns by selecting Freeze Pane. You will notice that the *Freeze* option you previously selected now displays *Unfreeze*. Click that option to unfreeze rows and columns.

Hiding and Unhiding Rows, Columns, and Worksheets

Hidden is the state of rows, columns, and sheets being invisible.

Figure 4.3 shows a worksheet with rows, columns, and a worksheet *hidden*, which is the process of making rows, columns, and sheets invisible. The hiding of these items in a worksheet is a common practice and is done for a variety of reasons. Often, it is done to conceal nonessential information, or information not needed at a particular time. At other times, confidential information is contained in a workbook and rows, columns, or sheets must be hidden to allow nonauthorized users to view a workbook. You might also hide rows or columns to make other rows or columns visible. Row and columns containing sensitive data or data that uniquely identifies an individual or product are hidden from colleagues or competitors. Social Security Numbers, salary, or rate of pay, pricing data, and trade secret information are some examples of data used in worksheets that might be hidden. Large workbooks might include worksheets that not all employees are authorized to view because of the classified nature of the data contained in the worksheet. Trade secret information or information specifically classified by the federal government are just two examples of why worksheets may be hidden.

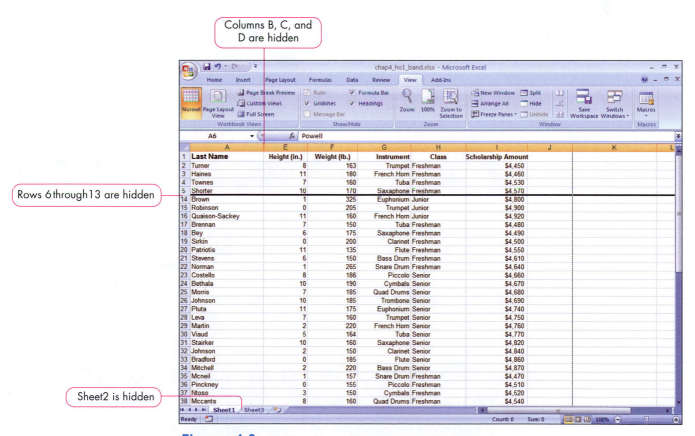

Figure 4.3 Hidden Rows, Columns, and Worksheet

Keep in mind that Hide is not a delete command. Hiding an element of a worksheet does not affect the data in that element, nor does it affect any other visible cell that might reference data in the hidden element. Formulas will still display correct results even when the references used in the formulas are hidden. To hide a particular row or column in a worksheet:

1. Select the row or column to be hidden.
2. Click the Home tab.
3. Open the Format menu in the Cells group and select Hide & Unhide.
4. Select the appropriate hide option.

To unhide rows or columns, repeat the above steps, except the rows or columns on either side of the hidden row or column must be selected and the appropriate unhide option is selected.

To hide a worksheet:

1. Make active the sheet to be hidden.
2. Click the Home tab.
3. Open the Format menu in the Cells group and select Hide & Unhide.
4. Select Hide Sheet.

To unhide a worksheet:

1. Click the Home tab.
2. Open the Format menu in the cells group and select Hide & Unhide.
3. Select Unhide Sheet. A dialog box appears asking which sheet is to be unhidden. Click the sheet to be unhidden and click OK.

TIP   Unhiding Rows and Columns

Hiding a row or column is easy: You select the row(s) or column(s) you want to hide, click the right mouse button, then select the Hide command from the shortcut menu. Unhiding a row or column is more challenging because you cannot see the target cells. To unhide a column, for example, you need to select the columns on either side. For example, select columns A and C if you are trying to unhide column B. To unhide column A, click in the Name box and type A1. Click Format in the Cells group on the Home tab, point to Hide & Unhide, and click Unhide Columns.

Protecting a Cell, a Worksheet, and a Workbook

The advent of networks and information sharing also introduced the need to protect data from being altered and from falling into the hands of the wrong person. When you post a spreadsheet on the company network, it becomes available to any user of the network. Network users can make any change to any worksheet in the workbook file. Excel has protection controls that, used with the proper restrictions, can ensure that the right people see only the right data. Unauthorized users will not be able to get into the spreadsheet. Authorized users can edit only those areas you give them access to. The formulas that calculate the visible values are confidential unless you choose to make them visible. The issue of protecting cells, worksheets, or workbooks is an important one because it can determine if users can change an element of a workbook. Generally, when a workbook is protected, the creator of the workbook controls if changes can be made to a file.

Lock and Unlock Cells

All cells in a workbook have a locked property that determines if changes can be made to a cell. This concept has no effect if a worksheet is not protected. On the other hand, once a worksheet is protected, if the locked property is on, all cells are locked, and no data can be entered. Locking cells allows you to prevent viewers of your worksheet from making any changes to the cells. You can unlock just those cells you permit others to change. For example, if you are working in a payroll department and have created an employee salary worksheet that lists pay rates, you may want to lock this data to prevent unauthorized users from changing their own pay rate. Similarly, you would want to lock the formulas for calculating gross pay. Table 4.1 illustrates the protect sheet and locked property. You can see that the Protect Sheet command must be on along with the Locked Property in order to prevent data from being entered. It is possible to allow data to be entered in some cells but not all.

1. Select the cells where entering or changing data will be allowed.
2. Click the Home tab, open the Format menu in the Cells group, and select Format Cells to open the Format Cells dialog box.
3. Select the Protection tab, clear the Locked check box, and click OK.
4. Click the Home tab, open the Format menu in the Cells group, and click Protect Sheet.
5. Select a password if desired and clear the *Select locked cells* check box.
6. Click OK.

To unprotect the sheet and unlock all cells, click the Home tab, open the Format menu in the Cells group, and select Unprotect Sheet.

Table 4.1 Protect/Lock Sheet Property

Protect Sheet	Locked Property On	Locked Property Off
Yes	No data can be entered.	Data can be entered.
No	Data can be entered.	Data can be entered.

Protect and Unprotect a Worksheet

The process of protecting a worksheet can be a two-step process, because the protection can allow users to only perform certain functions in the spreadsheet or allow users to only perform certain functions in certain cells. To protect a worksheet, follow this general procedure:

1. Click the Home tab and open the Format menu in the Cells group.
2. Click Protect Sheet.
3. Select a password if desired and click the options that users will be permitted in the worksheet. See Figure 4.4 for a display of the protect options.
4. Click OK.

It is recommended that you only use a protection password in cases requiring very tight security and that the password be placed in a safe location. Passwords can be up to 255 characters including letters, numbers, and symbols and are case sensitive. It is up to you to choose a suitably difficult password but not one that uses all 255 characters. If you should forget the password, it is gone; you cannot get into the locked file any more than the people you were trying to block in the first place.

To unprotect a worksheet:

1. Click the Home tab and open the Format menu in the Cells group.
2. Select Unprotect Sheet.

Figure 4.4 Protect Sheet Dialog Box

Protect a Workbook

Even though protecting a worksheet provides a relatively high level of protection, it does not prevent a criminal or vandal from changing the structure or windows of a workbook. This could include such things as deleting or renaming sheets. Protected workbooks prevent anyone from viewing hidden worksheets; moving, deleting, hiding, or changing the names of worksheets; and moving or copying worksheets to another workbook. The general procedure you use for protecting a workbook is as follows:

1. Click the Review tab and click Protect Workbook in the Changes group.
2. Click the boxes for the protection desired, as shown in Figure 4.5.
3. Click Protect Structure and Windows.
4. Enter a password, if desired, in the Protect Workbook dialog box.
5. Click OK.

Figure 4.5 Protect Workbook Dialog Box

TIP Protect the Formulas

The formulas in a well-designed worksheet should be based on a set of assumptions and initial conditions that are grouped together for ease of change. The user can change any of the initial values and see the effect ripple throughout the spreadsheet. The user need not, however, have access to the formulas and thus, the formulas should be protected. Remember, protection is a two-step process. First, you unlock the cells that you want to be able to change after the worksheet has been protected, and then you protect the worksheet.

Controlling Calculation

Calculation is the computing of formulas and the display of the results or values in the cells that contain the formulas. In Excel, the default recalculation takes place when the cells formulas refer to change. This default recalculation can be changed as circumstances warrant. Table 4.2 illustrates different recalculation schemes. These schemes all begin by clicking the Office Button, clicking Excel Options, and then clicking the Formulas category.

Table 4.2 Formula Recalculation Schemes

Recalculation Action	Steps
All dependent formulas every time a change is made to a value, formula, or name.	Click **Automatic** under Calculate Options in the Calculate performance section.
All dependent formulas except data tables every time a change is made to a value, formula, or name.	**Click Automatic except for data tables** under Calculate Options in the Calculate performance section.
Turn off automatic recalculation and recalculate open workbooks only when desired.	Click **Manual** under Calculate Options in the Calculate performance section.
Manually recalculate.	Click **Calculate Now** in the Calculation group on the Formulas tab, or press **F9**.

Printing Large Worksheets

Printing all or parts of a large worksheet presents special challenges to even veteran users of Excel. It is easy for you to make erroneous assumptions about what will print and be unpleasantly surprised. You must consider such things as Page Breaks, Page Orientation, Printing a selection, and the order in which pages print when printing all or part of a large worksheet. Figure 4.6 shows a worksheet that prints on six pieces of paper with just one column printing on page 5 and one row printing on pages 2, 4, and 6. You can adjust column widths, margins, and page orientation before printing and wasting paper.

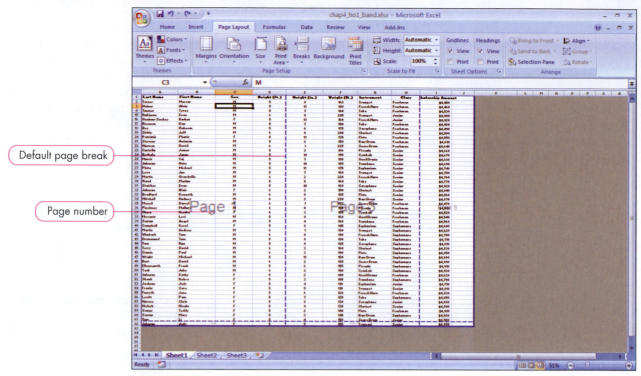

Default page break

Page number

Figure 4.6 Page Break Preview

Manage Page Breaks

The ***Page Break Preview***
shows where page breaks
occur and gives you the opportunity to change where the
page breaks.

The ***Page Break Preview*** command shows you where page breaks currently occur
and gives you the opportunity to change where the page breaks occur when a worksheet is printed. Figure 4.6 displays a Page Break Preview. The dashed blue line indicates where the default page breaks occur. To use the Page Break Preview command
and adjust page breaks:

1. Click Page Break Preview on the status bar. If the Welcome to Page Break
   Preview dialog box appears, check the *Do not show this dialog again* box and click
   OK.
2. A watermark shows the page numbers.
3. Move the dashed blue lines as appropriate to adjust the page breaks.

Change Page Orientation

Printing an entire worksheet on a single piece of paper is more efficient in terms of
paper use and provides the reader with the whole picture. The reader does not have
to shuffle pages in order to get to the totals or perhaps the summary portion of the
spreadsheet. One of the more efficient ways to have more of a worksheet printed on
a page is to change the page orientation. Page orientation can be either Portrait (tall)
or Landscape (wide). To change page orientation to print more of a worksheet on a
page:

1. Click Orientation in the Page Setup group the Page Layout tab.
2. Select Portrait or Landscape.

Print a Selection

Excel users working with large spreadsheets sometimes want to print only a portion of a worksheet. Printing a portion of a worksheet involves selecting an area to print prior to actually printing. Figure 4.7 shows a selected area of a worksheet and the Print dialog box with Selection as the print range. Complete the following steps to print a selection or range of a worksheet:

1. Select the portion of the worksheet you want to print.
2. Click the Page Layout tab, and then click the Page Setup Dialog Box Launcher in the Page Setup group.
3. Click Print, and then click Selection in the *Print what* section.
4. Verify the selection using Preview.

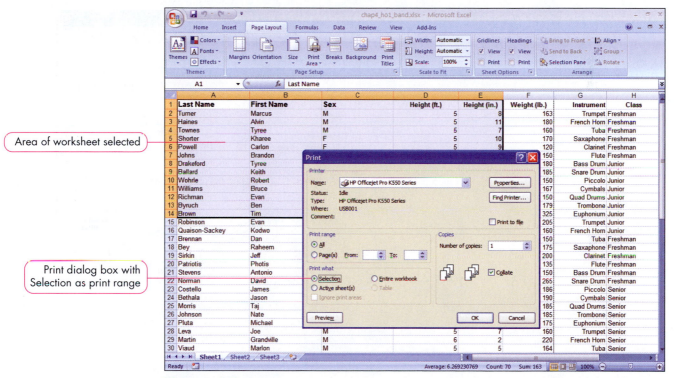

Figure 4.7 Printing a Selection

TIP   Set Print Areas

To set print areas, press and hold Ctrl as you click and drag to select one or more areas in the worksheet, and then click Print Area in the Page Setup group on the Page Layout tab and select Set Print Area. The print area is highlighted. The next time you execute the Print command, you will print just the print area(s), with each print area appearing on a separate page. To clear the print area, click Print Area in the Page Setup group on the Page Layout tab, and then select Clear Print Area.

Control Print Page Order

The complexity of large spreadsheets sometimes makes it necessary for you to change the order that pages will print. The print order may be changed because the data will make more sense if the order of pages printed is changed or to keep like data together. When you have four pages to print, you can print left to right, 1–2 and then 3–4, or you can print top to bottom, 1–3 and then 2–4. You choose which order to print based on your worksheet; data may be arranged wider than it is tall. You control the order in which pages are numbered and printed. To change the order of the printing of pages:

1. Click the Page Setup Dialog Box Launcher of the Page Layout tab.
2. Click the Sheet tab.
3. Change the *Page order* options, as appropriate, as shown in Figure 4.8.

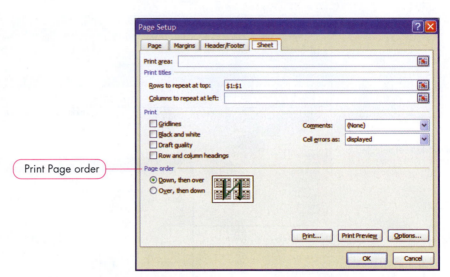

Figure 4.8 Page Setup Dialog Box

Hands-On Exercises

1 | Marching Band Roster

Skills covered: 1. Freeze and Unfreeze Rows and Columns **2.** Hide and Unhide Rows, Columns, and Worksheets **3.** Protect a Worksheet and a Workbook and Control Calculations **4.** Print a Large Worksheet

Step 1 **Freeze and Unfreeze Rows and Columns**	Refer to Figure 4.9 as you complete Step 1. **a.** Start Excel. Open the *chap4_ho1_band* workbook and save it as **chap4_ho1_band_solution** so that you can return to the original workbook if necessary. As you use the horizontal scroll bar to view the worksheet, note that some columns disappear. Rows also disappear when you use the vertical scroll bar. The worksheet is too large to fit on one screen and you must use Freeze Panes to keep parts of the worksheet in constant view. **b.** Click **cell B2**, the cell below the row you will freeze. Click the **View tab**, click **Freeze Panes** in the Window group, and select **Freeze Top Row**. Use the vertical scroll bar to see that the row data becomes visible while the row data labels remain constant. **c.** Click **cell B2**, the cell to the right of the column you will freeze. Click the **View tab**, click **Freeze Panes** in the Window group, and select **Freeze First Column**. Use the horizontal scroll bar to see that the first column data are always visible as other columns become visible. **d.** Click the **Freeze Panes** in the Window group and select **Unfreeze Panes**. Now that the panes are no longer frozen, use either scroll bar to see that the worksheet is again too large to view on one screen. **TROUBLESHOOTING:** Your screen definition settings may change your view of the spreadsheet and make freezing more or less important. **e.** Enter and format a heading: • Select **row 1**, click the **Home tab**, and click **Insert** in the Cells group to insert a new row. • Click in **cell A1** and type **State University Marching Band Roster**. • Select **cells A1:I1** and click **Merge & Center** in the Alignment group on the Home tab. • Point to the title and right-click the mouse to display the Mini toolbar. Click the **Bold** button and select a font size of **14**. • Click **Font Color** in the Font group and select **Dark Blue** from Standard Colors; similarly, open **Fill Color** and select the complement, **Dark Blue, Accent 1, Lighter 80%** from the blue theme colors. **f.** Save the workbook.

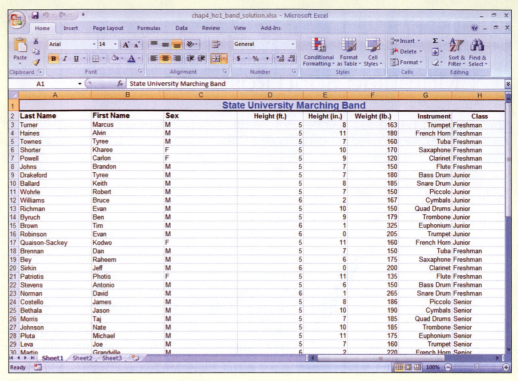

Figure 4.9 Freeze and Unfreeze Rows and Columns

Refer to Figure 4.10 as you complete Step 2.

a. Select **column F**. Click the **Home tab** if needed, click **Format** in the Cells group, select **Hide & Unhide**, and click **Hide Columns**.

Column F is hidden and a thick black line appears between columns E and G, indicating the location of the hidden column. When you begin the next step, the line disappears.

b. Select **row 6** and open **Format** in the Cells group, select **Hide & Unhide**, and click **Hide Rows**.

Row 6 is hidden, and a thick black line appears between rows 5 and 7, indicating the location of the hidden row.

c. Right-click the **Sheet2 tab** and select **Hide** to hide the sheet.

When a sheet is hidden, the sheet and sheet tab disappear, and there is no indication that a sheet is hidden, unlike a hidden row or column. Refer to Figure 4.10 and note the hidden row, column, and sheet.

d. Click the **Sheet1 tab**, select **columns E and G**, click **Format** menu in the Cells group, select **Hide & Unhide**, and click **Unhide Columns** to display the column again.

TROUBLESHOOTING: Note that the columns on either side of the hidden columns must be selected prior to unhiding. Rows above and below hidden rows must be selected prior to unhiding.

e. Selecting **rows 5** and **7**, click the **Home tab**, click **Format** in the Cells group, select **Hide & Unhide**, and click **Unhide Rows** to display row 6 again.

f. Click **Format** in the Cells group, select **Hide & Unhide**, click **Unhide Sheet** to see the Unhide dialog box, select **Sheet2**, and click **OK** to display Sheet2 again. Save the workbook.

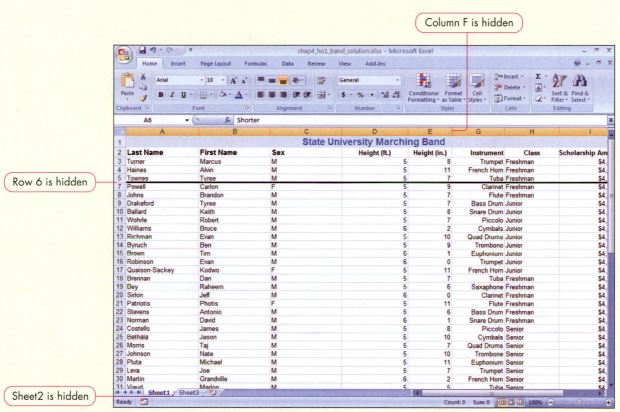

Figure 4.10 Hiding Rows, Columns, and Worksheets

Step 3
Protect a Worksheet and a Workbook and Control Calculations

Refer to Figure 4.11 as you complete Step 3.

a. Select **Sheet1** and select **cells G3:G63**, the cells that you want to edit.
   - Click **Format** in the Cells group, and then click **Format Cells** to open the Format Cells dialog box.
   - Click the **Protection tab**, click the **Locked check box** to deselect it, and click **OK**.
   - Select **Protect Sheet** from **Format** in the Cells group to see the Protect Sheet dialog box.
   - Check the **Select unlocked cells** option if necessary, uncheck the **Select locked cells**, and click **OK**.
   - You unlocked cells for editing purposes, and then protected or locked all other cells. The only data that you can change is a band member's instrument. Try to change any player's name or other statistic except their instrument and you will see the Microsoft Office Excel warning box.

You must unprotect the worksheet in order to unlock the cells you previously protected and before continuing with this exercise.

b. Click **Format** in the Cells group and click **Unprotect Sheet** to unprotect the worksheet again.

c. Click the **Review tab** and click **Protect Workbook** in the Changes group. Then click **Protect Structure and Windows**. The Protect Workbook dialog box is opened. Verify that a check mark appears in the **Structure** box and click **OK** to protect the workbook.

Remember you are the creator of the workbook and can make any changes. You have protected the workbook so that others cannot make changes.

TROUBLESHOOTING: If you enter a password in any dialog box, only those who know the password will be able to change data or perhaps open the workbook. If you forget the password, you cannot edit or perhaps cannot even open the workbook.

d. To unprotect the workbook, click **Protect Workbook** in the Changes group. Click **Protect Structure and Windows** to deselect it. Save the workbook.

e. Click the **Office Button**, click **Excel Options**, and then click **Formulas**.

Calculation options are displayed at the top of the Excel Options dialog box. You can use these options to change how and when Excel calculates formulas.

f. Click **Cancel** to close the Excel Options dialog box.

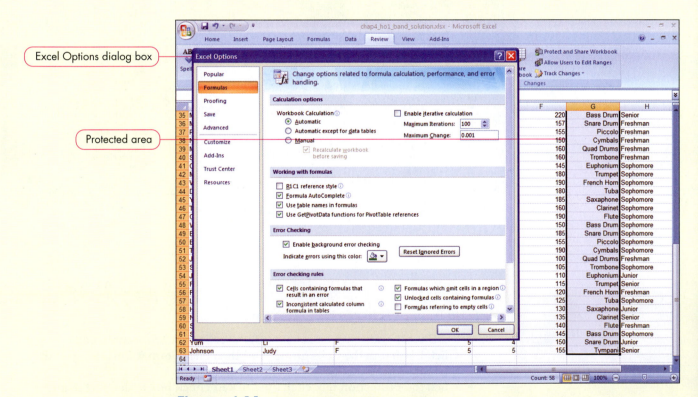

Figure 4.11 Protected Area of Worksheet

Step 4
Print a Large Worksheet

Refer to Figure 4.12 as you complete Step 4.

a. Click the **Page Break Preview** button on the status bar in the lower-right area of the window. If you see the Welcome to Page Break Preview dialog box, click **OK**.

You will use the Page Break Preview command to adjust the page breaks in a large spreadsheet.

b. Move the **blue dashed line** that separates pages 1 and 3 as well as pages 2 and 4 to the right to eliminate the page break.

c. Move the **blue dashed line** that now separates pages 1 and 2 down to eliminate the page break.

You will now see just page 1, as all page breaks have been eliminated.

d. Click the **Normal** button on the status bar to return to Normal view.

e. Click the **Page Layout tab**, click **Orientation**, and select **Landscape** to change the page orientation.

- Click the **Page Setup Dialog Box Launcher** on the Page Layout tab to launch the Page Setup dialog box.
- Click the **Print Preview** button and verify that the worksheet will print on one page.
- Click **Print** to print the worksheet.

Changing to landscape orientation enables more of the worksheet to fit on one page. You used the Print Preview feature to view how much data now fits on one page before printing and then printed the worksheet.

f. Select **cells A4:H10**, then click **Print Area** in the **Page Setup** group on the Page Layout tab.

- Select **Set Print Area**.
- Click the **Page Setup Dialog Box Launcher** on the Page Layout tab to launch the Page Setup dialog box.
- Click **Print Preview** and verify that your selection is correct.
- Click the **Print** button to print your selection.
- Click **Cancel** to close the Page Setup dialog box, if necessary.
- Click **Print Area** in the Page Setup group on the Page Layout tab and select **Clear Print Area**.

You selected just a specific portion or area of the worksheet and verified that the selection you wanted to print was correct. You then printed the selection and after printing, cleared the selection.

g. Click in **cell A28**, click **Breaks** on the Page Layout tab, and select **Insert Page Break**.

h. Select **column G**, click **Breaks** on the Page Layout tab, and select **Insert Page Break**. Click the **Page Break Preview** button on the status bar.

You placed page breaks above cell A28 and after Column F to print the worksheet on four pages.

i. Click the **Page Setup Dialog Box Launcher** on the Page Layout tab, click the **Sheet tab**, click **Over, then down button** in the *Page order* section, and then click **OK**.

j. Click the **Page Setup Dialog Box Launcher** on the Page Layout tab, click the **Print Preview** button to verify that you will print four pages, click **Print**, and then close the Print Preview window.

Before printing the four-page worksheet you changed the order in which the pages will print. (See Figure 4.12 and note that the Rows to repeat at top: box contains the default rows to print on each page.)

k. Save the workbook. Close the workbook and exit Excel if you do not want to continue with the next exercise at this time.

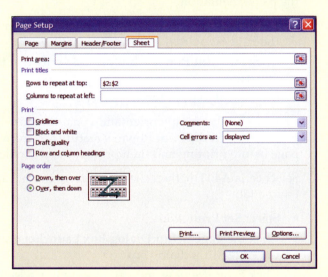

Figure 4.12   Print a Large Worksheet

Excel Data Tables

All enterprises, be they business, educational, or governmental, maintain data in the form of lists. Companies have lists of employees. Educational institutions maintain lists of students and faculty members. Governmental entities, such as the military, maintain extensive inventory lists. In this part of the chapter, we will present the fundamentals of table management, which is how Excel presents lists of data so that it can be manipulated by the program. This section begins with definitions of basic terms, such as *table*, *field*, and *record*, and then discusses the creation of tables; how to add, edit, or delete records in a table; and how to use the Find and Replace feature to change recurring data in a table. Formatting tables will be presented.

(All enterprises . . . maintain data in the form of lists.)

In the first part of this section, you learn how to distinguish between information and data and describe how one is converted into another. Sorting of data in tables will be explored, both in simple sorts and in multiple-level sorts. In the second part of this section, you will filter records in a table and insert column totals and summary reports with charts.

The concepts associated with tables in Excel are database concepts. These can be difficult concepts to understand in the abstract, so the following example may help to clarify things. As the Director of Human Resources at State University, you manually maintain employee data for the members of the university faculty. You maintain specifics about each employee such as name, salary, and faculty rank in an individual manila file folder that is stored in a file cabinet. The file folders have the faculty member's name on the tab, and they are sorted alphabetically by last name in the filing cabinet.

This example shows the basics of manual database management. Each item can be equated to a database term. The set of manila file folders corresponds to a file. Each folder can be equated to a record. Each item within the file folder equates to a field in a record. See Figure 4.13 for an example of a file cabinet analogy.

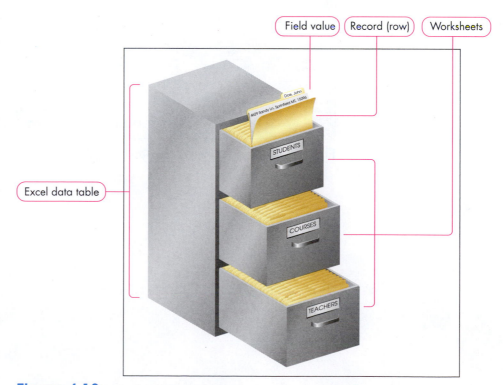

Figure 4.13 File Cabinet Analogy

A **table** is an area in the worksheet that contains rows and columns of similar or related information.

Excel maintains lists of data in the form of a table. A **table** is an area in the worksheet that contains rows and columns of similar or related information. A table can be used as part of a database or organized collection of related information, where the worksheet rows represent the records and the worksheet columns represent the fields in a record. The first row contains the column labels or field names. This identifies the data that will be entered in the columns. Each row in the table contains a record. Every cell in the table area, except the field names, contains a specific value for a specific field in a specific record. Every record (row) contains the same fields (columns) in the same order as every other record.

Figure 4.14 contains a college marching band roster. This roster contains nine fields in every record: Last Name, First Name, Sex, Height (ft.), Height (in.), Weight, Instrument, Class, and Scholarship Amount. Assigned field names should be meaningful and unique. Field names may contain up to 255 characters, but they should be kept short so the column does not become too wide and unwieldy to work with. How the fields are arranged is consistent from record to record. Last Name was chosen as the key so the records are in alphabetical order by that label.

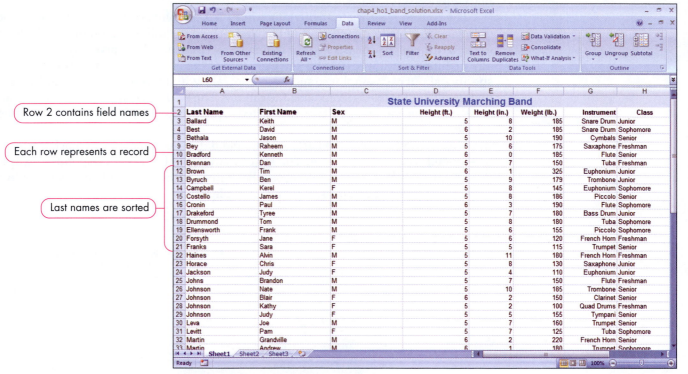

Figure 4.14 Marching Band Roster

Exploring Basic Table Management

Creating tables is a relatively straightforward task to complete in Excel. You choose the area in the worksheet that will contain the list, create the table, and then indicate that the table has labels or field names. Each field name must be unique to prevent confusion. Data for individual records are entered in the rows below the row of field names.

Once you have created a table, any field in any record can be edited, just as entries can be changed in a regular worksheet. The Insert Rows command allows additional rows (records); the Insert Columns command allows additional columns (fields); the Delete command allows deletion of rows or columns. Shortcut menus streamline many of these operations, and formatting can be accomplished from the contextual tab. The contents of the contextual tab are shown in the reference table. The table defines the Design tab, the groups it contains, and their general function.

Create and Use Tables

As described, the process for creating a table is clear-cut. Tables can be created either from data already in a spreadsheet, or a table may be created and then the data added. The steps for creating a table with or without data are similar. To create a table without data:

1. Select a range of cells on a sheet.
2. Click the Insert tab and click Table in the Tables group. The Create Table dialog box appears asking for the range of data for the table. Users should place a check mark in the box My table has headers. See Figure 4.15.
3. Click OK; a contextual Design tab becomes active once the table is created.

To create a table from already existing data on a sheet:

1. Select the range of cells on the sheet that contains the data.
2. Click the Insert tab and click Table in the Tables group. The Create Table dialog box described previously appears. Changes should be made as appropriate.
3. Click OK to complete the table creation and display the contextual Design tab. You will see that Excel automatically applies the default Table Style Medium 9 banded rows to your table. The contextual Table Tools tab is also the active tab, and each cell in the header row has sort arrows. See Figure 4.16 for the style, tab, and arrows.

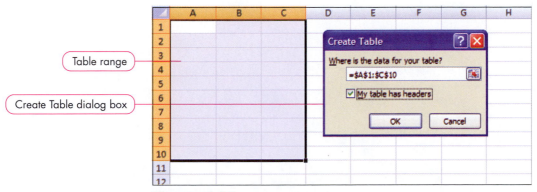

Figure 4.15 Define Table Area

Table Tools Design Groups and Description | Reference

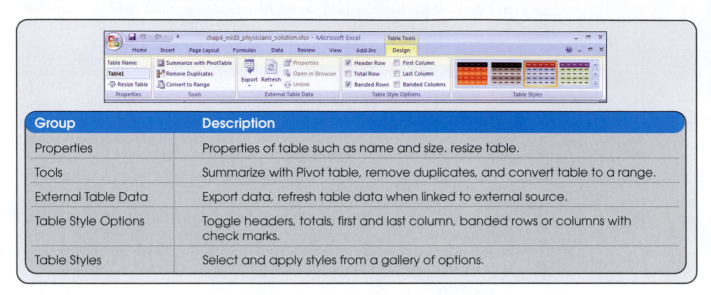

Group	Description
Properties	Properties of table such as name and size. resize table.
Tools	Summarize with Pivot table, remove duplicates, and convert table to a range.
External Table Data	Export data, refresh table data when linked to external source.
Table Style Options	Toggle headers, totals, first and last column, banded rows or columns with check marks.
Table Styles	Select and apply styles from a gallery of options.

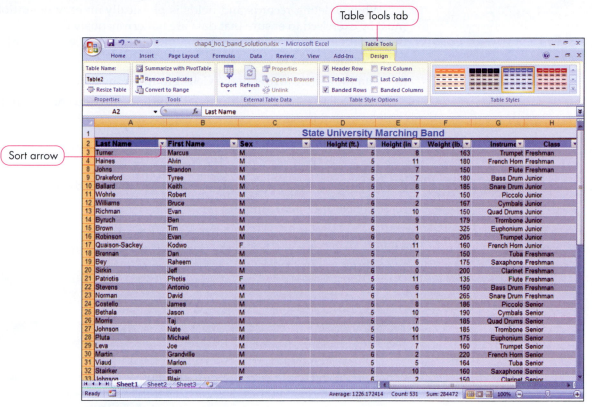

Table Tools tab

Sort arrow

Figure 4.16 Data Table

TIP Shortcut Key

Once the table range has been selected, you can press F9 to insert a table.

Add, Edit, or Delete Records and Fields

Once you have created a table, you will add, edit, or delete records. You will use previously learned Excel commands. It is possible to edit any field in any record in the same way you change entries in a spreadsheet.

1. Click the field (cell) of the data to be edited.
2. Edit the data as desired.
3. Accept the change by pressing Enter.

To add or delete records as your data table expands or contracts, several techniques are available. To add a record:

1. Select a cell in the record below where you want the new record inserted and open the Insert drop-down list in the Cells group on the Home tab.
2. Select Insert Table Rows Above.

If you wanted to insert a field (column) in a table, you would make active the field to the right of where the field is to be inserted and repeat the previous steps, except that the selection from the Insert drop-down list is Insert Table Columns to the Left.

While deleting records and fields is physically an easy operation, extreme care must be exercised to ensure that data are not erroneously deleted. If you accidentally delete data, use the Undo command immediately. To delete a record from a table:

1. Select the record to be deleted.

2. Open the Delete arrow in the Cells group on the Home tab.

3. Select Delete Table Rows. Multiple records, contiguous or noncontiguous, may be deleted in this manner.

To delete one or more fields from a table:

1. Select the column or columns to be deleted.

2. Open the Delete down arrow in the Cells group on the Home tab.

3. Select Delete Table Columns.

Again, extreme caution must be exercised when deleting records or fields. Make sure you have selected the desired row or column before initiating the delete procedures.

TIP   Edit Clear Versus Edit Delete

The Delete command in the Cells group on the Home tab deletes the selected cell, row, or column from the worksheet, and thus, its execution will adjust cell references throughout the worksheet. It is very different from Clear Contents in the shortcut menu, which erases the contents (and/or formatting) of the selected cells, but does not delete the cells from the worksheet and hence has no effect on the cell references in formulas that reference those cells. Pressing Delete erases the contents of a cell and thus corresponds to the Clear Contents command.

Use Find and Replace

The Find and Replace command can be valuable when some part of the data in a table changes and there are multiple occurrences of the data. Rather than editing the data individually in each record, Find and Replace allows global editing of data. For example, Figure 4.17 shows a school marching band roster. The field shown in column H is each player's class. Rather than going to each record to edit the class, Find and Replace is used to advance the class level at the end of each school year.

1. Select the field that is to be edited.

2. Select Replace from the Find & Select down arrow in the Editing group on the Home tab.

3. Enter the data to be changed in the *Find what* box.

4. Enter the data that will replace the changed data in the *Replace with* box.

5. The user can either look at each occurrence of the data to determine if the change is appropriate or click Replace All to replace all occurrences at one time.

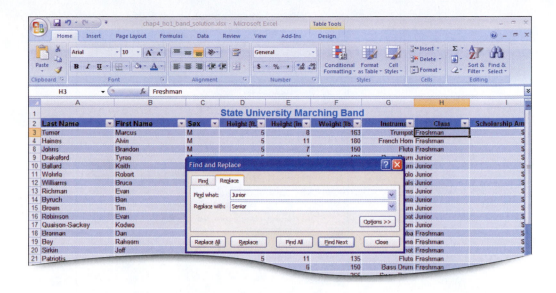

Figure 4.17 Find and Replace Data

TIP   Garbage In, Garbage Out (GIGO)

The information produced by a system is only as good as the data on which it is based. It is absolutely critical, therefore, that you validate the data that goes into a system, or else the associated information will not be correct. No system, no matter how sophisticated, can produce valid output from invalid input. In other words, garbage in—garbage out.

Format the Table

Formatting tables can make them more attractive and easier to read, and you can emphasize data. The standard types of formatting available in worksheets are available for you to use with tables. Some of these format options, such as cell height and width, are available in the Format down arrow of the Cells group on the Home tab. Other formatting options are available in the Cell Styles gallery of the Styles group on the Home tab (see Figure 4.18). Other formatting options are present in the Number, Alignment, and Font groups of the Home tab.

The Design contextual tab provides a variety of formatting options for tables. The Table Styles group presents a selection of predefined table styles. You can see the effect of each style on a table by pointing to the style. Your table will display the style as you move the mouse across the Table Style gallery.

The Table Style Options group, shown in Figure 4.19, contains a set of boxes to select specific format actions in a table. Table 4.3 lists the options and the effect when each is selected. Whatever formatting and formatting effects you choose to use, remember that oftentimes less is more. It is not good to apply so many formatting effects that the message you want to present with the data is obscured or lost.

Figure 4.18 Cell Styles Gallery

Figure 4.19 Table Style Options Group

Table 4.3 Table Style Options

Check Box Options	Action
Header Row	Turns on or off the header or top row of a table.
Totals Row	Turns on or off the totals or last row of a table.
First Column	Shows special formatting for the first column of a table.
Last Column	Shows special formatting for the last column of a table.
Banded Rows	Displays banded rows where even rows are differently formatted than odd rows.
Banded Columns	Displays banded columns where even columns are differently formatted than odd columns.

Sorting Data

The data in a table are easier to understand and work with if they are in some meaningful order. The marching band roster shown in Figure 4.20 is in no particular order, and it is difficult to locate individual band members. Parents would like the roster in alphabetical order so they can easily locate their children. Announcers and members of the media would like it arranged by name also. Instrument teachers would want it arranged by instrument so they can quickly identify the students they teach. University administrators want it arranged by scholarship amount so that they know who has been awarded how much.

Sorting arranges records in a table by the value in field(s) within a table.

The **sort command** puts lists in ascending or descending order according to specified keys.

Keys are the fields that records are sorted on.

Sorting arranges records in a table by the value of one or more fields within a table. The **sort command** puts lists in ascending or descending order according to specified keys. The most basic types of sorts are ascending, or low to high, and descending high to low, sequence. Putting a table in alphabetical order is considered an ascending sort. It is also possible to sort on more than one field at a time. An example of this with the marching band roster would be sorting alphabetically by class and then alphabetically by last name. The field or fields that you use to sort the table on are called keys. **Keys** are the fields that records are sorted on. Keys dictate the sequence of the records in the table; for example, if you want to put the marching band table in order by instrument, then instrument is the key field in the sort process.

Figures 4.21, 4.22, and 4.23 show the marching band roster worksheet sorted using three different keys. Figure 4.21 shows the roster sorted by last name. Note that the four Johnsons in the roster are not sorted in order. Figure 4.22 shows the same roster sorted by instrument. Finally, Figure 4.23 shows the roster sorted alphabetically by class in ascending order.

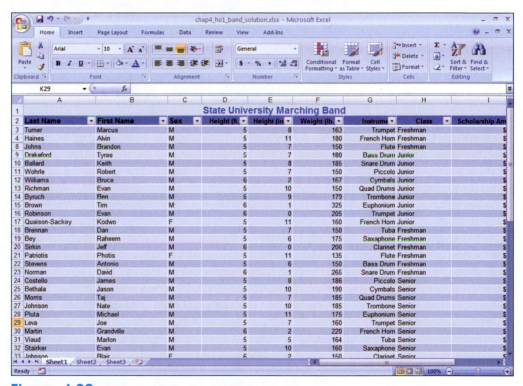

Figure 4.20 Data in No Particular Order

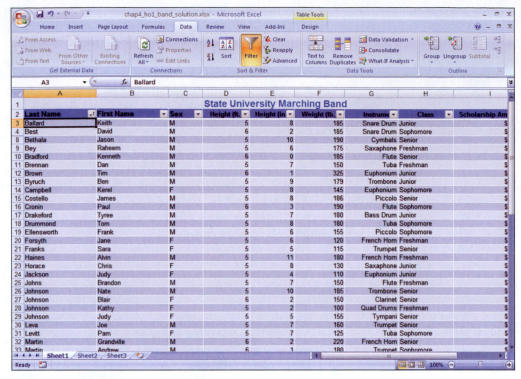

Figure 4.21 Sorted by Last Name

Figure 4.22 Sorted by Instrument

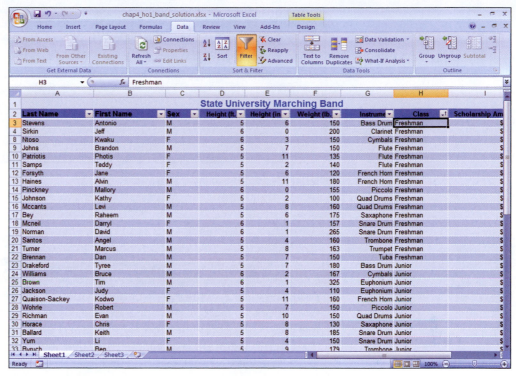

Figure 4.23 Alphabetically by Class in Ascending Order

Sort in Ascending or Descending Order

The most basic sorts are those done in ascending or descending order. An ascending order sort will sort text data alphabetically from A to Z, and numeric data in increasing order, or 1 to 100, for example. The descending order sort will sort text data in reverse alphabetical order from Z to A, and the numeric data in decreasing order, or 100 to 1. To accomplish this:

1. Click in any cell in the column to be sorted.

2. Click either Sort A to Z or Sort Z to A in the Sort & Filter group on the Data tab.

Perform a Multiple Level Sort

At times, sorting on only one field yields several records that have the same information—for example the same last name or the same class. Refer to Figure 4.21 for multiple Johnsons and Figure 4.23 for multiple members of the same class. The single key does not uniquely identify a record. You might need both last name and first name to uniquely identify an individual. Using multiple level sorts allows differentiation among records with the same data in the first key. For example, university administrators might sort on Class, Last Name, and First Name to see an alphabetical list of band members by class. Excel allows sorts on 64 different keys. To perform a multiple level sort:

1. Click in any cell in the table.

2. Click Sort in the Sort & Filter group on the Data tab. This opens the Sort dialog box.

3. Click the Add Level button and choose the first key from the Sort by drop-down list. Verify that the results are correct.

4. Continue to click the Add Level button and add keys until you have entered all desired sort keys. See Figure 4.24.

5. Click OK.

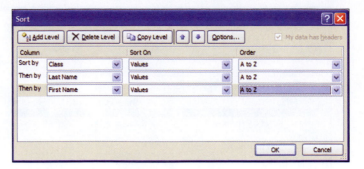

Figure 4.24 Sort Dialog Box

TIP Choose a Custom Sort Sequence

Alphabetic fields normally are arranged in strict alphabetical order. You can, however, choose a custom sort sequence such as the days of the week or the months of the year. Click Sort in the Sort & Filter group on the Data tab. Select Custom List from the Order drop-down list, choose a sequence other than the alphabetic, and then close the Custom Lists dialog box.

Filtering and Totaling Data

Data refer to facts about a specific record or sets of records.

Information is data that have been arranged in some form and are viewed as useful.

Data and **information** are not the same thing, although you often hear the two terms used interchangeably. Data refer to facts about a specific record or sets of records, such as a band member's name, his instrument, or his weight as reflected in the marching band roster you have been using. Information is data that have been arranged in some form and is viewed as useful. With the marching band roster, an example of data would be the entire list, but information is a list of members who play the flute. In other words, data are the raw material, and information is the final output produced based on that data.

Decisions in any organization, from businesses to marching bands, are based not just on raw data but on information. The military intelligence-gathering process is an analogy to the decision making process. Many pieces of intelligence data are gathered and analyzed prior to the preparation and dissemination of intelligence information. Similarly, a band director gathers data about such things as his members and their past performances before determining how many members who play which instruments need to be recruited.

In today's world, all organizations gather data that lead to information. The maintenance of data was discussed in some detail in the previous section. This final section of the chapter focuses on using data to create information.

Use AutoFilters

Filtering data using AutoFilter is a quick way to display a subset of data from a table. The filtered data display only the records that meet the criteria you, the Excel user, specify. Records that do not meet the specified criteria are hidden: Hidden records are not deleted; they are just not displayed. Figure 4.16 depicts the marching band roster we have been using, and Figure 4.25 shows the same roster filtered to show only those members in the band who are juniors. When you created a data table, Filter in the Sort & Filter group on the Data tab was highlighted. This default option indicates that the Filter command is available. To apply a simple AutoFilter to a data table, click the arrow in the column header. Either Text Filters or Number Filters will display according to the type of data in the column; see Figure 4.25. Remove the check mark from the Select All box, select the filter conditions(s) to be imposed, and click OK.

If the header column arrows are not visible:

1. Select the data table.

2. Click Sort & Filter in the Editing group on the Home tab.

3. Click Filter to show the arrows in each column header.

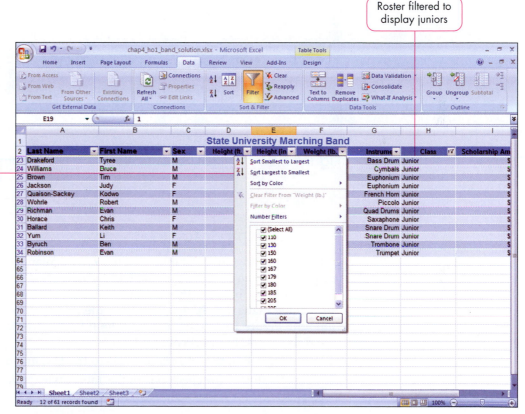

Figure 4.25 Filtered Roster

Use Multiple AutoFilters

Often, Excel users need to filter on more than one criteria to display the exact information required. Multiple AutoFilters can be used to return a more specific result. With AutoFilter, you can filter more than one criteria. Filters are additive, which means that each additional filter is based on the current filtered data and further reduces a data subset. To apply multiple AutoFilters you would repeat the steps described above until the subset of data is exactly what is desired. Figure 4.26 shows the marching band roster filtered to show only Snare Drum members who are also Juniors. Typically, you will filter from gross to fine. For example, if you wanted to identify the freshman female flute players, you would filter first by class (freshman), then by sex (F), and finally by instrument (flute).

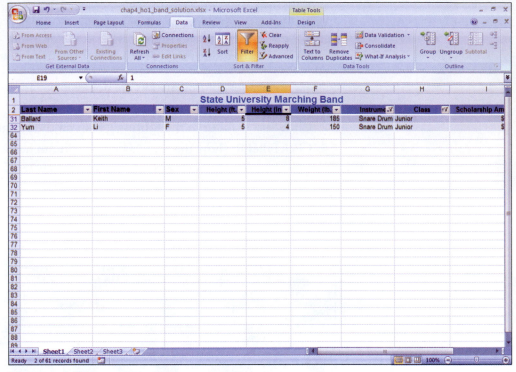

Figure 4.26 The Members Who Are Juniors and Play the Snare Drum

Insert Column Totals

Often, fields exist in data tables that require calculation in order to best display some or all of the data contained in the table. You can use Help to learn more about database functions that may be used in Excel. Here, however, you will find a simple column total. In the marching band roster, there is a field for each member's scholarship amount. Figure 4.27 shows a column total for the scholarships awarded to marching band members. To insert column totals:

1. Ensure a cell in the table is selected so the Design Tab is available.
2. Click the Total Row check box of the Table Style Options group on the Design tab.

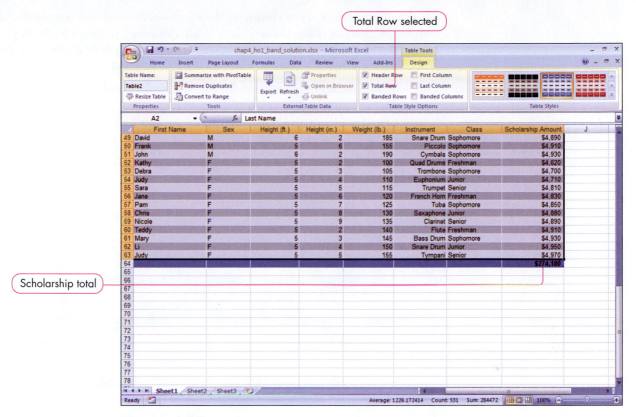

Figure 4.27 Scholarship Total

Create a Summary Report with a Chart

Creating a summary report computes subtotals for groups of records within a list. It is imperative you remember that the subtotals command will not function with data in tables. The records in the list are grouped according to value in a specific field such as Class. The subtotals command inserts a subtotal row into the list when the value of a designated field such as Class changes from one record to the next. Automatic row insertions are not permitted in a data table.

A grand total is displayed after the last record. The list must be in sequence by the field on which the subtotals will be grouped prior to executing the subtotals command. The list can be sorted while it is a data table or when it is a list. Figure 4.28 shows a summary report for scholarship amounts by class for the marching band. To create a summary report:

1. To make sure the data are a list and not a table, click Convert to Range in the Tools group on the Design tab as necessary, and click Yes in the warning box.
2. Click in the list and then click Subtotal in the Outline group on the Data tab.
3. Select the criteria and the Add subtotal categories as appropriate.
4. Click OK.

Creating a chart of the summary data follows the principles used in the previous chapter. A chart of the summary data is an ideal way to graphically depict the data from the summary report. See Figure 4.29 for an example of a pie chart showing the scholarship amount by class. To create a summary chart:

1. Select data fields to be charted. In the marching band example, it was necessary to select noncontiguous cells.
2. Click the Insert tab and open the Charts group.
3. Select the type of chart appropriate for the data and click OK.
4. Format and move the chart as appropriate.

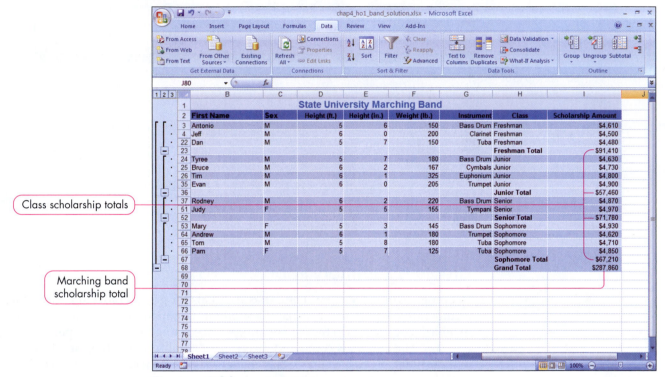

Figure 4.28 Scholarship Summary Report

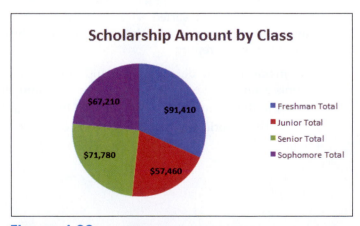

Figure 4.29 Chart of Summary Report

Hands-On Exercises

2 | Marching Band Roster Revisited

Skills covered: 1. Create a Table **2.** Add, Edit, or Delete Records, and Use Find and Replace **3.** Format a Table
4. Sort a Table **5.** Filter a Table **6.** Create Column Totals and a Summary Report **7.** Print the Completed Worksheet

---

Step 1
Create a Table

Refer to Figure 4.30 as you complete Step 1.

a. Open a new blank workbook.

b. Select **cells D2:G13**.

   You have selected the area that will be defined as a table.

c. With the Insert tab active, click **Table** in the Tables group to display the Create Table dialog box.

d. Verify that the range of cells in the **Where is the data for your table?** box is correct, click in the box for **My table has headers**, and click **OK**.

   You selected a blank area of the worksheet and formally defined it as a table. The contextual Design tab becomes active once the table is created. Refer to the reference table to see the Table Tools Design contextual tab and groups. Also note the default style is applied to the header row with banded rows.

e. Close Book1 without saving it.

f. Open the *chap4_ho1_band_solution* workbook. Save it as **chap4_ho2_band_solution**.

g. Select **cells A2:I63**, click the **Insert tab**, and click **Table**. Verify the range in the **Where is the data for your table?** box, make sure the **My table has headers** box is checked, and click **OK**.

   The data in the selected range are converted to a table with a clearly identifiable header row. Each column header cell contains an arrow that will be used later. The default table style is applied with banded rows. You will change the style later in the hands-on exercise.

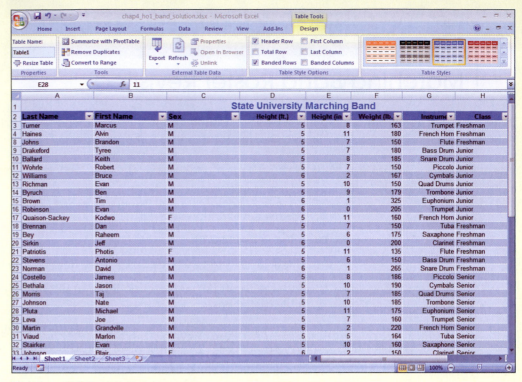

Figure 4.30 Table Created

Refer to Figure 4.31 as you complete Step 2.

a. Click in **cell F28**, type **195**, and press **Enter**.

   You changed Michael Pluta's weight to 195 from 175. Editing a single field is
   done in this manner everywhere in the table. Click the cell and type the change.

b. Click **cell A11**, click the **Home tab**, and click the **Insert** down arrow in the **Cells**
   group. Select **Insert Table Rows Above**. Type the following data for the new
   record:

Cell address	Data
A11	Thomas
B11	Joe
C11	M
D11	6
E11	3
F11	167
G11	Tuba
H11	Sophomore
I11	4550

You inserted a blank record for row 11 and entered all the data for that record.

c. Save the workbook with the new record.

d. Select **cells A11:I11**, open the **Delete** down arrow in the Cells group, and select **Delete Table Rows.**

You deleted Joe Thomas from the data table and now see that Robert Wohrle is record 11.

TROUBLESHOOTING: If you accidently press Delete, the entire record is deleted, but the blank row remains.

e. Select **cells H3:H63**, open the **Find & Select** down arrow in the Editing group, and select **Replace**.

f. In the **Find what** box, type **Sophomore**; in the **Replace with** box, type **Junior**.

g. Click the **Replace All** button and a Microsoft Office Excel message box appears, indicating the number of replacements made.

h. Click **OK**, and then click **Close** to close the Replace box.

You replaced all sophomores with juniors and would repeat this step for each class after graduation. Because this is a fictitious scenario, you will not replace other text.

TROUBLESHOOTING: If no replacements were made, verify the spelling in the Find text box. Remember that using Replace All allows Excel to make the decision to replace all occurrences automatically. You must click the Replace button to manually approve the replace if you do not want all replaced automatically.

i. Click **Undo** on the Quick Access Toolbar to undo the replace. Save the workbook.

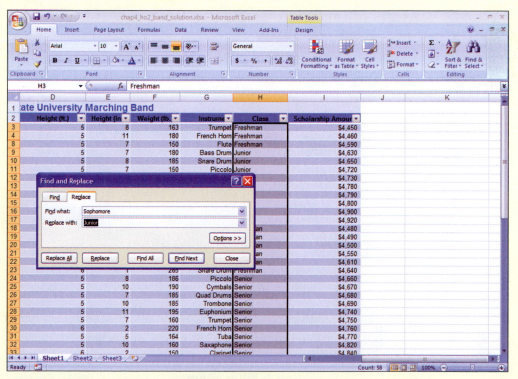

Figure 4.31 Edited Records

Step 3
Format a Table

You will explore the table style options group in this exercise by first changing the banding from rows to columns and then changing the style of the whole table. Refer to Figure 4.32 as you complete Step 3.

a. Click anywhere in the defined table, click the **Design tab**, and select **Banded Columns** in the Table Style Options group.

b. Remove the check mark from **Banded Rows** in the Table Style Options group.

c. Click the **More down arrow** in the Table Styles group to choose a visual style for the table from the **Gallery**.

Move the mouse over various table styles to preview the results. The live update is designed to provide you with a preview before making your final selection.

d. Click **Table Style Medium 7** (the last style in the first row of the Medium section).

e. Save the workbook.

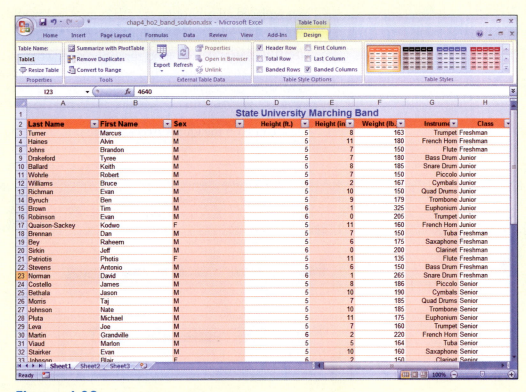

Figure 4.32 Formatting a Table

Step 4
Sort a Table

Refer to Figure 4.33 as you complete Step 4.

a. Click in any cell in **column H**, click the **Data tab**, and click **Sort A to Z** in the **Sort & Filter** group.

You have sorted the marching band roster alphabetically by Class (Freshman, Junior, Senior, Sophomore). Note this is an alphabetical sort, and there are several occurrences of the same last name in the roster.

b. Click **Sort** in the Sort & Filter group on the Data tab to open the Sort dialog box.

The Sort by Class option already exists because you last sorted using this key.

c. Click **Add Level**, click the **Then by** drop-down list, and select **Last name**.

d. Click **Add Level** again, click the **Then by** drop-down list, and select **First Name**. Click **OK** to perform the sort.

You sorted the marching band roster using multiple keys: alphabetically by Class, then by Last Name, and finally, by First Name.

e. Save the workbook.

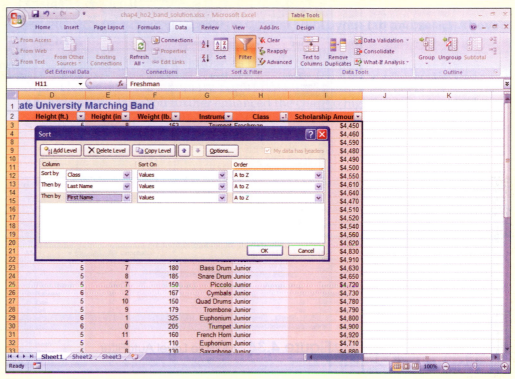

Figure 4.33 Multiple Level Sort

Step 5
Filter a Table

Refer to Figure 4.34 as you complete Step 5.

a. Click the column arrow for the **Class column** (column H). Remove the check mark from the **Select all** check box. Put a check in the **Junior** box and click **OK**.

This filter selected just the Junior members of the band and these are now the only data rows visible.

TROUBLESHOOTING: If the column headers do not display the Filter column arrows, click **Sort & Filter** in the Editing group on the Home tab and select **Filter**. Or you can click **Filter** in the Sort & Filter group on the Data tab. Either way, you will make the drop-down list visible in each column header.

b. Click the **Instrument** column arrow (column G) and **remove the check mark** for **Select all**. Place a check in the **Euphonium** box and click **OK**.

You have now reduced the Junior members to just those who play the Euphonium.

- Click the **Header/Footer tab,** click **Custom Header,** and type **Your Name** in the Left section, **Marching Band Roster** in the Center section, and your instructor's name in the Right section and click **OK.**

- Click the **Custom Footer** and use the icons to insert the date in the Left section and the page number in the Right section. Click **OK.**

- Click the **Margins tab** and select **Horizontally** and **Vertically** in the *Center on page* section.

- Click the **Sheet tab** and select **Over, then down** in the *Page order* section. Also check **Gridlines** in the *Print* section.

- Click **Print Preview** to make sure you have entered or selected the correct options.

- Click **Close Print Preview.**

It is important to view your worksheet before printing to verify your selections for headers and footers, page numbers, orientation, gridlines, and any other choices you make in the page setup dialog box.

c. Click **Page Break Preview** on the status bar and click **OK** in the Welcome message box.

d. Drag the vertical page break blue dashed line to the left so the page break is between columns E and F.

e. Drag the horizontal page break blue dashed line so it is between rows 36 and 37.

f. Click **Page Layout** view on the status bar and click **Page Setup Dialog Box Launcher** in the Page Layout tab.

g. Click **Print Preview** in the Page Setup dialog box to preview your spreadsheet.

h. Click **Print** and click **OK** to print your worksheet. Save the workbook and exit Excel.

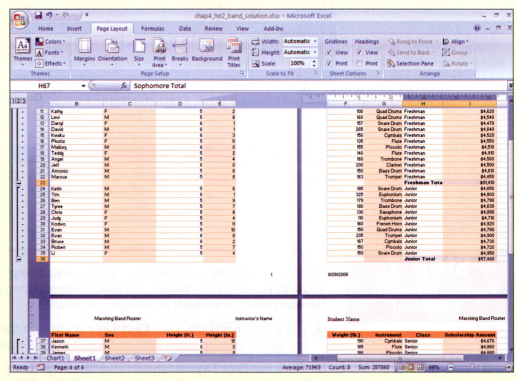

Figure 4.36 Page Layout View

Summary

1. **Freeze rows and columns.** Working with large worksheets, those that are too big for one monitor screen, can confuse users because they are not able to view the entire worksheet at one time. When working with a large worksheet, it is necessary to know how to view parts of the worksheet not visible, how to keep some parts of the worksheet always in view, and how to hide selected rows and columns. When a user is scrolling to parts of a worksheet not initially visible, some rows and columns disappear from view. It is sometimes valuable to be able to view row and column headings no matter where you scroll to, and this is done by freezing rows and columns.

2. **Hide and unhide rows, columns, and worksheets.** The hiding of rows and columns in a worksheet is a common practice and is done for a variety of reasons. It is done to conceal nonessential information, or information not needed at a particular time. There may be times when confidential information is contained in a worksheet, and rows, columns, or sheets must be hidden to allow nonauthorized users to view the worksheet.

3. **Protect a cell, a worksheet, and a workbook.** With the advent of networks and information sharing, the need evolved to protect data from change and from the wrong person. When you post a spreadsheet on the company network, it becomes available to any user of the network. They can make any change to any worksheet in the workbook file. Microsoft Excel 2007 has protection controls that, used with the proper restrictions, can ensure that the right people see only the right data.

4. **Control calculation.** Calculation is the computing of formulas and the display of the results or values in the cells that contain the formulas. In Excel, the default recalculation occurs when the cells that formulas refer to change. This default recalculation can be changed as circumstances warrant.

5. **Print large worksheets.** Printing all or parts of a large worksheet presents special challenges to even the veteran user of Excel. It is easy to make erroneous assumptions about what will print and be unpleasantly surprised. Users must consider such things as page breaks, page orientation, printing a selection, and the order in which pages will print when printing all or part of a large workbook.

6. **Explore basic table management.** Creating tables is a relatively straightforward task to complete in Excel. You choose the area in the worksheet that will contain the list, create the table, and then indicate that the table has labels or field names. Each field name must be unique to prevent confusion. Data for individual records are entered in the rows below the row of field names.

7. **Sort data.** The data in a table are often easier to understand and work with if they are in some meaningful order. Sorting arranges records in a table by the value of one or more fields within the table.

8. **Filter and total data.** Data and information are not the same thing, although you often hear the two terms used interchangeably. Data refer to facts about a specific record, such as a band member's name, his instrument, or his weight as reflected in the marching band roster you have been using. Information is data that have been arranged in some form viewed as useful. Creating a summary report computes subtotals for groups of records within a list. It is imperative that you remember that the subtotals command will not function with data in tables.

Key Terms

Multiple Choice

1. Which of the following lets you see and/or modify page breaks that will occur when the worksheet is printed?

   (a) The Page Break Preview command

   (b) The Page Setup command

   (c) The Page Breaks command

   (d) The Print Preview command

2. You are working with a large worksheet. Your row headings are in column A. Which command(s) should be used to see the row headings and the distant information in columns X, Y, and Z?

   (a) The Freeze Panes command

   (b) The Hide Rows command

   (c) The New Window command and cascade the windows

   (d) The Split Rows command

3. The command that lets you specify the order in which rows in a table appear is:

   (a) AutoFilter command

   (b) AutoFill command

   (c) Hide Rows command

   (d) Sort command

4. Columns A and B contain row headings, columns C through T contain the results of individual measurements you have taken, and columns U, V, and W contain summary and statistical information based on those measurements. What can you do to display and/or print only the row headings and the summary information?

   (a) Apply the outline feature.

   (b) Freeze rows and columns.

   (c) Hide columns C through T.

   (d) Hide columns A and B.

5. Which of the following options enables you to increase the number of columns that will be displayed on a printed worksheet?

   (a) Freezing panes

   (b) Changing from portrait to landscape orientation

   (c) Hiding columns

   (d) Using the Split command

6. You have used the AutoFilter command to display only certain rows. The other rows are not displayed. What has happened to them?

   (a) Nothing; the filtered rows are displayed in a new worksheet.

   (b) They have been written to a new worksheet.

   (c) They have been hidden.

   (d) They have been deleted.

7. All of the following statements regarding fields are true except:

   (a) Field names must be entered in the first row of the list.

   (b) Field names will change from record to record.

   (c) Field name must be unique.

   (d) Fields will be in the same order in every record.

8. Which of the following statements is true?

   (a) The Delete command can be used to delete a field, but not a record.

   (b) The Delete command can be used to delete a record, but not a field.

   (c) The Delete command erases the contents of the selected area, but does not delete it.

   (d) The Delete command can be used to delete either a record or a field.

9. You have a list of all the members of a club that you belong to. The worksheet contains other data as well. How can you be sure Excel recognizes the boundaries of the list?

   (a) Insert a comment in the upper-left corner of the list.

   (b) Insert a blank row between the field names and the data.

   (c) Insert a blank row and a blank column between the list and other data in the worksheet.

   (d) Type a row of dashes (- - -) after the last row of the list.

...continued on Next Page

10. You have a list of all the employees in your organization. The list contains employee name, office, title, and salary. You want to list all employees in each office branch. The branches should be listed alphabetically, with the employee earning the highest salary listed first in each office. Which is true of your sort order?

(a) Branch office is the primary sort and should be in ascending order.

(b) Salary is the primary sort and should be in descending order.

(c) Salary is the primary sort and should be in ascending order.

(d) Branch office is the primary sort and should be in descending order.

11. You have a list of all the employees in your organization. The list contains employee name, location, title, and salary. You want to list all employees in each location. The locations should be listed alphabetically, with the highest-paid employees listed first for each location. Which is true of your sort order?

(a) Sort by location ascending, then by salary ascending.

(b) Sort by location ascending, then by salary descending.

(c) Sort by salary descending, then by location ascending.

(d) Sort by location descending, then by salary ascending.

12. You have a list containing all the employees in your organization. You select the AutoFilter command, and then select New York from the location field. What is the result?

(a) The list is sorted by city, with New York first.

(b) The rows where the location is New York are written to another worksheet.

(c) The rows where the location is not New York are deleted.

(d) The rows where the location is not New York are hidden.

13. Which of the following statements about the AutoFilter command is true?

(a) Records that do not meet the criteria are deleted.

(b) If two criteria are entered, records must meet both conditions to be selected.

(c) Records that meet the selected criteria are copied to another worksheet.

(d) All of these statements are true.

14. How must the data be arranged before creating a summary report?

(a) In a table

(b) In a list

(c) In either a table or a list

(d) In a range

15. Which of the following will compute a summary function for groups of records within a list?

(a) The Advanced Filter command

(b) The Subtotals command

(c) The AutoFilter command

(d) The Totals command

16. You want to show total sales for each location. What should you do before executing the Subtotals command?

(a) Sort by Sales, in ascending order.

(b) Sort by Sales, in descending order.

(c) Sort by Sales, in either ascending or descending order, then by Location.

(d) Sort by Location, in either ascending or descending order.

Practice Exercises

1 West Transylvania Education Foundation Silent Auction

You are assisting the director of the Education Foundation as she prepares for the Chef's Table fundraising event. Your task is to record silent auction donations as they are delivered and prepare the printed report for the director. The completed worksheet is shown in Figure 4.37, and you will use this as a guide as you practice freezing panes, editing titles, protecting the worksheet, and hiding rows and columns.

a. Open the *chap4_pe1_auction* workbook and save it as **chap4_pe1_auction_solution** so that you can return to the original workbook if necessary. Use the horizontal scroll bar to view the worksheet, noting that some column headings disappear. Rows also disappear when you use the vertical scroll bar because the worksheet is too large to fit on one screen. You must use Freeze Panes to keep parts of the worksheet in constant view.

b. Click in **cell B3**, the cell below the row and the column to the right of the column you will freeze. Click the **View tab**, click **Freeze Panes** in the Window group, and click **Freeze Panes**. Use the vertical and horizontal scroll bars to see that the row and column data becomes visible while the row and column data labels remain constant.

c. Click **Freeze Panes** in the Window group and select **Unfreeze Panes**. Now that the panes are no longer frozen, use either scroll bar to see that the worksheet is again too large to view on one screen.

d. Edit and format a heading:
   - Click **cell A1**, select the words **Silent Auction Donor Listing** in the Formula Bar, click the **Home tab**, and then click **Cut** in the Clipboard group.
   - Right-click **row 2**, then select **Insert** from the shortcut menu to insert a new row.
   - Right-click **cell A2** and select **Paste** from the shortcut menu.
   - Select **cells A2:L2** and click **Merge & Center** in the Alignment group on the Home tab.
   - Select **cells A1:A2**, click the **Fill Color down arrow** to open the Theme Colors palette in the Font group on the Home tab, and choose **Blue**.
   - Open the **Font Color palette** in the Font group on the Home tab and choose **White, Background 1** for the title text.

e. Select **cells J4:J28**, the cells that you want to edit or protect.
   - Click **Format** in the Cells group on the Home tab and click **Format Cells** to open the Format Cells dialog box.
   - Select the **Protection tab** and clear the check mark from the **Locked box**. Click **OK**.
   - Select **Protect Sheet** in the Format drop-down list in the Cells group on the Home tab to see the Protect Sheet dialog box.
   - Check the **Select unlocked cells** option if necessary, and uncheck the Select locked cells. You unlocked cells for editing purposes and then protected or locked all other cells. The only data that you can change are Item Values in column J. Try to change any donor's name or other personal information.

f. Click **Format** in the Cells group and select **Unprotect Sheet**. Click **Format** in the Cells group and click **Protect Sheet**. Clear all check marks from the *Allow all users of this worksheet to* area and click **OK**. You must unprotect the worksheet in order to unlock the cells you previously protected and before continuing with this exercise.

g. Click **Format** in the Cells group and click **Unprotect Sheet**. Click the **Review tab**, and then click **Protect Workbook** in the Changes group. Click **Protect Structure and Windows** to open the Protect Structure and Windows dialog box. Place a check mark in the **structure** check box and click **OK**.

h. Click **Protect Workbook** in the Changes group and click **Protect Structure and Windows** to deselect it. Select **columns D** through **H** and click the **Home tab**. Open **Format** in the Cells group, select **Hide & Unhide**, and click **Hide Columns**. Columns D through H are hidden and a thick black line appears between columns C and I indicating the location of the hidden columns.

...continued on Next Page

i. Select **rows 6** through **12** and click **Format** in the Cells group, select **Hide & Unhide**, and click **Hide Rows**. Rows 6 through 12 are hidden, and a thick black line appears between rows 5 and 13, indicating the location of the hidden rows.

j. Click the **Sheet2 tab** to make it active, click the **Home tab**, and click **Format** in the Cells group. Select **Hide & Unhide**, then click **Hide Sheet** to hide Sheet2.

k. Add your name in **cell A30**. Click the **Page Layout tab**, click **Orientation**, and select **Landscape**. Click **Size**, select **More Paper sizes**, and pick **Fit to** 1 page. Click the **Margins tab**, then check to center the worksheet **horizontally**. Click the **Sheet tab**. Check the **Row and Column Headings** and **Gridlines**. Click **OK**. Print the worksheet, save the workbook, and exit Excel.

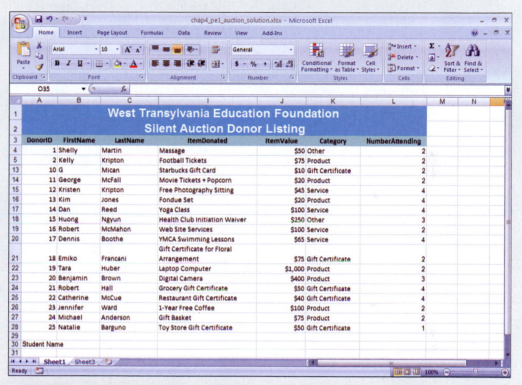

Figure 4.37   Silent Auction

2 West Transylvania Education Foundation Donor List

You are assisting the director of the Education Foundation as she prepares for the major funding event of the year. Your task is to format for printing and print the list of donors and their personal information so that they can receive an acknowledgement for income tax purposes. The completed worksheet is shown in Figure 4.38, and you will use this figure as a guide as you work with page breaks, page orientation, and control print order.

a. Open the *chap4_pe2_donor* workbook and save it as **chap4_pe2_donor_solution** so that you can return to the original workbook if necessary. You will use the Page Break Preview command to adjust the page breaks in a large spreadsheet.

b. Click the **Page Break Preview** button on the status bar in the lower-right area of the window. If you see the Welcome to Page Break Preview dialog box, click **OK**.

c. Move the **blue dashed line** that separates pages 1, and 2 to the right to eliminate the page break. You will now see just page 1 as all page breaks have been eliminated. Click the **Normal** button on the status bar to return to normal view.

d. Change the **Page Orientation** by clicking the **Page Layout tab** and click **Orientation**. Click **Landscape**.

...continued on Next Page

- Click the **Page Setup Dialog Box Launcher** on the Page Layout tab to launch the Page Setup dialog box.
- Click the **Header/Footer tab** and create a custom footer with **Your Name** in the center position.
- Click **Print Preview** and verify that the worksheet will print on one page.
- Click **Print** to print the worksheet.

e. Click in **cell A16**, open **Breaks** on the Page Layout tab, and select **Insert Page Break**. Select **column H**, open **Breaks** on the Page Layout tab, and select **Insert Page Break**. Click the **Page Break** Preview button on the status bar.

f. Click the **Page Setup Dialog Box Launcher** on the Page Layout tab.
- Click the **Sheet tab** and click the **Over, then down button** in the Page order section and verify that Gridlines and Row and column headings are selected.
- Click **Print Preview** and verify that you will print four pages.
- Click **Print**.

g. Save the workbook and exit Excel.

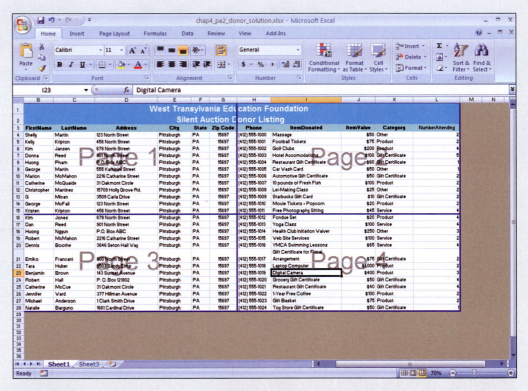

Figure 4.38 Education Foundation Donor List

3 XYZ Corporation Employee List

Your summer internship in the XYZ Corporation human resources department gives you the opportunity to practice your Excel skills. You are tasked with preparing a series of employee reports. You will use Excel and the data table feature to sort and filter the data into reports required by management. The data table you will work with is shown in Figure 4.39, and you will use this as a guide as you work with sorts and filters, but you will print several different pages.

a. Open the *chap4_pe3_xyz* workbook and save it as **chap4_pe3_xyz_solution** so that you can return to the original workbook if necessary. Select **cells A1:H156**, click the **Insert tab**, and click **Table**. Verify the range in the Where is the data for your table? text box, check **My table has headers**, and click **OK**. You defined the worksheet data as a table.

...continued on Next Page

b. Click anywhere in the defined table, click the **Design tab**, and then click **Banded Columns** in the Table Style Options group. Remove the check mark from **Banded Rows** in the Table Style Options group on the Design tab. Click the **More Command** button in the Table Styles group on the Design tab and select **Table Style Medium 12**.

c. Insert a new row above row 1 and type: **XYZ Corporation Employee List** in **cell A1**. Merge and center the title in **cells A1** through **H1**, and format the titles as **Comic Sans, 16, Bold**. Fill the title area with **Purple** color, and change the font color to **White, Background 1**. Select **cells F3:F157** and format as currency, no decimals.

d. Select **cell A11** and click the Insert down arrow in the Cells group. Select **Insert Table Rows Above**. Type the following data for the new record:

Cell address	Data
A11	12378
B11	Your Last Name
C11	Your First Name
D11	Your Gender
E11	Trainee
F11	37800
G11	Kansas City
H11	Excellent

e. Select **cells A17:H17**, open the **Delete** down arrow in the Cells group on the Home tab, and select **Delete Table Rows**. You deleted Maylou Sampieri from the data table.

f. Select **cells G3:G157**, click the **Find & Select** drop-down list in the Editing group on the Home tab, and select **Replace**. In the **Find what** box, type **Atlanta**; in the **Replace with** box, type **Miami**. The company moved its branch office. Click the **Replace All** button and a Microsoft Office Excel message box appears indicating the number of replacements made. Click **OK**, and then click **Close** to close the Replace box.

g. Select **cells A4:H11**, then open **Print Area** in the Page Setup group on the Page Layout tab. Click **Set Print Area**.
   • Click the **Page Setup Dialog Box Launcher** on the Page Layout tab to launch the Page Setup dialog box.
   • Click **Print Preview** and verify that your selection is correct. Click the **Print** button to print your selection.
   • Click **Print Area** in the Page Setup group on the Page Layout tab and select **Clear Print Area**.

h. Click in any cell in column G, click the **Data** tab, and click **Sort A to Z** in the Sort & Filter group. The table is sorted by branch office location.
   • Click **Sort** in the Sort & Filter group on the Data tab to open the Sort dialog box. Click **Add Level**, open the **Then by** drop-down list, and select **Last name**.
   • Click **Add Level** again, open the **Then by** drop-down list, and select **First Name**. Click **OK** to perform the sort. You sorted the employee list by location, last name, and finally by first name.

i. Select **cells A22:H39**, then open **Print Area** in the Page Setup group on the Page Layout tab. Click **Set Print Area**. Click the **Page Setup Dialog Box Launcher** on the Page Layout tab to launch the Page Setup dialog box. Click Sheet tab and select Row and column headings, then click **Print Preview** and verify that your selection is correct. Click the **Print** button to print your selection.

j. Click **Print Area** in the Page Setup group on the Page Layout tab and select **Clear Print Area**. Click the column arrow for **Title** (column E). **Remove the check mark** from the **Select all** check box. Put a check in the **Trainee** box and click **OK**. This filter selected just the Trainees in the corporation, and these are now the only data rows visible.

...continued on Next Page

k. Open the **Performance** column arrow (column H) and remove the check mark for **Select all**. Place a check in the **Excellent** box and click **OK**. You have reduced the Trainees to just those whose performance has been rated Excellent.

l. Click the **Page Setup Dialog Box Launcher** on the Page Layout tab to launch the Page Setup dialog box. Click the **Page tab** and select **Landscape** as well as **Fit to 1 page**. Click the **Header/Footer tab** and insert a custom footer with your name in the center section. Click the **Sheet** tab and select **Gridlines** and **Row and columns** headings, then click **Print Preview** and verify your changes. Click the **Print** button to print your filtered table.

m. Save and close the workbook.

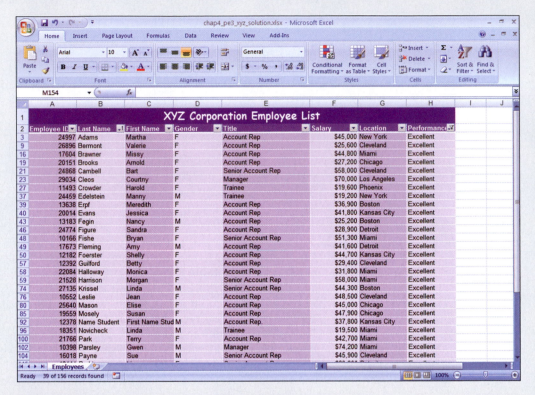

Figure 4.39 XYZ Corporation Employee List

4 Widget Employee List

As the director of Human Resources for the Widget Group, you will complete a worksheet that will show a total of salaries paid and further break down salaries by employee title. In addition, you will create a chart that shows salaries by job title. The worksheet and chart will help you assess salary outlays. The data table you will work with is shown in Figure 4.40, and you will use this as a guide as you work with sorts, summary reporting, and charting.

a. Open the *chap4_pe4_widget* workbook and save it as **chap4_pe4_widget_solution** so that you can return to the original workbook if necessary.

b. Click in any cell in column E, click the **Data tab**, and click **Sort A to Z** in the Sort & Filter group. The table is sorted by job title.

   • Click **Sort** in the Sort & Filter group on the Data tab to open the Sort dialog box. Click **Add Level**, open the **Then by** drop-down list, and select **Last Name**.

   • Click **Add Level** again, open the **Then by** drop-down list, and select **First Name**. Click **OK** to perform the sort. You sorted the employee list by job title, last name, and finally, by first name. The sort was the necessary first step in the creation of the summary report.

c. Click in any cell in column H, click the **Design tab**, and then check **Total Row** in the **Table Style Options** group. Scroll to see that you now have a total in cell H158 with a row label in A158. Make sure that any cell in the table is selected and that the table is

...continued on Next Page

sorted by Title before continuing. Click **Convert to Range** in the **Tools** group on the Design tab. Click **Yes** in the Microsoft Office Excel warning box.

d. Click the **Data tab**, and then click **Subtotal** in the Outline group to open the Subtotal dialog box. Open the drop-down list for the *At each change in* label and select **Title**. Open the drop-down list for *Use function* and select **Sum**. Make sure there is a check in **Salary**. If necessary, check **Replace current subtotals** and **Summary below data**. Click **OK**. Scroll through your list to see the Summary Report totals for Salaries for each Title group.

e. Select **cells A102** through **H108**, click the **Page Layout tab**, and then click **Print Area** in the Page Setup group. Click **Set Print Area**. Click the **Page Setup Dialog Box Launcher** on the Page Layout tab to launch the Page Setup dialog box. Click **Sheet tab** and select Row and columns headings, then click **Print Preview** and verify that your selection is correct. Click the **Print** button to print your selection.

f. Select **cells E101**, **H101**, **E108**, **H108**, **E143**, **H143**, **E161**, and **H161**. Remember to use Ctrl while selecting noncontiguous cells.
   - Click the **Insert tab**, open the **Column** drop-down list in the Charts group, and select **Clustered Column**.
   - Click the **Move Chart** button in the Location group on the **Design** tab to open the Move Chart dialog box. Click **New sheet** and click **OK**. Select the legend and delete it.

g. Click **Data Labels** in the Labels group on the Layout tab and select **Outside End**. Click **Chart** title on the Labels group on the Layout tab and select **Above Chart**. Type **Salary by Job Type** as the title of the chart. Save the file.

h. You will format the worksheet for printing by adding a custom header and footer. Click **Page Layout** view on the status bar, reduce the **Zoom** view to about **70%**, and scroll to view 10 pages. Click the **Page Setup Dialog Box Launcher** on the Page Layout tab to view the Page Setup dialog box. Select **Landscape**, and on the Header/Footer tab, click Custom header and type your name in the Left section, **The Widget Group** in the Center section, and your **Instructor's Name** in the Right section. Click **OK**.

i. Click the **Custom** footer button and use the icons to insert the date in the Left section and the page number in the Right section. Click **OK**. Click the **Margins tab** and select **Horizontally** and **Vertically** in the *Center on page* section. Make left and right margins .25". Click the **Sheet tab** and select check **Gridlines** in the **Print** section. Click **Print Preview** to make sure you have entered or selected these options.

j. Click Close Print Preview. Click **Print**, and then click **OK** to print your worksheet. Save and close the workbook.

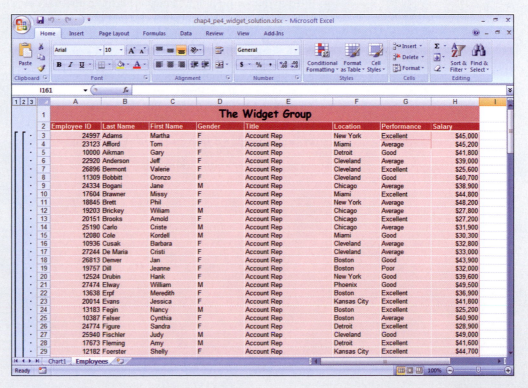

Figure 4.40 Widget Salary Analysis

...continued on Next Page

Weddings by Grace is in the final stages of a wedding plan, your task as Grace's assistant is to group the guests attending the wedding by table number. The guests already have been assigned to a table based on their reception card returns. In addition, you will prepare a summary report showing how many guests will be seated at each table. You will print a report for Grace. Figure 4.41 shows the completed worksheet. Use this figure as a guide as you complete your worksheet, which will include subtotals, sorting, hiding columns, and printing a large worksheet.

a. Open the *chap4_mid1_wedding* workbook and save it as **chap4_mid1_wedding_solution** so that you can return to the original workbook if necessary.

b. Freeze rows 1 and 2 so that they are always visible. In cell A80, which is the first blank cell at the bottom of the list of guests, add your name and that of your guest in the appropriate columns. Type **2** as the number attending; you will be sitting at Table 01. Click in **cell A81** and enter your instructor's name and guest. Your instructor will be sitting at Table 02 and **2** will attend.

c. Combine the Names in Column E, Guest Names. Use the formal forms of Address, for example; Mr. and Mrs. Joe Sutherland, Ms. Nancy Miles and Mr. Jack Wadsworth, Drs. Sam and Judy Grauer. (Hint: Use the Concatenate function.)

d. Click and drag to select the column headings for columns A, B, C, and D so that all four columns are selected. Right-click in any cell in the four selected columns and click **Hide** in the shortcut menu.

e. Click in **cell F3**. Sort the guests by table number in sequential order then last name and first name ascending.

f. Use the Subtotal command to display the associated subtotal dialog box. The subtotals should be calculated at each change in table; that is, use the Sum function to add the total to the Number field. Check the boxes to replace current subtotals and to place the summary below data.

g. Add a yellow fill color to highlight the cells that contain your name and your instructor's name. Merge and center the text in **cells E1:G1**. Increase the font size in the worksheet title to 48, change the font to Comic Sans MS, bold the title, and then Align Right. Add a clip art image and resize columns and rows as appropriate.

h. The worksheet looks better if it is centered and printed on two pages. Display the worksheet in Page Break Preview and adjust the break so that the guests at Table 08 start the second page. Use the Page Setup dialog box to repeat rows 1 and 2 on both pages and preview the pages to be sure that two pages will print. Adjust top and bottom margins if necessary. Print the completed worksheet.

i. Save and close the workbook.

...continued on Next Page

Figure 4.41 Weddings by Grace

2 The Job Search

As the personnel director, you maintain a list of applicants. You are searching for applicants for two different positions. For the first, the position requires people who are bilingual, do not require relocation, and are judged to be experienced. The second position is a directorship requiring no relocation. You will print a report of the qualified applicants for consideration by the vice president for Human Resources. Figure 4.42 shows the completed worksheet results of the second filter, and you will use the figure as a guide as you complete your worksheet. Your work will include converting data to a table, sorting the data, applying multiple filters, formatting the table, and formatting for printing.

a. Open the *chap4_mid2_jobsearch* workbook and save it as **chap4_mid2_ jobsearch_ solution** so that you can return to the original workbook if necessary.

b. Select **cells A2:H176** and convert the range of data to a data table. Sort by last name, and then by first name.

c. Click the **Bilingual** column arrow and select only those who are bilingual. Click the **Relocation** column arrow and select only those who do not have to be relocated. Finally, click the **Experience** column arrow and select only those who are judged to be experienced.

d. Format the title as shown in Figure 4.42.

e. You will format the worksheet in an attractive fashion. Use the Page Setup command to create a custom footer with your name, the date, and the name of the class you are taking. Display gridlines and row and column headings. Be sure the worksheet fits on one page. Print the worksheet.

f. Clear the three filters from the worksheet in order to initiate a second search for applicants who are applying for the position of "Director" and do not require relocation. Print this worksheet for your instructor and hand in both worksheets.

g. Save and close the workbook.

...continued on Next Page

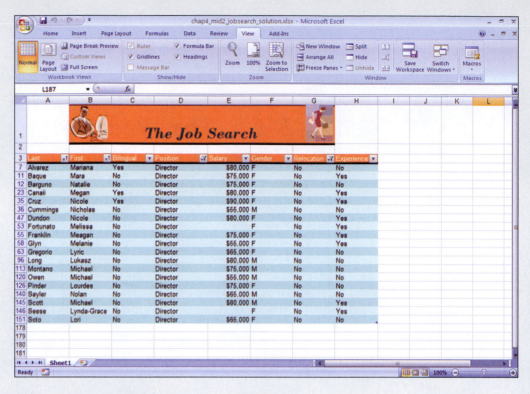

Figure 4.42 Job Search

3 Searching for a Doctor

You have just moved to Florida with your family and are searching for a doctor or doctors who can satisfy your family medical needs. You have obtained a list of more than 80 board-certified physicians from the state licensing agency. In this exercise, you will narrow the list using filters to a particular specialty, the city they practice in, and whether they take new patients. Furthermore, you will sort, format, and print the results for your family. Figure 4.43 shows the completed worksheet results. Use the figure as a guide as you complete your worksheet. You work will include converting data to a table, sorting the data, applying multiple filters, formatting, and formatting for printing.

a. Open the *chap4_mid3_physicians* workbook and save it as **chap4_mid3_ physicians_ solution** so that you can return to the original workbook if necessary.

b. Select **cells A1:H83** and convert the range of data to a data table.

c. Click the **City** column arrow and select only those who practice in Fort Lauderdale. Click the **Specialty** column arrow and select **Cardiology** and **Internal Medicine**. Finally, click the **New Patients** column arrow and select only those who accept new patients (TRUE).

d. Sort by specialty, last name, and then by first name.

e. Use the Page Setup command to create a custom header with your name, the date, and the name of the class you are taking. Display gridlines and row and column headings. Be sure the worksheet fits on one page. Print the worksheet.

f. Save and close the workbook.

...continued on Next Page

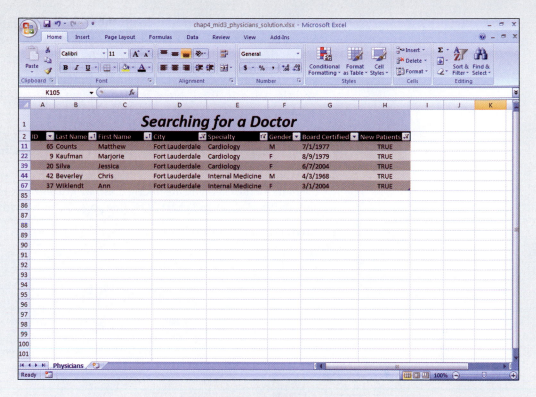

Figure 4.43 Searching for a Doctor

4 Population Analysis

Your geography professor has given you an assignment to analyze population data of the 50 states in the United States. In this exercise, you will determine the population density of each state, sort the states by geographic region, prepare a summary report showing the population by region, and prepare a chart illustrating the region populations. Finally, you will filter the list to show only those states in a particular geographic region and print both the chart and the filtered report. Figure 4.44 shows the filtered worksheet results with chart; use the figure as a guide as you complete your worksheet. The work you perform will include converting data to a table, sorting the data, applying multiple filters, creating a chart, formatting, and formatting for printing.

a. Open the *chap4_mid4_population* workbook and save it as **chap4_mid4_ population_ solution** so that you can return to the original workbook if necessary.

b. Click in **cell F2** and enter the formula to calculate population density (population divided by area). Copy the formula for all states. Format the population as number with 1 decimal.

c. Sort the range by region and then by state.

d. Create a summary report showing population subtotals by region. Use the Subtotal command to display the associated subtotal dialog box. The subtotals should be calculated at each change in region. Use the **Sum** function to add the total to the Population field. Check the boxes to replace current subtotals and to place the summary below data.

e. Add a fill color to highlight the cells that contain the region name and the region's total population. Create a clustered column chart on a separate sheet that shows total population by region. Be sure to format the chart in an aesthetically pleasing manner, include a descriptive title. Rename the Chart1 tab **Region Chart**.

...continued on Next Page

f. Insert a row on Sheet1, then type the title **Population Statistics**. Select **cells A2:F60** and convert the list of data to a data table. Format the table using one of the table styles and format the title of the worksheet to match.

g. Filter the table by clicking the Region column arrow and select only Middle Atlantic, Middle Atlantic Total, New England, New England Total, South Atlantic, South Atlantic Total.

h. Create a pie chart as an object on the worksheet showing total population by the three geographic regions. Format the chart so it is color coordinated with your data table.

i. Use the Page Setup command to create a custom footer with your name, the date, and the name of the class you are taking. Display gridlines and row and column headings. Be sure the worksheet and chart fit on one page. Print the worksheet and the region chart.

j. Save and close the workbook.

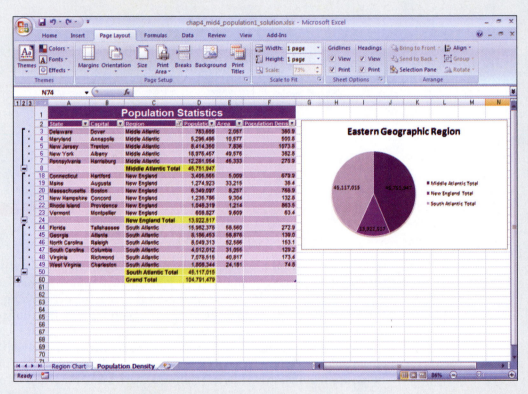

Figure 4.44 Population Analysis

Capstone Exercise

You are an intern with the Regional Realty Association and are analyzing the claim made by Alice Barr Realty that "we get your price." You have prepared a spreadsheet that shows data relating to three months' sales by Alice Barr Realty. You are going to determine the percent of asking price for each home sold that month. Determine which sales people have the most total sales and determine how many sales are made within the city of Miami. You will prepare an attractively formatted summary report for your boss and a chart showing the total sales by sales person.

Open and Save Worksheet

You must open a worksheet that lists home sales for three months.

a. Open the file *chap4_cap_barr*.

b. Save it as **chap4_cap_barr_solution**.

Calculate Percent of Asking Price and Format the Data

A formula is used to calculate the percent of asking price, and this formula is applied to all listed sales. You will format the list in an attractive and useful manner.

a. The percent of asking price is calculated by dividing the selling price by asking price. Enter the formula in column F.

b. Format columns D and E as currency, no decimals. Format columns G and H as dates so just the day and month (for example, 5-May) are visible. Change column F to a percentage with one decimal.

c. Widen columns to make all data and headings visible. Format titles as appropriate for the Regional Realty Association. Bold and center the column headings.

Sort the Data and Prepare the Summary Report and Chart

In order to sort the data by asking price and sales person, you must first convert the list to a data table. Once the data

are sorted, in order to prepare the summary report, you must convert the data table back into a range.

a. Convert the range to a data table.

b. Sort the data by selling agent and then by asking price.

c. Format the data table attractively.

d. Convert the data table back to a range.

e. Prepare a summary report showing total asking price and selling price by agent.

f. Use a fill color to highlight each sales person's total asking price and selling price.

g. Prepare a chart on a separate chart sheet that shows each sales person's total asking price and selling price. Include a title and a legend, and format the chart to compliment the worksheet. Rename the chart sheet tab Sales Analysis.

h. Print the chart.

Filter the Data Table and Print the Report

Your report should list just those properties sold in Miami by agent Carey, and you will use a filter to extract this data. Further, you must format before printing to make sure the report is documented and fits on one page.

a. Convert the range to a data table and filter the data table to show only those properties sold in Miami by agent Carey. Delete the Summary Total and Grand Total from the bottom of the filtered list.

b. Create a custom header with your name on the left and your instructor's name on the right. Change the orientation to landscape, center horizontally and vertically, and print gridlines and row and column headings. Preview your worksheet and make any necessary adjustments to print on one page. Save your changes, print the worksheet, and print the Sales Analysis chart.

Mini Cases

Use the rubric following the case as a guide to evaluate your work, but keep in mind that your instructor may impose additional grading criteria or use a different standard to judge your work.

Night on the Nile

GENERAL CASE

The University Museum is celebrating the 30th anniversary of founding with a glamorous "evening along the Nile River" theme that includes fine art, fine food, and lively entertainment featuring Egyptian dance and music. As a recent graduate and newly hired employee at the University Museum, you are tasked with maintaining the guest list, assigning guests to tables, and tracking payments for the fundraising dinner. Open the *chap4_mc1_nile* workbook and save it as **chap4_mc1_nile_solution**. You will convert the list to a data table and sort the data table. You will create a formula to calculate the total amount of revenue; the cost per person is $125. You will create a summary report to determine revenue by table and highlight the table totals. Format the completed worksheet as appropriate. Place your name somewhere in the worksheet. Be sure to use the Page Setup dialog box and tabs to create a custom header with the current date and page number, repeat the title rows on all pages, and center vertically and horizontally. Print the report. You will filter the report to determine who has not yet paid and then print this report as well.

Performance Elements	Exceeds Expectations	Meets Expectations	Below Expectations
Create and sort table	Table created correctly with headings.	Table created without headings.	No table created.
Create formula	Formula entered correctly.	Formula incorrectly used.	No formulas, numbers entered.
Summary report	Well formatted and easy to find totals.	Adequately formatted, difficult to identify totals.	No summary report.
Appropriate format for printing	All print format requirements met.	All but one print format requirement met.	Two or more print formats missing.

Census Data

RESEARCH CASE

Your geography professor has given you an assignment to analyze population data for the last three censuses. In this exercise, you use the census Web site to research the last three censuses, 1980, 1990, and 2000, to find the population for each of the 50 states. Once you determine the population of each state, you will sort the states by geographic region, prepare a summary report showing the population for all three censuses by region, and print the report. Finally, you will filter the list to show only those states in your geographic region. Prepare a chart illustrating the region populations and print both the chart and the filtered report. Open the *chap4_mc2_census* workbook and save as **chap4_mc2_census_solution**.

Performance Elements	Exceeds Expectations	Meets Expectations	Below Expectations
Research census statistics	All three censuses found.	Missing 2 censuses.	No census data.
Create and sort table	Table created correctly with headings.	Table created without headings.	No table created.
Summary report	Well formatted and easy to find totals.	Adequately formatted, difficult to identify totals.	No summary report.
Chart	Chart correctly prepared and attractively formatted.	Chart correctly prepared with no formatting.	No chart.
Printed formatted report	Both summary report and chart printed.	Either summary report or chart printed.	Nothing printed.

Peer Tutoring

DISASTER RECOVERY

Your service-learning project, tutoring students, is coming to an end, but you must provide assistance with data tables, summary reports, and summary charting in your final session. The assignment your tutoring student is working to complete is for a Political Science course that is analyzing the 2004 Presidential Election. Open the spreadsheet *chap4_mc3_tutoring* and save it as **chap4_mc3_tutoring_solution**, then find three errors. Correct the errors and explain how the errors might have occurred and how they can be prevented. Include your explanation in the cells below the spreadsheet. Review formula creation, summary report creation, and chart creation.

Performance Elements	Exceeds Expectations	Meets Expectations	Below Expectations
Identify 3 errors	Identified all 3 errors.	Identified 2 errors.	Identified 0 errors.
Correct 3 errors	Corrected all 3 errors.	Corrected 2 errors.	Corrected 1 or fewer errors.
Explain the error	Complete and correct explanation of each error.	Explanation is too brief to fully explain error.	No explanations.
Prevention description	Prevention description correct and practical.	Prevention description but obtuse.	No prevention description.

Data to Information

Data Tables, Conditional Formatting, PivotTables, and PivotCharts

Objectives

After you read this chapter, you will be able to:

1. Design tables based on data table theory **(page 305)**.

2. Import data from text files and other sources **(page 306)**.

3. Apply conditional formatting **(page 309)**.

4. Apply advanced filtering and sorting methods **(page 319)**.

5. Create and use range names **(page 324)**.

6. Use database functions **(page 327)**.

7. Create and delete PivotTables and PivotCharts **(page 341)**.

8. Format, sort, filter, subtotal, and refresh a PivotTable **(page 345)**.

Hands-On Exercises

Exercises	Skills Covered
1. **GEE AIRLINES HUMAN RESOURCES DEPARTMENT** (page 314) **Open:** chap5_ho1_hremployee.txt and chap3_ho1_hremployee.accdb **Save as:** chap5_ho1_hremployee_solution.xlsx	• Use the Text Import Wizard • Apply and Clear Conditional Formatting • Import Access Data • Apply Color Scales and Icon Sets Conditional Formatting
2. **GEE AIRLINES HUMAN RESOURCES DEPARTMENT REVISITED** (page 332) **Open:** chap5_ho1_hremployee_solution.xlsx (from Exercise 1) **Save as:** chap5_ho2_hremployee_solution.xlsx (additional modifications)	• Use Date Arithmetic • Sort and Filter with Conditional Formatting • Use Custom AutoFilter • Create a Criteria Range and Use an Advanced Filter • Define a Named Range • Set Up a Summary Area and Use DAVERAGE • Use DMAX, DMIN, DSUM, and DCOUNT Functions • Change the Criteria
3. **EYE FIRST ADVERTISING DEPARTMENT SALES** (page 350) **Open:** chap5_ho3_salesrep.xlsx **Save as:** chap5_ho3_salesrep_solution.xlsx	• Create a PivotTable • Complete the PivotTable • Modify the Source Data and Refresh the PivotTable • Pivot the Table • Create a PivotChart • Change and Enhance the PivotChart • Complete the PivotChart • Create a Web Page from a PivotTable • Change Underlying Data

CASE STUDY

Legal Specialties

Your proficiency with Excel and data analysis has landed you an internship with a new national law firm with headquarters in Pennsylvania. The partners in the firm are in the process of recruiting lawyers to join their firm, although the real recruiting will start next month. The practice has just gotten started and fewer than 100 lawyers have signed on.

Before proceeding further, however, the partners want to analyze the lawyers already in the firm to be sure that they recruit the right specialties in the right geographic areas. Accordingly, the founder of the practice has provided you with the *chap5_case_law* file, Legal Specialties workbook containing existing data. The record for each lawyer in the workbook contains seven fields: the lawyer's first name and last name; the city in which he or she practices; the lawyer's specialty, gender, and date

of passing the bar; and an indication of whether the lawyer is accepting new clients. The founder believes an analysis of this data will provide the information he is seeking to make the necessary regional hires.

The multiple fields provide the potential for detailed analysis, for example, identifying the female lawyers in a designated specialty in a particular city or who passed the bar after a specific date. Perhaps the founder wants to locate all the criminal lawyers in the firm working in Erie for a client living in Erie. Another analysis might be to determine if any divorce lawyers who passed the bar after 2004 are accepting new cases.

Your Assignment

- Read the chapter carefully and pay close attention to sections that demonstrate creating and using data and information as well as the creation and use of PivotTable reports and PivotChart reports. Open the *chap5_case_law* file, which contains the collected data for the law firm.

- Examine the list of lawyers to determine which specialties and/or which cities are underrepresented. How would you display the data for analysis? Is a simple PivotTable report embedded on the worksheet the solution? Or is this best accomplished by creating a simple PivotTable, on its own worksheet, with the specialty in the row area and the city in the column area? What range name would you create when you are searching the data table? Consider how you would sort the data. Would you sort by last name plus first name plus city? How many levels of sort would be appropriate? Is it better to display the data using a filter with one or more filters applied?

- Count the number of lawyers for each combination of city and specialty. The founder of the practice is visually oriented and has requested a chart, as opposed to a table of numerical data. As you review the chapter, consider if conditional formatting might be used to enhance the information for the founder of the practice.

- Determine who the most experienced lawyers are in the firm. Use conditional formatting to indicate the most experienced lawyers. The head of the law firm would like to know which member most recently passed the bar exam and which member first passed the bar. Use appropriate database functions to determine the most experienced and least experienced lawyers.

- Print the completed workbook. The workbook should contain three worksheets: the complete list of participating lawyers, the PivotTable report, and the corresponding PivotChart report. Print the PivotChart in landscape orientation. Be sure that all of the fields for each lawyer fit on one page; this worksheet will still require a second page, and thus the first several rows with the column headings and descriptive information should appear on both pages.

- Create a custom footer that includes your name, a page number, and your instructor's name. Print the worksheet as displayed. Save the workbook as **chap5_case_law_solution**.

Table Management

People often refer to data and information as if the words refer to the same thing. In fact, however, data and information are different. If the terms were put on a continuum, it would be easy to say that you start with data and end with information. Data are facts about a specific record. Information is data put into a useful form by a user.

> All organizations maintain data in order to produce information that is used to make informed decisions.

A series of names is data, but sorting the list alphabetically and adding the title *Class Roster* to the list of names transforms data into useful information. Another example, the date July 4, 1776, is data; stating that the Declaration of Independence was signed on July 4, 1776, becomes information.

All organizations maintain data in order to produce information that is used to make informed decisions. Data are converted to information through a combination of database functions and commands discussed in this chapter. You can prepare many reports from a data table in Excel using database functions and commands such as custom sorts, advanced filters, and other specialized reporting techniques. In this section, you design tables based on data table theory, import text files, and apply conditional formatting.

Designing Tables Based on Data Table Theory

Often, data tables are created from existing files, and little or no thought is put into the creation of a data table that will be used for complex data analysis. A poorly designed table may result in flawed analysis or make it impossible to generate the information a company requires. Just as you spent time planning a spreadsheet, you should plan the elements of a data table. You should think about who will use the data table, what types of reports will be produced, and what types of searches might be done. As a general rule, the more thorough your planning process is, the fewer changes will be needed to the table after it is created and in use. Though it is not always necessary, it can be helpful to set up a small table with your field names and sample data. You can then create field names that are descriptive of their function in your table.

Below are some guidelines that can make the construction of a data table more efficient:

- The top row should contain the field names for the data table.
- Field names should be short, descriptive, and easy to remember.
- Formatting the field names makes them easy for users to identify.
- Each column should contain the same type of information for each row in the table.
- Though a table can be just part of a worksheet, it helps to separate it from other elements of the spreadsheet.

Importing Data from Text Files and Other Sources

Importing is the process of inserting data from another application. As you work in an organization, you will probably need to import data created in another format or in another application into an Excel table. This often occurs when data are stored on a mainframe computer, an Access database table, or another source and are then analyzed on a PC. Though it is possible to import text files as an external data range where the data remains outside Excel, generally, you will want to import a text file by opening it, forgoing the conversion that is necessary when importing a file as an external data range.

Depending on your future needs, you may want to import files using the Open dialog box. Doing so imports the original data but does not maintain a connection to the original data. Changes in the original data do not update in Excel. If you want to maintain a connection to the original data, use the commands in the Get External Data group on the Data tab to import data from several supported source formats, such as text files, Access database tables, Web data, and other sources. When you want to maintain a connection to the data source, use the Data Connection Wizard to create the connection. To see existing data connections, click Existing Connections in the Get External Data group on the Data tab. You will want to maintain a connection to live data when using a just-in-time inventory system. Just-in-time inventory systems are commonly found in retail establishments and hospital pharmacies. If you use Excel with library circulation systems, you might maintain a live data connection. Maintaining the connection is a way to use current data without repeating the copy-and-paste or import steps each time you analyze the data.

Import a Text File

Text files, distinguished by the .txt file extension, contain ordinary textual characters with no formatting, graphical characters, or sound and video data. Text files are made up of letters, digits, and punctuation, including spaces. Comma Separated Value (CSV) files contain fields separated by commas and rows separated by a newline character. Both text and CSV-formatted files are used to exchange data between different applications. The CSV format is the standard for moving data between applications.

Text file data are often imported into Excel for use in a spreadsheet. Individual data elements are separated by a delimiter. A ***delimiter*** is a character used to separate one column from another in the text file. Fields are arranged in rows, and when imported into Excel fields become columns. The most common delimiters in a text file are commas or tabs. Figure 5.1 shows a comma-delimited text file and the Excel workbook created when the text file is imported.

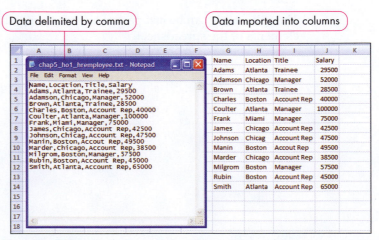

Figure 5.1 Comma-Delimited Text File and Data Imported into Excel

You can import and convert a text file created in another application into an Excel workbook. To import a text file, display the Open dialog box, select Text Files from the *Files of type* drop-down list, and then double-click the text file that contains data you want to import. If the file is a .csv file, Excel automatically converts the file and opens it. If the file is a .txt file, the Text Import Wizard appears, prompting you for information about the external data, and then converts the data into an Excel workbook during these three major steps:

1. Select *Delimited* or *Fixed width* based on how the text is formatted and set the *Start import at row* value to where you want the data to begin (see Figure 5.2). A fixed-width text file is one where fields are aligned and spaces are used to separate the fields. If the text file contains a title or extraneous data extending across multiple columns, you would not import from row 1; you would start importing from the row that contains the data. Click Next at the bottom of the Text Import Wizard – Step 1 of 3 dialog box.

2. Do one of the following in the Text Import Wizard – Step 2 of 3 dialog box, and then click Next.

   • If the text file is delimited, check the appropriate delimiter symbol, such as Tab (see Figure 5.3).

   • If the text file is fixed-width, move the column break lines to where the columns begin and end and click Next.

3. Select a *Column data format* for the columns to be imported, then click the *Do not import column* option to skip a specific column in the Text Import Wizard – Step 3 of 3 dialog box (see Figure 5.4). Click Finish.

TIP Connecting to a Text File

If you click From Text in the Get External Data group on the Data tab, you import the text file with a connection to the original text file. This approach, in contrast to the previous method, enables you to refresh the data in Excel to match any changes made to the original text file, as long as the text file is in the same location.

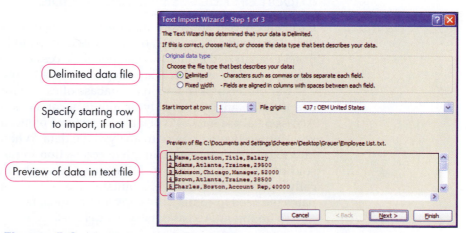

Figure 5.2 Step 1 Text Import Wizard

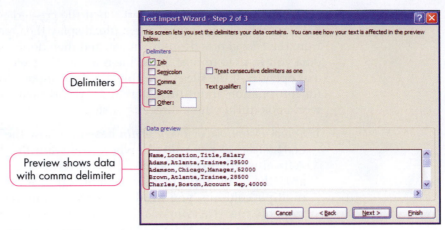

Figure 5.3 Step 2 Text Import Wizard

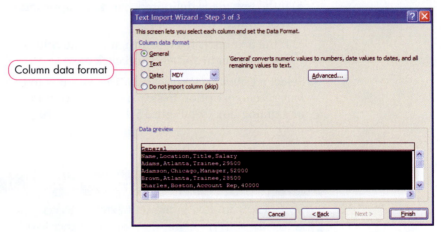

Figure 5.4 Step 3 Import Text Wizard

Import an Access Database Table

Excel and Access are two programs in the Microsoft Office 2007 Suite. As you work with Microsoft Office 2007, often you will need to import an Access database into Excel to analyze the data in more detail. Access databases may be imported in three ways: as a table, as a PivotTable Report, or as a PivotChart and Pivot Table Report.

Car dealerships maintain a database of cars in inventory and cars sold, but may use Excel to analyze weekly or monthly car sales data. The ability to import the Access database into a PivotTable Report or PivotChart and PivotTable Report gives you unprecedented power to analyze the data. When importing an Access database into Excel, you can maintain a live connection to the data. This way when cars are sold or added to inventory, in the above example, the Excel spreadsheet automatically updates. Furthermore, maintaining a connection to the Access database eliminates the need to continually copy and paste data from Access to Excel.

To import an Access database into Excel:

1. Click From Access in the Get External Data group on the Data tab.
2. In the Select Data Source dialog box, locate the Access file to be imported, select it, and click Open.
3. Choose a table from the list of Access tables and click OK.
4. In the Import Data dialog box (see Figure 5.5), select how you want to view the data in your workbook and where you want to put the data, and click OK.

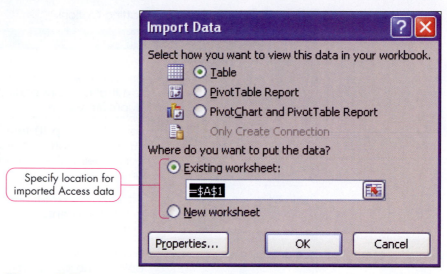

Specify location for imported Access data

Figure 5.5 Import Access Data Dialog Box

Import Data from Other Sources

Data can be imported from sources other than text files and Access databases. The From Other Sources command in the Get External Data group lists several types of sources. The other sources are listed and summarized in Table 5.1.

Table 5.1 Importing Data from Other Sources

Source	Definition
SQL Server	Create a connection to an SQL Server Table and import data as a table or PivotTable report.
Analysis Services	Create a connection to an SQL Server Analysis Services cube. Import data as a table or PivotTable report.
XML Data Import	Open or map an XML file into Excel.
Data Connection Wizard	Import data for an unlisted format by using the Data Connection Wizard or OLEDB.
Microsoft Query	Import data for an unlisted format by using the Microsoft Query Wizard and ODBC.

Applying Conditional Formatting

Conditional formatting applies specific formats to cells that contain particular values.

When the data in a cell meet specified conditions, the formatting that appears in that cell is referred to as conditional formatting. *Conditional formatting* is used to apply specific formats automatically to cells that contain particular values or content. For example, you might want to identify cells containing the year 2009 by applying a different fill color to those cells. You would use conditional formatting for this task. Conditional formatting makes it easy to highlight interesting cells or ranges of cells, emphasize unusual or duplicate values, or visualize data using data bars, color scales, or icon sets. For example, you might have every cell that contains a test score below 60% turn red. A baseball coach might want to highlight cells with batting averages above 300 in green. Conditional formatting is another way to visualize data. In conditional formatting, if the condition is true, the cell is formatted automatically based on that condition. If it is false, the cell is not formatted based on that condition. If you change a value in a conditionally formatted cell, Excel examines the new value to see if it should apply the conditional formatting. Table 5.2 lists and describes a number of different conditional formats that you can apply.

Table 5.2 Conditional Formatting Options

Conditional Formatting	Display Description
Highlight Cells Rules	Formats cells if values are greater than, less than, between two values, or equal to a value. Formats text that contains particular letters, a specific date, or duplicate values.
Top/Bottom Rules	Formats the top 10 items, the top 10%, bottom 10 items, bottom 10%, values above the average, or values below the average. This is used in education and economics statistics.
Data Bars	Displays gradient-filled horizontal bars in which the bar length represents the value in relation to other values in the column.
Color Scales	Formats different cells with different colors, assigns one color to the lowest value, another color to the highest value, and a blend of these colors to all other values.
Icon Sets	Uses an icon from the icon palette to indicate values. Sometimes used to show progress in contests. Only Excel's predefined icon set is used.

Data bars are gradient-colored bars that help you visualize the value of a cell relative to other cells.

Data bars help you visualize the value of a cell relative to other cells, as shown in Figure 5.6. The width of the gradient data bar represents the value in a cell, with a wider bar representing a higher value and a shorter bar a lower value. Data bar conditional formatting is used when identifying high and low values in large amounts of data. Excel locates the largest value and makes it the widest data bar. Excel then finds the smallest value and makes it the smallest data bar. If you change the values in your worksheet, Excel automatically updates the widths of the data bars. Data bars are used to view large values in relation to small values, are most useful when working with a big range of values, and are more effective with wider columns than narrow columns.

	A	B	C	D	E	F
1				WCCC Challenge		
2		Monday	Tuesday	Wednesday	Thursday	Friday
3	Joe Smith	14	16	19	45	36
4	Frank Thomas	4	22	54	110	90
5	Tom Jones	30	45	44	25	20
6	Leona Riley	8	6	6	17	1
7	Jane Doe	12	13	10	6	15
8	Kathy Bena	74	7	16	19	25
9	Anna Genwich	33	26	20	35	35
10	Tom Albaugh	4	29	6	10	10

Figure 5.6 Data Bars Conditional Formatting

Color scales format cells with colors based on the relative value of a cell compared to other cells.

Color scales format cells with different colors based on the relative value of a cell compared to other adjacent cells. Cells may be formatted using a two-color scale. This scale assists in comparing a range of cells using gradations of two colors. The shade of the color represents higher or lower values. Cells may also be formatted with a three-color scale. This scale helps you compare a range of cells by using gradations of three colors. The shade of the color represents the high, middle, or lower values. Figure 5.7 shows an example of color scales conditional formatting. The color scale, unlike data bars, uses shading to visualize relative values. Use color scales to understand variation in the data to identify trends, for example to view good stock returns and weak stock returns.

Figure 5.7 Color Scales Conditional Formatting

Icon sets are little graphics or symbols that display in cells based on the cell contents.

Icon sets are little graphics or symbols that display in cells and are used to classify data into three to five categories, based on the contents of the cells. The categories are separated by a threshold value. Each icon represents a range of values. The category range is assigned an icon that displays in a cell. The icons are effective when you want to annotate or present data that are quickly readable and understandable. Figure 5.8 shows a worksheet formatted with a variety of icon sets. In most worksheets, however, you would limit the icon sets to only one or two to avoid overwhelming the reader.

Figure 5.8 Icon Sets Conditional Formatting

To apply a conditional format, select the cells, click Conditional Formatting in the Styles group on the Home tab, and select the specific conditional formatting style you want to apply. For example, a weather tracker may have a spreadsheet containing the temperatures for each day of a month. She might want to conditionally format cells that contain temperatures between 70 and 75 degrees. To apply this conditional formatting, she would select Highlight Cells Rules, and then select Between. In the Between dialog box, she would type 70 in the *Format cells that are BETWEEN* and 75 in the *and* box. She would then select the type of conditional formatting.

Table 5.3 describes why you would use conditional formatting for particular types of cells.

Table 5.3 Why format?

Format What	Why
Cells that contain text, number, or date or time values	This type of formatting easily finds specific cells based on a comparison operator. This is a powerful conditional format with many options.
Only top- or bottom-ranked values	You can find the highest and lowest values in a range of cells based on a specified cutoff point and then apply formatting.
Only values above or below average	You can find and conditionally format a range of cells above or below an average or a standard deviation.
Only unique or duplicate values	This applies conditional formatting to cells that have a value that appears only once or cells that have a value that appears more than once.
Using a formula to determine which cells to format	In more complex conditional formatting, you can use logical formulas to specify the formatting criteria.

Clearing conditional formatting can be done in two ways, depending on where you want the conditional formatting removed. To remove conditional formatting from an entire sheet, click Conditional Formatting in the Styles group on the Home tab, select Clear Rules, and select Entire Sheet. To remove conditional formatting from a range of cells, a table, or a PivotTable, select the range of cells, table, or PivotTable first. Then click Conditional Formatting, select Clear Rules, and Selected Cells, This Table, or This PivotTable, as appropriate.

Create Conditional Formatting Rules

You can apply conditional formatting with either Quick Formatting or Advanced Formatting using the Conditional Formatting Rules Manager dialog box. Quick Formatting uses the options in Conditional Formatting in the Styles group on the Home tab. To apply Quick Formatting, select a range of cells or ensure that the active cell is in a table or PivotTable report. Then select the appropriate command from the Conditional Formatting drop-down list based on Table 5.2. Quick Formatting is a speedy way to apply formatting, but you cannot use it when a formula is used to determine which cells to format.

Use Advanced Formatting

The principles used with advanced formatting are similar to those used in Quick Formatting but use the Conditional Formatting Rules Manager dialog box, which provides much closer control of the conditional formatting (see Figure 5.9). To apply advanced formatting:

1. Select a range of cells or ensure the active cell is in a table or PivotTable report.
2. Click Conditional Formatting in the Styles group on the Home tab and select Manage Rules to display the Conditional Formatting Rules Manager dialog box (see Figure 5.9).
3. Click New Rule to display the New Formatting Rule dialog box (see Figure 5.10).
4. Select a new rule in the *Select a Rule Type* section.
5. Use the *Format Style* list box in the *Edit the Rule Description* section, which changes based on the general rule you select in Step 4.
6. Make appropriate choices to complete the conditional formatting.

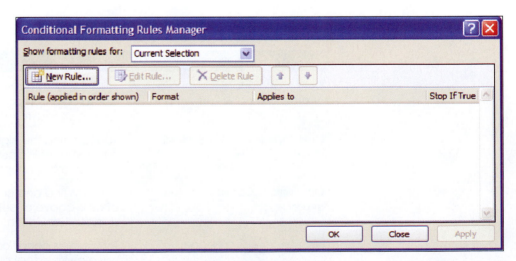

Figure 5.9 Conditional Formatting Rules Manager

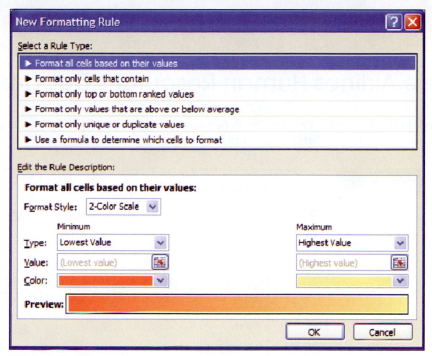

Figure 5.10 New Formatting Rule Dialog Box

Use Formulas in Conditional Formatting

Excel provides a vast number of conditional formatting options. If you need to create a complex conditional formatting rule, you can select a rule that uses a formula to format cells. For example, you might want to format gross pay cells for individuals who earn more than $10 an hour **and** who worked 5 or more overtime hours in a week to analyze your payroll budget. Figure 5.11 shows the conditional formatting applied to the gross pay column.

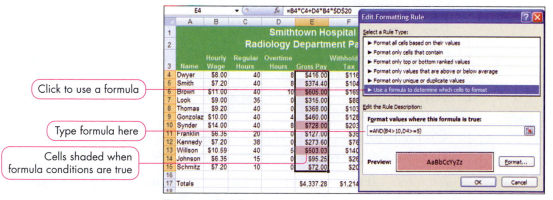

Figure 5.11 Formula-Based Conditional Formatting

To create a formula-based conditional formatting rule, select the data, click Conditional Formatting, and then select New Rule. In the New Formatting Rule dialog box, select *Use a formula to determine which cells to format* and then type the formula in the *Format values where this formula is true* box. In the previous example, the AND function requires that the hourly wage in column B be more than $10 and the overtime hours in column D be equal to or greater than 5. When both conditions are true, the cells are formatted with the fill color.

Hands-On Exercises

1 | Gee Airlines Human Resources Department

Skills covered: 1. Use the Text Import Wizard **2.** Apply and Clear Conditional Formatting **3.** Import Access Data **4.** Apply Color Scales and Icon Sets Conditional Formatting

Step 1 Use the Text Import Wizard	Refer to Figure 5.12 as you complete Step 1.

a. Start Excel, click the **Office Button**, and click **Open**.

b. Select **Text Files** from the *Files of type* drop-down list and open the *chap5_ho1_hremployee* file.

You began the process of importing a text file. The Text Import Wizard opens automatically. The wizard recognizes that the file is in delimited format.

c. Click **Next**.

d. Click the **Tab check box** to deselect this delimiter and click the **Comma check box**.

Each field is now shown in a separate column.

e. Click **Next**.

You do not need to change the default format (general) of any of the fields.

f. Click **Finish**.

You see the employee list in an Excel workbook, and the sheet tab is now named *chap5_ho1_hremployee*.

g. Select **cells A1:E1**, click **Bold** in the Font group on the Home tab, and click **Center** in the Alignment group.

These formats distinguish the field names from the data records.

h. Click the **Fill Color down arrow** in the Font group and select **Orange Accent 6, Lighter 60%**.

i. Select **cells A1:E14**, click the **Format down arrow** in the Cells group, and select **AutoFit Column Width**.

j. Select **cells E2:E14**, click the **Number Format down arrow** in the Number group, and select **Currency**. Click **Decrease Decimal** twice in the Number group.

You formatted the salary values as currency with no decimals (see Figure 5.12).

k. Save the workbook as **chap5_ho1_hremployee_solution**. Click the **Save as type drop-down arrow** and select **Excel workbook**. Click **Save**.

TROUBLESHOOTING: You opened a text file and it is assumed you will save a text file. If you use the Save As dialog box, you must use the *Save as type* drop-down arrow to select the Excel workbook file type. You can also point to Save As after clicking the Office Button, and then select Excel Workbook to save.

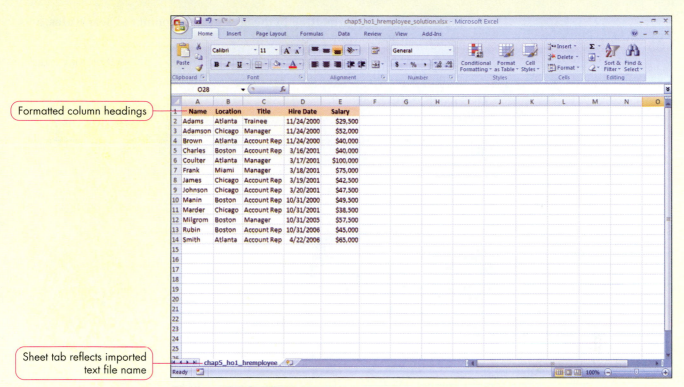

Formatted column headings

Sheet tab reflects imported text file name

Figure 5.12 Import Text File

Exporting Data from Excel

You began the exercise by importing data from a text file into an Excel workbook. You can also go in the opposite direction; that is, you can export the data in an Excel worksheet into a CSV, comma-separated value or text file, or an XML document. Click the Office Button, select Save As, and select Other Formats. Then specify the file type, e.g., a text file, by selecting the type of file you want from the *Save as type* drop-down list.

Step 2
Apply and Clear Conditional Formatting

Refer to Figure 5.13 as you complete Step 2.

a. Select **cells E2:E14** and click **Conditional Formatting** in the Styles group on the Home tab.

Conditional Formatting enables you to analyze your data. In this case, you want to select and highlight those employees whose salary is above $60,000.

b. Point to **Highlight Cells Rules** and select **Greater Than** to open the Greater Than dialog box.

c. Type $**60,000** in the **Format cells that are GREATER THAN** box.

d. Click the **with drop-down arrow**, select **Light Red Fill**, and click **OK**.

You highlighted with light red fill color those salaries greater than $60,000 in the entire data table.

e. Click **Conditional Formatting** in the Styles group, point to **Clear Rules**, and select **Clear Rules from Entire Sheet**.

You cleared all conditional formatting from the data table so it is not brought into the next exercise.

f. Save the workbook.

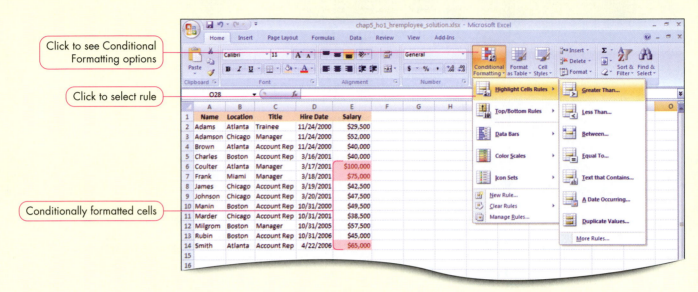

Figure 5.13 Conditional Formatting

Step 3
Import Access Data

Refer to Figure 5.14 as you complete Step 3.

a. Click **From Access** in the Get External Data group on the Data tab and open the *chap5_ho1_hremployee* file.

The Import Data dialog box opens so you can select how you want to view the data and where they are placed.

b. Verify that Table is selected, click **New worksheet** to place the data on a new worksheet, and click **OK**.

The data are imported as a table and display the Excel table characteristics. The table contains banded rows and a header row.

c. Double-click the **Sheet2 tab** and type **Access Data** to rename the tab.

d. Click **Table Style Medium 7** in the Table Styles group on the Table Tools Design tab.

The data are formatted with the Table Style Medium 7 style. This style applies a dark orange fill and white font color to the column headings. Every other row is formatted with a light orange color.

e. Save the workbook.

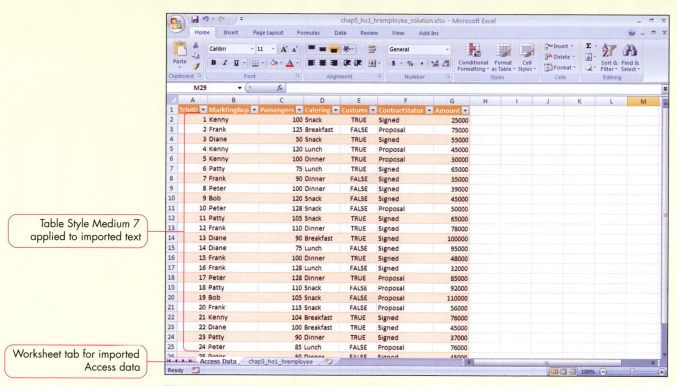

Table Style Medium 7 applied to imported text

Worksheet tab for imported Access data

Figure 5.14 Imported Access Data

Step 4
Apply Color Scales and Icon Sets Conditional Formatting

Refer to Figure 5.15 as you complete Step 4.

a. Select **cells C2:C28** and click **Conditional Formatting** in the Styles group on the Home tab.

You will now apply conditional formatting to the Access data you previously imported.

b. Select **Color Scales** and click **Blue – Yellow – Red Color Scale**

You applied the Color Scales to the number of passengers column and now see which Marketing Reps booked the most passengers and which Marketing Reps booked the fewest passengers.

c. Select **cells G2:G28** and click **Conditional Formatting** in the Style group.

d. Select **Icon Sets** and click **3 Flags**.

You can now clearly see that green flags highlight the flights generating the most revenue and the red flags highlight the flights generating the least revenue.

e. Save the *chap5_ho1_hremployee_solution* workbook and keep it onscreen if you plan to continue to the next hands-on exercise. Close the workbook and exit Excel if you do not want to continue with the next exercise at this time.

Color Scales

Icon Sets

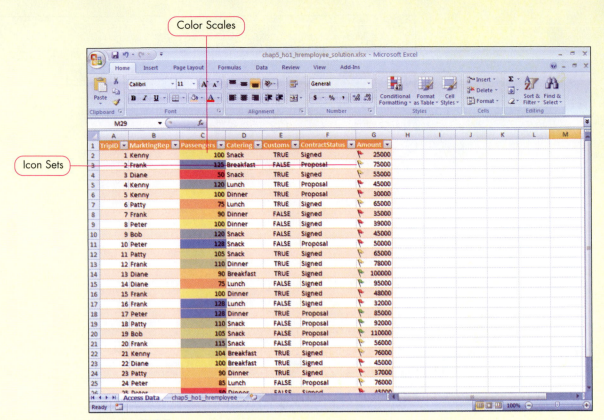

Figure 5.15 Conditional Formatting

Data Management

Once information has been placed in a range and the range converted to a data table, you can perform more complex data management analyses, such as using advanced data filters with defined criteria ranges, database functions to perform calculations on the information in the data table, and defined names to make the use of database functions more efficient. The items discussed are sequential; in other words, to better understand the concepts of data management the steps will work best if completed in the order presented.

In this section, you learn how to apply specialized sorting and filtering, extract specific data using advanced filtering techniques, define and use range names, and use database functions.

Applying Advanced Filtering and Sorting Methods

Data become more useful and important when they are organized or sorted and they can be reduced in volume by selecting a subset of data that meets specific conditions. For example, a teacher wants to know which students earned an "A," which students earned a "B," and so on in her sections of College Writing. A production manager wants an alphabetical list of employees working first, second, and third shifts arranged by shift. A bank manager wants a list of customers with CDs maturing in December. These are examples of information used to make decisions. It is data that are sorted and extracted using specific conditions to make them meaningful.

You have previous experience in simple filtering and sorting. However, you may need more complex sorting and filtering conditions. For example, you may want to filter records based on conditional formatting you applied, or you may want to create an advanced filter and place these extracted records together in a different location.

Sort and Filter Using Conditional Formatting

Excel provides several useful ways to organize and extract data using filters and conditional formatting. Once data are conditionally formatted, you can sort or filter the data to match the conditional formatting. For example, you might want to sort a table that has been conditionally formatted with a fill color based on ranges of housing costs. Sorting by color places all the records with the same color together for easy reference. To sort by color, click the filter drop-down arrow for the field that you want to sort, select Sort by Color, and select the formatting color or icon set. Cells containing that color are displayed at the top of the list. The Sort dialog box enables you to sort with more than one color at a time.

You can also set a filter based on conditional formatting. For example, assume that you applied the flags icon set. You can filter the records to show only records that have a particular flag color. To filter by conditional formatting, click the filter drop-down arrow for the field that you want to filter, select Filter by Color, and select the conditional formatting color or icon set. Figure 5.16 shows the Gee Airlines flights generating the most revenue. The filter displays only those amounts containing the green flags.

Sort and Filter by Cell Attributes

Another way you can visually present data is to sort by a cell attribute, such as cell color or font color. To sort by cell attributes, display the Sort dialog box, select the column for sorting, specify the cell attribute, such as Cell Color from the *Sort On* drop-down list, and select the order. You can filter records based on cell attributes. For example, Figure 5.17 depicts a worksheet filtered to show only the cells that are red. These cells also represent the flights with the fewest passengers.

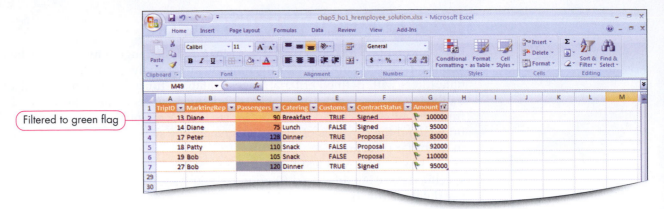

Figure 5.16 Filter by Conditional Formatting—Icon Set

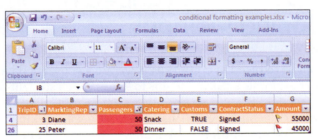

Figure 5.17 Filter by Conditional Formatting—Cell Color

Filter Data with Number Filters

Data can be filtered by using predefined number filters. Figure 5.18 shows the menu of options you can use to apply to numeric data. If you want a list of all flights carrying more than 50 passengers, you would use a number filter to obtain the data. If you want a list of flights producing less than $25,000 in revenue, you would use a number filter.

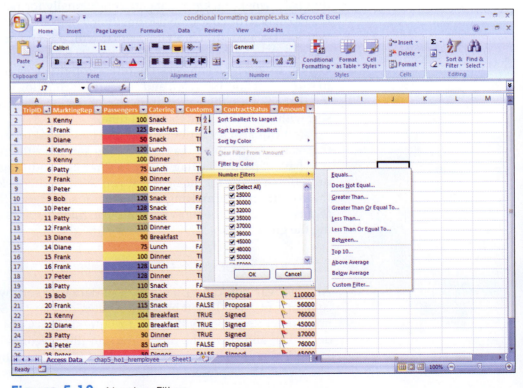

Figure 5.18 Number Filters

You can create custom filters by using a combination of different number filters. For example, if you want to see all the flights with more than 75 passengers but fewer than 100 passengers, you would create a custom filter.

Define a Criteria Range

A **criteria range** is an area separate from the data table and specifies the conditions used to filter the table.

Although the AutoFilter provides a variety of ways to filter data, you may need to create an advanced filter with more complex criteria. Before you can use Excel's advanced filtering capability, you must define a criteria range. A **criteria range** is an area that specifies the conditions to filter the table. A criteria range is independent of the table and exists as a separate area on a worksheet, typically above or below the main table. A criteria range must be at least two rows deep and one column wide.

(A criteria range is independent of the table and exists as a separate area on a worksheet.)

The most basic criteria range you use has two rows and as many columns as in the table. The first row contains the field names as they appear in the table, and the second row contains the conditions (e.g., values) you are looking for. See Figure 5.19 for an example of a basic criteria range. The database is filtered to show only records in which the location is Atlanta.

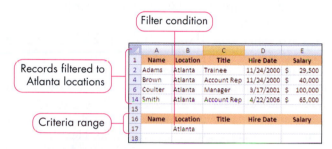

Figure 5.19 Criteria Range

Multiple values in the second row create an AND condition, which requires that records selected meet both conditions. Spelling is particularly important because variations in spelling or misspelled words will not meet the criteria. If you want to select those employees named Smith AND who have a pay period of 10, you would enter Name and PayPeriod in the first criteria row and Smith and 10 immediately below the respective labels in the second criteria row. Figure 5.20 shows multiple criteria that filter the records to display all Account Reps located in Atlanta. Note that *both* conditions must be met. Account Reps in other cities are not listed and other job titles in Atlanta are not listed.

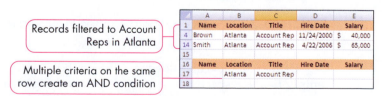

Figure 5.20 Criteria Range

When values are entered in multiple rows, an OR condition is created. Returned records are those meeting either condition. Figure 5.21 shows an OR condition with Atlanta listed on one row and Account Reps listed on a different row. Running the advanced filter displays all Atlanta employees (regardless of job titles) and all Account Reps (regardless of location), compared to the previous AND condition that required that both conditions be met.

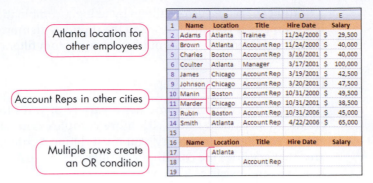

Atlanta location for other employees

Account Reps in other cities

Multiple rows create an OR condition

Figure 5.21 Criteria Range

You can combine AND and OR conditions for more specific filters. For example, you might want to show Account Reps in Atlanta *or* any employee in Boston. The Account Reps and Atlanta create an AND condition and are placed on one row. Boston is placed on the next row to form an OR condition.

Relational operators are symbols used to compare cell contents to another cell or specific value. Relational operators include <, >, <=, >=, <>, and =. They may be used with date or numeric fields to return records within a designated range. Recall that you used relational or comparison operators in the conditional test argument of an IF function, such as = IF(B10<B1,B10*.05,B10*.10), in which the value of cell B10 is compared to see if it is less than the value of cell B1.

Figure 5.22 shows three sets of criteria ranges. The first criteria range shows the less than relational operator used with a date. This condition displays records in which the date is *before* 3/16/2001. The second criteria range shows the greater than relational operator used with numerical data. This condition displays records in which the salary is greater than $40,000. The third criteria range establishes a boundary for the same field by repeating the field within the criteria range. This condition identifies salaries that are greater than or equal to $40,000 and less than or equal to $60,000.

A *relational operator* is a symbol used to compare cell contents to another cell or value.

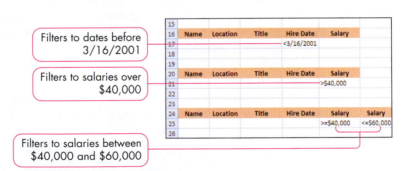

Filters to dates before 3/16/2001

Filters to salaries over $40,000

Filters to salaries between $40,000 and $60,000

Figure 5.22 Relational Operators Used in Criteria Ranges

Using equal (=) and unequal (<>) symbols selects records with empty and non-empty fields, respectively. An equal with nothing after it will return all records with no entry in the designated field (see Figure 5.23). An unequal (<>) with nothing after it will select all records with an entry in the field. An empty row in the criteria range returns every record in the list.

Relational operator identifies missing data

Figure 5.23 Criteria Range

TIP   The Top 10 AutoFilter

Use the *Top 10 AutoFilter* option to see the top or bottom 10, or for that matter any number of records in a list. You just turn the AutoFilter condition on, click the down arrow in the designated field, select Number Filters, and select Top 10 to display the associated dialog box. You specify the records you want to view. You can also specify a percentage, as opposed to a number—for example, the top 10% of the records in a list.

Apply the Advanced Filter

After you create the criteria range, you are ready to apply the advanced filter. Instead of displaying the AutoFilter drop-down arrows, the Advanced command displays the Advanced Filter dialog box. This dialog box enables you to filter the table in place or copy the selected records to another area in the worksheet, specify the list range, specify the criteria range, or display unique records only. Excel uses the separate criteria range in the Advanced Filter dialog box as the source for the advanced criteria.

    To set an advanced filter:

1. Create a criteria range.
2. Click a cell in the data table.
3. Click Advanced in the Sort & Filter group on the Data tab.
4. Click *Filter the list, in-place* to filter the range by hiding rows that do not match your criteria. If you want to copy the rows that match your criteria to another area of the worksheet, click *Copy to another location*, click in the Copy to box, and then click the upper-left corner cell where you want to paste.
5. Enter the criteria range, including the criteria labels, in the *Criteria range* box, and then click OK. Figure 5.24 shows the Advanced Filter dialog box with an example advanced command setup.

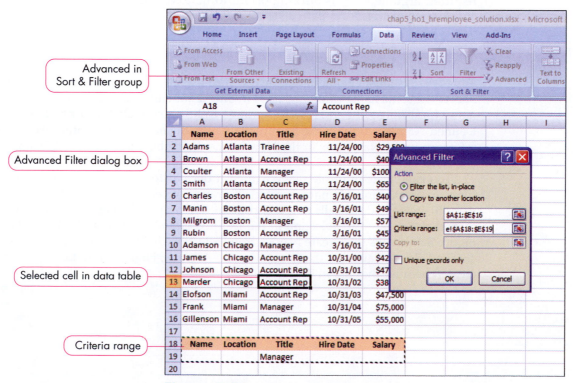

Figure 5.24   Advanced Filter

TIP   Filter the List in Place

Use the Advanced Filter command to filter the list in place and display the records that meet the current criteria. Click anywhere in the list, click the Data down arrow, select the Filter command, and then choose Advanced Filter to display the Advanced Filter dialog box. Click the option to filter the list in place, and then click OK to display the selected records. You have to execute this command each time the criteria change.

Creating and Using Range Names

A *range name* is a word or string of characters that represents a cell, range of cells, or constant value.

In previous sections, you used a range of cells such as A1:E15 in formulas, functions, and data tables. You can create a *range name*, a word or string of characters, to represent a cell, range of cells, or constant value. For example, the name EmployeeList represents a cell or range of cells such as A1:E15. After assigning a name to a range of cells, you can use that name to reference cells in formulas and functions. A range name can be up to 255 characters long but must begin with a letter or underscore. It can be a mixture of upper or lowercase letters, numbers, periods, and underscores, but a range name cannot have blank spaces or special characters. Furthermore, a range name should not look like a cell address, such as B15.

Once you define a range name, it automatically adjusts for insertions or deletions within a range. For example, if you assign the name EmployeeList to the range A1:E15 and delete a row in the range, the definition changes to A1:E14. In a similar fashion, if a column is added the definition would change to A1:F15. Names are used in formulas and serve as documentation while helping to clarify formula components. A name can be used in any formula or function instead of cell addresses. This is of particular value when using database functions but is useful for all functions. A range name can represent a single cell; B15, for example, is state sales tax and in the formula = stax*B2, stax is used to document the worksheet. When using database functions, it is easier to create the function when you can use range names for the required arguments. It is also important to note that names used in formulas are absolute references.

Create a Range Name

Range names must be unique within a workbook. When a name is created for use in Sheet1 the same name cannot be used in Sheet2 to refer to different cells. To create a name for a range of cells, select the range to be named, click Define Name in the Defined Names group on the Formula tab, type the name you want to use for your reference in the Name box in the New Name dialog box (see Figure 5.25), and then click OK.

You can create multiple range names at once instead of creating one name at a time. To create multiple names, select the range of cells containing the names you want to create and the cells that will contain the formulas using the names. You can then click Create from Selection in the Defined Names group on the Formulas tab. Figure 5.26 shows the Create Names from Selection dialog box with the *Left column* checked. This means that the range names—Average, Highest, and Lowest—will be created because they are in the left column.

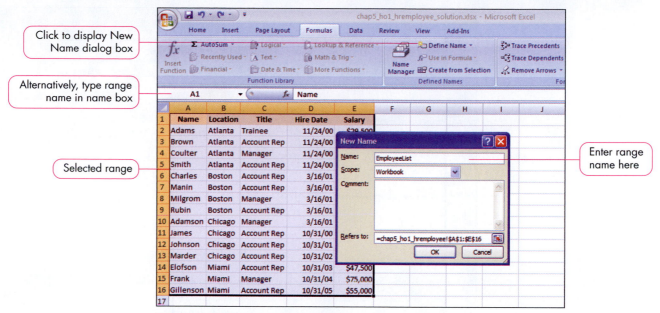

Figure 5.25 Naming a Range

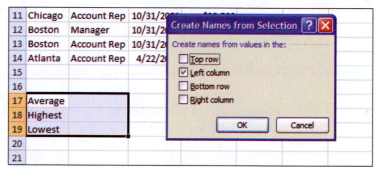

Figure 5.26 Create Range Names from Selection

> **TIP** **Name Range Shortcuts**
>
> Excel provides several other methods when you want to name a range. You can select the range, click in the Name box (left side of the Formula Bar), type the name, and press Enter. You can right-click the selected range, select *Name range* from the shortcut menu, and fill in the New Name dialog box entries. Or you can click Name Manager in the Defined Names group on the Formulas tab and click New. Fill in the New Name dialog box entries as above.

Modify and Delete a Range Name

How often do you type something and discover that you made a mistake? Maybe the word is incorrect or more often the name does not represent the data in the cells. You can use the Name Manager dialog box to edit existing range names, delete existing range names, and create new range names. Figure 5.27 shows the Name Manager dialog box that displays when you click Name Manager in the Defined Names group on the Formulas tab. If you want to edit or delete an existing name, click the name and click either Edit or Delete, respectively. When you click Edit, another dialog box opens so you can type the correct name and change the cell reference, if necessary.

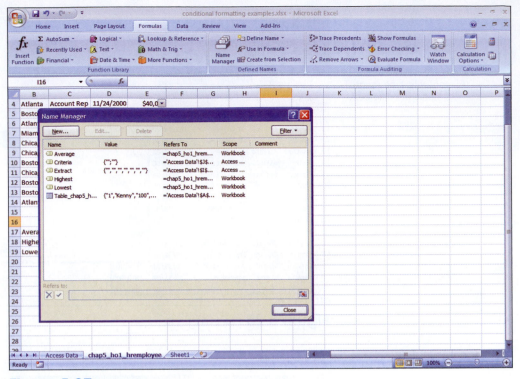

Figure 5.27 Edit or Delete a Range Name

Insert a Table of Range Names

After creating several range names in a workbook, you might want to display an alphabetical list of the range names. A good location for an alphabetical list of range names would be a separate sheet within the workbook, such as the documentation sheet. To insert a list of range names, click Use in Formula in the Defined Names group on the Formulas tab, and select Paste Names. Figure 5.28 shows the Paste Name dialog box. Click Paste List. Excel then pastes an alphabetical list of range names starting in the active cell (see Figure 5.29). The first column displays the range names, and the second column displays the worksheet name and cell reference. Note that this is not a linked operation. If you add or change any of the listed range names, you must Paste Names again to update the list.

Figure 5.28 Paste Name Dialog Box

Figure 5.29 List of Range Names

Use Range Names in Formulas

After you create a range name, you can use that range name instead of cell references in formulas. For example, assume that cell C15 contains a purchase amount and cell C5 contains the sales tax amount. Instead of typing =C15*C5 to calculate the sales tax, you can type =C15*stax, assuming that cell C5 has been named *stax*. The *stax* range name is an absolute reference to cell C5. If you need to copy the formula down the column for other purchases, you do not have to worry about creating an absolute reference like you would by typing =C15*$C$5. When you copy the formula =C15*stax, the copied formula for the next row is =C16*stax. Furthermore, as you build a formula and click a cell that is range-named, Excel will automatically substitute the range name for the cell address in the formula.

> ### TIP   AutoComplete Formulas with Range Names
>
> When you start typing a range name within a formula, the Formula AutoComplete feature displays a list of possible functions or range names. For example, if you type =C15*s, you will see a list of functions that start with *s*. As you continue typing, you will see the appropriate range name. You can then double-click the range name to enter it in the formula.

Using range names in formulas is helpful when you need to create formulas that reference a cell or a range of cells on a different worksheet. Instead of typing the worksheet name and cell references, you can use the range name. Because the range name creates an absolute reference to a cell or range of cells, the range-name reference in a formula is absolute. The Formula Bar in Figure 5.30 displays the database function DAVERAGE with one range name for an argument. EmployeeList is the name used for the database.

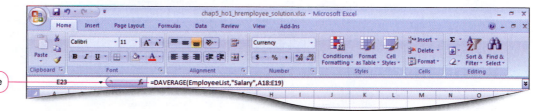

Formula using named range

Figure 5.30   Range Names in a Formula

If you create range names after creating formulas, you can update the formulas to use range names rather than cell references. Select the cells that contain formulas that you want to update and click the Define Name down arrow in the Defined Names group on the Formulas tab. In the Apply Names dialog box, select the applicable range names for the formulas you have selected, select appropriate options, and click OK. Use Help to learn about the other options in the Apply Names dialog box.

Using Database Functions

The *database functions* analyze data for selected records in a table.

The *database functions* analyze data only for selected records in a table. These functions are similar to statistical functions (SUM, AVERAGE, MAX, MIN, COUNT) except that database functions are exclusively used for database tables; these functions affect only records that satisfy the specified criteria. Data not meeting the specified criteria are filtered out and are not included in the function calculations. Database functions, as with all functions, return a value and save you time because you do not have to construct the underlying mathematical formula. All database functions use a criteria range that defines the search parameters. Using range names can simplify the construction of database functions.

Database functions have three arguments:

1. **Database**. The database range is the entire table, including column headings and all columns, on which the function operates. The database reference may be represented by a range name. In the DAVERAGE function shown in Figure 5.30, the database range is EmployeeList, which refers to cells A1:E16.

2. **Field**. The field is the column in the database that contains the values operated on by the function. You can enter the name of the column heading in quotation marks, such as "Salary" in the DAVERAGE function shown in Figure 5.30. Alternatively, you can enter the number that represents the location of that column within the table. For example, if the Salary column is the sixth column in the table, you can enter a 6 for the Field.

3. **Criteria**. The criteria range defines the conditions to be met by the function. This range must contain at least one column label and a cell below the label that specifies the condition. The criteria range is A18:E19 in the DAVERAGE function shown in Figure 5.30. The criteria range may include more than one column with conditions for each column label. The criteria may be defined by a range address or by a range name.

The summary shown in Figure 5.31 is based on the salaries for only the managers, not all employees. Each database function includes the criteria range in cells A18:F19 as the third argument. The criteria range limits the calculations to just the managers.

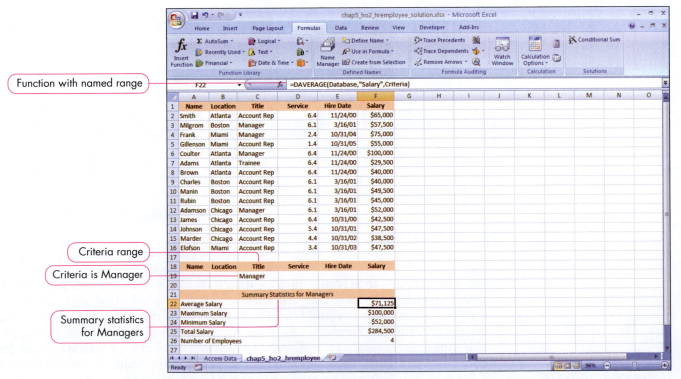

Figure 5.31 Database Functions

To insert a database function, you can click Insert Function between the name box and the Formula Bar, click the *Or select a category* drop-down arrow, select Database, and then click the desired database function in the *Select a function* list box. Figure 5.32 shows the database functions in the Insert Function dialog box.

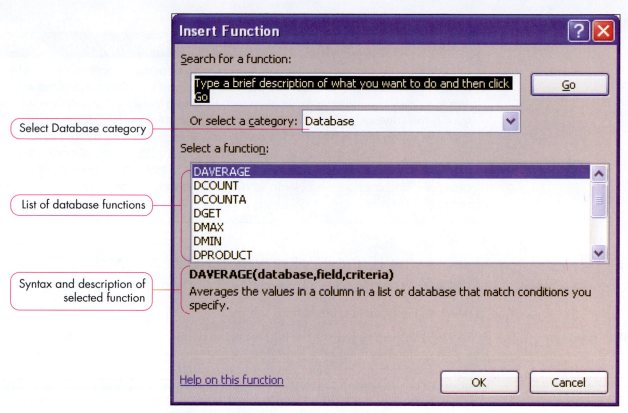

Figure 5.32 Database Functions

Alternatively, you can type =D in a cell and then select the appropriate database function from the Formula AutoComplete list. The reference box on page 332 lists and describes some common database functions.

Calculate a SUM with the DSUM Function
DSUM Function | Reference

DSUM(database,field,criteria)

The **DSUM function** sums the numeric entries in a field in a database that match specified conditions.

The **DSUM function** adds up or sums the numeric entries in a field of records in a list or database that match conditions you specify. For example, you might want to calculate the total amount that one specific employee was paid over 32 pay periods, or you might want to find the total salaries paid for employees in Boston. In Figure 5.31, the DSUM function is used to calculate the total salary of all managers.

Calculate an Average with the DAVERAGE Function
DAVERAGE Function | Reference

DAVERAGE(database,field,criteria)

The **DAVERAGE function** determines the average of numeric entries in a field of records in a database that match specified conditions.

The **DAVERAGE function** determines the arithmetic mean, or average, of numeric entries in a field of records in a list or database that match conditions you specify. For example, you might want to use DAVERAGE to determine the average number of hours that interns worked during a pay period or the average GPA of psychology majors. In Figure 5.31, the DAVERAGE function is used to calculate the average salary of all managers.

Identify the Highest Value with the DMAX Function
DMAX Function | Reference

DMAX(database,field,criteria)

The **DMAX function** determines the highest value in a field of records in a database that match specified conditions.

The *DMAX function* returns the highest value of numeric entries in a field of records in a list or database that match conditions you specify. For example, you can use the DMAX function to determine the maximum number of hours worked during pay period 10 or the highest number of points scored by a basketball player in a particular game. In Figure 5.31, the DMAX function is used to calculate the highest salary within the list of all managers.

Identify the Lowest Value with the DMIN Function
DMIN Function | Reference

DMIN(database,field,criteria)

The **DMIN function** returns the lowest value of numeric entries in a field of records in a database that match specified conditions.

The *DMIN function* returns the lowest value of numeric entries in a field of records in a list or database that match conditions you specify. For example, you can use the DMIN function to determine the lowest number of patients in a hospital during April, or the lowest score on a statistics test for male students. In Figure 5.31, the DMIN function is used to calculate the lowest salary of all managers.

Identify the Total Number with the DCOUNT Function
DCOUNT Function | Reference

DCOUNT(database,field,criteria)

The **DCOUNT function** counts the cells that contain numbers in a field of records in a database that match specified conditions.

The *DCOUNT function* counts the cells that contain numbers in a field of records in a list or database that match conditions you specify. For example, you can use the DCOUNT function to count the number of pay periods where the hours are greater than 8 but less than 6 or count the number of females who participated in a market research study. In Figure 5.31, the DCOUNT function is used to count the number of managers in the database.

Database Functions | Reference

Name	Syntax	Definition
DSUM	DSUM(database,field,criteria)	Calculates the total of values in a field that meets the specified condition(s).
DAVERAGE	DAVERAGE(database,field,criteria)	Determines the mathematical average of values in a field that meets the specified condition(s).
DMAX	DMAX(database,field,criteria)	Identifies the largest value in a field that meets the specified condition(s).
DMIN	DMIN(database,field,criteria)	Identifies the smallest value in a field that meets the specified condition(s).
DCOUNT	DCOUNT(database,field,criteria)	Counts the number of records for a field that meets the specified condition(s).
DCOUNTA	DCOUNTA(database,field,criteria)	Counts the number of records that contain values (nonblank) in a field that meets the specified condition(s).
DPRODUCT	DPRODUCT(database,field,criteria)	Multiplies the values within a field that meets the specified condition(s).
DSTDEV	DSTDEV(database,field,criteria)	Calculates the standard deviation for values in a field that meets the specified condition(s).
DVAR	DVAR(database,field,criteria)	Estimates the sample population variance for values in a field that meets the specified condition(s).
DVARP	DVARP(database,field,criteria)	Estimates the entire population variance for values in a field that meets the specified condition(s).

Hands-On Exercises

2 | Gee Airlines Human Resources Department Revisited

Skills covered: 1. Use Date Arithmetic **2.** Sort and Filter with Conditional Formatting **3.** Use Custom AutoFilter **4.** Create a Criteria Range and Use an Advanced Filter **5.** Define a Named Range **6.** Set Up Summary Area and Use DAVERAGE **7.** Use DMAX, DMIN, DSUM, and DCOUNT Functions **8.** Change the Criteria

Step 1
Use Date Arithmetic

Refer to Figure 5.33 as you complete Step 1.

a. Open the *chap5_ho1_hremployee_solution* workbook, save it as **chap5_ho2_hremployee_solution**, and rename the chap5_ho1_hremployee sheet tab as **chap5_ho2_hremployee**.

b. Right-click the **column D heading** and select **Insert** from the shortcut menu.

The column of hire dates has been moved to column E and a new empty column is inserted.

c. Click **cell D1**, type **Service**, and press **Enter**.

d. Click **cell D2** and type **=(Today()-E2)/365**, as shown in Figure 5.33, and press **Enter**.

The years of service for Adams, the first employee, are displayed in cell D2.

e. Click **cell D2**, then click **Decrease Decimal** in the Number group on the Home tab several times to display the length of service with only one decimal.

f. Drag the fill handle in **cell D2** to the remaining cells in that column, **cells D3:D14**.

You copied the formula to compute the length of service for the remaining employees. You do not have to format the cells because you copied the format with the formula.

TROUBLESHOOTING: Your results will differ because the TODAY function returns the current date when Excel calculates the function. Figure 5.33 displays the result based on a previous date.

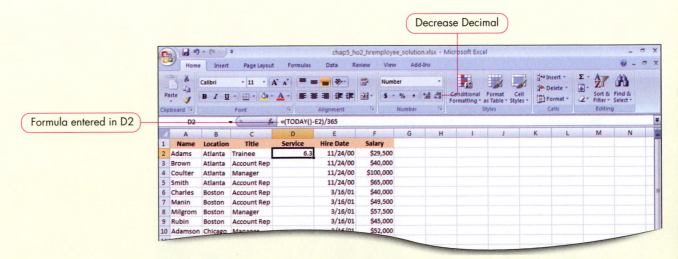

Figure 5.33 Calculate Years of Service

TIP Date Arithmetic

Excel stores a date as an integer or serial number, starting with January 1, 1900; that is, January 1, 1900, is stored as the number 1, January 2, 1900, as the number 2, and so on. This enables you to use dates in an arithmetic computation. An employee's service, for example, is computed by subtracting the hire date from the Today() function and dividing the result by 365. For greater precision in dealing with leap years, divide the result by 365.25.

Step 2
Sort and Filter with Conditional Formatting

Refer to Figure 5.34 as you complete Step 2.

a. Click any cell in the list and click **Filter** in the Sort & Filter group on the Data tab.

You now see the down arrows to the right of each field name. These are used with all Filters.

b. Select **cells F2:F14**, click **Conditional Formatting** in the Styles group on the Home tab, and select **Icon Sets**, as shown in Figure 5.34.

You will apply conditional formatting to the Salary field. This represents the first step in the sort and filter process.

c. Click **3 Traffic Lights** (Unrimmed) on the Icon Sets palette.

You applied conditional formatting to the salaries, with green representing the highest and red representing the lowest.

d. Click the **Salary drop-down arrow**, select **Sort by Color**, and click the yellow **Traffic Light Cell Icon**.

You sorted your data table by yellow, the middle salary group.

e. Click the **Salary drop-down arrow** a second time, click **Filter by Color**, and select **Red** in the Filter by Cell Icon list.

The display changes to show only those employees who meet the filter. The row numbers for the visible records are blue, showing that some records are ignored. The pull-down for Salary now displays the filter symbol, indicating it is part of the filter condition.

f. Click the **Salary drop-down arrow** a third time, click **(Select All)** to remove the filter condition on location, and click **OK**.

You removed the filters so all data are again displayed.

g. Click **Conditional Formatting** in the Styles group, select **Clear Rules**, and click **Clear Rules from Selected Cells**.

You removed the filter and the conditional formatting rules so you can proceed to the next hands-on step.

h. Save the workbook.

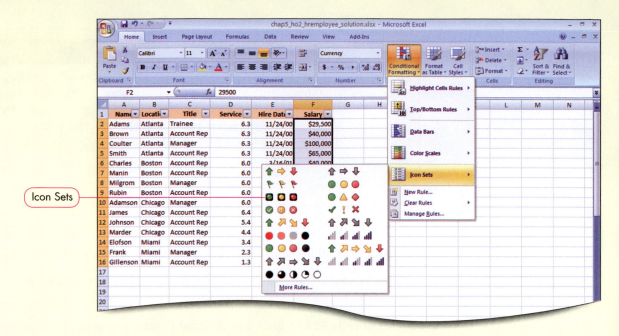

Figure 5.34 Conditional Formatting Icon Sets

Step 3
Use Custom AutoFilter

Refer to Figure 5.35 as you complete Step 3.

a. Click the **Salary drop-down arrow** and click **Custom Filter** from the Number Filters list.

The Custom AutoFilter dialog box is displayed, as shown in Figure 5.35, and you can create a custom AutoFilter.

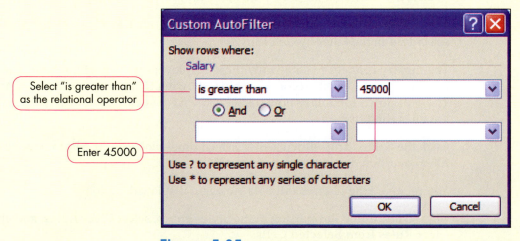

Figure 5.35 Custom AutoFilter

b. Click **is greater than** as the relation operator in the drop-down in the left box for **Salary**.

c. Type **45000** in the text box for the salary amount and click **OK**.

The list changes to display only those employees whose title is Account Rep and Manager and who earn more than $45,000.

d. Click **Filter** in the Sort & Filter group on the Data tab.

You toggled the AutoFilter command off and removed the arrows next to the field names to cancel all filter conditions. All of the records in the list are now visible.

e. Save the workbook.

Step 4
Create a Criteria Range and Use an Advanced Filter

Refer to Figure 5.36 as you complete Step 4.

a. Click and drag to select **cells A1:F1**, then click **Copy** in the Clipboard group on the Home tab.

A moving border appears around the selected cells.

b. Click **cell A18**, click **Paste** in the Clipboard group, and press **Esc** to cancel the moving border.

TROUBLESHOOTING: The field names in the criteria range must be spelled exactly the same way as in the associated list. The best way to ensure the names are identical is to copy the entries from the list to the criteria range.

c. Click **cell C19** and type **Manager**.

d. Click anywhere in the employee list, then click **Advanced** in the Sort & Filter group on the Data tab to display the Advanced Filter dialog box shown in Figure 5.36.

The list range is already entered because you selected a cell in the list before executing the command.

e. Click in the **Criteria Range** text box, and then click and drag **cells A18:F19**.

A moving border appears around the cells in the worksheet, and the corresponding cell reference is entered in the dialog box, as shown in Figure 5.36.

f. Check to make sure **Filter the list, in-place** is selected and click **OK**.

The display changes to show just the managers. Now only rows 3, 4, 6, and 9 are visible.

g. Click **cell B19**, type **Atlanta**, and press **Enter**.

h. Click **Advanced** in the Sort & Filter group.

The Advanced Filter dialog box already displays the cell references for the list and criteria range.

i. Click **OK**.

The display changes to show just the manager in Atlanta. Only row 6 is visible because it is the only row meeting the criteria.

j. Click **Clear** in the Sort & Filter group.

You have removed all filter conditions and the entire list is visible.

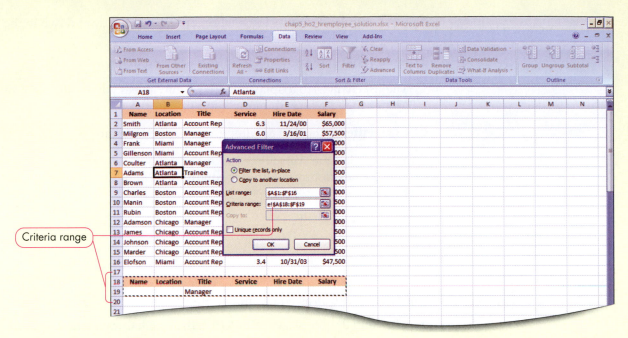

Criteria range

Figure 5.36 Advanced AutoFilter

Step 5
Define a Named Range

Refer to Figure 5.37 as you complete Step 5.

a. Click and drag to select **cells A1:F14**.

b. Click **Name Manager** in the Defined Names group on the Formulas tab to open the Name Manager dialog box, and then click **New** to show the New Name dialog box.

c. Type **Database** in the name box and click **OK** to display the Name Manager dialog box again.

The Name Manager dialog box contains two range names: Database, which you just defined, and Criteria, which was defined automatically when you specified the criteria range in Step 4.

d. Click **Close** in the Name Manager dialog box.

e. Click **cell I1**, type **Range Names**, and press **Enter**.

f. Click **Use in Formula** in the Defined Names group on the Formulas tab and select Paste Names.

g. Click **Paste List**.

You pasted the list of range names in your worksheet for future reference.

h. Save the workbook.

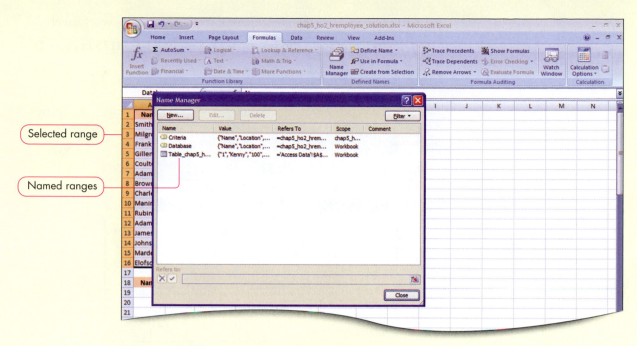

Figure 5.37 Name a Range in the Name Manager Dialog Box

Selected range

Named ranges

Step 6
Set Up a Summary Area and Use DAVERAGE

Refer to Figure 5.38 as you complete Step 6.

a. Click **cell A21**, type **Summary Statistics for Managers**, press **Enter**, and then select **cells A21:F21**.

b. Click **Merge & Center** in the Alignment group on the Home tab.

c. Click **Fill Color** in the Font group and select **Orange Accent 6, Lighter 60%** from the Theme Colors palette.

d. Enter the labels for **cells A22:A26** as shown in Figure 5.38.

You created and formatted an area in your worksheet for summary statistics from your database.

e. Click **cell B19** and press **Delete**.

The criteria range is now set to select only managers.

f. Click **cell F22** and click **Insert Function** in the Function Library group on the Formulas tab to display the Insert Function dialog box.

g. Select **Database** from the Category list, select **DAVERAGE** as the function name, and then click **OK** to open the Function Arguments dialog box shown in Figure 5.38.

You selected the DAVERAGE function and are now ready to enter the arguments for the function.

h. Enter the function arguments as shown below:

Argument	Type Text:
Database	Database
Field	Salary
Criteria	Criteria

TROUBLESHOOTING: Database and Criteria are range names you previously created and are typed exactly as you created them. Salary will appear in quotes in the Formula Bar and must be typed within quotes when typing the formula because it is a text field name and is also typed exactly as it appears in the column heading.

i. Click **OK** to enter the DAVERAGE function into the worksheet.

If the function was entered correctly, you will see 71125 in cell F22.

j. Save the workbook.

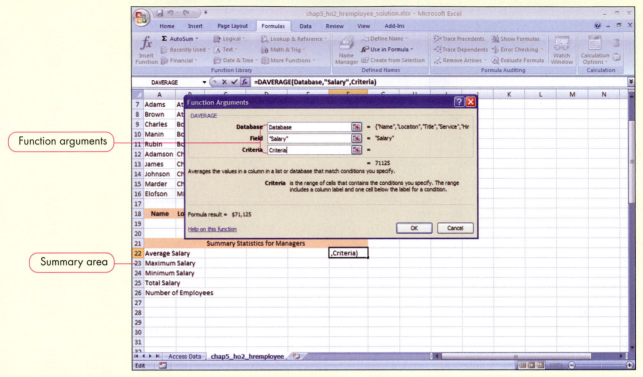

Figure 5.38 Summary Area

Step 7

Use DMAX, DMIN, DSUM, and DCOUNT Functions

Refer to Figure 5.39 as you complete Step 7.

a. Enter the DMAX, DMIN, DSUM, and DCOUNT functions in **cells F23:F26**. Use **Insert Function** in the Function Library group on the Formulas tab to enter each function individually as shown below.

Cell	Function
F23	=DMAX(Database,"Salary",Criteria)
F24	=DMIN(Database,"Salary",Criteria)
F25	=DSUM(Database,"Salary",Criteria)
F26	=DCOUNT(Database,"Salary",Criteria)

The computed values are shown in Figure 5.39.

b. Format **cells F22:F25** as **currency** with **zero** decimals.

c. Click and drag the border between **columns F and G** to widen column F if necessary. Save the workbook.

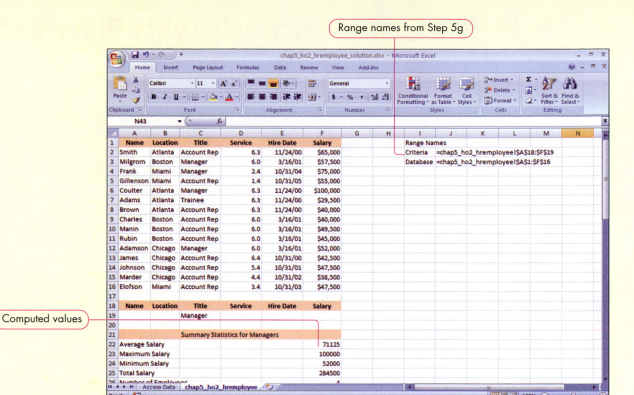

Figure 5.39 Database Functions

Refer to Figure 5.40 as you complete Step 8.

a. Click in the **Name box**, type **B19**, and press **Enter** to make cell B19 the active cell.

b. Type **Chicago** to change the criteria to Chicago managers and press **Enter**.

The values displayed by the DAVERAGE, DMIN, DMAX, and DSUM functions change to $52,000, reflecting the one employee, Adamson, who meets the current criteria, a manager in Chicago. The value displayed by the DCOUNT function changes to 1 to indicate one employee, as shown in Figure 5.40.

c. Click **cell C19** and press **Delete**.

The average salary changes to $45,125, reflecting all employees in Chicago.

d. Click **cell B19** and press **Delete**.

The criteria range is now empty. The DAVERAGE function displays $52,300, which is the average salary of all employees in the database.

e. Click **cell C19**, type **Manager**, and press **Enter**.

The average salary is $71,125, the average salary for all managers.

f. Save and close the workbook.

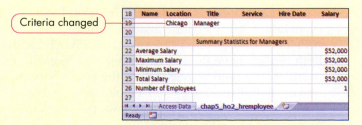

Figure 5.40 Change the Criteria

Data Analysis with PivotTables and PivotCharts

A **PivotTable** is a way to quickly summarize large amounts of data.

A *PivotTable* is a powerful, interactive data mining feature that enables you to quickly summarize and analyze large amounts of data in tables. You can also specify the type of calculations you need to analyze the data. PivotTables give you the ability to quickly summarize long lists of data by categories. The concept that led to today's pivot table came from Lotus Development Corporation with a spreadsheet program called Lotus Improv. Improv was envisioned in 1986 by Pito Salas. Salas realized that spreadsheets have patterns of data and by designing a tool that could recognize these patterns, you could quickly build advanced data models.

When using a PivotTable, you can calculate summary information without writing a formula or copying a single cell. The best thing about PivotTables is their flexibility in data analysis: They enable you to arrange them dynamically as your data

> The best thing about PivotTables is their flexibility in data analysis . . .

needs require. This dynamic process of rearranging a PivotTable is known as "pivoting" your table. You turn the same information around and look at it from different angles to identify relationships between variables. A PivotTable is an interactive way to summarize large amounts of data and to analyze numerical data in depth. They are especially designed for the following:

- Querying large amounts of data in user-friendly ways.
- Subtotaling numeric data, summarizing data, and creating custom calculations.
- Expanding and collapsing levels of data to facilitate focusing.
- Pivoting or moving rows to columns or columns to rows to see different summaries of data.

If you were working for a marketing company, you would create a PivotTable using census data to summarize the data based on gender, ethnic groups, or geographic location. This is particularly valuable with marketing companies' increased emphasis on data mining for target advertising.

Figure 5.41 shows the relationship between the data tools and the PivotTable. In a PivotTable, each column or field in the source data becomes a PivotTable field that summarizes multiple rows of information. A value field provides the values to be summarized, and a grand total is calculated.

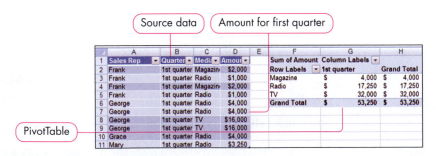

Figure 5.41 Data Table with PivotTable

A **PivotChart** is a graphical representation of data in a PivotTable.

A *PivotChart* is an interactive graphical representation of the data in a PivotTable. A PivotChart enables you to visually present the data in a report. A PivotChart always has an associated PivotTable that has a corresponding layout. Both reports have fields that correspond to each other, and when you change the position of a field in one report, the corresponding field in the other report also moves. Both PivotTables and PivotCharts enable you to make informed decisions based on the data. Figure 5.42 shows the specialized elements in a PivotChart that correspond to the PivotTable.

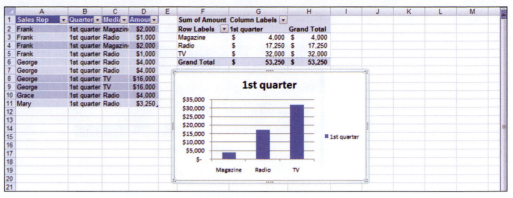

Figure 5.42 PivotTable and PivotChart

Creating and Deleting PivotTables and PivotCharts

The PivotTable command displays the Create PivotTable dialog box, and the PivotChart report command displays the Create PivotTable with PivotChart dialog box. Both commands are in Insert PivotTable in the Tables group on the Insert tab. Both dialog boxes have similar interfaces, but the difference is that the Create PivotTable dialog box creates a PivotTable only, whereas the Create PivotTable with PivotChart dialog box creates a PivotChart and an associated PivotTable.

Create a PivotTable or PivotChart

Before creating a PivotTable, you must think about the design of the data table itself. Make sure to use meaningful column headings, accurate data, and most importantly, do not leave any blank rows in your data table. One column must have duplicate values, such as names of cities, states, or departments. The duplicate values are used to create categories for organizing and summarizing data. Another column must have numeric values to produce quantitative summaries, such as averages or sums. To create a PivotTable or PivotChart, you need to connect to a data source and specify the report's location. To create the report:

1. Select a cell in a named range of cells or in an Excel table. Make sure the range of cells has column headings.
2. To create a PivotTable, click Insert PivotTable in the Tables group on the Insert tab to display the Create PivotTable dialog box. To create a PivotTable and PivotChart, click PivotChart in the Insert PivotTable list, in the Tables group on the Insert tab, to display the Create PivotTable with PivotChart dialog box.
3. Choose the data to be analyzed by clicking *Select a table or range*. If you selected a cell in a range or table, the range of cells or table name reference shows in the Table/Range box (see Figure 5.43). Otherwise, you will have to type a range of cells or a table name reference in the Table/Range box.
4. To place a PivotTable in a new worksheet, click New Worksheet. To place it on an existing worksheet, select Existing Worksheet and type the first cell in the range where the PivotTable will be located. Generally, it is beneficial to place PivotTables and PivotCharts on new sheets so that the original data source is separated from the manipulated data in the PivotTable or PivotChart.
5. Click OK. An empty PivotTable appears on the left side of the worksheet, and the PivotTable Field List window appears on the right side of the window so that you can add fields, create a layout, and customize the PivotTable.

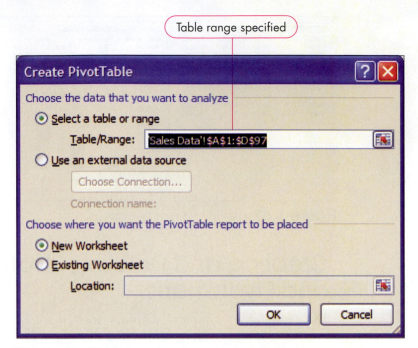

Figure 5.43 Create PivotTable Dialog Box

To create a PivotChart report from an existing PivotTable report:

1. Click the PivotTable.
2. Click a chart type in the Charts group on the Insert tab. You may select any type of chart, except a scatter, bubble, or stock chart.

Delete a PivotTable or PivotChart

If you no longer need a PivotTable or PivotChart, you can delete it. Deleting PivotTables and PivotCharts requires only a few steps. To delete a PivotTable, click the PivotTable. Click Select in the Actions group on the Options tab, select Entire PivotTable, and then press Delete. To delete a PivotChart, select the PivotChart and press Delete. Deleting the PivotChart does not delete the associated PivotTable.

> ### TIP   Customize the PivotTable
>
> Right-click anywhere in a PivotTable to display a shortcut menu and select PivotTable Options to display the PivotTable Options dialog box. The default settings work well for most tables, but you can customize the table in a variety of ways. You can, for example, suppress the row or column totals or display a specific value in a blank cell. You can also change the formatting for any field within the table by right-clicking the field and selecting the Format Cells button from the resulting menu.

Add Fields to a PivotTable or PivotChart

The PivotTable Field List window (see Figure 5.44) is used to add fields to a PivotTable or a PivotChart. It is also used to remove and rearrange fields. The PivotTable Field List window displays two sections:

1. A field section at the top shows fields from an external data source. You use this section to add and remove fields.
2. A layout section at the bottom is used to arrange and reposition fields as Report Filter, Row Labels, Column Labels, and Values.

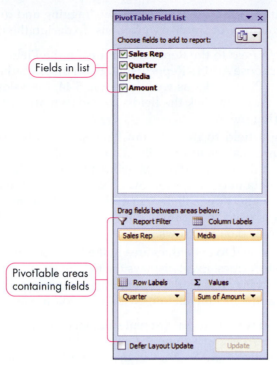

Figure 5.44   PivotTable Field List

To create a quick PivotTable, check the fields in the *Choose fields to add to report* section of the PivotTable Field List window. Excel arranges the fields based on their data types. Text fields are typically used for row labels, and numeric fields are typically used for column labels. Although the default layout might be acceptable in some situations, you might want to control where fields appear in the PivotTable. Table 5.5 lists and describes the areas of a PivotTable, and Table 5.6 lists and describes the areas of a PivotChart.

Table 5.5   Areas of a PivotTable Report

Area	Description
Values	Display summary numeric data.
Row Labels	Display fields on the left side of the report to organize data into categories, with each row summarizing one particular category.
Column Labels	Display fields as columns at the top of the report to organize data into categories, with each column summarizing one particular category.
Report Filter	Filters the entire report based on the selected item in the report filter.

Table 5.6   Adding Fields to PivotChart Reports

PivotChart Report	Description
Valued	Displays summary numeric data.
Axis Field (categories)	Displays fields in an axis on the chart.
Legend Fields (series) Labels	Displays fields in the legend for the chart.
Report Filter	Filters the entire report based on the selected item in the report filter.

You can organize PivotTables by dragging and dropping data fields to different rows, columns, or summary positions. To design the PivotTable, do the following:

1. Drag a field to the Report Filter area in the Field List or right-click a field name and choose Add to Report Filter. Excel displays the field in the Report Filter area in the PivotTables as well. In Figure 5.44, the Sales Rep field is used to filter the data. You can click the field's drop-down arrow to select a particular value for filtering the data.

2. Drag a field to the Column Labels or right-click a field and choose Add to Column Labels to organize data into columns. Drag a field to the Row Labels area of the Field List or right-click a field and choose Add to Row Labels to organize data into groups on rows. Excel displays the field in the respective Column Labels and Row Labels area of the PivotTable as well. In Figure 5.44, the Media field is used to organize data into columns, and the Quarter field is used to organize data into rows.

3. Drag a field to the Values area in the Field List or right-click a field and choose Add to Values. Excel displays the field in the Values area of the PivotTable as well. In Figure 5.44, the Amount field is used as the Values field. The default function will sum amounts within the column and row categories.

If you want to use a different summary function instead of SUM, you can change it. To do so, click in a value within the PivotTable, click the PivotTable Tools Options tab, and click Field Settings in the Active Field. Alternatively, you can right-click a value in the PivotTable to display the Value Field Settings dialog box. The dialog box enables you to select other calculation types, such as Count, Average, Max, and Min. Furthermore, you can create your own custom calculations, such as percentage differences or running totals. You should explore the different options in the Value Field Settings and experiment with the available options.

In addition to selecting different summary functions and customizing calculations, you can create a calculated field. Similar to a calculated field in Access, a calculated field is a user-defined field that does not exist in the original data source. It derives its values based on performing calculations on other original data source fields. To create a calculated field, select a cell within the PivotTable, click the PivotTable Tools Options tab, and click Formulas in the Tools group. Then select Calculated Field to display the Insert Calculated Field dialog box. Use Excel Help to learn more about creating calculated fields in PivotTables.

TIP   The Page Field

A page field adds a third dimension to a PivotTable. Unlike items in the row and column fields, however, the items in a page field are displayed one at a time. Creating a page field on Quarter, for example, lets you view the data for each quarter separately, by clicking the down arrow on the Page field list box, then clicking the appropriate quarter.

You can rearrange or reposition existing fields in both PivotTables and PivotCharts by using one of the four areas at the bottom of the layout section. To rearrange fields, click and drag the field between the field and layout sections and between the different areas or click the field name in one of the areas, and then select one of the commands from Table 5.7.

Table 5.7 Rearrange Fields in PivotTables and PivotCharts

Command	Moves the Field . . .
Move Up	up one position in the area
Move Down	down one position in the area
Move to Beginning	to the beginning of the area
Move to End	to the end of the area
Move to Report Filter	to the Report Filter area
Move to Row Labels	to the Row Labels area
Move to Column Labels	to the Column Labels area
Move to Values	to the Values area

To remove a field, click the field name in the layout section, and then click Remove Field or clear the check box next to each field name in the field section. Alternatively, you can click and hold a field name in the layout section and drag it outside the PivotTable Field List.

Formatting, Sorting, Filtering, Subtotaling, and Refreshing a PivotTable

After you create a PivotTable, you will format it to enhance its information value. You will sort and filter your table to best analyze the data. Because PivotTables contain numeric data, you will generally subtotal and total the values. It is important to note that when your original data table data change, the PivotTable does not. PivotTables and PivotCharts are NOT dynamic; you must refresh the reports.

Format the PivotTable

Formatting PivotTables is primarily done in the PivotTable Tools Design tab. The dynamic Design palette shown in Figure 5.45 displays a wide variety of preset formats that are used to format PivotTables. In addition, the PivotTable Style Options group provides several other tools such as Banded rows and Banded columns for further formatting of the PivotTable.

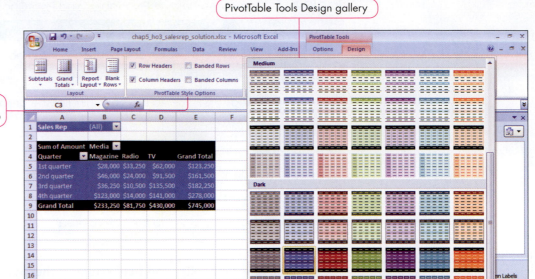

Figure 5.45 Tools for Formatting PivotTables

TIP   Design and Design Time

Excel provides a wide variety of design options in tools, galleries, and styles, but you must remember that less can be better. You do not have to choose all options, all colors, or all styles for all elements in your PivotTable or PivotChart. Further, some visually impaired people have difficulty distinguishing red and green colors. Use these colors sparingly.

Sort and Filter the PivotTable

PivotTables can be as complicated as the original data on which the PivotTable is based. Sorting and filtering the PivotTable make the data more manageable and easier to analyze. This simplifies the data analysis in the PivotTable. To sort or filter a PivotTable, click the drop-down arrow for a particular column heading. Figure 5.46 shows the Sort and Filter option lists available for PivotTables. The sorting and filtering options are similar to how you sort regular data tables.

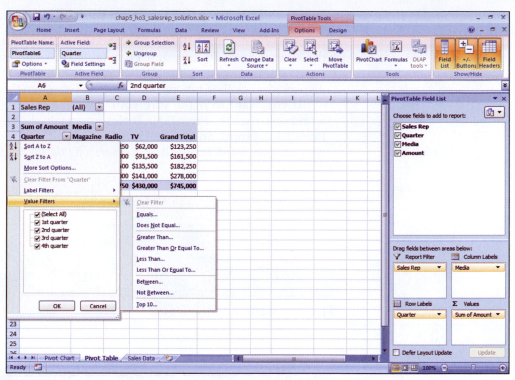

Figure 5.46 PivotTable Sort and Filter Options

Subtotal the PivotTable

By default, the values area consolidates data by showing subtotals for each category. You can customize PivotTable subtotals using the Subtotals command in the Layout group on the Design tab. Figure 5.47 displays the three subtotal options. When your PivotTable is large, displaying the subtotals at the top of the group draws attention to the totals and enables you to scroll to view all of the supporting data if necessary.

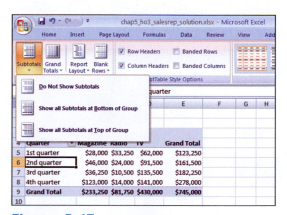

Figure 5.47 PivotTable Subtotals

Refresh the PivotTable and PivotChart

Excel does not update PivotTables and PivotCharts automatically when you change the source data. To refresh a PivotTable or PivotChart, right-click any cell in a PivotTable and select Refresh. Alternatively, with the PivotTable Tools contextual tab displayed, click the Options tab and click Refresh in the Data group (see Figure 5.48).

If you want to make sure your PivotTable is up-to-date when you open the workbook, click the PivotTable Tools Option tab, click the Options down arrow in the PivotTable group, and select Options. In the PivotTable Options dialog box, click the Data tab, select *Refresh data when opening the file*, and click OK.

Figure 5.48 PivotTable Tools

TIP   Format the Data Series

Why settle for a traditional bar chart when you can change the color, pattern, and shape of its components? Right-click any column to select a data series and display a shortcut menu, then select Format Data Series to display a dialog box in which you can customize the appearance of the vertical columns. We warn you that it is addictive and that you can spend much more time than you intended initially. Set a time limit and stop when you reach it.

PivotTable/PivotChart Tools | Reference

PivotTable Tools Tab and Group	Description
Options PivotTable Active Field Group Sort Data Actions Tools Show/Hide	The basic PivotTable tab. Contains basic editing functions for PivotTables. As with all groups, pull-down areas are available and do increase functionality.
Design Layout PivotTable Style Options PivotTable Styles	Brings together all format functions in one area. Includes ability to change the layout and styles within the PivotTable. Also enables the user to change the pre-defined style.

PivotChart Tools

Design Type Data Chart Layouts Chart Styles Location	Contains all functions associated with chart appearance and design. Allows the type of chart to be changed and placement of the chart in a different location
Layout Current Selection Insert Labels Axes Background Analysis Properties	Extensive coverage of layout functions for charts. This tab contains another option for adding shapes and also areas to change label elements and both axes and gridlines. The Analysis group is essential in advanced charting.
Format Current Selection Shape Styles WordArt Styles Arrange Size	Contains a wide variety of quick formatting tools. The shape styles and WordArt styles contain handy tools to quickly format those elements in charts. The Arrange items are valuable when working with text boxes and shapes.
Analyze Active Field Data Show/Hide	Contains all tools for analyzing the data in a PivotChart. Enables the user to refresh the chart when data are updated.

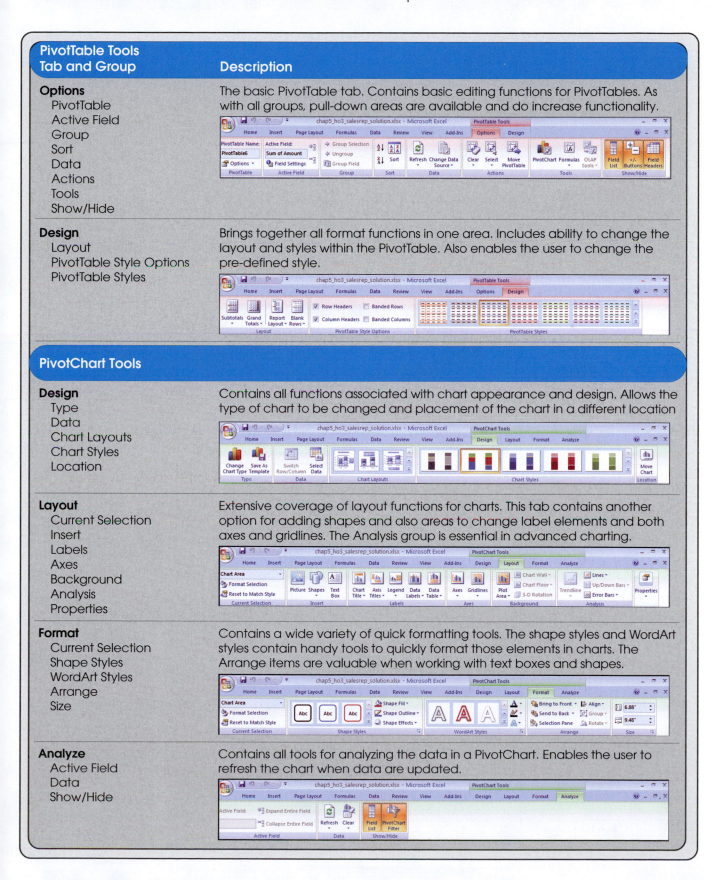

Hands-On Exercises

3 | Eye First Advertising Department Sales

Skills covered: 1. Create a PivotTable **2.** Complete the PivotTable **3.** Modify the Source Data and Refresh the PivotTable **4.** Pivot the Table **5.** Create a PivotChart **6.** Change and Enhance the PivotChart **7.** Complete the PivotChart **8.** Create a Web Page from a PivotTable **9.** Change Underlying Data

---

Step 1
Create a PivotTable

Refer to Figure 5.43 and Figure 5.49 as you complete Step 1.

a. Start Excel and open the *chap5_ho3_salesrep* workbook and save it as **chap5_ho3_salesrep_solution** so that you will be able to return to the original workbook.

The workbook contains a list of sales records for an advertising agency. Each record displays the name of the sales representative, the quarter in which the sale was recorded, the media type, and the amount of the sale.

b. Click anywhere in the list of sales data and click **PivotTable** in the Tables group on the Insert tab to open the Create PivotTable dialog box, as shown in Figure 5.43.

c. Verify that the **Select a table or range** is selected and that the **Table/Range** is Sales Data!$A$1:$D$97.

The Table/Range is the range for your data table and will be the basis for your PivotTable.

d. Verify that **New Worksheet** is selected and click **OK**. You will see Sheet1 (the PivotTable sheet) and the PivotTable Field List pane.

The option to put the PivotTable into a new worksheet was already selected. One additional sheet has been added to the workbook, but the PivotTable is not yet complete.

e. Save the workbook.

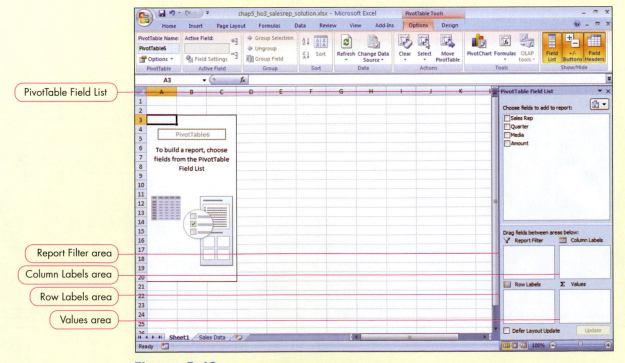

Figure 5.49 New PivotTable Placeholder

Step 2
Complete the PivotTable

a. Verify that the **Sheet1 tab** is selected and complete the PivotTable as follows:
Drag the **Media** field to the Row Labels area.

- The Media field box is checked and the field is simultaneously moved to the Row Label area in the PivotTable.
- Drag the **Sales Rep** field to the Column Labels area.
- The Sales Rep field box is checked and the field is simultaneously moved to the Column Labels area in the PivotTable.
- Drag the **Quarter** field to the Report Filter area.
- The Quarter field box is checked and the field is simultaneously moved to the Report Filter area in the PivotTable.
- Drag the **Amount** field to the Σ Values area.

The Amount field box is checked and the field is simultaneously moved to the Values area in the PivotTable, where it changes to the Sum of the Amount. You should see the total sales for each sales representative for each type of media within the PivotTable.

b. Double-click the **Sheet1 tab** (the worksheet that contains the PivotTable), type **PivotTable** as the new name, and press **Enter**.

You renamed the worksheet so it is more descriptive of its contents.

c. Click **cell B3**, type **Sales Rep**, and press **Enter**.

d. Click **cell A4**, type **Media**, and press **Enter**.

You changed the headings in the PivotTable to reflect the data labels in the data table.

e. Select the PivotTable by clicking and dragging **A1:J8**. Click **Format** in the Cells group on the Home tab and select **AutoFit Column Width**.

You changed the width of the columns to best display the report data.

TROUBLESHOOTING: If you click in a cell not in the PivotTable, the PivotTable Field List pane closes and the PivotTable tools are no longer available. Click anywhere in the PivotTable to redisplay the PivotTable Field List pane and the PivotTable tools.

f. Save the workbook.

Step 3
Modify the Source Data and Refresh the PivotTable

Refer to Figure 5.50 as you complete Step 3.

a. Click the **Sales Data sheet tab**, click **Find & Select** in the Editing group on the Home tab, and then click **Replace** to display the Find and Replace dialog box.

You will replace Peter's name within the list of transactions with your own name.

b. Type **Peter** in the *Find what* box and type **Your First Name and First Initial** of your last name in the *Replace with* box.

c. Click **Replace All**, click **OK** after the replacements have been made, and close the Find and Replace dialog box.

You used Find and Replace to replace all occurrences of Peter with your own name.

d. Click the **Pivot Table tab** to return to the PivotTable.

The name change is not yet reflected in the pivot table because the table must be manually refreshed whenever the underlying data changes.

e. Click anywhere in the PivotTable, click **Refresh** in the Data group on the Options tab, and then click **Refresh All** to update the PivotTable.

TROUBLESHOOTING: You must click Refresh All to update the PivotTable whenever the underlying data changes.

You should see your name as one of the sales representatives.

f. Save the workbook.

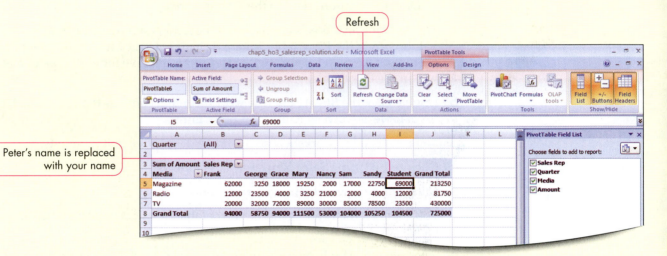

Figure 5.50 Modified Sales Data

Step 4

Pivot the Table

Refer to Figure 5.51 as you complete Step 4.

a. Click and drag the **Quarter** field to the **Row Labels area**.

You can change the arrangement of a PivotTable by dragging fields from one area to another. After moving the Quarter field, the Report Filter area is now empty and you can see the breakdown of sales by quarter and media type.

b. Click and drag the **Media** field to the **Column Labels area**, and then drag the **Sales Rep** field to the **Report Filter area**.

c. Click **cell A4**, type **Quarter**, and press **Enter**.

d. Click **cell B3**, type **Media**, and press **Enter**.

Your PivotTable should match the one in Figure 5.51. You pivoted the table by dragging the Media and Sales Rep fields. You then manually changed the labels.

e. Right-click anywhere in the PivotTable, click the **Sum of Amount drop-down arrow**, and select **Value Field Settings** to display the Value Field Settings dialog box.

The Value Field Settings dialog box enables you to select a different calculation function, such as Average. In addition, you use this dialog box to specify the number format.

f. Click **Number Format** in the Value Field Settings dialog box, and then choose **Currency** and **zero** decimal places.

g. Click **OK** to close the Format Cells dialog box and click **OK** a second time to close the Value Field Settings dialog box.

h. Save the workbook.

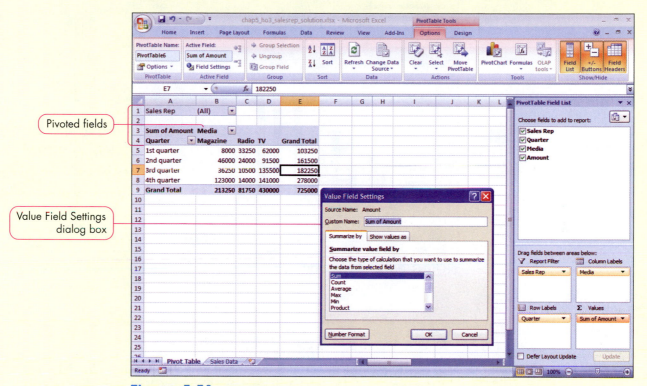

Figure 5.51 Pivoted Table

Step 5
Create a PivotChart

Refer to Figure 5.52 as you complete Step 5.

a. Click anywhere in the PivotTable and click **PivotChart** in the Tools group on the Options tab.

> **TROUBLESHOOTING:** You must make sure the PivotTable is active before you can create a PivotChart report.

b. Click **Clustered Column**, the first chart in the first row, in the Insert Chart dialog box and click **OK**.

You created a PivotChart that is displayed on the PivotTable sheet. The PivotChart shows total sales for all sales reps by media for each quarter. The PivotChart Filter pane displays the active fields on the PivotChart. The PivotChart Tools context tab displays four tools tabs you will use to enhance the appearance of the chart and to analyze your data.

c. Save the workbook.

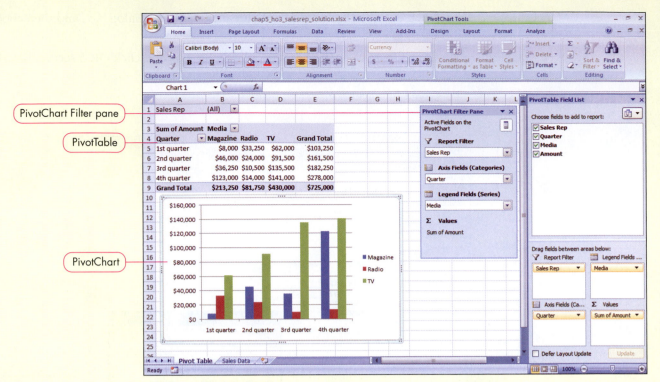

PivotChart Filter pane

PivotTable

PivotChart

Figure 5.52 PivotChart

Step 6	
Change and Enhance the PivotChart	

Refer to Figure 5.53 as you complete Step 6.

a. Verify that the PivotChart is selected and click **Change Chart Type** in the Type group on the Design tab to open the Change Chart Type dialog box.

b. Click **Stacked Column** and click **OK**.

You changed the chart type to better show total media sales by quarter.

c. Click **Move Chart** in the Location group on the Design tab to open the Move Chart dialog box.

d. Click **New sheet**, type **Pivot Chart** in the text box, and click **OK**.

You placed the PivotChart on a separate sheet and simultaneously renamed the sheet tab. Moving the chart expands the visible chart area for effective analysis.

e. Close the PivotTable Field List pane if necessary and close the PivotChart Filter pane.

f. Click **Chart Title** in the Labels group on the Layout tab and select **Above Chart**.

g. Type **Advertising Revenue by Quarter and Media Type**.

h. Click **Axis Titles** in the Labels group on the Layout tab and select **Primary Vertical Axis Title** and **Rotated Title**.

i. Type **Total Revenue**.

You added a title and labeled the Y axis to better identify the data.

j. Save the workbook.

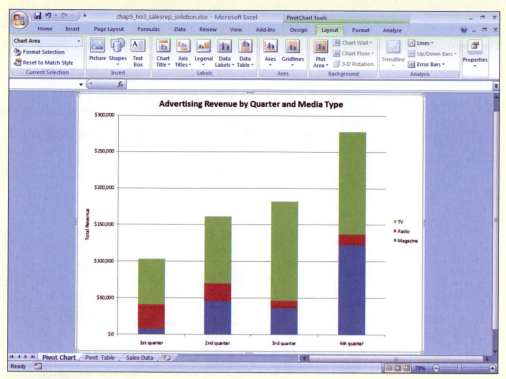

Figure 5.53 PivotChart on New Sheet

Step 7
Complete the PivotChart

a. Click the **Pivot Table sheet tab**, press and hold **Ctrl**, and click the **Sales Data sheet tab**.

You selected the Sales Data sheet and the Pivot Table sheet. Both worksheets are selected and both will be affected by the next command.

b. Click **Margins** in the Page Setup group on the Page Layout tab, select **Custom Margins**, and click the **Horizontally check box** in the *Center on page* section.

c. Click the **Header/Footer tab**, click **Custom Footer**, type **Your Name** in the Left section, click in the Right section, click **Insert Page Number**, and click **OK**.

d. Click the **Sheet tab**, click the **Gridlines check box**, and click the **Row and column headings check box** in the *Print* section.

e. Click **Print Preview** to verify that the PivotTable and the Sales Data will print correctly.

f. Close **Print Preview** and save the workbook.

Step 8
Create a Web Page from a PivotTable

Refer to Figure 5.54 as you complete Step 8.

a. Click the **Sales Data sheet tab** to deselect the two tabs and click the **PivotTable tab**.

b. Click and drag to select the entire PivotTable.

If you have difficulty selecting the table, click and drag from the bottom-right cell to the top-left cell.

c. Click the **Office Button** and select **Save As** to open the Save As dialog box.

d. Click the **Save as type drop-down arrow** and select **Web Page (∗.htm; ∗.html)**. Click **Publish: PivotTable**, and then click **Publish** to open the Publish as Web Page dialog box.

The selected PivotTable is going to be saved as a Web page, but first, you must enter a title and make the Web page interactive.

e. Click **Change** to open the Set Title dialog box, type **Advertising Agency Solution**, and then click **OK**.

f. Click the **AutoRepublish every time this workbook is saved check box** and click the **Open published web page in browser check box**.

g. Check that your settings match those in Figure 5.54 and click **Publish** to publish the PivotTable.

h. View the Web page in your browser and leave the browser open as you continue to Step 9.

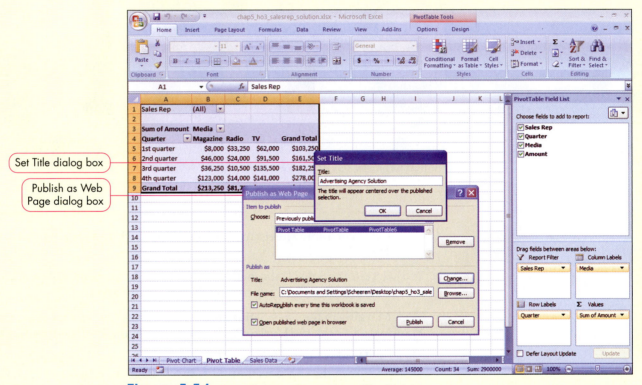

Figure 5.54 Create Web Page from PivotTable

Step 9
Change Underlying Data

Refer to Figure 5.55 as you complete Step 9.

a. Click the Excel button on the Windows taskbar to return to Excel and click the **Sales Data worksheet**.

b. Click **cell D18**, type **22000**, and press **Enter**.

You changed your magazine sales in the first quarter from $2,000 to $22,000.

c. Click the **Pivot Table sheet tab**, click anywhere in the PivotTable, click **Refresh** in the Data group on the Options tab, and select **Refresh All**.

The magazine sales in the 1st quarter increase to $28,000, and the grand total changes to $233,250.

d. Save the workbook, click **Enable the AutoPublish**, and then click **OK** in the Microsoft Office dialog box.

e. Return to Internet Explorer, then click **Refresh** on the browser toolbar to update the Web page (see Figure 5.55).

The numbers within the Web PivotTable change to reflect the change in magazine sales. If the numbers do not refresh, close Internet Explorer, reopen it, and then reopen the Web page from the Exploring Excel folder.

f. Return to Excel and click **PivotTable Tools Options tab**, click the **Options down arrow** in the PivotTable group, and select **Options**.

g. Click the **Data tab** in the PivotTable Options dialog box, select **Refresh data when opening the file**, and click **OK**.

Your PivotTable will automatically refresh when the workbook is opened and the PivotTable will display accurate results.

h. Close Internet Explorer. Close Excel. Click **Yes** if prompted to save the changes.

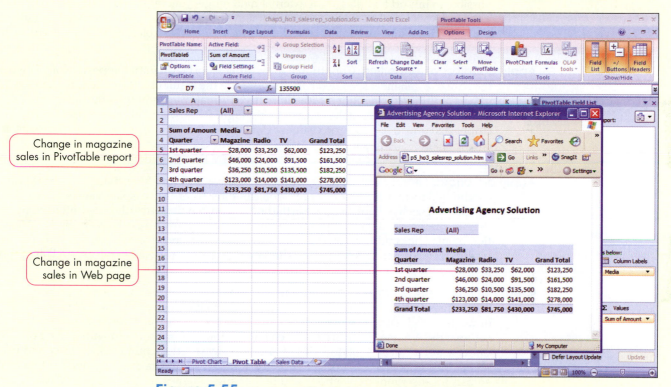

Figure 5.55 Updated PivotTable and Web Page

Summary

1. **Design tables based on data table theory.** Often, data tables are created from existing files and little or no thought is put into the creation of a data table that will be used for complex data analysis. Just as you spent time planning a spreadsheet, you should plan the elements of a data table. You should think about who will use the data table, what types of reports will be produced, and what types of searches might be done. As a general rule, the more thorough your planning process, the fewer changes will be needed to the table after it is created and in use.

2. **Import data from text files and other sources.** You have some options for importing data created in another format or in another application into an Excel table. This often occurs when data are collected on a mainframe computer and are then analyzed on a PC. Whereas it is possible to import text files as an external data range, generally, you will want to import a text file by opening it, forgoing the conversion that is necessary when importing a file as an external data range. You can import data from Access data tables and from sources such as the World Wide Web.

3. **Apply conditional formatting.** Conditional formatting is formatting that appears in a cell when the data in a cell meet specified conditions or are the result of a formula. It is used to impose additional conditions with alternative formats depending on the value of a cell. Conditional formatting makes it easy to highlight interesting cells or ranges of cells, emphasize unusual values, or visualize data using data bars, color scales, or icon sets. In conditional formatting, if the condition is true, the cell formatting is based on that condition. If it is false, the cell is not formatted based on that condition.

4. **Apply advanced filtering and sorting methods.** You can sort and filter data tables based on conditional formatting. For example, you can filter records to display values with a particular icon set, such as a green flag. Furthermore, you can perform advanced filtering by defining a criteria range for specifying multiple conditions. You can create an AND condition by placing conditions on the same row or you can create an OR condition by placing conditions on separate rows in the criteria range. Use relational operators, such as < and >, to restrict the filtered records.

5. **Create and use range names.** Creating a name, a word or string of characters representing a cell, range of cells, or constant value, equates the name, such as EmployeeList, to a cell or range of cells such as A1:E15. This name can then be used to reference cells in later commands. A name can be up to 255 characters long but must begin with a letter or underscore. It can be a mixture of upper or lowercase letters, numbers, periods, and underscores, but cannot have blank spaces. Once you have defined a range name, it automatically adjusts for insertions or deletions within the range. Names are used in formulas and serve as documentation while helping to clarify formula components. After creating range names, you can paste an alphabetical list of range names into a documentation worksheet for reference.

6. **Use database functions.** The database functions operate only on the selected records in a table. Their functions are similar to statistical functions (SUM, AVERAGE, MAX, MIN, COUNT) except that they only affect records that satisfy the criteria.

7. **Create and delete PivotTables and PivotCharts.** A PivotTable provides the most flexibility in data analysis. A PivotTable divides records in a list into categories and computes statistics for those categories. A PivotTable summarizes, analyzes, explores, and presents summary data. A PivotChart enables you to visually present the data in a report. Both PivotTable and PivotChart enable you to make informed decisions based on the data.

8. **Format, sort, filter, subtotal, and refresh a PivotTable.** Once you make a PivotTable, you format it to enhance its information value. You sort and filter your table to best analyze the data. You can even change subtotal options and select other summary functions, such as Average. Because PivotTables contain numeric data, you will often have to subtotal and total the values. It is important to note that when your original data changes, the PivotTable does not. PivotTables and PivotCharts are NOT dynamic; you must refresh the reports.

Key Terms

Peer Tutoring

DISASTER RECOVERY

Your volunteer service learning project involves tutoring students in Excel. Open the spreadsheet *chap5_mc3_donor*, save it as **chap5_mc3_donor_solution**, and find five errors. Correct the errors and explain how the errors might have occurred and how they can be prevented. Use Excel Help to locate information about possible errors and to assist you in the explanation of the error. Use Help to find the correct steps used to prevent the error. Include your explanation in the cells below the spreadsheet.

Performance Elements	Exceeds Expectations	Meets Expectations	Below Expectations
Identify and correct five errors	Identified and corrected all five errors.	Identified and corrected four errors.	Identified and corrected three or fewer errors.
Explain the errors	Complete and correct explanation of each error.	Explanation is too brief to fully explain error.	No explanations.
Prevention description	Prevention description correct and practical.	Prevention description present but obtuse.	No prevention description.
PivotTable created	Correct data used and identified.	Incorrect data used.	No PivotTable.
PivotTable formatted	Easy to read and analyze data.	Difficult to read and interpret data.	No formatting.
Identify sources	Two sources identified and correctly cited.	One source identified and correctly cited.	No sources identified or sources not cited.

Data Tables and Amortization Tables

Revisiting Data Tables and Amortizing

Objectives

After you read this chapter, you will be able to:

1. Separate and combine text **(page 379)**.
2. Manipulate text with functions **(page 381)**.
3. Identify and remove duplicate rows **(page 387)**.
4. Group and subtotal data **(page 388)**.
5. Work with windows **(page 391)**.
6. Use conditional functions **(page 399)**.
7. Create nested IF functions **(page 401)**.
8. Use AND, OR, NOT, and IFERROR functions **(page 402)**.
9. Define the amortization table **(page 409)**.
10. Use functions in amortization tables **(page 410)**.

Hands-On Exercises

Exercises	Skills Covered
1. IT DEPARTMENT STRING MANIPULATION (page 383) **Open:** chap6_ho1_textstrings.xlsx **Save as:** chap6_ho1_textstrings_solution.xlsx, chap6_ho1_textstrings_solution.txt, and chap6_ho1_textstrings2_solution.xlsx	• Convert Text to Columns • Use PROPER and CONCATENATE Functions to Create a User ID List • Use LOWER and CONCATENATE Functions to Create E-Mail Addresses • Use SUBSTITUTE Function to change E-Mail Addresses
2. AJAX COLLEGE BAND (page 394) **Open:** chap6_ho2_band.xlsx **Save as:** chap6_ho2_band_solution.xlsx	• Convert Text to Columns • Identify and Remove Duplicate Rows • Subtotal the Data • Group and Ungroup Data • Use Multiple Windows
3. CLASSIC CARS AND SECURITY (page 404) **Open:** chap6_ho3_classiccars.xlsx **Save as:** chap6_ho3_classiccars_solution.xlsx	• Use SUMIF, AVERAGEIF, and COUNTIF Functions • Use SUMIFS, AVERAGEIFS, and COUNTIFS Functions • Nest the AND Function in an IF Function • Nest the OR Function in an IF Function • Nest the IF Function
4. PURCHASE A NEW HOUSE (page 413) **Open:** chap6_ho4_amortization.xlsx **Save as:** chap6_ho4_amortization_solution.xlsx	• Enter the Loan Parameters • Enter Formulas for the First Payment • Name a Cell • Add the IF Functions • Enter the Formulas for the Second Payment • Complete the Payment Schedule • Complete the Summary Area and Print

CASE STUDY

Refinance Your Home

You purchased your first home three years ago. It is in a good neighborhood, your neighbors are friendly, you have a large yard for your dog, and you are at home. You took out a 30-year mortgage for $300,000 at 7.5%, which resulted in a monthly payment of just under $2,100. You have paid approximately $75,000 to the bank (principal and interest) during the three years you have lived in the house, but are shocked to learn that you still owe approximately $291,000 on the mortgage. In other words, you have paid approximately $65,000 in interest and only $10,000 in principal.

The good news is that interest rates are at or near their lowest level in 40 years. You have been approached by multiple mortgage brokers about the benefits of refinancing, yet you still have doubts about whether you should refinance. You know that your monthly payment will go down, but you will incur additional closing costs of 4% to obtain the new loan on the remaining principal of $291,000. You plan to roll the closing costs into the new mortgage to avoid an out-of-pocket

expense. You can obtain either a 15- or 30-year mortgage and you want to explore the advantages of each. Is it possible that the lower interest rates on a new 15-year loan could keep your payments at the same level as your existing 30-year mortgage? Further, you will pay an extra amount each month in order to pay the loan off sooner. What impact will the extra payments have on the term of your mortgage? What is your payment for a 20-year mortgage or a 40-year mortgage?

Your Assignment

- Read the chapter carefully and pay close attention to information on how to create and use a loan amortization workbook. Your workbook will enable you to enter an additional payment each month, reducing the total time of your mortgage.

- Open the *chap6_case_house* file and save it as **chap6_case_house_solution**. You notice that the column headings are combined in cell A12. Convert the text into columns, splitting text at the appropriate delimiter.

- Look at the Rate Comparison worksheet, which displays various financial institutions, rates, and points. However, the table contains duplicate information. Remove duplicate rows. As you build the amortization table, try out different terms and rates based on the data in the Rate Comparison worksheet.

- Compare your existing mortgage to a new 15-year mortgage at 5%. It should show the monthly payment, the savings per month, and the total interest over the life of each loan. It should also determine the number of months to break even on the new 15-year mortgage. Incorporate nested IF functions and date functions to perform the calculations.

- Use the completed workbook to enter extra payments each month to reduce the term of the mortgage.

- Experiment with different interest rates to see the impact each has on the mortgage. Test your work for both a 20- and 40-year mortgage, extending the workbook if necessary.

- Split the worksheet windows to view the top five and last five payments.

- Create a custom footer that includes your name, a page number, and your instructor's name. Print the worksheet as displayed and with formulas visible. Save the completed workbook.

Tables

All enterprises—business, education, health care, or government—maintain data in the form of lists. Companies have lists of employees. Educational institutions maintain lists of students and faculty members. Governmental entities, such as the military, maintain extensive inventory lists. The concepts associated with tables in Excel are database concepts.

Excel maintains lists of data in the form of a table. A table is an area in the worksheet that contains rows and columns of similar or related information. A table can be used as part of a database or organized collection of related information, where the worksheet rows represent the records, and the worksheet columns represent the fields in a record. The first row contains the column labels or field names, such as *First Name*, *Last Name*, *Address*, *City*, *State*, and *Zip Code*. This identifies the data that will be entered in the columns. Each row in the table contains a record. Every cell in the table area, except the field names, contains a specific value for a specific field in a specific record. Every record (row) contains the same fields (columns) in the same order as the other records. For example, if cell A1 contains *First Name* as the column heading, all records contain first names in the first column.

Tables and table theory were introduced in a previous chapter, and in this chapter you will continue to explore tables and manipulate table data. In this section you will convert text to columns and remove duplicate rows from tables. You will work with separating and combining text, features that are sometimes necessary to work with data in tables. You will use a function to join text and use functions to convert text from one case to another. These actions will yield more accurate and meaningful data.

Separating and Combining Text

Often, colleagues share data files with each other in organizations. Sharing Excel workbooks helps others update budgets and prepare financial reports. Although you might receive a workbook that contains data you need, it might not be formatted the way you need it. Specifically, you might need to convert text to columns, combine text entries, or remove duplicate rows.

Convert Text to Columns

You previously learned how to import text files into a workbook using the Text Import Wizard. As you completed the wizard, you had to select the delimiter type to separate data into columns as they were imported. After you import the text file data, you might find that data are combined into one column when they should be separated into two columns. In other situations, a colleague might send you an Excel workbook in which data are combined into one column but need to be separated so that you can manipulate them.

> You can use the Text to Columns command to . . . separate *Sam Jones* into two columns—one column for first name and one column for last name.

For example, a column might combine first and last names, such as Sam Jones. You need to sort the list alphabetically by last name, but you cannot do that as long as the first and last names are combined. You can use the Text to Columns command to split the contents in one column into separate columns. For example, you can use Text to Columns to separate *Sam Jones* in two columns—one column for first name and one column for last name. Figure 6.1 shows first and last names combined in Column A and the results after converting text into two columns.

The Convert Text to Columns Wizard is very similar to the Text Import Wizard. To place the first and last names in different cells:

1. Select the column containing the text you want to split.
2. Click Text to Columns in the Data Tools group on the Data tab.
3. Use the Convert Text to Columns Wizard to distribute the data (see Figure 6.2). As with the Import Text Wizard, you must specify the file type and click Next.

4. Specify the delimiters, such as a Tab or Space, in the Convert Text to Columns Wizard – Step 2 of 3. The data shown in Figure 6.2 are delimited by spaces. The wizard can use the space to separate the first and last names in this example. Click Next.

5. Select the type of data, such as General, in the Convert Text to Columns Wizard – Step 3 of 3 and click Finish.

It is important to allow enough columns to the right of the column to be split so data are not overwritten. If you have a first name, middle name, and last name all in one column and you separate to get a first name column, middle name column, and last name column, you must have three empty columns. If your columns are not empty, Excel will overwrite existing data.

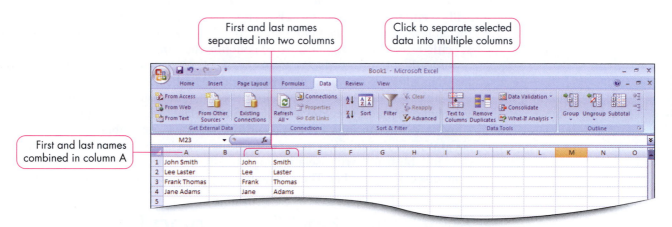

Figure 6.1 Combined Names and Separated Names

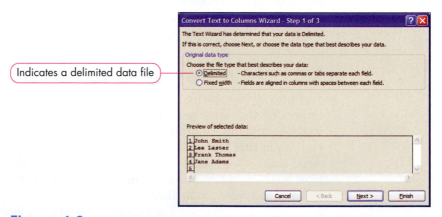

Figure 6.2 Convert Text to Columns Wizard

Combine Text into One Cell
CONCATENATE Function | Reference

CONCATENATE(text1,text2, . . .)

Text labels are often referred to as text strings. A text string is any entry in a cell that is not used for calculation. Both 2008 and 3/15/2008 are text strings when used as labels. Name is a label but the cell contents might be Jane Doe, and both are text strings. Often, you want to combine two or more text strings located in two or more cells into just one string in one cell. For example, you must make an account name and want to combine last name with first name. Perhaps you would even include a comma and a space after the comma. The *CONCATENATE function* joins two or

The **CONCATENATE function** joins two or more text strings into one text string.

more text strings into one text string and permits you to include the comma or space separators in the text string. If first name is in cell A4, last name in cell B4, and the result in cell C4, you would enter =CONCATENATE(B4,", ",A4) in cell C4. Note the comma and space included inside the quotes to produce *Doe, Jane*. When constructing a CONCATENATE function, be careful to place any commas and spaces correctly so that you get the desired result. See Figure 6.3 for an example of the CONCATENATE function. The text items can be strings of text, numbers, or single-cell references, but Excel enables you to join up to only 255 text items into a single text item.

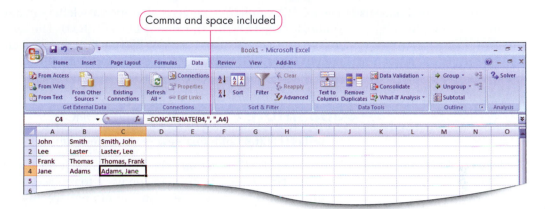

Figure 6.3 Concatenation—Join Text Strings

 **Another Way**

Use the ampersand (&) operator instead of the CONCATENATE function to join text items. For example, =A4&B4 returns the same value as =CONCATENATE(A4,B4).

Manipulating Text with Functions
PROPER Function | Reference

PROPER(text)

The **PROPER function** capitalizes the first letter in a text string and any other letters in text that follow any character other than a letter.

Excel has several functions that are specifically designed to enable you to change or manipulate text strings. Often, a spreadsheet is created with names typed in all lowercase letters, all uppercase letters, or some combination. The **PROPER function** capitalizes the first letter of a text string and any other letters in a text string that follow any character other than a letter and converts all uppercase or all lowercase so just the first letter of a string is uppercase. The PROPER function converts all other letters to lowercase. The syntax for the PROPER function is PROPER(text). The text argument is a text string that must be enclosed in quotation marks, a formula that returns text, or a reference to a cell that contains text that you want to partially capitalize. For example, if you receive a spreadsheet with song titles including the song "hello I must be going" you could use the PROPER function to convert the text string to "Hello I Must Be Going."

UPPER Function | Reference

UPPER(text)

The **UPPER function** converts text to uppercase letters.

The **UPPER function** converts text strings to uppercase letters. The syntax for the UPPER function is UPPER(text). The text argument is the text to be converted to uppercase and can be a reference or text string. You use this function when a cell or range contains text in lowercase letters and you need the text to be formatted in all uppercase letters. Often you will want to standardize your text strings to be all uppercase and will use the UPPER function to convert columns of text to all uppercase. When searching a table, you will get skewed results if your search criteria include uppercase text but your data are in lower or mixed case.

LOWER Function | Reference

LOWER(text)

The **LOWER function** converts all uppercase letters to lowercase.

The **LOWER function** converts all uppercase letters in a text string to lowercase. The syntax for the LOWER function is LOWER(text). The text argument is text you want to convert to lowercase. The LOWER function does not change characters in text that are not letters. E-mail addresses and computer user IDs are typically used in lowercase. You can use the LOWER function to convert text not already in lowercase.

SUBSTITUTE Function | Reference

SUBSTITUTE(text,old_text,new_text,instance_num)

The **SUBSTITUTE function** substitutes new text for old text in a text string.

The **SUBSTITUTE function** substitutes new text for old text in a text string. You use the SUBSTITUTE function when you want to replace specific text in a text string. You would use this function when you want to replace any text in a specific location in a text string. For example, colleges that become universities can use the SUBSTITUTE function to substitute the string "college" with "university" in the title of all workbooks. The syntax for the SUBSTITUTE function is SUBSTITUTE(text, old_text,new_text,instance_num). Text is the text or reference to a cell that is to be substituted for. Old_text is the text to be replaced, new_text is the text you want to replace old_text with. Instance_num specifies which occurrence of old_text you want to replace with new text. When instance_num is specified, only that instance is changed. If you do not include instance_num, all occurrences are changed. For example, if your text string was February 1, 2011, you could use =SUBSTITUTE(A4,"1","2",3) to produce February 1, 2012. Excel will replace the third instance of "1" with a "2." Review Figure 6.4 for examples of the text functions in row 6.

Nested functions are functions within another function.

The text functions are often used in combination or as nested functions. Nesting is a technique that lets you put one function inside another. **Nested functions** are functions within another function. For example, you can nest a CONCATENATE function inside an UPPER function argument. For example, =UPPER(CONCATE-NATE(B4,", ",A4)) concatenates the contents of cells B4, a comma and a space, and the contents of cell A4. The concatenated result is then converted to uppercase.

	A	B	C	D	E	F	G	H	I	J	K	L	M
1	John	Smith	Smith, John	SMITH, JOHN	smith, john	February 1, 2011		February 1, 2012					
2	Lee	Laster	Laster, Lee	LASTER, LEE	laster, lee								
3	Frank	Thomas	Thomas, Frank	THOMAS, FRANK	thomas, frank								
4	Jane	Adams	Adams, Jane	ADAMS, JANE	adams, jane								
5													
6	Function Used			=UPPER(C1)	=LOWER(C1)			=SUBSTITUTE(F1,"1","2",3)					
7													

Figure 6.4 Text Functions

Hands-On Exercises

1 | IT Department String Manipulation

Skills covered: 1. Convert Text to Columns **2.** Use PROPER and CONCATENATE Functions to Create a User ID List **3.** Use LOWER and CONCATENATE Functions to Create E-Mail Addresses **4.** Use SUBSTITUTE Function to Change E-Mail Addresses

---

Step 1 Convert Text to Columns	Refer to Figure 6.5 as you complete Step 1.

a. Open the *chap6_ho1_textstrings* workbook and save it as **chap6_ho1_textstrings_solution** so you can return to the original workbook if necessary.

You notice that the names of students in the IT department are in one cell in first name, last name order. You must convert the text into columns.

b. Select **cells A3:A76** and click **Text to Columns** in the Data Tools group on the Data tab.

You selected the names of all students.

c. Verify that **Delimited** is selected in the *Original data type* section in the Convert Text to Columns Wizard – Step 1 of 3 dialog box and click **Next**.

d. Click the **Space check box**, remove the check from the **Tab check box** in the *Delimiters* section in the Convert Text to Columns Wizard – Step 2 of 3 dialog box, and click **Next**.

The combined data are separated by a space; therefore, you must use the space to delimit the data.

e. Verify that the **General** option is selected in the *Column data format* section, the **Destination** box contains **$A$3**, the *Data preview* is correct, and then click **Finish**.

f. Click **OK** if prompted *Do you want to replace the contents of the destination cells?*

You will see that Excel separated the name data into columns A and B.

g. Type **First Name** in **cell A2** and press **Enter**.

h. Save the workbook.

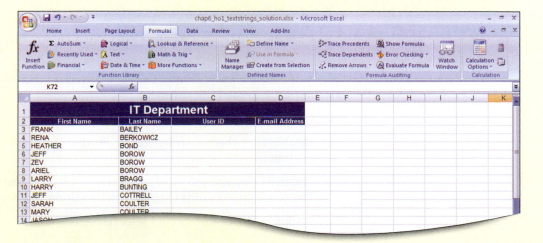

Figure 6.5 Separated First and Last Names

Step 2

Use PROPER and CONCATENATE Functions to Create a User ID List

Refer to Figure 6.6 as you complete Step 2.

a. Click in **cell C3**.

b. Type **=PROPER(CONCATENATE(B3,".",A3))**.

You created a nested function that will first join last name and first name with a period separating the two. Excel then converted the uppercase text to proper case.

TROUBLESHOOTING: Make sure your parentheses match before pressing Enter.

c. Press **Enter**.

d. Click in **cell C3** and copy through **cell C76**.

Excel created a list of User IDs for all employees in the IT Department.

e. Save the workbook.

TROUBLESHOOTING: If you reverse the nested functions, use the PROPER function twice: =CONCATENATE(PROPER(B3),".",PROPER(A3)).

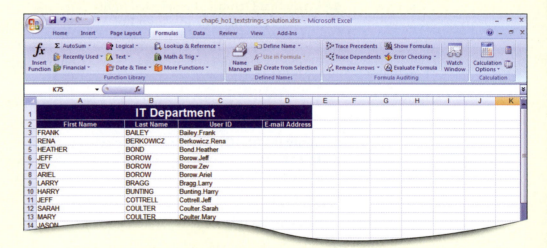

Figure 6.6 User ID List

Step 3

Use LOWER and CONCATENATE Functions to Create E-Mail Addresses

Refer to Figure 6.7 as you complete Step 3.

a. Click in **cell D3**. Type **=LOWER(CONCATENATE(A3,"_",B3,"@myschool.edu"))** and press **Enter**.

You used the LOWER and CONCATENATE functions to create e-mail addresses for those in the IT department.

b. Click in **cell D3** and copy the formula through **cell D76**.

c. Double-click the border between columns D and E to AutoFit the contents of column D.

You used functions to manipulate text to produce the results shown in Figure 6.7. The results in columns C and D are functions and not text.

d. Click the **Office Button** and select **Save As**.

e. Click the **Save as type drop-down arrow**, select **Text (Tab delimited) (∗.txt)**, and click **Save**.

If you want to use the results of your text manipulation in another application, you must convert the function produced results to text data. When you save your workbook as a text file, Excel automatically converts the contents of cells to text and formatted numbers and removes all worksheet formatting. You could use the Paste Special Values to convert small amounts of function-produced data to text.

TROUBLESHOOTING: You will see a Microsoft Excel warning box when you save the file as a text file. You are warned that you could lose some functions when converting to a text file. The warning box is shown in Figure 6.7.

f. Click **Yes**.

g. Close the text file.

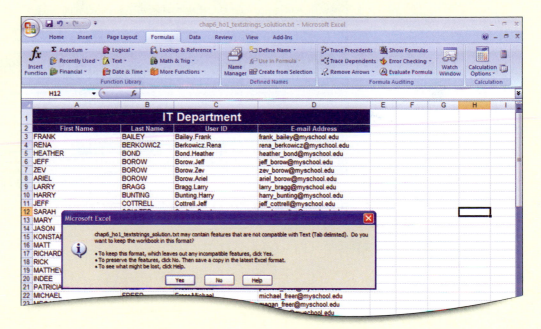

Figure 6.7 E-Mail Addresses

Step 4

Use SUBSTITUTE Function to Change E-Mail Addresses

Refer to Figure 6.8 as you complete Step 4.

a. Open the file **chap6_ho1_textstrings_solution.txt** you just created.

The Text Import Wizard automatically opens.

b. Verify that **Delimited** is selected in the *Original data type* section and click **Next**.

c. Click the **Tab check box** in the *Delimiters* section, remove the check from the **Space check box**, and click **Next**.

d. Verify that **General** is selected in the *Column data format* section and click **Finish**.

You imported a text file into Excel.

e. Click the **Office Button**, select **Save As**, click the **Save as type drop-down arrow**, select **Excel Workbook (∗.xlsx)**, and save the file as **chap6_ho1_textstrings2_solution**.

f. Click in **cell E2**, type **New E-mail Address**, and press **Enter**.

This is the column where you will use the SUBSTITUTE function to convert all e-mail addresses to the new e-mail address.

g. Format the worksheet as shown in Figure 6.8.

h. Click in **cell E3**, type **=SUBSTITUTE(D3,"myschool.edu","mynewschool.com")**, and press **Enter**.

i. Click in **cell E3** and copy the formula through **cell E76**.

j. Double-click the border between columns E and F to AutoFit the text.

Using the SUBSTITUTE function you were able to have Excel replace the old school e-mail address with a new address.

k. Save and close the workbook.

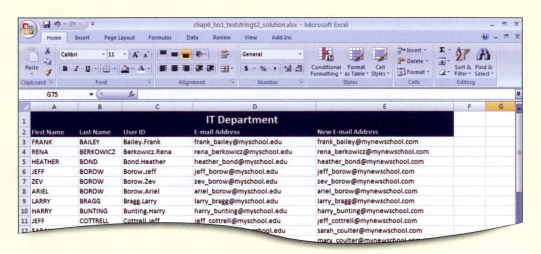

Figure 6.8 New E-Mail Addresses

Data Analysis and Windows

Previously, you learned the difference between data and information and will continue to learn new techniques to help you analyze data. Data analysis is the process of methodically applying statistical and logical techniques to describe, summarize, and compare data.

In this section, you learn how to identify and remove duplicate rows, group and subtotal data, and manipulate windows. These techniques individually and collectively are used to prepare and present data for analysis.

Identifying and Removing Duplicate Rows

Despite the best efforts to check data, duplicate values can slip into data tables. Often, you can see duplicate values if the table is small. However, if the table is large, it may involve considerable scrolling to identify these duplicates. For example, assume you are hosting a formal dinner for your organization. You believe that your assistant entered duplicates for some of your guests. You need to identify the duplicate rows so that you do not assign the same guests to multiple tables. Review Figure 6.9 to see how it is possible to assign the same two people to two different tables.

Using conditional formatting techniques, discussed previously, it is possible to identify duplicates.

1. Select the column in a table that is to be checked for duplicates.
2. Click the Home tab, and then click Conditional Formatting in the Styles group.
3. Point to Highlight Cell Rules, and then select Duplicate Values to open the Duplicate Values dialog box. You then choose the formatting that will show duplicate values and click OK.

Excel highlights all values that are duplicated in the selected column(s). This is a dynamic option and continues to work even as records with duplicated values are added. Figure 6.9 shows duplicate rows. Excel 2007 automates the removal of duplicate rows.

1. Click any cell in a table.
2. Click Remove Duplicates in the Data Tools group on the Data tab.
3. The Remove Duplicates dialog box prompts you to select the columns that may contain duplicates.
4. Click OK. A report of the number of duplicates found and deleted is shown in the dialog box in Figure 6.10.

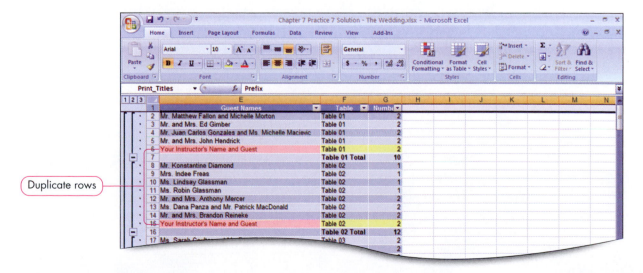

Figure 6.9 Worksheet with Duplicate Rows

Figure 6.10 Remove Duplicates Dialog Box

Grouping and Subtotaling Data

Grouping is often used to compress data for presentation or analysis by different groups of people. For example, in the manufacturing process, production managers are primarily concerned with daily production figures. The production reports are detailed, showing the finest granularity of items produced. The next level of supervisor is not concerned with the finer details of daily production, but instead, uses the monthly production figures. The president of the company is interested in viewing the quarterly production figures. Excel's grouping feature enables you to create the reports used by various people in the organization.

Group and Ungroup Data

A way to simplify complex worksheets containing formulas is to group data. Grouping enables you to consolidate related rows or columns into single units. Once you have consolidated the rows or columns into a group, you can collapse the group to make it easier to view only what you want to see. Figure 6.11 shows the details and three groups for quarterly, monthly, and daily sales by salesperson for a clothing store.

To group data, select the rows or columns to be grouped. Then click Group in the Outline group on the Data tab. It is now possible to collapse the group by clicking the minus sign in the margin area.

To ungroup this data and expand the group, select all columns or rows that were grouped and click Ungroup in the Outline group on the Data tab. Excel will not create an outline or group data if no formulas exist in the worksheet. Grouping data in a worksheet with no formulas produces one level, not a detailed outline.

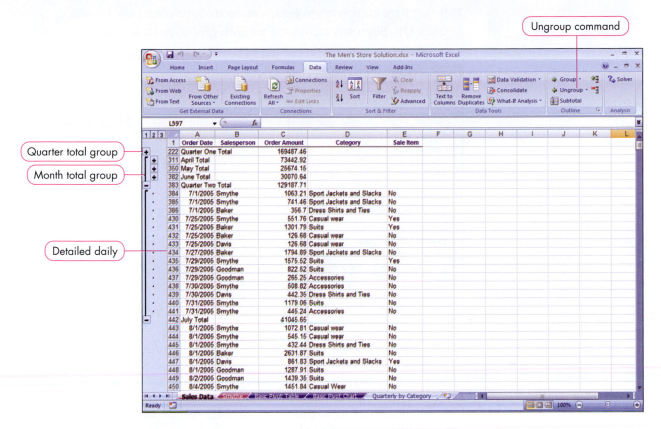

Figure 6.11 Grouped Data

Subtotal Data

The **Subtotal command** inserts
a subtotal row where the value
of the designated field changes.

The **Subtotal command** uses a summary function such as SUM, AVERAGE, or COUNT to compute subtotals within a sorted data list. The records are grouped according to the value of a specific field, such as location, and the Subtotal command inserts a subtotal row where the value of the designated field changes. A grand total is displayed after the last record. The records must be in sequence by the field on which the subtotals will be grouped prior to executing the Subtotal command. Referred to as control break reports, the subtotals provide summary totals used in data analysis. For example, a multinational organization will compare several data from individual countries. The organization will review the data from just one country. Figures 6.13, 6.14, and 6.15 show all data, city totaled data, and a grand total, respectively. The data are grouped and totaled.

To add automatic subtotals:

1. Sort the data in the group field. Do this by selecting a cell in the column and clicking Sort A to Z in the Sort & Filter group on the Data tab. The subtotal option in Excel will produce erroneous or not useful results if the data are not sorted first.

2. Select a cell containing data.

3. Click Subtotal in the Outline group of the Data tab to open the Subtotal dialog box.

4. Click the *At each change in* drop-down arrow and select the column heading for the column used as the group field. If you select the incorrect field for the change, Excel will produce a total in every cell.

5. Click the *Use function* drop-down arrow and select the function you want to apply to the data.

6. Check the appropriate field in the *Add subtotal to* list for each field you want to total, as shown in Figure 6.12. You can use all functions for columns that contain numerical data. For text fields, you can only count the number of rows within the group.

7. Select *Page break between groups* as needed for your page breaks.
8. Click OK. Subtotals are added for each group, as shown in Figure 6.12.

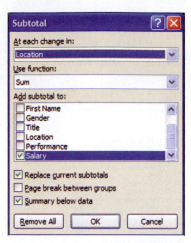

Figure 6.12 Subtotal Dialog Box

Summary information can be displayed with different levels of detail, as shown in Figures 6.13, 6.14, and 6.15. A minus sign indicates that the group has been collapsed, while the plus sign indicates that more detail is available. You can click the symbol (1, 2, 3, etc.) above the plus or minus signs to collapse or expand the amount of detail. Another way to change the detail level is to click Show Detail or Hide Detail in the Outline group of the Data tab.

Figure 6.13 Table with All Data Visible

Figure 6.14 Table with Summary Totals—Less Data Visible

Figure 6.15 Table with Least Data Visible

Working with Windows

Often, you will have multiple workbooks open at one time. When you want to compare data from one workbook to another or when you want to combine data from several individual workbooks in one comprehensive workbook, you will need to have several workbooks open at one time. Maybe you have first-quarter sales open to compare to last year's first-quarter sales. It is easy to compare the data when you can view these worksheets side by side on your screen. You can work with multiple workbooks visible in multiple windows on your screen. Refer to the View tab shown in Figure 6.16.

Figure 6.16 The View Tab

Open and Arrange Windows

When you have several Excel windows open at the same time, you might have an occasion when you want to see more than one window at a time. Accountants, for example, will compare your last year's tax return to this year's tax return in separate windows and on the screen at the same time. Teachers will have your research paper open and their grade book open at the same time and visible in separate windows on the screen.

To open and arrange windows, click Arrange All in the Window group on the View tab. Select one of the options from the Arrange Windows dialog box, and then click OK. The arrangement of windows can be changed as often as necessary to view the data with which you must work.

Split a Window

Splitting a window is the process of dividing a worksheet window.

When you work with very large, complex worksheets, you may need to view different sections at the same time. For example, you may need to look at input data on rows 5 and 6 and see how changing the data affects overall results on row 150. To see these different worksheet sections at the same time, you can split the worksheet window. **Splitting a window** is the process of dividing a worksheet window into two or four resizable panes so you can view widely separated parts of a worksheet at the same time. All window panes are part of the one worksheet. Any changes you make to one window affect the entire worksheet.

A **splitter control** is the two-headed arrow in the scroll bar used to divide a window into panes.

To do this, click Split in the Window group on the View tab. To resize these split panes, you can drag the horizontal or vertical splitter controls. A **splitter control** is the two-headed arrow at the bottom of the vertical scroll bar and at the right of the horizontal scroll bar and it is used to resize the panes. As you drag the splitter control, you see a gray bar that shows where the window pane will be divided. You drag the horizontal splitter bar to divide the window pane into upper and lower (horizontal) panes. You can drag the vertical splitter bar to split the window pane into left and right (vertical) window panes. Within each window pane, you can scroll to the desired area you wish to see. When you split the worksheet vertically, synchronized scrolling is on. If you scroll any pane, the cells in the other panes move. If you have different worksheets visible in the panes, you can use the Synchronous Scrolling command in the Window group on the View tab to turn off synchronous scrolling and scroll just one pane at a time. Figure 6.17 shows both the beginning summary area and bottom of a large worksheet.

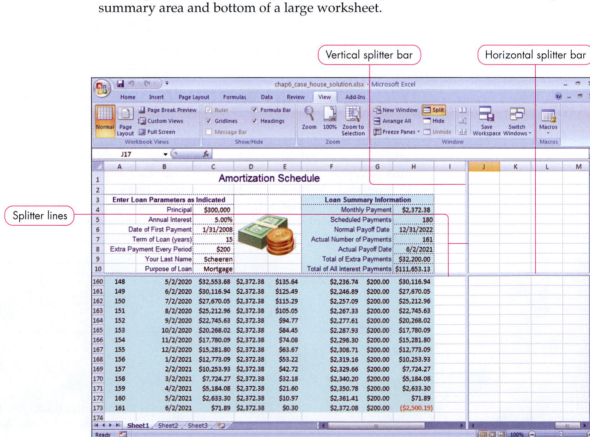

Figure 6.17 Split Window

Change the View in a Single Window

You can view multiple worksheets or multiple workbooks in the same window. To do this, either arrange the windows so all are visible and click one to make it active or click a sheet tab to make it active. Then you may click many of the view options on the View tab, as shown in Figure 6.16. The options you select are only in effect for the active window. Figure 6.18 shows multiple views of the same workbook.

If your job requires you to open the same workbooks all the time and you always arrange the workbook windows the same way, you will find the custom workspace feature beneficial. To use the feature, you will first open and arrange the windows for your needs. Click Save Workspace in the Window group on the View tab, enter a file name, and click Save. The file is saved with the .XLW extension to distinguish the file from workbook files.

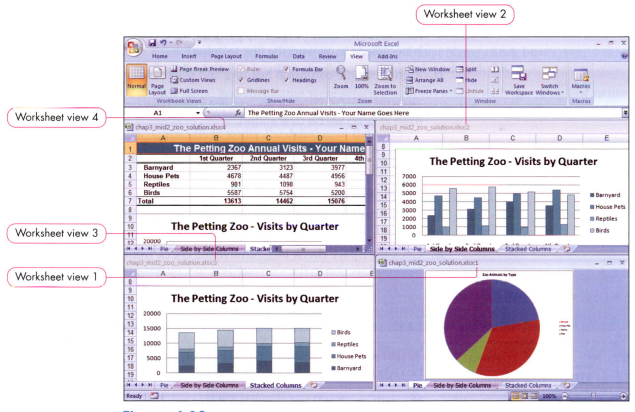

Figure 6.18 Multiple Views

g. While viewing the pie chart, click **New Window** in the Window group on the View tab.

You have opened a second window.

h. Click **Arrange All** in the Window group, click **Horizontal** in the Arrange Windows dialog box, and click **OK**.

i. Click the **Sheet1 tab** in the top window to view the worksheet.

You have two windows visible on the screen. One displays the chart and one shows the grouped sheet.

j. Save and close the workbook.

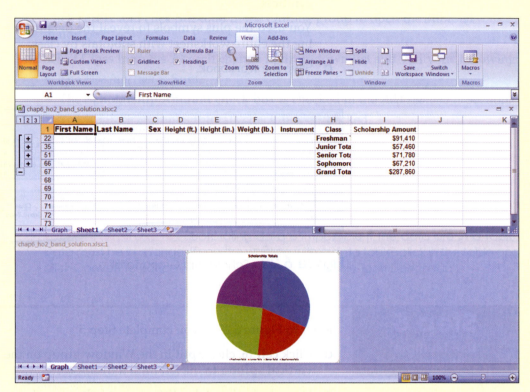

Figure 6.23 Multiple Windows

TIP **Print Preview Versus Page Break Preview**

The Print Preview command displays a worksheet as it will be printed including the header and/or the footer. The Page Break Preview, however, lets you see and/or modify the page breaks by dragging the breaks, which are indicated by a solid or dashed blue line, to allow more or less on any given page. Click Page Break Preview in the status bar to see the worksheet with the intended page breaks. Click Normal to return to the familiar view of a spreadsheet.

Conditional and Logical Functions

Functions are powerful tools that are built-in formulas you do not have to create yourself. This section will discuss the use of more complex functions. You will use conditional functions to SUM, AVERAGE, or COUNT data based on particular conditions or criteria. In the payment tables, you will use functions that include nested IF and the use of AND, OR, and NOT. The IFERROR function that is used primarily with error checking will be introduced, as well as several text-manipulation functions. Logical functions are a category of function in Excel and are one of the workhorses in workbook use. Accountants, teachers, statisticians, and managers use logical functions on a regular basis. In this section, you use conditional and logical functions.

> (. . . use conditional functions to SUM, AVERAGE, or COUNT data based on particular conditions or criteria.)

Using Conditional Functions

When you created formulas with SUM, COUNT, and AVERAGE functions, you summed, counted, or averaged all values in a range of cells. Two sets of three functions expand the power of the SUM, COUNT, and AVERAGE functions. The first set is SUMIF, COUNTIF, and AVERAGEIF, which return the total, count, or average for one criterion. For example, you might want the total sales for just one particular salesperson from the whole sales force, or you might want to know the number of blue bicycles manufactured last year from a rainbow of colors produced. The second set of functions is SUMIFS, COUNTIFS, and AVERAGEIFS. These functions return a total, count, or average based on two criteria. For example, you can use the SUMIFS function to determine the total sales for a salesperson for the weeks in the first quarter, or you might want the total of blue bicycles manufactured the first two weeks of this month.

Use SUMIF, COUNTIF, and AVERAGEIF Functions
SUMIF Function | Reference

SUMIF(range,criteria,sum_range)

The *SUMIF function* adds the cells specified by a given criterion.

The *SUMIF function* is similar to the SUM function except that it enables you to calculate a sum of values in a range that satisfies a specific condition you specify instead of calculating the sum of an entire range. SUMIF is often called a conditional sum because it sums the values that meet a particular condition. In the syntax for the SUMIF function, the range is the range of cells that are evaluated by criteria. Cells in the range must be numbers, range names, arrays, or references that contain numbers. The criteria are expressed in the form of a number, expression, or text that defines which cells will be added. The sum_range argument includes the actual cells to add if their corresponding cells in the range match the criteria.

COUNTIF Function | Reference

COUNTIF(range,criteria)

The *COUNTIF function* counts the number of cells within a range that meet the given criterion.

The *COUNTIF function* calculates the number of cells in a range that match the specified criteria rather than the number of all cells in a range that would be calculated using the COUNT function. The COUNTIF function is often referred to as a conditional count. In the syntax for COUNTIF the range is one or more cells to count, and can include numbers or range names, arrays, or references that contain numbers. The criteria are expressed in the form of a number, expression, cell reference, or references that contain numbers. When using criteria, you can test if:

- a cell matches a specific value.
- a cell is greater than (>) or less than (<) a specific number.
- a cell matches, or is greater or less than, a number in another cell.
- the text in a cell matches a pattern.

AVERAGEIF Function | Reference

AVERAGEIF(range,criteria,average_range)

The **AVERAGEIF function** returns the average of all the cells in a range that meet a given criterion.

The third function in the group of functions is the **AVERAGEIF function**. This function calculates the average, or arithmetic mean, of all cells in a range that meet criteria you specify. The range in the syntax for AVERAGEIF is one or more cells to average and may include names, arrays, or references that contain numbers. The criteria are expressed in the form of a number, expression, cell reference, or text that defines which cells are averaged. The average range is the set of cells to average. Review cells B22, B26, and B30 shown in Figure 6.24 to see examples of the SUMIF, AVERAGEIF, and COUNTIF functions, respectively.

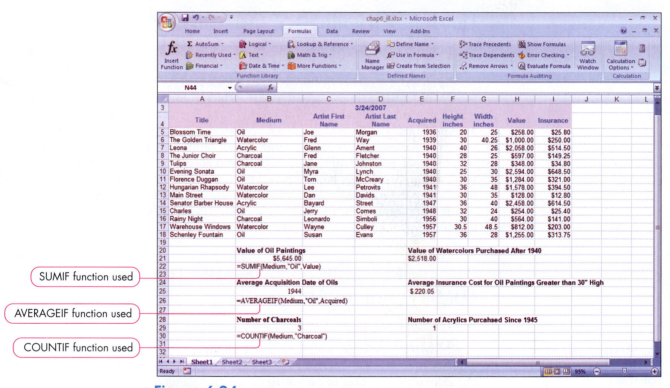

Figure 6.24 Logical Functions

Use SUMIFS, COUNTIFS, and AVERAGEIFS Functions

SUMIFS Function | Reference

SUMIFS(sum_range,criteria_range1,criteria1,criteria_range2,criteria2. . .)

COUNTIFS Function | Reference

COUNTIFS(range1,criteria1,range2,criteria2. . .)

AVERAGEIFS Function | Reference

AVERAGEIFS(average_range,criteria_range1,criteria1,criteria_range2,criteria2. . .)

The three functions described in this section are the logical outgrowth of the SUM, COUNT, and AVERAGE, and SUMIF, COUNTIF, and AVERAGEIF functions. The actions for the functions are the same as their counterparts except that you can use

The **SUMIFS function** adds the cells in a range that meet multiple criteria.

The **COUNTIFS function** counts the number of cells within a range that meet multiple criteria.

The **AVERAGEIFS function** returns the average of all the cells that meet multiple criteria.

multiple conditions. The SUMIFS function sums cells in a range that meet multiple criteria. The sum_range in the syntax is the first argument in the **SUMIFS function** but the last argument in the SUMIF function. This function allows up to 127 criteria to be evaluated. The **COUNTIFS function** counts the number of cells in a range that meet multiple criteria. Up to 127 criteria can be evaluated with the function. The **AVERAGEIFS function** calculates the average of all cells meeting up to 127 criteria. These functions are useful when you want to answer such questions as: What is the total value of the watercolors in the collection that were acquired before 1940? Perhaps you want to know the average insurance cost for oil paintings that are larger than 30 inches or how many acrylic paintings were acquired before 1945. Review cells E22, E26, and E30 shown in Figure 6.25 to see examples of the SUMIFS, AVERAGEIFS, and COUNTIFS functions, respectively.

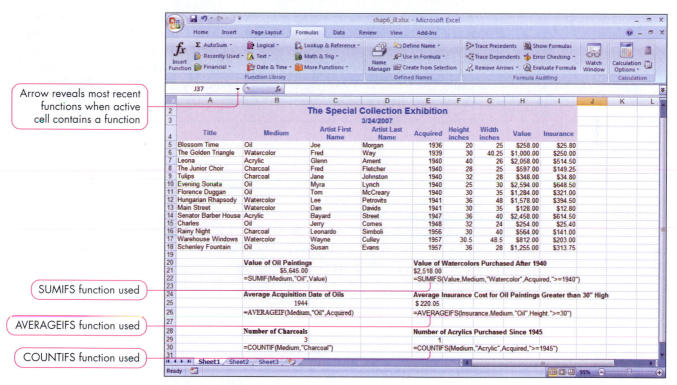

Figure 6.25 Logical Functions

Creating Nested IF Functions

The IF function enables two possible formulas: The logical text is true and the first formula is used or the logical test if false and the second formula is used. You can expand the power of the IF by choosing more than two options, by nesting multiple IF statements in one formula. Nesting is done by placing one function within another. Excel permits up to 64 IF statements in one formula. As previously stated, nesting functions is a technique that permits you to place one function inside another. A nested IF can be used to calculate taxable earnings, for example, IF year-to-date pay minus total earnings is less than the FICA limit, then zero taxable earnings, else IF year-to-date pay is greater than the FICA limit, then FICA limit minus the total of (year-to-date pay minus total earnings), else total earnings.

The following formula is another example of nested IFs: =IF(A20<500,A20*2%, IF(A20>10000,A20*5%,A20*3%)). In this case, the formula calculates commission when the total sales value is in cell A20. If the sales are less than $500, the commission is 2%; if sales are above $10,000, the commission is 5%; the commission is 3% in all other instances. If the first condition is met, Excel carries out the calculation. If the first condition is not met, Excel moves on to the second condition, which is actually a second IF statement. The use of multiple IF statements can be very confusing and you should exercise care when using them.

Using AND, OR, NOT, and IFERROR Functions

The AND, OR, NOT, and IFERROR functions are examples of logical functions that expand the power of Excel. They are often used with conditional functions. You would use the AND function to test when more than one condition is met. For example, if a salesperson earns a $10 bonus for each snow blower sold on Sunday you would use the AND function to test both conditions. The OR function tests whether any of the arguments are true. Using the same example, a salesperson earns a $10 bonus for selling snow blowers any day of the week or selling anything on Sunday. NOT functions reverse the logic; true becomes false and false becomes true. It is not recommended that you use the NOT function.

AND Function | Reference

AND(logical1,logical2,. . .)

The ***AND function*** returns true when all arguments are true and returns false when one or more arguments are false.

The ***AND function*** accepts two or more conditions and returns true if all conditions are true and false if any of the conditions are false. The syntax of the function is AND(logical1,logical2,. . .). If an array or reference argument contains text or empty cells, those values are ignored. If there are no logical values in the specified range, AND returns the #VALUE! Error.

OR Function | Reference

OR(logical1,logical2,. . .)

The ***OR function*** returns true if any argument is true and returns false if all arguments are false.

The ***OR function*** also accepts two or more conditions and returns true if any of the conditions are met. It returns a false only if all conditions are false. The syntax for the OR function is OR(logical1,logical2,. . .). Up to 255 conditions can be tested that can be either true or false. Table 6.1 shows examples of OR functions:

Table 6.1   Examples of OR Functions

Formula	Result
=OR(TRUE)	One argument is true, returns true.
=OR(1+1=1,2+2=5)	All arguments are false, returns false.
=OR(TRUE,FALSE,TRUE)	At least one argument is true, returns true.

NOT Function | Reference

NOT(logical)

The **NOT function** reverses the value of its argument.

The *NOT function* reverses the value of its argument. You would use NOT when you want to make sure a value is not equal to a particular value. The syntax of the NOT function is NOT(logical). If logical is false, not returns true, and if the logical is true, NOT returns false. Table 6.2 shows examples of NOT functions.

Table 6.2 Examples of NOT Functions

Formula	Result
=NOT(FALSE)	Returns true, the reverse of false.
=NOT(1+1=2)	Returns false as the reverse of an equation that returns true.

IFERROR Function | Reference

IFERROR(value,value_if_error)

The **IFERROR function** returns a value you specify if a formula evaluates to an error.

The *IFERROR function* is a function used in error checking. IFERROR checks an indicated cell and displays a value specified if a formula evaluates to an error. If there is no error, the IFERROR function returns the value of the formula. This function is used to trap and handle errors in formulas. The syntax of the IFERROR function is IFERROR(value,value_if_error). In the syntax, value is the argument that is checked for an error, and value_if_error is the value to return if the formula evaluates to an error. #N/A, #VALUE!, #REF!, #DIV/0!, #NUM!, #NAME?, and #NULL! are the types of errors evaluated.

period is less than for the previous period because the beginning balance is less. Remember that interest is paid on the remaining balance. As each month's beginning balance decreases, so does the monthly interest. The payment remains the same with less payment going toward interest and more toward principal. This process continues until the loan is paid off.

Figure 6.32 shows the amortization worksheet for a home mortgage of $300,000 at 6.25% for 30 years. This loan has one other parameter: an optional extra payment of $100 per month. Paying an extra $100 per month enables the borrower to pay off the loan in 313 rather than 360 payments. Making an extra payment is a good strategy if you can afford it. Many home buyers choose a 30-year mortgage to keep the monthly payment low but opt to make extra payments to reduce the length of the mortgage and the interest paid.

This reduction in interest can be substantial—in our case, over $50,000 over the life of the mortgage. The borrower will pay $31,300 or 313 payments of $100 each, in early payments. This is money that the borrower would have paid during the life of the mortgage but elected to pay early to reduce the total amount of interest.

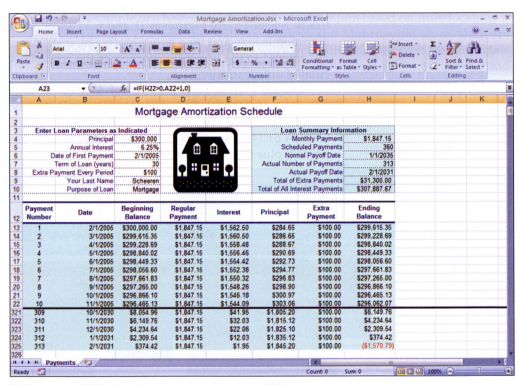

Figure 6.32 The House Amortization Table

Using Functions in Amortization Tables

You can use several functions to help build an amortization table. These functions deal with the calculation of payment dates, the actual number of payments, and the actual payoff date of a loan.

Use YEAR, MONTH, and DAY Functions

Calculating payment dates in Excel is more complicated than you might expect because Excel stores dates as integers (serial numbers) that are equivalent to the number of days that have elapsed since January 1, 1900. Stated another way, January 1, 1900, is stored as day one, January 2, 1900, is stored as day two, and so on. This makes it possible to determine a past or future date by adding or subtracting the number of days to your date. Excel, in these calculations, also accounts for differing numbers of days in months, such as 31 days in March, 30 days in April, or 28 days in February, except in leap year.

Your paycheck is issued weekly, biweekly, or perhaps monthly. You can use Excel to calculate your pay dates for the entire year if you use date functions. These functions work with serial numbers and you can easily add numbers to a date to produce a new date. For example, if your first paycheck is dated January 13, 2008, and you add 14, you will find that your next biweekly pay date is January 27, 2008. Figure 6.33 shows the serial number 42265 in cell A1, formatted as a date in cell B1, and the results of the YEAR, MONTH, and DAY functions in cells B2 through B4.

YEAR Function | Reference

YEAR(serial_number)

MONTH Function | Reference

MONTH(serial_number)

DAY Function | Reference

DAY(serial_number)

The YEAR function returns the year corresponding to a date.

The MONTH function returns the month represented by a serial number.

The DAY function returns the day of a date represented by a serial number.

The functions DAY, MONTH, and YEAR return the numeric day, month, and year. The *YEAR function* returns the year corresponding to a date. The *MONTH function* returns the month represented by a serial number, and the *DAY function* returns the day of a date represented by a serial number. For example, if you have a date in cell B1, the function =MONTH(B1) returns the numeric month of the date in cell B1. Similarly, =MONTH(B1)+1 will add one to the numeric month shown in cell B1. The reference box on page 424 summarizes these functions.

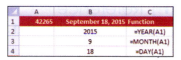

Figure 6.33 YEAR, MONTH, and DAY Functions

Use Match and Index Functions
MATCH Function | Reference

MATCH(lookup_value,lookup_array,match_type)

The MATCH function returns the relative position of an item in an array that matches a specified value in a specified order.

The MATCH and INDEX functions are functions commonly used with amortization tables showing payment schedules for loans. The *MATCH function* returns the relative position of an item in an array that matches a specified value in a specified order. The MATCH function returns the position in the list where the match occurs, which is the actual payment number where the zero balance is reached. A MATCH function has three arguments:

1. The value being looked up, typically a zero ending balance.
2. An associated cell range, the cells containing the balance at the end of each period.
3. The type of match; is it an exact match or not? The type of match is 1, 0, or -1.

Functions Used | Reference

Name	Syntax	Definition
CONCATENATE	CONCATENATE(text1,text2,...)	Joins two or more text strings into one text string.
PROPER	PROPER(text)	Capitalizes the first letter in a text string.
UPPER	UPPER(text)	Converts text to uppercase letters.
LOWER	LOWER(text)	Converts all uppercase letters to lowercase.
SUBSTITUTE	SUBSTITUTE(text,old_text,new_text, instance_num)	Substitutes new_text for old_text in a text string.
SUMIF	SUMIF(range,criteria,sum_range)	Adds the cells specified by a given criterion.
COUNTIF	COUNTIF(range,criteria)	Counts the number of cells within a range that meet the given criterion.
AVERAGEIF	AVERAGEIF(range,criteria, average_range)	Returns the average of all the cells in a range that meet a given criterion.
SUMIFS	SUMIFS(sum_range,criteria_range1, criteria1,criteria_range2, criteria2...)	Adds the cells in a range that meet multiple criteria.
COUNTIFS	COUNTIFS(range1,criteria1,range2, criteria2...)	Counts the number of cells within a range that meet multiple criteria.
AVERAGEIFS	AVERAGEIFS(average_range, criteria_range1,criteria1, criteria_range2,criteria2...)	Returns the average of all the cells that meet multiple criteria.
AND	AND(logical1,logical2,...)	Returns true when all arguments are true and returns false when one or more arguments are false.
OR	OR (logical1,logical2,...)	Returns true if any argument is true and returns false if all arguments are false.
NOT	NOT(logical)	Reverses the value of its argument.
IFERROR	IFERROR(value,value_if_error)	Returns a value you specify if a formula evaluates to an error.
YEAR	YEAR(serial_number)	Returns the year of a date. The year is shown as an integer from 1900 to 9999.
MONTH	MONTH(serial_number)	Returns the month of a date as a serial number. The month is shown as an integer from 1 (January) to 12 (December).
DAY	DAY(serial_number)	Returns the day of a date as a serial number. The day is shown as an integer from 1 to 31.
MATCH	MATCH(lookup_value, lookup_array,match_type)	Returns the relative position of an item in an array that matches a specified value in a specified order.
INDEX	INDEX(array,row_num, column_num)	Returns a value or the reference to a value within a table or range.
ROUND	ROUND(number, num_digits)	Rounds a value to a specified number of digits.

Summary

1. **Separate and combine text.** Converting text to columns enables you to convert information in a single column, such as a name, into two columns so the names could be sorted by both first and last name. On the other hand, if data are stored in multiple cells, you can use the CONCATENATE function to join the text strings together.

2. **Manipulate text with functions.** Functions can be used to change the case of text strings. The PROPER function capitalizes the first letter in a text string and converts remaining characters to lower-case. The UPPER function converts all letters in a text string to uppercase. The LOWER function converts all letters in a text string to lowercase. The SUBSTITUTE function substitutes new text for existing text in a text string.

3. **Identify and remove duplicate rows.** Large lists or tables might contain duplicate records. The duplicate data can cause inaccurate statistical analysis. To ensure that only unique records are contained in the table, you can remove duplicate rows. The process deletes records that are exact duplicates, yet leaves the original record.

4. **Group and subtotal data.** Grouping is a way to simplify complex worksheets. Grouping enables you to consolidate related rows or columns into single units. After you consolidate the rows or columns into a group, you can collapse the group to make it easier to view only what you want to see. The Subtotal command uses a summary function such as SUM, AVERAGE, or COUNT to compute subtotals within the data table. The records are grouped according to the value of a specific field, such as location, and the Subtotal command inserts a subtotal row where the value of the designated field changes. A grand total is displayed after the last record. The records must be in sequence by the field on which the subtotals will be grouped prior to executing the Subtotal command.

5. **Work with windows.** Often, you will have multiple workbooks open at one time. It is easy to compare the data when you can view these worksheets side by side on your screen. You can even split a large worksheet into multiple panes to view different parts of the worksheet at the same time.

6. **Use conditional functions.** When you created formulas with SUM, COUNT, and AVERAGE functions, you summed, counted, or averaged all values in a range of cells. Two sets of three functions expand the power of the SUM, COUNT, and AVERAGE functions. The first set is SUMIF, COUNTIF, and AVERAGEIF, which return the total, count, or average for one criterion. The second set of functions is SUMIFS, COUNTIFS, and AVERAGEIFS. These functions return a total, count, or average based on two criteria.

7. **Create nested IF functions.** When multiple conditions need to be evaluated to determine the correct action, you can nest functions within an IF statement. A nested IF function can include a second IF function to help evaluate multiple conditions. Other functions can also be nested in an IF function.

8. **Use AND, OR, NOT, and IFERROR functions.** These logical functions are used with conditional expressions. The AND function determines if both conditions are true, while the OR function determines if either condition is true. The NOT function reverses the value of true and false conditions, and the IFERROR function is used in error checking.

9. **Define the amortization table.** One of the most commonly used applications for Excel is to determine a payment or amortization schedule for a loan. The amortization schedule shows the date of each loan payment, the amount of each payment that goes to principal and interest, and the remaining balance, which eventually reaches zero.

10. **Use functions in amortization tables.** Several functions are available to help create amortization tables. The YEAR function returns the year for a date, the MONTH function returns the month represented by a serial number, and the DAY function returns the day represented by a serial number. You can use the MATCH function to return the relative position of an item in an array, and the INDEX function returns a value within a table. Finally, the ROUND function rounds a value to a specified number of digits.

Key Terms

Multiple Choice

1. A(n) _____ is used to display how a loan is being repaid, and displays the date, amount of principal, and amount of interest for each payment.

   (a) Template
   (b) Amortization schedule
   (c) MATCH function
   (d) AND function

2. The _____ function returns True if all its arguments are true.

   (a) MATCH
   (b) IF
   (c) INDEX
   (d) AND

3. All of the following are required arguments to the DATE function except:

   (a) The cell containing the date
   (b) The year portion of the date
   (c) The month portion of the date
   (d) The day portion of the date

4. All of the following are required arguments for the MATCH function except:

   (a) The value you are looking up
   (b) The cell range you are looking in
   (c) The number of rows in the cell range you are looking in
   (d) The type of match

5. Cell G12 contains the date 12/19/2008. Which of the following will return the date 1/19/2009?

   (a) =DATE(YEAR(G12),MONTH(G12)+1,DAY(G12))
   (b) =DATE(YEAR(G12)+1,MONTH(G12)+1,DAY(G12))
   (c) =G12 + MONTH(1)
   (d) =MONTH(G12)+1

6. The INDEX function returns:

   (a) The position in a list where a match occurs
   (b) The number of cells in the list
   (c) The cell in the list that contains the desired value
   (d) The value in the cell being looked up

7. The MATCH function returns:

   (a) The cell in the list where a match occurs
   (b) The number of cells in the list
   (c) The position in a list where a match occurs
   (d) The column in the list that contains the desired value

8. The _____ function shows the amount of a loan payment that is applied towards principal repayment.

   (a) PMT
   (b) PPMT
   (c) MATCH
   (d) IPMT

9. Assume that cell E12 contains the date February 26, 2008. Which of the following will display the date February 25, 2008?

   (a) =DATE(E12) – 1
   (b) =DATE(YEAR(E12), MONTH(E12), DAY(E12)–1)
   (c) =DATE(YEAR(E12), MONTH(E12), DAY(E12–1))
   (d) =DATE(YEAR(E12)–1, MONTH(E12)–1, DAY(E12)–1)

10. You created a workbook on December 12, 2007, and entered the Today() function in cell B5. You modified and saved the workbook on December 19, 2007. On January 3, 2008, you opened the workbook again. What is displayed in cell B5?

    (a) December 19, 2007
    (b) December 12, 2007
    (c) January 3, 2008
    (d) It depends on how you created the Today() function.

11. The IPMT function returns the amount of a(n):

    (a) Periodic payment
    (b) Periodic payment that is applied towards principal
    (c) Periodic payment that is applied towards interest
    (d) Extra payment

12. The primary benefit of using the ROUND function rather than formatting values as currency is:

    (a) Ease of working with fractional numbers
    (b) Increases precision in numbers
    (c) Easier to use than the number format
    (d) Gives you less control when copying values

13. Which of the following statements is true?

    (a) The Delete command can be used to delete a record, but not a field.

    (b) The Delete command erases the contents of the selected area, but does not delete it.

    (c) The Delete command can be used to delete either a record or a field.

    (d) The Delete command can be used to delete a field, but not a record.

14. You have created a named range called MyCDs that is equivalent to the range A1:E19. What is the extent of the range if you subsequently delete row 1 and delete column C?

    (a) A1:D18

    (b) A1:E19

    (c) A1:E18

    (d) A1:D19

15. Which of the following causes a named range to be adjusted automatically?

    (a) Inserting a row within the range

    (b) Deleting a row within the range

    (c) Either inserting or deleting a row within the range

    (d) Neither inserting nor deleting a row within the range

16. Which of the following enables you to create several named ranges at once?

    (a) The Insert Name Define command

    (b) The Insert Name Create command

    (c) The Name Box

    (d) The Go To command

Practice Exercises

1 Ajax Medical Society Donors

Your work as Event Coordinator with the state medical society enables you to demonstrate your expertise with Excel. The workbook shown in Figure 6.42 is the completed list of donors to the medical society major fund-raising event. You will convert name text to columns, remove duplicate records, use conditional functions, subtotal data, create a chart, and view the results in several different window arrangements.

a. Open the *chap6_pe1_donations* workbook and save it as **chap6_pe1_donations_ solution** so that you can return to the original workbook if necessary.

b. Convert text to columns for column B by completing the following tasks:

- Right-click **column C** and select **Insert** to insert a new column.

- Select **cells B3:B31** and click **Text to Columns** in the Data Tools group on the Data tab to start the Convert Text to Columns Wizard.

- Verify that **Delimited** is selected in the *Original data type* section and click **Next**.

- Click the **Space check box**, remove the check from the **Tab check box** in the *Delimiter* section, and click **Next**.

- Verify that **General** is selected in the *Column Data Format* section, that **Destination is $B$3**, that Data Preview is correct, and then click **Finish**.

- Type **First Name** in **cell B2** and type **Last Name** in **cell C2**.

c. Convert text to columns for column E using the following specifications:

- Right-click **column F** and select **Insert** from the menu to insert a new column. Repeat the step to insert a second column.

- Select **cells E3:E31** and click **Text to Columns** in the Data Tools group on the Data tab to launch the Convert Text to Columns Wizard.

- Verify that **Delimited** is selected in the *Original data type* section and click **Next**.

- Click the **Space check box** and click **Next**.

- Verify that **General** is selected in the *Column Data Format* section, that **Destination** is **$E$3**, that Data Preview is correct, and then click **Finish**.

- Type **State** in **cell F2** and type **Zip Code** in **cell G2**.

- Click the **Select All** box to select the entire worksheet, click **Format** in the Cells group on the Home tab, and click **AutoFit Column Width**.

d. Remove duplicate rows by completing the following tasks:

- Click **column B** to select it.

- Click **Remove Duplicates** in the Data Tools group of the Data tab.

- Verify that **Expand the selection** is selected in the Remove Duplicates Warning box and click **Remove Duplicates**.

- Click **Unselect All**, click the **DonorID check box**, verify that the **My data has headers check box** is selected, and click **OK**.

- Click **OK** to verify the deletion of 4 rows with 26 unique remaining.

...continued on Next Page

e. Create a SUMIF function that determines the total of product contributions by completing the following tasks:

- Click in **cell B35**, then click **Insert Function** in the Functions group on the Formulas tab to open the Insert function dialog box.

- Type **SUMIF** in the **Search for a function** text box, click **Go**, click **SUMIF** in the **Select a function** list, and click **OK** to display the Function Arguments dialog box.

- Type **J3:J30** in the **Range** box, **Product** in the **Criteria**, and **K3:K30** in the **Sum_range** box. Click **OK**.

f. Create a SUMIFS function to determine the total of product contributions greater than $400 by completing the following:

- Click in **cell E35**, then click **Insert Function** in the Functions group to open the Insert Function dialog box.

- Type **SUMIFS** in the **Search for a function** text box, click **Go**, click **SUMIFS** in **the Select a function** list, and click **OK**.

- Enter the following in the Function Arguments dialog box: **K3:K30** in the **Sum_range** box, **J3:J30** in the **Criteria_range1** box, **Product** in the **Criteria1** box, **K3:K30** in the **Criteria_range2** box, and **>400** in the **Criteria2** box. Click **OK**.

- Format **cell E35** as **Currency** with **0** decimal places.

g. Create an AVERAGEIFS function to determine the average value of the restaurant gift certificates by completing the following tasks:

- Click in **cell B38** and click **Insert Function** in the Functions group on the Formulas tab to open the Insert function dialog box.

- Type **AVERAGEIFS** in the **Search for a function** text box, click **Go**, click **AVERAGEIFS** in the **Select a function list**, and click **OK**.

- Enter the following in the Function Arguments dialog box: **K3:K30** in the **Average_range** box, **J3:J30** in the **Criteria_range1** box, **Gift Certificate** in the **Criteria1** box, **I3:I30** in the **Criteria_range2** box, and **Restaurant Gift Certificate** in the **Criteria2** box. Click **OK**.

h. Create an AVERAGEIF function to determine the average value of the service donations by completing the following tasks:

- Click in **cell E38**, then click **Insert Function** in the Functions group to open the Insert function dialog box.

- Type **AVERAGEIF** in the **Search for a function** text box, click **Go**, click **AVERAGEIF** in the **Select a function** list, and click **OK**.

- Enter the following in the Function Arguments dialog box: **J3:J30** in the **Range** box, **Service** in the **Criteria** box, and **K3:K30** in the **Average_range** box. Click **OK**.

- Format **cell E38** as **Currency** with **2** decimal places.

i. Create a COUNTIF function to determine the number of service items donated by completing the following tasks:

- Click in **cell B41**, then click **Insert Function** in the Functions group on the Formulas tab to open the Insert function dialog box.

- Type **COUNTIF** in the **Search for a function** text box, click **Go**, click **COUNTIF** in the **Select a function** list, and click **OK**.

- Enter the following in the Function Arguments dialog box: **J3:J30** in the **Range** box and **Service** in the **Criteria** box. Click **OK** and format **cells B35** and **B38** as **Currency**.

...continued on Next Page

j. Create a COUNTIFS function to determine the number of gift certificates valued at more than $50 by completing the following tasks:

- Click in **cell E41** and click **Insert Function** in the Functions group to open the Insert Function dialog box.

- Type **COUNTIFS** in the **Search for a function** text box, click **Go**, click **COUNTIFS** in the **Select a function** list, and click **OK**.

- Enter the following in the Function Arguments dialog box: **J3:J30** in the **Criteria_range1** box, **Gift Certificate** in the **Criteria1** box, **K3:K30** in the **Criteria_range2** box, and **>50** in the **Criteria2** box. Click **OK**.

k. Subtotal the data using the following specifications:

- Click in **column J**, click the **Data tab**, and click **Sort A to Z** in the Sort & Filter group.

- Click **cell K3** and click **Subtotal** in the Outline group to open the Subtotal dialog box.

- Click the **At a change in drop-down arrow**, then select **Category**.

- Verify that the **Use function** is set to **Sum**.

- Uncheck **Category** and check **ItemValue**, if necessary, in the *Add subtotal to* section.

- Verify that the **Replace current subtotals check box** is checked.

- Verify that the **Summary below data check box** is checked.

- Click **OK**.

l. Split the worksheet window by completing the following tasks:

- Click **Split** in the Window group on the View tab and drag the vertical splitter to the left until it disappears.

- Drag the **horizontal splitter** to just below **row 2**.

- Click **Split** again to return to the original single window.

m. Group and ungroup data by completing the following tasks:

- Click the **minus symbol** to the left of **rows 11**, **16**, **26**, and **31**.

- Click the **minus symbol** to the left of **row 32**.

n. Create a chart:

- Click the **plus symbol** to the left of row 32.

- Select **cells J11:K31**, click **Bar** in the Chart group on the Insert tab, and click **Clustered Bar** from the Chart Gallery.

o. To enhance the bar chart:

- Click **Style 14** in the Chart Styles group on the Design tab.

- Click **Layout tab**, click **Chart Title** in the Labels group, and select **Above Chart**.

- Type **Donations** and press **Enter**.

- Click **Legend** and select **None** to remove the legend.

p. Click **Move Chart** in the Location group on the Design tab, select **New sheet** in the Move Chart dialog box, type **Graph**, and click **OK**.

...continued on Next Page

q. View multiple windows by completing the following tasks:

- While viewing the bar chart, click **New Window** in the Window group on the View tab.

- Click **Arrange All** in the Window group, click **Horizontal** in the Arrange Windows dialog box, and click **OK**.

- Click the **Sheet1 tab** in the top window to view the worksheet in that window with the chart in the second window below.

r. Create a custom footer that includes your name, a page number, and your instructor's name. Print the worksheet as displayed and with formulas visible. Save, print, and close the workbook.

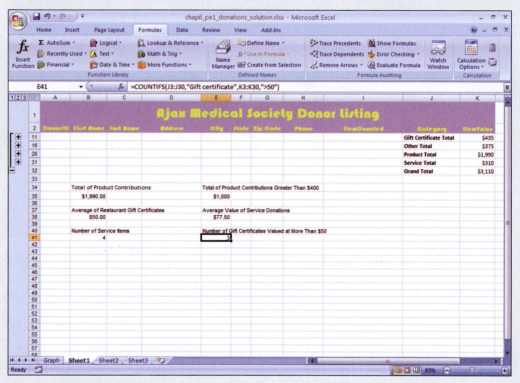

Figure 6.42 Medical Society Fundraiser

2 Finding the Month and Day

The workbook in Figure 6.43 illustrates the table lookup function in conjunction with date functions. You will create the workbook and use functions to determine the month and day of the week for a given birth date. Format the workbook as shown in Figure 6.43.

a. Create a new workbook:

- Open a blank workbook.

- Click in **cell A1**, type **Finding the Month and Day**, and merge and center the title over **cells A1:D1**.

- Click in **cell A3** and type your birth date.

- Click in **cell A4** and type **You were born on a**.

- Click in **cell C4** and type **in the month of**.

...continued on Next Page

- Click in **cell B3** and type your birth date in the form **MM/DD/YYYY** to test your formulas.

- Click in **cell A9**, type **1**, press **Enter**, type **2**, and then use AutoFill to enter the numbers shown in Figure 6.43.

- Click in **cell B9**, type **Sunday**, press **Enter**, and use AutoFill enter the days of the week.

- Click in **cell C9**, type **1**, press **Enter**, type **2**, and then use AutoFill to enter the numbers shown in Figure 6.43.

- Click in **cell D9**, type **January**, press **Enter**, and use AutoFill enter the months of the year.

b. Name the ranges:

- Click in **cell B3**, click **Name Manager** in **the Defined Names** group on the Formulas tab, and click **New** in the Name Manager dialog box.

- Type **birthdate** in the **Name** text box, verify that Workbook appears in **Scope** and that =Sheet1!$B$3 appears in **Refers to**, and click **OK** to return to the Name Manager dialog box.

- Click **New**, type **DayofWeek**, click in the **Refers to** box, select **cells A9:B15**, and click **OK** to return to the Name Manager dialog box.

- Click **New**, type **MonthofYear**, click in the **Refers to** box, select **cells C9:D20**, and click **OK** to return to the Name Manager dialog box.

- Click **Close** to close Name Manager dialog box.

c. Click in **cell B8** and type the formula **=IF(Birthdate<>"",WEEKDAY(B3),"")**. You used an IF function with a variation of the DAY function to determine the day of the week on which you were born.

d. Click in **cell D8** and type the formula **=IF(Birthdate<>"",MONTH(B3),"")**. You used an IF function with a variation of the MONTH function to determine the month in which you were born.

e. Click in **cell B4** and type the formula **=IF(Birthdate<>"",VLOOKUP(B8,DayofWeek,2),"")**.

f. Click in **cell D4** and type **=IF(Birthdate<>"",VLOOKUP(D8,MonthofYear,2),"")**.

g. Create a custom footer that includes your name, today's date, and your instructor's name. Print the worksheet as displayed and with formulas visible. Save the file as **chap6_pe2_dates_solution** and close the workbook.

...continued on Next Page

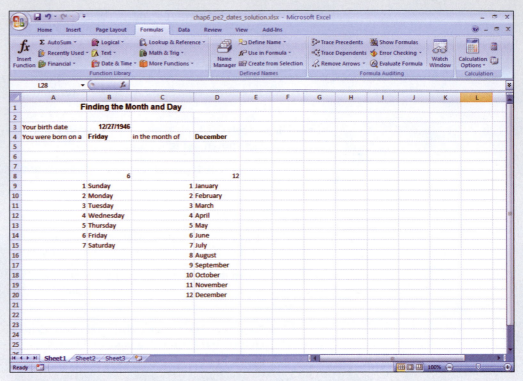

Figure 6.43 Display Birth Day and Month

3 Pay Off Your Credit Card

You have found that during your college years you have run up considerable credit card debt. In an effort to discharge this debt, you have resolved to pay it all off. The workbook in Figure 6.44 resembles the amortization table completed in Hands-On Exercise 4 except the interest is much higher. Refer to Figure 6.44 as you complete the exercise.

a. Open the *chap6_pe3_debt* workbook and save it as **chap6_pe3_debt_solution**.
b. Drag the clip art out of the way, click in **cell D7** and type **=AND(C5>0,C6>0,C7>0,OR(C4>0,C8>0))**. Drag the clip art back into place.
c. Type the parameters shown in Figure 6.44 into **cells C4:C7**.
d. Click **Name Manager** in the **Defined Names** group on the **Formulas tab** to see the ranges that are already named in the workbook. You will use these in your formulas. Close the dialog box.
e. Create the formulas for the first payment beginning in row 14:

- Click in **cell A14** and type **=IF(DataEntered,1,0)**.

- Click in **cell B14** and type **=IF(A14>0,C6,0)**. Format **cell B14** as Short Date.

- Click in **cell C14** and type **=IF(A14>0,C4,0)**.

- Click in **cell D14** and type **=IF(A14>0,($C$5/12)*C14,0)**. The interest is charged on the unpaid balance at the beginning of the period.

- Click in **cell E14** and type **=IF(A14>0,$C$8,0)**.

- Click in **cell F14** and type **=IF(A14>0,D14+$C$7*(C14+E14),0)**. The minimum payment is the interest due plus the minimum percent required by the credit card company, which is computed on the initial balance plus the new charges.

- Click in **cell G14** and type **=IF(A14>0,$C$9,0)**.

...continued on Next Page

- Click in **cell H14** and type **=IF(A14>0,C14+D14+E14-F14-G14,0)**.

- Format **cells C14:H14** as Currency and verify that your results match Figure 6.44.

f. Create the formulas for the second payment:

- Click in **cell A15** and type **=IF(H14>0,A14+1,0)**.

- Click in **cell B15** and type **=IF(A15>0,DATE(YEAR(B14),MONTH(B14)+1,DAY(B14)),0)** to compute the date of the next payment. Format **cell B15** as Short Date.

- Click in **cell C15** and type **=IF(A15>0,H14,0)**. Format **cell C15** as Currency.

- Copy the formulas from **cells D14:H14** to **cells D15:H15**.

- Copy **cells A15:H15** to the remaining payments (through row 193, where you see payment 180).

g. Click the **Office Button**, click **Excel Options**, and click **Advanced** to view Advanced Options for Working with Excel.

h. Scroll through the options to see *Display options for this worksheet* and remove the check from **Show a zero in cells that have zero value**, then click **OK**.

i. Create a custom footer that includes your name, today's date, and your instructor's name. Select **cells A1:H19** and print the selection as displayed with formulas visible. Save and close the workbook.

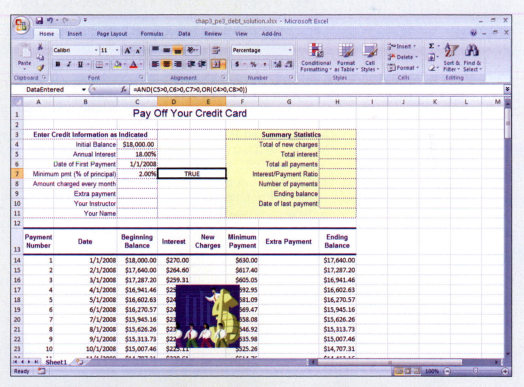

Figure 6.44 Credit Card Debt

...continued on Next Page

This exercise continues the development of the credit card worksheet by computing the summary information. Figure 6.45 shows the completed summary information which you will use for reference.

a. Open the completed workbook, *chap6_pe3_debt_solution*, from the previous exercise and save it as **chap6_pe4_debt_solution**.

b. Select **cell G13**, click **Unmerge Cells** in the Alignment group, type **Extra Payment** in **cell G13**, and type **Ending Balance** in **cell H13**.

c. Click in **cell C9** and type **$25.00** for the extra payment you feel you can make to pay the debt off early.

d. Type the following formulas in the summary area beginning with **cell H4**:

- Click in **cell H4** and type **=SUM(NewCharges)**. The range name has already been defined in the workbook. An IF statement is not required in the formula because zero values are suppressed.

- Click in **cell H5** and type **=SUM(Interest)**.

- Click in **cell H6** and type **=SUM(MinimumPayment,ExtraPayment)**.

- Click in **cell H7** and type **=IF(H6>0,H5/H6,0)**.

- Click in **cell H8** and type the formula shown in Figure 6.45 to compute the number of payments. The nested IF calculates the number of payments only if all of the data have been entered. The range name EndingBalance refers to the balance after the 180th payment when the table ends; that is, if a zero balance is not reached at this point, there are 180 payments.

- Click in **cell H9** and type **=IF(H8>0,INDEX(PaymentTable,H8,8),0)**.

- Click in **cell H10** and type **=IF(H8>0,INDEX(PaymentTable,H8,2),"")**.

e. Click in **cell H11** and type a formula to determine if you are still in debt, or are debt free: **=IF(DataEntered,IF(H9<=0,"Congratulations, you are debt free!","You are still in debt!"),"")**. You should see the values in Figure 6.45.

f. Create a custom footer that includes your name, a page number, and your instructor's name. Print the worksheet as displayed and with formulas visible.

g. Save and close the workbook.

...continued on Next Page

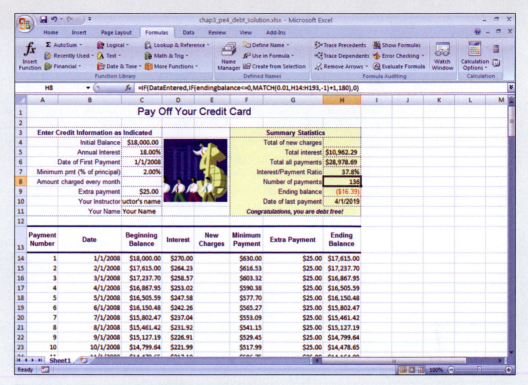

Figure 6.45 Credit Card Debt Continued

Congratulations, you have been awarded a summer internship position with the Nix Mortgage Corporation. Your summer internship assignment is to open the partially completed workbook and complete it to match Figure 6.46. The workbook in Figure 6.46 is used to analyze employee salary with respect to job title. The corporation is considering downsizing, and your boss asked you to prepare a summary showing the total salaries of the managers and account reps. He wants to know the total salary of the account reps working in Miami and the total salary of the managers working in Boston. He also wants to know how many employees might be affected in Chicago and Atlanta. Further, he wants a report of the average salary by location and a chart to show visually the average salary for the job titles.

a. Open the *chap6_mid1_salary* workbook and save it as **chap6_mid1_salary_solution** so you can return to the original workbook if necessary. Sort the data by job title. This is the first step required to prepare the summary report. Create range names for all columns of data in the worksheet.

b. Use conditional functions to determine the total salary of all managers, the average salary of the account reps, the number of employees working in Chicago, the total salary of the account reps working in Miami, the average salary of the managers working in Boston, and the number of trainees working in Atlanta. Format appropriate values as Currency with 2 decimal places.

c. Click anywhere in the data and create a subtotal report showing the salary totals for each job title. Make sure you subtotal when Title changes, use the SUM function, and subtotal on Salary. The resulting summary report did not give you the data required by your boss.

d. Sort the data by city, and then create a subtotal that shows average salary by city. Make sure you subtotal when Location changes, use the AVERAGE function, and subtotal on Salary.

e. Reduce the report displayed to display just the city average salaries. Use this data to create a pie chart displayed on a separate sheet. Make sure you include a title, data labels, and a legend on your chart.

f. Make all the data visible on Sheet1 and create a new window for this data. Arrange your windows vertically.

g. Create a custom footer that includes your name, today's date, and your instructor's name. Print the worksheet as displayed and with formulas visible. Close the workbook.

...continued on Next Page

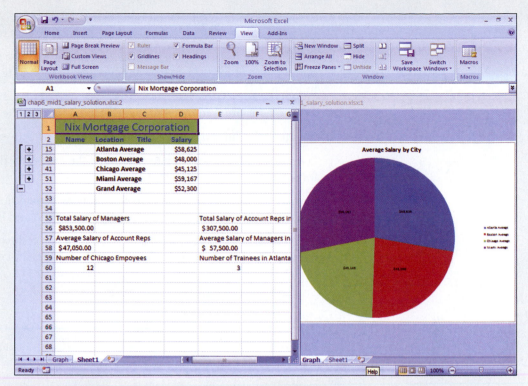

Figure 6.46 NIX Mortgage Corporation Salary Analysis

2 Nested IFs and Other Functions

As a graduate assistant, you are tasked with maintaining your professor's grade book. Dr. Smith decided to drop the lowest test grade if the student has taken all five exams. Students are allowed to take the course for credit only and, thus, the formula to compute the semester grade must determine whether the student elected this option, and if so, whether the student has passed. Figure 6.47 shows the completed version of a grade book that uses a variety of Excel functions. These functions are used individually and in conjunction with one another. This challenging exercise provides you with the opportunity to practice and apply your skill with the text-to-columns operation, concatenate functions, nested IFs, and other functions.

a. Open the *chap6_mid2_gradebook* workbook and save it as **chap6_mid2_gradebook_ solution**.

b. Click in **cell A4** and freeze panes.

c. Join students' names—last name, comma, first name—in column A, and then delete column B.

d. Use the appropriate command to separate the test scores in column B to columns B through G and suppress the zeros in the columns.

e. Click in **cell G4** and type the formula to compute the student's test average, and drop the lowest grade if the student has taken all five exams.

   The professor also wants you to round the calculated average. Alex Pons, for example, would get a C rather than a B if his average were not rounded. Click in **cell H4** and enter the function that rounds the student's score to zero decimal places. The zero indicates the number of decimal places in the rounded number.

...continued on Next Page

f. Create a formula in cells J3 through J18 that calculates the students' grade and displays the word *Pass* when students are taking the course for credit only and pass.

g. Use the Rank function to determine each student's rank in class according to the computed value of his or her semester average. Use Help to learn how to enter the Rank function.

h. Copy the formulas in row 4 to the remaining rows in the worksheet.

i. Calculate the summary statistics for each exam, as shown in rows 21 through 25.

j. Use the COUNTIF function to determine the grade distribution. The entry in cell K22, for example, is COUNTIF($J$4:$J$19,"=F").

k. Format the worksheet in attractive fashion, as shown in Figure 6.47. You are required to use conditional formatting to display grades of A and F in blue and red, respectively.

l. Create a custom footer that includes your name, today's date, and your instructor's name. Print the worksheet as displayed and with formulas visible. Close the workbook.

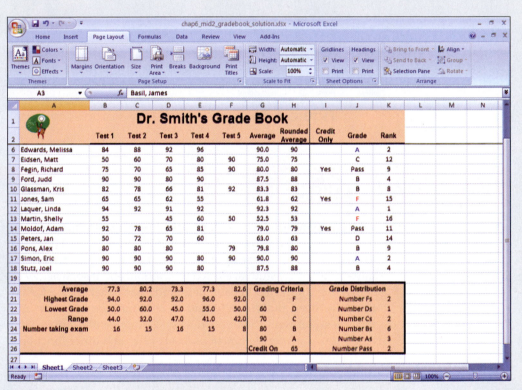

Figure 6.47 Professor's Grade Book

...continued on Next Page

Your father, the owner of The Golf Shoppe, asked for your help with Excel. He recently purchased a new dump truck and wants to create an amortization schedule to see what his monthly payments will be for the life of the loan. The final amortization table is shown in Figure 6.48 and should be used as you complete this exercise.

a. Open the *chap6_mid3_dumptruck* workbook and save it as **chap6_mid3_dumptruck_solution**. Enter the loan parameters as shown in the table below:

Principal	50000
Annual Interest	8%
Date of First Payment	2/1/2008
Term of Loan (years)	4
Your Last Name	Your name
Purpose of Loan	Truck Loan

b. Enter formulas in **cell G4** and **cell G5** to calculate the monthly payment and the total number of monthly payments. Enter formulas in row 13 for the first payment.

c. Create and type AND and IF functions in **cell C7:D7**, **cell A13**, **cell B13**, **cell C13**, **cell G4**, and **cell G5**. These functions prevent an error message from displaying before all data is entered in the worksheet.

d. Type the formulas in row 14 for the second payment. Hint: These are IF functions that show second payment information only if there is a balance after the first payment.

e. Complete the payment schedule for the life of the loan or when there is a zero balance.

f. Change the annual interest rate and the term of the loan to see the changes made to the amortization schedule.

g. Create a custom footer that includes your name, a page number, and your instructor's name. Select the first 20 rows of the worksheet and print the selection as displayed and with formulas visible. Close the workbook.

...continued on Next Page

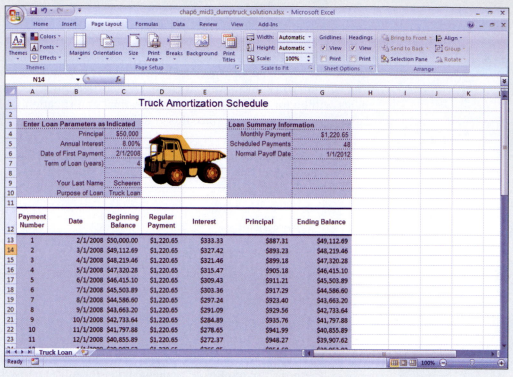

Figure 6.48 The Golf Shoppe Dump Truck Amortization

4 Planning for Retirement

Compound interest is called the eighth wonder of the world. It can work against you, as in the case of credit card and other debt. It works in your favor if you are able to save periodically toward retirement, especially when you begin saving at an early age. The best time to start is when you begin your first job, because the longer your money is invested, the more time it has to grow. Assume, for example, that you begin saving $25 a week at age 22 and that you continue to save for 45 years until you reach age 67, the regular retirement age under Social Security. Let us further assume that you earn an annual return of 8%, which is the historic rate of return for a broad-based investment in the stock market. When you retire, you will have contributed a total of $58,500, but your money will have grown to more than $540,000. The compound interest you earned on your money accounts for almost 90% of your nest egg. Let us say that you delay for 10 years and that all other parameters are the same. Your total contribution is $45,500 ($13,000 less), but your nest egg will be only $241,000, less than half of what you would have had if you had contributed the additional 10 years. Use Figure 6.49 for reference as you complete the retirement worksheet. The summary portion of the worksheet is complete; all of the formulas have already been entered. You will enter the parameters in the blue-shaded input area, **cells C4:C8**, to see your retirement projection.

a. Open the *chap6_mid4_retirement* workbook and save it as **chap6_mid4_retirement_ solution**. Enter the required data in **cells C4:C8**, as shown in Figure 6.49.

b. Enter the appropriate formulas to complete the amortization schedule for **cells C11:G55**. Hint: Some formulas involve the use of functions while others are simple formulas.

...continued on Next Page

c. Format values as **Currency** with zero decimals, **Percentages** with two decimals, and dates as **Short Dates** where appropriate.

d. Create a custom footer that includes your name, a page number, and your instructor's name. Select the first 20 rows of the worksheet and print the selection as displayed and with formulas visible. Close the workbook.

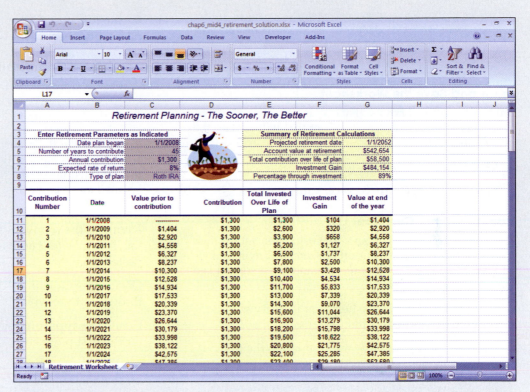

Figure 6.49 Retirement Planning

Capstone Exercise

As the owner of the JAS Bakery, you are a jack of all trades. You develop the recipes, make the recipes, market your baked goods, and manage the business. Your business has been very successful, and you are now considering an expansion of your business. In this exercise, you are going to modify your customer list, analyze your sales totals for the past year, and prepare an amortization schedule for the loan you are applying for that will allow you to expand.

Open and Save the Worksheet

You must open a workbook that contains three worksheets: customers, product sales, and a sheet that will contain the amortization schedule.

a. Open the file *chap6_cap_bakery*.

b. Save it as **chap6_cap_bakery_solution**.

Manipulate the Customer List

You have collected data about your customers, but the data is not in a form that you can sort or search in any meaningful way. You have duplicate records and must sort on last name as well as zip code.

a. Use the Excel feature to help you identify and remove duplicate records.

b. Use the appropriate feature to separate the first and last names into two columns.

c. Use the appropriate feature to separate the city, state, and zip code in column D into separate columns. Remember to insert columns to accommodate the expanded data.

d. Sort the customer list by last name in alphabetical order.

e. Insert a title for your customer list, add column headings, and format the worksheet in a professional fashion. Create a custom footer that includes your name, a page number, and your instructor's name.

Summarize Sales Data

You must provide a financial summary and will create a summary report of your sales for the year. Your goal is to determine which month has the best sales.

a. Click the Product Sales sheet tab to review your sales data. Insert an appropriate title at the top of the worksheet.

b. Use the Subtotal command to average annual product sales.

c. Use the Subtotal command to total sales by month.

d. Format the worksheet to highlight the monthly totals.

e. Create a custom footer that includes your name, a page number, and your instructor's name.

Create a Loan Amortization

The bakery is doing well and you want to expand your facility to better serve your customers and to increase profits. To do this, you want to secure a small business loan to expand the bakery facility. You will use the BusinessLoan sheet to complete the amortization schedule to see what your monthly payment will be, how many monthly payments you must make, the date of the final payment, and total of all interest payments.

a. Create the formulas to determine Monthly Payment, the number of Scheduled Payments, and the Payoff Date. These formulas involve the use of nested IFs.

b. Create a formula in **cell D6** to suppress zeros throughout the worksheet.

c. Create the appropriate formulas in **cells A13:G13** for the first payment.

d. Create the appropriate formulas in **cells A14:G14** for the second payment. Hint: You cannot copy all formulas.

e. Copy **cells A14:G14** through **cells A72:G72**.

f. Format all cells with the appropriate format for dates, percents, and currency.

Print the Workbook

Before printing the reports, you see they are missing the standard footers. Create a custom footer that contains your name, page number, and your instructor's name. Print the completed workbook.

a. Select the CustomerList, ProductSales, and BusinessLoan sheet tabs and create a custom footer with your name on the left, the page number in the middle, and your instructor's name on the right.

b. Change the page orientation to landscape.

c. Print the workbook with displayed values.

d. Save your changes and close the workbook.

Mini Cases

Use the rubric following the case as a guide to evaluate your work, but keep in mind that your instructor may impose additional grading criteria or use a different standard to judge your work.

Upper Saddle River Gallery

GENERAL CASE

As the owner of the Upper Saddle River Gallery, you must calculate information about the collection. Specifically, you need the value of all oil paintings, the average acquisition date of all paintings, the number of charcoal works, the value of watercolor pieces purchased after 1940, the insurance value of oil paintings greater than 30 inches in height, and the number of acrylic paintings purchased since 1945. You also want to divide the artist names into two columns so you can search on last name only. Open the *chap6_mc1_art* workbook and save it as **chap6_mc1_art_solution**. Your assignment is to open the workbook and use appropriate conditional functions to calculate the required information.

Performance Elements	Exceeds Expectations	Meets Expectations	Below Expectations
Text manipulation	Labeled names in two columns.	Names in two columns.	Names not separated.
Conditional functions	Three completed.	Two completed.	One or none completed.
Conditional functions with more than one criterion	Three completed.	Two completed.	One or none completed.

Celebrity Birthdays

RESEARCH CASE

You will use the workbook *chap6_mc2_celebrities* to compare your age to that of several celebrities. The finished workbook will be a sophisticated spreadsheet using a nested IF function and conditional formatting. Open the partially completed version, *chap6_mc2_celebrities*, and use the Web to locate the birth date of the listed celebrities. You may want to begin your search at birthdays.celebhoo.com. Row C will contain the formula to calculate the amount the celebrity is older or younger than you. Column D will contain a formula to determine the difference in your ages. Column E will have a formula that produces the word *years*. Save your workbook as **chap6_mc2_celebrities_solution**.

Performance Elements	Exceeds Expectations	Meets Expectations	Below Expectations
Research birth dates for celebrities	Identified 17 birth dates.	Identified 14 birth dates.	Identified fewer than 14 birth dates.
Correct function in column C	Yes.	Yes.	No.
Correct formula in column D	Yes.	Yes.	No.
Calculation of your age	Completed using a formula.	Typed age (no formula used).	No entry.

Peer Tutoring

DISASTER CASE

Your volunteer service learning project involves tutoring students in Excel. Open the spreadsheet *chap6_mc3_sales* and save it as **chap6_mc3_sales_solution**. You will find four major errors in subtotals, duplicate names, and page break anomalies. Correct the errors and explain how the errors might have occurred and how they can be prevented. Include your explanation in the cells below the spreadsheet.

Performance Elements	Exceeds Expectations	Meets Expectations	Below Expectations
Identify four errors	Identified all four errors.	Identified three errors.	Identified two or fewer errors.
Correct four errors	Corrected all four errors.	Corrected three errors.	Corrected two or fewer errors.
Explain the error	Complete and correct explanation of each error.	Explanation is too brief to fully explain error.	No explanations.
Prevention description	Prevention description correct and practical.	Prevention description but obtuse.	No prevention description.

Data Consolidation, Links, and Formula Auditing

Worksheet References, File Linking, and Auditing Formulas

Objectives

After you read this chapter, you will be able to:

1. Consolidate data from multiple worksheets (**page 445**).
2. Define the three-dimensional workbook (**page 446**).
3. Create three-dimensional formulas (**page 450**).
4. Link workbooks (**page 462**).
5. Create the documentation worksheet (**page 464**).
6. Restrict values to a drop-down list (**page 474**).
7. Validate data (**page 475**).
8. Audit formulas (**page 477**).
9. Set up a Watch Window (**page 480**).

Hands-On Exercises

Exercises	Skills Covered
1. CONSOLIDATING BEST RESTAURANT CORPORATE SALES (page 454) **Open:** chap7_ho1_new_york.xlsx, chap7_ho1_chicago.xlsx, and chap7_ho1_philadelphia.xlsx **Save as:** chap7_ho1_summary_solution.xlsx	• Begin a New Workbook and Open Individual Workbooks • Copy Workbook Data • Verify the Copy Procedure • Insert a Worksheet • Create a 3-D Formula • Arrange Windows and Change Data • Edit Grouped Worksheets • Format Grouped Worksheets
2. CONSOLIDATING WORKBOOKS FOR CORPORATE SALES AND ADDING DOCUMENTATION (page 468) **Open:** chap7_ho2_new_york.xlsx, chap7_ho2_chicago.xlsx, and chap7_ho2_philadelphia.xlsx **Save as:** chap7_ho2_linking_solution.xlsx	• Open the Workbooks and Use AutoFill • Link Files and Copy Cell Formulas • Change the Data • Work with Comments and Documentation Worksheets
3. JAS MANUFACTURING (page 482) **Open:** chap7_ho3_jas.xlsx **Save as:** chap7_ho3_jas_solution.xlsx	• Trace Precedents • Audit a Region's Quarterly Sales and Remove Cell Error Indicators • Correct a Cell Formula and Trace a Cell's Dependents • Use Error Checking • Create a Watch Window • Validate Data

CASE STUDY

Judy's Luxury Ice Cream Shoppe

Judy's Luxury Ice Cream Shoppe offers old-fashioned, homemade ice cream in a comfortable setting that has a strong appeal to young families. The first store was opened three years ago in Madison, Wisconsin. Everyone loves ice cream, and the store was an instant hit. Two other stores in other Wisconsin communities quickly followed, both with similar success.

Judy Scheeren, the owner of Judy's Luxury Ice Cream Shoppe, has received an unsolicited offer to sell the three stores. Judy has bigger plans, however, and wants to expand further before selling out at what she hopes will be a much better price. She knows that she needs

Case Study

to evaluate the overall performance of the chain before opening additional stores, and thus she is especially interested in the comparative results of the various ice cream products she sells. Each store in the three cities sells the same variety of ice cream products, and each store maintains its own spreadsheet reflecting store sales by quarter.

Each store manager has entered the sales data for last year in a separate workbook. Because of your experience as an Excel consultant, Judy hired you to consolidate sales data to assist her in making an informed decision.

Your Assignment

- Read the chapter carefully and pay close attention to data consolidation, workbook linking, and formula auditing topics that demonstrate the techniques you will use to complete the case study.
- Consolidate the data into a single workbook that shows the total sales for each quarter and each ice cream category. The information should be shown in spreadsheet form as well as in graphical form. Create a drop-down list to choose from three cities, and include an appropriate input message and error message. You will create a summary workbook with multiple worksheets, one for each store location, a summary, a chart, and a documentation sheet. After consolidating the data, determine which store has the highest quarterly sales and which store has the lowest quarterly sales.
- Use the Formula Auditing tools on the Formulas tab to verify all of your formulas. Accurate financial information is a major concern to Judy as she will use your results to expand her business. Verify and change any formatting to make a consistent appearance among all worksheets and the chart.
- Begin by opening and reviewing the completed workbooks for the individual stores: *chap7_case_madison*, *chap7_case_milwaukee*, and *chap7_case_greenbay*. The *chap7_case_summary* workbook is partially complete and will become the final workbook.
- Print the completed summary workbook for Judy, your supervisor, to show both displayed values and cell formulas. Print the associated chart as well as the documentation sheet. Save the workbook as **chap7_case_summary_solution**.

Data Consolidation

Some of the most powerful tools in Excel are those that enable you to consolidate data from more than one workbook or more than one worksheet within a workbook into either a summary workbook or a summary worksheet. If you are the marketing manager for a national corporation and want each branch manager to report to you on a quarterly basis, you would need to consolidate the data received in some meaningful way, such as on a consolidated spreadsheet. You would then analyze the data, perhaps comparing product sales from each city. Which city has the greatest or lowest sales? Which product is the best-selling product? This situation is depicted graphically in Figure 7.1. This figure shows separate reports for Chicago, Philadelphia, and New York, all leading to a summary report for the corporation. Once a workbook is consolidated, you have the summary as well as the detailed spreadsheets available in one workbook.

Which city has the greatest or lowest sales? Which product is the best-selling product?

In this section, you consolidate data from multiple worksheets into one workbook, work with three-dimensional references, and control calculations in workbooks.

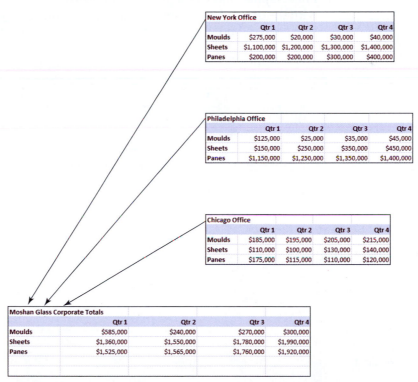

New York Office

	Qtr 1	Qtr 2	Qtr 3	Qtr 4
Moulds	$275,000	$20,000	$30,000	$40,000
Sheets	$1,100,000	$1,200,000	$1,300,000	$1,400,000
Panes	$200,000	$200,000	$300,000	$400,000

Philadelphia Office

	Qtr 1	Qtr 2	Qtr 3	Qtr 4
Moulds	$125,000	$25,000	$35,000	$45,000
Sheets	$150,000	$250,000	$350,000	$450,000
Panes	$1,150,000	$1,250,000	$1,350,000	$1,400,000

Chicago Office

	Qtr 1	Qtr 2	Qtr 3	Qtr 4
Moulds	$185,000	$195,000	$205,000	$215,000
Sheets	$110,000	$100,000	$130,000	$140,000
Panes	$175,000	$115,000	$110,000	$120,000

Moshan Glass Corporate Totals

	Qtr 1	Qtr 2	Qtr 3	Qtr 4
Moulds	$585,000	$240,000	$270,000	$300,000
Sheets	$1,360,000	$1,550,000	$1,780,000	$1,990,000
Panes	$1,525,000	$1,565,000	$1,760,000	$1,920,000

Figure 7.1   Consolidating Data from Multiple Worksheets

Consolidating Data from Multiple Worksheets

You are able to reconcile corporate totals for each product in each quarter with the amounts provided by each branch office. For example, consider the sales of moulds in the first quarter. The Chicago office sold $185,000, the Philadelphia office $125,000, and the New York office $275,000. The corporation sold a total of $585,000 worth of moulds during the first quarter ($185,000 + $125,000 + $275,000 = $585,000). The New York, Philadelphia, and Chicago offices sold $1,100,000, $150,000, and $110,000 worth of sheets in the first quarter, for a corporation total of $1,360,000.

Another example of the value of data consolidation would be in the creation of an extensive grade book for a professor. Each class would have a separate workbook and each student would have a separate worksheet within the workbook. The professor then creates a summary worksheet that summarizes the entire class's performance during the course. In this case, the professor might use averages rather than sums in the consolidated worksheet. Businesses with 5 to 10 employees use data consolidation for payroll, with each sheet representing one employee. Collectively, the workbook is the payroll workbook.

Chapter 7 presents two ways to consolidate the Moshan Glass corporate totals data shown in Figure 7.1. One way is to use the three-dimensional capabilities of Excel, where one workbook contains multiple worksheets. The workbook contains a separate worksheet for each branch and a summary worksheet that holds the consolidated corporate data. Another way to accomplish this is to maintain the data for each branch office in separate workbooks and create a summary workbook that uses file linking to reference cells in the other workbooks. Advantages and disadvantages for each technique are discussed in the chapter.

Defining the Three-Dimensional Workbook

The workbook shown in Figure 7.2 contains four worksheets. The title bar displays the name of the workbook, Corporate Sales, and the four tabs at the bottom of the workbook window display the names of each worksheet: Summary, New York, Philadelphia, and Chicago. The drill-down concept begins with the Summary sheet, with the details behind the summary in the individual sheets. This is a three-dimensional effect, and when you create formulas, you will reference specific worksheets.

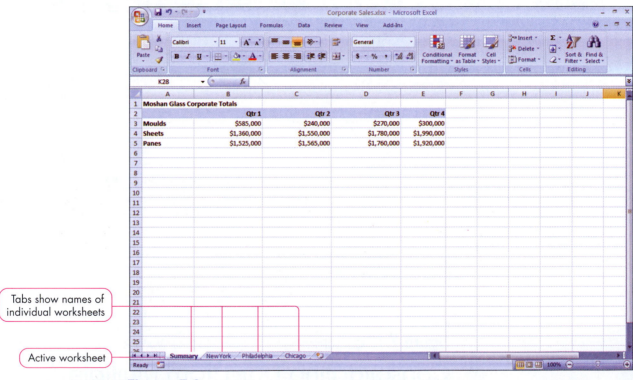

Figure 7.2 Worksheets Used in Consolidation

The Summary worksheet shows the total amount of each product sold during each quarter. The data in this worksheet reflect the amounts shown in Figure 7.1. Each entry in the Summary worksheet is the sum of the corresponding entries in the worksheets of the individual cities. Because the worksheets for the individual cities are not visible in the example in Figure 7.2, it may be useful and convenient to open multiple windows to see the individual city worksheets while you view the Summary worksheet.

Figure 7.3 shows the four worksheets in the Corporate Sales workbook. A different sheet is displayed in each window. The sheet tab indicates the worksheet displayed in the tiled view. The individual windows are smaller than the view in Figure 7.2, but the view does show how the Summary worksheet consolidates the data from each worksheet. The New Window command is used to open each additional window in

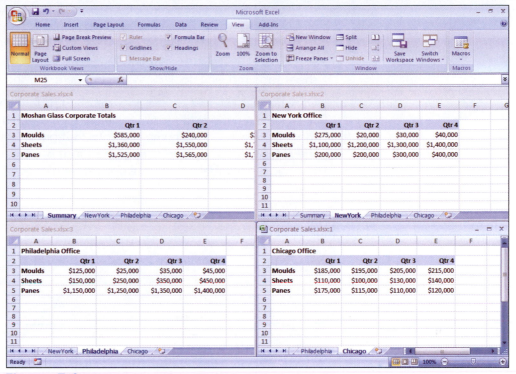

Figure 7.3 All Workbook Worksheets Open and Tiled

the same workbook. After all desired windows are open, you use the Arrange All command to tile or cascade all open windows.

Just one window is active at a time, and all commands apply only to the active window. To make a different window active, click in that window.

Copy Worksheets

Figure 7.3 shows a workbook that summarizes the data in individual worksheets. Placing the data in each worksheet can be accomplished in several ways. You could type the data in each worksheet as you receive the workbooks from each branch office. This is the most inefficient way to accomplish the task, however. It is more effective to enter the data by using one of two copy techniques. The first copy technique is to copy the data from the individual workbooks received from the branches into the appropriate sheets of the Corporate Sales workbook.

Another way to copy data is to copy worksheets from one workbook into another. To do this:

1. Select the sheets you want to move or copy.

2. Click Format in the Cells group on the Home tab.

3. Click Move or Copy Sheet in the Organize Sheets section.

4. Click the workbook to which you want to copy the selected sheets in the *To book* list.

5. In the *Before sheet* list, either click the sheet before which you want to insert the copied list or click Move to end to insert the copied sheet after the last sheet in the workbook.

6. Select the *Create a copy* check box.

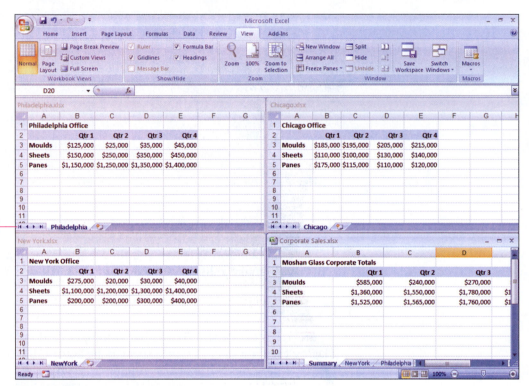

Figure 7.4 Multiple Workbooks

Use Multiple Workbooks

At first glance, Figure 7.4 is the same as Figure 7.3, but with one major difference. Figure 7.3 shows four different worksheets from the same workbook, but Figure 7.4 shows four different workbooks. Three workbooks contain only one worksheet; each worksheet has the sales data for the branch city. The fourth workbook contains four worksheets and is the workbook displayed in Figure 7.3.

Each technique has advantages and disadvantages. The single workbook shown in Figure 7.3 is easier for the manager to use as all of the data are in one file. The disadvantage is that the worksheets have to be maintained in remote locations and that several people have to have access to the same workbook. The multiple workbooks shown in Figure 7.4 make it easier to maintain the data, but four separate files are required for summary data.

Change Formula Recalculation, Iteration, or Precision

Calculation is the process of computing formulas and then displaying the results as values in the cells that contain the formulas. As calculation goes on, you can perform other actions in Excel. The program interrupts calculation to perform these actions, and then continues to calculate. Calculation can take more time if any of the following conditions exist:

- The workbook has a large number of formulas.
- The worksheets contain data tables or functions that automatically recalculate each time you enter data and the workbook is recalculated.
- The worksheets contain links to other worksheets or workbooks, and those data are updated.

To change when a worksheet or workbook recalculates, click the Office Button, click Excel Options, and click the Formulas category. In the *Calculation options* section, choose a Workbook Calculation option. Table 7.1 lists the Workbook Calculation options.

Table 7.1   Recalculation Options

To	Click
Recalculate all dependent formulas each time you make a change to a value, formula, or name.	Automatic
Recalculate all dependent formulas, except data tables, each time you make a change to a value, formula, or name.	Automatic except for data tables
Turn off automatic recalculation and recalculate open workbooks only when you do so explicitly.	Manual

TIP   Manual Calculation

When manual calculation is enabled, you can recalculate either the workbook or the worksheet. Click Calculate Now in the Calculate group on the Formulas tab to calculate the entire workbook. Click Calculate Sheet in the Calculate group on the Formulas tab to calculate the current worksheet.

Iteration is the repeated recalculation of a worksheet until a specific numeric condition is met.

Iteration is the repeated recalculation of a worksheet until a specific numeric condition is met. Iteration entries determine how long Solver works to solve a problem, and you will learn more about this topic later. To change the number of times Excel iterates a formula, click the Office Button, click Excel Options, and click the Formulas category (see Figure 7.5). Select the Enable iterative calculation check box in the *Calculation options* section. Type the number of iterations in the Maximum Iterations box. The higher the number, the more times Excel needs to recalculate the worksheet. To set the maximum amount of change you will accept between recalculation results, type the amount in the Maximum Change box.

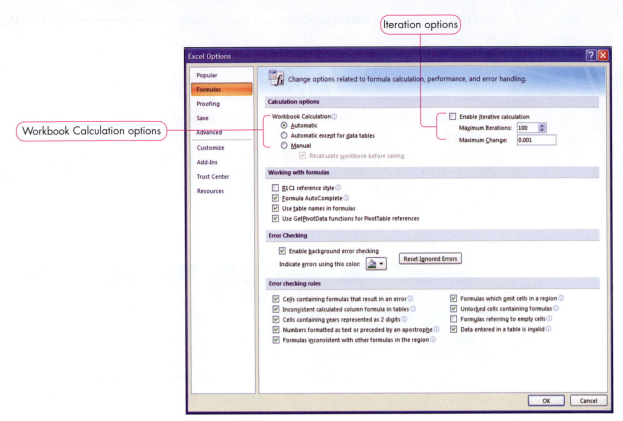

Figure 7.5 Formulas Section of Excel Options Dialog Box

Precision is a measure of the degree of accuracy for a calculation.

Precision is a measure of the degree of accuracy for a calculation. Excel stores and calculates 15 significant digits of precision. Precision defines how exact the calculation needs to be. The smaller the number (the more zeros after the decimal), the greater the precision. You will learn more about precision and iteration in a later chapter. To change the Precision settings, click the Office Button, click Excel Options, and then click the Advanced category. Select the workbook you want in the *When calculating this workbook* section. Select the Set precision as displayed check box.

Creating Three-Dimensional Formulas

You have read about and used cell references in earlier chapters where you refer to a particular cell in a worksheet by its cell reference or cell address. Cell B3 is cell B3 no matter what worksheet or workbook you work with; people who work with spreadsheets understand this cell reference naming convention. This issue becomes more complicated when you work the multiple worksheets in the same workbook. Each worksheet contains a cell B3, and if you want to reference a cell in another worksheet, a naming scheme must exist.

A *worksheet reference* is a reference to a cell in a worksheet not currently active.

If you want to reference a cell or cell range in a worksheet that is not active, you need to begin the cell address with a *worksheet reference*. A worksheet reference is a reference to a cell in a worksheet not currently active. An example of a worksheet reference is Philadelphia!B3, which references cell B3 in the Philadelphia worksheet. Worksheet references may also be used with cell ranges to simplify functions and formulas. The worksheet reference NewYork!B2:E5 references cells B2 through E5 in the NewYork worksheet. Failure to include a worksheet reference defaults to the cell reference in the active worksheet. In the following examples, note that the name of the worksheet is NewYork, not New York.

Review Figure 7.6 for an example of how worksheet references are used on the Summary worksheet. Each entry on the Summary worksheet calculates the sum of the corresponding cells in the NewYork, Philadelphia, and Chicago worksheets. The following formulas would be entered in cell B3:

=NewYork!B3+Philadelphia!B3+Chicago!B3

        Chicago is the worksheet reference

      Philadelphia is the worksheet reference

NewYork is the worksheet reference

In a worksheet reference, an exclamation point separates the worksheet reference from the cell reference. Worksheet references are always absolute references; however, the cell reference may be either relative (NewYork!B3), absolute (NewYork!$B$3), or mixed (NewYork!$B3 or NewYork!B$3).

This combination of relative cell references and constant worksheet references enables you to enter the formula once (in cell B3), and then copy it to the remaining cells in the worksheet. You enter the formula in cell B3 to calculate total sales for moulds in the first quarter, and then you copy that formula to the other cells in row 3, C3 through E3, to obtain the totals for moulds in the second, third, and fourth quarters. Similarly, you then copy the entire row, cells B3 through E3, to rows 4 and 5 to generate totals for Products 2 and 3 in all four quarters.

The correct use of relative and absolute references in the original formula in cell B3 is what makes it possible to copy the cell formulas. Look at the formula that was copied from cell B3 into cell C3:

=NewYork!C3+Philadelphia!C3+Chicago!C3

        Chicago is the worksheet reference

      Philadelphia is the worksheet reference

NewYork is the worksheet reference

The worksheet references, such as NewYork!, remain absolute, but the cell references adjust for the new location of the formula, cell C3. The same kind of adjustment is made in all of the other copied formulas.

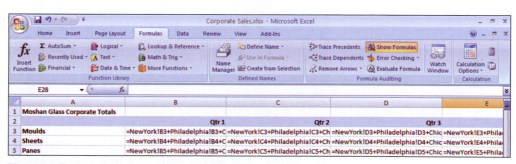

Figure 7.6 Worksheet References

Define a Three-Dimensional Formula

A *three-dimensional (3-D) formula* is a formula that refers to the same cell or range in multiple worksheets.

A formula or function that refers to the same cell or range in multiple worksheets is called a *three-dimensional (3-D) formula*. The individual reference to a cell on multiple worksheets is called a 3-D cell reference. It is a convenient way to reference several identically structured worksheets in which the cells in each worksheet contain the same type of data, such as when you consolidate sales information from different branches into the Summary worksheet. You can type a 3-D reference directly into a cell formula or function, but using the point-and-click method is more efficient. To enter a 3-D reference in a cell formula, type = in the cell that will contain the cell reference. To reference a cell in another worksheet, click the tab for that worksheet and then click the cell or range of cells to be referenced.

An example of a 3-D formula is =SUM(Philadelphia:Chicago!B3) that sums cell B3 in the Philadelphia, NewYork, and Chicago worksheets. The sheet range is specified with a colon between the beginning and ending worksheets. An exclamation point follows the last worksheet, before the cell reference. Worksheet references are constant and do not change when a formula is copied. Cell references may be relative or absolute.

Three-dimensional references used in the Summary worksheet are an alternative method to compute totals for each product-quarter combination. To calculate the corporate sales for Product 1 in quarter 1 in cell B3, you would create the following function:

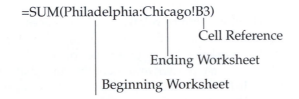

The 3-D formula includes all worksheets starting with Philadelphia and ending with Chicago, including in-between worksheets, such as NewYork. The reference automatically adds any worksheets that are subsequently added between Philadelphia and Chicago and similarly adjusts for worksheets that are deleted. The cell reference is relative so that the formula can be copied from cell B3 in the Summary worksheet to the remaining cells in row 3. The formulas can then be copied to the appropriate cells in rows 4 and 5.

You can also create 3-D formulas using functions, such as SUM or AVERAGE. To create a 3-D formula using a function:

1. Click the cell where you will enter the function.
2. Type =, type the name of the function, such as SUM, and then type an opening parenthesis.
3. Click the tab for the first worksheet to be referenced, such as Philadelphia.
4. Hold down Shift and click the tab for the last worksheet to be referenced, such as Chicago.
5. Select the cell or range of cells that you want to reference, such as cell C3.
6. Complete the formula and press Enter.

Group Worksheets

Worksheets in a workbook are often similar to one another in content or formatting. The formatting in the four worksheets shown in Figure 7.3 is identical. Although you can format worksheets individually, it is more efficient to format a group of worksheets than it is to format the worksheets individually.

Excel is capable of grouping worksheets to format or enter data in multiple worksheets at the same time. After worksheets are grouped, anything you do in one worksheet is done to the other worksheets in the group. Examples of what you can do to grouped worksheets might include:

- Entering row and column labels
- Formatting data
- Entering formulas to compute row and column totals
- Setting identical headers and footers, margins, and other layout options

You must remember to ungroup worksheets to enter data in a specific worksheet. To group worksheets in a workbook:

1. Click a worksheet tab.
2. Press and hold Ctrl as you click the worksheet tab for each worksheet to be included in the group. The grouped worksheet tabs display as white and the word *Group* appears in the title bar.
3. To ungroup, click any worksheet tab.

TIP Selecting Text

You can use Shift to select contiguous sheets and use Ctrl to select non-contiguous sheets. Remember also that you can use Shift to select contiguous cells and use Ctrl to select non-contiguous cells.

Hands-On Exercises

1 | Consolidating Best Restaurant Corporate Sales

Skills covered: 1. Begin a New Workbook and Open Individual Workbooks **2.** Copy Workbook Data **3.** Verify the Copy Procedure **4.** Insert a Worksheet **5.** Create a 3-D Formula **6.** Arrange Windows and Change Data **7.** Edit Grouped Worksheets **8.** Format Grouped Worksheets

Step 1 **Begin a New** **Workbook and Open** **Individual Workbooks**	Refer to Figure 7.7 as you complete Step 1. **a.** Start Excel and delete all worksheets except Sheet1: • Click the **Sheet2 tab** and press **Shift** as you click the **Sheet3 tab**. • Right-click the **Sheet3 tab** and select **Delete**. You grouped and then deleted Sheet2 and Sheet3 from the workbook. The workbook should contain only Sheet1. **b.** Save the workbook as **chap7_ho1_summary_solution**. **c.** Click the **Office Button** and click **Open** to display the Open dialog box. **d.** Click the *chap7_ho1_new_york* workbook, then press and hold **Ctrl** as you click the *chap7_ho1_chicago* and *chap7_ho1_philadelphia* workbooks. You used Ctrl to select all three workbooks at the same time. **e.** Click **Open** to open the selected workbooks. The selected workbooks are open in individual windows. **f.** Click the **View tab** and click **Arrange All** in the Window group to display the Arrange Windows dialog box. Make sure **Tiled** is selected in the dialog box, and then click **OK**. You should see four open workbooks, as shown in Figure 7.7. Your workbooks may be arranged differently.

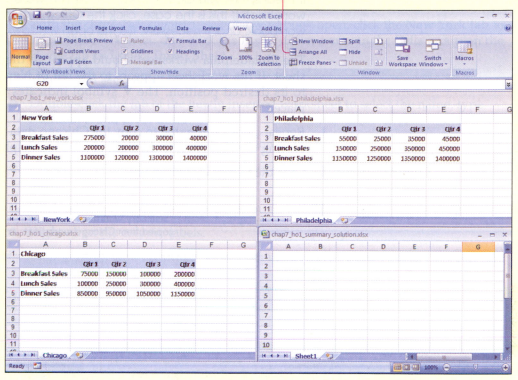

Figure 7.7 Opening Individual Workbooks

Step 2
Copy Workbook Data

Refer to Figure 7.8 as you complete Step 2.

a. Click the **chap7_ho1_new_york** workbook and select **cells A1:E5**.

b. Click **Copy** in the Clipboard group on the Home tab and click **cell A1** of the Summary workbook.

c. Click **Paste** in the Clipboard group on the Home tab.

You copied the New York office financial data and pasted it in the Summary workbook.

d. Right-click the **Sheet1 tab** in the Summary worksheet window and select **Rename**.

e. Type **New York** and press **Enter**.

You changed the worksheet tab from Sheet1 to New York.

f. Click in the **chap7_ho1_philadelphia** workbook to make it active.

g. Click the **Philadelphia tab**, then press and hold **Ctrl** as you drag the tab to the right of the New York tab in the Summary workbook.

You will see a tiny spreadsheet with a plus sign as you drag the tab. The plus sign indicates that the worksheet is being copied; the ▼ symbol indicates where the worksheet will be placed.

h. Release the mouse, and then release Ctrl.

The worksheet from the Philadelphia workbook should have been copied to the Summary workbook and appears as Philadelphia in that workbook.

Workbook Linking and Documentation

Workbook linking is another way to consolidate data. Earlier you worked with worksheet references that consolidate data within one workbook. When you link workbooks, you consolidate the data from several workbooks into another workbook. External references can be used effectively when you want to merge data from several workbooks, when you want to create different views of your data, or when you want to streamline large, complex models.

> (*External references can be used effectively when you want to merge data from several workbooks . . . .*)

Documenting a workbook means that you include such elements as the author, subject, and location of the workbook, and you define formulas used in the workbook. These and other elements used to document a workbook become essential when large, complex workbooks are created and accessed by several people. Though you know what is in a workbook, others who work with it may not. Auditors use documentation when they verify accuracy of formulas. These are examples of the value of workbook documentation.

In this section, you learn how to link workbooks and create a documentation worksheet.

TIP   Pointing to Cells in Other Worksheets

A worksheet reference can be typed directly into a cell formula, but it is easier to enter the reference by pointing. Click in the cell that is to contain the reference, then enter an equal sign to begin the formula. To reference a cell in another worksheet, click the tab for the worksheet you want to reference and click the cell or cell range you want to include in the formula. Complete the formula as usual, continuing to first click the tab whenever you want to reference a cell in another worksheet.

Linking Workbooks

Linking uses formulas that reference cells in other workbooks.

Linking in Excel uses formulas that reference cells in other workbooks. Linking in Excel and the other Office applications enables you to paste a copy of an object so that it keeps its connection to the original object. Linking is established by the creation of external references that refer to a cell or range of cells in another workbook. Linking enables you to make a change in one workbook and see the change in another workbook. You use a dependent workbook that contains the external references and reflects data in the source workbooks. Linking is used to update workbooks so that the data are consistent across the application. The dependent workbook, the Linking Worksheet in Figure 7.14, contains the external references and reflects, or is dependent on, the data in one or more source workbooks. The source workbooks—Philadelphia, New York, and Chicago—contain data that are referenced by the dependent workbook.

Figure 7.15 shows the use of linking in the example you have been working with. You have four separate workbooks; each contains one open worksheet. The Linking Worksheet is the dependent workbook and uses external references to obtain summary totals. The Philadelphia, New York, and Chicago workbooks are the source workbooks. Cell B3 is the active cell in the Linking Worksheet. The contents are displayed in the Formula Bar. Corporate sales for the first quarter are calculated by summing the corresponding values in the source workbooks. Workbook names are displayed in square brackets to indicate that they are external references.

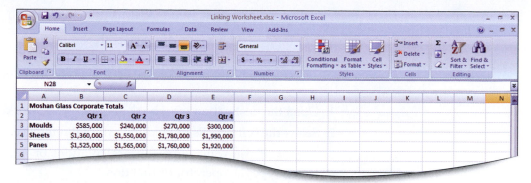

Figure 7.14 Summary Linking Workbook

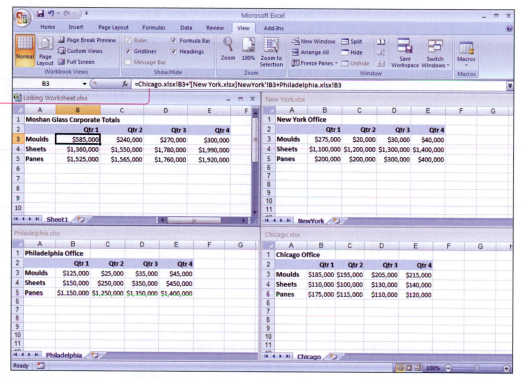

Figure 7.15 Tiled Linking Workbooks

The formulas to compute corporate totals for moulds in the second, third, and fourth quarters contain similar external references. Workbook references, like sheet references, are absolute, but cell references may be relative or absolute. This enables the formula to be copied to remaining cells in the row to calculate the totals for moulds in the remaining rows after the formula is completed in cell B3.

Formulas with external references are displayed in two ways, depending whether the source workbook is open or closed. When the source is open, the external reference includes the workbook name in square brackets, the worksheet name, an exclamation point, and the cells on which the formula depends.

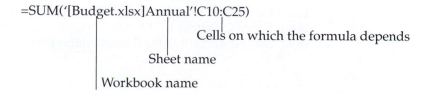

=SUM('[Budget.xlsx]Annual'!C10:C25)

Cells on which the formula depends

Sheet name

Workbook name

When the source is not open, the external reference includes the entire path to the workbook file as shown in the following example.

$$=SUM('C:\backslash Reports\backslash[Budget.xlsx]Annual'!C10:C25)$$

Complete path

To create an external reference between cells in different workbooks:

1. Open the destination workbook and all source workbooks.
2. Select the cell or cells to hold the external reference.
3. Type =. If you want to perform calculations or functions on the external references, type the operator or function.
4. Switch to the source workbook and click the worksheet that contains the cells you want to link to.
5. Select the cells you want to link to.
6. Return to the destination workbook and press Enter.

> **TIP** **Drive and Folder Reference**
>
> An external reference is updated regardless of whether the source workbook is open. The reference is displayed differently depending on whether or not the source workbook is open. The references include the path, the drive, and folder if the source workbook is closed; the path is not shown if the source workbook is open. The external workbooks must be available to update the summary workbook. If the location of the workbooks changes, as may happen if you copy the workbooks to a different folder, click Edit Links in the Connections group on the Data tab.

Creating the Documentation Worksheet

A ***documentation worksheet*** describes the contents of each worksheet within the workbook.

This Excel textbook emphasizes design of worksheets through the isolation of assumptions and initial conditions on which the worksheet is based. A *documentation worksheet* describes the contents of each worksheet within the workbook. Documenting a workbook and the worksheets in the workbook is important because spreadsheets are very often used by individuals other than the person who created them. You, the author, know what is in the workbook, but others may not. Everyone who works with a workbook, including anyone who has never seen it before, needs to be able to recognize the purpose and the structure of the workbook. Even if you do not share the workbook with others, you may forget some aspects of it as time passes and will appreciate documentation.

The best way of documenting a workbook is by creating a documentation worksheet that describes the contents of each worksheet within a workbook. Figure 7.16 shows a sample documentation worksheet created for some of the examples in this chapter. A documentation worksheet may contain some or all of the following information: author, date of creation, date of last modification, description of the workbook, list of sheets in the workbook, and description of each sheet.

A documentation worksheet should be attractively formatted and take advantage of color and font size to call attention to the title of the workbook. Remember, though, not to format to the point that the message is lost. Other users appreciate clear, concise, and attractive documentation.

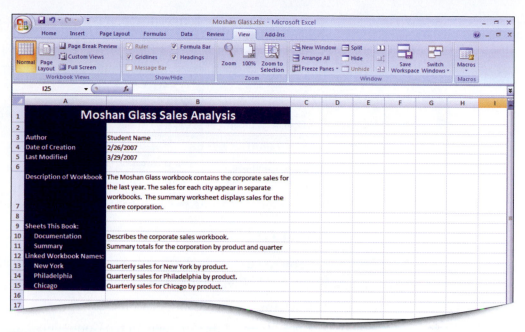

Figure 7.16 Documentation Worksheet

Insert, Edit, and Delete Comments

Using comments is one of the easiest ways for Excel users to share or collaborate in their work and to provide additional documentation beyond that contained in the documentation worksheet. Comments, which appear as yellow boxes, can be used to indicate a possible error, ask a question, or make a suggestion. Comments are frequently used to clarify formulas, describe cell contents, or indicate any assumptions. When you are using comments, you are not changing the worksheet itself, even though the comments do become part of the worksheet. Excel does not limit the number of comments that can be placed in a workbook; however, a cell may have only one comment. To create a new comment:

1. Click the cell to which you want to add a comment.
2. Click New Comment in the Comments group on the Review tab.
3. Type the comment.
4. Click the cell again after you have typed the comment to finish the insert comment process.

The cell with the comment contains a red triangle in the upper-right corner, as shown in Figure 7.17.

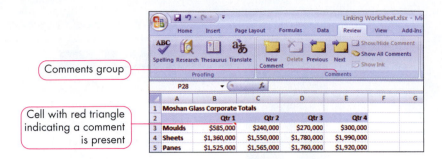

Figure 7.17 Comments

You can use either the Comments group on the Review tab or the shortcut menu to edit an existing comment (see Figure 7.18). To edit a comment:

1. Click the cell containing the comment.
2. Click Show/Hide Comment in the Comments group on the Review tab.
3. Click in the comment and edit it as desired.
4. Right-click on the comment and select Exit Edit Text or click in the cell containing the comment.

Alternatively,

1. Click in the cell containing the comment to finish the edit process.
2. Click Show/Hide Comment in the Comments group of the Review tab to hide the comment.

Note that you can format comment text by selecting Format Comment from the shortcut menu associated with the comment. To delete a comment, click Delete in the Comments group of the Review tab after clicking in the cell with the comment or right-click the cell and select Delete Comment.

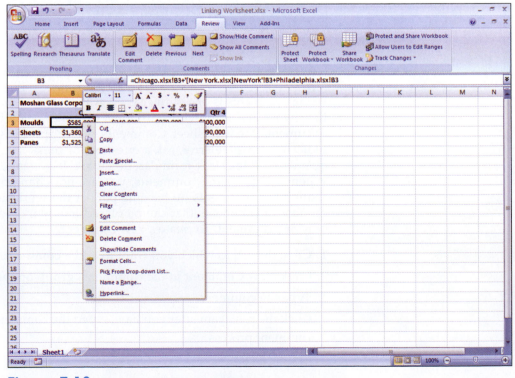

Figure 7.18 Comments Shortcut Menu

Print Comments

When you print a worksheet, comments do not print by default. You do have two options when you choose to print comments. The first option is that they may be printed if they are not hidden on the worksheet itself. This option would cause parts of the worksheet to be covered or hidden by the visible comments. The second option is to print the comments on a separate sheet.

To print comments, click the Page Setup Dialog Box Launcher on the Page Layout tab. Click the Sheet tab and select either *At end of sheet* or *As displayed on sheet* from the Comments drop-down arrow, as shown in Figure 7.19. Click OK.

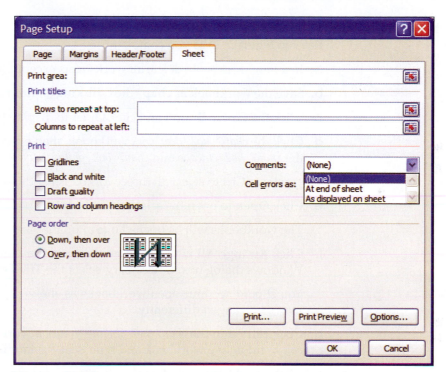

Figure 7.19 Page Setup Dialog Box with Comments Print Choices

Hands-On Exercises

2 | Consolidating Workbooks for Corporate Sales and Adding Documentation

Skills covered: 1. Open the Workbooks and Use AutoFill **2.** Link Files and Copy Cell Formulas **3.** Change the Data **4.** Work with Comments and Documentation Worksheets

<table>
<tr>
<td>

Step 1

Open the Workbooks and Use AutoFill

</td>
<td>

Refer to Figure 7.20 as you complete Step 1.

a. In a new workbook, delete all worksheets except **Sheet1**.

b. Save the workbook as **chap7_ho2_linking_solution**.

c. Click the **Office Button** and click **Open** to display the Open dialog box.

d. Click the *chap7_ho2_new_york* workbook, then press and hold **Ctrl** as you click the *chap7_ho2_chicago* and *chap7_ho2_philadelphia* workbooks.

You used Ctrl to select all three workbooks at the same time.

e. Click **Open** to open the selected workbooks.

The workbooks will be opened one after another.

f. Click **Arrange All** in the Window group on the View tab to display the Arrange Windows dialog box. If necessary, select the **Tiled option**, and then click **OK**.

You should see four open workbooks as shown in Figure 7.20. Your workbooks may be arranged differently.

g. Click **cell A1** in the *chap7_ho2_linking_solution* workbook to make this the active cell in the active workbook and type **Best Restaurant Corporate Sales**.

h. Click **cell B2**, type **Qtr 1**, click **cell B2**, and drag the fill handle over **cells C2:E2**.

A border appears to indicate the destination range. Cells C2 through E2 now contain the labels Qtr 2, Qtr 3, and Qtr 4, respectively.

i. Right-align the entries in **cells B2:E2**, and reduce the column widths so you can see the entire worksheet in the window.

j. Click **cell A3**, type **Breakfast Sales**, **Lunch Sales** in **cell A4**, and **Dinner Sales** in **cell A5**.

</td>
</tr>
</table>

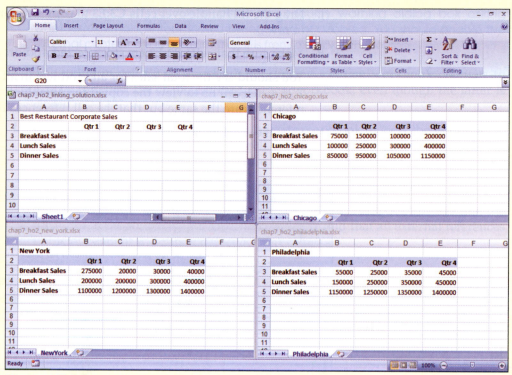

Figure 7.20 Setup for Linking

<table>
<tr><td>**Step 2**
Link Files and
Copy Cell Formulas</td><td>

Refer to Figure 7.21 as you complete Step 2.

a. Click **cell B3** of the *chap7_ho2_linking_solution* workbook and type =.

You will now create the formula by pointing.

b. Click in the window for the New York workbook and click **cell B3**.

The Formula Bar should display =[chap7_ho2_new_york.xlsx]NewYork!$B$3. But you must make the cell reference relative.

c. Press **F4** until the cell reference changes to B3.

d. Type +, click in the window for the Philadelphia workbook, and click **cell B3**.

The formula expands to include:
+[chap7_ho2_philadelphia.xlsx]Philadelphia!$B$3.

e. Press **F4** until the cell reference changes to B3.

f. Type +, click in the window for the Chicago workbook, and click **cell B3**.

The formula expands to include +[chap7_ho2_chicago.xlsx]Chicago!$B$3.

g. Press **F4** until the cell reference changes to B3.

h. Press **Enter**.

The formula is complete, and you should see 405000 in cell B3 of the *chap7_ho2_linking_solution* workbook.

i. Click **cell B3**.

The entry on the Formula Bar should match the entry in Figure 7.21.

</td></tr>
</table>

b. Click in any cell.

Clicking in another cell after you finish entering the comment closes the comment box. The text of the comment is no longer visible, but a tiny red triangle is visible in cell B3. When you point to cell B3, you will see the text of the comment.

c. Click **cell B3**, click **Edit Comment** in the Comments group, delete the word **four** and type **three**, and click in any cell.

You realize that just three cities have sales and edited the comment appropriately. The following steps will add the documentation worksheet.

d. Click the **Home tab**, click the **Insert down arrow** in the Cells group, and select **Insert Sheet**.

e. Double-click the new worksheet tab, type **Documentation**, and press **Enter**.

You inserted a new worksheet and named it Documentation.

f. Double-click the **Sheet1 tab**, type **Summary** to rename the sheet, and press **Enter**.

g. Click the **Documentation sheet** tab and type the descriptive entries in column A as shown in Figure 7.23, type your name in **cell B3**, click **cell B5** and type **=Today()**, and press **Enter**. Left-align the date.

h. Increase the width of column B as shown in Figure 7.23, click **cell B7**, and type the descriptive entry shown below:

The Best Restaurants Corporate Sales workbook contains the corporate sales for the last year. The sales for each city appear in separate workbooks. The summary worksheet displays sales for the entire corporation.

Do not press Enter until you complete the entire entry. Do not be concerned if the text in cell B7 appears to spill into the other cells in row 7.

i. Press **Enter** when you have completed the entry.

j. Right-click **cell B7**, select **Format Cells**, click the **Alignment** tab in the Format Cells dialog box, click the **Wrap text check box**, and click **OK**.

You wrapped the descriptive text to the cell width, making the text more readable.

k. Right-click **cell A7**, select **Format Cells**, select **Top** from the Vertical alignment drop-down arrow, and click **OK**.

You aligned the label in cell A7 with the top of the cell to facilitate readability.

l. The following will format the Documentation sheet to enhance its appearance:

- Click **cell A1**, type **Best Restaurants Corporate Sales Analysis**, and change the font size to **20 point**.
- Click and drag to select **cells A1:B1**, then click **Merge & Center** in the Alignment group.
- Check that **cells A1:B1** are still selected and press and hold **Ctrl** while you select **A2:A15**.
- Click **Dark Blue** from the Fill Color down arrow and click **Bold** in the Font group.
- With cells A1:B1 and A2:A15 selected, click **White** from the Font Color down arrow.
- Click outside the selected cells to see the effects of the formatting change. You should see white letters on a dark blue background.
- Widen column A as necessary.

Refer to Figure 7.23 as you complete the text entries in cells B10 through B15.

m. Save and close the workbook. Exit Excel if you do not want to continue with the next exercise at this time.

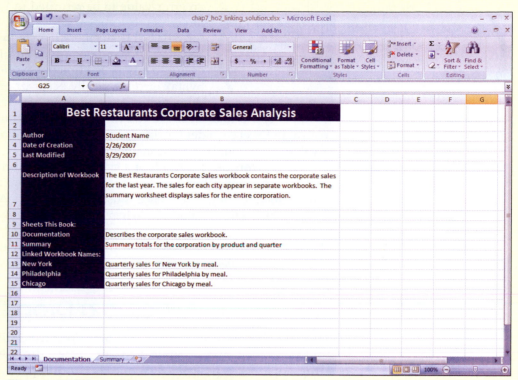

Figure 7.23 The Documentation Worksheet

Workbook Auditing

Errors can occur in a worksheet in several ways, and different forms of errors will occur in a worksheet. Sometimes, it is just an incorrectly entered formula that causes an error value to be returned in Excel. More difficult to detect are errors that appear correct but are not because an incorrect formula has been entered. A *syntax error* is an error that occurs because a formula or function violates correct construction, such as a misspelled function name or illegal use of an operator. Syntax errors typically occur prior to the execution of a procedure and must be corrected for the procedure to continue. An example of a syntax error is a run-time error; a program halts until the error is corrected. In Excel consider the divide by zero error a syntax error. Attempting to divide a value by zero violates basic mathematical syntax.

Logic errors are the result of a syntactically correct formula but logically incorrect construction, which produces inaccurate results. Logic errors occur when the wrong operator or cell reference is used in a formula. An example of a logic error is one in which a formula divides when it should multiply two cells.

This section discusses validating data, which enables you to set rules to guide data entry in particular cells, and formula auditing, which enables you to review the way your formulas are constructed and how they behave in a spreadsheet.

> More difficult to detect are errors that appear correct but are not because an incorrect formula has been entered.

A *syntax error* is an error that violates correct construction of a formula.

A *logic error* is an error that produces inaccurate results.

Restricting Values to a Drop-Down List

To make data entry a bit easier or to limit spreadsheet items to certain defined items and thereby be more accurate, you can create a drop-down list of valid entries. The drop-down list is assembled from cells in other parts of the workbook. When you create a drop-down list, it displays an arrow in the cell, and information is entered by clicking the down arrow and then clicking the desired entry. You can choose from just those entries provided. You cannot enter invalid data. To create a drop-down list:

1. Create a list of valid entries in a single column or row without blank cells.
2. Click Data Validation in the Data Tools group on the Data tab to show the Data Validation dialog box.
3. Click the Settings tab, click the Allow drop-down arrow, and select List.
4. Enter a reference to the list in the source box. See Figure 7.24.
5. Make sure that the In-cell dropdown check box is selected and that the Ignore blank check box is clear or selected.

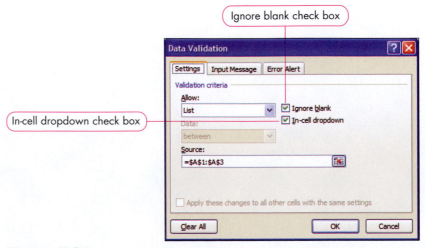

Figure 7.24 Data Validation Dialog Box

Validating Data

Data validation enables you to restrict values that can be entered into a cell. It warns and prevents people other than you from entering "wrong" data in a cell. Data validation enables you to specify and correct the kind of data that can be entered, specify an input message warning people when they click a cell that only specific types of data can be entered in that cell, and specify error messages that appear when others persist and attempt to enter incorrect data. All of these tasks are accomplished using the Data Validation dialog box. You access this dialog box by clicking Data Validation in the Data Tools group on the Data tab.

Specify Data Validation Criteria

In the Settings tab of the Data Validation dialog box, you set the values that are permitted in a cell. In the Allow list box, you specify the type of data permitted in a cell. These types include Any value, Whole number, Decimal, Date, Time, and Text length. For example, if you specify Decimal and you enter a whole number, Excel will not permit you to enter a whole number and will display an error message.

You then set the data range in the Data list box. The data range is not available if you select List from the Allow drop-down arrow in the dialog box. You will set the parameters and then specify the Minimum and Maximum values permitted. You would create a drop-down list if the valid grades were A, B, or C, or valid zip codes were 15601, 15697, or 15146. Figure 7.25 shows a validation rule in which the cell contents must be (a) a whole number and (b) between a minimum and maximum value, which are stored respectively in cells F4 and F6.

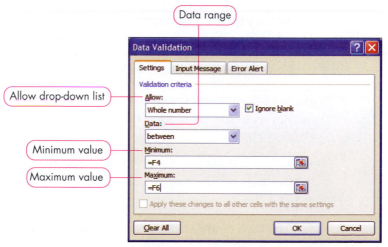

Figure 7.25 Settings Tab of the Data Validation Dialog Box

TIP   Circle Text

The Data Validation down arrow list contains an item called Circle Invalid Data. When this item is clicked, circles appear around cells that contain invalid data. When the data are corrected, the circles disappear. Data Validation rules must be defined for the cells before the Circle Invalid Data option can be invoked.

Create an Input Message

Input messages are descriptive text or instructions for data entry. You add input messages to cells, and they are displayed when a user moves to a cell that has some data entry restriction. Input messages consist of two parts: a title and an input message (see Figure 7.26). Generally, input messages should be a bit more than just a description of the data validation settings and should explain or show something about the data that can be entered in the cell. For example, an input message might be *Enter hire date in the form: mm/dd/yyyy.* or *Enter Employee name: last name, first name.*

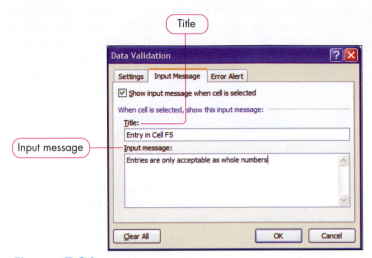

Figure 7.26 Input Message Tab of the Data Validation Dialog Box

Create an Error Alert

Sometimes, no matter how descriptive you are, users will attempt to enter invalid data in a cell. Instead of using Excel's default error message, you have the ability to create your own user-friendly message using the Error Alert tab (see Figure 7.27). The error alert message should be polite and should clearly state what the error is. Cryptic, nondescriptive alert messages do not help users understand the data entry problem. You are creating a worksheet that someone else will use. Data entry people are not necessarily familiar with Excel, nor are they familiar with the business. You should design input messages and error alerts for the novice Excel user and the new employee. In the Error Alert tab in the Data Validation dialog box, you have three styles of error alert:

1. Stop—Prevents the user from entering invalid data.
2. Warnings—Will accept invalid data.
3. Information—Will accept invalid data.

   You then create a title and descriptive message to complete the Error Alert.

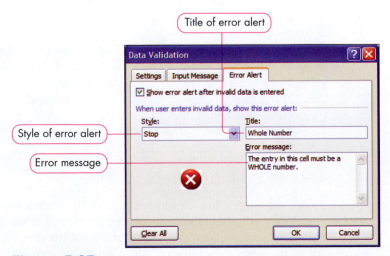

Figure 7.27 Error Alert Tab in the Data Validation Dialog Box

Auditing Formulas

To this point, you have reviewed material pertaining to invalid entry of new data. However, a worksheet might contain instances where formulas have been entered incorrectly and Excel returns error messages. Even harder to detect are instances where the formula is correct but it is the wrong formula for the application. This is a common logic error. If Excel cannot perform the calculations called for by a formula in a cell, an error value is displayed in the cell. *Formula auditing* enables you to display or trace relationships between cells and formulas. Table 7.2 displays Excel error values and the source of the error. In Excel 2007, all auditing of formulas is done using commands in the Formula Auditing group on the Formulas tab, as shown in Figure 7.28.

Formula auditing enables you to display or trace relationships between cells and formulas.

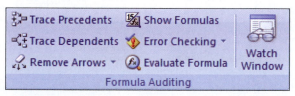

Figure 7.28 The Formula Auditing Group

Table 7.2 Excel Errors and Source of Error

Error Value	Source
#DIV!0!	Formula contains a number divided by zero.
#NAME?	Failure to recognize text in a function, such as misspelling a function name or range name.
#N/A	Value not available to the formula.
#NULL!	Formula requires cell ranges to intersect and they do not.
#NUM!	Invalid numbers used in a formula.
#REF!	Cell reference in a formula no longer valid.
#VALUE!	Incorrect type of argument used in formula.

Trace Precedents and Dependents

Often when auditing formulas, it is difficult to locate the source of an error in a formula when the formula uses precedent or dependent cells. *Precedent cells* are cells that are referred to by a formula in another cell, such as hourly wage and regular hours being referred to by a formula to calculate gross pay. *Dependent cells* contain formulas that refer to other cells such as the formula for gross pay depending on the hourly wage and regular hours. You use the Trace Precedents and Trace Dependents commands to graphically display, using tracer arrows, the relationship between these cells and formulas (see Figure 7.29). The tracer arrows help you identify cells that are causes of errors. An error message icon may also display with an explanation of the possible error, and the down arrow list contains possible fixes. To trace precedents:

Precedent cells are cells referred to by a formula in another cell.

Dependent cells contain formulas that refer to other cells.

1. Select the cell that contains the formula for which you will find precedent cells.
2. Click Trace Precedents in the Formula Auditing group of the Formulas tab.

Blue arrows show cells with no errors. Red arrows show cells that cause errors. To remove tracer arrows, click Remove Precedent Arrows in the Formula Auditing group on the Formulas tab. To trace dependent cells:

1. Click the cell for which you will find dependents.
2. Click Trace Dependents in the Formula Auditing group on the Formulas tab.

Again, blue arrows show cells with no errors and red arrows show cells that cause errors.

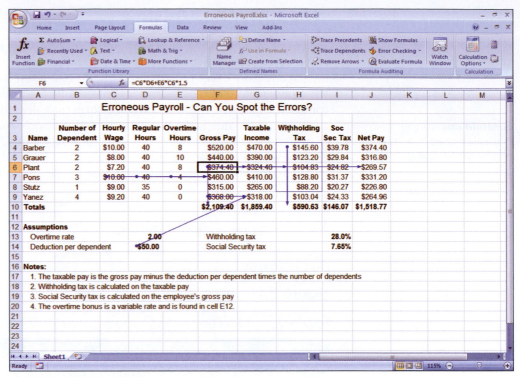

Figure 7.29 Trace Precedents

TIP | Remove Tracer Arrows

Click Remove Arrows from the down arrow in the Formula Auditing group on the Formulas tab. You may remove all tracer arrows or just precedent or dependent tracer arrows.

Check For and Repair Errors

When the tracing of precedents or dependents shows errors in formulas, or if you want to check for errors that have occurred in formulas anywhere in a spreadsheet, you can use the Error Checking command in the Formula Auditing group on the Formulas tab. When an error is identified in a cell by the Error Checking command, the Error Checking dialog box appears, as shown in Figure 7.30.

Figure 7.30 Error Checking Dialog Box

This identifies the cell with an error and describes the error. When you click the Help on this error button, Excel transfers you to the section of Excel Help that describes the error. Clicking Show Calculation Steps opens the Evaluate Formula dialog box, as shown in Figure 7.31. This dialog box graphically displays an evaluation of the formula and shows which part of the evaluation will result in an error.

Clicking Ignore Error either moves to the next error or indicates that Error Check is complete. When you click Edit in the Formula Bar, you can correct the formula in the Formula Bar.

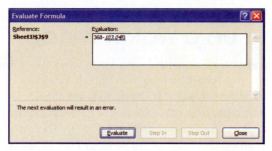

Figure 7.31 Evaluate Formula Dialog Box

TIP **The Formulas Are Color-Coded**

The fastest way to change the contents of a cell is to double-click in the cell and make the changes directly in the cell rather than to change the entries on the Formula Bar. Note, too, that if the cell contains a formula as opposed to a literal entry, Excel will display each cell reference in the formula in a different color that corresponds to the border color of the referenced cells elsewhere in the worksheet. This makes it easy to see which cell or cell range is referenced by the formula. You can also click and drag the colored border to a different cell to change the cell formula.

Evaluate a Formula

Using nested formulas can make it difficult to understand the evaluation of the formula. Understanding how a nested formula calculates is hard because there are intermediate calculations and logical tests. You can use the Evaluate Formula dialog box to view different parts of a nested formula and view how they are evaluated in the order the formula is calculated. To use the Evaluate Formula dialog box:

1. Select the cell to be evaluated.
2. Click Evaluate Formula in the Formula Auditing group on the Formulas tab to see the Evaluate Formula dialog box, as shown in Figure 7.31.
3. Click Evaluate to examine the value of the reference that is underlined.
4. If the underlined part of the formula is a reference to another formula, click Step In to display the other formula in the Evaluation box.
5. Click Step Out to return to the previous cell and formula.
6. Continue until the entire formula has been evaluated.
7. Click Close to end the evaluation.

Avoid Circular References

A ***circular reference*** is a formula that contains a cell reference that relies on its own value.

A ***circular reference*** happens when you create a formula that relies on its own value. The reliance can be either direct or indirect. For example, if you enter the formula =A3+10 in cell A3, you create a circular reference. For this formula to work, Excel needs to add 10 to the current value of cell A3. This formula, however, changes the value of A3 and means Excel needs to recalculate the formula. Without correction this process creates an endless loop, never producing a value. Circular references inevitably lead to invalid data. The most common way you will inadvertently create a circular reference is to begin your formula with the active cell, the cell that contains a value, rather than an empty cell that will display the result.

Setting Up a Watch Window

When you are working with a very large worksheet, formulas in cells that are not visible can be "watched" using the Watch Window box. You do not need to keep scrolling to different parts of the worksheet if you are using Watch Window. Among the new features in Excel 2007 is the greatly expanded worksheet; you now have many more rows and columns to work with. Computer screens are not large enough to display all of the cells of these larger worksheets. The Watch Window feature enables you create a small window so you can view the formula calculation. You can conveniently inspect, audit, or confirm formula calculations involving cells that are not displayed on the screen. You can double-click a cell in the Watch Window to quickly jump to that cell. To add cells to the Watch Window:

1. Select the cell or cells you want to watch.
2. Click Watch Window in the Formula Auditing group on the Formulas tab.
3. Click Add Watch in the Watch Window toolbar.
4. Select the cells to be watched in the Add Watch dialog box and click Add Watch.
5. The Watch Window dialog box shows the watch, as shown in Figure 7.32.

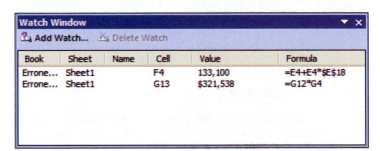

Book	Sheet	Name	Cell	Value	Formula
Errone...	Sheet1		F4	133,100	=E4+E4*$E$18
Errone...	Sheet1		G13	$321,538	=G12*G4

Figure 7.32 The Watch Window

TIP   Changes to Watched Cells

Anytime you make a change to the watched cell, the Watch Window dialog box shows you the current value of the watched cell or cells.

Comments and Auditing Commands | Reference

Icon	Command	Description
	New Comment	Inserts a new comment in the active cell
	Edit Comment	Opens comment for active cell so that you can edit the comment
	Delete	Deletes the comment for the active cell
	Previous	Navigates to and displays the previous comment in the worksheet
	Next	Navigates to and displays the next comment in the worksheet
	Show/Hide Comment	Shows (or hides) the comment for the active cell
	Show All Comments	Displays all comments in the worksheet
	Trace Precedents	Displays arrows to show what cells have an impact on the current cell's value
	Trace Dependents	Displays arrows to show what cells are affected by (dependent upon) the current cell's value
	Remove Arrows	Removes the arrows that trace precedents and/or dependents
	Show Formulas	Displays formulas in the worksheet
	Error Checking	Checks worksheet for common errors within formulas
	Evaluate Formula	Launches the Evaluate Formula dialog box to evaluate each part of a specific formula to debug it
	Watch Window	Monitors values of particular cells while changes are made to the worksheet

Hands-On Exercises

3 | JAS Manufacturing

Skills covered: 1. Trace Precedents **2.** Audit a Region's Quarterly Sales and Remove Cell Error Indicators **3.** Correct a Cell Formula and Trace a Cell's Dependents **4.** Use Error Checking **5.** Create a Watch Window **6.** Validate Data

Step 1 **Trace Precedents**	Refer to Figure 7.33 as you complete Step 1. **a.** Open the *chap7_ho3_jas* workbook and save it as **chap7_ho3_jas_solution** so that you can return to the original workbook if necessary. The partially completed workbook contains errors that you will identify and correct. **b.** Click the **Quarterly Summary** tab. You will see the seven regions for the JAS Manufacturing Company and Quarterly Sales Summary totals. **c.** Click **Formulas tab**, click **cell C12**, and click **Trace Precedents** in the Formula Auditing group. Tracer arrows are displayed and a box encompasses the range of cells included in the formula. An error alert is displayed because the range is incorrect. **d.** Verify that cell C12 is selected, click the Formula Bar to edit the formula as **=SUM(C4:C10)**, and press **Enter**. **e.** Save the workbook.

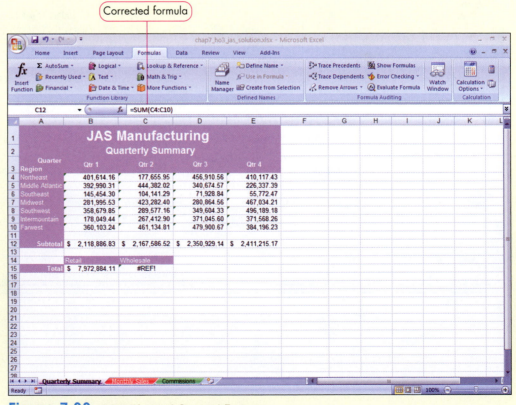

Figure 7.33 Identify and Correct Errors

Step 2
Audit a Region's Quarterly Sales and Remove Cell Error Indicators

a. Click **cell B10** and click **Trace Precedents** in the Formula Auditing group.

The tracer arrow points to a worksheet icon indicating that the cell refers to another worksheet.

b. Double-click the **tracer arrow** to view the Go To dialog box.

The dialog box displays the cell references on which the formula may depend.

c. Click the first cell reference listed in the dialog box and click **OK**.

The Monthly sales worksheet opens and one of the cell ranges is highlighted. This shows the relationship between the quarterly worksheet and the summary worksheet.

d. Click the **Quarterly Summary tab**, point to the Error message box, and click the drop-down arrow to display options for resolving the error.

You can review the options available for correcting errors in the list. Excel anticipates what you might do and in this case, the formula is correct as entered.

e. Click and drag to select **cells B4:E10**, click the down arrow for the Error message box, and select **Ignore Error**.

f. Click any cell to deselect the cell range and click **Remove Arrows** from the Formulas Auditing group.

You removed the green triangles which indicated possible errors in cells.

g. Save the workbook.

TROUBLESHOOTING: Double-clicking a tracer arrow is an efficient way to locate dependent or precedent cells on either the current worksheet or another worksheet.

Step 3
Correct a Cell Formula and Trace a Cell's Dependents

Refer to Figure 7.34 as you complete Step 3.

a. Click **cell C9** in the **Monthly Sales** worksheet.

b. Click the **Error message box drop-down arrow**.

The error message Number Stored as Text means that cell C9 contains text instead of a value. The formula in the Formula Bar begins with an apostrophe ('). You will correct the formula after tracing the cell's dependents.

c. Click **Trace Dependents** in the Formula Auditing group.

d. Double-click the **tracer arrow**, click the first item in the list, and click **OK** in the Go To dialog box.

e. Verify that **cell C9** on the **Quarterly Summary** sheet is selected and click **Trace Dependents** in the Formula Auditing group.

By tracing dependents on both worksheets, you see the relationship between the data on the Monthly Sales worksheet and the Quarterly Summary worksheet.

f. Click the **Monthly Sales tab** and click **Remove Arrows** in the Formula Auditing group.

g. Click **cell C9**, click the **Error message drop-down arrow**, and select **Convert to Number**.

Excel converted the text string to a value.

h. Save the workbook.

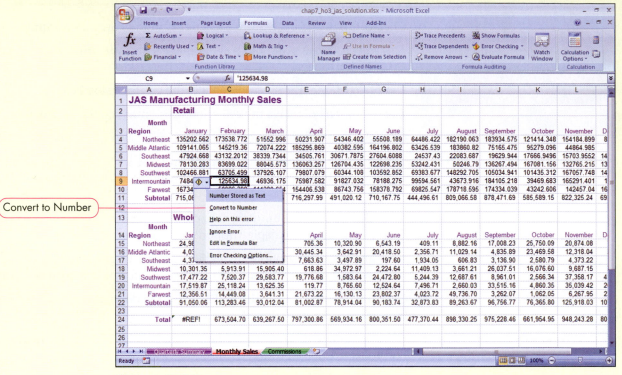

Figure 7.34 Error Message Shortcut Menu

Step 4
Use Error Checking

Refer to Figure 7.35 as you complete Step 4.

a. Click **cell C15** on the **Quarterly Summary tab**.

b. Click **Error Checking** in the Formula Auditing Group to open the Error Checking dialog box.

c. Click **Help on this error** to open Excel Help to display possible solutions to the error, as shown in Figure 7.35.

d. Close the Help window, click **Next** twice, and then click **OK** to acknowledge that the error check of the entire sheet is complete.

e. Click the **Error Checking down arrow** on the Formula Auditing group and select **Trace Error**.

The tracer error points to a worksheet icon indicating that the error source is on another worksheet.

f. Double-click the **tracer arrow**, click the first item in the Go to list, and click **OK**.

Cell N24 on the Monthly Sales worksheet becomes the active cell.

g. Click the **Error Checking down arrow** in the Formula Auditing group and select **Trace Error**.

A red tracer arrow leads from cell B24 through and including cell N24. The arrow indicates that the root of the error is in cell B24.

h. Verify that cell B24 is selected and type **=B11+B22** and press **Enter**.

The red tracer arrow becomes a blue tracer arrow and the dependent formulas are correct.

i. Click **Remove Arrows** in the Formula Auditing group.

j. Format the worksheets as **Currency** with **2** decimal places.

k. Save the workbook.

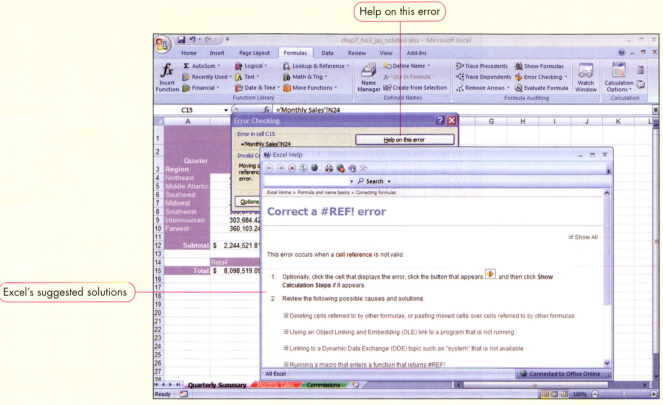

Figure 7.35 Error Checking Dialog Box with Excel Help

Step 5
Create a Watch Window

Refer to Figure 7.36 as you complete Step 5.

a. Click **cell N11** on the Monthly Sales sheet, then press and hold **Ctrl** while clicking **cell N24**.

These cells are not visible without scrolling through the worksheet and to view them, you will set up a Watch Window.

b. Click **Formulas tab** and click **Watch Window** in the Formula Auditing group.

c. Click **Add Watch** in the Watch Window dialog box and verify that **cells N11** and **N24** are displayed in the Add Watch dialog box. See Figure 7.36.

d. Click **Add**.

The Add Watch box closes but the Watch Window box remains open so you can easily jump to any of the cells in the Watch Window box.

e. Click **cell B10**, type **170000**, and press **Enter**.

Cells N11 and N24 were not visible, but you viewed the changes to these cells when you entered a new value in B10.

f. Close the Watch Window box, click **Undo** on the Quick Access Toolbar, and save the workbook.

e. Click **Calculate Sheet** in the Calculation group continually or press **F9** (recalculate) continually to see the spreadsheet go through multiple iterations, eventually settling on steady state values of $400,000 and $1,600,000 for the profit sharing and net income, respectively. Note that the profit sharing value of $400,000 is 25% of the net income value of $1,600,000.

f. Close the Watch Window and create a custom footer containing your name, today's date, and your instructor's name.

g. Print the completed workbook. Save and close the workbook.

h. Restore Calculation Settings:
   - Open a blank workbook.
   - Click the **Office Button**.
   - Select **Excel Options**.
   - Click **Formulas**.
   - Select **Automatic** in the Calculation options section.
   - Remove the check from **Enable iterative calculations**.
   - Type **100** in the Maximum Iterations box and click **OK**.

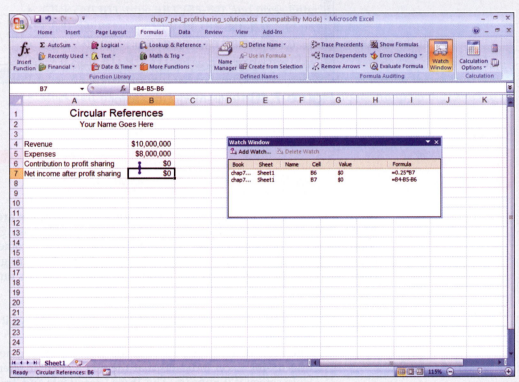

Figure 7.41 Circular Reference

Mid-Level Exercises

1 Professor's Grade Book—Link Worksheets

The workbook shown in Figure 7.42 displays a documentation worksheet that includes exam results for multiple sections of an introductory computer course. It also contains an individual worksheet for each section of the course. Your assignment as the professor's teaching assistant is to open the partially completed workbook, compute the test averages for each section, and then create the summary worksheet.

a. Open the *chap7_mid1_linkprofessor* workbook and save it as **chap7_mid1_link professor_solution** so that you can return to the original workbook if necessary.

b. Group the worksheets.

c. Create a formula to calculate the average on the first test for the students in Section 1. Copy the formula to **cells C10** and **D10**. The sections have different numbers of students, but the last student in every section appears in row 8 or before. The Average function ignores empty cells within the designated range, and you can use the same function for all four worksheets.

d. Check that the worksheets are still grouped and apply the same formatting to each worksheet.

e. Merge and center the name of the section in the first row and use bold text and a fill color. Change the color of the worksheet tab to match the formatting in the worksheet. You will not see the color change until you ungroup the worksheets.

f. Ungroup the worksheets and insert a blank worksheet for the summary, as shown in Figure 7.42. Enter the title and column headings as shown in rows 1 and 2.

g. Click **cell A3** of the summary worksheet and use a formula to display the section names in **cells A3:A6**.

h. Click **cell B3** of the summary worksheet and use a formula to display the average test score for Test 1 in Section 1. Copy the formula in **cell B3** to **cells C3** and **D3** of the summary worksheet. Enter the test grades for the other sections in similar fashion.

i. Format the summary worksheet using the same colors, fonts, and font sizes as the section sheets.

j. Insert a new sheet and create a documentation worksheet, making sure to include: Your Name as Author, Date of creation, Date of last modification, Description of the workbook, List of sheets in the workbook, and Description of each sheet.

k. Create a custom footer containing your name, a page number, and your instructor's name. Print the completed workbook. Save and close the workbook.

...continued on Next Page

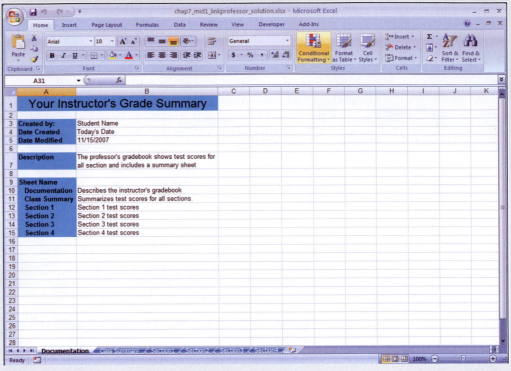

Figure 7.42 Linking Professor's Grade Sheets

2 The Plumber Corporation—Grouping Sheets

Your new job with The Plumber Corporation allows you to demonstrate your expertise with Excel. The workbook shown in Figure 7.43 contains a separate worksheet for each month of the year as well as a summary worksheet for the entire year. Each monthly worksheet tallies the expenses for five divisions in each of four categories to compute a monthly total for each division. The summary worksheet is designed to display the total expense for each division. However, only the months of January, February, and March are complete. Your assignment is to open the partially completed workbook and complete it as indicated below.

a. Open the *chap7_mid2_plumbercorp* workbook and save it as **chap7_mid2_plumber corp_solution**.

b. Insert a new worksheet for April to the right of the March worksheet and enter the appropriate row and column headings. Assume that Division 1 spends $100 in each category, Division 2 spends $200 in each category, Division 3 spends $300 in each category, and so on. Change the worksheet tab to April.

c. Group the sheets for January through April and calculate the expense total by division and by category.

d. Format the worksheet in an attractive fashion, making sure you include bold text, borders, and shaded cells as appropriate. Values are Currency with 0 decimal places. Change the color of the worksheet tab. Ungroup the worksheets and view the various monthly worksheets to verify that the formulas and formatting appear in each worksheet.

e. Click the worksheet tab for the summary worksheet. Insert a column for April to the right of the column for March. Click **cell B3**, type =, click in the January worksheet, click **cell F3** (the cell that contains the January total for Division 1), and press **Enter**. Enter the formulas for the remaining months for Division 1 in similar fashion.

...continued on Next Page

f. Create formulas to calculate year-to-date totals by division and totals by month. Copy the formulas in **cells B3:F3** to the remaining rows in the summary worksheet. Format the summary worksheet in the same manner as the monthly worksheets.

g. Use Page Setup to create a custom footer for all worksheets that includes your name, the name on the worksheet tab, and your instructor's name. Print the worksheet for April and the summary worksheet for your instructor as displayed and with formulas visible. Save and close the workbook.

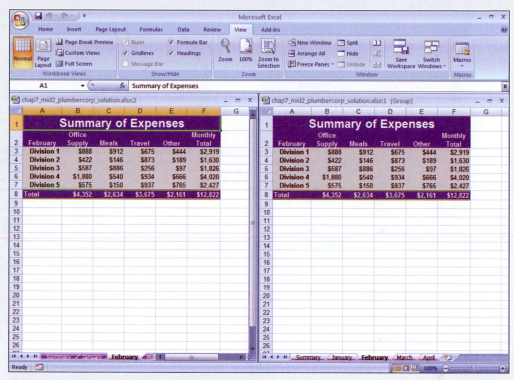

Figure 7.43 The Plumber Corporation

3 The Golf Shoppe Payroll

Your father, the owner of The Golf Shoppe, asked for your help with Excel. The worksheet shown in Figure 7.44 displays an erroneous version of a worksheet that computes the payroll for The Golf Shoppe. The worksheet is nicely formatted but your father wants you to make it more eye-catching. Several calculations are in error, and your assignment is to find the errors and correct the worksheet. You can "eyeball" the worksheet to find the mistakes, but you will use Formula Auditing techniques. Follow the guidelines below to correct the worksheet.

a. Open the *chap7_mid3_golfpayroll* workbook, save it as **chap7_mid3_golfpayroll_solution**, and print the worksheet prior to making any corrections.

b. Calculate the pay. The gross pay is the regular pay, hourly wage times regular hours, plus the overtime pay, hourly wage times the overtime hours times the overtime rate. The overtime rate is entered as an assumption within the worksheet.

c. Calculate the net pay, which is the gross pay minus the deductions, the withholding tax, and the Social Security tax.

d. Calculate the taxable income, which is the gross pay minus the deduction per dependent multiplied by the number of dependents.

e. Calculate the withholding tax, which is based on the individual's taxable income. The Social Security tax is based on the individual's gross pay.

...continued on Next Page

f. Format the worksheet in an attractive manner using fill colors, font colors, font sizes, and alignment.

g. Insert comments to describe the gross pay, taxable income, withholding tax, net pay, and total gross pay.

h. Create a custom footer that includes your name, today's date, and your instructor's name. Print the corrected worksheet with displayed values, comments, and cell formulas. Save and close the workbook.

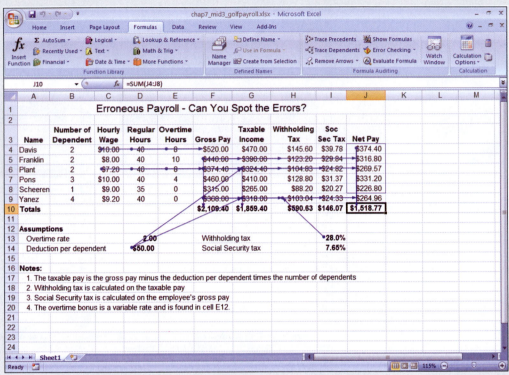

Figure 7.44 The Golf Shoppe Payroll

4 J&W Bank Mortgage Calculator

As the manager trainee of the J&W Bank, you must create a Mortgage Calculator in Excel. The worksheet shown in Figure 7.45 should be completely flexible in that it accepts the user's input in the shaded cells, and then it computes the associated monthly payments in the body of the worksheet. It also introduces the Evaluate Formula tool in the Formula Auditing group on the Formulas tab. The Evaluate Formula tool enables you to step through the calculation of any formula within a worksheet. Your assignment is to create the worksheet as shown in Figure 7.45. This worksheet is protected so users can change only the shaded input values. You may want to review material on the PMT function, mixed references, and protecting worksheets.

a. Open the *chap7_mid4_jwbank* workbook and save it as **chap7_mid4_jwbank_solution**.

b. Click in **cell B8** and enter the formula =E4; the initial interest rate in the body of the spreadsheet is taken from the user's input in cell E4. Click in **cell C8** and enter the formula to calculate the incremental increases in interest rates, and copy the formula to the remaining cells in this row. Enter parallel formulas in **cells A9** to **A19** to compute the values for the principal amounts that will appear in the table. Check that your formulas are correct by changing the input parameters in rows 4 and 5. Any changes to the input parameters should be reflected in row 8 and/or column A.

c. Develop an appropriate PMT function for cells B9:G19. Remember to use mixed references in cell B9.

d. Use Evaluate Formula to evaluate formulas within the workbook to see how this tool can help you to understand how a formula works.

e. Format the completed worksheet to include eye-appealing fill color, font size, and font color, and values as Percent with 2 decimals or Currency with 2 decimals. You do not have to match the formatting shown exactly, but you are to shade the input parameters.

f. Unlock **cells B4:B6** and **cells E4:E5**, and then protect the completed worksheet. DO NOT USE a password for your worksheet.

g. Create a custom footer that includes your name, a page number, and your instructor's name.

h. Print the worksheet two ways, once with displayed values and once with the cell formulas. Use landscape orientation. Save and close the workbook.

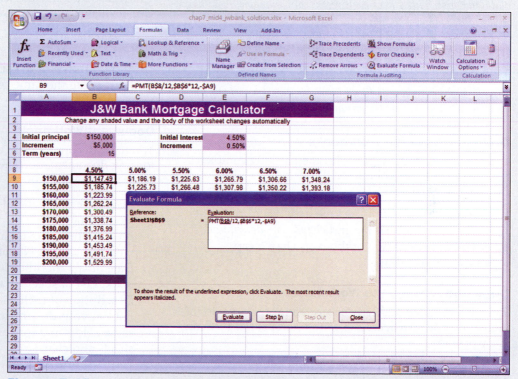

Figure 7.45 Mortgage Calculator

Capstone Exercise

Bruno's Pizza offers a tasty pizza at a "steal" of a price, with a strong appeal to the college and family crowds. Their pizzas are generously proportioned and made with a homemade spicy pizza sauce to create a unique zesty flavor, and their list of toppings includes some of the most off-the-wall but healthy selections around. This tried-and-true proven product offering, combined with great customer service, keeps their pizzas flying out the door! Bruno's Pizza has expanded from its initial restaurant downtown to two additional sites elsewhere in the city.

The owner, Joe Bruno, wants to evaluate the overall performance of the chain before expanding further. He is especially interested in the comparative results of three dining categories: dine-in, pickup, and delivery. Joe knows you are studying Excel at the local college and asked for your help in return for a small stipend and all the pizza you can eat. You have already prepared a template and distributed it to each restaurant manager, who has entered the sales data for last year. Your next task is to consolidate the data into a single workbook that shows the total sales for each quarter and each dining category. The information should be shown in tabular as well as graphical form. You will also create a documentation sheet so that Joe will know exactly what you have created. Make sure you audit all formulas, trace precedents and dependents, and evaluate the formulas for accuracy.

Open and Save the Workbooks

You must open four workbooks: the partially completed Summary and the completed Westside, Eastside, and Downtown workbooks.

a. Open the files: *chap7_cap_summary*, *chap7_cap_westside*, *chap7_cap_eastside*, and *chap7_cap_downtown*.
b. Save the Summary workbook as **chap7_cap_summary_solution**.

Copy and Arrange the Worksheets

You have collected quarterly sales data for three modes of dining from the managers and want to summarize them on one worksheet.

a. Copy the Eastside, Westside, and Downtown worksheets into the Summary workbook.
b. Tile the four worksheets so you can see all of the data.

Summarizing Dining Categories by Quarter

You must provide a summary report of the dining category sales by quarter for the year so Joe Bruno knows exactly what each location is doing.

a. Create formulas to calculate sales by dining category and quarter for all locations on the Summary sheet.
b. Calculate grand totals by quarter and by dining category.

Audit Formulas

Before giving your financial report to Joe Bruno, you must verify the accuracy of your formulas and results. You will use the tools in the Formula Auditing group on the Formulas tab to verify your results.

a. Trace Precedents and Dependents on the Summary worksheet.
b. Use Error Checking to determine if there are errors in your formulas and to trace any errors.
c. Use Evaluate Formula to verify the results of your formula.

Create Chart

Joe Bruno is more of a visual person, and you want to present your data in an alternate way. You will create a chart visualizing your summary data.

a. Create a chart on a separate sheet.
b. Include a title, legend, and data labels on your chart.
c. Format the chart to coordinate with your summary chart using the same colors, fonts, font sizes, and clip art.

Document Workbook

You must document your workbook with a professional-looking documentation sheet before Joe Bruno can reimburse you for your work.

a. Insert a new sheet and rename the sheet tab Documentation.
b. Include the following on your documentation worksheet: Your Name as Author, Date of creation, Date of last modification, Description of the workbook, List of sheets in the workbook, and Description of each sheet.
c. Format your documentation worksheet using the same colors and font as used in the other worksheets and chart.
d. Hide the gridlines on the documentation sheet.

Print the Workbook

As part of the documentation process, you recognize that each worksheet in the workbook must include standard footers. Create a custom footer that contains your name, page number, and your instructor's name. Print the completed workbook.

a. Group the worksheets and create a custom footer with your name on the left, the page number in the middle, and your instructor's name on the right.
b. Add the custom footer to the chart sheet.
c. Print the workbook as displayed, and print the Summary worksheet with formulas displayed. Save and close the workbook.

Mini Cases

Use the rubric following the case as a guide to evaluate your work, but keep in mind that your instructor may impose additional grading criteria or use a different standard to judge your work.

Leason International Security Sales Summary

GENERAL CASE

Each branch manager of Leason International Security creates an identically formatted workbook with the sales information for his or her branch office. Your job as marketing manager is to consolidate the regional quarterly sales information into a single workbook, and then graph the results appropriately. The branch data are to remain in the individual workbooks; that is, the formulas in your workbook are to contain external references to the sales information workbooks. Begin by opening the individual workbooks: *chap7_mc1_foreign*, *chap7_mc1_eastern*, and *chap7_mc1_western* and saving them as: **chap7_mc1_foreign_solution**, **chap7_mc1_eastern_solution**, and **chap7_mc1_western_solution**. Enter the appropriate formulas to total the data for each product and each quarter. Begin a new workbook and save it as **chap7_mc1_summary_solution**. You will use the summary workbook to reflect the quarterly totals for each branch through external references to the individual workbooks. Any change in the individual workbooks should be automatically reflected in the consolidated workbook. Be sure to include a documentation worksheet in your summary workbook.

Performance Elements	Exceeds Expectations	Meets Expectations	Below Expectations
Consolidate with accurate formulas	All formulas correct.	One formula incorrect.	Two or more formulas incorrect.
Chart	Chart accurate, includes title and legend.	Chart accurate but missing either title or legend.	No chart.
Documentation worksheet	Four or more major documentation items included.	Two or more major documentation items included.	No documentation worksheet.

Watch Window

RESEARCH CASE

Use Excel Help to research the concept of Watch Windows. You are specifically looking for information about when they are used and what their purpose is. You want to know where they are most effectively and efficiently used. You will open and use the *chap7_mc2_mines* workbook to practice what you learn about Watch Windows. Save the workbook as **chap7_mc2_mines_solution**. Your final workbook will include a Watch Window with watches on three cells containing formulas. Include a brief paragraph summarizing the use of Watch Windows. Print the workbook.

Performance Elements	Exceeds Expectations	Meets Expectations	Below Expectations
Watch Window	Watching three or more cells.	Watching two cells.	No Watch Window.
Summary	Complete and inclusive.	Either incomplete or not inclusive.	No summary.
Print	Includes standard footer data.	No footer included.	No printout.

Find and Fix the Errors

DISASTER RECOVERY

A friend of yours has asked for your help. He has created a grade book to use with his student teaching experience. The grade book is well formatted and easy to read, but it contains some fundamental errors. You are to correct the errors and complete any additional processing requirements for your colleague. Use the tools in the Formula Auditing tools to identify and correct the errors. Open the workbook *chap7_mc3_studentteaching* and save it as **chap7_mc3_student teaching_solution.** You will create a VLOOKUP function and find three major errors. Correct the errors and explain how the errors might have occurred and how they can be prevented. Include your explanation in the form of comments in the appropriate cells in the spreadsheet.

Performance Elements	Exceeds Expectations	Meets Expectations	Below Expectations
VLOOKUP function	Correct with accurate results.	Formula incorrectly applied.	No VLOOKUP.
Identify and correct errors	Identified and corrected all three errors.	Identified and corrected two errors.	Identified and corrected one or no errors.
Explain the error	Complete and correct explanation of each error.	Explanation is too brief to fully explain error.	No explanations.
Prevention description	Prevention description correct and practical.	Prevention description, but obtuse.	No prevention description.

What-If Analysis
Using Spreadsheets for Decision Making

bjectives

After you read this chapter, you will be able to:

1. Create a one-variable data table **(page 507)**.

2. Create a two-variable data table **(page 509)**.

3. Solve problems with Goal Seek **(page 515)**.

4. Use Scenario Manager **(page 516)**.

5. Load the Solver Add-In **(page 528)**.

6. Solve problems with Solver **(page 529)**.

Hands-On Exercises

Exercises	Skills Covered
1. CAN YOU AFFORD IT? (page 511) **Open:** chap8_ho1_suv.xlsx **Save as:** chap8_ho1_suv_solution.xlsx	• Use Functions and Formulas • Create a One-Variable Data Table • Create a Two-Variable Data Table
2. PURCHASE GOLF CARS AND MANUFACTURE GOLF CLUBS (page 520) **Open:** chap8_ho2_gss.xlsx **Save as:** chap8_ho2_gss_solution.xlsx	• Insert a Function and Use Goal Seek • Apply Conditional Formatting • Define Cell Names • Create the Scenarios • View Scenarios • Create a Scenario Summary Report • Create a Scenario PivotTable Report
3. FAL COMPUTER MANUFACTURING (page 535) **Open:** chap8_ho3_optimization.xlsx **Save as:** chap8_ho3_optimization_solution.xlsx	• Install Solver and Enter Cell Formulas • Set Target, Set Adjustable Cells, and Enter Constraints • Solve the Problem • View and Print the Report

CASE STUDY

Hideaway Retirement and Golf Community

Your Uncle Bill was lucky. He made his money with the Internet boom, and then sold out early in 2000 before the market crash. Since then, Bill has played innumerable rounds of golf and dropped his handicap to 5. He can play only so much golf, however, and he is ready for a new challenge, which came upon him quite unexpectedly when he learned that one Hideaway Retirement and Golf Community golf course was for sale.

Bill is thinking of making an offer to buy the club to maximize the return on his investment and is using Excel to create a six-year financial forecast. He plans to offer $2.5 million for the club and intends to spend another $1 million immediately for such capital improvements as redoing the greens and enhancing the driving range. The spreadsheet he developed is typical of other financial forecasts, but it includes a limitation on membership. The membership currently totals 130 and he expects to add members each year, capping membership at 250. Bill does not plan to charge an initiation fee, but he has set the initial annual dues rather steeply at $15,000. Capping the membership will ensure that members will always be able to get a tee time, and Bill hopes that this will justify the cost. At the end of his six-year plan, his goal is to maximize the return on his investment.

Case Study

Your Assignment

- Read the chapter carefully and pay close attention to the financial forecast and demonstrations of the use of Scenario Manager in the workbook.

- Open the partially completed *chap8_case_community* workbook and create the appropriate formulas in the body of the worksheet. Compute the rate of return at the end of years two through six of the forecast.

- Use Goal Seek to determine the increase in golf memberships and the annual increase in dues.

- Use Scenario Manager to construct Status Quo, Optimistic, and Pessimistic scenarios to reflect the rate of return in the year 2013.

- Create a Scenario Summary report and a Scenario PivotTable report reflecting the internal rate of return in the year 2013.

- Format the workbook, including the Scenario Summary report and the Scenario PivotTable report, with a professional look suitable for presentation to potential investors.

- Apply conditional formatting to format the cells containing the internal rate of return so investors can easily distinguish between profit and loss.

- Group the worksheet and create a custom footer that includes your name, today's date, and your instructor's name. Print the worksheet as displayed and with formulas visible. Save the workbook as **chap8_case_community_solution**.

One- and Two-Variable Data Tables

(A powerful feature . . . what-if analysis.)

The power of the Excel spreadsheet has been demonstrated to you as we have moved through the textbook. This chapter examines three very powerful Excel tools that will enable you to perform what is known as "what-if" analysis. *What-if analysis* enables you to optimize conditions by changing variables or values within a worksheet. A *variable* is a value that you can change, or vary, to see how those changes impact other values. Business people create spreadsheets with variables, such as advertising costs, to see how the variables affect results, such as sales. The power of using Excel is that all you need to do is change the values or variables; Excel does the rest. What-if analysis enables you to see how changes in variables, the items that can change in a worksheet, affect calculated results.

What-if analysis is the process that enables you to see how changes in variables affect calculated results.

A variable is a value that you can change to see how those changes impact other values.

Remember that Excel is a tool, not a solution. You must plan, design, and define the variables and worksheet areas before using Excel. The pencil-and-paper planning process will reduce your frustration when Excel does not produce the results you expect. Although this process may not be necessary when working with one- and two-variable data tables, you will spend some time thinking about how you want Excel to work with your variables. Changing one variable, such as price, might affect another piece of data, such as sales. Just because you can use Excel to solve problems does not necessarily mean the solution is the correct one. Your design and setup process can produce incorrect or unexpected results.

In this section, you learn how to create one- and two-variable data tables as data analysis tools. You will learn how to design the data tables, insert formulas, and complete the data tables to compare the results for different values of the variables.

Creating a One-Variable Data Table

A variable is something, such as price, that can vary or change. If one variable can be controlled directly (such as the selling price of apples), then it is called an independent variable, whereas the remaining variable (in this case the number of apples bought) is called a dependent variable. Using data tables is a method of doing what-if analysis. A *one-variable data table* is a data analysis tool that enables you to analyze different values of *one* variable to compare *one or more* calculated results that are affected by the variable. For example, if you use the interest rate as a variable, you can compare several interest rate values, such as 4%, 4.5%, 5%, 5.5%, and 6%, to see how changing the interest rate impacts the monthly payment on a car loan. The monthly payment is a calculated result that is partly dependent on the interest rate. Because the one-variable data table can display calculated results for more than one outcome, you can also display how different values of the interest rate variable affect total interest paid over the life of the loan, and the total amount to repay a loan. When you create one-variable data tables, you are concerned with two elements:

A one-variable data table is a data analysis tool that provides various results based on changing one variable.

- *Input cells*—the cells that contain the different values of the variable you want to use to test to see their effects on the calculated value(s) for the what-if analysis.

- *Result cells*—the cells that contain the outcome values derived from formulas that reflect the different values of the variable that are contained in the input cells.

Input cells are the cells that contain the values to be modified for what-if analysis.

Result cells contain the outcome values to be modified.

Figure 8.1 shows a sample of a one-variable data table for the purchase of a car. The variable is the interest rate for the car loan. The input cells contain different values, such as 6% and 6.5%, for the interest rate variable. The result cells contain formulas to calculate the monthly payment, total payment, and total interest paid. The data table shows the input values as the possible different interest rates, while the result values show the respective monthly payments, total payments, and total interest paid for the respective interest rates. When using a one-variable data table you want to see all the results when just one element or variable changes.

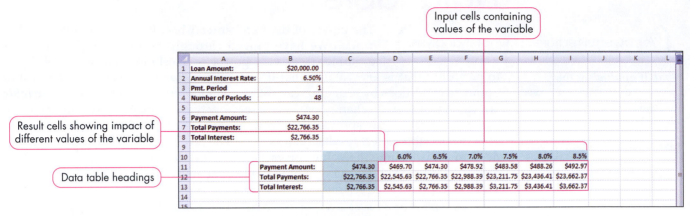

Figure 8.1 One-Variable Data Table

Set Up the One-Variable Data Table

A data table summarizes important input and output cell values in multiple what-if analyses in one rectangular cell range. A one-variable data table enables you to specify one input variable that Excel changes to produce the data table. You must decide if you want the values for the input cell to appear in a column or in a row. In Figure 8.1, the input cells containing values for the interest rate variable are displayed horizontally in cells D10:I10. Labels are entered in cells B11:B13 to describe the contents of the result cells that will be generated.

Add Formulas to the One-Variable Data Table

After you enter values in the input cells for the variable, you will create the formula to determine the initial result. Create the one-variable data table and enter the formula:

1. Create the headings that describe the result cells either vertically on the left side of the table or horizontally above the result cells. In Figure 8.1, the headings are Payment Amount, Total Payments, and Total Interest in cells B11:B13. These headings are labels used to indicate what will be in the rows.

2. Create one or more formulas to perform the calculation. Typically, the original formulas are located elsewhere in the worksheet, and the table contains cell references to the original data. Be sure to use cell references and not literal values. For example, in Figure 8.1, cells B6:B8 are the cells containing formulas generating the original monthly payment, total payments, and total interest. In a data table in which the different values of the variable are listed horizontally, you enter cell references to the formulas in the column between the descriptive labels and the column containing the first value of the variable. For example, cell C11 contains =B6 to refer to the cell containing the formula that generates the original monthly payment, cell C12 contains =B7 to refer to the cell containing the formula that generates the original total payment, and C13 contains =B8 to refer to the cell containing the formula that generates the original total interest. Note that these cell references go to the *left* of the column for the first value of the interest rate variable.

3. Select the entire data table, except the descriptive labels; for example, to generate the one-variable data table shown in Figure 8.1, you would select C10:I13.

4. Click the What-If Analysis down arrow in the Data Tools group on the Data tab and select Data Table.

5. Type the address of the cell to be changed in the Data Table dialog box as shown in Figure 8.2. The input cell refers to the *original* value of the variable, which is stored outside the data table. In this case, the original interest rate on which the formulas are based is located in cell B2. If the different values of the variable are listed horizontally in one row, like in Figure 8.1, you enter the input cell reference in the *Row input cell* box. If the different values of the variable are listed vertically down one column, you enter the input cell reference in the *Column input cell* box.

6. Click OK.

In Figure 8.1, column C contains the values of the current results, which are identical to the results shown in column E. You can hide column C to avoid the appearance of duplication; however, you should not delete column C because doing so would destroy the results of the one-variable data table.

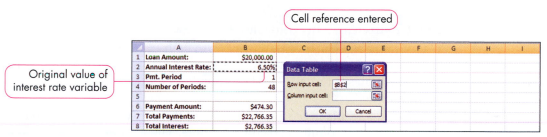

Figure 8.2 Data Table Dialog Box

Creating a Two-Variable Data Table

The second option used with what-if analysis in Excel is the two-variable data table. You can determine the affect of *two variables* on a single formula result by using a two-variable data table. A two-variable data table, like a one-variable data table, is rectangular and the result cells contain formulas that compute result values. The major difference between one- and two-variable data tables is in the result. You must decide if you want Excel to consider one variable and produce several results, or if you want Excel to use two variables but produce only one result.

Set Up the Two Variables in the Table

A **two-variable data table** summarizes the effects that two variables have on one result.

A *two-variable data table* summarizes important input and output cell values in multiple what-if analyses in one rectangular cell range. A two-variable data table enables you to specify two input variables that Excel changes to produce the data table. In a two-variable data table, the first variable must be in the left column of the table, and the second variable must be in the top row of the data table.

For example, instead of comparing results of *only* the interest rate variable, you might want to compare the combination of two variables—different interest rates and different loan amounts. However, you can select only *one* result instead of multiple results. For example, you would have to decide which result is the most important based on the two variables. In the case of a car loan, the most important result might be to compare the effects on different monthly payments.

Add a Formula to the Table

The two-variable data table enables you to change two input cells, but it shows only one result cell. For the car loan example, the interest rate and the loan amount are the two variables, and the monthly payment is the one result. Therefore, the two-variable data table can reference only one result cell—monthly payment—in which the original formula is stored in cell B6 in the example. Figure 8.3 shows a completed two-variable data table.

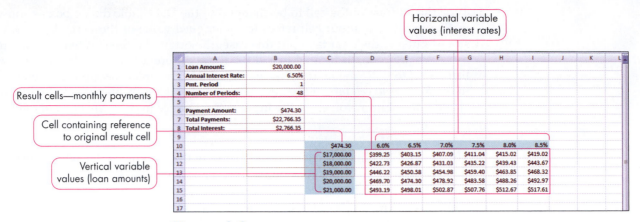

Figure 8.3 Two-Variable Data Table

The steps to create a two-variable data table are:

1. Create the data table with the appropriate headings, which indicate the different values of the two variables. The headings shown in Figure 8.3 are different interest rates (in row 10) and the numbers representing the amount of the loan (in column C).

2. Create a formula in the top-left corner of the two-variable data table, at the intersection of the column and row headings. The formula should reference the cell containing the original result formula. In this case, cell C10 contains =B6, the cell containing the original formula to calculate the monthly payment.

3. Select the entire data table, including the column and row headings that contain the different values for the two variables. In this case, you would select C10:I15.

4. Click the What-If Analysis down arrow in the Data Tools group on the Data tab and select Data Table.

5. Type the cell that contains the original value for the horizontal variable in the *Row input cell* box, and type the cell that contains the original value for the vertical variable in the *Column input cell* box. For example, the original horizontal (interest rate) variable value is stored in cell B2, and the original vertical (loan) variable value is stored in B1 (see Figure 8.4).

6. Click OK.

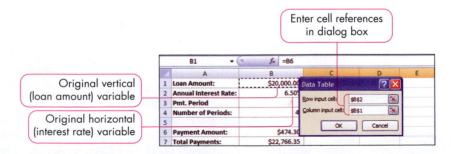

Figure 8.4 Data Table Dialog Box

TIP   Speed Up Calculation

When automatic calculation is turned off, you must manually recalculate the workbook by pressing F9 or using the Calculate Now command. This speeds up calculation in variable data tables. To change workbook calculation, click the Office Button, click Excel Options, click the Formulas category, and click Calculation Options. Choose the Workbook Calculation option you want and click OK.

Hands-On Exercises

1 | Can You Afford It?

Skills covered: 1. Use Functions and Formulas **2.** Create a One-Variable Data Table **3.** Create a Two-Variable Data Table

---

Step 1
Use Functions and Formulas

Refer to Figure 8.5 as you complete Step 1.

a. Open the *chap8_ho1_suv* workbook and save it as **chap8_ho1_suv_solution** so you can return to the original workbook if necessary.

b. Click **cell B6** and type **=PMT(B2*(B3/12),B4,-B1)**.

You used the PMT function to calculate the monthly payment amount and should see $474.30 in cell B6. Parts of the worksheet are already formatted.

c. Click **cell B7** and type **=B6*B4** to calculate the total payments.

d. Click **cell B8** and type **=B7-B1** to calculate the total amount of interest over the life of the loan.

You have now entered the loan parameters you will apply in the one-variable data table.

e. Save the workbook.

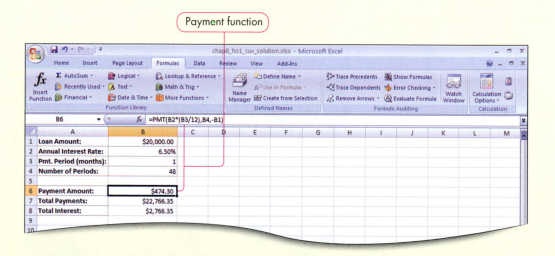

Figure 8.5 Loan Parameters

Step 2
Create a One-Variable Data Table

Refer to Figure 8.6 as you complete Step 2.

a. Select **cells A6:A8** and copy them to **cells B11:B13**.

You copied the labels to describe the results that will be generated in rows 11, 12, and 13 in your one-variable data table.

b. Click **cell C11** and type **=B6**.

c. Click **cell C12** and type **=B7**.

d. Click **cell C13** and type **=B8**.

TROUBLESHOOTING: Copying the contents of cells B6:B8 will produce inaccurate results because you did not use absolute cell references in the original formulas. Using absolute cell references in the original formulas will prevent the what-if analysis from working.

In cells C11:C13, you entered formulas that simply reference the cells that contain the original result cells for the monthly payment, total payments, and total interest. Excel will use these formulas to construct the results for the different values of the interest rate variable.

e. Click **cell D10** and type **.06**.

The first value of the variable is 6%. You enter the value as a decimal point, which then will format all the values as percentages.

f. Click **cell E10** and type **.065**.

g. Select **cells D10:E10** and use AutoFill to fill cells through **I10**.

To create a sequence of values you must enter the first two values before using AutoFill. You entered the different values of the interest rate variable. These values of the one variable are used to see how they affect the three results.

h. Format **cells D10:I10** as **Percentage** with **2** decimal places.

i. Select **cells C10:I13**.

These are the cells making up the one-variable data table. You should not select the row labels in column B.

j. Click the **Data tab**, click **What-If Analysis** in the Data Tools group, and select **Data Table** to open the Data Table dialog box.

k. Click **cell B2**.

$B$2 appears in the *Row input cell* box in the Data Table dialog box.

l. Click **OK**.

You should see the completed one-variable data table that shows how changes in the interest rate for the loan affect the monthly payment, total payments, and the total interest.

m. Format **cells D11:I13** as **Currency** with **2** decimal places.

n. Save the workbook.

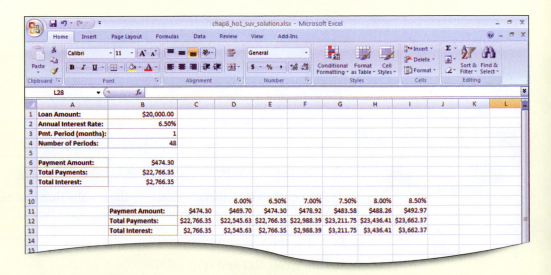

Figure 8.6 One-Variable Data Table

TIP   Hide Formula Cells

To create a one-variable data table, you must enter formulas in the first column of the data table. In this case, cells C11:C13 contain formulas that refer to the original cells (i.e., B6:B8) containing formulas. After you generate the data table, the formula cells C11:C13 in the data table look extraneous. Therefore, you should consider hiding the formulas column in the data table for real situations. You should not simply delete the formulas column of a two-variable data table; doing so deletes all result cells.

Step 3
Create a Two-Variable Data Table

Refer to Figure 8.7 as you complete Step 3.

a. Click **cell B15** and type **=B6**.

Copying the contents of B6 will "seed" the two-variable data table with monthly payment amount. Changes in the monthly payment are the result of changes in both variables.

b. Click **cell C15** and type **.06**.

c. Click **cell D15** and type **.065**.

d. Select **cells C15:D15** and use AutoFill to fill cells through **I15**.

You just filled in the different values for the interest rate variable.

e. Format **cells C15:I15** as **Percentage** with **2** decimal places.

f. Click **cell B16** and type **17000**.

The first value of the loan variable is $17,000. You will enter the remaining values before formatting them.

g. Click **cell B17** and type **18000**.

h. Select **cells B16:B17** and use AutoFill to fill cells through **cell B20**.

The values of the loan variable range from $17,000 to $21,000.

i. Format **cells B16:B20** as **Currency** with **2** decimal places.

You have now completed the setup required for the two-variable data table.

j. Select **cells B15:I20**.

These are the cells making up the two-variable data table. Note that the two-variable data table has a value in the top-left corner cell of the table. The one-variable data table does not.

k. Click **What-If Analysis** in the Data Tools group on the Data tab and select **Data Table** to open the Data Table dialog box.

l. Click **cell B2**.

$B$2 appears in the *Row input cell* box in the Data Table dialog box.

m. Click in the **Column input cell** box and click **cell B1**.

$B$1 appears in the *Column input cell* box in the Data Table dialog box.

TROUBLESHOOTING: You must enter cell references in both the Row input cell and Column input cell boxes in the Data Table dialog box for the two-variable data table to work. Both entries represent data from the loan parameter area of your worksheet.

n. Click **OK**.

You should see the completed two-variable data table that shows how changes in the interest rate and the loan amount affect the monthly payment.

o. Format **cells C16:I20** as **Currency** with **2** decimal places.

p. Save and close the workbook.

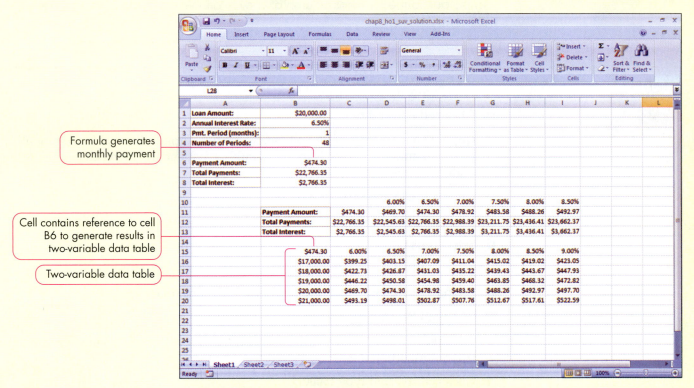

Figure 8.7 Two-Variable Data Table

Annotations on figure:
- Formula generates monthly payment
- Cell contains reference to cell B6 to generate results in two-variable data table
- Two-variable data table

	A	B	C	D	E	F	G	H	I
1	Loan Amount:	$20,000.00							
2	Annual Interest Rate:	6.50%							
3	Pmt. Period (months):	1							
4	Number of Periods:	48							
5									
6	Payment Amount:	$474.30							
7	Total Payments:	$22,766.35							
8	Total Interest:	$2,766.35							
9									
10			6.00%	6.50%	7.00%	7.50%	8.00%	8.50%	
11		Payment Amount:	$474.30	$469.70	$474.30	$478.92	$483.58	$488.26	$492.97
12		Total Payments:	$22,766.35	$22,545.63	$22,766.35	$22,988.39	$23,211.75	$23,436.41	$23,662.37
13		Total Interest:	$2,766.35	$2,545.63	$2,766.35	$2,988.39	$3,211.75	$3,436.41	$3,662.37
14									
15		$474.30	6.00%	6.50%	7.00%	7.50%	8.00%	8.50%	9.00%
16		$17,000.00	$399.25	$403.15	$407.09	$411.04	$415.02	$419.02	$423.05
17		$18,000.00	$422.73	$426.87	$431.03	$435.22	$439.43	$443.67	$447.93
18		$19,000.00	$446.22	$450.58	$454.98	$459.40	$463.85	$468.32	$472.82
19		$20,000.00	$469.70	$474.30	$478.92	$483.58	$488.26	$492.97	$497.70
20		$21,000.00	$493.19	$498.01	$502.87	$507.76	$512.67	$517.61	$522.59

TIP   Formatting the Top Left Cell

The top-left cell of a two-variable data table must contain a reference to the cell in which the original result formula is stored. In this case, cell B15 contains a reference to cell B6, the cell containing the original monthly payment result. After you generate the two-variable data table, this value looks out of place. You can format the top-left cell by applying the White font color to hide the value, or you can create a custom number format that displays text. To create a custom number format that appears as a descriptive label, display the Format Cells dialog box, click Custom in the Category, type the text enclosed in quotation marks in the Type box, such as "Loan", and then click OK. The custom number format appears as a label in the top-left cell of the two-variable data table. You should not simply type the descriptive label in the top-left cell of a two-variable data table; doing so replaces all result cells with that text.

Goal Seek and Scenario Manager

Scenario Manager uses several sets of assumptions to see quickly the results of a scenario.

Goal Seek is a method for finding one-time solutions to problems.

(*. . . Goal Seek* is a method for finding solutions to problems . . .)

Scenario Manager is designed for you to work with several sets of assumptions, called scenarios, to quickly compare the results of multiple scenarios. Each scenario represents different sets of what-if conditions that can be considered when assessing the outcome of a spreadsheet model. Using *Goal Seek* is a method for finding solutions to problems such as determining how many of a product you can buy given the amount of money you have in the bank. Goal Seek automates a manual trial-and-error process. Rather than inputting values into Excel to calculate result values, Goal Seek works backwards in your worksheet by computing an unknown value that produces the optimized result you want. Both Goal Seek and Scenario Manager enable you to forecast, or predict, what results will (or may) occur when values or variables change.

In this section, you learn when and how to use both Goal Seek and Scenario Manager, two what-if analysis tools, to assist you in making decisions.

Solving Problems with Goal Seek

Goal Seek enables you to work backwards to solve a problem. For example, when you want to buy a car, you start by thinking what is the most you can pay a month, such as $200. You can use Goal Seek to determine the most you can borrow to keep that monthly payment. Goal Seek enables you to set the end result to determine the input to produce the result. The primary advantage of Goal Seek is the dialog box that enables you to change your goals and parameters relatively easily. You can find many different possible ways to solve a problem. Excel uses the same type of iterative approach to obtain the solution you indicate.

To use Goal Seek, consider the car loan example shown in Figure 8.8. You want to keep the payment to $200. Before using Goal Seek, you should set up the worksheet and enter preliminary values and the formulas that are dependent on those values.

1. Select the cell containing the formula for which you want a desired result.

2. Click What-If Analysis in the Data Tools group on the Data tab.

3. Select Goal Seek to open the Goal Seek dialog box.

4. Enter the cell reference for the cell to be optimized in the *Set cell* box.

5. Enter the result you want to achieve in the *To value* box.

6. Enter the cell reference that contains the value of the variable to be adjusted in the *By changing cell* box as shown in Figure 8.9 and click OK.

7. When an answer appears, click OK to accept the change or Cancel to return to the original data.

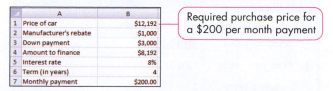

Required purchase price for a $200 per month payment

Figure 8.8   Car Loan Example

Figure 8.9 Goal Seek Dialog Box

Using Scenario Manager

Scenario Manager enables you to specify multiple sets of assumptions, called scenarios, to quickly see the results of any given scenario. Each scenario represents different sets of what-if conditions to be considered in assessing the outcome of spreadsheet models. Scenarios are saved for a specific worksheet within the workbook and are available when the workbook is opened. When you compare Goal Seek to Scenario Manager, you will see that Goal Seek returns one result, indicating rather simple goals. Scenario Manger, on the other hand, enables you to design more sophisticated analysis. You design multiple scenarios for Excel to solve.

Figure 8.10 shows the Scenario Manager dialog box. It contains several scenarios that have been created. Each scenario is stored under its own name and is made up of a set of cells whose values change from scenario to scenario. Figures 8.11 and 8.12 show two examples of scenarios using the same variables but with different values for each variable. After creating scenarios, you can generate a Scenario Summary to compare the results of the different scenarios.

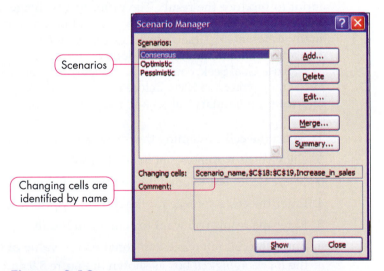

Figure 8.10 Scenario Manager Dialog Box

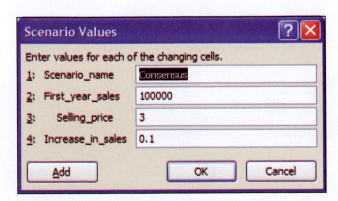

Figure 8.11 Example 1 Scenario

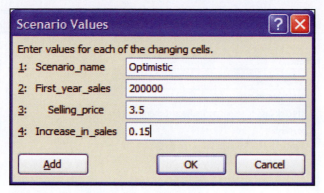

Figure 8.12 Example 2 Scenario

Create Scenarios

You can create scenarios for any worksheet; each worksheet can contain its own set of scenarios. You create scenarios to perform multiple calculations on the same set of data in the same worksheet. Before you start the Scenario Manager, identify cells that contain the variables you want to change or manipulate. For example, you might want to manipulate the values for these variables: loan, interest rate, and term of the loan. The cells that contain these variables are known as the changing cells because you change the values to compare the results. After identifying the variables you want to change, identify one or more cells containing formulas that generate results you want to compare. For example, you might want to see the effects of the variables on monthly payment, total amount paid, and total interest paid.

Scenario Manager enables you to perform more sophisticated what-if analysis than variable tables. Similar to a one-variable table, Scenario Manager enables you to compare multiple results. However, the one-variable table is restricted to only one variable, whereas you can specify multiple variables in Scenario Manager. A two-variable data table is restricted to only two variables and only one result. You should analyze what type of analysis you want to perform and then decide which analysis tool is most appropriate for the situation.

Creating scenarios uses the Scenario Manager dialog box and the Add Scenario dialog box. To create a scenario:

1. Click What-If Analysis in the Data Tools group on the Data tab.
2. Select Scenario Manager to display the Scenario Manager dialog box.
3. Click Add to open the Add Scenario dialog box, as shown in Figure 8.13.
4. Enter a meaningful name in the *Scenario name* box.
5. Enter the input cells for the scenarios in the *Changing cells* box. These are the cells containing variable values that Scenario Manager will adjust or change to display the results. You can have up to 30 variables. The changing cells are identical cell references for all the scenarios you want to compare.

   By default, Excel enters the name of the person who created the scenarios in the Comment box. The name is the user name specified in the Excel Options dialog box and can be added to, deleted, or changed.

6. Click a Protection option if they are available. The Protection options are only active when the worksheet is protected and the Scenario's option was chosen in the Protect Sheet dialog box.
7. Click OK to display the Scenario Values dialog box, which lists the changing cell references that you specified in the previous dialog box. In each respective box, type the value you want to use for that particular scenario.
8. Click Add to add another scenario and specify its values. After you enter values for the last scenario, click OK to return to the Scenario Manager dialog box.

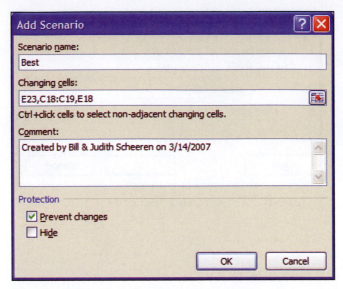

Figure 8.13 Add Scenario Dialog Box

View Scenarios

After you create all scenarios, you will want to view each of them. To view your scenarios, click What-If analysis in the Data Tools group on the Data tab, select Scenario Manager, highlight the name of the scenario you want to view in the Scenarios list, and click Show. Excel places the corresponding value into the changing cell and calculates and shows the results for the scenario.

Generate a Scenario Summary Report

A **scenario summary report** is a condensed version of the scenario results.

When you create several scenarios, you can document the work by creating a scenario summary report. A **scenario summary report** is a condensed, organized version of the scenario parameters and results. The summary report appears in the form of a worksheet outline (see Figure 8.14) and enables you to compare the results based on different values specified by the respective scenarios. For example, you can see that the values for the Optimistic scenario produce the highest result.

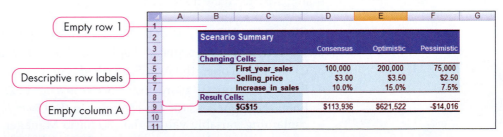

Figure 8.14 The Summary Report

To create a scenario summary report:

1. Click What-If Analysis in the Data Tools group on the Data tab.
2. Select Scenario Manager, and then click Summary (see Figure 8.15).
3. Click Scenario Summary and enter the reference for the cell(s) that refer to cells whose values change in the scenarios in the *Result cells* box.
4. Click OK. The scenario summary report appears on a separate worksheet.

After Excel generates the scenario summary report, you should clean it up. Typically, you should delete the blank row and column. In addition, you should replace cell references with descriptive labels in the report. For example, you could replace $G$15 with a meaningful label, such as Fifth Year Earnings Before Taxes. Furthermore, you can format the scenario summary to match the spreadsheet theme.

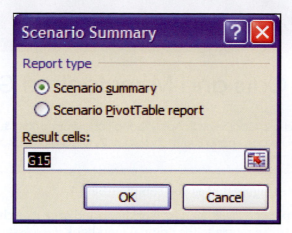

Figure 8.15 Scenario Summary Dialog Box

Generate a Scenario PivotTable Report

If you defined many scenarios with multiple result cells, a Scenario PivotTable report may give you more flexibility in your analysis of outcomes. A PivotTable report is an interactive way to summarize data. In Figure 8.16, the scenario PivotTable summarizes data contained in the scenario summary report. It shows the Consensus scenario, the Optimistic scenario, and the Pessimistic scenario. Using the PivotTable summarizes a great deal of data into just 12 cells. To create a scenario PivotTable report:

1. Click What-If Analysis in the Data Tools group on the Data tab.
2. Select Scenario Manager, and then click Summary.
3. Click Scenario PivotTable Report and enter the cell references for the cells whose values change in the scenario in the *Result cells* box.
4. Click OK. The scenario PivotTable report appears on a separate sheet.

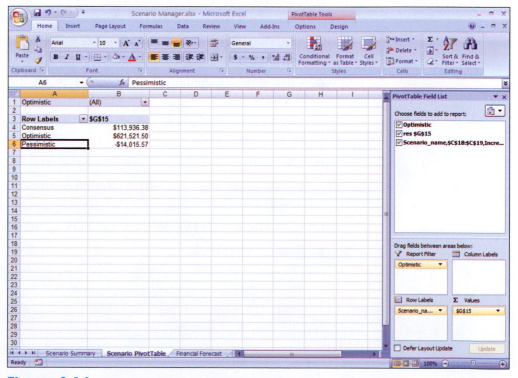

Figure 8.16 Scenario PivotTable Report

Hands-On Exercises

2 | Purchase Golf Cars and Manufacture Golf Clubs

Skills covered: 1. Insert a Function and Use Goal Seek **2.** Apply Conditional Formatting **3.** Define Cell Names **4.** Create the Scenarios **5.** View Scenarios **6.** Create a Scenario Summary Report **7.** Create a Scenario PivotTable Report

Step 1
Insert a Function and Use Goal Seek

Refer to Figure 8.17 as you complete Step 1.

a. Open the *chap8_ho2_gss* workbook and save it as **chap8_ho2_gss_solution** so you can return to the original workbook if necessary.

You notice that the workbook contains two worksheets. The Goal Seek worksheet is used to determine how much you can borrow to purchase new golf cars. The Scenario worksheet is used to determine earnings based on sales forecast.

b. Click **cell B10** on the Goal Seek worksheet, type **=PMT(B8/12,B9*12,-B7)**, and press **Enter**.

You typed the PMT function to determine the monthly payment for the golf cars.

c. You can reduce the monthly payment in various ways:

- Click **cell B4** and change the price of the golf cars to **$60,000**.

The monthly payment drops to $1,382.38.

- Change the interest rate to **6%** and the term of the loan to **5** years.

The payment drops to $1,094.72. You can reduce the payment still further by using the Goal Seek command to fix the payment at a specified level.

d. Click **cell B10**, the cell containing the formula for the monthly payment.

e. Click **What-If Analysis** in the Data Tools group on the Data tab and select **Goal Seek** to display the dialog box shown in Figure 8.17.

f. Verify that **Set cell** contains **B10**. Click in the **To value** box and type **950**, the desired payment.

g. Click in the **By changing cell** box and type **B4**, the cell containing the price of the cars.

Cell B4 is the cell whose value will be determined using the Goal Seek analysis tool.

h. Click **OK**.

Goal Seek returns a successful solution consisting of $52,514 and $950 in cells B4 and B10, respectively.

i. Click **OK** to accept the solution and to close the Goal Seek Status dialog box.

j. Save the workbook.

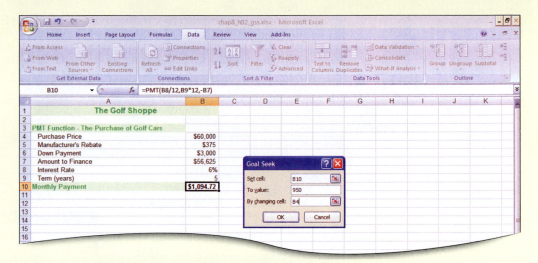

Figure 8.17 PMT Function and Goal Seek

Step 2
Apply Conditional Formatting

Refer to Figure 8.18 as you complete Step 2.

a. Click the **Scenario worksheet tab**, select **cells C15:G15**, click **Conditional Formatting** in the Styles group on the Home tab, select **Highlight Cells Rules**, and click **Greater Than** to open the Greater Than dialog box.

You are going to apply formatting to those cells that display earnings greater than $425,000.

b. Click in the **Format cells that are GREATER THAN** box and replace the value with **425000**.

c. Open the **with drop-down arrow** and select **Custom Format** to open the Format Cells dialog box.

d. Click the **Font tab**, change the font style to **Bold** and the font color to **Green**, and click **OK** twice.

You set the relationships for condition 1 and will now set the relationships for condition 2.

e. Make sure **cells C15:G15** are selected, click **Conditional Formatting** in the Styles group, select **Highlight Cells Rules**, and click **Less Than** to open the Less Than dialog box.

You are going to apply formatting to those cells that display a loss.

f. Click in the **Format cells that are LESS THAN** box and replace the value with **0**.

TROUBLESHOOTING: The Format Cells that are . . . text box will display the current value in the selected cell. You must replace this value with your condition value.

g. Open the **with drop-down arrow** and select **Custom Format** to open the Format Cells dialog box.

h. Click the **Font tab**, change the font style to **Bold** and the font color to **Red**, and click **OK**. Click **OK** again to save your changes and to exit the dialog box.

You set the relationships for condition 2, as shown in Figure 8.18. You conditionally formatted the cells to display earnings in red when you lose money. You will also test your conditions.

i. Click **cell C19**, change the selling price to **90**, and press **Enter**.

The earnings before taxes are displayed in red since they are negative for the last three years.

j. Click **Undo** on the Quick Access Toolbar to return the initial sales price to 125.00.

k. Save the workbook.

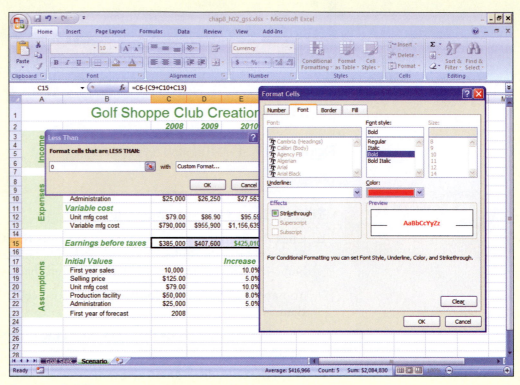

Figure 8.18 Conditional Formatting

Step 3
Define Cell Names

Refer to Figure 8.19 as you complete Step 3.

a. Click **cell C18** and click **Define Name** in the Defined Names group on the Formulas tab to display the New Name dialog box, as shown in Figure 8.19.

You are going to define names for several cells for documentation of your formulas. Using names is often easier than using cell references. First_year_sales is already entered as the default name, because this text appears as a label in the cell immediately to the left of the active cell. Underscores were added between the words because blanks are not permitted in a cell name.

b. Click **OK** to accept the name.

Name the other cells that will be used in various scenarios.

c. Use **Selling_price** as the name for **cell C19**.

d. Enter names of **Increase_in_sales** for **cell E18** and **Scenario_name** for **cell E23**.

TROUBLESHOOTING: Cell E23 is currently empty but will contain the names of various scenarios.

e. Click **OK** to close the New Name dialog box.

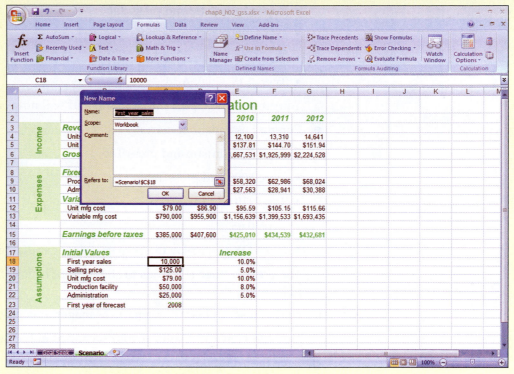

Figure 8.19 Cell Name

Refer to Figure 8.20 as you complete Step 4.

a. Click **cell E23**, type the word **Consensus**, press **Enter**, and click **cell E23** to make it the active cell.

You want to emphasize the name of your scenario on the worksheet.

b. Create the Consensus scenario with these specifications:

- Click **What-If Analysis** in the Data Tools group on the Data tab and select **Scenario Manager** to open the Scenario Manager dialog box.

- Click **Add** to display the Add Scenario dialog box shown in Figure 8.20.

- Type **Consensus** in the **Scenario name** box.

- Click in the **Changing cells** box.

    Cell E23 (the active cell) is already entered as the first cell in the scenario.

- Type a **comma**, then type **C18**, **C19**, and **E18** as the remaining cells in the scenario and click **OK**.

TROUBLESHOOTING: You must make a list of cell references, separating each with a comma and not using a space after the comma.

You should see the Scenario Values dialog box with the values of this scenario already entered from the corresponding cells in the worksheet.

c. Click **Add** to add a second scenario called **Optimistic**.

The changing cells are already entered and match the Consensus scenario.

d. Click **OK** to again display the Scenario Values dialog box so you can type the values for Optimistic, the second scenario.

- Type **Optimistic** and press **Tab**.
- Type **12000** and press **Tab**.
- Type **150** and press **Tab**.
- Type **0.15**. Click **Add**.

You created the Optimistic scenario and will now create the Pessimistic scenario.

e. Enter a Pessimistic scenario:

- Type **Pessimistic** and press **Tab**.
- Type **8000** and press **Tab**.
- Type **110** and press **Tab**.
- Type **0.05**.
- Click **OK** to display the Scenario Manager dialog box.

You created three scenarios to show profit or loss from the sale of custom-made golf clubs.

f. Click **Close** to close the Scenario Manager dialog box.

You will view the results of your scenarios in the next step.

g. Save the workbook.

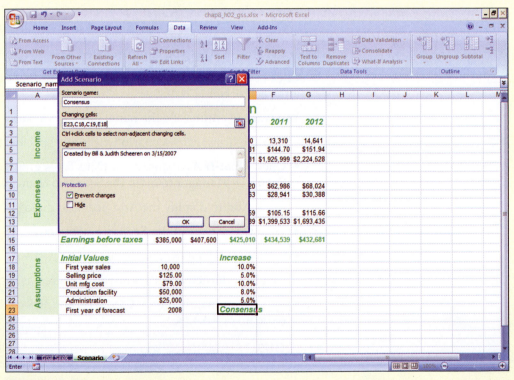

Figure 8.20 Create Scenarios

Refer to Figure 8.21 as you complete Step 5.

a. Click **What-If Analysis** in the Data Tools group on the Data tab, and select **Scenario Manager** to open the Scenario Manager dialog box.

The three scenarios—Consensus, Optimistic, and Pessimistic—should be listed, corresponding to the scenarios that were created in Step 4.

b. Click the **Optimistic** scenario and click **Show** to display the financial forecast under the assumptions for the Optimistic scenario. See Figure 8.21.

TROUBLESHOOTING: You could double-click the scenario name to display the forecast for the selected scenario.

c. Double-click the **Pessimistic** scenario to see the changes made to the worksheet showing the forecast for the Pessimistic scenario.

d. Double-click the **Consensus** scenario to return to this scenario.

By clicking the various scenarios, you can see how easy it is to change multiple assumptions at one time by storing the values in a scenario.

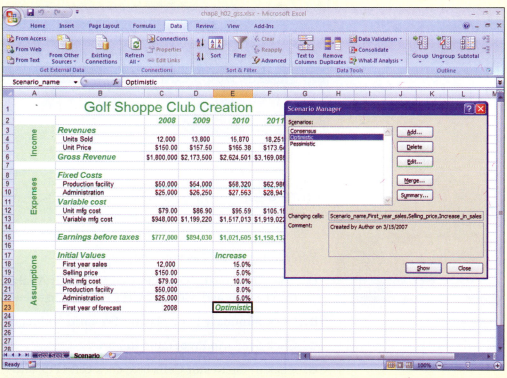

Figure 8.21 The Optimistic Scenario

Refer to Figure 8.22 as you complete Step 6.

a. Verify that the Scenario Manager dialog box is still open and click **Summary** to display the Scenario Summary dialog box.

b. Click **Scenario Summary**.

c. Click in the **Result Cells** box, click **cell G15**, and click **OK**.

Cell G15 contains the earnings before taxes in the fifth year of the forecast. You should see a Scenario Summary on a new worksheet. Each scenario has its own column in the worksheet. The changing cells, identified by name rather than cell reference, are listed in column C. The Scenario Summary worksheet is an ordinary worksheet to the extent that it can be modified like any other worksheet. The summary is actually the important component of the Scenario Manager, in as this is the output used to make decisions. The information shown in the Scenario Summary is analyzed and used to determine the product mix and selling price to maximize profit.

d. Click the header for **row 6**, then press and hold **Ctrl** while you select **rows 12** through **14**.

e. Right-click the selected cells and select **Delete** to delete the rows.

f. Delete columns A and the Current Values column and delete the blank Row 1.

You cleaned up the summary report by deleting the duplicate and empty rows and column.

g. Edit cell B9 from the $G$15 label to **2012 Earnings Before Taxes**, and then widen column B.

h. Save the workbook.

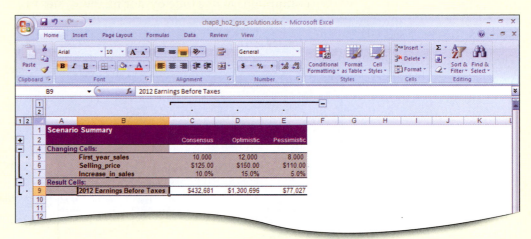

Figure 8.22 Scenario Summary

Refer to Figure 8.23 as you complete Step 7.

Step 7
Create a Scenario PivotTable Report

a. Select the Scenario worksheet, click **What-If Analysis** in the Data Tools group on the Data tab, and select **Scenario Manager** to open the Scenario Manager dialog box.

b. Click **Summary** to display the Scenario Summary dialog box.

c. Click **Scenario PivotTable Report**.

d. Click in the **Result Cells** box, click **cell G15**, and click **OK**.

Cell G15 contains the earnings before taxes in the fifth year of the forecast. You should see a PivotTable report on a new worksheet. Each scenario has its own row in the worksheet. The changing cells, identified by the column heading, $G$15, are listed in column B. The PivotTable Report worksheet is an ordinary worksheet to the extent that it can be modified like any other worksheet.

e. Format **cells B4:B6** as **Currency** with **2** decimal places.

f. Click **cell A1**, type **Scenarios** to change the title, and press **Enter**.

g. Group the sheets and create a custom footer with your name, today's date, and your instructor's name.

h. Print, save, and close the workbook.

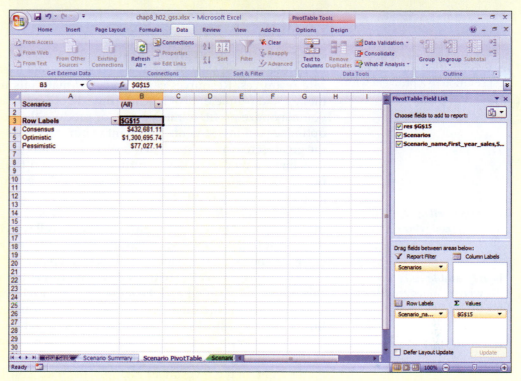

Figure 8.23 Scenario PivotTable Report

TIP Scenario Manager

You can return to the Scenario Manager to add or modify an individual scenario, after which you can create a new scenario summary. You must, however, execute the command when the original worksheet is displayed on the screen. Note, too, that each time you click the Summary button within the Scenario Manager, you will create another summary worksheet called Scenario Summary 2, Scenario Summary 3, and so on. You can delete the extraneous worksheets by right-clicking the worksheet tab, then clicking the Delete command.

Solver

Solver is an add-in program
for Excel that searches for the
best solution to a problem with
several variables.

Solver is an add-in program for Excel that searches for the best or optimum solution to a problem with several variables. Solver is a tool used to find the best way to allocate resources. Resources can be the raw materials used in a production facility, money, and people time or machine time. In order to determine the optimal solution, you maximize profit, minimize cost, or produce the best quality. When you want to optimize your investments, you want to purchase the stocks and bonds that give you the greatest return at a particular level of risk. You could also determine the least risk to achieve a predetermined return. Solver is used to find the answer to such questions. When using Solver, you must specify three items or parameters: target cell, adjustable cells, and constraints.

The *target cell* specifies the
goal or the cell whose value
will change.

The *target cell* specifies the goal—the cell whose value you want to maximize, minimize, or set to a specific value. The target cell typically contains a formula that is directly or indirectly based on the adjustable cells and constraints. In the investment example, the target is the most profit you can make.

The *adjustable cells* are the
cells whose values are adjusted
until the constraints are satisfied.

The *adjustable cells* are the cells whose values are adjusted or changed until the constraints are satisfied and the target cell reaches its optimum value. The changing cells are typically cells that contain values, not formulas. In the investment scenario, this is the mix of stocks and bonds purchased to achieved the maximum profit.

The *constraints* specify the
restrictions.

The *constraints* specify the restrictions. Each constraint is made up of a cell or range of cells on the left, a relational operator, and a numeric value or cell reference on the right. In the investment example, the main constraint is the amount of money you have to invest. Obviously, if you are not limited in the amount you can invest, the amount of profit can extend to infinity. A secondary constraint is the level of risk you are willing to accept. The constraints always appear in alphabetical order by cell reference, regardless of the order in which they were entered.

The Solver parameters are shown in the Solver Parameters dialog box in Figure 8.24.

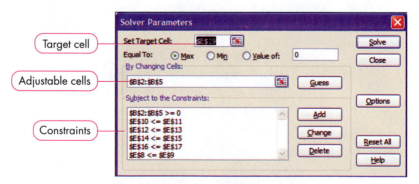

Figure 8.24 Solver Parameters Dialog Box

In this section, you learn how to load the Solver add-in. Then you use Solver to set a target that needs to be solved, select changing cells, and create constraints.

Loading the Solver Add-In

Created by Frontline Systems, Solver is an add-in program that extends the capability of Excel. Solvers or optimizers are frequently used in operations management to allocate scarce resources. It is too narrow an application to be part of the Excel program, as not all users need the extended capability of Solver. Therefore, you must install Solver before you can use it. To install Solver:

1. Click the Office Button.
2. Click Excel Options.
3. Click Add-Ins, select Excel Add-ins from the Manage list, and click Go.

4. Click Solver Add-in in the Add-Ins available list and click OK, as shown in Figure 8.25.

Solver appears in the Analysis group on the Data tab, as shown in Figure 8.26.

Figure 8.25 Excel Add-Ins

Figure 8.26 Solver Command in Analysis Group on Data Tab

Solving Problems with Solver

Solver is the best choice to solve more complex problems. It can be used for complex equation solving and for constrained optimization where a set of constraints is specified and you want the outcome to be minimized or maximized. With Solver, you are able to change the value of several cells at once to achieve the desired result.

Before using Solver, it is a good idea to work with paper and pencil to (1) Define the problem on paper—include decision variables, describe the function to be optimized, and list all the constraints; (2) Enter the problem into an Excel spreadsheet—in general use a 2-dimensional layout for constraints; (3) Solve the problem using Solver; and (4) Generate a summary report.

You would use Solver to determine the lowest shipping costs to ship goods from a manufacturing plant to a warehouse. The goal is to minimize the shipping cost by analyzing routes and the amounts to ship from each plant to each warehouse to meet regional demand while not exceeding manufacturing capacity. Obviously, it will cost more to ship a long distance rather than a short distance, but unless manufacturing capacity and demand are unlimited, these factors must be taken into consideration.

Define a Problem

When you want to define a problem in Solver, the worksheet should have one or more input variables and one or more formulas that show a solution in a single cell. Each input variable may have certain constraints. For example, if a business wants to maximize profits, a constraint may be its production capacity. Another example where Solver is useful is to determine product mix. In this case, a drug company wants to maximize monthly profit but cannot produce above a certain level. It also must consider the amount of resources available and the amount of product that can be sold.

Solver uses identified input ranges, output cells, and constraints. Solver can minimize or maximize the input cell or set the output cell to a particular value. Solver will stop at the first solution unless you direct it to do otherwise. To define a Solver problem:

1. Click Solver in the Analysis group on the Data tab. This opens the Solver Parameters dialog box. A completed Solver Parameters dialog box is shown in Figure 8.24.

2. Enter the cell you want Solver to optimize in the Set Target Cell box.

3. Select one of the three Equal To options to choose the kind of optimization you want. If you select Value of, you must enter a value in the text box. In the drug company example, the company would use Max because it wants the highest possible profit. If a company wants to minimize costs, use the Min option.

4. Enter the cell references that should be modified by Excel to reach the target in the By Changing Cells box.

5. The constraints for the drug company are that the produce mix has a limited amount of resources available and it will not produce any more of the product than can be sold. If constraints will be used in your Solver problem, add each constraint as follows and iterate each:

   a. Click Add to the right of the Subject to the Constraints box. This opens the Add Constraint dialog box.

   b. Enter the cell reference, the operator to test the cell references, and the constraint the cell needs to match, as shown in Figure 8.27.

   c. Click OK to add the constraint.

6. Click Solve to begin the Solver process. When Solver completes the process, the Solver Results dialog box appears (see Figure 8.28). If Solver cannot reach an optimal solution, it may be because you have an error in your logic or the constraints do not allow sufficient elasticity to achieve a result. For example, a constraint between 10 and 11 does not allow sufficient elasticity or a constraint greater than 20 but also less than 10 is illogical.

7. Click Keep Solver Solution to keep the changed values or click Restore Original Values to return to the original values.

8. Choose a Solver report from Reports list if desired. Reports appear on a separate worksheet. The reports show how Solver arrived at an answer.

Figure 8.27 Change Constraint Dialog Box

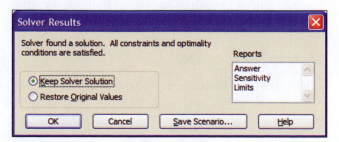

Figure 8.28 Solver Results Dialog Box

9. Click Save Scenario and type a name for the scenario in the Scenario Name box to save the adjusting cell values as a Scenario that can be displayed later.
10. Click OK to return to your worksheet.

To change or delete a constraint, click the constraint you want to change or delete in the Solver Parameters dialog box. Then click Change and make the desired changes or click Delete to delete the constraint. Should your results be unreasonable or unrealistic, you might have to change your constraints or delete a parameter.

Step Through Solver Trial Solutions

It is possible to closely monitor the trial solutions that Solver arrives at prior to reaching the final solution. Solver is a mathematical modeling operation and you can determine solutions using the associated mathematics. However, stepping through Solver enables you to view the steps Solver performs.

1. After you have defined a Solver problem, click Options in the Solver Parameters dialog box.
2. Select the Show Iteration Results check box in the Solver Options dialog box to see the values of each trial solution, as shown in Figure 8.29, and click OK.
3. Click Solve in the Solver Parameters dialog box.
4. When the Show Trial Solution dialog box appears, either:

   • Click Stop to stop the solution process and display the Solver Results dialog box, or

   • Click Continue to continue the solution process and move to the next trial solution.

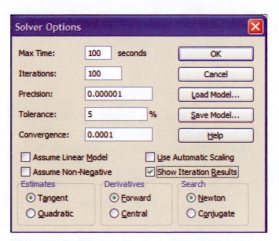

Figure 8.29 Show Iteration Results

Save a Solver Model

When you use Solver, Excel keeps track of your settings, and when you save a workbook, it saves only the most recent Solver settings. In some cases, you may want to save more than the most recent Solver settings. You must save the Solver target value, the changing cells, and the constraints.

Saving a Solver model places the information in a small block of cells on a worksheet. The number of cells required to save the Solver model is dependent on the number of constraints in the model. To save a Solver model:

1. Click Options on the Solver Parameters dialog box.
2. Click Save Model in the Solver Options dialog box.
3. Click the Select Model Area box, and then click in the worksheet where the first cell is to be placed. Make sure the worksheet has sufficient empty cells so the Solver information does not overwrite Excel data.
4. Click OK to return to the Solver options dialog box.
5. Click OK (or Cancel) to return to the Solver Parameters dialog box. Figure 8.30 shows Solver model data stored on a worksheet.

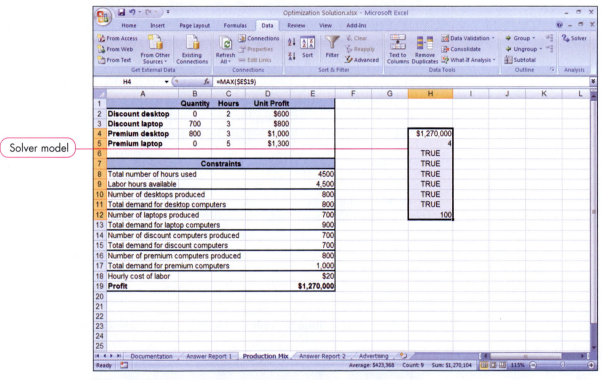

Figure 8.30 Save Solver Model

Restore a Solver Model

If you want to use an existing Solver model with new or updated data, you must return to a previous Solver Model. When you want to return to and use a Solver model that you previously created and restore it, do the following:

1. Click Options in the Solver Parameters dialog box.
2. Click Load Model in the Solver options dialog box.

3. Click in the Select Model Area box and then select the worksheet cells that contain the Solver data. All cells with the Solver data must be selected as indicated by the dashed box in Figure 8.31.

4. Click OK or Cancel to return to the Solver Options dialog box.

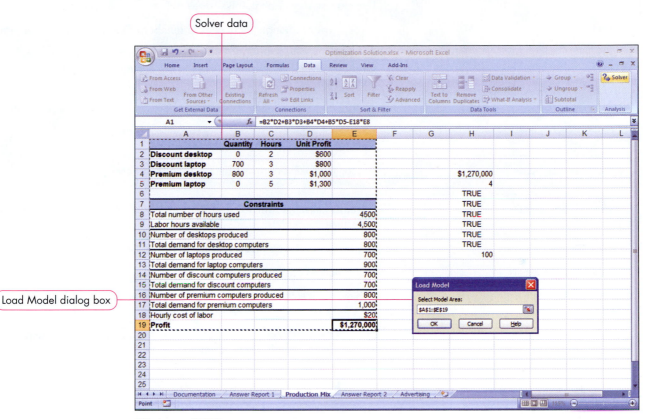

Figure 8.31 Restore Solver Model

TIP   Review the Terminology

Solver is an optimization technique that enables you to maximize or minimize the value of an objective function, such as profit or cost. The formula to compute the objective function is stored in the target cell within the worksheet. Other cells in the worksheet contain the variables or adjustable cells. Another set of cells contains the value of the available resources or constraints. This type of optimization problem is referred to as linear programming.

Configure Solver

The predefined options used by Solver are generally sufficient for most problems. It may, at times, be necessary to change one or more of the Solver options when Solver will not arrive at a solution. To access the Solver Options dialog box, click Options in the Solver Parameters dialog box. The Solver Options dialog box is shown in Figure 8.29 and the Reference material describes Solver options.

Excel Solver Options | Reference

Option	Description
Max Time	Specifies in seconds the maximum time Solver will spend on a problem. This may be increased if Solver does not arrive at a solution.
Iterations	Enables you to change the maximum number of trials Solver will perform.
Precision	Specifies how close the Cell Reference and Constraint formulas must be to satisfy a constraint. Specifying less precision may speed up the problem-solving process.
Tolerance	Designates the maximum percentage of error allowed for integer solutions.
Convergence	Enter a value between 1 and 0, specifying the amount of change to allow in nonlinear problems before Solver stops.
Assume Linear Model	Speeds the solution process but only if all relationships in the model are linear.
Assume Non-Negative	Solver assumes a lower value of 0 for adjustable cells that do not specify lower-limit constraints.
Use Automatic Scaling	Used when problems involve large differences in magnitude.
Show Iteration Results	Solver pauses and displays results after each trial.
Estimates, Derivatives, and Search Group boxes	Control some technical aspects of solutions. Generally not changed.
Load Model	Displays the Load Model dialog box, in which you can specify a range of cells that contains a set of Solver parameters to be loaded.
Save Model	Displays the Save Model dialog box so you can specify the range of cells, in which Excel saves model parameters.

TIP   The Greater-Than-Zero Constraint

One constraint that is often overlooked is the requirement that the value of each adjustable cell be greater than or equal to zero. Physically, it makes no sense to produce a negative number of products in any category. Mathematically, however, a negative value in an adjustable cell may produce a higher value for the target cell. Hence, the nonnegativity (greater than or equal to zero) constraint should always be included for the adjustable cells.

Hands-On Exercises

3 | FAL Computer Manufacturing

Skills covered: 1. Install Solver and Enter Cell Formulas **2.** Set Target, Set Adjustable Cells, and Enter Constraints **3.** Solve the Problem **4.** View and Print the Report

---

Step 1
Install Solver and Enter Cell Formulas

Refer to Figure 8.32 as you complete Step 1.

a. Start Excel, open the *chap8_ho3_optimization* workbook, and save it as **chap8_ho3_optimization_solution** so that you will be able to return to the original workbook.

Some areas of the workbook are preformatted and represent summary areas you will complete as you work through the following steps.

b. Click the **Office Button** and click **Excel Options**.

c. Click **Add-Ins**, select **Excel Add-ins** from the Manage list, and click **GO**.

d. Check **Solver Add-in** in the Add-Ins available list and click **OK**.

You installed Solver and the Solver command is now available in the Analysis group on the Data tab.

e. Click **cell E8**, type **=B2*C2+B3*C3+B4*C4+B5*C5**, and press **Enter**.

The total number of hours worked in cell E8 is derived by multiplying the quantity in column B by the respective hours in column C and summing the hours for the four products. View Figure 8.32 to see your formula for the total number of hours used in production. You will see zeros in some cells because the quantity produced is a function of Solver.

f. Enter the formulas in the cells as shown in the table:

Cell	Formula
E10	=B2+B4
E12	=B3+B5
E14	=B2+B3
E16	=B4+B5
E19	=B2*D2+B3*D3+B4*D4+B5*D5-E18*E8

g. Save the workbook.

TROUBLESHOOTING: Solver is an optional component of Microsoft Excel, and it may not be installed on your system. If you are working on a computer at school, your instructor should be able to notify the network administrator to correct the problem. If you are working on your own computer, follow the instructions in Step 1 to install Solver.

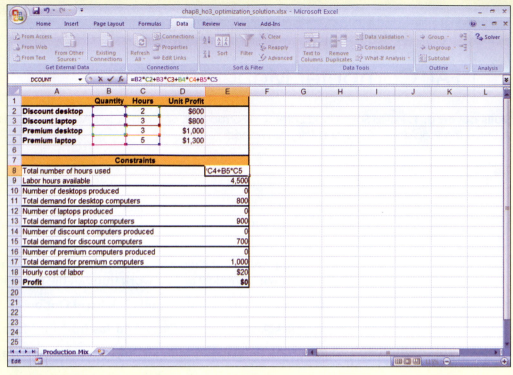

Figure 8.32 Cell Formulas

Step 2

Set Target, Set Adjustable Cells, and Enter Constraints

Refer to Figure 8.33 as you complete Step 2.

a. Click **Solver** in the Analysis group on the Data tab to display the Solver Parameters dialog box.

b. Click in the **Set Target Cell** box and click **cell E19**.

You set the target cell and the Max option button is selected by default.

c. Click in the **By Changing Cells** box, select **cells B2:B5**, and click **Add** to open the Add Constraint dialog box.

Throughout the rest of Step 2, you will add the constraints for the Solver problem. If you type the cell references, remember they must be absolute.

d. Verify the insertion point is in **Cell Reference** and click **cell E8**.

e. Verify the <= constraint is selected, click **Constraint**, and click **cell E9**.

Cell E8 contains the formula to compute the total number of hours used. The <= constraint is the default constraint, and cell E9 will contain the value of the constraint.

f. Click **Add** to complete the first constraint and add another constraint.

g. Add the constraints as shown in the table below:

Constraint to enter:	Click to complete:
E10<=E11	ADD
E12<=E13	ADD
E14<=E15	ADD
E16<=E17	ADD

h. Select **cells B2:B5**, click the **relational operators down arrow**, and select **>=**.

i. Type **0** in Constraint and click **OK**.

The production quantities for all computers must be greater than or equal to zero.

TROUBLESHOOTING: Click Add to complete the current constraint and display an empty dialog box to enter another constraint. Click OK only when you have completed the last constraint and want to return to the Solver Parameters dialog box to solve the problem.

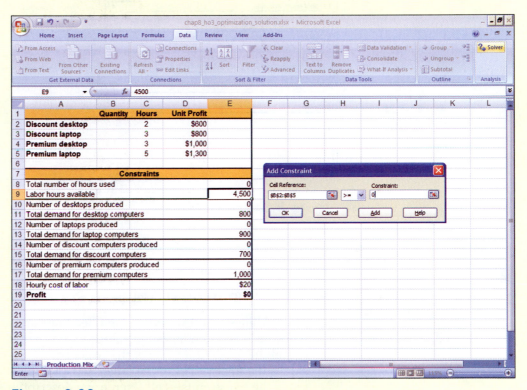

Figure 8.33 Target, Adjustable Cells, and Constraints

Step 3
Solve the Problem

If the settings shown in the Solver Parameters dialog box in Figure 8.34 do NOT match your settings, complete one or more of the following:

- Click the **Set Target Cell** box and **click $E$19**, the target cell in the worksheet, to change the target cell.
- Select the constraint and click **Change** to edit a constraint.
- Select the constraint and click **Delete** to delete a constraint.

a. Click **Solve**.

You should see the Solver Results dialog box, indicating that Solver has found a solution. The maximum profit is $1,270,000. The option button to Keep Solver Solution is selected by default.

b. Click **Answer** in the Reports list and click **OK**.

You will see the report being generated and the Solver Results dialog box closes automatically. Excel inserts a worksheet called Answer Report 1 and stores the Solver results there.

c. Save the workbook.

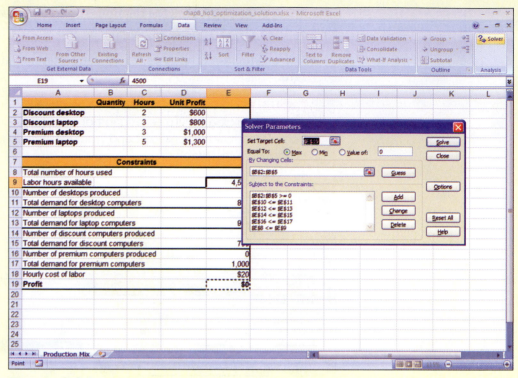

Figure 8.34 Problem Solution

Refer to Figure 8.35 as you complete Step 4.

Step 4
View and Print the Report

Refer to Figure 8.35 as you complete Step 4.

a. Click the **Answer Report 1** tab.

The gridlines and row and column headings are suppressed by default for this worksheet. Solver adjusts the values in the changing cells B2, B3, B4, and B5 to obtain the maximum value of the target cell E19 of $1,270,000. The Solver report shows the final values of the target cell and adjustable cells. In addition, it displays the constraints—cell references, descriptions, current values, formulas, binding/not binding, and slack.

b. Click **cell A1**, type **FAL Computer Production Answer Report**, and press **Enter**.

c. Format the answer report as shown in Figure 8.35.

d. Group the worksheets and create a custom footer that includes your name, today's date, and your instructor's name.

e. Print the workbook.

f. Save and close the workbook.

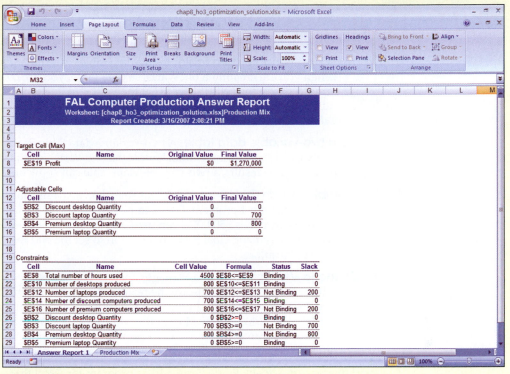

Figure 8.35 The Solver Report

View Options

Any worksheet used to create a spreadsheet model will display gridlines and row and column headers by default. Worksheets containing reports, however, especially reports generated by Excel, often suppress these elements to make the reports easier and more appealing to read. To suppress (or display) these elements, click the View tab and either click to add the check or click to remove the check for the options in the Show/Hide group.

Summary

1. **Create a one-variable data table.** Using data tables is a method of doing what-if analysis. When you are creating a one-variable data table, you are concerned with two elements: input cells are the cells that contain the values to be modified for what-if analysis. Result cells contain the values to be modified. In a one-variable data table, you observe different values for one variable on one or more results affected by the variable.

2. **Create a two-variable data table.** A two-variable data table enables you to compare results for two variables at the same time. Unlike the one-variable data table that enables you to compare multiple results, a two-variable data table can show only one result.

3. **Solve problems with Goal Seek.** The Goal Seek data analysis tool is designed to enable you to work backwards with a problem. For example, when you want to buy a car, you think the most you can pay a month is $500. You can use Goal Seek to determine the most you can borrow to keep that payment. Goal Seek enables you to set the end result to determine the input to produce the result.

4. **Use Scenario Manager.** Scenario Manager enables you to specify multiple sets of assumptions, called scenarios, to see quickly the results of any given scenario. Each scenario represents different sets of what-if conditions to be considered in assessing the outcome of spreadsheet models. Scenarios are saved with the workbook and are available when the workbook is opened. You can generate scenario summary reports to compare and contrast the results of different scenarios to determine the optimal course of action.

5. **Load the Solver Add-In.** Solver is an add-in program for Excel that searches for the best solution to a problem with several variables. Solver can be used to find a line that best fits data or minimizes production costs for a particular product. When using Solver, you must specify three items or parameters. The target cell specifies the goal, the cell whose value you want to maximize, minimize, or set to a specific value. The adjustable cells are the cells whose values are adjusted until the constraints are satisfied and the target cell reaches its optimum value. The constraints specify the restrictions. Each constraint is made up of a cell or range of cells on the left, a relational operator, and a numeric value or cell reference on the right. The constraints always appear in alphabetical order, regardless of the order in which they were entered.

6. **Solve problems with Solver.** Solver is the best choice to solve more complex problems. It can be used for complex equation solving and for constrained optimization where a set of constraints is specified and you want the outcome to be minimized or maximized. With Solver, you are able to change the value of several cells at once to achieve the desired result.

Key Terms

Multiple Choice

1. You want to purchase a new car. You have used the PMT function and determined that the amount of the monthly payment will be $450. You can only afford $350 per month. Which of these features will help you determine either the purchase price of the car you can buy or the amount of the down payment you must come up with to reduce the monthly payment to $350?

   (a) The Scenario Manager
   (b) The VLOOKUP function
   (c) The Function Wizard
   (d) The Goal Seek

2. When using the Goal Seek command, how many parameters can you change at a time?

   (a) 1
   (b) 2
   (c) 3
   (d) All of them, if necessary

3. You are creating a financial forecast. What is a good reason for isolating the initial conditions and assumptions from the body of the forecast?

   (a) To allow the forecast to be updated automatically if the initial assumptions change
   (b) To prevent inaccurate information from being entered into the forecast
   (c) To keep invalid formulas from being entered into the forecast
   (d) To keep the forecast accurate regardless of formulas entered into the forecast

4. You are developing a financial forecast. Where would you most likely use absolute references?

   (a) When referring to the assumptions about the rate of change in the formulas for the first year
   (b) When referring to the values from the first year in the formulas for the second year
   (c) When referring to the assumptions about the rate of change in the formulas for the second year
   (d) When referring to the initial conditions in the formulas for the first year

5. Cell B17 contains the formula =B12*B14 and displays the value of 100,000. When you change cell B12, the value changes to 90,000 and the font in cell B17 changes from red to blue. What is the most likely explanation?

   (a) Conditional formatting has been applied to cell B17.
   (b) Your computer has the dreaded Red-To-Blue virus.
   (c) Conditional formatting has been applied to cell B12.
   (d) Conditional formatting has been applied to cell B14.

6. A(n) _____ is a limitation on the values that a cell can have.

   (a) assumption
   (b) constraint
   (c) objective
   (d) result

7. The _____ cell must always contain a formula.

   (a) changing
   (b) constraint
   (c) precedent
   (d) result

8. Solver can be used for _____ in which goal seeking or back solving is used.

   (a) constrained optimization
   (b) equation-solving
   (c) linear programming
   (d) resource allocation

9. For the Solver to reach a feasible solution, users need to specify _____.

   (a) changing cells
   (b) constraints
   (c) precedent values
   (d) slack values

10. Which of the following is the most useful and popular Solver report?

    (a) Answer report
    (b) Constraint report
    (c) Limits report
    (d) Sensitivity report

11. Whose characteristics does the second section of an Answer report describe?

    (a) Changing cells
    (b) Constraints
    (c) Precedent values
    (d) Target cells

12. A _____ summarizes key input and output cell values of multiple what-if analysis in a single, rectangular cell range.

    (a) data table
    (b) data criterion
    (c) data range
    (d) data report

13. What is the combination of values assigned to one or more variable cells in a what-if analysis called?

    (a) One-variable data table

    (b) PivotTable

    (c) Scenario

    (d) Two-variable data table

14. Which of the following dialog boxes is accessed to change the name of an existing scenario?

    (a) Add Scenario

    (b) Edit Scenario

    (c) Change Scenario

    (d) Rename Scenario

15. To apply a scenario's values to the designated changing cells, users need to:

    (a) Click the scenario in the Scenario Manager dialog box.

    (b) Double-click the scenario in the Scenario Manager dialog box.

    (c) Right-click the scenario in the Scenario Manager dialog box.

    (d) Triple-click the scenario in the Scenario Manager dialog box.

16. Which of the following tools outline each scenario by displaying changing cells and result cells in a separate worksheet?

    (a) Break-even analysis

    (b) Cost-Volume-Profit analysis

    (c) Data table

    (d) Scenario summary

17. Which of the following statements is true when using the Scenario Manager to produce a scenario summary report?

    (a) Users need to select all changing cells in the report manually and the result cells they want to include.

    (b) The Scenario Manager automatically includes all changing cells in the report and the result cells users want to include.

    (c) The Scenario Manager automatically includes all changing cells in the report, but users must select the result cells they want to include.

    (d) The Scenario Manager automatically includes all the result cells in the report, but users must select the changing cells they want to include.

Practice Exercises

1 Advertising the Worldwide Fitness Centers

The director of marketing at the Worldwide Fitness Center has a total of $125,000 in the weekly advertising budget. The director wants to establish a presence in both magazines and cable television, and requires a minimum of four magazine ads and ten cable TV ads each week. Each magazine ad costs $10,000 and is seen by one million readers. Each cable TV commercial costs $5,000 and is seen by 250,000 viewers. Your task is to determine how many ads of each type should be placed to reach at least 10 million customers at minimum cost. The workbook shown in Figure 8.36 is the completed solution to minimize costs. You will use Solver to achieve the goal of minimizing costs. Note that you cannot purchase a fractional part of an ad, and you will have to impose an integer constraint. You will have to relax a constraint because the integer constraint presents an infeasible solution.

a. Use paper and pencil to determine the target and the adjustable data and to define the constraints. Sketch the design of your final workbook before beginning to use Excel.

b. Open the *chap8_pe1_advertising* workbook and save it as **chap8_pe1_advertising_ solution** so that you can return to the original workbook if necessary.

c. Enter the formulas:

- Click **cell E6** and type **=B2*C2+B3*C3**.

- Click **cell E10** and type **=B2*D2+B3*D3**.

d. Set the target, enter adjustable cells, and enter the constraints:

- Click the **Data tab** and click **Solver** in the Analysis group to display the Solver Parameters dialog box.

- Click in the **Set Target Cell** box, click **cell E6,** and click **Min** in the Equal To area.

- Click the **By Changing Cells** box, select **cells B2:B3**, and click **Add** to open the Add Constraint dialog box.

- Click **Cell Reference** and click **cell E6**.

- Verify the <= constraint is selected, click **Constraint**, and click **cell E7**.

- Click **Add** to complete the first constraint and to add another constraint.

- Add three constraints as shown in the table below:

Constraint to enter:	Click to complete:
E10>=E11	ADD
B2>=E8	ADD
B3>=E9	OK

e. Click **Solve**, click **OK**, and save the workbook.

f. Impose an integer constraint:

- Click **Solver** in the Analysis group to display the Solver Parameters dialog box.

- Click **Add** to add a constraint in the Add Constraint dialog box.

- Select **cells B2:B3**, select **int** from the drop-down arrow, and click **OK**.

- Click **Solve** and note that Solver could not find a solution to satisfy existing constraints.

- Click **Cancel** to close the dialog box, return to the worksheet, and relax a constraint to achieve a better mix of ads.

...continued on Next Page

g. Relax a constraint:

- Click **cell E9**, type **9**, and press **Enter**.
- Click **Solver** in the Analysis group and click **Solve** to see a solution.

h. Click **Answer** in the Reports list and click **OK** to generate the Answer report on a new sheet tab.

i. Format the report as shown in Figure 8.36, duplicating the formatting as closely as possible.

j. Group the worksheets and create a custom footer that includes your name, today's date, and your instructor's name. Save, print, and close the workbook.

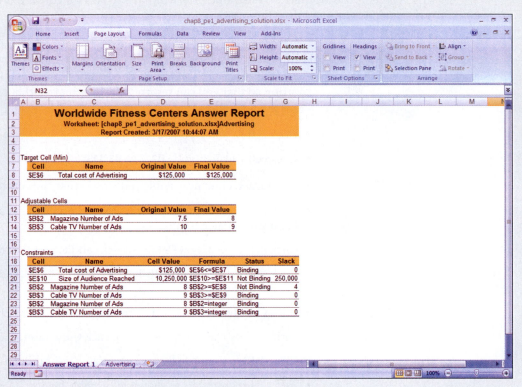

Figure 8.36 Worldwide Fitness Centers

2 The GLHS Art Gallery Budget

The workbook in Figure 8.37 illustrates the budget for the GLHS Art Gallery. After one year of extensive renovation, the gallery will soon open to the public. The avant garde gallery is located in the cultural area of the city and includes state-of-the-art education programs, generous studio space for resident artists, and excellent display facilities. The only income the gallery has to cover expenses is monthly membership dues, and the board of directors must determine the new monthly dues. Because this is a nonprofit gallery, it is important that the gallery be as close as possible to break-even each year. The gallery's charter does impose one constraint: that there not be more than 4,500 members at one time. Figure 8.37 shows the budget with both a one- and two-variable data table. Your task is to create the one-variable data table to determine funding for various membership levels. You will also create a two-variable data table to analyze members and dues to determine the break-even point.

a. Open the *chap8_pe2_glhs_budget* workbook and save it as **chap8_pe2_glhs_budget_solution** so that you can return to the original workbook if necessary.

b. Begin to create a one-variable data table by typing the data in the cells as indicated in the following table:

...continued on Next Page

Cell	Data
G6	Total Revenues
G7	Total Expenses
G8	Income
I6	=D19
I7	=D20
I8	=D21
G5	Members
I5	4000
J5	4100

c. Select **cells I5:J5** and use AutoFill to fill cells through **N5**.
d. Format **cells I6:N8** as **Currency** with **2** decimal places.
e. Select **cells I5:N8**, click the **Data tab**, click **What-If Analysis** in the Data Tools group, select **Data Table** to open the Data Table dialog box, click **cell D14**, and click **OK**.
f. Widen columns as necessary to fully display the values and save the workbook.
g. Begin to create a two-variable data table by typing the data in the cells as indicated in the table below:

Cell	Data
G12	=D21
G13	4000
G14	4100
H12	35
I12	38

h. Select **cells G13:G14** and use AutoFill to fill cells through **G18**.
i. Select **cells H12:I12** and use AutoFill to fill cells through **M12**.
j. Format **cells H12:M18** as **Currency** with **0** decimal places.
k. Select **cells G12:M18**, click the **Data tab**, click **What-If Analysis** in the Data Tools group, select **Data Table** to open the Data Table dialog box, and click **cell D14**.
l. Click **Column input cell** box, click **cell D15**, and click **OK**.
m. Highlight the cell containing the breakeven amount.
n. Create a custom footer that includes your name, today's date, and your instructor's name. Save, print, and close the workbook.

...continued on Next Page

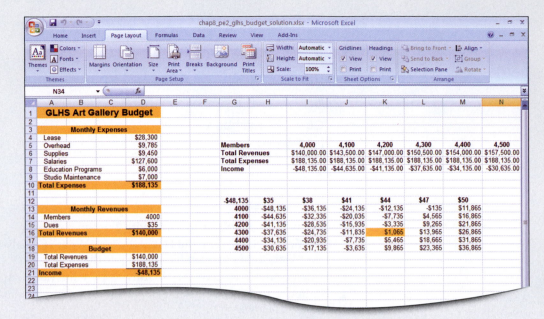

Figure 8.37   GLHS Art Gallery Budget

3 Ziegler's Posey Shoppe

Mary Ziegler, your sister-in-law, wants to take her flower store online and has asked for your help. You have investigated online Web-hosting packages and now must use Goal Seek to determine the total dollar volume of credit card sales Mary needs to get a monthly profit of $50,000. Refer to Figure 8.38 as you complete the exercise.

    a. Open the *chap8_pe3_poseyshoppe* workbook and save it as **chap8_pe3_poseyshoppe_ solution** so you can return to the original workbook if necessary.

    b. Complete the worksheet by typing the values and formulas in the cells as indicated in the table below:

Cell	Data
C4	75
C7	49.95
C9	=(1.99%*G5)+(0.25*G8)
C10	14.50
C14	=G6-C11-C4

    c. You want to increase the profit by increasing credit sales.

    d. Click **cell C14**, the cell containing the formula for the monthly profit.

    e. Click the **Data tab**, click **What-If Analysis**, and select **Goal Seek** to display the dialog box.

    f. Click in the **To value** box and type **50000**, the desired profit.

    g. Click in the **By changing cell** box, type **G5**, the cell containing the monthly credit card sales, and click **OK**.

...continued on Next Page

h. Click **OK** to accept the solution and to close the Goal Seek Status dialog box.

i. Create a custom footer that includes your name, today's date, and your instructor's name. Select **cells A1:G14** and print the selection on one page as displayed and with formulas visible. Save and close the workbook.

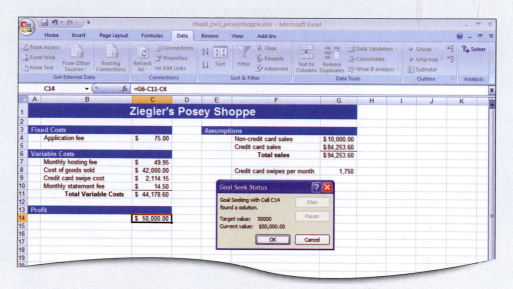

Figure 8.38 Ziegler's Posey Shoppe

4 The Janesway Coal Company

Figure 8.39 displays a five-year financial forecast for a coal mine owned by a company in which you are interested in investing. The initial investment of $20,000,000 is substantial, but so is the return on the investment. You will use Scenario Manager to construct three different scenarios to determine the chances of recouping your investment and making a profit. Figure 8.39 shows the completed summary information you will use for reference.

a. Open the *chap8_pe4_mining* workbook and save it as **chap8_pe4_mining_solution** so you can return to the original workbook if necessary.

b. You create three scenarios, each with five input variables, in **cells C23:C27**. The descriptive labels for these cells are found in the adjacent cells B23:B27. You can create all five cell names at once:

- Select **cells B23:C27**.

- Click **Create from Selection** in the Define Names group on the **Formulas tab**.

- Verify that the Left column check box in the Create Names from Selection dialog box is selected and click **OK**.

c. Click **cell H20**, click the **Name** box, type **FiveYearRateOfReturn**, and press **Enter**.

d. Work with Scenario Manager:

- Click the **Data tab**, click **What-If Analysis** in the Data Tools group, and select **Scenario Manager** to open the Scenario Manager dialog box.

- Click **Add** to open the Add Scenario dialog box.

- Type **Consensus** in the Scenario Name box.

- Click the **Changing Cells** box; if necessary delete H20.

- Select **cells C23:C27** and click **OK**. You should see the Scenario Values dialog box with the values for this scenario already entered.

...continued on Next Page

- Click **Add** to enter a **Pessimistic** scenario using the values from the summary shown in Figure 8.39.

- Add the **Optimistic** scenario in similar fashion. The Scenario Manager dialog box should still be open with three scenarios listed.

e. Click **Summary**, verify that Scenario Summary is selected, click the **Result Cells** box, click **cell H20**, and then click **OK** to create the Scenario Summary worksheet.

f. Edit the labels in the changing and result cells to avoid showing underscores or lack of spaces.

g. Group the worksheets and create a custom footer that includes your name, today's date, and your instructor's name. Save, print, and close the workbook.

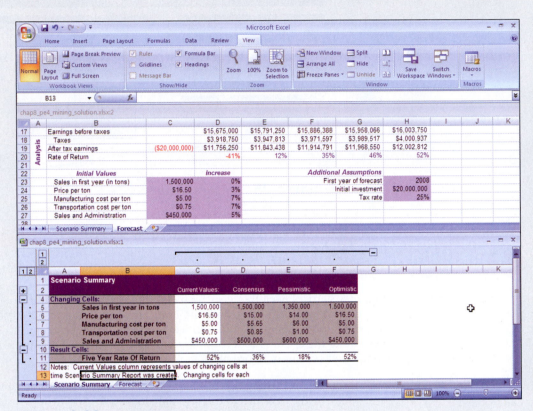

Figure 8.39 The Janesway Coal Company

Your parents want to invest in the ABC Racquet Club as a way to generate income during their retirement years. They have given you some data that are used to prepare a six-year financial forecast for the club. Your parents asked you to complete the workbook, include a report, and show possible levels of profitability over the six years. Your task is to complete the workbook and use Scenario Manager to construct consensus, optimistic, and pessimistic scenarios. Note that the club begins each year with some existing members from the previous year. It can add 100 members per year without overtaxing the facilities but has a maximum membership of 1,000. Open the partially completed workbook and refer to Figure 8.40 as you finish the workbook.

a. Open the *chap8_mid1_investment* workbook and save it as **chap8_mid1_investment_solution** so you can return to the original workbook if necessary.

b. Develop the formulas for the first year of the forecast (column C) based on the assumptions and initial conditions at the bottom of the spreadsheet. The MIN function used in **cell C5** reflects the limitation in total membership. Note that even the first year of the forecast, **cell C2**, is entered as a formula so that the forecast can be easily changed if necessary.

c. Develop the formulas for the second year based on the values in year one and the assumed rates of increase at the bottom of the worksheet. Use an appropriate combination of relative and absolute references so that these formulas can be copied to the remaining columns in the worksheet. Note there is a cap on the annual dues, and the MIN function should be used in conjunction with this formula.

d. Copy the formulas for year two, in column D, to the remaining years of the forecast, columns E through H.

e. Enter the formula to display the initial investment in **cell B17**, then click **cell C19** and enter the function to calculate the internal rate of return at the end of year one. Compute the rate of return for the remaining years.

f. Format the completed worksheet as shown in Figure 8.40. You are to display dollar amounts with the currency symbol. Use conditional formatting to display negative returns in red and positive returns in blue.

g. Select the cells that contain the variable inputs for the initial values and additional assumptions, **cells B22:C26, D22:D23**, and **H22:H26**. Use Aqua, Accent 5, Lighter 80% as the fill color.

h. Create three scenarios, each with four input variables, in **cells B23, C22, D22**, and **D23**. Select **cell B23**, and then use the Name box to give it a descriptive name. Assign descriptive names to **cells C22, D22**, and **D23**. Sample names appear in the Scenario Summary worksheet in Figure 8.40. The scenario summary also has two result cells, E19 and H19, which should be named **ReturnAfterThreeYears** and **ReturnAfterSixYears**.

i. Click **What-If Analysis** and select **Scenario Manager**. Click **Add** to display the Add Scenario dialog box. Type **Consensus** in the Scenario Name box. Click the **Changing Cells** box, and then select **cells B23, C22, D22**, and **D23**. Click **OK**. You should see the Scenario Values dialog box with the values for this scenario already entered. Click the **Add** button to enter an Optimistic scenario and take the values from the summary in Figure 8.40. Add the Pessimistic scenario in similar fashion.

j. The Scenario Manager dialog box should be open with three scenarios listed. Click **Summary**, click the **Result Cells** box, and select **cells E19** and **H19**, placing a comma between the cell references. Click **OK** to create the Scenario Summary worksheet.

k. Paste the defined Names on the Scenario Summary worksheet in **cell I2**.

...continued on Next Page

l. Delete the blank row 1 and the blank column A. Edit the labels in the changing cells and result cells to show spaces.

m. Group the worksheets and create a custom footer that includes your name, a page number, and your instructor's name. Print the workbook as displayed and with formulas visible. Save and close the workbook.

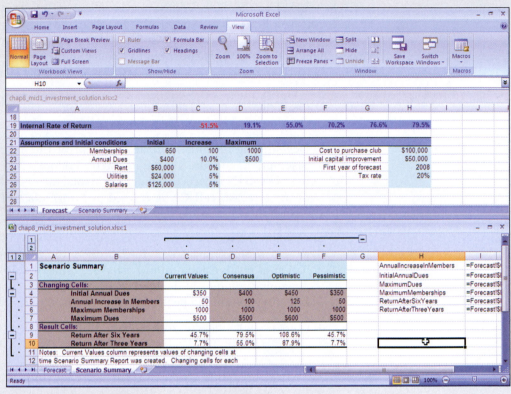

Figure 8.40 ABC Racquet Club Financial Analysis

2 Advanced degree—how much does it cost?

Now that you are ready to graduate with your bachelor's degree, you have decided that an advanced degree would be valuable to have before seeking employment in your field of study. Your task is to determine how much money you must earn in the summer before you begin school based on several scholarships you have applied for but have not yet been awarded. Use Figure 8.41 as a guide as you complete the exercise. Your task is to determine the amount needed beyond the scholarships and your parents' contribution for the first semester. You will use a one-variable data table to obtain a determination of your options. The worksheet already has suggested expenses to get you started.

a. Open the *chap8_mid2_gradschool* workbook and save it as **chap8_mid2_gradschool_ solution** so you can return to the original workbook if necessary.

b. Complete the formulas in **cells D5, D19, D22, D23**, and **D24**.

c. Enter the headings: **Scholarship, Total Sources**, and **Amount Needed** in **cells F6:F8**.

d. Enter the formulas for scholarships, total sources, and amount needed in **cells H6:H8**.

e. Enter the scholarship amounts: **$11,000, $13,000, $15,000**, and **$17,000** in **cells I6:L6**.

f. Create the data table to reflect the different amounts of scholarships by selecting **cells H6:L8** and select **Data Table** from the What-If Analysis list.

...continued on Next Page

g. Select **cell** D3 as the row input cell.

h. Format the completed worksheet matching Figure 8.41 as closely as possible. You are to display dollar amounts with the currency symbol and 0 decimal places. Use conditional formatting to display negative amounts in red.

i. Create a custom footer that includes your name, today's date, and your instructor's name. Print the worksheet as displayed and with formulas visible. Save and close the workbook.

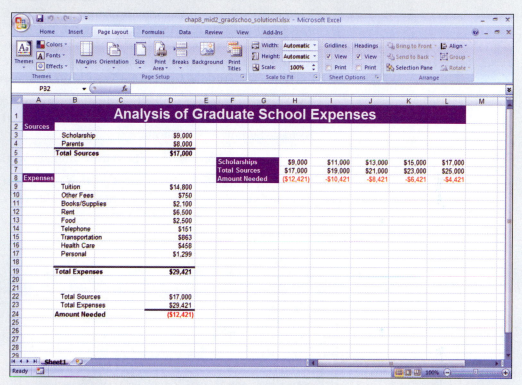

Figure 8.41 Graduate School Expenses

3 The Olde Tyme Sign Shoppe

You and your partner are the sole proprietors of the Olde Tyme Sign Shoppe, a business specializing in the creation of custom signs. The business lost $5,000 last year, and you are concerned about the future of the business. You currently produce two types of signs: ink-jet signs and vinyl signs. You and your partner believe you need to continue to offer both types of signs to move forward with the business. Your father, a successful entrepreneur, suggested you create a spreadsheet to analyze income and expenses for the year just ended, and then project these numbers for a three- or four-year period. Your assignment is to complete the forecast by creating the missing formulas, when you will see that the business earns under $3,000 in the fourth year according to the Status Quo scenario. You will create three new scenarios, one for your partner who wants to focus on ink-jet signs, one for your father who wants to control costs, and one for yourself because you want to move to a smaller location. Combine the results in a scenario summary. Use Figure 8.42 for reference as you complete your tasks.

a. Open the *chap8_mid3_signs* workbook and save it as **chap8_mid3_signs_solution** so you can return to the original workbook if necessary.

b. Enter formulas in **cells C4**, **C6**, **C8**, **C11**, **C12**, **C13**, **C15**, **C16**, **C17**, and **C19** to calculate the Income, Total Expenses, and Earnings before taxes for the year 2009. Use the percent of change values provided in the Assumption area of the worksheet.

...continued on Next Page

c. Copy the formulas through column E to see the results through 2011 maintaining the status quo.

d. Create descriptive names for **cells C23:C33**. Sample names appear in the Scenario Summary worksheet shown in Figure 8.42. The scenario summary has one result cell, E19, which should be named **FourthYearProfit**. Use the Scenario Manager to create the Status Quo scenario with three input variables in **cell ranges C22:C25, C27:C29**, and **C31:C33**.

e. Create the next three scenarios. Click **Add** to display the Add Scenario dialog box. Type **Ink-Jet Focus** in the Scenario Name box. Click **Changing Cells** box, and then select **cell ranges C22:C25, C27:C29**, and **C31:C33**. Click **OK**. You should see the Scenario Values dialog box with the values for this scenario already entered. Click the **Add** button to enter a **Move Location** scenario and take the values from the summary in Figure 8.42. Add the **Control Costs** scenario in similar fashion.

f. The Scenario Manager dialog box should be open with four scenarios listed. Click **Summary**, click the **Result Cells** box, and select **cell E19**. Click **OK** to create the Scenario Summary worksheet.

g. Paste the defined names on the Scenario Summary worksheet in **cell I2**.

h. Group the worksheets and create a custom footer that includes your name, today's date, and your instructor's name. Print the workbook as displayed and with formulas visible. Save and close the workbook.

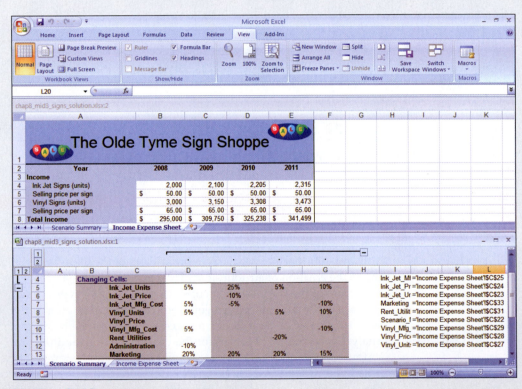

Figure 8.42 The Olde Tyme Sign Shoppe

4 Stained Glass Windows, LLC

The Stained Glass Windows Company manufactures and sells two sizes of stained glass windows: the Circle Rose window and the Rectangle Theme door window. The glass and frame are actually manufactured elsewhere and assembled by the Stained Glass Windows Company. The Circle Rose

...continued on Next Page

window takes, on average, 17 hours of labor to assemble with 9.8 feet of solder and glass equal to one full sheet. The Rectangle Theme door window requires 12.5 hours of labor, uses 20 feet of solder, and glass equal to one full sheet. Based on company history, you have determined that the Circle Rose window generates a profit of $500 per window, and the Rectangle Theme door window generates $435 per window. You want to expand the company to produce more windows but you have limited resources. Your next production period requires 3,250 labor hours, 3,290 feet of solder, and 222 total sheets of glass. Your task is to use Solver to determine how many Circle Rose and Rectangle Theme windows to build to maximize your profit. Refer to Figure 8.43 for reference as you complete the workbook.

a. Open the *chap8_mid4_glass* workbook and save it as **chap8_mid4_glass_solution** so you can return to the original workbook if necessary. Enter the required constraint data in **cells C4:D6**, as shown in Figure 8.43.

b. Enter the appropriate formula to calculate total profit in **cell D18**. Enter the formulas in **cells C10:C12**. The formulas multiply the resources for each type of window and the number of windows made. Initially the results will be zero because no windows are produced.

c. Using Solver, Set Target Cell to **cell D18**, select **MAX**, and enter **C15:D15** in By Changing Cells. Use Add to add the appropriate constraints in the Solver Parameters dialog box. Note that your allocated resources must be less than the available resources. The quantity produced must be an integer and there cannot be zero produced for either type of window.

d. Solve the problem and create an Answer report on a new sheet. Format the answer report matching Figure 8.43 as closely as possible.

e. Group the worksheets and create a custom footer that includes your name, today's date, and your instructor's name. Print the workbook as displayed and with formulas visible.

f. Save and close the workbook.

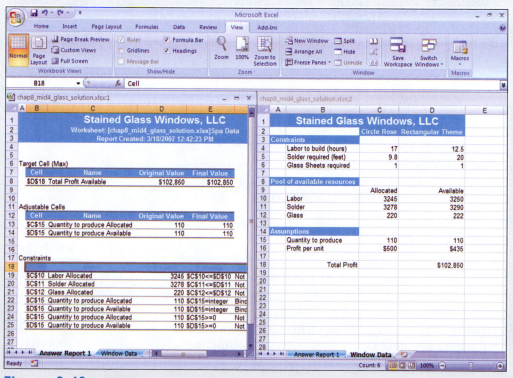

Figure 8.43 Stained Glass Windows, LLC

Capstone Exercise

You have applied to be Professor Judy's graduate assistant next year and she has asked you to demonstrate your expertise with Excel. Graduate assistants typically support a professor by teaching classes, updating grade books, and assisting in the preparation of class assignments. You must successfully complete all of the challenges in the partially completed workbook she has given you. These challenges will test your knowledge of one- and two-variable data tables, Goal Seek, Scenario Manager, and Solver. Your first challenge involves creating one- and two-variable data tables. Your second challenge is to use Goal Seek. Your third challenge uses Scenario manager and conditional formatting, and finally you will use Solver. Make sure to format the worksheets appropriately for each challenge.

Open and Save the Workbook

You must open the workbook and review each challenge as indicated by the sheet tabs.

a. Open the file *chap8_cap_challenge*.

b. Save the workbook as **chap8_cap_challenge_ solution**.

One- and Two-Variable Data Tables

You will use a function to determine a monthly payment. You will determine the difference in monthly payment based on changes in interest rate, and determine how changes in interest rate and loan amount affect the monthly payment. Select the One- and Two-Variable sheet tab.

a. Type the PMT function in **cell B6**, making sure to use the current interest rate and time periods.

b. Create a one-variable data table in **cells B10:I13** with varying rates of interest beginning with 6% and ending with 8.5%, increasing by .5%.

c. Create a two-variable data table in **cells B15:I20** with varying interest rates and loan amounts. Interest rates increase by .5% beginning with 6% and ending with 9%. Loan amounts begin at $30,000 and end at $34,000, increasing by $1,000.

d. Format appropriate cells as **Currency** with 2 decimals. Insert the title **One and Two Variable Data Tables** and format it for your worksheet.

e. Save the workbook.

Use Goal Seek

Your next challenge is on the Goal Seek tab. You will use Goal Seek to determine what the purchase price of snow removal equipment will be if the monthly payment is limited to $1,000.

a. Use the PMT function in **cell B10** to determine the monthly payment for the snow removal equipment.

b. Use Goal Seek to determine what the purchase price of the snow removal equipment will be if the monthly payment is $1,000.

c. Save the workbook.

Scenario Manager and Conditional Formatting

Select the Scenario Manager sheet tab to see your next challenge. You will use Scenario Manager to create three scenarios—Consensus, Optimistic, and Pessimistic—as well as a Scenario Summary report. A Scenario PivotTable report is also needed as part of the data analysis. Finally, you must apply conditional formatting so that earnings above $425,000 are highlighted.

a. Use Scenario Manager to create the **Consensus** scenario; the Changing cells are **E23**, **C18:C19**, and **E18**. The values for the changing cells are: **Consensus, 10000, 125,** and **0.1**.

b. Create the scenario for **Optimistic** using the same changing cells, but the values are: **Optimistic, 12,000, 150,** and **0.15**.

c. Create the scenario for **Pessimistic** using the same changing cells, but the values are: **Pessimistic, 8,000, 110,** and **0.05**.

d. Create the Scenario Summary report and the Scenario PivotTable report with the result in **cell G15**. Format the Scenario PivotTable report values as **Currency** with 2 decimal places, change the labels in **cells A1**, **A3**, and **B3**, and widen columns as needed to view the data.

e. Conditionally format **cells C15:G15** on the Scenario Manager sheet so that earnings before taxes are greater than $425,000 are highlighted.

f. Save the workbook.

Use Solver

Your final challenge is on the Solver sheet tab where you will find another worksheet for the United Manufacture of Widgets and Gadgets. This time, you must use Solver to determine what the optimum manufacturing mix among discount and premium widgets and gadgets is to maximize profits.

a. Click the **Solver** sheet tab and enter the formulas in the cells as shown in the table:

Cell	Formula
E8	=B2*C2+B3*C3+B4*C4+B5*C5
E10	=B2+B4
E12	=B3+B5
E14	=B2+B3
E16	=B4+B5
E19	=B2*D2+B3*D3+B4*D4+B5*D5-E18*E8

b. Set the target cell to cell **E19** and the changing cells to **B2:B5**.

c. Enter the following constraints:

Constraint to enter:	Click to complete:
E8<=E9	ADD
E10<=E11	ADD
E12<=E13	ADD
E14<=E15	ADD
E16<=E17	ADD

d. Select **cells B2:B5**, click the relational operators down arrow and select >=, type **0** in Constraint, and click **OK**.

e. Solve the problem and create the Answer report. Use **United Manufacture** as the title of the answer report.

f. Group the sheets and create a custom footer that includes your name, today's date, and your instructor's name. Print the workbook as displayed and with formulas visible. Save and close the workbook.

Mini Cases

Use the rubric following the case as a guide to evaluate your work, but keep in mind that your instructor may impose additional grading criteria or use a different standard to judge your work.

A Penny a Day

GENERAL CASE

What if you had a rich uncle who offered to pay you "a penny a day," and then double your salary each day for the next month? It does not sound very generous, but you will be surprised at how quickly the amount grows. Create a simple worksheet that enables you to use the Goal Seek command to answer the following questions. On what day of the month (if any) will your uncle pay you more than one million dollars? How much money will your uncle pay you on the 31st day? Your assignment is to create the worksheet using appropriate formulas, use Goal Seek, and create comments to annotate your results. Save the worksheet as **chap8_mc1_penny_solution**.

Performance Elements	Exceeds Expectations	Meets Expectations	Below Expectations
Formula	Correct formula.	Incorrect formula.	No formula.
Goal Seek	Used correctly.	Used incorrectly.	No Goal Seek.
Comments	Three comments.	One or two comments.	No comments.

Master's Degree

RESEARCH CASE

You have applied to several graduate schools to obtain a master's degree. Search the Web to locate more information about what your expenses will be when you attend a school across the country. The partially completed workbook contains suggested expense categories that you may have while in graduate school. It lists two possible sources to pay for graduate school, scholarships and your parents' contribution, but your contribution is missing. You will use the workbook *chap8_mc2_masters* with a data table to determine your contribution based on a parents' contribution of $8,000 and scholarships of $10,000, $12,000, $14,000, and $16,000. Open the *chap8_mc2_masters* workbook and use the Web to locate tuition, fees, and any other college charges for a college or university of your choice. Determine your contribution. Save the workbook as **chap8_mc2_masters_ solution**.

Performance Elements	Exceeds Expectations	Meets Expectations	Below Expectations
Research college expenses	All accurate expenses for listed college.	Most expenses accurate for listed college.	Inaccurate expenses for listed college.
One-variable data table	Correctly constructed.	Incorrectly constructed.	No data table.
Conditional formatting	Yes.	Yes.	No.

Advertising Costs

DISASTER RECOVERY

Your mother used Solver to determine a breakeven point for her advertising business, but the results are not what she expected. The parameters are incorrect in Solver, causing inaccurate results. She has asked you to review her work, identify the problems, and fix the problems. Create an Answer report that is valid for her business. The goal of the Solver is to minimize the total cost of the advertising. Open the *chap8_mc3_mom* workbook and save it as **chap8_mc3_mom_solution.** You will find four major errors with Solver. Correct the errors, then explain how the errors might have occurred and how they can be prevented. Include your explanation in the cells below the spreadsheet.

Performance Elements	Exceeds Expectations	Meets Expectations	Below Expectations
Identify four errors	Identified all four errors.	Identified three errors.	Identified two or fewer errors.
Correct four errors	Corrected all four errors.	Corrected three errors.	Corrected two or fewer errors.
Explain the error	Complete and correct explanation of each error.	Explanation is too brief to fully explain error.	No explanations.
Prevention description	Prevention description correct and practical.	Prevention description but obtuse.	No prevention description.

Collaboration and Workbook Distribution

Sharing, Distributing, and Working with Excel Options

Objectives

After you read this chapter, you will be able to:

1. Track changes **(page 561)**.
2. Enable simultaneous changes by multiple users **(page 564)**.
3. Save workbooks in different formats **(page 567)**.
4. Copy data to Word and PowerPoint **(page 571)**.
5. Finalize documents **(page 579)**.
6. Prepare workbooks for distribution **(page 581)**.
7. Understand Excel options **(page 588)**.
8. Work with the Quick Access Toolbar **(page 593)**.
9. Add add-ins **(page 595)**.

Hands-On Exercises

Exercises	Skills Covered
1. **COLLABORATE AND SHARE** (page 573) **Open:** chap9_ho1_sharing.xlsx **Save as:** chap9_ho1_sharing_solution.xlsx, chap9_ho1_sharing_solution.xls, chap9_ho1_sharing_solution.pdf, chap9_ho1_word_solution.docx, and chap9_ho1_powerpoint_solution.pptx	• Track Changes • Enable Simultaneous Changes by Multiple Users • Save a Workbook in Different Formats • Send a Workbook by E-Mail • Copy Data to Word and PowerPoint
2. **DISTRIBUTE AND SECURE WORKBOOKS** (page 584) **Open:** chap9_ho2_housing.xlsx **Save as:** chap9_ho2_housing_solution.xlsx	• Finalize a Document • Prepare a Workbook for Distribution • Add a Digital Signature and Mark a Workbook as Final
3. **CUSTOMIZE EXCEL** (page 597) **Open:** chap9_ho3_options.xlsx **Save as:** chap9_ho3_options_solution.xlsx	• Change Excel Options • Add and Remove Items from the Quick Access Toolbar • Install, Use, and Remove Add-Ins

CASE STUDY

Reckie Memorial Art Gallery

You are the curator of the Reckie Memorial Art Gallery. Currently, you are planning a traveling exhibition of selected art works to be displayed at local schools, senior citizen centers and community centers. As curator, you are responsible for completing the development and implementation of the traveling exhibition.

Your assistants have prepared some preliminary data in an Excel workbook. The responsibilities for the exhibition include the distribution of a workbook to the agencies. You will use Excel to finalize the workbook prepared by your administrative assistant. In the process, you have to work with Track Changes, insert comments as explanation for the agencies, allow simultaneous changes, save the workbook in a different format, send the workbook by e-mail, copy data to PowerPoint for your kickoff meeting, and prepare the workbook for distribution.

Case Study

Your Assignment

- Read the chapter carefully and pay close attention to information on how to use Track Changes, save in different formats (including sending the workbook via e-mail), work with the Quick Access Toolbar, finalize the workbook, and prepare the workbook for distribution.

- Allow the workbook to be updated by the various agencies receiving the exhibition. Save the workbook as a PDF, **chap9_case_gallery_solution.pdf**, so an agency that does not have Excel can view the workbook. E-mail the workbook to all your agencies. Prepare a PowerPoint presentation, including the chart you have created, for your kickoff meeting. Save the presentation as **chap9_case_gallery_powerpoint.pptx**. At all stages of your work, make sure you capture the screen and paste your results in the workbook.

- Prepare the workbook for distribution to the directors of the agencies and prepare a copy of the traveling exhibition workbook for your board of directors. Make sure you are the only one able to change the workbook data. Add workbook properties and run Compatibility Checker on the workbook. Also use Document Inspector and restrict permission to the workbook.

- Create a digital signature with an appropriate purpose statement, making sure your name is displayed in the *Signing as* label, if possible.

- Open *chap9_case_gallery*, which contains the partially completed traveling exhibition workbook and save it as **chap9_case_gallery_solution**. When you have completed the requirements, create a custom footer that includes a page number and your instructor's name. Print the workbook.

Excel Collaboration and Workbook Sharing

Collaboration in Excel has become an integral part of financial forecasting. *Collaboration* involves group editing of the same workbook. The creator of the workbook makes the final decisions after all edits and comments are made by those

(Collaboration in Excel has become an integral part of financial forecasting.)

in the reviewing group. It has become very common for one person to create an initial workbook and then share it with others who are working on a project. In the business world, with employees scattered around the world and often working from home, distributing workbooks electronically for review and editing is the norm. Workbook collaboration can take several forms. One method is that each person working on a project can make changes or suggestions in different workbooks, and then the workbooks can be merged. A second method of collaboration is to create a shared workbook that gives all collaborators access to the same file.

In this chapter, you will work with Track Changes, workbook sharing, and workbook distribution. In this section, you will track changes, share workbooks, save workbooks in a variety of formats, and work with Excel in other Office applications.

Tracking Changes

You gained some experience in collaboration when you inserted comments in worksheet cells. Although comments are helpful for posing questions or suggestions, you may also want others to make changes within the cells to see the effects of those changes. When you are collaborating, you can use the Track Changes feature to make it easier for people to work together. *Track Changes* monitors all additions, deletions, and formatting changes made in a workbook and enables you to accept or reject those changes. You should use the Track Changes feature when you want to:

- Be able to easily recognize changes made by another person who is reviewing or editing a workbook.
- Have the final decision on changes others made to a workbook.
- Share the completed workbook with others.

People in various organizations can make use of the Track Changes collaboration tool. For example, when a hospital administrator develops a budget, he or she can circulate a proposed budget. Department heads can insert rows and change budget values for their respective departments, but the changes affect the entire budget. Another example is a stock brokerage firm senior analyst who circulates a financial report, asking each broker to make changes or suggestions about the listed stocks. In these examples, the hospital administrator and the senior analyst of the stock brokerage firm have the final authority to implement or reject the changes.

Activate Track Changes

When you want to track changes made by users, you need to activate the Track Changes feature on the Review tab. It is important to remember that when Track Changes is activated, so is workbook sharing. You cannot activate the Track Changes feature without turning on workbook sharing. *Workbook sharing* occurs when a workbook is placed on a network server so that several people can simultaneously edit the workbook.

To activate Track Changes, click Track Changes in the Changes group on the Review tab. Select Highlight Changes to open the Highlight Changes dialog box (see Figure 9.1). Click the *Track changes while editing check box*, click other options you want, and click OK. Click Yes when you are prompted to save the workbook.

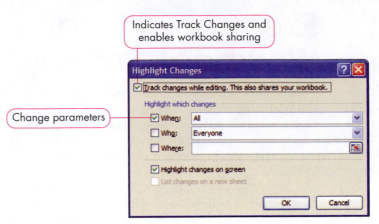

Indicates Track Changes and enables workbook sharing

Change parameters

Figure 9.1 Highlight Changes Dialog Box

When a cell is edited or changed with Track Changes on, a small blue triangle appears in the top-left corner of the cell. When you position the mouse pointer on that cell, you see a yellow message box, similar to a comment box, about the change made to that cell. The message displays the name of the person who made the change, the date and time the change was made, and the type of change made. For example, in Figure 9.2, Bill & Judith Scheeren changed the value of cell J8 from 58 to 64 at 2:30 PM on March 30, 2007. Note the yellow box is similar to a comment box, except you can edit comment boxes, and they are indicated by a red triangle in the top-right corner in a cell.

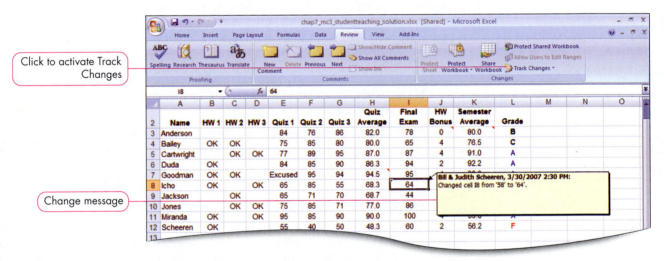

Click to activate Track Changes

Change message

Figure 9.2 Track Change Message

When Track Changes is turned on, some Excel features are disabled. Disabled commands are dimmed on the Ribbon. You cannot do the following tasks when you turn on Track Changes:

- Merge cells together or split merged cells into several cells.
- Apply, change, or remove conditional formatting.
- Format a list as a data table.
- Delete, protect, and unprotect worksheets.
- Change the tab color for worksheets.
- Insert PivotTables, tables, pictures, clip art, shapes, SmartArt, and charts.
- Insert text boxes, WordArt, signature lines, objects, and symbols.
- Insert, edit, or remove hyperlinks.

- Apply a background.
- Import or link external data, display connections, or edit links.
- Add, modify, or remove data validation rules.
- Create, edit, delete, or view scenarios.
- Group, ungroup, or subtotal tables.
- Record, edit, or assign macros.

TIP Turning Off Track Changes

If you turn off Track Changes, the workbook is no longer shared. In addition, the history of changes made is lost, and other users who are sharing the workbook will not be able to save the changes they have made.

Highlight, Review, Accept, and Reject Changes

When changes are made with Track Changes turned on, each cell changed contains a blue triangle in the top-left corner. If you close the workbook and open it again, the blue triangles indicating changes disappear, showing the need to highlight changes. You can make several different choices in the Highlight Changes dialog box to configure highlighting. Click the When drop-down arrow to select *Since I last saved*, *All*, *Not yet reviewed*, or *Since date*. Click the Who drop-down arrow to select changes made by *Everyone*, *Everyone but Me*, you, or another person. Click Where, and then select a range of cells to indicate whether changes are made to those respective cells. By default, the *Highlight changes on screen check box* is selected to ensure that changes are designated onscreen. Click *List changes on a new sheet* if you want to display a list of changes on a new worksheet within the workbook.

Reviewing, accepting, and rejecting changes are processes that enable you to review the changes others have made and decide if you want to accept or reject them. When you accept a change, the change is no longer indicated by the blue triangle; the change is accepted as part of the worksheet. When you reject a change, the suggested change is ignored, meaning the change is removed from the worksheet. For example, if someone made a change by deleting a row and you reject that change, the row is restored. In the above hospital example, the hospital administrator may reject the Radiology department's proposed budget value as being too high but might accept the Housekeeping department's budget value because it is realistic to fund the needs of that department.

The *change log* lists particular types of changes made to a workbook.

An option associated with Track Changes is the change log. The *change log* is a new sheet that lists the changes made to the workbook, such as value changes, inserted and deleted columns and rows, and some formula changes. Changes made to formulas with dependent values are not listed. The log does not track font changes or hiding/unhiding columns or rows. For example, Figure 9.3 shows a change log in a new worksheet named History. The change log shows the dates, times, new and original values, and other details about all the changes.

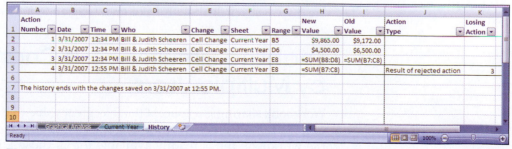

Figure 9.3 Change Log

To review changes so that you can accept or reject them:

1. Click Track Changes in the Changes group on the Review tab.
2. Click Accept/Reject Changes to show the Select Changes to Accept or Reject dialog box.
3. Indicate the changes you want to review in the When, Who, and Where lists. Excel always ignores changes that have already been accepted.
4. Click OK to open the Accept or Reject Changes dialog box, which shows the changes being reviewed (see Figure 9.4). The dialog box shows only one change at a time. Specifically, it shows who made each change on what date and at what time. It also indicates the type of change, such as changing the cell contents from one value to another.
5. Click Accept to accept an edit to make it part of the workbook, or click Reject to discard the edit and reinstate the original value. Rejecting discards the edit and removes it from the log. Although you can accept or reject all changes at one time, this action is not advisable, as you should review each change individually to determine whether the respective change is appropriate.

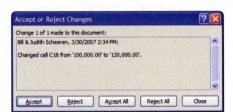

Figure 9.4 Accept or Reject Changes Dialog Box

Review, Edit, Show, and Delete Comments

Often, collaborators using the same workbook will add comments to the workbook as well as changes. Reviewing and deleting comments is a matter of moving from comment to comment and deciding whether the comment should be retained. If a comment has not been addressed or is needed to document a worksheet, you should keep it. If you made a change recommended by a comment, you can then delete the comment.

To review comments, click a cell that contains a comment. The Comments group on the Review tab (see Figure 9.2) contains actions you can take for comments. You can edit or delete a comment. When you click Previous or Next, Excel goes directly to the cell containing the previous or next comment, respectively, and displays its comment. Click Show All Comments to display all comment boxes. If all comment boxes are displayed, click Show All Comments again to hide all comment boxes.

Enabling Simultaneous Changes by Multiple Users

Workbook sharing is a concept that has great value to Excel users: It enables multiple users to modify an Excel workbook simultaneously. Workbook sharing works when the workbook file is readily available for all those who need it. For example, the shared workbook might be stored on an organization's internal network.

Major issues can arise when more than one person tries to make changes to an Excel workbook when workbook sharing is not enabled. If you want to work on an Excel workbook that someone else is currently using, the File in Use dialog box appears, warning that the file is in use and that you may open a read-only copy of the document (see Figure 9.5). You can click Read Only to view the workbook contents but not save the changes back to the original file name, you can click Notify to open the workbook in read-only mode and be notified when the workbook is no longer being used, or you can click Cancel to not open the workbook.

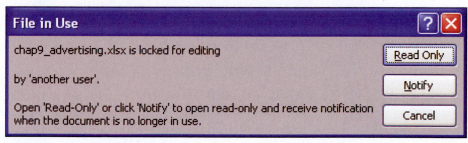

Figure 9.5 File in Use Dialog Box

The biggest problem with making changes to workbooks that are not shared arises when the original workbook does not become available in a reasonable period of time. For example, if someone else is working on a workbook late Friday afternoon and does not close the workbook when leaving for the weekend, that workbook is unavailable until that person returns and closes the workbook, perhaps on Monday. When you try to save the shared workbook, the File Changed dialog box appears. Your only choices are to discard your work or save the workbook with a different name and attempt to reconcile changes later.

Many network sharing options function only in a network environment. The following discussion describes some of the options, but you cannot implement them unless you are actually working in a networked environment and have selected the appropriate network sharing options. This applies to an organization's internal network drive or a home network. To turn on workbook sharing:

1. Click Share Workbook in the Changes group on the Review tab to display the Share Workbook dialog box.
2. Click the *Allow changes by more than one user check box*, and then click the Advanced tab (see Figure 9.6). The Advanced tab provides options for you to verify or change settings for workbook sharing.
3. In the *Update changes* section, determine how often you will be informed about changes.
4. Select one of the settings in the *Conflicting changes between users* section.
5. Click OK.

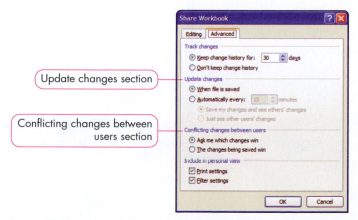

Figure 9.6 Share Workbook Dialog Box

It is possible to see who is currently working on a shared workbook by again clicking Share Workbook in the Changes group on the Review tab, and then clicking the Editing tab. You then see a list of all current users of the shared workbook. Conflicts can arise when several users are working with shared workbooks. If multiple users attempt to change the same cell at the same time, a Conflict Resolution dialog box is displayed for the second user. The change is resolved based on the settings you select in the Shared Workbook dialog box. When several people on a network are sharing a workbook and are making changes to the workbook, the last person to make changes decides which changes to accept. This becomes a problematic situation when the last person is the least knowledgeable about Excel or the particular workbook application.

Send a Workbook by E-Mail

If you do not store a workbook on a shared network drive, you can e-mail the workbook to others so that they can collaborate on the contents of the workbook. While it is possible to send an Excel workbook as an attachment to an e-mail message, it is often more convenient to send the e-mail directly from Excel, as long as Outlook is your e-mail client. Outlook must be configured before you can directly send workbooks as e-mail attachments.

To send an Excel workbook by e-mail via Outlook, open the workbook you want to send, click the Office Button, and select Send. Select E-mail to open the Outlook Send Mail window (see Figure 9.7). You will see that the workbook is automatically attached. Enter an e-mail address in the To box and type an appropriate subject. Compose a message that informs the recipient of the workbook attachment and what you want the recipient to do with the workbook. Click Send to send the e-mail message with the attached Excel workbook.

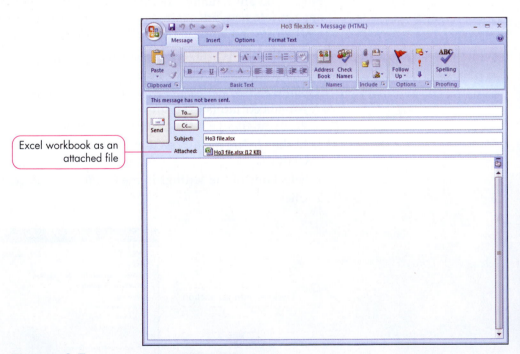

Excel workbook as an attached file

Figure 9.7 Outlook Send Mail Window

Publish to a SharePoint Server

In addition to sharing Excel workbooks by attaching them to e-mail messages, you might want to set up a SharePoint Server through a Microsoft Windows 2003 Server. The SharePoint server enables you and your colleagues to share documents, such as Excel workbooks. In addition, an administrator can set up permissions that enable different methods of accessing files for different people. For example, some people may have full rights to open and save files, whereas other people might be able to open but not save changes to files back to the SharePoint server.

The Publish option on the Office menu enables you to publish documents for other people. Use Help and explore Microsoft's Web site for additional information on how to publish Excel workbooks to a SharePoint server.

Saving Workbooks in Different Formats

When you save a workbook in Excel 2007, you save the workbook in the default 2007 file format, which ends with the .xlsx extension. Previous releases of Excel saved workbooks in the .xls extension. The primary reasons that the .xlsx file format is better than the .xls format are that the .xlsx files are smaller in size because Office 2007 uses a built-in compression feature; content images and macros are stored separately to enable increased probability of data recovery if a file becomes corrupted; and Office 2007 uses XML (eXtensible Markup Language), a standardized way of tagging data so that programs can automatically extract data from workbooks.

Although you use the default .xlsx file format when you save most Excel 2007 workbooks, you might need to save a workbook in another format. Excel enables you to save workbooks in many different formats. Some of the most popular formats are Excel 97–2003 workbook (.xls), Web page (.html), template (.xlt), text-delimited (.txt), and PDF.

Save Workbooks for Previous Versions of Excel

As Excel 2007 proliferates, more and more users will be using it and saving workbooks as xlsx files. Until this proliferation is complete, however, some users will continue to use previous versions of Excel. You can open a workbook saved in Excel 2003 format within Excel 2007 and then save it in the new .xlsx format. However, Excel 2007 workbooks are not by default backward compatible with previous versions of Excel. If you need to send a workbook to someone who is using a previous version of Excel, you can save the workbook in the old .xls format by following these steps:

1. Click the Office Button and position the mouse over Save As.
2. Select Excel 97–2003 Workbook (*.XLS) in the *Save a copy of the document* menu (see Figure 9.8).
3. Click Save in the Save As dialog box to save the workbook.

Figure 9.8 Save a Copy of the Document Menu

You are then warned that the workbook will be opened in Compatibility mode (see Figure 9.9). Compatibility mode tries to stop you from using features that are not supported in older versions of Excel. It generally is not a problem, and you may not even know you are in Compatibility mode, but Compatibility mode has a few restrictions:

- Able to use only 65,536 rows in a grid instead of 1,048,576.
- Some new functions, such as SUMIFS, are not supported.
- Some PivotTable features are not available.

Figure 9.9 Compatibility Mode Warning Message Box

If you open an Excel 2003 workbook in Excel 2007, you see the words *Compatibility Mode* on the right side of the file name in the Excel title bar.

TIP   Opening an XLSX File

Users of previous Excel versions can open an Excel 2007 file by downloading a free patch from Microsoft's Web site. The patch provides backward compatibility for collaboration with users using older versions of Microsoft Office. Search the http://office.microsoft.com Web site for the Office Compatibility Pack.

Save Workbooks as PDFs

Sometimes you may want to save an Excel workbook so those who do not have Excel can display and print the file. The most common and best way to enable non-Excel users to display and print Excel workbooks is to save the Excel file in *Portable Document Format (PDF)*, a standard file format that preserves the formatted data, including images, as originally intended in the source program. PDF files can be viewed correctly on various computer systems and platforms, even if the user does not have the source program. Saving a workbook as a PDF file saves the formatting

The *Portable Document Format (PDF)* is a universal file format that preserves a document's original data and formatting for multi-platform use.

that you used in an Excel workbook and enables non-Windows users to display and print the file because Adobe Systems Incorporated designed PDF as a universal format file.

Saving as a PDF file requires an add-in from www.microsoft.com/downloads. Search the downloads site for PDF and click the 2007 Microsoft Office add-in Microsoft Save as PDF or XPS to download that add-in. An *add-in* is an independent computer program that you can add to enhance the functionality of Excel. After you download the PDF add-in, it appears in the *Save as type* drop-down list in the Save As dialog box. You also see a Publish as PDF dialog box when you click the Office Button and select PDF from the *Save a copy of the document* menu. This brings up the Publish as PDF dialog box or the Publish as PDF or XPS dialog box. From within that dialog box, click Options to display the Options dialog box, which contains settings that control the quality of the PDF file and other options (see Figure 9.10).

An *add-in* is a computer program that is added to Excel to enhance functionality.

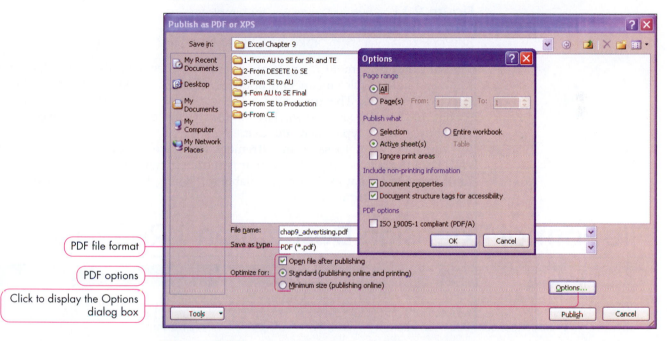

Figure 9.10 Publish as PDF or XPS Dialog Box and Options Dialog Box

Save an Excel Workbook as a Template

A *template* is a partially completed workbook that is used to create other workbooks.

Templates are partially completed workbooks that are used to create other workbooks. A template generally contains formulas and formatting or themes but no specific data. If your job involves a lot of spreadsheet analysis, you will find yourself creating and modifying the same types of spreadsheets frequently. Instead of creating a new workbook for regular data analysis, you should consider saving a workbook as a template. For example, if you need to create a monthly budget workbook, you can create a budget template and use it as a foundation to create each month's budget. You can enter values and formulas in a template and save the template as a regular workbook.

To create a template, you first create the file you want to save as a template, and then you follow these steps:

1. Click the Office Button and select Save As.
2. Select Excel Template (*.xltx) from the *Save as type* drop-down list. Your template is saved to the Templates folder (see Figure 9.11). You may select another location, if appropriate.
3. Click Save to save the workbook as a template.

Templates folder location

Template file type

Figure 9.11 Save As Dialog Box for Templates

Save Excel Workbooks in Other Formats

Several other document formats are available when you are using the Save As command in the Office menu. One option is to save a workbook as an Excel Macro-Enabled Workbook. This option saves the workbook in the XML-based and macro-enabled file format (.xlsm). If you have added macros to a spreadsheet, Excel prompts you to use this file type when you save.

You may want to save an extremely large workbook in the Excel Binary Workbook format because this format is more efficient than .xlsx. The Reference Table lists file format extensions available for saving Excel workbooks and a brief description of the formats.

File Format Extension Description | Reference

Extension	Format	Description
.xlsx	Excel Workbook	The default Office Excel 2007 XML-based file format.
.xls	Excel 97–Excel 2003 Workbook	The Excel 97–Excel 2003 binary file format.
.xml	XML Spreadsheet 2003	XML spreadsheet 2003 file format.
.xltx	Template	The default Office Excel 2007 file format for an Excel template.
.xslm	Excel Workbook (code)	The Office Excel 2007 XML-based and macro-enabled file format. Stores VBA macro code.
.xltxm	Template (code)	The Office Excel 2007 macro-enabled file format for an Excel template. Stores VBA macro code.
.xlam	Excel Add-In	The Office Excel 2007 XML-based and macro-enabled Add-In, a supplemental program that is designed to run additional code. Supports the use of VBA projects.
.csv	CSV (comma delimited)	Saves a workbook as a comma-delimited text file for use on another Windows operating system and ensures that tab characters, line breaks, and other characters are interpreted correctly. Saves only the active sheet.
.pdf	Portable Document Format	A fixed-layout file format that preserves document formatting and enables file sharing. The PDF format ensures that when the file is viewed online or printed, it retains exactly the format intended and that data in the file cannot be easily changed.
.html	Web Page and Single File Web Page	Web Page file formats (.htm, .html) and Single File Web Page file formats (.mht, .mhtml) can be used for exporting Excel data that are viewed in a Web browser.

Copying Data to Word and PowerPoint

Microsoft Office 2007 is designed so that each application serves a specific purpose. For example, Excel is used for quantitative analysis, and Word is used to create word processing documents. Although each application has its own purpose, sometimes you need data created in another program. You might want to include part of an Excel worksheet in a Word document or in a PowerPoint slide show. For example, you might need to create a budget, write a status report about the budget, and prepare a presentation to discuss the budget at a meeting. You would use Word to compose the status report, Excel to create the budget, and PowerPoint to create the presentation. Although you could create a budget table directly in Word or PowerPoint, you know that Excel is more robust for quantitative analysis. After creating the budget in Excel, you can copy the spreadsheet data into the status report in Word and into the PowerPoint slide show.

Embedding is the process of inserting an object or data into a file.

Embedding is the process of inserting an object or data from a source program into a destination program; it does not create a link to the original source data. If you make changes in the embedded object in Word, the changes are *not* made in the original Excel workbook. To embed an Excel workbook in Word:

1. Select and copy the cell range in the Excel workbook.
2. Open Microsoft Word.
3. Click the Paste down arrow in the Clipboard group on the Home tab and select Paste Special.
4. Select the Paste option, choose Microsoft Office Excel Worksheet Object in the Paste Special dialog box (see Figure 9.12), and click OK.

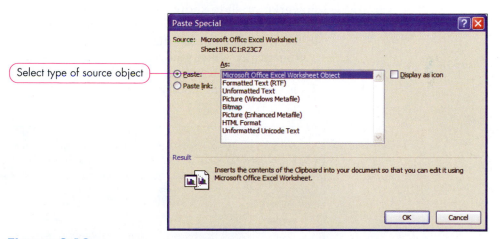

Figure 9.12 Paste Special Dialog Box

You can also copy and paste Excel data into PowerPoint. When you paste a range of Excel data in PowerPoint, the data are pasted as text. The formulas are no longer formulas; they are converted to values. However, you can embed a worksheet into a PowerPoint presentation and preserve the formulas. To do this, display the Paste Special dialog box and select Microsoft Office Excel Worksheet Object. The data are embedded as an object. You can double-click the object and edit data and formulas as you normally do in Excel. Figure 9.13 shows Excel data embedded in a PowerPoint slide.

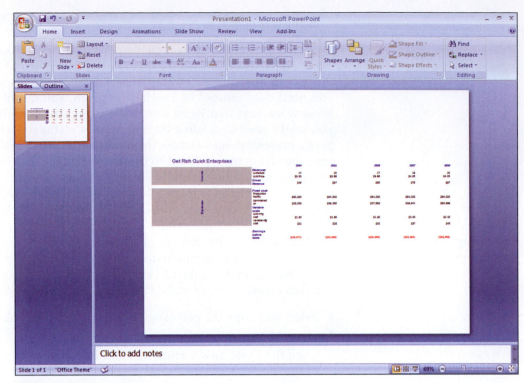

Figure 9.13 Excel Data Pasted into PowerPoint

In addition to copying worksheet data, you can copy an Excel chart into a PowerPoint slide show. To do this, select and copy your chart in Excel. Open PowerPoint and click Paste in the Clipboard group on the Home tab. You do not have to use the Paste Special dialog box to paste the chart; it is embedded as an object automatically when you paste it. Figure 9.14 shows a chart created in Excel and pasted onto a PowerPoint slide. After you embed the chart, you can use the Chart Tools Design tab to modify it within PowerPoint.

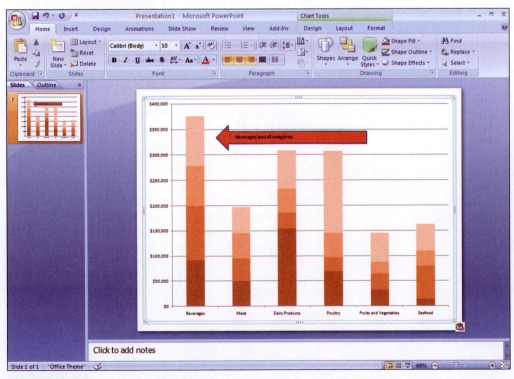

Figure 9.14 An Excel Chart in PowerPoint

Hands-On Exercises

1 | Collaborate and Share

Skills covered: 1. Track Changes **2.** Enable Simultaneous Changes by Multiple Users **3.** Save a Workbook in Different Formats **4.** Send a Workbook by E-Mail **5.** Copy Data to Word and PowerPoint

Step 1 Track Changes

Refer to Figure 9.15 as you complete Step 1.

a. Open the *chap9_ho1_sharing* workbook and save it as **chap9_ho1_sharing_solution** so you can return to the original workbook if necessary.

> **TROUBLESHOOTING:** Make sure you open the workbook from a location in which you can make changes. If you open the workbook from a shared school network drive or an FTP site, you may not be able to use the Track Changes feature.

b. Click the **Review tab**, click **Track Changes** in the Changes group, and select **Highlight Changes** to open the Highlight Changes dialog box.

c. Check **Track changes while editing**, if it is not already selected, remove any checks from the *Highlight which changes* section, and click **OK**.

You activated Track Changes by opening the dialog box and selected the parameters you want to use. You are now ready to accept or reject changes made to the workbook.

d. Click the **Track Changes down arrow** in the Changes group and select **Accept/ Reject Changes** to open the Select Changes to Accept or Reject dialog box.

e. Verify that the **When check box** is the only check box selected and click **OK** to open the Accept or Reject Changes dialog box.

The default When option is *Not yet reviewed*, which means that only those changes that have not been reviewed will be displayed. The Accept or Reject Changes dialog box indicates the first change, *Change 1 of 3 made to this document*. It shows the name of the person who made the change and the date and time the change was made. It also shows that cell B5 was changed from $4,500.00 to $9,865.00.

f. Click **Accept**.

When you accept the change, Excel keeps the changed value in cell B5 and displays the next change that was tracked. The second change was changing the value of cell D6 from $9,865.00 to $4,500.00.

g. Click **Accept** to accept the change in cell D6.

Your acceptance of the change made to cell D6 automatically moves you to the next change for your consideration. The third change indicates a formula change from =SUM(E3:E7) to =SUM(B3:F7). The original function is correct, not the change, so you should not accept that change.

h. Click **Reject** to reject the change made to the formula in cell E8.

You rejected the change in cell E8, and the formula was returned to the original.

i. Click **cell E4** and review the comment.

You defer action on this comment for now.

j. Click **Next** twice in the Comments group on the Review tab to see the comment in cell B7, and then click **Delete** in the Comments group after reviewing the second comment.

k. Save the workbook.

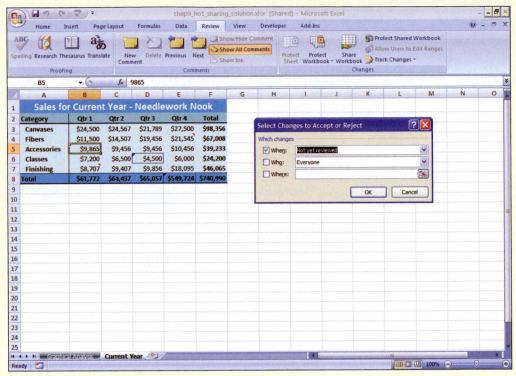

Figure 9.15 Accept or Reject Changes Dialog Box

Step 2

Enable Simultaneous Changes by Multiple Users

Refer to Figure 9.16 as you complete Step 2.

a. Click **Share Workbook** in the Changes group on the Review tab to open the Share Workbook dialog box.

b. Click the **Allow changes by more than one user at the same time check box**, if it is not already selected, and click the **Advanced tab**.

The Advanced tab enables you to verify or change settings for workbook sharing.

> **TROUBLESHOOTING:** If your computer is not part of a network, you will not see more than one user, yourself, in the *Who has the workbook open now* section on the Editing tab in the Share Workbook dialog box.

c. Verify that **Keep change history for 30 days** is selected in the *Track changes* section.

d. Verify that **When file is saved** is selected in the *Update changes* section.

e. Verify that **Ask me which changes win** is selected in the *Conflicting changes between users* section.

f. Verify that both check boxes are selected in the *Include in personal view* section.

g. Click **OK**.

h. Save the workbook.

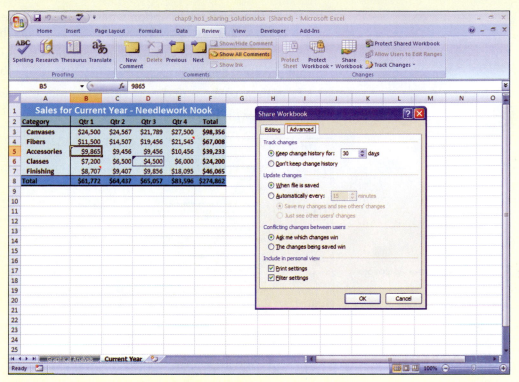

Figure 9.16 Share Workbook Dialog Box Advanced Tab

Step 3
Save a Workbook in Different Formats

Refer to Figures 9.17 and 9.18 as you complete Step 3.

a. Click the **Office Button**, position the mouse pointer over **Save As**, and select **Excel 97–2003 Workbook**.

You will save the workbook in a previous version of Excel so that those using an earlier version can open your workbook. Note the file extension is .xls instead of .xlsx.

b. Click **Save**, click **Continue** to accept the Microsoft Office Excel–Compatibility Checker dialog box summary, and click **OK** to close and reopen the workbook in Compatibility Mode.

If your chart contains a SmartArt graphic, you will lose it because it is not compatible with the earlier version of Excel. The title bar then displays chap9_ho1_sharing_solution.xls [Shared] [Compatibility Mode].

c. Save and close the shared *chap9_ho1_sharing_solution.xls* workbook.

d. Open the Office 2007 *chap9_ho1_sharing_solution* workbook again.

You can use the Open dialog box to look at the Type column to distinguish between different versions and file formats for Excel workbooks.

e. Click **Save As** in the Office menu to open the Save As dialog box.

TROUBLESHOOTING: You will not be able to complete this step if the PDF converter is not installed on your system. Check with your instructor to see if you must download and install the PDF converter before proceeding.

f. Click the **Save as type drop-down arrow** and select **PDF (*.pdf)**.

g. Click **Options** and verify that **All** is selected in the *Page range* section, **Entire workbook** is selected in the *Publish what* section, and both check boxes are checked in the *Include non-printing information* section. Click **OK**.

h. Verify that the **Save in** option will save the PDF file where you usually save your files, and click **Save** to save the file as **chap9_ho1_sharing_solution.pdf**.

You saved the entire workbook in Portable Document File (PDF) format. If you have Adobe Reader on your system, you can view both pages of your workbook.

i. Print the workbook and close Adobe Reader if necessary.

j. Save the workbook in Excel.

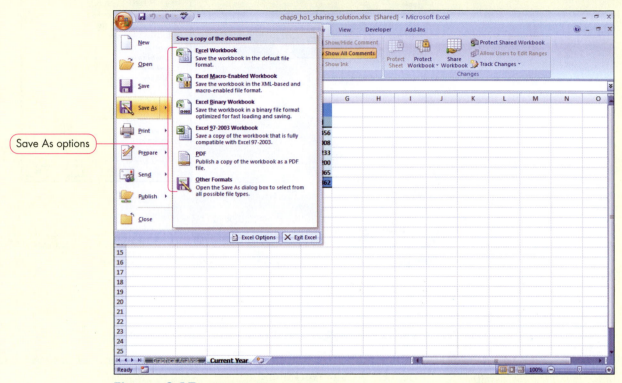

Figure 9.17 Save As File Format List

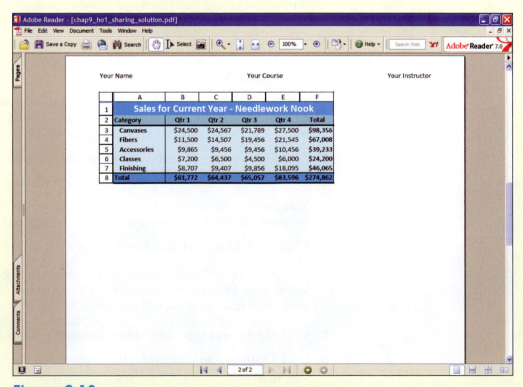

Figure 9.18 Excel Workbook Saved in PDF Format

Refer to Figure 9.19 as you complete Step 4.

a. Click the **Office Button**, position the mouse pointer over **Send**, and click **E-mail**.

> **TROUBLESHOOTING:** If Outlook is not configured on your PC, consult your instructor before proceeding.

b. Type your instructor's e-mail address in the To box and type **Here is the file you asked for** in the body area.

c. Verify that *chap9_ho1_sharing_solution.xlsx* is listed in the Attached box.

d. Click **Send**.

You sent your workbook to your instructor as an attached file.

e. Click **Share Workbook** in the Changes group on the Review tab to open the Share Workbook dialog box.

f. Click the **Editing tab** in the dialog box, click the **Allow changes by more than one user at the same time check box** to deselect this option, and click **OK**.

You began the process of removing the sharing from the workbook for the next step because charting is disabled when a workbook is shared.

g. Click **Yes** to verify removing the workbook from shared use.

h. Save the workbook.

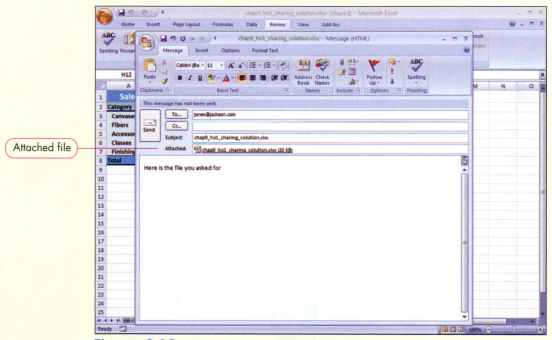

Attached file

Figure 9.19 Workbook as E-Mail Attachment

Refer to Figure 9.20 as you complete Step 5.

a. Select **cells A1:F8**.

b. Click the **Home tab** and click **Copy** in the Clipboard group.

c. Open a new document in Microsoft Word, type your name, and press **Enter**.

d. Click the **Paste down arrow** in the Clipboard group and select **Paste Special**.

The Paste Special dialog box opens so that you can select the appropriate method for pasting the Excel data into the Word document.

e. Click **Microsoft Office Excel Worksheet Object** and click **OK**.

You copied and pasted a selection from your workbook into a Word document. The data you pasted into Word are not dynamic. You cannot see any changes made to the workbook in the Word document, nor can you see any changes made to the Word document in your workbook.

f. Print and save the Word document as **chap9_ho1_word_solution** and close Word.

g. Click the **Graphical Analysis tab** to make your chart sheet active.

The Graphical Analysis tab contains a chart you want to include in a PowerPoint slide show.

h. Click the chart to make it active and click **Copy** in the Clipboard group.

i. Open Microsoft PowerPoint, then type the title **Needlework Nook Sales Chart** in the *Click to add title* placeholder.

j. Click and type your name in the *Click to add subtitle* placeholder.

k. Click **New Slide** in the Slides group, then type the title **Quarterly Sales** in the *Click to add title* placeholder.

l. Click the *Click to add text placeholder* and click **Paste** in the Clipboard group.

You created an opening slide, and then pasted your chart into the second slide in the presentation.

TROUBLESHOOTING: Make sure you click the *Click to add text* placeholder. If you click the slide itself and paste the chart, it will paste on the entire slide, covering the title as well. If this happens, click Undo and try again.

m. Print and save the PowerPoint presentation as **chap9_ho1_powerpoint_solution** and close Microsoft PowerPoint.

The data you pasted into PowerPoint are not dynamic. You cannot see any changes made to the workbook in the presentation, nor can you see any changes made to the presentation in your workbook.

n. Save the workbook and close Excel if you are not continuing to the next hands-on exercise.

Figure 9.20 Excel Chart Pasted into PowerPoint Slide

Workbook Distribution

(... protecting a workbook from viruses and other actions that can damage the integrity of a workbook.)

At this point, you may think you have completed all the tasks associated with the preparation of a workbook. While you have done much work, some steps involved in finalizing documents and preparing workbooks for distribution are yet to be covered. When you are preparing workbooks to be distributed to other users, either for update or for comment only, it is important that you do it in such a way that other users can perform the operation you want them to be able to while at the same time protecting a workbook from viruses and other actions that can damage the integrity of a workbook. The hospital administrator in the earlier example would submit the final budget to the department managers for comment only. As another example of workbook distribution, a national sales manager might send a product sales workbook to regional managers for updating.

In this section, you will examine steps that are used to finalize documents. Specifically, you will learn how to create document properties and check the compatibility of a workbook's contents. Next, you will take steps to prepare the workbook for distribution. Specifically, you will learn how to inspect documents for items to remove prior to distributing a workbook to others.

Finalizing Documents

After you finalize a workbook, the figures presented cannot be changed; the workbook is read only. Two general areas involved in finalizing Excel workbooks or documents are setting the properties of the document and running Compatibility Checker to determine what properties of Excel will be available when you save the document in an older version of Excel. *Compatibility Checker* is an operation to examine, locate, and find solutions to compatibility issues between Excel 2007 and earlier versions.

Compatibility Checker is an operation to examine, locate, and find solutions to compatibility issues between Excel 2007 and earlier versions.

View and Edit Workbook Properties

A valuable source of documentation for Excel workbooks is setting workbook properties. A *property* is a collection of metadata associated with a file. In Excel, properties include general statistics such as file name, location, size, and date and time created or modified. Properties further include optional summary information, such as title, subject, author, manager, company, category, keywords, comments, and hyperlink base for the workbook. When a workbook contains multiple worksheets, they are listed as contents in the Properties box. You can also customize workbook properties by choosing from a list or creating your own properties.

A **property** is a collection of metadata associated with a file.

When you click the Office Button, select Prepare, and then select Properties, a panel opens below the Ribbon (see Figure 9.21). The panel contains some data about the document, such as its author and title. You can edit the data here, or you can add, change, or delete data in the Properties dialog box. You can open the Properties dialog box, shown in Figure 9.22, by clicking the Document Properties drop-down arrow and selecting Advanced Properties. Table 9.1 summarizes the contents of the five tabs in the Properties dialog box. Document properties are a valuable part of the documentation process and are often used in forensic examination of documents.

Document Properties panel

Figure 9.21 Document Properties

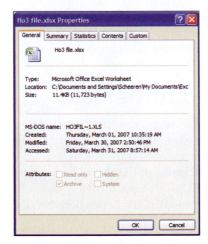

Figure 9.22 File Properties Dialog Box

Table 9.1 Properties Dialog Box Tabs

Tab	Contents
General	Shows general information about the file, such as name, size, location, and date created. This information cannot be changed.
Summary	Contains nine fields that can be modified. Some of the fields are duplicated from the Properties panel.
Statistics	Shows more unchangeable information about the file.
Contents	Shows the sheet names and named ranges in the workbook.
Custom	Stores a range of information about the file.

Run Compatibility Checker

Compatibility Checker enables you to check for features that are not supported in earlier versions of Excel. This is especially important when others who will be using a workbook do not have Excel 2007. When you click the Office Button, select Prepare, and then select Run Compatibility Checker, the Microsoft Office Excel–Compatibility Checker dialog box opens (see Figure 9.23). Each new version of Excel added features not available in the previous versions. When you use a feature such as SmartArt in Excel 2007 and save the workbook as a previous version, your previously editable SmartArt graphic is no longer editable. If you used new functions such as SUMIFS, the old Excel version will display errors instead of values.

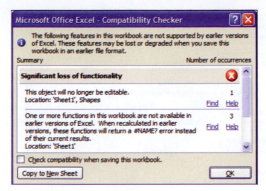

Figure 9.23 Compatibility Checker Dialog Box

The Summary section lists all the compatibility issues found and includes features of Excel 2007 that are not supported in earlier versions of Excel. Examples are Smart Art diagrams that are converted to pictures, table formatting is lost, some new functions are not supported, and charts may appear without drawing objects or without color schemes.

To display the Compatibility Checker results in a more readable fashion, click Copy to New Sheet. To continue to check compatibility, select the *Check Compatibility when saving this workbook* check box.

Preparing Workbooks for Distribution

Often, workbooks are distributed to other individuals within or outside an organization. For example, budget workbooks may be distributed by an Accounting office to various cost center departments for review. As another example, in school districts, teachers submit grade books to the principal for review. Before you release your documents for distribution to others, you must perform a few tasks. You should protect your workbook from change, protect your formulas from change, and check for compatibility issues with earlier versions of Excel. These and other workbook distribution issues are grouped in the Prepare option of the Office menu.

Use Document Inspector

The ***Document Inspector*** checks Excel files for hidden data and personal information.

The ***Document Inspector***, a new feature introduced in Excel 2007, checks Excel files for hidden data and personal information that may be contained in a file. This tool finds information that you may not want to share with others. For example, you might not want your name associated with the workbook you created and want the Document Inspector to remove it. You should exercise care when removing items identified by the Document Inspector because they may be, unbeknownst to you, crucial to the workbook. Always make a backup copy of a workbook prior to running the Document Inspector.

To open the Document Inspector (see Figure 9.24), open the Office menu, select Prepare, and select Inspect Document. If you have not recently saved your workbook, Excel will prompt you to save it. Click the Inspect button and Excel will display the results of the inspection.

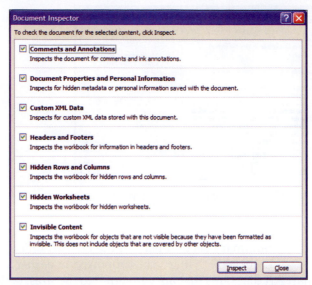

Figure 9.24 Document Inspector Dialog Box

Restrict Permission

The Restrict Permission feature enables you to grant people access to a workbook while restricting their ability to print, copy, or edit the workbook. The underlying "principle of least privilege" gives the user just enough power to accomplish the tasks required—but no more. This principle, first used in software design, also applies to workbook sharing. Unless you are working on a large network, this feature is generally not used. If you are on a network and want to restrict users' rights, you must have the Windows Rights Management client and Information Rights Management (IRM) installed on your computer. You will restrict users from changing values, formulas, or labels because changing any data will change results. Those who use your workbook must also be authorized to print a workbook. Your workbook may contain sensitive, proprietary, or personal data and should not be printed, copied, or edited. The Restrict Permission feature is not available unless you are connected to a server.

Add a Digital Signature

A *digital signature* is an electronic notation in a document to authenticate the contents.

A digital signature can be likened to a signature on a paper document. A *digital signature* is an electronic notation in a document to authenticate the contents. You use a digital signature to ensure that a workbook is authentic and that the content has not been changed since the signature was added. Your signature is valid until you make changes and save the file again. For example, a professor would want to ensure that grades are valid and have not been changed since the grade book was completed. The professor's signature would authenticate the grades.

To digitally sign a workbook, you must obtain a certificate from a certified authority who can verify your signature. If you review the links at the Microsoft Office Marketplace Web site, you can choose a signature service. This is similar to having your signature notarized. You can create your own digital ID to ensure that no one has tampered with your workbooks, but others will not be able to verify the signature's authenticity. Digital signatures may be either visible or invisible.

Mark a Workbook as Final

Excel enables you to mark a document as final. This makes two changes to the workbook:

- The workbook becomes read-only and cannot be saved with the same name.
- The workbook becomes view-only, so nothing can be changed. Most Ribbon commands are disabled.

To make a workbook final, click the Office Button, click Prepare, and then select Mark As Final. A warning box appears, indicating that the file will be saved and marked as final, as shown in Figure 9.25. Marking a workbook as final prohibits anyone from changing anything.

Figure 9.25 Mark As Final Verification Box

Hands-On Exercises

2 | Distribute and Secure Workbooks

Skills covered: 1. Finalize a Document **2.** Prepare a Workbook for Distribution **3.** Add a Digital Signature and Mark a Workbook as Final

Step 1
Finalize a Document

Refer to Figure 9.26 as you complete Step 1.

a. Open the *chap9_ho2_housing* workbook and save it as **chap9_ho2_housing_solution** so you can return to the original workbook if necessary.

b. Click the **Office Button**, select **Prepare**, and select **Properties** to display the Document Properties panel.

c. Type your name in the Author text box in the Document Properties panel.

d. Type **Housing**, **Forest College**, and **Revenue** in the Keywords text in the Document Properties panel.

   You entered your name and three keywords as document properties. When you save the workbook, these become a permanent part of the file. They are used to quickly locate the document later.

e. Click the **Document Properties drop-down arrow** and select **Advanced Properties** to open the Properties dialog box.

   You are able to review more detailed properties in the Properties dialog box as well as make more changes.

f. Verify that the Summary tab is active, click in the **Company** box, and type **Forest College**.

g. Click in the **Comments** box and type **This is a workbook for this year's and next year's housing costs.**

h. Click the **Custom tab**, click **Checked by**, type your name in the Value box, and click **Add**.

i. Click **Date completed**, type **Today's Date** in the Value box, click **Add**, and click **OK**.

   You added two more properties to your document. These will serve as more documentation for the workbook.

j. Press and hold **Alt** while pressing **PrtScn**, click **cell A17**, click **Paste**, and resize the image so the bottom boundary is row 28.

   You electronically captured the screen and pasted the image into your worksheet. The image represents documentation for your instructor.

k. Click the **Office Button** and click **Run Compatibility Checker** from the Prepare menu to display the Microsoft Office Excel–Compatibility Checker dialog box.

l. Click **Copy to New Sheet** to create a compatibility report on a new worksheet.

m. Click the **This Year tab**, close the Document Properties panel, and save the workbook.

   You created a compatibility report that describes features lost or not supported by earlier versions of Excel.

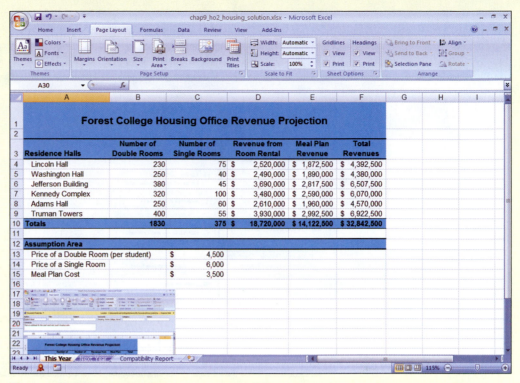

Figure 9.26 Worksheet After Compatibility Checker and Document Properties Used

---

Step 2
Prepare a Workbook for Distribution

Refer to Figure 9.27 as you complete Step 2.

a. Click the **Office Button**, select **Prepare**, and select **Inspect Document** to display the Document Inspector dialog box.

b. Click **Inspect**.

The Document Inspector results show that there are document properties, personal information, and headers and footers (see Figure 9.27).

c. Click **Remove All** for Header and Footers.

You removed the custom footer from your workbook but kept all document properties associated with the workbook.

d. Press and hold **Alt** while pressing **PrtScn**, and then click **Close** to close the Document Inspector dialog box.

e. Click **cell D17**, click **Paste**, and resize the image so the bottom boundary is row 28.

f. Click the **Office Button**, select **Prepare**, and select **Restrict Permission**. Then select **Restricted Access** to display the Microsoft Office Information Rights Management (IRM) dialog box.

g. Click **No** to close the dialog box unless your instructor indicates otherwise.

TROUBLESHOOTING: Before you can proceed, you must install the extra-cost Windows Rights Management client. You must also have a .NET Passport account. Check with your instructor to see if you should download the software and install it on your computer.

h. Save the workbook.

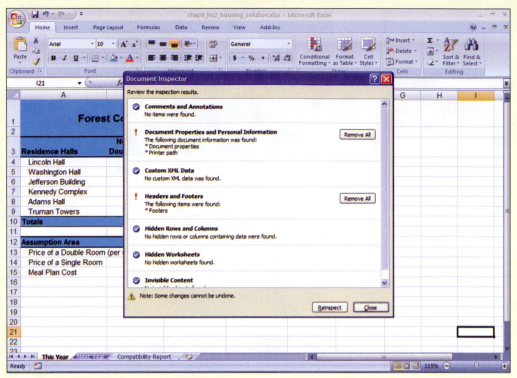

Figure 9.27 Document Inspector Dialog Box

<table>
<tr><td rowspan="2">**Step 3**
Add a Digital Signature and Mark a Workbook as Final</td></tr>
</table>

Step 3
Add a Digital Signature and Mark a Workbook as Final

Refer to Figure 9.28 as you complete Step 3.

a. Click the **Office Button**, select **Prepare**, and select **Add a Digital Signature** to display the Microsoft Office Excel dialog box for digital signatures. Click **OK** to open the Get a Digital ID dialog box.

> **TROUBLESHOOTING:** A digital ID is associated with the computer on which it was created. Check with your instructor before proceeding.

b. Click **Create your own digital ID** and click **OK** to open the Create a Digital ID dialog box.

c. Type your name in the Name text box.

d. Type your e-mail address in the E-mail address text box.

e. Type the name of your college in the Organization text box.

f. Type the city and state where your college is located in the Location text box.

g. Click **Create** to open the Sign dialog box.

h. Type **Validation** in the Purpose for signing this document dialog box and click **Sign**.

i. Click **OK** in the Signature Confirmation dialog box.

You created a digital signature that is saved with your workbook, but your signature will disappear when the workbook is edited. A Signatures pane opens in the workbook window, as shown in Figure 9.28.

> **TROUBLESHOOTING:** Note that this is not a valid digital signature until you register it with a Certificate Authority. The signature is a digital ID and is associated with the computer on which it was created.

j. Click the **Office Button** and click **Mark as Final** from the Prepare menu to open the Microsoft Office Excel information box.

The information box presents a warning indicating that marking your workbook as final invalidates the signatures in the workbook.

k. Click **Yes** to mark the workbook as final.

l. Click **OK** after reading the Microsoft Office Excel message about finalizing the document.

m. Save the workbook and note that the Signature pane now indicates that your signature is invalid.

n. Close the workbook and exit Excel if you are not going to continue on at this time.

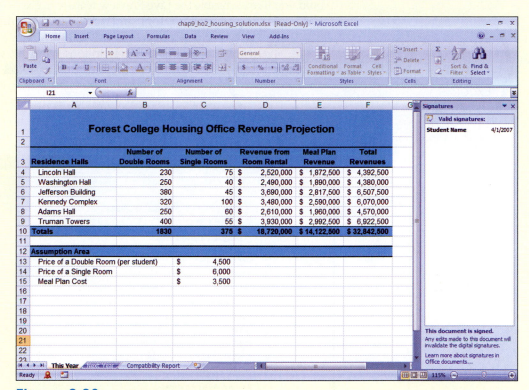

Figure 9.28 Digital Signatures

Excel Options and Add-Ins

Rather than requiring you to go to several different places in the Excel interface to change defaults or to set Excel options, Microsoft centralized and simplified such things as Excel options and the Quick Access Toolbar. In addition, Excel continues to provide the capability to work with add-ins, or something that is added to Excel to give it added functionality.

In this section, you will review some of the Excel options for changing default settings. You will also customize the Quick Access Toolbar and work with add-ins.

Understanding Excel Options

Would you like to disable the Live Preview feature in Excel? Would you like to change the default font and font size? Would you like to change your AutoCorrect options? You can change these and other standard settings in the Excel Options window, which you access by clicking the Office Button and clicking Excel Options. The Excel Options dialog box (see Figure 9.29) is a centralized area where you can change the look, behavior, and calculation options in Excel.

> Excel Optionsis . . . a centralized area where you can change the look, behavior, and calculation options in Excel.

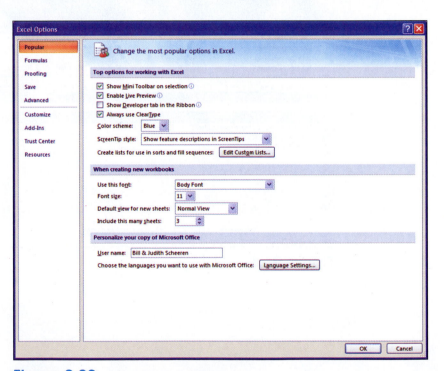

Figure 9.29 Excel Options Window

Set Excel Defaults

The first time you open Excel, you see and work with Excel's preset look, behavior, and calculation options. These are also referred to as the Excel defaults. Nearly everyone will customize, or change, these default settings to meet their own individual needs or the needs of their organization. Every time you go into the Excel Options dialog box and change something, you are changing the Excel defaults. It should be noted that if you are using Excel in a computer lab or other academic environment, you may not be able to change the Excel defaults, or, if you can change them, they may return to the default settings when you log off or shut down the computer.

Customize with Excel Options

Instead of the familiar tabs, when you open the Excel Options window, you see nine categories. When you choose one of the categories, the settings you can change appear in the right portion of the window. The following text summarizes the Excel Options window settings and includes a figure for each of the nine categories.

The Popular category is the category most often used and is displayed when you open Excel Options. It contains the most commonly used settings, such as color schemes, custom fonts, default fonts, and the number of sheets in a new workbook. See Figure 9.29 for a more complete view of the Popular category options.

The Formulas category (see Figure 9.30) contains options related to formulas, including control of calculations, error checking rules, and formula settings. You would work with these settings, for example, if you have a very large worksheet and want to change the calculation setting to manual to recalculate after all data entry.

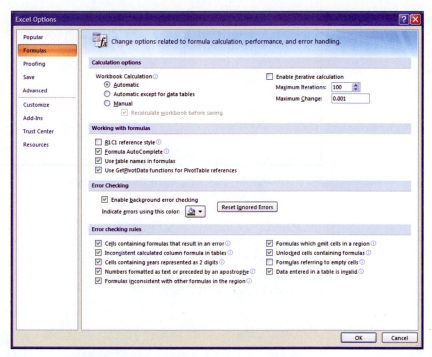

Figure 9.30 Excel Options Formulas Category

The Proofing category (see Figure 9.31) contains the spell check options and a link to the AutoCorrect dialog box. Some people find the AutoCorrect feature annoying and disable it. Others add frequently used words to the AutoCorrect feature.

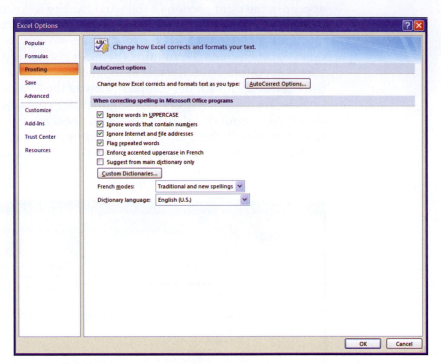

Figure 9.31 Excel Options Proofing Category

The Save category (see Figure 9.32) shows methods for saving, AutoRecover settings, legacy colors, and Web server options. In a networked organization, you might be required to save all workbooks in a particular location on the corporate server. Maybe you want to always save your files in the .xls format. You make both of these types of changes in the Save category.

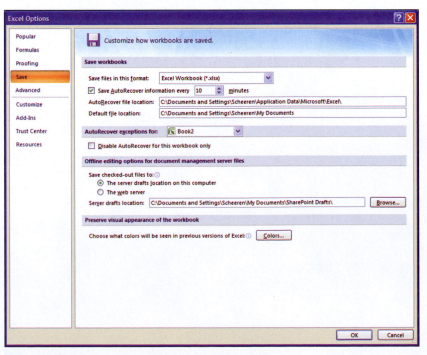

Figure 9.32 Excel Options Save Category

The Advanced category (see Figure 9.33) contains a wide variety of Excel options, including editing, display, and general options. It is a good idea to use Excel for some time before making any changes in the Advanced category as these settings affect the way you use the interface. You can use this category to change the display of the worksheet, the display of images, and the basics of Excel.

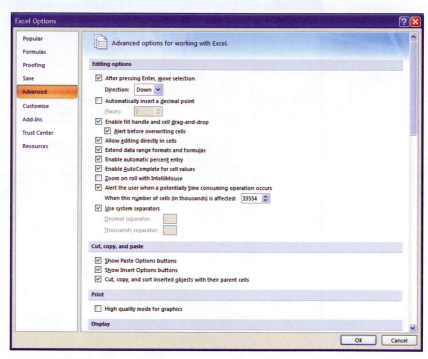

Figure 9.33 Excel Options Advanced Category

The Customize category (see Figure 9.34) contains icons used to customize the Quick Access Toolbar, which is discussed more thoroughly in the next section. You can add frequently used commands to the Quick Access Toolbar to save yourself some time.

Figure 9.34 Excel Options Customize Category

The Add-Ins category (see Figure 9.35) shows the available and installed add-ins and smart tags. New add-ins can be installed using the button at the bottom of this category. Add-ins are programs created by Microsoft and third-party software companies to enhance or extend the functionality of Excel.

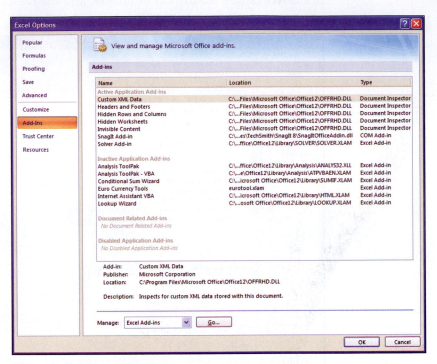

Figure 9.35 Excel Options Add-Ins Category

The Trust Center category (see Figure 9.36) links to information about protecting privacy and implementing security, and it links to the Microsoft Trust Center.

The Resources category (see Figure 9.37) links to Office updates, diagnostics, and other information. It is worth spending some time reviewing each of the links to learn more about Excel.

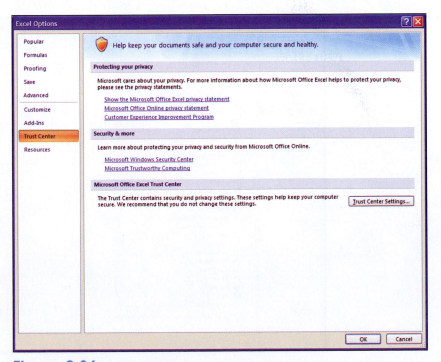

Figure 9.36 Excel Options Trust Center Category

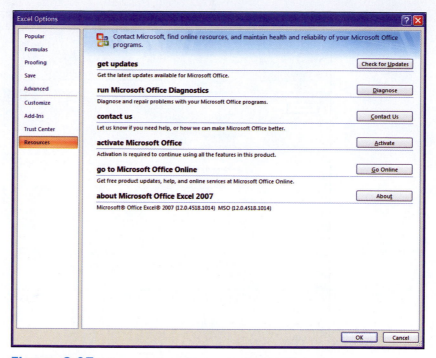

Figure 9.37 Excel Options Resources Category

Working with the Quick Access Toolbar

Past versions of Excel enabled you to customize areas of the Excel window; you could make changes such as moving toolbars, rearranging buttons, and changing the order of items in a menu. Excel 2007 restricts your ability to customize, and the Ribbon is nearly impossible to change. However, you can change the Quick Access Toolbar, which is shown in Figure 9.38. There are two reasons to add buttons to the Quick Access Toolbar:

- To make commands you use frequently more accessible.
- To add commands you frequently use that are not on the Ribbon.

As its name suggests, the Quick Access Toolbar gives you quick access to the functions you use most frequently, so you do not have to wend your way through the cumbersome Office Button menus. It is incredibly simple to add commands to the Quick Access Toolbar.

Quick Access Toolbar

Figure 9.38 Quick Access Toolbar

Add Items

In the previous section, you saw that you can use the Customize category in Excel Options to add items to the Quick Access Toolbar. In the following steps, you use the Excel Options dialog box, but you access it differently:

1. Click the down arrow on the Quick Access Toolbar and select More Commands (see Figure 9.39). The Excel Options dialog box appears.

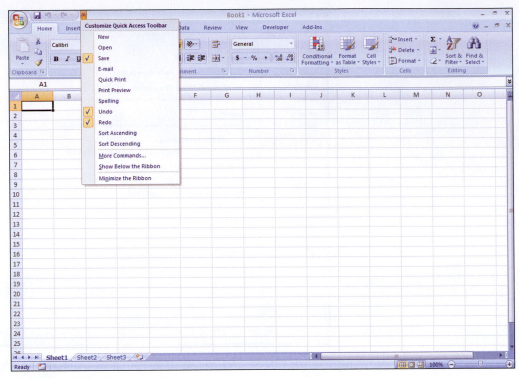

Figure 9.39 Customize Quick Access Toolbar

2. Choose a category from the *Choose commands from list*. The categories are briefly summarized in Table 9.2.

Table 9.2 Customizing the Quick Access Toolbar

Category	Contents
Popular Commands	Contains the commands Excel considers the most often used.
Commands not in the Ribbon	Contains commands not important enough to be on the Ribbon. Also contains commands used in previous versions of Excel.
All Commands	Shows all commands that can be added to the Quick Access Toolbar.
Macros	Shows all macros in open workbooks.

3. Select a command from the list and click Add.
4. Click OK.

Remove Items

You may need to add commands to the Quick Access Toolbar for the short term. For example, a project might require frequent sorting. After you finish the project, you may no longer need to sort your worksheet data as frequently, so you can remove the Sort command from the Quick Access Toolbar. You can easily remove items from the Quick Access Toolbar. Right-click the item to be removed and select Remove from Quick Access Toolbar, as shown in Figure 9.40.

Figure 9.40 Quick Access Toolbar Context List

Adding Add-Ins

In the most generic form, an add-in is a part of a program that gives the program more functionality. Excel add-ins provide new worksheet functionality that you can use as you would any other feature in Excel. Previously, you installed and used the Solver add-in. In a best-case scenario, add-ins interface seamlessly with the original Excel program. Excel contains several already available add-ins, and additional add-ins can be downloaded from http://office.microsoft.com, where you can also find detailed descriptions and tutorials.

List and Describe Add-Ins

Seven primary add-ins are included with Excel 2007. Table 9.3 lists and describes these add-ins. As you review the table, note the very specific and somewhat limited uses for the add-ins. You will use only the add-ins that you need to use; they were developed for specific applications.

Table 9.3 Excel Add-Ins

Add-In	Description
Analysis ToolPak	Contains sophisticated statistical and engineering tools, such as ANOVA.
Analysis ToolPak–VBA	Provides VBA functions for the Analysis ToolPak.
Conditional Sum Wizard	Assists in creating formulas that add values based on a condition.
Euro Currency Tools	Converts and formats euro currency.
Internet Assistant VBA	Enables the publishing of data to the Web.
Lookup Wizard	Assists in creating formulas to look up data.
Solver Add-In	Assists in using a number of numeric methods for solving and optimizing equations.

Install Add-Ins

Add-ins are programs and must be installed before you can use them. Add-ins are listed and installed in the Excel Add-ins Manager. To install add-ins:

1. Click the Office Button and click Excel Options.
2. Select the Add-Ins category from the Excel Options dialog box.
3. Select Excel Add-ins from the Manage list and click Go. This opens the Add-Ins dialog box (see Figure 9.41).
4. Click the check box for the add-in to be installed and click OK.
5. To remove an add-in, remove the check mark from the add-in and click OK.

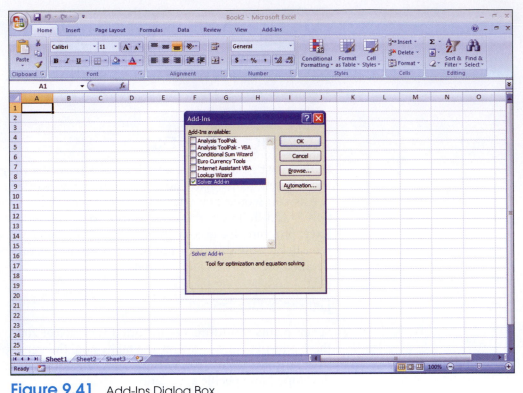

Figure 9.41 Add-Ins Dialog Box

Hands-On Exercises

3 | Customize Excel

Skills covered: 1. Change Excel Options **2.** Add and Remove Items from the Quick Access Toolbar **3.** Install, Use, and Remove Add-Ins

---

Step 1
Change Excel Options

Refer to Figure 9.42 as you complete Step 1.

a. Click the **Office Button** and click **Excel Options** to open the Excel Options window.

b. Make the following changes in the Popular window:

- Change Color scheme to **Silver**.
- Change Use this font to **Arial**.
- Change Font size to **12** and click **OK**.
- Click **OK** to acknowledge the warning message.

c. Exit Excel and restart Excel to see the changes in the interface.

d. Open the *chap9_ho3_options* workbook and save it as **chap9_ho3_options_solution**.

You used the Popular Options window to customize the Excel default interface by changing the overall color scheme to silver, the default font to Arial, and the font size to 12. Before the font and size changes could take effect, you had to exit and then restart Excel.

e. Click **cell A1** and type your last name.

f. Click **cell B1** and type your first name.

You should see your name in 12-point Arial.

g. Save the workbook.

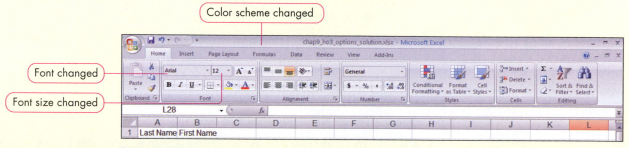

Figure 9.42 Change Interface Defaults

Step 2
Add and Remove Items from the Quick Access Toolbar

Refer to Figure 9.43 as you complete Step 2.

a. Click the **Quick Access Toolbar down arrow** and click **Spelling** to add it to the Quick Access Toolbar.

The Spelling icon now appears in the Quick Access Toolbar. You can add those features you use frequently. Note that adding spelling to the Quick Access Toolbar does not remove it from the Review tab.

b. Click the **Quick Access Toolbar down arrow** and click **More Commands** to open Customize Options.

c. Click **Open** in the left list box, click **Add** to add Open to the list in the right list box, and click **OK**.

The Open icon now appears on the Quick Access Toolbar, as shown in Figure 9.43.

TROUBLESHOOTING: If you are working in a lab, you may not be able to customize your Quick Access Toolbar. Check with your instructor for further instructions.

d. Right-click the **Open** icon on the Quick Access Toolbar and select **Remove from Quick Access Toolbar**.

This illustrates the ease of removing items from the Quick Access Toolbar. You will sometimes add to the Quick Access Toolbar items that have limited use. Rather than leave them on the Quick Access Toolbar, you can delete them when you have finished using them.

e. Save the workbook.

Additions to the Quick Access Toolbar

Figure 9.43 Customized Quick Access Toolbar

Step 3
Install, Use, and Remove Add-Ins

Refer to Figure 9.44 as you complete Step 3.

a. Click the **Office Button** and click **Excel Options**.

b. Click **Add-Ins**, verify that Excel Add-Ins is in the Manage text box, and click **Go** to open the Add-Ins dialog box.

c. Check **Euro Currency Tools** in the Add-Ins available list and click **OK**.

TROUBLESHOOTING: You may have to click OK to install Euro Currency Tools if it is not already installed. Check with your instructor for further instructions.

You find Euro Conversion and Euro Formatting in the Solutions group on the Formulas tab.

d. Click the **Formulas tab**, select **cells A3:A9**, click **Euro Formatting** in the Solutions group, and widen column A as necessary.

You converted the values to Euro currency format.

e. Click **Euro Conversion** in the Solutions group to open the Euro Conversion box.

f. Click in **Destination range**, select **cells B3:B9**, and select EUR-Euro in the *From* section drop-down arrow.

g. Select **IEP-Irish Pound** in the *To* section drop-down arrow.

Although the Irish Pound was discontinued in 2002, you notice that the Euro Currency Tools add-in provides an option for converting currency to Irish Pounds. Therefore, you just tried out the option to see if it still works.

h. Verify that Currency appears in the *Output Format* section drop-down arrow and click **OK**.

You have converted a column of values to Euro format and then converted the Euro values to Irish pounds.

i. Save and close the workbook but do not exit Excel.

j. Click the **Office Button**, click **Excel Options**, click **Add-Ins**, click **Go**, remove the check from **Euro Currency Tools** in Add-Ins available, and click **OK**.

k. Right-click **Spelling** in the Quick Access Toolbar and select **Remove from Quick Access Toolbar**.

l. Click the **Office Button**, click **Excel Options**, change the Color scheme to **Blue**, change the Font to **Body Font**, change the Font size to **11**, and click **OK** twice.

m. Exit Excel.

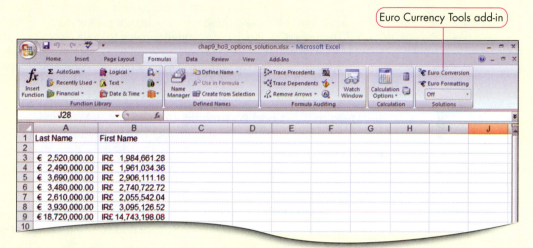

Figure 9.44 Euro Currency Tools Add-In

Summary

1. **Track changes.** When you are collaborating, you can use Track Changes to make it easier for groups of people to work together. Change tracking enables you to monitor and accept or reject changes made by others who are reviewing, editing, or working with the same workbook.

2. **Enable simultaneous changes by multiple users.** Workbook sharing enables more than one person to modify an Excel workbook at one time. Workbook sharing is appropriate when the workbook file is readily available for all those involved to access it, such as a location on an organization's network.

3. **Save workbooks in different formats.** Excel 2007 introduced the new .xlsx file format for Excel workbooks. As Excel 2007 proliferates, more and more users will be using it and saving workbooks as .xlsx files. Until this proliferation is complete, however, some users will continue to use older versions of Excel, and these versions are not backward compatible with the new file format. A user can download a compatibility patch to open Excel 2007 files in previous versions. However, you may want to save an Excel workbook so those who do not have Excel 2007 can read and print the file without downloading the compatibility patch. The most common and best way to enable non-Excel users to display and print Excel files is to save an Excel workbook as a Portable Document Format (PDF) file.

4. **Copy data to Word and PowerPoint.** Pasting an Excel workbook in a Microsoft Word document is also known as embedding. If you make changes in an embedded object in Word, the changes are *not* made in the original workbook. You can copy and paste Excel data and charts into PowerPoint as well. The default Paste option does not retain formulas; you must use the Paste Special dialog box and select Microsoft Office Excel Object to embed data as an editable object and maintain formulas.

5. **Finalize documents.** Two general areas involved in finalizing Excel workbooks or documents are setting the properties of the document and running Compatibility Checker to determine what properties of Excel will be available when you save the document in an older version of Excel. These are the key components of finalizing a document.

6. **Prepare workbooks for distribution.** In organizations, the Accounting office distributes budget spreadsheets to various cost center departments for review. In school districts, teachers submit grade books to the principal for review. Before you release your documents for distribution to others, you must perform a few tasks. These are grouped in the Prepare option of the Office menu.

7. **Understand Excel options.** The Excel Options window, which is accessed by clicking the Office Button and choosing Excel Options, is a centralized area where you can change the look, behavior, and calculation options in Excel.

8. **Work with the Quick Access Toolbar.** Past versions of Excel enabled you to customize areas of the Excel window, including moving toolbars, rearranging buttons, and changing the order of items in a menu. Excel 2007 restricts your ability to customize; the Ribbon is nearly impossible to change. However, Excel 2007 enables you to change the Quick Access Toolbar.

9. **Add add-ins.** In the most generic form, an add-in is a part of a program that gives the program more functionality. Excel add-ins provide new worksheet functions that you can use as you would use any other feature in Excel. Previously, you installed and used the Solver add-in. In a best-case scenario, add-ins interface seamlessly with the original Excel program. Excel contains several add-ins, and additional add-ins can be downloaded from http://office.microsoft.com.

Key Terms

Multiple Choice

1. In your group that is going to share an Excel workbook, you are the only one who has upgraded to Excel 2007. Before you share the workbook you should:

   (a) Print a backup copy.

   (b) Run the Compatibility Checker.

   (c) Have no concerns about whether they can open your document.

   (d) Place all the documents on a CD.

2. How can you tell if a document is not an Excel 2007 document?

   (a) The title bar is a different color.

   (b) The status bar includes the text [Compatibility Mode].

   (c) The title bar includes [Compatibility Mode] after the file name.

   (d) The file extension is XLSX.

3. Which tab contains the Track Changes command?

   (a) Review

   (b) View

   (c) Home

   (d) Data

4. Which of the following Excel features is disabled if Track Changes is turned on?

   (a) Save a workbook

   (b) Format cells

   (c) Create a Web page

   (d) Merge cells

5. Which of the following is not an option when accepting or rejecting changes?

   (a) Delete all

   (b) Accept

   (c) Accept all

   (d) Reject

6. Who gets to decide who has the last call on what changes are accepted?

   (a) The first person to make a change

   (b) Anyone who makes a change

   (c) Cannot be determined

   (d) The last person to make a change

7. Which of the following is a restriction in Excel Compatibility mode?

   (a) 1,048,576 rows are available.

   (b) SUMIF is not supported.

   (c) Long formulas are omitted.

   (d) All PivotTable features are not available.

8. Partially completed workbooks used to create other workbooks are known as:

   (a) Files

   (b) Templates

   (c) PDF documents

   (d) Workbooks

9. What e-mail client must be used to automatically send on Excel document as an attachment?

   (a) AOL

   (b) Works

   (c) Outlook

   (d) SMTP

10. Where is the Compatibility Checker located?

    (a) Office Button

    (b) Home tab

    (c) Compatibility tab

    (d) Review tab

11. Which of the following is a new feature in Excel 2007?

    (a) Document Sharing

    (b) Digital Signature

    (c) Security Certificates

    (d) Document Inspector

12. Which of the following does not apply to a document when it is marked final?

    (a) It is write-only.

    (b) It is read-only.

    (c) It is view-only.

    (d) All of the above.

Multiple Choice Continued...

13. Which of the following is a category in Excel Options?

(a) Customize

(b) Set-up

(c) Personal

(d) Preview

14. Which of the following is not an option in the Document Inspector?

(a) Remove comments

(b) Remove metadata

(c) Remove the signature

(d) Remove range names

15. A Certificate Authority is a company that:

(a) Issues digital signatures.

(b) Verifies a certificate's validity.

(c) Manages versions of certified software.

(d) Issues identity theft warnings.

16. Restricting access to a spreadsheet enables you to accomplish all of the following except:

(a) Mark a document as final.

(b) Set an access password for a document.

(c) Protect a document.

(d) Create a signature.

Practice Exercises

1 Lee Art Museum Fundraiser

As the director of the Lee Art Museum, you are planning a fundraising event but must update your donor list. Several individuals and organizations have already donated items to your fundraiser. Since these donations were made, the donors, items donated, and the value of the items have changed. In the partially completed workbook, you will use Track Changes to note the changes in item value, the changes in donated items, and changes in donors. You will also add comments related to these changes. Use Figure 9.45 as a guide as you complete this exercise.

a. Open the *chap9_pe1_contributions* workbook and save it as **chap9_pe1_contributions_solution** so that you can return to the original workbook if necessary.

b. To work with Track Changes:

- Click the **Review tab**.
- Click the **Track Changes down arrow** and select **Highlight Changes**.
- Check **Track changes while editing** and remove the check from the **When check box**.
- Click **OK** and click **OK** again to save the workbook as a shared workbook.

c. Insert the following:

- Click **cell B13** and type **George**.
- Click **cell E6** and type **600**.
- Click **cell D26** and type **1-Month Free Gas**.

d. Insert comments as follows:

- Click **cell B13**, click **New Comment** in the Comments group, and type **We found his first name**.
- Click **cell E6**, click **New Comment**, and type **Value of the golf clubs has increased**.

e. Save the workbook.

f. Click **Show All Comments** in the Comments group.

g. Click the **Track Changes down arrow** in the Changes group on the Review tab and select **Highlight Changes**. Check **List changes on a new sheet** and click **OK**.

h. Group the workbook and create a custom footer that includes your name, today's date, and your instructor's name. Print and close the workbook.

...continued on Next Page

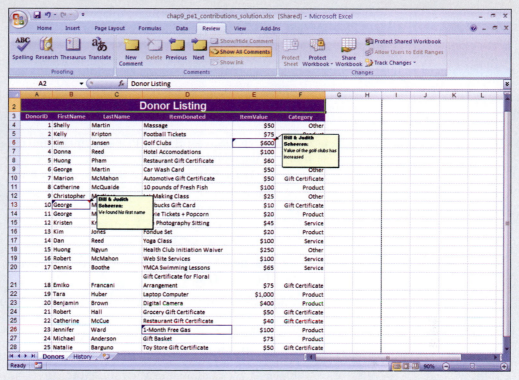

Figure 9.45 Lee Art Museum Changes

2 Nationwide Computer Sales Analysis

As the director of sales for Nationwide Computer, you need to prepare a workbook for distribution to your regional sales managers so they can make any necessary changes. You will save the workbook both in a previous version of Excel and as a PDF so those using older versions of Excel or who do not have Excel can view your work. You will e-mail the workbook to your sales managers. You will incorporate the final product sales data in a presentation to the board of directors. Refer to Figure 9.46 as you work through this exercise.

a. Open the *chap9_pe2_computer* workbook and save it as **chap9_pe2_computer_solution** so that you can return to the original workbook if necessary.

b. Click the **Review tab** and click **Share Workbook** in the Changes group to open the Share Workbook dialog box.

c. Click the **Allow changes by more than one user check box**, click the **Advanced tab**, and verify that:

   • **Keep change history for 30 days** is selected in the *Track changes* section.

   • **When file is saved** is selected in the *Update changes* section.

   • **Ask me which changes win** is selected in the *Conflicting changes between users* section.

   • Both options are selected in the *Include in Personal view* section and click **OK**.

d. Click the **Office Button**, position the mouse pointer over **Save As**, and click **Excel 97–2003 Workbook**.

e. Click **Save**, click **Continue** to accept the Compatibility Checker dialog box summary, and click **OK** to close and reopen the workbook in Compatibility mode.

f. Close the shared *chap9_pe2_computer_solution.xls* file and open the Microsoft Office Excel Worksheet *chap9_pe2_computer_solution*.

   TROUBLESHOOTING: If you did not install the PDF Add-in in the hands-on exercise, it must be installed to continue.

...continued on Next Page

g. Click **Save As** in the Office menu to open the Save As dialog box.

h. Click the **Save as type drop-down arrow** and select **PDF (*.pdf)**.

i. Click **Options** and verify that:

- **All** is selected in the *Page range* section.

- **Entire Workbook** is selected in the *Publish what* section.

- Both check boxes are checked in the *Include non-printing information* section.

j. Click **OK**, click **Save**, print the PDF document, and close Adobe Reader if necessary to return to the workbook.

k. Click the **Office Button**, point to **Send**, and click **E-mail**.

l. Type your instructor's e-mail address in the To box and a short message in the body area, then click **Send**.

m. Click the **Review tab** and click **Share Workbook** in the Changes group to open the Share Workbook dialog box.

- Remove the check from the *Allow changes by more than one user at the same time* section and click **OK**.

- Click **Yes** to verify removing the workbook from shared use.

n. To copy the worksheet to Word:

- Select **cells A1:F6** and click **Copy** in the Clipboard group on the Home tab.

- Open a new document in Microsoft Word and type your name.

- Click the **Paste down arrow** in the Clipboard group and select **Paste Special** to open the Paste Special dialog box.

- Click **Microsoft Office Excel Worksheet Object** and click **OK**.

- Save the Word document as **chap9_pe2_word_solution**, print the document, and close Microsoft Word.

o. Click the **Sales by Product tab** to make your chart sheet active.

- Click the chart to make it active and click **Copy** in the Clipboard group.

- Open Microsoft PowerPoint and type the title **Sales by Product**.

- Click and type your name as the subtitle.

- Click **New Slide** from the Slides group and type the title **Product Sales by City**.

- Click in the bottom placeholder on the slide and click **Paste** from the Clipboard group.

- Save the PowerPoint presentation as **chap9_pe2_powerpoint_solution** and close Microsoft PowerPoint.

p. Create a custom footer that includes your name, today's date, and your instructor's name. Print and close the workbook.

...continued on Next Page

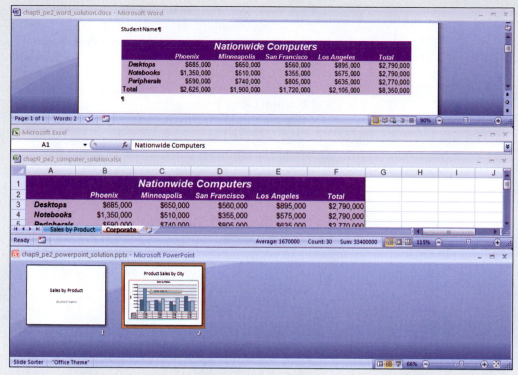

Figure 9.46 Nationwide Computer Sales Analysis

3 Frank's Baseball Card Emporium

You are the accountant for your brother Frank, who owns and operates Frank's Baseball Card Emporium, a rapidly growing hobby store that currently has three locations. Figure 9.47 displays the second quarter sales as well as the first quarter sales totals. Frank has asked you to prepare the workbook for distribution to himself and each manager at the three locations. Make sure you are the only one who is able to change the workbook data. You will add workbook properties and run Compatibility Checker on the workbook. Further, you will use Document Inspector, restrict permission to the workbook, and add your digital signature to the workbook. Figure 9.47 shows the completed workbook you will use for reference.

a. Open the *chap9_pe3_franks* workbook and save it as **chap9_pe3_franks_solution** so you can return to the original workbook if necessary.

b. Click the **Office Button** and click **Properties** from the Prepare menu to display the Document Properties panel. In this panel:

- Type your name in the Author text box.

- Type **Sales by Location** in the Subject text box.

- Type **Frank, Baseball, Cards,** and **Collectables** in the Keywords text box.

- Type **This workbook shows second quarter comparison with the first quarter**. in the Comments box.

c. Click the **Office Button** and click **Run Compatibility Checker** from the Prepare menu to display the Microsoft Office Excel–Compatibility Checker dialog box.

d. Click **Copy to New Sheet** to create a compatibility report on a new worksheet and Close the dialog box.

e. Click the **Second Quarter tab**, close the Document Properties panel, and save the workbook.

f. Click the **Office Button**, click **Prepare**, select **Inspect Document**, and select **Inspect**.

g. Press and hold **Alt** while pressing **PrtScn**, and then click **Close** to close Document Inspector without making changes.

...continued on Next Page

h. Click the **Compatibility Report** tab, click cell **A10**, click **Paste**, and resize the image so the bottom boundary is row 25.

i. Click the **Office Button**, click **Restrict Permission** from the Prepare menu, and select Restricted Access to display the Microsoft Office Information Rights Management (IRM) dialog box.

j. Press and hold **Alt** while pressing **PrtScn**, and then click **No** in response to the Microsoft Office box.

k. Click the **Compatibility Report tab**, click cell **C10**, click **Paste**, move and resize the image to fit, and save the workbook.

l. Group the worksheets and create a custom footer that includes your name, today's date, and your instructor's name. Save the workbook.

m. Click the **Office Button**, select **Prepare**, select **Mark as Final** to open the Microsoft Office Excel information box, click **Yes** to mark the workbook as final, and click **OK**.

n. Print and close the workbook.

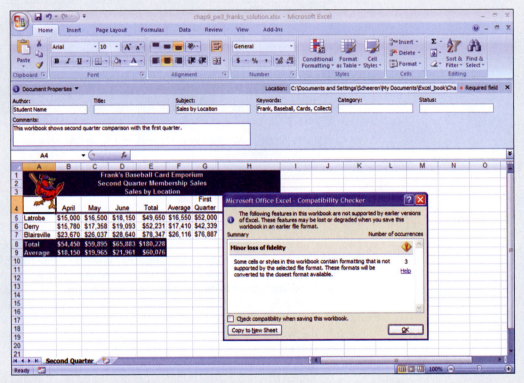

Figure 9.47 Frank's Baseball Card Emporium

4 The Analysis ToolPak Add-In

The degree to which you will benefit from the analysis tools in Excel depends in part on your proficiency with statistics. Even if you are not a statistician, however, you can use a few basic techniques, as shown in Figure 9.48. This worksheet uses three tools to perform some basic analysis: You will generate random numbers, descriptive statistics, and a histogram.

a. Open a new workbook and save it as **chap9_pe4_statistics_solution**.

b. Click the **Office Button**, click **Excel Options**, click **Add-Ins**, verify that Excel Add-ins is in the Manage text box, and click **Go** to open the Add-Ins dialog box.

c. Check the **Analysis ToolPak box** and click **OK**.

d. Verify that Data Analysis is in the Analysis group on the Data tab.

e. Click **Data Analysis** in the Analysis group to open the Data Analysis dialog box.

...continued on Next Page

f. Scroll down the list of analysis tools, select **Random Number Generation**, and click **OK** to display the Random Number Generation dialog box, where you specify the type of random numbers you want to generate.

g. Make the following changes in the Random Number Generation dialog box:

  • Type **1** as the Number of Variables.

  • Type **200** as the Number of Random Numbers.

  • Choose **Normal** as the Distribution.

  • Verify that Mean = **0** and that Standard deviation = **1**.

  • Type **A2** as the output range and click **OK**.

h. Click **cell A1** and type **Random Number** as the column heading.

i. Click **Data Analysis**, scroll down the list of analysis tools until you can select **Descriptive Statistics**, and click **OK** to display the Descriptive Statistics dialog box.

j. Make the following changes in the Descriptive Statistics dialog box:

  • Enter **A1:A201** as the input range.

  • Check the **Labels in the first row** box.

  • Type **C1** as the Output range.

  • Check the **Summary statistics** box.

  When you finish making these changes, click **OK**.

k. Enter the lower bounds for the histogram you are about to create in cells F1 through F13, as shown in Figure 9.48.

l. Execute the Data Analysis command again and specify **Histogram** as the analysis tool.

m. Enter the following:

  • Type **A2:A201** as the Input range.

  • Type **F2:F12** as the Bin range.

  • Type **C17** as the Output range.

n. Format the worksheet as shown in Figure 9.48.

o. Create a custom footer that includes your name, today's date, and your instructor's name. Print, save, and close the workbook.

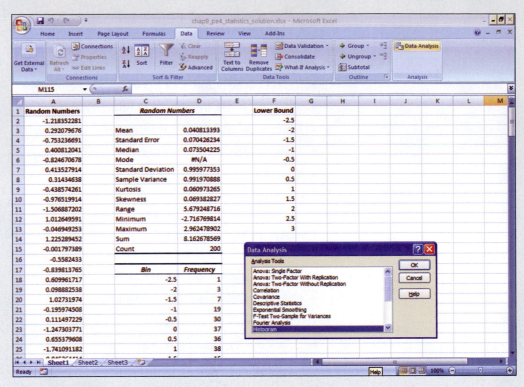

Figure 9.48 Statistical Analysis

Mid-Level Exercises

1 Horace County Medical Association

The Horace County Medical Association has appointed you as its system administrator. Your first task is to update the physician specialty directory. Included in the workbook are the physicians' names, the cities in which they work, their medical specialties, and the dates they became board certified. As part of the update process, you will make changes to elements of the list and add comments to the list where needed. Refer to Figure 9.49 as you finish the workbook for this exercise.

a. Open the *chap9_mid1_ama* workbook and save it as **chap9_mid1_ama_solution** so you can return to the original workbook if necessary.

b. Turn on **Track Changes** and change Adam Dunn's first name to **Jack**, Neil Watson's city to **Allentown**, Jessica Wall's specialty to **Obstetrics**, and Becky Young's board certificate date to **September 26, 1989**.

c. Type the comment **Jack verified this** in **cell C15** and type the comment **Dr. Watson moved his practice this year** in **cell D29**.

d. Save the workbook, show all comments, and list the changes on a new sheet.

e. Group the worksheets and create a custom footer that includes your name, today's date, and your instructor's name. Print and close the workbook.

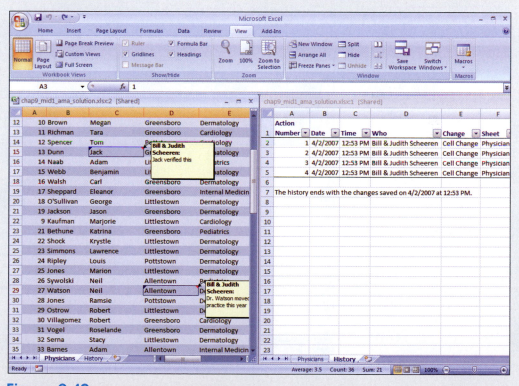

Figure 9.49 Horace County Medical Association Records

2 Analyses of Visitors to a Historical Site

You are the director of the national historical site in your hometown. With government funding at a premium, you have decided to be proactive and prepare data showing the large number of visitors to your historical site. You will allow the workbook to be updated by other employees because they have the most current figures you need. You will save the workbook as a PDF file so

...continued on Next Page

those who do not have Excel can view and print the workbook. You will e-mail the workbook to your superior, prepare a Word document showing the worksheet, and create a PowerPoint presentation that includes the chart you have created. Use Figure 9.50 as a guide as you complete the exercise.

a. Open the *chap9_mid2_history* workbook and save it as **chap9_mid2_history_solution** so that you can return to the original workbook if necessary.

b. Share the workbook, make sure to allow changes by more than one user, and verify the appropriate options in the Advanced tab of the Share Workbook dialog box.

c. Save the workbook as **PDF**, print the PDF document, and close Adobe Reader, if necessary.

d. E-mail the workbook to your instructor.

e. Copy the worksheet to a Word document, print it, and save the Word document as **chap9_mid2_word_solution**.

f. Copy the data chart to a new PowerPoint presentation, save the presentation as **chap9_mid2_powerpoint_solution**, print the presentation, and close PowerPoint.

g. Share the workbook and allow others to update it.

h. Create a custom footer that includes your name, today's date, and your instructor's name. Print and close the workbook.

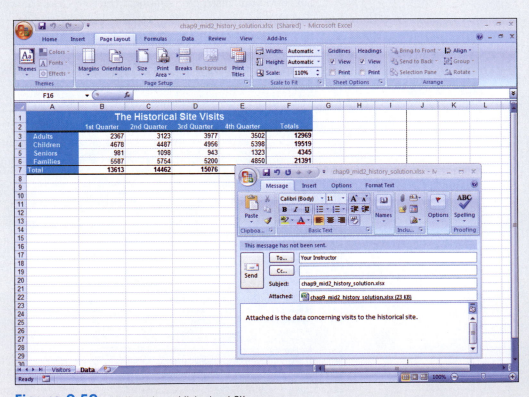

Figure 9.50 Visitors to a Historical Site

3 Finalizing Sales at The Golf Shoppe

You are the business manager for The Golf Shoppe, and it is time to finalize the yearly sales report for the investors. Figure 9.51 displays the source data used to create the PivotTable and chart included in the workbook. The corporate headquarters has asked you to prepare the workbook for distribution to them and to all salespersons. After you make sure you are the only one able to change the workbook data, you will add workbook properties and run the Compatibility Checker on the

...continued on Next Page

workbook. Further, you will use Document Inspector and restrict permission to the workbook. Figure 9.51 shows the completed workbook you will use for reference as you complete your tasks.

a. Open the *chap9_mid3_golf* workbook and save it as **chap9_mid3_golf_solution** so you can return to the original workbook if necessary.

b. Change the document properties to include your name as Author, **Annual Sales** as the Subject, **Golf Shoppe, golf, golf clubs** as keywords, and **This workbook shows annual sales for 2008.** in the Comment area.

c. Run Compatibility Checker and copy the compatibility report to a new worksheet.

d. Run Document Inspector, copy the Document Inspector box, and paste it on the Source Data sheet, reducing the image to fit in 4 columns by 17 rows.

e. Restrict permission so only you can make changes to the workbook. Copy the dialog box and paste it below the Document Inspector image. Remember to click **No** in the Microsoft Office Information Rights Management (IRM) dialog box.

f. Create a custom footer on all worksheets that includes your name, today's date, and your instructor's name. Save the workbook.

g. Mark the workbook as final. Print and close the workbook.

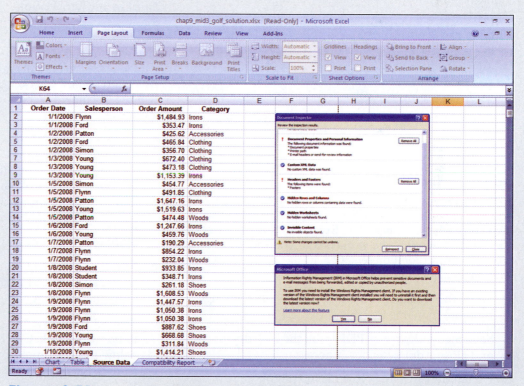

Figure 9.51 Finalizing Sales at The Golf Shoppe

You are the owner of jean jane's designer clothing and must prepare your annual salesperson sales report for distribution to your silent partners. You will use Excel to finalize the workbook prepared by your accountant. In the process, you will work with Track Changes, inserting comments as explanation for your partners; allow simultaneous changes; save the workbook in a different format; send the workbook by e-mail; copy data to PowerPoint for your sales meeting; and prepare the workbook for distribution.

Open and Save the Workbook

You will open the workbook and begin to prepare your finalized workbook.

a. Open the *chap9_cap_design* workbook.

b. Save the workbook as **chap9_cap_design_solution**.

Track Changes and Work with Comments

You have to make changes suggested by your accountant and include comments explaining the changes.

a. Use Track Changes to change Franklin's first quarter sales to $85,000, Dane's fourth quarter sales to $15,000, and correct the third quarter total formula.

b. Add a comment to the third quarter total sales, explaining how you corrected the formula.

c. Comment on Dane's sales in the fourth quarter.

d. Save and print the workbook with all comments visible.

Workbook Sharing

You will allow your employees to update the workbook. You will save the workbook as a PDF file so one of your investors, who does not have Excel, can view the workbook. You will e-mail the workbook to your investors and prepare a PowerPoint presentation, including the chart you have created, for your next sales meeting.

a. Share the workbook, making sure to allow changes by more than one user.

b. Save the workbook as **PDF**, print the PDF document, and close Adobe Reader, if necessary.

c. E-mail the workbook to your instructor.

d. Copy the chart to a new PowerPoint presentation, save the presentation as **chap9_cap_powerpoint_solution**, print the presentation, and close PowerPoint.

e. Share the workbook and allow others to update it.

f. Create a custom footer that includes your name, today's date, and your instructor's name. Print the workbook.

g. Save the workbook and turn off workbook sharing.

Quick Access Toolbar and Add-Ins

You want to make using Excel a little easier for the people you are sharing the workbook with. To that end, you will add and remove items from the Quick Access Toolbar. You will add the Euro Currency Tools add-in because you are thinking about marketing your clothing line in Europe.

a. Add **E-mail** and **Print Preview** to the Quick Access Toolbar.

b. Add the **Euro Currency Tools** add-in to Excel.

c. Capture your screen, making sure the Euro Conversion commands are visible on the Formulas tab, and paste the image below sales data. Resize the image so it prints on the same page as the sales data.

d. Remove the Euro Currency Tools add-in, E-mail, and Print Preview from the Quick Access Toolbar.

Finalize the Workbook

The silent partners have asked you to prepare the workbook for distribution to themselves and all salespersons. After you make sure you are the only one able to change the workbook data, you will add workbook properties and run the Compatibility Checker on the workbook. Further, you will use Document Inspector and restrict permission to the workbook.

a. Change the document properties to include your name as Author, **Quarterly Sales by Sales Person** as Subject, **jean jane** and **clothing** as keywords, and **This workbook shows a quarterly sales summary.** in the Comment area.

b. Run Compatibility Checker and copy the compatibility report to a new worksheet.

c. Run the Document Inspector, copy the Document Inspector box, and paste it on the sales data sheet, reducing the image to fit.

d. Restrict permission so only you can make changes to the workbook. Copy the dialog box and paste it below the Document Inspector image. Remember to click **No** in the Microsoft Office Information Rights Management (IRM) dialog box.

e. Create a custom footer on all worksheets that includes your name, today's date, and your instructor's name. Save the workbook.

f. Mark the workbook as final. Print and close the workbook.

Mini Cases

Use the rubric following the case as a guide to evaluate your work, but keep in mind that your instructor may impose additional grading criteria or use a different standard to judge your work.

Track Changes and Share Workbook

GENERAL CASE

You received a shared workbook, *chap9_mc1_apartmentrental*, from one of your clients, an apartment rental manager, and you must update the workbook. You use Track Changes and include comments to indicate what you change or correct. After correcting the changes, you note that the document properties are not all correct, and you must update them to reflect your status as a corporate accountant. Make sure to include keywords and comments. Document your work by capturing the window and pasting it below the corporate worksheet. Copy the Corporate Summary worksheet, place it in a Word document, and save the document as **chap9_mc1_word**. Save the final workbook as **chap9_mc1_apartmentrental_solution**.

Performance Elements	Exceeds Expectations	Meets Expectations	Below Expectations
Correct errors noted in Track Changes	Two errors identified and corrected.	One error identified and corrected.	No errors identified.
Comments	Two relevant, descriptive comments.	Two relevant comments.	One comment.
Document properties	Five document properties entered.	Four document properties entered.	Three or fewer document properties entered.
Word document	Includes worksheet summary.	Includes chart.	No Word document.

Excel Add-In

RESEARCH CASE

This chapter introduced you to Excel add-ins, and you are interested in finding out about different add-ins. Choose one of the unused add-ins from the list in this chapter, and then search Excel Help and the Web for a description to identify the purpose of your add-in. Include several examples, listing when, where, and who would use your add-in. Finally, create detailed instructions that anyone can follow to use your add-in. Nicely format your report in Word and include an image showing your add-in command on the appropriate tab. Save the workbook as **chap9_mc2_addin_solution**.

Performance Elements	Exceeds Expectations	Meets Expectations	Below Expectations
Search Help and the Web	Appropriate information located, and report indicates comprehension.	Appropriate information located.	No information found.
Summarize and communicate	Report clearly written and could be used as directions.	Report clear, but directions inadequate.	No report or poorly written.
Screen capture	Image clearly shows add-in.	Image included, but no add-in visible.	No image included.

You are the statistician for the Community Senior League Women's Basketball team. Your goal is to make all corrections to the finalized basketball season summary workbook, *chap9_mc3_bb*. Use comments liberally to indicate the corrections needed in the workbook. Make sure to include appropriate document properties (author, keywords, and title), save the workbook as **chap9_mc3_bb_solution**, and print your solution. Also save the workbook as a PDF file: **chap9_mc3_bb_solution.pdf**.

Performance Elements	Exceeds Expectations	Meets Expectations	Below Expectations
Remove read-only format	Yes.	Yes.	No.
Document properties	Three appropriately completed properties.	Two completed properties.	No properties.
Correct formulas for errors	Four correct formulas.	Three correct formulas.	Two or fewer correct formulas.
Save in PDF format and print	Saved and printed in PDF format.	Saved PDF, but no PDF printed.	No PDF file.

Templates, Styles, the Web, and Macros

Automating Workbooks

bjectives

After you read this chapter, you will be able to:

1. Work with existing templates, themes, and styles **(page 619)**.

2. Create and apply custom styles for advanced formatting **(page 623)**.

3. Create and use a template **(page 626)**.

4. Create a Web page **(page 636)**.

5. Create Web queries **(page 642)**.

6. Create a macro with the Macro Recorder **(page 650)**.

7. Create macro buttons **(page 654)**.

8. Work with macro security **(page 656)**.

9. Understand the basics of VBA **(page 658)**.

Hands-On Exercises

Exercises	Skills Covered
1. USE AND CREATE THEMES, STYLES, AND TEMPLATES (page 629) **Open**: chap10_ho1_styles.xlsx and chap10_ho1_world.xlsx **Save as**: chap10_ho1_styles_solution.xlsx, chap10_ho1_amortization_solution.xlsx, chap10_ho1_world_template_solution.xltx, and chap10_ho1_world_solution.xlsx	• Apply Styles to Workbook Data • Use and Modify Themes in Workbooks • Create and Modify a Style in a Workbook • Use an Existing Template • Protect a Workbook • Create and Save a Template • Test the Template
2. QUERY THE WEB AND CREATE A WEB PAGE (page 645) **Open**: chap10_ho2_stocks.xlsx **Save as**: chap10_ho2_stocks_solution.xlsx and chap10_ho2_stocks_solution.htm	• Open the Stock Portfolio and Complete the Web Query • Compute the Gain or Loss, Copy the Formulas, and Format the Workbook • Insert Hyperlinks, an Image, and a SmartArt Graphic in the Workbook • Save as a Web Page
3. WORK WITH MACROS AND VISUAL BASIC FOR APPLICATIONS (page 659) **Open**: none **Save as**: chap10_ho3_macros_solution.xlxm	• Create the Macro • Run the Macro • Use the Visual Basic Editor • Create and Use the Erase Macro • Step Through the Macro and Print the VBA Code • Add a Custom Button and Print the Workbook

CASE STUDY

Vacation Parks Incorporated

Your first position after graduation is in the comptroller's office at the national headquarters of Vacation Parks Incorporated, an international corporation that owns and manages amusement parks around the globe. The tasks associated with your new position include communicating attendance information to each of the parks. Since the park Web page is open to the public, and therefore viewable by former and potential customers, it is important that the page have a good look and feel and that it be informative. Your work becomes an important part of marketing the parks worldwide.

Case Study

To that end, you will modify an existing workbook by changing an already applied style, applying a theme for a uniform look and feel for all worksheets in the workbook. You decide to create a template that you will use to add attendance statistics as they become available. As you prepare the workbook, you realize that the corporate logo should be inserted on all sheets in your workbook. The comptroller requested a graphic depicting the top-level corporate hierarchy, so you plan to insert a SmartArt graphic on a separate sheet. In addition, the comptroller requested that you create a Web page. Finally, you will create a macro to create the company standard headers and footers. You will create four files: an Excel solution workbook, an Excel template, a Web page file, and a macro-enabled Excel workbook.

Your Assignment

- Read the chapter carefully and pay close attention to styles, themes, templates, Web page creation, and macros, as they demonstrate the techniques you will use to complete the case study.

- Modify an existing workbook by changing an already applied style and apply a theme for a uniform look and feel for all worksheets in the workbook.

- Create a template that you will use to add attendance statistics as they become available. Protect the workbook but allow for appropriate data entry. Insert the corporate logo on all sheets in your workbook.

- Insert a SmartArt graphic on a separate sheet, depicting the top-level corporate hierarchy, and create a Web page of the entire workbook.

- Create a macro that inserts the company standard headers and footers on all pages of the workbook.

- Begin by opening and reviewing the partially completed workbook for Vacation Parks Incorporated, *chap10_case_parks*, which will become the final workbook.

- Print the completed workbook and the Web page for your supervisor. Save the workbook as **chap10_case_parks_solution**.

Worksheet Automation

Through the early chapters of Excel, you reviewed a large number of Excel techniques and routines. Nearly all of these require a specific sequence of steps in order to successfully complete tasks. The repetitive tasks that can be generalized or abstracted can often be automated, using various techniques that you will study in this chapter. Using predefined document settings or a template will automate some of your work, enabling you to be more productive.

(*. . . techniques that could simplify tasks and, in effect, automate some worksheet operations.*)

In this section, you will learn some techniques that could simplify tasks and, in effect, automate some worksheet operations. You will work with existing templates, themes, and styles to automate some of the formatting tasks. Then you will create your own template and create your own styles to satisfy your individual needs or creative uses for formatting.

Working with Existing Templates, Themes, and Styles

Excel has several tools that can assist you in automating your creation and formatting of worksheets. Corporations use logos as the basis for the creation of a corporate identity. A logo, however, is just one piece of the corporate identity. A standard document look and feel, or corporate identity, applies to workbooks. You can use Excel tools such as templates, themes, and styles to create a corporate identity. These tools are available for you to use in your Excel workbooks to make some formatting tasks easier and to standardize the look and feel of your workbooks.

Select a Template

A template is a partially completed workbook that is used as a model to create other workbooks that have the same structure and purpose. A template typically contains formulas and formatting but no data or only sample data. Templates help ensure consistency and standardization for similar workbooks, such as detailed income statements for all 12 months of a year. Templates reside in a special folder so the latest templates are available for you to use. Templates use a different file extension (.xltx) than a regular Excel workbook (.xlsx). Later in this section, you will work with templates in more depth. Here, you will select an already created template to save time in setting up an Excel worksheet.

When you install Microsoft Office 2007, several common templates are installed for your use. You can use existing templates to create billing statements, expense reports, loan amortizations, personal monthly budgets, sales reports, blood pressure trackers, and time cards. To create a workbook based on one of these existing templates, you do that in conjunction with opening a blank workbook. When you click the Office Button and click New, rather than selecting Blank Workbook, you have several template selections available on the left side of the New Workbook dialog box, as shown in Figure 10.1.

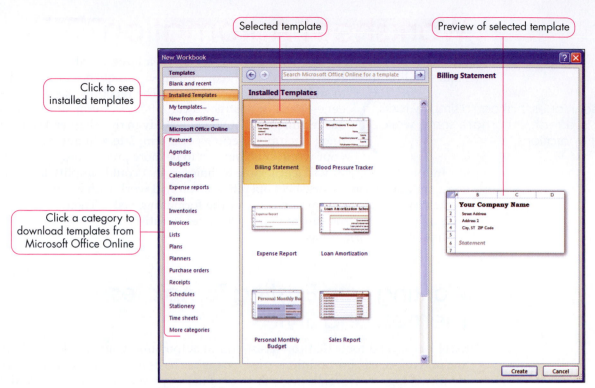

Selected template

Preview of selected template

Click to see installed templates

Click a category to download templates from Microsoft Office Online

Figure 10.1 New Workbook Dialog Box

The Templates pane contains these categories:

- **Blank and recent**—Enables you to either create a blank workbook, which is the default template when you start a new workbook, or select a recently applied template so that you can quickly find and apply it to another workbook.

- **Installed Templates**—Contains a small set of templates that are part of the standard Excel installation.

- **My templates**—Displays the New dialog box so that you can choose from custom templates you have already created.

- **New from existing**—Displays the New from Existing Workbook dialog box so that you can create a new workbook based on a workbook that already exists.

- **Microsoft Office Online**—Displays category links to a Web site from which you can download the templates. For example, you can download templates to create agendas, budgets, calendars, schedules, and more.

To download templates from Microsoft Office Online, click one of the categories of templates listed under the Microsoft Office Online category in the New Workbook dialog box. Click a template to preview it on the right side of the dialog box. After identifying a template you want, click Download to create a new workbook based on the template. You may be prompted to click Continue when Microsoft verifies that you are a registered user of a legitimate license of Microsoft Office 2007. See Figure 10.2.

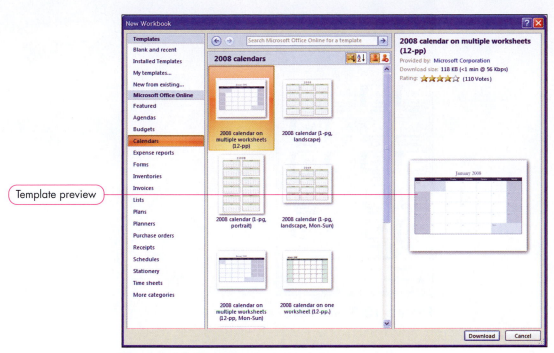

Template preview

Figure 10.2 Online Templates

Apply a Document Theme

A ***document theme*** is a
defined set of colors, fonts,
lines, and fill effects applied to
an entire workbook or to specific items in a workbook.

A ***document theme*** is a defined set of colors, fonts, lines, and fill effects that can be
applied to an entire workbook or to specific items in a workbook. Themes are a combination of three things—fonts, colors, and effects that are prepackaged and can be
applied to a worksheet to change its appearance. Broken down in more detail, a
theme consists of the following elements:

- **Fonts**—A theme contains one font for headings and another font for all other
  elements.

- **Colors**—A theme has a palette of 12 complementary colors that are applied to
  text and background fills used in the Themed Cell styles. The complementary
  colors make up the whole theme and show as background or text color when you
  apply the theme to an already styled cell.

- **Effects**—Shapes and hand-drawn graphics are altered here. This has no effect if
  you have no shapes on the worksheet.

You can apply themes to existing worksheets that use Themed Cell styles. In
effect, you must have created a worksheet and used Themed Cell styles when you created the worksheet. You will often create and use themes that represent the business
"look and feel." Most businesses have a style that encompasses a logo, trademark, or
the use of both in all corporate stationary and all print and non-print advertising
material. You will use themes in workbooks to match the corporate "look and feel."

To select a predefined theme, click Themes in the Themes group on the Page
Layout tab to show the Themes gallery (see Figure 10.3). When you move your
mouse over any theme, the Live Preview changes your worksheet to match the
theme. You then click a theme to select it and apply it to the previously themed worksheet. You can make a previously themed worksheet by first applying Themed Cell
styles to one or more cells in the worksheet. You then apply a theme from the Themes
palette on the Themes group. After you apply a theme, you can customize the
theme's colors, fonts, and effects by clicking the respective command in the Themes
group on the Page Layout tab.

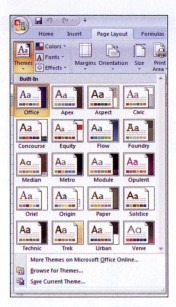

Figure 10.3 Themes Gallery

Insert a Background

A ***background*** is an image placed behind the worksheet data.

Excel enables you to use graphics as the background of a worksheet. The effect is similar to placing a background on a Web page. A ***background*** is an image placed behind the worksheet data. For example, you might want to use the corporate logo as your background, or you might want a *Confidential* graphic image to remind viewers that the worksheet contains corporate trade secrets. Remember that just as with Web page backgrounds, the images can overpower the message of the workbook. Use discretion when inserting background images. A subtle, pale image is less likely to distract a workbook user than a bright, vividly colored image. To add a background to a worksheet:

1. Click Background in the Page Setup group on the Page Layout tab to display the Sheet Background dialog box.
2. Select the picture file to be used as a background. You can use picture files, such as jpeg or bitmap files, for your background image. Choose an image with a light background so that the data on your worksheet will remain readable. Dark images make it more difficult to read the worksheet data.
3. Click Insert.

   The image, like background images in Web pages, is tiled across your worksheet (see Figure 10.4). The background image is for screen display only; it does not print. Notice that Delete Background replaces Background in the Page Setup group after you insert a background for a specific worksheet.

Delete Background replaced Background command

Background image

Figure 10.4 A Worksheet with a Background Image

TIP Delete Background Image

To delete a background picture, click Delete Background in the Page Setup group on the Page Layout tab.

Apply a Style

It is possible to impose Excel's defined styles on cells or ranges of cells. This feature, along with Excel's installed themes, gives you quick access to common formatting choices. A *style* is a set of formatting options applied to cells. When formatting a title for a worksheet, typically you will select a font, a font size, an enhancement such as bold, a font color, and a fill color for the cell. You can make all these changes by choosing a cell style and save time.

A *style* is a set of formatting options applied to cells.

To apply a style to a cell or range of cells, click Cell Styles in the Styles group on the Home tab to display the Cell Styles gallery. Select the cell style to be applied to a cell and click it. You can apply more than one style to a cell to get the right mix of formatting techniques.

Creating and Applying Custom Styles for Advanced Formatting

The discussion of styles in the previous section dealt with predefined styles. Here, you will create, modify, and remove custom cell styles. A style is a set of formatting characteristics stored under a specific name. The advantage of saving formatting characteristics as a style is that when you change the definition of the style, all cells defined by that style change automatically. Corporate styles use colors and fonts to make the corporate image. You will create and apply your custom styles to impose the corporate image on all worksheets. Using your custom styles saves time when you begin each workbook.

Create Styles

Creating a custom style that can be used in all your Excel workbooks is based on the formatting already in an existing cell. After you create and name a style, you can use it over and over again to build a corporate look. For example, if you are an editor for a textbook series, you might want to create styles for formatting different headings to outline a chapter, as shown in Figure 10.4. The first-level headings are red and bold; the second-level headings are blue, bold, and indented three times; and the third-level headings are green, bold, and indented six times. By creating custom styles, the editor can apply those styles to see the hierarchy of topical headings for all chapters in the textbooks.

To create a new style:

1. Click the cell that contains the desired formatting.
2. Click Cell Styles in the Styles group on the Home tab and select New Cell Style at the bottom of the gallery to open the Style dialog box (see Figure 10.5).
3. Type the name for your new style in the *Style name* box.
4. Select the style options you want in the *Style Includes (By Example)* section of the Style dialog box.
5. Click Format to open the Format Cells dialog box and select the formats just as you would format an individual cell. You can select number, alignment, font, border, fill, and protection formats.
6. Click OK to close the Format Cells dialog box and click OK to close the Style dialog box.

The custom style you created is now in the *Custom* section of the Cell Styles palette, as shown in Figure 10.6.

Figure 10.5 Style Dialog Box

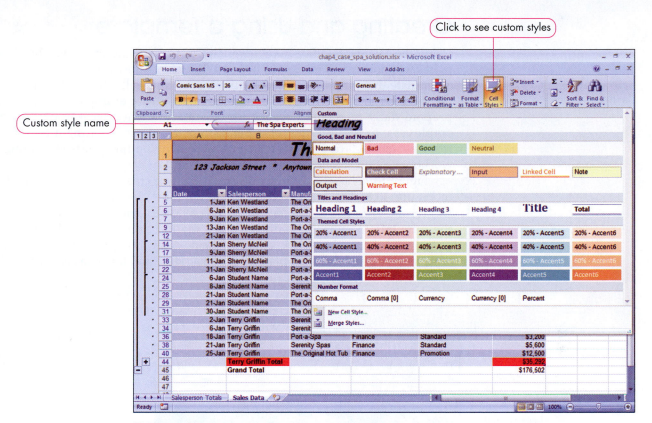

Figure 10.6 Custom Style Added to Palette

Modify and Remove Cell Styles

As you create different custom styles, you may discover that you are consistently overriding the styles you created. For example, the art department might change the "standard" corporate font, or the weight of the font, so it is now bold. This should indicate that the style needs to be modified. To modify a style, right-click it in the *Custom* section of the Cell Styles palette and select Modify. This again opens the Style dialog box and enables you to make the changes needed in the style.

Occasionally, you may find that you no longer need a style and you want to delete it. To delete a style, right-click the style in the *Custom* section of the Cell Styles palette and select Delete. The style is deleted.

TIP Use Styles in Other Workbooks

When you create your own styles, the styles are saved with the workbook in which you created the styles. However, you will probably want to apply those styles in other workbooks as well. To do this, open the workbook that contains the custom styles and open the workbook in which you want to apply those custom styles. Click Cell Styles in the Styles group on the Home tab. Select Merge Styles at the bottom of the Cell Styles gallery to display the Merge Styles dialog box. In the *Merge styles from* list, select the name of the workbook that contains the styles you want and click OK. When you click Cell Styles, the custom styles appear.

Creating and Using a Template

Using the Microsoft Office Excel templates can be a great time saver, but these templates will not always meet your needs. When this is the case, you will want to create a template that meets your exact requirements. You will often find yourself creating the same structured workbook on a regular basis. For example, you might have to prepare daily medicine dosages for hospital patients, weekly payroll data for employees, or monthly travel-expense logs. However, creating a new workbook from scratch each time is time-consuming. When you find yourself creating routine workbooks, you should develop and use a template.

Figure 10.7 shows a payroll workbook that was created from the template shown in Figure 10.8. The formatted template contains the employees' names, hourly wages, and formulas to calculate the gross pay, taxes, and net pay. A manager can use the template to enter the values for the regular and overtime hours worked to quickly determine the weekly payroll. The next several figures illustrate how to create a template, protect a template so the basic style and formulas cannot be changed, and use the template you create.

Hours entered for current week

Template formulas display calculated results

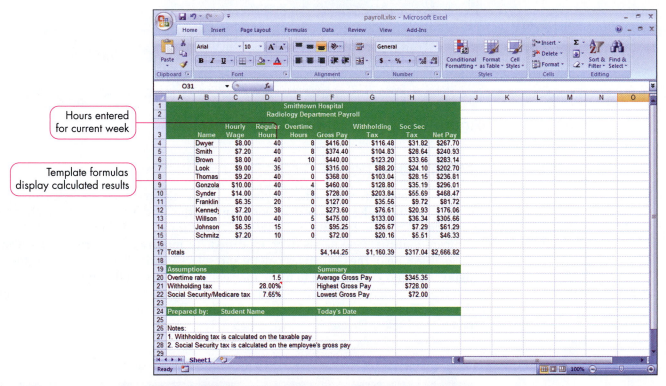

Figure 10.7 Payroll Workbook

TIP   Trap Errors with the IFERROR Function

Formulas used in workbooks display zeros or error messages when you remove values to create a template. You can use the IFERROR function to trap errors and display a zero in a cell. You used the IFERROR function when you created payment schedules or amortized a loan. When you use the function, you can prevent Excel error messages from displaying in a cell.

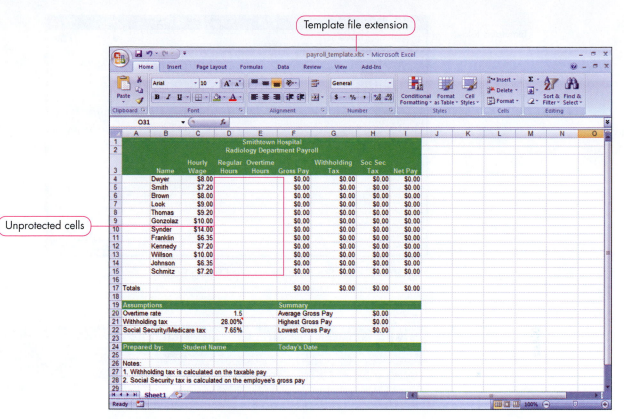

Figure 10.8 Payroll Template

Create a Template

The creation of a custom template is a short process. As Figures 10.7 and 10.8 show, a template contains items such as text, formatting, and formulas but does not contain variable data, as you can see from the blank data entry area. Some considerations that you should understand when you are creating a template include:

- Keep in mind that a template should be, in essence, a blank form.
- Create formulas so they will not change. For example, use absolute references whenever necessary and use cell references, not values, in the formulas.
- Use the appropriate function to trap errors.
- Include instructions for the template.
- Turn off worksheet gridlines for clarity.
- Apply appropriate formatting to the template.
- Give worksheets meaningful names and delete worksheets that are not used.

After you finalize your custom template, you need to save it. To save a workbook as a template, click the Office Button and select Save As. In the Save as type drop-down arrow, select Excel Template (*.xltx). This will save your template to the Templates folder (see Figure 10.9). Type the name of your template and click Save.

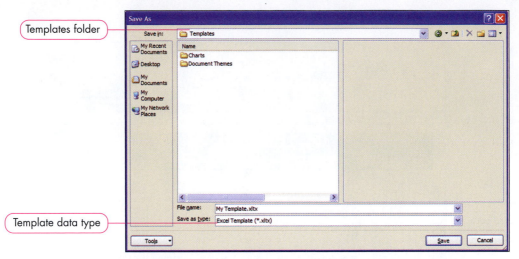

Templates folder

Template data type

Figure 10.9 Save As Template Dialog Box

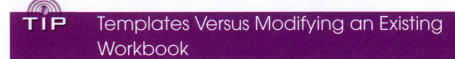

TIP Templates Versus Modifying an Existing Workbook

When you create similar workbooks on a regular basis, you should create and use a template rather than open the previous workbook, change it, and save it with the new name. Often when people do this, they accidentally delete the previous workbook because they inadvertently use the same file name.

Protect a Template

Most templates are based on protected worksheets that enable users to change only a limited number of cells on the worksheet. For example, users would typically not be able to change formulas on a worksheet. The payroll example permits data entry of the regular hours worked and the overtime hours for the listed employees. Protecting worksheets prevents modification of formulas and text but enables you to change values in unprotected cells. Remember that protecting worksheets involves two steps. First, you unlock the cells that can be changed in the worksheet. Second, you protect the worksheet. Locking or unlocking cells has no effect if the worksheet has not been protected. Protecting the template is typically the final step in the creation of a custom template.

Use a Template

Using either a custom template or predefined template is nearly the same as using a regular workbook. The differences are in the Open process and the Save As process. To open a template to begin working on it, click the Office Button and select New. Select My Templates in the New Workbook dialog box (refer to Figure 10.1) to display the New dialog box, click the custom template, and click OK. Take care when opening templates created with previous versions of Excel, as they may have security issues. Further, enhancements in Excel 2007 could make older templates unreliable.

The template opens a new Excel workbook. The default workbook name is almost identical to the template name, with a number, such as 1, at the end. You can make changes filling in the workbook. When you complete your work and want to save the workbook, use the Save As dialog box to specify the location and file name.

Hands-On Exercises

1 | Use and Create Themes, Styles, and Templates

Skills covered: 1. Apply Styles to Workbook Data **2.** Use and Modify Themes in Workbooks **3.** Create and Modify a Style in a Workbook **4.** Use an Existing Template **5.** Protect a Workbook **6.** Create and Save a Template **7.** Test the Template

<table>
<tr>
<td>

Step 1
Apply Styles to Workbook Data

</td>
<td>

Refer to Figure 10.10 as you complete Step 1.

a. Open the *chap10_ho1_styles* workbook and save it as **chap10_ho1_styles_solution** so you can return to the original workbook if necessary.

b. Select **cells A1:F45**, click **Cell Styles** in the Styles group, and select **40% - Accent2**.

You applied a style color to the entire worksheet as the first step in formatting the workbook.

c. Click **cell A1**, click **Cell Styles** in the Styles group, and select **Title** in the *Titles and Headings* section.

d. Apply styles to the cells as follows:

- **Cells A2:A3** are **Heading 1**.
- **Cells A4:F4** are **Heading 2**.
- **Cells A5:F45** are **Heading 4**.
- **Cells F5:F45** are **Accounting with 0 decimals**.

e. Center **cells A1:F3**.

You applied styles to the workbook data to finish the first step in working with themes.

f. Save the workbook.

</td>
</tr>
</table>

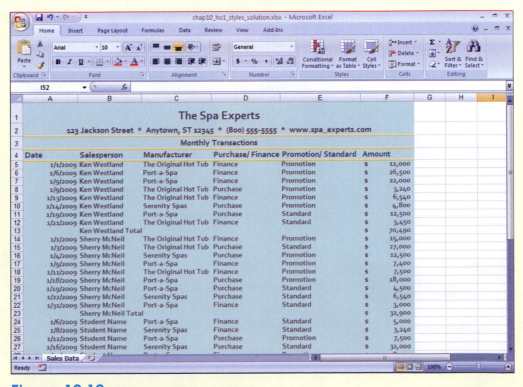

Figure 10.10 Styles Applied to a Workbook

Step 2

Use and Modify Themes in Workbooks

Refer to Figure 10.11 as you complete Step 2.

a. Click the **Page Layout tab** and click **Themes** in the Themes group.

b. Click **Median** as your first theme.

Notice that both the color and font have changed to match the new theme.

c. Click **Themes** in the Themes group and click **Technic** as your second theme. Resize columns as necessary.

d. Click **Colors** in the Themes group and click **Oriel** as the new theme color.

e. Click **Fonts** in the Themes group and click **Concourse** as the new font, then resize columns as necessary.

You modified an existing theme by changing the original color and font of the theme.

TROUBLESHOOTING: Remember that less is better, and you should not spend inordinate amounts of time experimenting with theme colors and fonts.

f. Select **cells A4:F4** and center the headings.

g. Save the workbook.

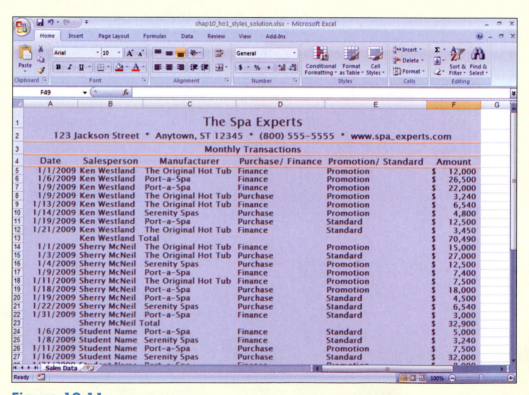

Figure 10.11 Modified Theme

Step 3

Create and Modify a Style in a Workbook

Refer to Figure 10.12 as you complete Step 3.

a. Click the **Home tab**, click **cell F5**, click **Cell Styles** in the Styles group, and select **New Cell Style** to open the Style dialog box.

b. Type **Money** in the Style name box and click **Format**.

c. Click the **Number tab**, if necessary, click **Currency** in the *Category* section, select **2 decimal places**, click **OK**, and click **OK** to close the Style dialog box.

You created a new style, Money, as Currency rather than Accounting and selected 2 decimal places for display.

d. Select **cells F5:F45**, click **Cell Styles** in the Styles group, and click **Money** in the *Custom* section.

The Amount column changed to Currency with 2 decimal places.

e. Click **cell A1** and click **Cell Styles** in the Styles group.

f. Right-click **Title** and select **Modify** to open the Style dialog box.

g. Click **Format** to open the Format Cells dialog box, click **Font** tab, and make the following selections:

- **Arial Black** font
- **Italic** font style
- **26** font size

h. Click **OK** in each dialog box and adjust the height of row 1 as necessary.

You modified the default Title style.

i. Save and close the workbook.

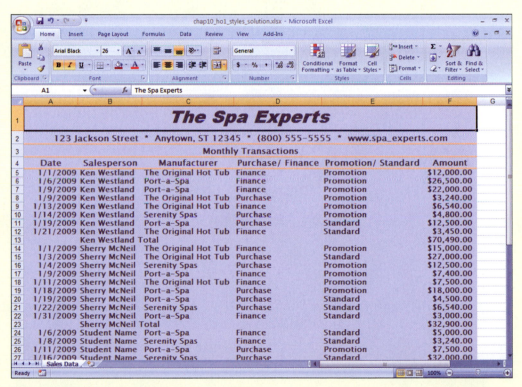

Figure 10.12 Modified Style

Step 4
Use an Existing Template

Refer to Figure 10.13 as you complete Step 4.

a. Click the **Office Button**, click **New**, click **Installed Templates**, click **Loan Amortization** in Installed Templates, and click **Create**.

b. Save the workbook as **chap10_ho1_amortization_solution**.

You are going to use a supplied template to see what your payment schedule would be if you purchase a house.

c. Enter the following values:

- Type **300000** in **cell D5**.
- Type **6.25%** in **cell D6**.
- Type **30** in **cell D7**.
- Type **13** in **cell D8**.
- Type **01/01/2009** in cell **D9**.
- Type **300** in **cell D10**.
- Type **Your Name** in **cell C12**.

Note that the workbook is already styled and formatted for currency and date values. The formulas in cells A18:J282 are protected, and you cannot change them. You are also making an extra payment each year.

d. Save and close the workbook.

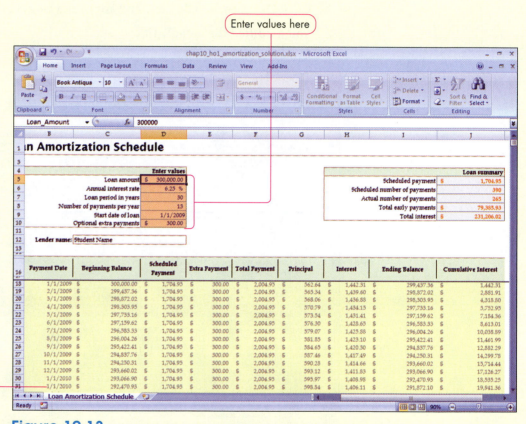

Figure 10.13 Amortization Template

Step 5
Protect a Workbook

Refer to Figure 10.14 as you complete Step 5.

a. Open the *chap10_ho1_world* workbook.

You will make changes to an existing workbook before saving it as a template.

b. Double-click **cell D19**, select and copy the formula, excluding the =, click the **Formulas tab**, click **Logical** in the Function Library group, and select **IFERROR** from the list of logical functions.

c. Press **Ctrl+V** to paste the copied formula in the **Value** box, type **0** in the **Value_if_error** box, and click **OK**.

> **TROUBLESHOOTING:** If Excel does not let you paste the copied formula in the Value box, type IRR(C18:D18,-0.35) in the Value box.

You copied the original formula and pasted it in the IFERROR function to produce a nested function that will trap Excel errors and display a 0 instead of the error message. The function looks like this: =IFERROR(IRR(C18:D18,-0.35),0).

d. Copy the formula through **cell H19**.

e. Select **cells C22:D26** and press and hold **Ctrl** as you select **cells H22:H24**.

f. Click the **Home tab**, click **Format** in the Cells group, and select **Format Cells** to open the Format Cells dialog box.

g. Click the **Protection tab**, clear the **Locked check box**, and click **OK**.

You unlocked the cells that are used for data entry in the final template.

h. Click the **Review tab** and click **Protect Sheet** in the Changes group to open the Protect Sheet dialog box.

i. Verify that the **Protect worksheet and contents of locked cells check box** is selected, verify that the **Select unlocked cells check box** is selected, and click **OK** to close the dialog box.

You protected your formulas and formatting. Only the data entry cells are unlocked and available to users.

j. Ensure that cell protection works by trying to change the formula in any of the protected cells in the upper part of the spreadsheet.

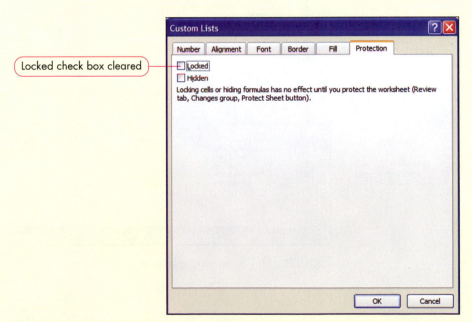

Figure 10.14 Custom Lists Dialog Box Protection Tab

Step 6
Create and Save a Template

Refer to Figure 10.15 as you complete Step 6.

a. Select **cells C22:D26**, press and hold **Ctrl** as you select **cells H22:H24**, and press **Delete** to delete the contents of the cells.

b. Click the **Office Button**, select **Save As**, click the **Save as type drop-down arrow**, and select **Excel Template (*.xltx)**.

c. Type **chap10_ho1_world_template_solution** in the File name box and click **Save** to save the template.

TROUBLESHOOTING: If you are using your own computer, Excel will save your template in the Templates folder unless you indicate another location. If you are using a lab computer, follow your professor's instructions for saving files.

You saved the protected workbook as a template for use by others.

d. Close the workbook.

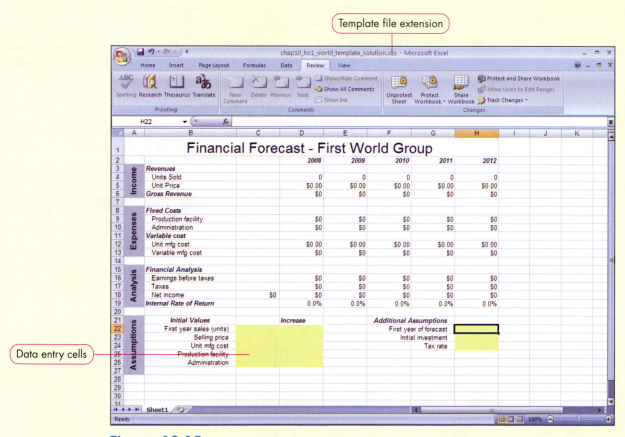

Figure 10.15 Workbook Template Solution

Step 7
Test the Template

Refer to Figure 10.16 as you complete Step 7.

a. Open your template *chap10_ho1_world_template_solution* and save it as **chap10_ho1_world_solution**.

You now have an Excel workbook file, *chap10_ho1_world_solution*, and a *chap10_ho1_world_template_solution* file.

b. Type the initial values in the shaded assumption area, as shown in Figure 10.16.

As you enter each successive value, additional calculations are displayed in the body of the worksheet, as shown in Figure 10.16.

c. Create a custom footer containing your name, today's date, and your instructor's name. Print the completed workbook. Save and close the workbook.

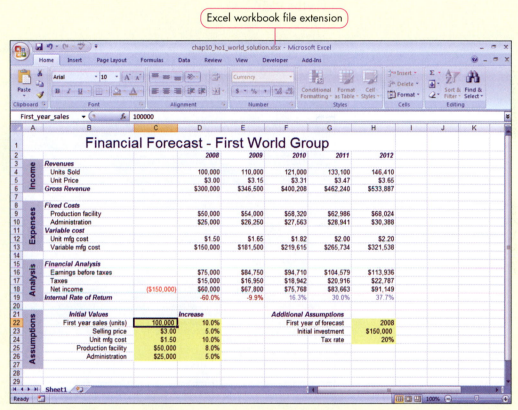

Figure 10.16 Completed Workbook Based on Template

Web Pages and Queries

With the advent of networking and the development of Internet technologies, businesses display vital corporate information in Virtual Private Networks on Web pages.

Excel has a relationship with the Internet in three ways. First, you can insert a hyperlink, or a reference to another document, in an Excel worksheet, and then just click the hyperlink to open your browser and view the document. Second, you can save a workbook as a Web page and view it in your browser, as shown in Figure 10.17. With the advent of networking and the development of Internet technologies, businesses display vital corporate information in Virtual Private Networks on Web pages. Third, you can download information from the Web into an Excel workbook, using a Web query. Remember that Web queries are not dynamic: You have to refresh periodically to make sure the data are current. For example, investors and business analysts use Web queries to download current stock market information for analysis. In addition, international businesses frequently need to address currency conversion and obtain updates to currency rates via the Web.

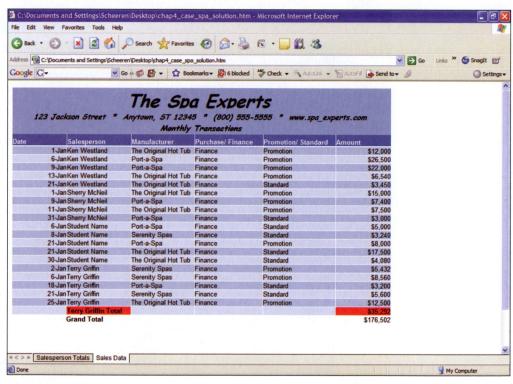

Figure 10.17 Excel Workbook Viewed as a Web Page

In this section, you will create a Web page that includes hyperlinks, pictures, and SmartArt graphics. Further, you will learn to set up a workbook for a Web query.

Creating a Web Page

The basic creation of a Web page from an Excel workbook involves nothing more than saving the Excel workbook as a Web page. However, additions such as hyperlinks, pictures, and SmartArt graphics make Web pages more effective. Previewing the Web page in a browser is also recommended to see how the Web page will look on the Internet. Many businesses communicate with their employees via intranets, where information, such as payroll or benefits, is displayed as a Web page. Businesses communicate with customers by posting information, including price lists and catalog data, to the Web in the form of Web pages. Teachers communicate with parents and students by creating Web pages for assignments and school information.

Insert, Modify, and Remove a Hyperlink

Hyperlinks are links in an application or Web page.

Hyperlinks are electronic markers in an application or Web page that enable you to move to other files or locations. In Excel, hyperlinks can be used for three basic purposes:

- To display a Web page
- To display a different application file, such as a Word file
- To display another worksheet or different location on a large worksheet in Excel

In this chapter, you will consider adding hyperlinks to a Web page. To create a hyperlink to a Web site from Excel:

1. Click in the cell that will contain the hyperlink. You are limited to one hyperlink per cell.
2. Click Hyperlink in the Links group on the Insert tab to open the Insert Hyperlink dialog box.
3. Click Existing File or Web Page in the *Link to* section and type the Web address in the *Address* section, as shown in Figure 10.18.
4. Click ScreenTip and enter the appropriate text to describe the link.
5. Click OK. A hyperlink is created that links to a Web site.

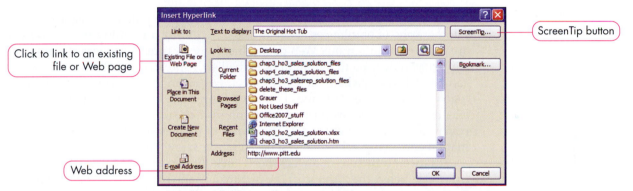

Figure 10.18   Insert Hyperlink Dialog Box

To modify a hyperlink, right-click the hyperlink and select Edit Hyperlink to open the Edit Hyperlink dialog box (see Figure 10.19). Make the desired modifications in this dialog box. Note that if you left-click the hyperlink, your computer will open the browser and retrieve the Web page.

Figure 10.19   Edit Hyperlink Dialog Box

To delete a hyperlink, right-click the hyperlink and choose Remove Hyperlink from the shortcut menu (see Figure 10.20). This removes the hyperlink but not the words describing the hyperlink.

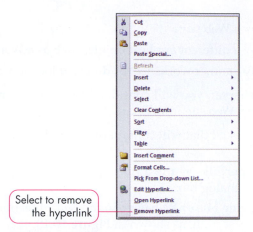

Select to remove the hyperlink

Figure 10.20 Hyperlink Shortcut Menu

Insert a Picture

Pictures of corporate headquarters are often used to enhance business Web pages. Photographs of employees, such as a team winning a monthly productivity award, are often used in intranet Web pages. Inserting Pictures, photographs as opposed to clip art, can be used to highlight or embellish a spreadsheet. Pictures are objects that can be placed anywhere on a worksheet. For example, you could insert a corporate logo picture, images of homes you are selling if the Web page is part of a real estate site, or corporate logos for each stock on a stock summary Web page. Pictures may cover data but never change it. The choice of images should be based on their information enhancing value, not just because you know how to insert a picture.

To insert a picture in a worksheet, click Picture in the Illustrations group on the Insert tab. Select the location of the picture and the picture to be inserted in the Insert Picture dialog box, as shown in Figure 10.21. Click Insert.

Figure 10.21 Insert Picture Dialog Box

When the picture is inserted and active on the worksheet, the Picture Tools Format tab is available, as shown in Figure 10.22. This tab enables you to format the inserted picture by adjusting brightness and other image enhancements. You can add borders, shading, or three-dimensional effects to pictures. If you use more than one picture or add a callout or drawing object, you create layers and must arrange your images using the Arrange options on the Picture Tools tab. Use the Size options to resize and crop your picture. Click in any cell to deselect the image and hide the Picture Tools Format tab.

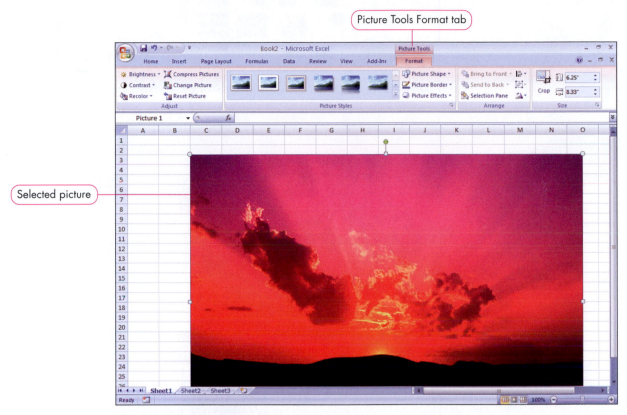

Figure 10.22 Picture Tools Format Tab

Insert a SmartArt Graphic

SmartArt is a graphic organizer diagram that visually presents information to communicate a message.

SmartArt is a new feature in Excel 2007 and is a graphic organizer diagram that visually presents information to communicate a message. It enables you to create and place business graphics—such as hierarchy charts, relationship charts, or process charts—in Excel. You can depict management structure graphically by using hierarchy charts. Medical processes are often depicted graphically, using any one of a variety of several process chart examples. Product production lends itself well to process charts. Educators might use the graphic organizer for mind mapping. All these examples could be used on either intranet or Internet Web pages. Care must be exercised when creating a SmartArt graphic because these graphics are relatively generic and do not always enhance the information value of a workbook. The Reference Table shows the SmartArt categories and descriptions. To create a SmartArt diagram:

1. Click SmartArt in the Illustrations group on the Insert tab.
2. Choose the diagram you want to use, as shown in Figure 10.23, and click OK.
3. Click any [Text] and type your text. If your image includes bullets, press the down arrow to move from bullet to bullet. Some SmartArt enables you to insert images by clicking the icon of the image to open the Insert Picture dialog box. See Figure 10.24 for an example of a text-based SmartArt graphic.
4. Move your SmartArt graphic to the desired location in your workbook.

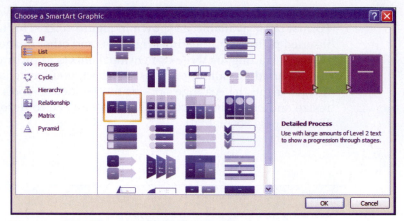

Figure 10.23 Choose a SmartArt Graphic Dialog Box

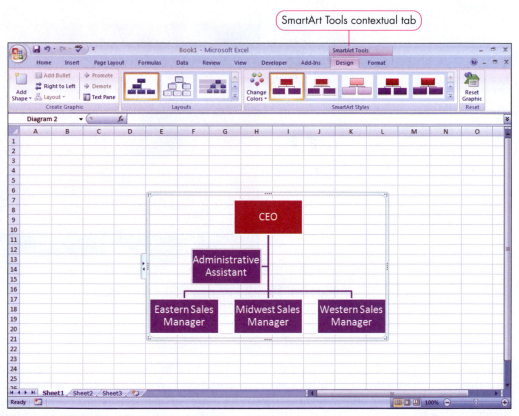

Figure 10.24 Inserted SmartArt Graphic

SmartArt Categories, Descriptions, and Examples | Reference

Category	Description	Example
List	Use to show nonsequential information because arrows are not used between shapes	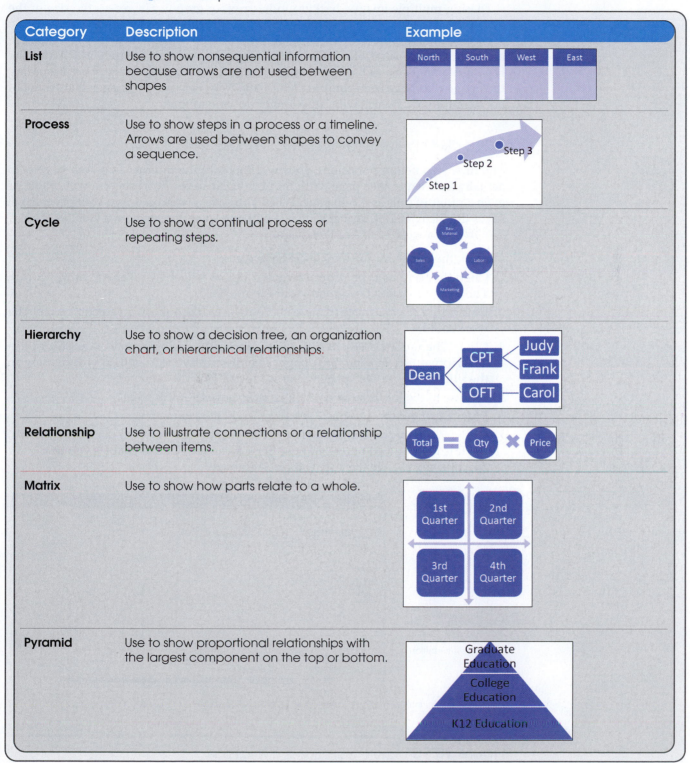
Process	Use to show steps in a process or a timeline. Arrows are used between shapes to convey a sequence.	
Cycle	Use to show a continual process or repeating steps.	
Hierarchy	Use to show a decision tree, an organization chart, or hierarchical relationships.	
Relationship	Use to illustrate connections or a relationship between items.	
Matrix	Use to show how parts relate to a whole.	
Pyramid	Use to show proportional relationships with the largest component on the top or bottom.	

Format a Web Page

It is important for you to realize and understand that just because a workbook or spreadsheet looks fine in Excel, it may not look good when the Web page is published to the Internet. Different browsers can display Web pages differently, and even things such as the resolution of your monitor can affect the display of a Web page.

As a general rule, simplicity should be the watchword for your Web pages. Less is often more. Aim to use no more than two fonts, and take care with font sizes and font color as browsers are not created equal. In addition, using combinations of bold, italic, and underline can detract from your Web page and make reading it difficult.

Using multiple images, backgrounds, or other graphics increases the size of the Web page file and makes downloading slow for those with dial-up connections. Typically, photographs are saved as .jpg files for Web usage with an average file size of 78KB. On the other hand, the average .gif file is approximately 10KB and the HTML file might be 4KB. Keep in mind, these file sizes are average sizes, assuming the image files have been compressed. Many Web sites contain images that have not been compressed, which will cause longer download time.

Save as a Web Page

The final step before publishing your workbook to the Internet as a Web page is to actually save it as a Web page. With Excel, you can save a worksheet, a workbook, or even a range of cells as a Web page. When you save a workbook as a Web page, Excel saves the file in HTML format so that it will be viewed correctly in a Web browser.

To save a workbook as a Web page:

1. Click the Office Button and select Save As.
2. Click the Save as type drop-down arrow and select Web Page (*.htm; *.html). The Save As dialog box is shown in Figure 10.25.
3. Determine if you want to save the entire workbook or a selection from the workbook.
4. Click Change Title to open the Set Page Title dialog box so you can add a descriptive title to your Web page. The descriptive title, which will display in the title bar of the Web page window, documents the Web page.
5. Browse to the location where you want to save the Web page.
6. Enter the file name for your Web page in the File name box.
7. Click either Save or Publish. Save enables you to view the Web page in a browser, but it is not updated unless you use Save As again. Publish enables you to dynamically change the data and the Web page.

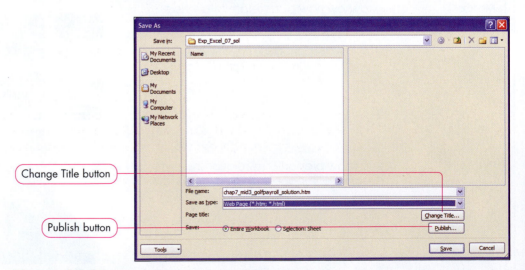

Figure 10.25 Save a Workbook as a Web Page

Creating Web Queries

The Internet—and, more specifically, the Web—provides a wealth of information. Government agencies, corporations, hospitals, colleges and universities, and individuals are just a few examples of entities that upload current information daily.

A **Web query** enables Excel to go to a particular Web site to obtain Web-based information.

Figure 10.26 shows a worksheet with a stock portfolio displayed. The top section shows basic information about stocks, and the bottom portion contains the data about the stocks that were obtained from the Internet to determine the current price of each stock. These data were obtained using a **Web query** that enables Excel to go to a particular Web site to obtain Web-based information. Web queries let you extract data from tables on a Web page.

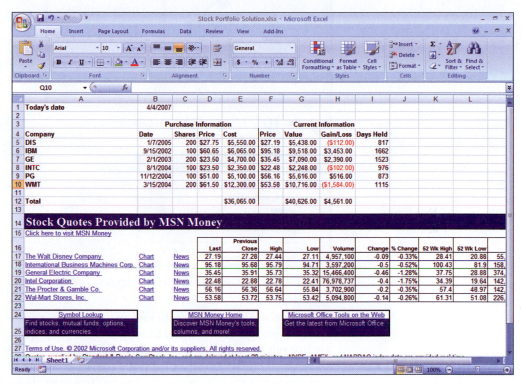

Figure 10.26 Results of a Web Query

Import Web Data

Before setting up a Web query, you should be aware of the limitations of Web queries. A Web query is tied to a specific Web address. If the Web address changes, you must change the Web query and URL to ensure that you have the most accurate information and citation. The information downloaded is based on the structure of the Web page. If the Web page is redesigned to display data in a table structure, for example, and your query is based on data displayed in free form, you will get unexpected results when you refresh your data. If you have to log in to a Web site, the query generally will not work because it has no accommodation made for the storage of your login and password.

To create a Web query:

1. Determine where you will get the data on the Web; that is, locate the correct URL for the Web page containing the information you want to include in your workbook.
2. Click From Web in the Get External Data group on the Data tab. This opens the New Web Query dialog box (see Figure 10.27).
3. Type the Web address in the Address box and click Go to display the Web page.
4. Navigate to the specific data you want to use in your workbook.
5. Select the table containing the data you want to extract.
6. Click the Import button at the bottom right of the New Web Query dialog box to open the Import Data dialog box (see Figure 10.28).
7. Choose where the data should go and click OK. Note the use of absolute cell reference in the Existing worksheet box.

Depending on the speed of your connection, it may take a few minutes to download the data.

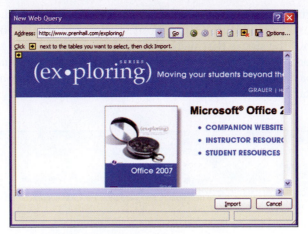

Figure 10.27 New Web Query Dialog Box

Figure 10.28 Import Data Dialog Box

If you are going to create and use multiple queries, it is more efficient to create all your queries at one time. Excel stores all your queries and makes them available for use when you click Existing Connections in the Get External Data group on the Data tab. The Existing Connections dialog box lists your current connections, and you can select the one you want to use. You then click Open to import data. You can also browse the Web to locate new data sources to add to your existing connections.

Refresh a Web Query

In order for your data to be current, you need to refresh a query periodically. The easiest way to refresh your query is to click Refresh All in the Connections group on the Data tab. If you have more than one query in a worksheet, it is better to click Connections in the Connections group on the Data tab to open the Workbook Connections dialog box, as shown in Figure 10.29. You see all your connections and can then select the connection to be refreshed as needed.

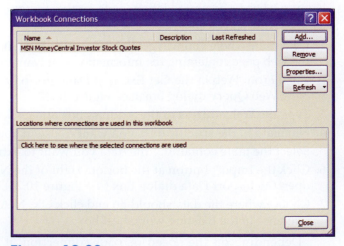

Figure 10.29 Workbook Connections Dialog Box

Hands-On Exercises

2 | Query the Web and Create a Web Page

Skills covered: 1. Open the Stock Portfolio and Complete the Web Query **2.** Compute the Gain or Loss, Copy the Formulas, and Format the Workbook **3.** Insert Hyperlinks, an Image, and a SmartArt Graphic in the Workbook **4.** Save as a Web Page

Step 1 **Open the Stock Portfolio and Complete the Web Query**	Refer to Figure 10.30 as you complete Step 1. **a.** Open the *chap10_ho2_stocks* workbook and save it as **chap10_ho2_stocks_solution** so you can return to the original workbook if necessary. You are going to include a Web query in a workbook to retrieve current stock prices from the Internet. This exercise requires an Internet connection. **b.** Click in **cell B5**, the cell containing the date on which the shares of DIS were purchased. Cell B5 contains the date 1/7/2005 (no equal sign). This is a "fixed" date, meaning that its value will not change from one day to the next. **c.** Click the **Data tab** and click **Existing Connections** in the Get External Data group to open the Existing Connections dialog box, as shown in Figure 10.30. **d.** Click the **MSN MoneyCentral Investor Stock Quotes** query and click **Open** to open the Import Data dialog box. The Import Data dialog box prompts you for information about the Web query. **e.** Verify that **Existing worksheet** is selected, click **cell A14**, and click **OK**. You indicated the location within the current worksheet where the Web query data will be displayed. **f.** Select **cells A5:A10**, click the **Use this value/reference for future refreshes check box**, and click **OK**. You indicated which cells contain the stock symbols used in your query. When you click OK, your system pauses as Excel goes to the Web to retrieve the information, provided you have an Internet connection. You should then see the current stock quotes provided by MSN MoneyCentral Investor. **TROUBLESHOOTING:** Do not be concerned if the column widths change as a result of the query; you can widen them later. **g.** Save the workbook.

Figure 10.30 Existing Connections Dialog Box

<table>
<tr><td rowspan="2">

Step 2

Compute the Gain or Loss, Copy the Formulas, and Format the Workbook
</td><td>

Refer to Figure 10.31 as you complete Step 2.

a. Enter the formulas to calculate the gain or loss:

- Click **cell E5** and type **=C5*D5** to multiply the original cost by the number of shares.

- Click **cell F5** and type **=D17**, which is the cell containing the current price of DIS.

- Click **cell G5** and type **=C5*F5** to multiply the number of shares by the current price.

- Click **cell H5** and type **=G5-E5**. Today's value minus the cost is used to determine your profit or loss.

- Click **cell I5** and type **=$B$1-B5** to determine how many days you have held the stock.

TROUBLESHOOTING: If necessary, change the format in cell I5 to reflect a number rather than a date.

b. Select **cells E5:I5** and copy the formulas through **cell I10**.

You copied your formulas to finish the calculation area of your stock portfolio workbook.

c. Click **cell E12** and enter the SUM function to determine the total cost of your investments.

d. Copy the formula in cell E12 to cells G12 and H12.

The displayed value in cell E12 should be 36065. The displayed values in cells G12 and H12 depend on the current stock prices. The value of your portfolio will vary depending on the current price of your stocks.

e. Select **cells D5:H12** and format as **Currency**.

f. Select all the cells that contain labels—**cell A1, cells A3:I4, A5:A10**, and **cell A12**—and click Bold.

g. Select **cells B3:E3** and click **Merge & Center**.
</td></tr>
</table>

h. Select **cells F3:I3** and click **Merge & Center**.

i. Adjust the column widths, if necessary, and save the workbook.

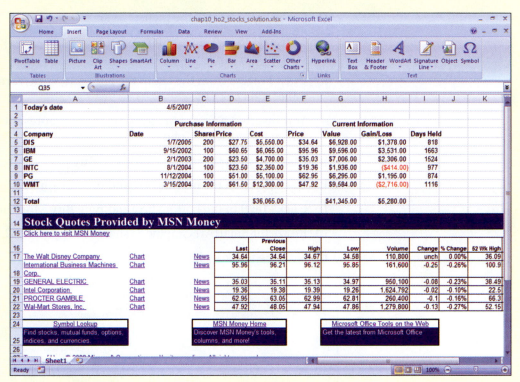

Figure 10.31 Final Stock Portfolio Workbook

Step 3
Insert Hyperlinks, an Image, and a SmartArt Graphic in the Workbook

Refer to Figure 10.32 as you complete Step 3.

a. Click **cell K4** and type **Company Web Links**.

b. Enter the following labels in the cells indicated below:
- **Walt Disney** in **cell K5**
- **IBM** in **cell K6**
- **General Electric** in **cell K7**
- **Intel** in **cell K8**
- **Procter & Gamble** in **cell K9**
- **Wal-Mart** in **cell K10**

c. Click **cell K5**, click the **Insert tab**, and click **Hyperlink** in the Links group to open the Insert Hyperlink dialog box.

d. Type **corporate.disney.go.com** in the Address box and click **OK**.

You entered the URL in the Insert Hyperlink dialog box to create a live link in your workbook.

e. In a similar manner, type the following URLs in the cells indicated below:
- **www.ibm.com** in **cell K6**
- **www.ge.com** in **cell K7**
- **www.intel.com** in **cell K8**
- **www.pg.com** in **cell K9**
- **www.walmart.com** in **cell K10**

f. Click **cell J12**, click **Picture** in the Illustrations group, locate and click the picture **stock.jpg**, and click **Insert**.

You inserted a picture that represents stocks.

g. Resize and relocate the picture as shown in Figure 10.32.

h. Click **cell J5** and click **SmartArt** in the Illustrations group to open the Choose a SmartArt Graphic dialog box.

i. Click **Process** from the list in the left pane, click **Vertical Process** in the middle pane, and click **OK**.

You inserted a SmartArt graphic that is representative of the process used to manage a stock portfolio.

j. Click **[Text]** in the top box and type **Buy**.

k. Click **[Text]** in the middle box and type **Evaluate**.

l. Click **[Text]** in the bottom box and type **Buy More or Sell**.

m. Resize the SmartArt Graphic as shown in Figure 10.32. Widen column J if necessary.

n. Save the workbook.

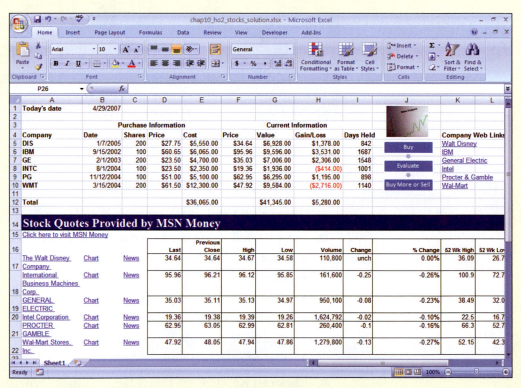

Figure 10.32 Links and Art in a Workbook

Refer to Figure 10.33 as you complete Step 4.

a. Click the **Office Button** and select **Save As** to open the Save As dialog box.

You will use the Save As option to convert your workbook to a Web page that can be viewed in any Web browser.

b. Click the **Save as type drop-down arrow** and select **Web Page (*.htm; *.html)**.

c. Verify that **Entire workbook** is selected and the file name is *chap10_ho2_stocks_ solution.htm*.

Note that your file has the extension .htm, which indicates a Web page.

d. Click **Change Title**, type **Student Investments**, click **OK**, and click **Save**.

You converted your workbook to a Web page.

e. Click **Yes** in the Microsoft Office warning box.

f. Exit Excel and open your Web browser.

g. Open the file *chap10_ho2_stocks_solution.htm* in your Web browser.

Your investment Web page is displayed in the browser window.

h. Review your Web page and close the browser.

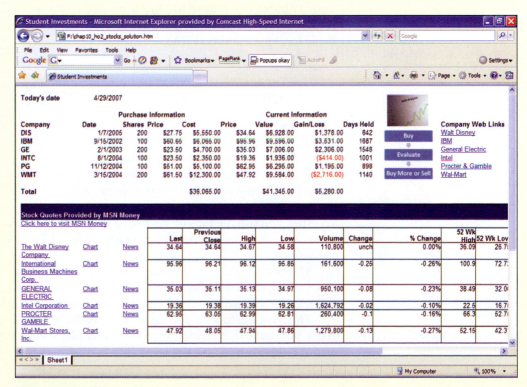

Figure 10.33 A Web Page

Macros and VBA

Have you ever used the same tabs and clicked the same sequence of commands repetitively when creating your workbook? Although the sequence may be easy to execute, it is a burden to continually repeat the same mouse clicks or keystrokes. If you can think of any task that you do repeatedly, whether in one workbook or in a series of workbooks, you are a candidate to use macros. A macro is used to automate such repetitive tasks as printing or inserting often used complex formulas. Specifically, the following tasks are easily automated using macros:

(Have you ever used the same tabs and clicked the same sequence of commands repetitively when creating your workbooks?)

- Insert a group of often-used cells.
- Analyze a selection of cells.
- Apply specific print formats.
- Apply consistent formatting.

A *macro* is a set of instructions that tells Excel which commands to execute.

Visual Basic is a programming language used to create macros.

A *macro* is a set of instructions that tells Excel which commands to execute. It is, for all purposes, a program, and its instructions are written in *Visual Basic*, a programming language. You do not have to be a programmer to write macros; instead, you use the Macro Recorder within Excel to record your commands, keystrokes, and mouse clicks, and let Excel write the macros for you.

In this section, you will learn how to use the Macro Recorder to record a macro. You will also learn how to play a macro, test a macro, create macro buttons, and review macro security issues. Finally, you will gain a basic understanding of Visual Basic for Applications (VBA).

Creating a Macro with the Macro Recorder

The Macro Recorder stores Excel commands, in the form of Visual Basic instructions, within a workbook. Visual Basic for Applications (VBA) is a subset of Visual Basic that is built into Microsoft Office. To use the Macro Recorder, click the Macros down arrow in the Macros group and select Record Macros. From that point until you stop recording, every command you execute will be stored by the recorder. It does not matter whether you execute commands from drop-down arrows via the mouse or whether you use the tabs or keyboard shortcuts. The Macro Recorder captures every action you take and stores the equivalent Visual Basic statements in a macro within the workbook.

The two ways to create a macro are by creating the macro manually, using VBA, or by using the Excel Macro Recorder. The easiest way is to use the Macro Recorder, but this method sacrifices the power and flexibility that VBA brings to the mix.

The .xlsx file format you have been working with is perfectly satisfactory for the work you have done so far. However, this file format is not able to store macros. To address this issue, Excel has two other file formats that do store macros:

- XLSM files are macro enabled workbooks. They are stored using XML.
- XLSB files are workbooks stored in binary format. This format is often used for very large spreadsheets.

The Macro Recorder, which is the way you will create and record macros in this chapter, has some issues you must keep in mind:

- Everything you do once you begin recording a macro becomes part of the macro. If you click something in error, you have to edit the code to correct it.
- Take your time and be sure the action is correct. No time limit exists in the macro record process.
- Try to ensure your macros are broad enough to apply to a variety of situations.

It is important to determine if your macro should contain absolute cell references or relative cell references. You would generally use absolute references if the data are always in the same position, such as adding custom footer information at the bottom of documents. Relative references are used when you want to repeat a task in several places, such as with the imposition of formatting.

Figure 10.34 illustrates a simple macro to enter your name and class in cells A1 and A2 of the active worksheet. The macro is displayed in the Visual Basic Editor (VBE), which is used to create, edit, execute, and debug Excel macros. VBE is a separate application that is accessible from any application in Microsoft Office.

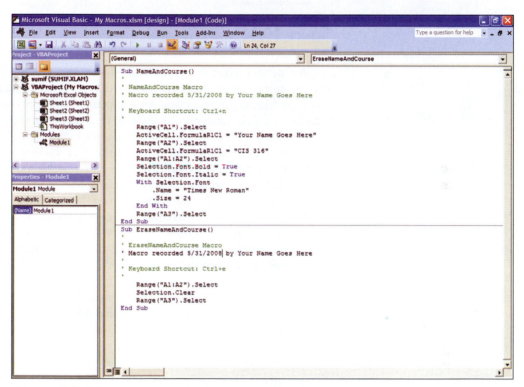

Figure 10.34 Visual Basic Application Editor Display of a Macro

The left side of the VBE window, shown in Figure 10.35, contains the Project Explorer, which is similar in concept and appearance to the Windows Explorer except that it displays only open workbooks and/or other Visual Basic projects. The Visual Basic statements for the selected module (Module1 in Figure 10.36) appear in the Code window in the right pane. A Visual Basic module consists of one or more procedures, each of which corresponds to an Excel macro. In this example, Module1 contains the NameAndCourse procedure, which corresponds to the Excel macro of the same name. Module1 is stored in the My Macros.xlsm workbook.

Figure 10.35 Project Explorer

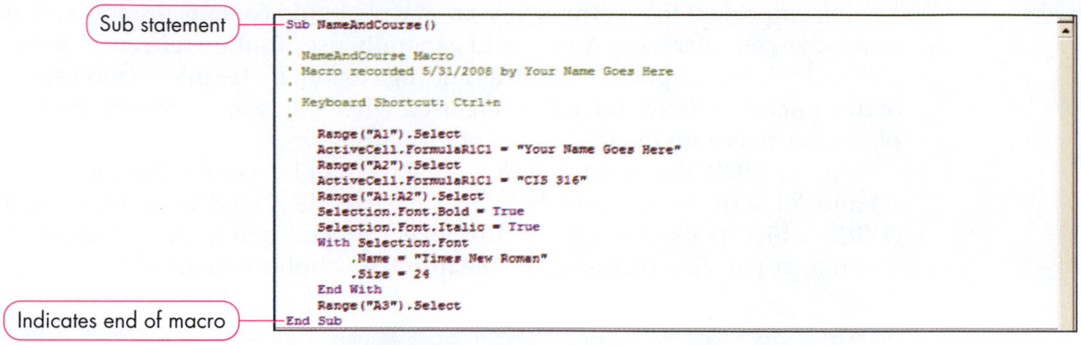

Sub statement

Indicates end of macro

```
Sub NameAndCourse()
'
' NameAndCourse Macro
' Macro recorded 5/31/2008 by Your Name Goes Here
'
' Keyboard Shortcut: Ctrl+n
'
    Range("A1").Select
    ActiveCell.FormulaR1C1 = "Your Name Goes Here"
    Range("A2").Select
    ActiveCell.FormulaR1C1 = "CIS 316"
    Range("A1:A2").Select
    Selection.Font.Bold = True
    Selection.Font.Italic = True
    With Selection.Font
        .Name = "Times New Roman"
        .Size = 24
    End With
    Range("A3").Select
End Sub
```

Figure 10.36 Code Window

A macro consists of Visual Basic statements created through the Macro Recorder. You are not expected to be able to write the Visual Basic procedure yourself. You just open the Macro Recorder and let it capture the Excel commands for you. It is important, however, to understand a macro and to see its statements.

A macro always begins and ends with the Sub and End Sub statements. The Sub statement contains the name of the macro—for example, NameAndCourse in Figure 10.36. Spaces are not allowed in a macro name. The End Sub statement is physically the last statement and indicates the end of the macro. Sub and End Sub are Visual Basic keywords and appear in blue.

Comments provide information about a macro, but do not affect its execution and are considered documentation.

The next several statements begin with an apostrophe, appear in green, and are known as comments. *Comments* provide information about the macro, but do not affect its execution and are considered documentation. The results of a macro are the same, even if the comments are included. Comments are inserted automatically by the recorder to document the macro name, its author, and shortcut key (if any). You can add comments (a comment line must begin with an apostrophe), or delete or modify existing comments. You can also add comments at the end of a statement by typing an apostrophe and then adding the explanatory text.

Every other statement in a macro is a Visual Basic instruction that was created as a result of an action taken in Excel. For example, the statements

    Range ("A1").Select
    ActiveCell.FormulaR1C1="Darren Krein"

select cell A1 as the active cell, and then enter the text "Darren Krein" in the active cell. These statements are equivalent to clicking in cell A1 of a worksheet, typing the indicated entry in the active cell, and then pressing Enter to complete the entry. Similarly, the statements

    Range ("A2").Select
    ActiveCell.FormulaR1C1="CIS 316"

select cell A2 as the active cell, and then enter the text entry "CIS 316" into that cell. The concept of select-then-do applies to statements within a macro. The statements

    Range ("A1:A2").Select
    Selection.Font.Bold = True
    Selection.Font.Italic = True

select cells A1:A2, and then change the font for the selected cells to bold italic. The With statement enables you to perform multiple actions on the same object. All commands between the With and the corresponding End With statement are executed collectively. The statements

    With Selection.Font
        .Name = "Times New Roman"
        .Size = 24
    End With

format the selected cells (A1:A2) with 24-point Times New Roman. The last macro statement, Range ("A3").Select, selects cell A3, deselecting all other cells.

Create (Record) the Macro

The actual creation or, more specifically, the recording of a macro is a relatively straightforward process. The trick is to be careful and thorough when creating a macro to ensure that it does not have to be edited and to ensure that it performs the task it is designed to do. Before recording a macro, you should plan it first and make sure you know the sequence of tasks you want to perform. After planning a macro, you are ready to record it. To create a macro:

1. Click Record Macro in the Macros down arrow in the Macros group of the View tab to open the Record Macro dialog box, as shown in Figure 10.37.
2. Type a name for the macro in the Macro name box. Macro names cannot include spaces or special characters and must start with a letter.
3. Create a keyboard shortcut, if desired, for your macro in the Shortcut key box. Exercise caution because many Ctrl+ shortcuts are already used in Excel. To be safe, it is best to use Ctrl+Shift+ for keyboard shortcuts for macros.
4. Select a location to store the macro from the Store macro in drop-down arrow.
5. Click OK to start recording the macro.
6. Determine whether to use relative or absolute cell references in the macro. Click Use Relative References from the Macros drop-down list in the Macros group on the View tab to use relative references.
7. Perform the actions to be recorded in the macro.
8. To stop recording the macro and save it, click Stop Recording in the Macros down arrow list in the Macros group in the View tab.

Figure 10.37 Record Macro Dialog Box

Play or Test a Macro

Just as the process for creating a macro is straightforward, so is the process for testing a macro by playing it. Playing a macro means running, or executing, the macro. When you run a macro, Excel performs the tasks in the sequence in which you recorded the steps. To test a macro:

1. Select the location where the macro will be tested. It is often good policy to test a macro in a new, blank workbook.
2. Click View Macros from the Macros down arrow in the Macros group on the View tab to open the Macro dialog box, as shown in Figure 10.38.
3. Select the macro from the list and click Run. Macros may be deleted using the Macro dialog box.

Figure 10.38 Macro Dialog Box

Creating Macro Buttons

For the most part, it will be a rare macro that is so all-encompassing that it would rate a place on the Quick Access Toolbar. On the other hand, you may create a macro that is frequently used in a particular workbook. The easiest way to deal with this issue is to attach a macro to a button on a worksheet. That way when other people use the spreadsheet, they can click the button and run the macro.

Creating a button on a worksheet requires two steps because the Developer tab must be on the Ribbon, and it is not one of the default installation options. To place the Developer tab on the Ribbon, click the Office Button and click Excel Options. Choose the *Popular* section and check Show Developer tab in the Ribbon, as shown in Figure 10.39. Click OK to close the Excel Options dialog box.

Show Developer tab on the Ribbon

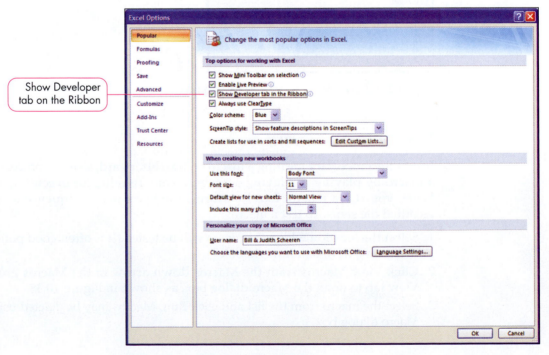

Figure 10.39 Popular Options

When the Developer tab is on the Ribbon, you are ready to add a macro button to the spreadsheet. These are the steps:

1. Click the Developer tab, click Insert in the Controls group, and select Button from Form Controls. See Figure 10.40.
2. Drag the + to draw the button on the worksheet. When the drawing is completed, the Assign Macro dialog box opens, as shown in Figure 10.41.
3. Select the macro to be attached to the button and click OK.
4. Right-click the button and choose Edit Text to change the default text to more descriptive text.
5. Click the worksheet to complete the button, as shown in Figure 10.42.
6. Click the button to execute the linked macro.

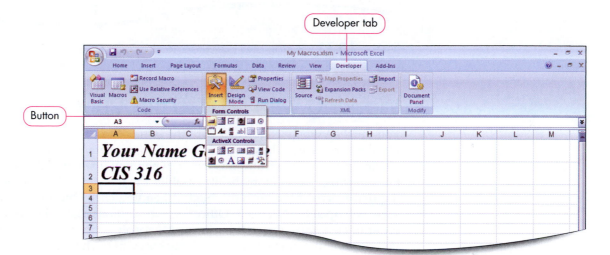

Figure 10.40   Form Controls

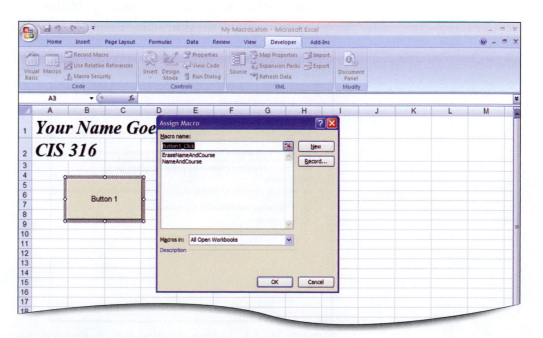

Figure 10.41   Assign Macro Dialog Box

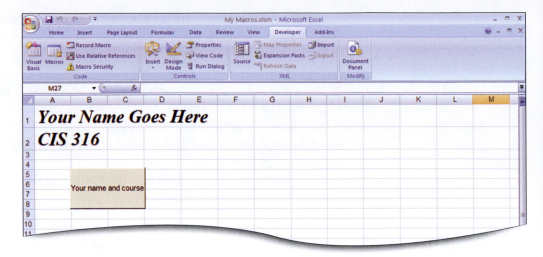

Figure 10.42 Button and Executed Macro

Working with Macro Security

You must be vitally concerned with the issue of macro security. The proliferation of Excel macro viruses has made it a dangerous operation to open spreadsheets that contain macros. To counter this threat, when you open an Excel workbook that contains macros, Excel automatically disables the macros and displays a security warning that macros have been disabled. When you click Options on this warning message, you open the Microsoft Office Security Options dialog box (see Figure 10.43). In order to customize the settings in the Microsoft Office Security Options dialog box, you can use the Trust Center, which enables you to change settings to make it easier to work with macros. The Trust Center can direct Excel to:

- Trust files in particular folders.
- Trust workbooks created by a trusted publisher.
- Lower security settings to allow macros.

Figure 10.43 Microsoft Office Security Options Dialog Box

To open the Trust Center, you can either click Open the Trust Center in the Microsoft Office Security Options dialog box or click the Office Button and then click Excel options. You can also select Trust Center in the Excel Options window and click Trust Center Settings to open the Trust Center dialog box (see Figure 10.44). The Trust Center dialog box displays the sections described in Table 10.1 on the left side of the dialog box.

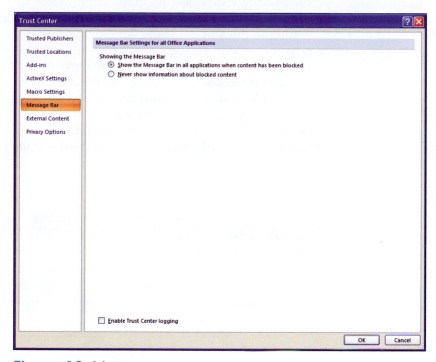

Figure 10.44 Trust Center Dialog Box

Table 10.1 Trust Center Options

Item	Description
Trusted Publishers	Directs Excel to trust digitally signed workbooks by certain creators.
Trusted Locations	Enables you to select places on your computer to store workbooks.
Add-ins	Enables you to decide which add-ins will be supported.
ActiveX Settings	Enables you to adjust how Excel deals with ActiveX controls.
Macro Settings	Enables you to decide how Excel deals with macros.
Message Bar	Enables you to decide when Excel shows the message bar when it blocks macros.
External Content	Enables you to decide how Excel deals with links to other workbooks and data from other sources.
Privacy Options	Enables you to deal with non-macro privacy issues.

Understanding the Basics of VBA

Originally, Excel macros were nothing more than recorded keystrokes. In earlier versions of Excel, you turned on the Macro Recorder to capture the associated keystrokes, and then you "played back" those keystrokes when you ran the macro. Starting with Office 95, the recorded keystrokes were translated into Visual Basic commands, which gave macros the potential to be much more powerful because you could execute Visual Basic programs from within Excel. Microsoft Office uses a subset of Visual Basic known as Visual Basic for Applications (VBA).

You can think of the Macro Recorder as a shortcut to generate VBA code. When you have that code, you can modify the various statements, using techniques common to any programming language. You can move or copy statements within a procedure or search for one character string and replace it with another. Finally, you can insert additional VBA statements that are beyond the scope of ordinary Excel commands. You can, for example, display information to the user in the form of a message box any time during the execution of the macro. You can also accept information from the user in a dialog box called an input box, for subsequent use in the macro.

TIP   Simplify the Macro

The Macro Recorder usually sets all possible options for an Excel command or dialog box, even if you do not change those options. It is suggested that you make a macro easier to read in VBA by deleting the unnecessary statements. Take a minute, however, to review the statement prior to removing them, so that you can see the options available.

Hands-On Exercises

3 | Work with Macros and Visual Basic for Applications

Skills covered: 1. Create the Macro **2.** Run the Macro **3.** Use the Visual Basic Editor **4.** Create and Use the Erase Macro **5.** Step Through the Macro and Print the VBA Code **6.** Add a Custom Button and Print the Workbook

Step 1 Create the Macro	Refer to Figure 10.45 as you complete Step 1.

a. Start Excel, click the **Office Button**, click **Excel Options**, check **Show Developer tab in the Ribbon**, and click **OK**.

It is necessary to have the Developer tab installed before you can create macro buttons.

b. Click the **Office Button** and select **Save As** to open the Save As dialog box.

c. Click **Excel Macro-Enabled Workbook (*.xlsm)** from the Save as type drop-down arrow.

d. Type **chap10_ho3_macros_solution** in the File name box and click **Save**.

You must save your workbook in the Macro Enabled format for the macros to be available for use.

e. Click the **View tab**, click the **Macros down arrow** in the Macros group, and select **Record Macro** to display the Record Macro dialog box.

You will create a macro to enter your name and your instructor's name in cells A1 and A2, respectively.

f. Type **NameAndInstructor** as the name of the macro.

TROUBLESHOOTING: Remember that spaces are not allowed in the name of a macro.

g. Click the **Shortcut Key check box** and type a lowercase **n**.

Ctrl+n should appear as the shortcut. If you see Ctrl+Shift+N, it means you typed an uppercase N rather than a lowercase letter. Correct the entry to a lowercase n.

h. Type today's date and your name as the person who created the macro in the **Description** box.

i. Verify that **Store macro in This Workbook** is selected and click **OK**.

j. Click the **Macros down arrow** in the Macros group and select **Use Relative References** to turn on relative references in your macro.

TROUBLESHOOTING: The Relative References option is a toggle command. You select it to turn it on, and you select it again to turn it off. You want the cell references in your first macro to be relative. You want to click in any cell, run the macro, and see your name and instructor's name in that cell.

k. Execute the following macro steps to record your macro:

- Click **cell A1** even if it is already selected and type Your Name.
- Click **cell A2** and type your instructor's name.
- Select **cells A1:A2**.
- Click **Bold** and click **Italic**.

- Change the font size to **14**.
- Click **cell A3** to deselect all other cells prior to ending the macro.
- Click the **View tab**, click the **Macros down arrow**, and select **Stop Recording**.

You created a simple macro to enter your name and your instructor's name in cells A1 and A2. You formatted both cells with bold and italic.

TROUBLESHOOTING: To stop recording your macro at any time, click Stop Recording in the Macro down arrow in the Macros group.

l. Save the workbook.

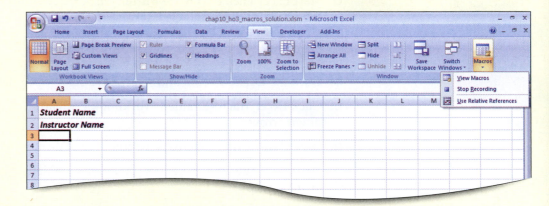

Figure 10.45 Macro Execution and Stop Recording Options

Step 2
Run the Macro

Refer to Figure 10.46 as you complete Step 2.

a. Select **cells A1:A2**, click the **Home tab**, and click **Delete** in the cells group.

Before you run or test your macro, you should remove the contents and formatting from cells A1 and A2.

b. Click the **View tab**, click the **Macros down arrow** in the Macros group, and select **View Macros** to open the Macro dialog box.

c. Click **NameAndInstructor** and click **Run**.

Your name and your instructor's name are entered in cells A1 and A2 and then formatted according to the instructions in the macro you just recorded.

d. Click **cell G8** and press **Ctrl+n**, the keyboard shortcut, to rerun the NameAndInstructor macro.

Your name and instructor should appear in cells G8 and G9, but this time you used the keyboard shortcut you assigned to your macro.

e. Save the workbook.

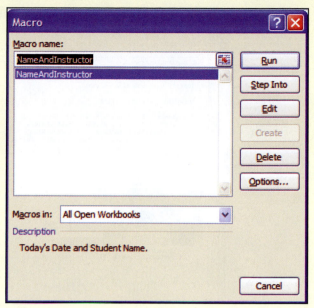

Figure 10.46 Macro Dialog Box

TIP   Macro Errors

If your macro contains errors or otherwise does not perform as designed, delete the macro and begin recording again. Editing an incorrect macro or one that does not perform as designed requires programming skills that are beyond the scope of this text.

Step 3
Use the Visual Basic Editor

Refer to Figure 10.47 as you complete Step 3.

a. Click the **Developer tab** and click **Visual Basic** in the Code group to open the Microsoft Visual Basic Editor.

You can use Alt+F11 to open the VBA editor.

b. If necessary, click the **Maximize button** in the Code window.

c. Change the NameAndInstructor macro by changing the font name and size to Times New Roman and 24, respectively, as shown in Figure 10.47.

d. Select the next nine statements, as shown in Figure 10.47.

e. Press **Delete** to delete these statements from the macro.

You changed the font and font size and deleted the character enhancement code lines that were not used in this macro.

f. Press **Alt+F11** to toggle back to the Excel workbook.

g. Clear the entries and formatting in any cells as you did earlier, click **cell A1**, and run the NameAndInstructor macro again.

Your name and your instructor's name should again be entered in cells A1 and A2 but in a different and larger font. If the macro does not execute correctly, press Alt+F11 to toggle back to the Visual Basic Editor to correct your macro.

h. Save the workbook.

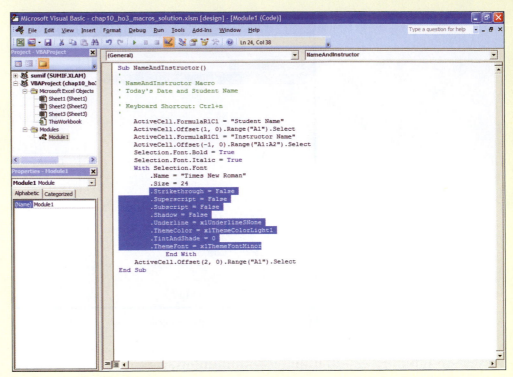

Figure 10.47 Visual Basic Code

Step 4
Create and Use the Erase Macro

a. Click the **View tab**, click the **Macros down arrow** in the Macros group, and select **Record Macro** to display the Record Macro dialog box.

   You will create a macro to erase your name and your instructor's name from your worksheet.

b. Type **EraseNameAndInstructor** as the name of the macro.

c. Click the **Shortcut Key check box** and type an uppercase **E**.

   Ctrl+Shift+E appears as your shortcut.

d. Type today's date and your name as the person who created the macro in the **Description** box.

e. Verify that **Store macro in This Workbook** is selected and click **OK**.

f. Verify that **Use Relative References** in the Macros down arrow in the Macros group is off (that is, not selected).

g. Execute the following macro steps to record your macro:

   - Select **cells A1:A2**.
   - Click the **Home tab** and click **Delete Cells** in the Cells group.
   - Click **cell A3** to deselect all other cells prior to ending the macro.
   - Click the **View tab**, click the **Macros down arrow** in the Macros group, and select **Stop Recording**.

   You created a simple macro to erase your name and your instructor's name in cells A1 and A2.

h. Click **cell A1** and press **Crtl+n** to insert the names in cells A1 and A2.

   You need to reenter your name and your instructor's name to test the newly created EraseNameAndInstructor macro.

i. Press **Ctrl+Shift+e** to erase the names from cells A1 and A2.

Cells A1 and A2 should again be empty. You can press Ctrl+n and Ctrl+Shift+e repeatedly to enter and then erase your name and your instructor's name. End this step after you erase the data.

j. Save the workbook.

Step 5
Step Through the Macro and Print the VBA Code

Refer to Figure 10.48 as you complete Step 5.

a. Click the **Visual Basic window** to make it active.

b. Close the Project pane and the Properties pane.

The Visual Basic code window fills the screen.

c. Right-click an empty area of the Windows taskbar and select **Tile Windows Vertically**.

You have vertically tiled both your workbook and the VBA code window.

d. Click in **cell A1**.

e. Click an insertion point in front of the first Sub in the VBA window.

f. Press **F8** to begin the step through process.

You will press F8 for each line of code in your first module and see each line execute in the open workbook window.

g. Press **F8** until you reach the End Sub line of code.

Both names again appear in cells A1 and A2.

h. Click an insertion point in front of the second Sub in the VBA window.

i. Press **F8** to begin and to step through the code.

Both names are erased from the workbook.

j. Click **File** in the VBA window, select **Print**, and click **OK** to print your VBA code.

k. Close the VBA window, maximize the workbook window, and save your workbook.

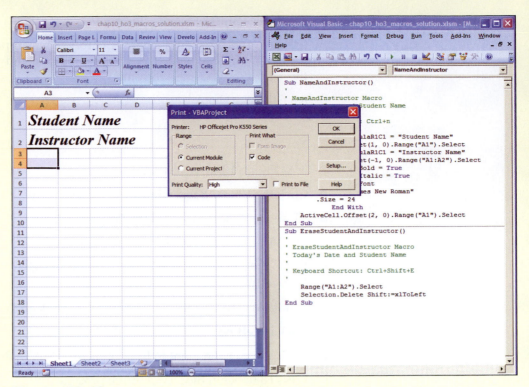

Figure 10.48 Step Through and Print VBA

Step 6

Add a Custom Button and Print the Workbook

Refer to Figure 10.49 as you complete Step 6.

a. Click the **Developer tab** and click **Button (Form Control)** from the Insert down arrow in the Controls group.

b. Use the cross-hair to draw a button over **cells B4:C7**.

The Assign Macro dialog box opens when you finish drawing the button.

c. Select **NameAndInstructor** from the list of available macros and click **OK**.

You created a button that will execute the NameAndInstructor macro.

d. With the button selected, highlight the text and type **Name and Instructor Macro**.

e. Click **cell A1** to deselect the button.

f. Click your **Name and Instructor Macro** button.

Your name and your instructor's name appear in cells A1 and A2.

g. Capture the workbook window, paste the image in **cell F1**, and move and resize the image below your button, as shown in Figure 10.49.

TROUBLESHOOTING: Use PrtScn (Print Screen) to capture the active window and Paste to paste the image.

h. Create a custom footer with your name, today's date, and your instructor's name. Save, print, and close the workbook.

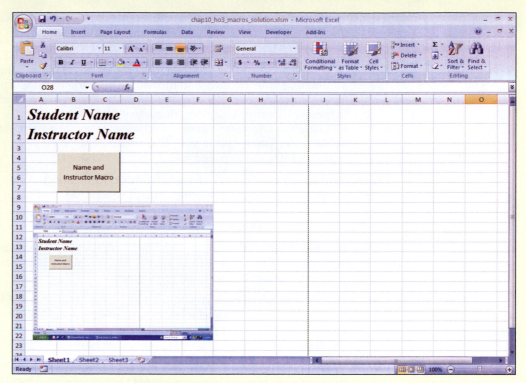

Figure 10.49 Custom Button

Summary

1. **Work with existing templates, themes, and styles.** Excel has several tools that can assist you in automating your creation and formatting of worksheets. Corporations use logos as the basis for the creation of a corporate identity. The logo, however, is just one piece of the corporate identity. A standard document look and feel, applies to workbooks. You use Excel tools such as templates, themes, and styles to create a corporate identity. These tools are available for you to use in your Excel documents to make some formatting tasks easier and to standardize the look and feel of your workbooks.

2. **Create and apply custom styles for advanced formatting.** A style is a set of formatting characteristics stored under a specific name. The advantage of saving formatting characteristics as a style is that when you change the definition of the style, all cells defined by that style change automatically.

3. **Create and use a template.** Using predefined templates can be a great time saver, but the predefined templates will not always meet your needs. When this is the case, you will want to create a template that meets your exact requirements.

4. **Create a Web page.** The basic creation of a Web page from an Excel workbook involves nothing more than saving the Excel workbook as a Web page. However, additions such as hyperlinks, pictures, and SmartArt graphics make Web pages more effective. Previewing a Web page in a browser is recommended so that you can see how the Web page will look on the Internet.

5. **Create Web queries.** Using a Web query enables Excel to go to a particular Web site to obtain Web-based information. Web queries are not perfect. You may have to face a number of issues with Web queries. For example, they are tied to specific Web addresses. If the Web address changes, you must change the Web query and URL to ensure that you have the most accurate information and citation. The information downloaded is based on the structure of the Web page. If the Web page is redesigned to display data in a table structure, for example, and the query is based on data displayed in free form, you will get unexpected results when you refresh the data. If you have to log in to a Web site, the query generally will not work because no accommodation is made for the storage of your login name and password.

6. **Create a macro with the Macro Recorder.** Macros are programs that perform a series of steps in any workbook automatically. Specifically, the following tasks are easily automated using macros: insert a group of often used cells, analyze a selection of cells, apply specific print formats, apply consistent formatting. The two ways to create a macro are either by creating the macro manually using VBA or by using the Excel Macro Recorder. The easiest way is to use the Macro Recorder, but this method sacrifices the power and flexibility that VBA brings to the mix.

7. **Create macro buttons.** For the most part, it will be a rare macro that is so all-encompassing that it would rate a place on the Quick Access Toolbar. On the other hand, you may create a macro that is frequently used in a particular workbook. The easiest way to deal with this issue is to attach a macro to a button on a worksheet. That way users of the spreadsheet can click the button and run the macro.

8. **Work with macro security.** The issue of macro security is vitally important. The proliferation of Excel macro viruses has made it dangerous to open spreadsheets that contain macros. To counter this threat, when you open an Excel workbook that contains macros, Excel automatically disables the macros and displays a message that security warning macros have been disabled.

9. **Understand the basics of VBA.** Originally, Excel macros were nothing more than recorded keystrokes. In earlier versions of Excel, you turned on the Macro Recorder to capture the associated keystrokes and then "played back" those keystrokes when you ran the macro. Starting with Office 95, the recorded keystrokes were translated into Visual Basic commands, which gave macros the potential to be much more powerful because you could execute Visual Basic programs from within Excel. Microsoft Office uses a subset of Visual Basic known as Visual Basic for Applications (VBA). You can think of the Macro Recorder as a shortcut to generate VBA code. When you have that code, you can modify the various statements, using techniques common to any programming language. You can, for example, move or copy statements within a procedure or search for one character string and replace it with another.

Key Terms

Multiple Choice

1. You have written a set of instructions that tells Excel which commands to perform. What you have written is known as:

    (a) The Visual Basic Editor

    (b) A macro

    (c) A command

    (d) The Code window

2. Which programming language is used to create Excel macros?

    (a) XML

    (b) VBA

    (c) VB.NET

    (d) C#.NET

3. What happens if you insert an apostrophe (') at the beginning of a line in an Excel macro?

    (a) The statement is displayed in red to signify that it has been changed.

    (b) At runtime, the macro pauses prior to executing the statement.

    (c) At runtime, the line is ignored.

    (d) At runtime, the entire macro is executed, one line at a time.

4. In the Visual Basic Editor, the VBA statements are displayed in the:

    (a) Project Explorer

    (b) Immediate pane

    (c) Macro recorder

    (d) Code window

5. Which of the following statements must be used to define the end of a macro?

    (a) Close

    (b) End Sub

    (c) End Macro

    (d) Stop

6. What is the purpose of the Step Into command?

    (a) It executes one macro statement at a time.

    (b) It enables you to pause the macro and select cells in the worksheet to which macro commands apply.

    (c) It enables you to pause the macro and edit incorrect formulas in the worksheet.

    (d) It enables you to specify input parameters to the macro.

7. How do you select a macro button to rename, move, or size it?

    (a) Point to the button, click the left mouse button, and follow the shortcut menu.

    (b) Point to the button, double-click the left mouse button, and follow the shortcut menu.

    (c) Point to the button, hold-down the Ctrl key, and click the left mouse button.

    (d) Point to the button, click the right mouse button, and select Options from the shortcut menu.

8. What is the best way to enter the current price of a stock into an Excel worksheet?

    (a) Copy the price directly from today's copy of *The Wall Street Journal*.

    (b) Save the worksheet as a Web page.

    (c) Create a Web query, and then refresh the query to obtain the current price.

    (d) Use Internet Explorer to locate a Web page that contains the current price.

9. Excel and Internet Explorer are both open and display the "same" worksheet. You make a change in the Excel file that is not reflected in the Web page. What is the most likely explanation?

    (a) The two files are not linked to one another.

    (b) The files are stored locally, as opposed to on a Web server.

    (c) You did not refresh the Web page in Microsoft Excel.

    (d) You did not refresh the Web page in Internet Explorer.

10. Which of the following best describes how to protect a worksheet but still enable the user to change the values of various cells within the worksheet?

    (a) Protect the entire worksheet, and then unlock the cells that are to change.

    (b) Protect the entire worksheet, and then unprotect the cells that are to change.

    (c) Lock the cells that are to change, and then protect the entire worksheet.

    (d) Unlock the cells that are to change, and then protect the entire worksheet.

11. What is the easiest way to change the formatting of five cells that are scattered throughout a worksheet, each of which has the same style?

   (a) Select the cells individually, and then click the appropriate buttons on the Formatting toolbar.

   (b) Select the cells at the same time, and then click the appropriate buttons on the Formatting toolbar.

   (c) Change the format of the existing style.

   (d) Reenter the data in each cell according to the new specifications.

12. When you create a new workbook based on a template called Expense Account but see Expense Account1 displayed on the title bar, what is the most likely explanation?

   (a) You are the first person to use this template.

   (b) Some type of error must have occurred.

   (c) All is in order. Excel has appended the number to differentiate the workbook from the template on which it is based.

   (d) The situation is impossible.

13. Which of the following best describes how a macro is to be recorded and executed?

   (a) A macro is recorded once and executed once.

   (b) A macro is recorded once and executed many times.

   (c) A macro is recorded many times and executed once.

   (d) A macro is recorded many times and executed many times.

14. Which statement must contain the name of the macro?

   (a) The Sub statement at the beginning of the macro

   (b) The first comment statement

   (c) Both (a) and (b)

   (d) Neither (a) nor (b)

15. Which of the following is not true regarding a customized button that has been inserted as an object onto a worksheet and assigned to an Excel macro?

   (a) Point to the customized button and then click the left mouse button to execute the associated macro.

   (b) Point to the customized button and then click the right mouse button to select the macro button and simultaneously display a shortcut menu.

   (c) Point to the customized button, and then press and hold Ctrl as you click the left mouse button to select the button.

   (d) Point to the customized button, press and hold Ctrl, and click the right mouse button to execute the associated macro.

16. You want to create a macro to enter your name in the active cell (which will vary whenever the macro is used) and enter the name of the course you are taking in the cell immediately below. The best way to do this is to:

   (a) Select the cell for your name, turn on the Macro Recorder with absolute references, type your name, press the down arrow, and type the course.

   (b) Turn on the Macro Recorder with absolute references, select the cell for your name, type your name, press the down arrow, and type the course.

   (c) Select the cell for your name, turn on the Macro Recorder with relative references, type your name, press the down arrow, and type the course.

   (d) Turn on the Macro Recorder with relative references, select the cell for your name, type your name, press the down arrow, and type the course.

Practice Exercises

1 Maintenance Department Payroll

The Smithtown Junior College is attempting to streamline and automate college functions as much as possible. To that end, you must create a macro for the head of maintenance to use when preparing the department payroll. Included in the macro will be steps to preview the workbook and print a selection. As the newest employee in the Accounting department, it is your task to create, test, and debug the macro, if necessary, for use by the Maintenance department. Use Figure 10.50 for reference as you complete the guidelines below. Make sure you save the workbook as a macro-enabled workbook so you can fully test the macro.

a. Open the *chap10_pe1_maintenancemacro* workbook and save it as **chap10_pe1_maintenancemacro_solution.xlsm**.

b. Click the **View tab**. Then click **Macros** in the Macros group and select **Record Macro** to display the Record Macro dialog box. Make the following changes:

- Type **PrintWorkbook** as the name of the macro.

- Click the **Shortcut Key check box** and type an uppercase **P**.

- Type today's date and your name as the person who created the macro in the **Description** box.

- Verify **Store macro in This Workbook** is selected and click **OK**.

c. Execute the following macro steps to record your macro:

- Select cells **A1:I24** even if they are already selected.

- Click the **Office Button** and select **Print** to open the Print dialog box.

- Click **Selection** in the *Print what* section and click **OK**.

- Click the **View tab**, click the **Macros down arrow** in the Macros group, and select **Stop Recording**.

d. Run the macro to test it:

- Click the **View tab**, click **Macros down arrow**, and select **View Macros** in the Macros group to open the Macro dialog box.

- Click **PrintWorkbook** and click **Run**.

- Click any range of cells and press the keyboard shortcut **Ctrl+Shift+P** to run your macro again.

e. Save the workbook.

f. Click the **Developer tab**, click **Button (Form Control)** from the Insert down arrow in the Controls group, and create a button for your macro, as follows:

- Use the cross-hair to draw a button over **cells K4:K5**.

- Select **PrintWorkbook** from the list of available macros and click **OK** twice.

- With the button selected, highlight the text and type **Print Payroll**.

- Click any cell to deselect the button.

- Click the **Print Payroll** button to test it.

g. Capture the workbook window, paste the image in **cell A30**, and move and resize the image as shown in Figure 10.50. Print and close the workbook.

...continued on Next Page

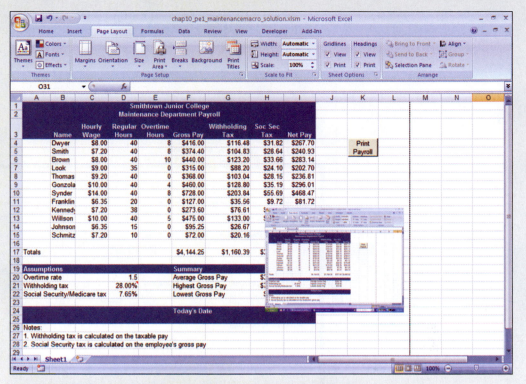

Figure 10.50 Maintenance Department Payroll Macro

2 Student Study Schedule

This chapter introduced you to the concept of using workbooks containing formulas, labels, and formatting but no data. A template is a useful and convenient workbook created by someone else and tailored to a specific application. You will create a study schedule to help organize time. This schedule can be used by any college student who has time management issues. In order for the worksheet to be used by anyone, you will have to protect areas that should not be changed by the casual user. Use Figure 10.51 for reference as you complete the workbook.

   a. Open the *chap10_pe2_timecard.xltx* template and save it as a workbook named **chap10_pe2_timecard_solution**.

   b. Complete the Student and Miscellaneous sections as follows:

- Type your name in **cell E10.**

- Type your student number in **cell I11**.

- Type the note shown in Figure 10.51 in **cell M9**.

   c. Complete the Course Information sections as follows:

- Type the name of the first course you are taking in **cell D20**.

- Type the study hours for the week, using Figure 10.51 as a model. Note that the total hours are calculated automatically.

- Enter the data for your remaining courses in similar fashion.

- Type **Study Hours** in **cell P5**.

- Rename the sheet tab **Study Schedule**.

   d. Select the data entry cells E10, I10, M9, E16, G16, and D20:P35 and unlock them. Click the **Review tab** and click **Protect Sheet** in the Changes group. Remove the check from Select locked cells and click **OK**.

...continued on Next Page

e. Create a custom footer containing your name, today's date, and your instructor's name. Use landscape orientation and print the completed workbook. Save and close the workbook.

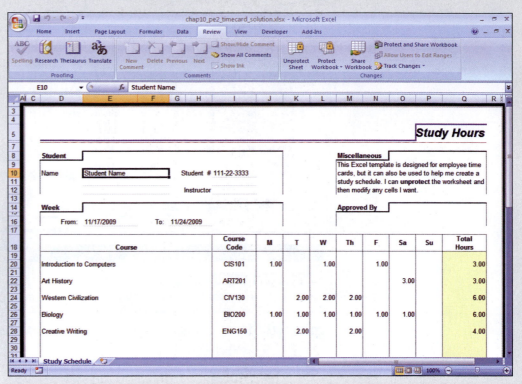

Figure 10.51 Study Schedule from Template

3 Tri-State Bank

Many businesses today are going multinational. They purchase raw material, they sell products, their employees travel, and they exchange information with foreign countries on a regular basis. No standard currency system exists, creating a demand for currency conversion. Businesses need to convert U.S. dollars to Japanese yen, Chinese yuan, and many other foreign currencies. As the assistant to the foreign banking vice president at Tri-State Bank, your task is to create a currency conversion workbook. You will use a Web query to collect current currency conversion data and display them in your workbook. Microsoft Office includes a Web query to determine the exchange rates for popular currencies, as shown in Figure 10.52. The workbook you will open contains two worksheets with formulas for two parallel sets of conversions: from British pounds to dollars, and from dollars to British pounds. Use Figure 10.52, the Pounds worksheet, for reference as you complete your task.

a. Open the *chap10_pe3_currency* workbook and save it as **chap10_pe3_currency_solution** so you can open the workbook again.

b. Import data from a Web query as follows:

- Click **cell A13**.

- Click the **Data tab** and click **Existing Connections** in the Get External Data group.

- Select **MSN MoneyCentral Investor Currency Rates**.

- Click **Open**.

...continued on Next Page

c. Use the conversion data as follows:

- Click **cell B11**, type **=B23**, and press **Enter**.

- Click **cell E11**, type **=1/B11**, and press **Enter** to calculate the reciprocal of the contents of cell B11.

- Click **cell B6** and type **=$B$11*A6**. Copy the formula through **cell B9**.

- Click **cell E6** and type **=D6*$E$11**. Copy the formula through **cell E9**.

d. Format the worksheet to match Figure 10.52. Be sure to use the appropriate currency symbols for dollars and pounds. Add your name and today's date, as shown.

e. Click the **Euro worksheet tab** for the Euro (European Currency) worksheet and enter the formulas for the appropriate conversion from Euros to dollars and vice versa. (Note that you do not have to enter the query on this worksheet because you can reference the values in the existing query.) The entry in cell B11 of the Euro worksheet is Pounds!B33 on the worksheet. Remember that the query changes continually so you may have to adjust the cell reference.

f. Format the Euro worksheet and include the European currency symbol, as appropriate.

g. Group the sheets and create a custom footer containing your name, today's date, and your instructor's name. Print the completed workbook. Save and close the workbook.

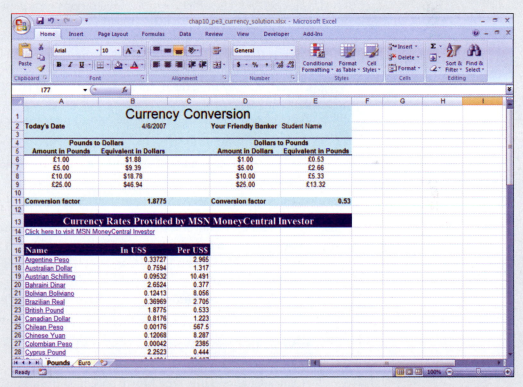

Figure 10.52 Currency Conversion

4 Morrison Green Solutions

You are the chief financial officer for Morrison Green Solutions, an environmental solutions provider. Your board of directors has asked you to prepare a statement of earnings comparing this year to last year. Further, the board of directors has indicated that the information should be available on the Web. Your task is to complete the workbook by applying a visually appealing theme, including a hyperlink to the corporate headquarters, inserting an appropriate picture that reflects the company's mission, and inserting a SmartArt graphic depicting the corporate hierarchy. Finally, you must create the Web page. Refer to Figure 10.53 as you complete your tasks.

...continued on Next Page

a. Open the *chap10_pe4_green* workbook and save it as **chap10_pe4_green_solution**.

b. Select, apply, and modify a theme as follows:

  • Click the **Page Layout tab** and click **Themes** in the Themes group.

  • Click **Flow** as the first theme.

  • Click **Themes** in the Themes group and click **Metro** as the final theme.

  • Click **Colors** in the Themes group and click **Module** as the new theme color.

  • Click **Font** in the Themes group, click **Median** as the new font, and resize columns as necessary.

c. Insert a hyperlink as follows:

  • Click **cell A20**.

  • Type **Morrison Green Solutions Web Site**.

  • Click the **Insert** tab and click **Hyperlink** in the Links group.

  • Type **www.prenhall.com/exploring** in the Address box and click **OK**.
  • Test the link by clicking it.

d. Click **cell A1**, click **Picture** in the Illustrations group on the Insert tab, locate and click the picture **green.jpg**, and click **insert**.

e. Resize and relocate the picture as shown in Figure 10.53.

f. Click **cell A22** and click **SmartArt** in the Illustrations group to open the Choose a SmartArt Graphic dialog box.

g. Click **Hierarchy** from the list in the left pane, click **Horizontal Hierarchy** in the middle pane, and click **OK**.

h. Type the text shown in Figure 10.53 and change the background color as follows:

  • Click the graphic to select it.

  • Click the **Design tab** and click the **Change Colors down arrow** in the SmartArt Styles group.

  • Click **Colored Fill Accent 4**.

i. Resize and move the SmartArt graphic as shown in Figure 10.53.

j. Create a custom footer containing your name, today's date, and your instructor's name. Print the completed workbook. Save the workbook.

k. Create the Web page:

  • Click the **Office Button** and select **Save As** to open the Save As dialog box.

  • Click the **Save as type drop-down arrow** and select **Web Page (*.htm; *.html)**.

  • Verify that **Entire Workbook** is selected and that the file name is *chap10_pe4_green_solution.htm*.

  • Click **Change Title**, type **Morrison Green Solutions**, click **OK**, and click **Save**.

  • Click **Yes** in the Microsoft Office warning box.

l. Exit Excel, open your Web browser, and open the file *chap10_pe4_green_solution* in your Web browser.

m. Review your Web page, print your Web page, and close the browser.

...continued on Next Page

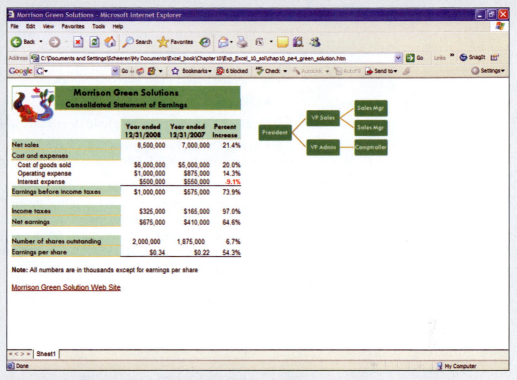

Figure 10.53 Morrison Green Solutions Web Page

5 Student Grade Sheet

As the instructor of a basic computer applications course, you want to provide a grade sheet to each student. Your course has four learning units: Word, Excel, Access, and PowerPoint. You require students to complete selected activities in the *Exploring Office 2007* textbook. You weight each activity within each learning unit and calculate a learning unit score by weighted average of activities. The workbook should find an average of the four unit scores and display the appropriate letter grade. You designed the initial workbook, and now you need to complete it and save it as a template. Figure 10.54 shows the template used to enter grades for one student.

    a. Open the *chap10_pe5_grade* workbook and save it as a template named **chap10_pe5_grade_solution**.

    b. Create the formula to calculate the weighted unit score for the Word unit:

- Click **cell C13**.

- Type **=(B8*C8) + (B9*C9) + (B10*C10) + (B11*C11) + (B12*C12)** and press **Enter**.

- Edit the formula in the formula bar, click in the **B8** reference, and press **F4** to make B8 absolute so that it does not change when you copy the formula.

- Make the B9, B10, B11, and B12 references absolute within the formula and press **Enter**.

    c. Click **cell C13** and use the fill handle to copy the formula to **cells D13:F13**.

    d. Click in **cell B3**, type **=AVERAGE(C13:F13)**, and press **Enter** to create the formula to calculate the mathematical average of the weighted unit scores.

    e. Click **cell B4**, type **=VLOOKUP(B3,GRADES,2)**, and press **Enter** to create the vertical lookup function that looks at the average score in B4, compares it to the lookup table in cells B16:D20 that is range-named as GRADES, and returns the respective letter grade.

    f. Designate the areas of the worksheet in which the user will be able to enter data:

- Select **cells B1:B2** and press and hold down **Ctrl** while you select **cells C8:F12**.

- Click the **Home tab**, click **Format** in the Cells group, and select **Lock Cells** to deselect it, that is, unlock it.

...continued on Next Page

g. Protect the rest of the worksheet from being altered by the user:

- Click the **Review tab** and click **Protect Sheet** in the Changes group.
- Make sure the **Protect worksheet and contents of locked cells check box** is selected.
- Make sure the **Select unlocked cells check box** is selected.
- Click **OK**.
- Select **cells B1:B2** and press and hold down **Ctrl** while you select **cells C8:F12**.
- Click in **cell C13** and try to press **Delete** to make sure you see the message that that cell is protected. Click **OK** to acknowledge the message.

h. Save and close the template with the changes.

i. Open the *chap10_pe5_grade_solution.xltx* template and save it as a regular workbook named **chap10_pe5_jones_solution.xls**.

j. Type **Terry Jones** in **cell B1** and **105** in **cell B2**. Try to type **A** in **cell B4** and click **OK** when you see the message about the cell being protected.

k. Enter the following values in the respective cells:

Word	Excel	Access	PowerPoint
100	95	100	100
100	100	100	100
90	85	75	100
95	75	80	95
85	80	70	95

l. Save, print, and close the workbook.

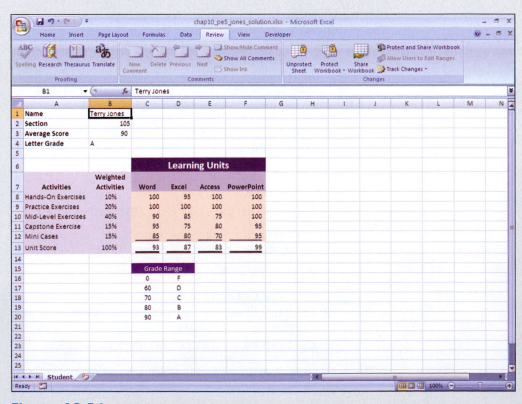

Figure 10.54 Grades for Terry Jones

As the top sales associate with Duke Real Estate and the only sales associate in the office with Excel experience, you want to prepare an Excel template that can be used to keep track of monthly sales. The template will allow you to enter a list of the properties sold, including the size, list price, and selling price. The template will automatically calculate the price per square foot, your commission, and the net amount to the seller, both as dollars and percentage of list price. The workbook shown in Figure 10.55 displays the finished workbook. You will open a partially completed workbook, enter the relevant formulas, and format the workbook before saving it as a template. You will protect the workbook prior to saving it as a template. As the final step, you will enter the data shown in Figure 10.55 to test your template.

a. Open the *chap10_mid1_realestate* workbook.

b. Calculate the price per square foot by dividing the selling price by size. The percentage of list price is calculated by dividing the selling price by the list price. Use an absolute reference to determine sales commission so the formula can be copied to other rows. Trap Excel error messages and display zeros instead.

c. Enter the appropriate SUM function in **cell B14** to compute the total square feet. Copy the formula to the remaining cells in the row.

d. Use the appropriate functions to calculate the values in the summary area.

e. Format the worksheet as shown in Figure 10.55, making sure you use a theme and display all dollar amounts with the currency symbol and no decimal places. Display percentages with the percent symbol and one decimal place. Use a date function to display the current date in the cell below the heading.

f. Protect the worksheet but remember that **cells A5:D12** are data entry cells.

g. Save the workbook as a template named **chap10_mid1_realestate_solution.xltx**.

h. Open the template, enter the following data in the cells as shown in Figure 10.55, and save it as **chap10_mid1_realestate_solution**.

Size	List Price	Selling Price
1200	85000	79600
2500	190000	185000
3600	375000	350000
4500	550000	540000
3500	390000	350000
3000	350000	325000
2250	275000	260000
1200	150000	150000

i. Create a custom footer containing your name, today's date, and your instructor's name. Print the completed workbook using landscape orientation. Save and close the workbook.

...continued on Next Page

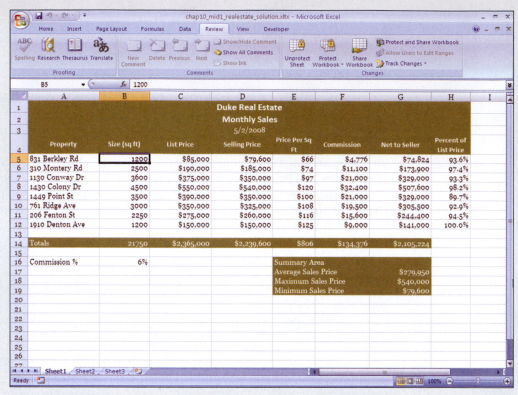

Figure 10.55 Real Estate Template

2 The S & S Banquet Hall

Your new job with S & S Banquet Hall requires you to maintain a workbook for inventory of the main banquet room. The person who created the workbook applied many cell styles and formats that have destroyed the integrity of the information. Your task is to create and edit a theme and create and edit a style appropriate for the inventory workbook and S & S Banquet Hall. Use Figure 10.56 as your model, but you may choose to use themes and styles that are more appropriate. Open the workbook and complete it as indicated here.

a. Open the *chap10_mid2_inventory* workbook and save it as **chap10_mid2_inventory_ solution**.

b. Apply the **Equity** theme to the workbook.

c. Change the **Color** of the theme to **Origin**.

d. Change the **Font** of the theme to **Verdana**.

e. Apply cell styles to rows 1 through 3 and 16 through 21 so that the labels and values in the selected cells display appropriately, as shown in Figure 10.56.

f. Create a new cell style to display the heading using the **Britannic Bold** font and **28** points, making sure to maintain the same fill color while changing the font color.

g. Format the **Purchase Price** and **Cost** values as **Currency** with **2** decimal places.

h. Create a custom footer containing your name, today's date, and your instructor's name. Print the completed workbook. Save and close the workbook.

...continued on Next Page

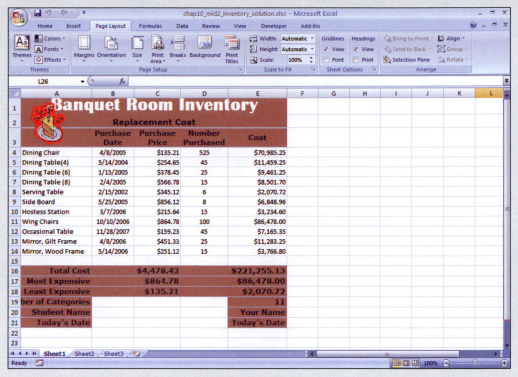

Figure 10.56 S & S Banquet Hall Inventory

3 Population Statistics Web Page

Your political science professor has assigned you the task of creating a Web page depicting the population of the United States. You are to include the names of the sates, the state capitals, the geographic region for each state, and the population, area, and population density for each state. You add a hyperlink to the U.S. Census Bureau and a picture that represents the state in which you were born. Use Figure 10.57 for reference as you complete this exercise.

a. Open the *chap10_mid3_population* workbook and save it as **chap10_mid3_population_solution**.

b. Insert a row below the title row with no fill and insert a hyperlink to the U.S. Census Bureau.

c. Insert clip art appropriate to the state in which you were born, resize it if necessary, and make the clip art a link to the official Web page of the state in which you were born.

d. Create a custom footer that includes your name, today's date, and your instructor's name. Print and save the workbook.

e. Save the workbook as a Web page, making sure to include a title, and save the entire workbook as **chap10_mid3_population_solution.htm**. Print all pages.

f. Exit Excel, open your Web browser and your Web page, scroll to view the whole Web page, test your links, print all pages, and close the browser.

...continued on Next Page

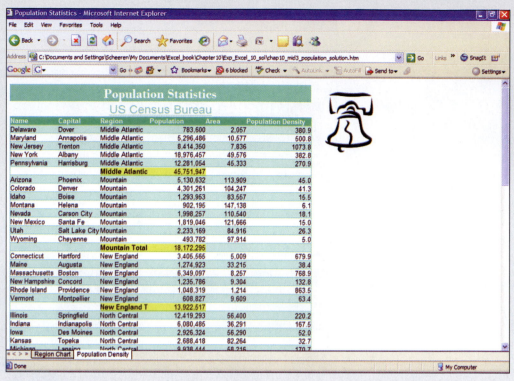

Figure 10.57 Population Statistics Web Page

4 Employee List

You are a data analyst for the Human Resources department for the XYZ Corporation, which has offices in Boston, Chicago, Cleveland, Detroit, Kansas City, Los Angeles, Miami, New York, Phoenix, and San Francisco. A majority of the employees are account representatives. Other positions include managers, senior account representatives, and trainees. You developed a workbook that lists employee data, including gender, job title, salary, city location, and performance evaluation. Because you constantly look at data from different perspectives, you want to create macros that can sort and subtotal data. After creating three macros, you want to create buttons that can be clicked to execute the macros. Figure 10.58 shows the location of the macro buttons. The worksheet data reflect the top rows of the data, based on the Performance-Gender sort. Notice that Excellent is listed first.

a. Open the *chap10_mid4_employees* workbook and save it as a macro-enabled file named **chap10_mid4_employees_solution**.

b. Create a macro named **LocationLastSubtotal** that does *not* use relative references, uses the shortcut key **L**, with an appropriate description, and does the following:

- Removes all existing subtotals.
- Sorts by location and then by last name, both in alphabetical order.
- Uses the Subtotal feature to create a SUM subtotal for Salaries by Location.

c. Create a macro named **TitleSalarySubtotal** that does *not* use relative references, uses the shortcut key **T**, with an appropriate description, and does the following:

- Removes all existing subtotals.
- Sorts by title in alphabetical order and then by salary, with the highest salaries listed first for each title.
- Uses the Subtotal feature to create an AVERAGE subtotal for Salaries by Title.

...continued on Next Page

d. Create a macro named **PerformanceGender** that does *not* use relative references, uses the shortcut key **P**, with an appropriate description, and does the following:

- Removes all existing subtotals.
- Sorts by performance, by using a custom sort that arranges performance in this sequence: Excellent, Good, Average, Poor. The secondary sort is by gender, with females listed first.
- Uses the Subtotal feature to create a COUNT subtotal by Performance.

e. Create a macro button for the **LocationLastSubtotal** macro. The button text should display **Location-Name** and **Ctrl-Shift-L**. Place the button on the worksheet as shown in Figure 10.58.

f. Create a macro button for the **TitleSalarySubtotal** macro. The button text should display **Title-Salary** and **Ctrl-Shift-T**. Place the button on the worksheet as shown in Figure 10.58.

g. Create a macro button for the **PerformanceGender** macro. The button text should display **Performance-Gender** and **Ctrl-Shift-P**. Place the button on the worksheet as shown in Figure 10.58.

h. Click the buttons in sequence to test that they run the respective macros.

i. Use the keyboard shortcuts to run each macro.

j. Edit one of the macros to display the VBA code. Print the VBA code and close the Code window.

k. Save and close the workbook.

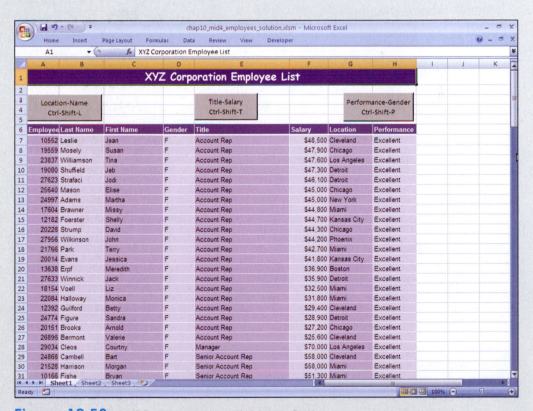

Figure 10.58 XYZ Employee List with Macro Buttons

Capstone Exercise

Little League baseball has a long history in your community. The teams have even made it all the way to Williamsport, Pennsylvania, to play in the Little League World Series. The commissioner of your local Little League has appointed you the official league statistician because of your expertise with Excel. Your task is to automate score keeping and record keeping as much as possible. Team scorekeepers now use laptop computers to keep score during the games. Parents have requested that team and league results be made available on the Web. In addition, the parents would like family statistics when their children play in the league.

The tasks associated with the position of league statistician include changing an existing style, applying a theme for a uniform look and feel for each team, and creating a template for each team scorekeeper to use. You will insert appropriate team pictures, insert SmartArt graphics, and create a Web page, per the parents' request. Finally, you will create a macro to automate the printing of the score sheets. You will create four files: an Excel solution file, an Excel template file, a Web page file, and a macro-enabled Excel file.

Open and Save the Workbook

You must open the workbook that you used to maintain statistics for your siblings. This is the foundation for your tasks.

a. Open the *chap10_cap_llbaseball* workbook.

b. Save the workbook as **chap10_cap_llbaseball_solution**.

Create and Apply a Style

Parents and scorekeepers would like you to highlight player names to make them more readable. Scorekeepers believe this change will make score keeping more efficient during the game.

a. Create a style titled Players to change the current font specifications for the listed players.

b. Apply your new style, Players, to the player names.

c. Save the workbook.

Examine and Apply a Theme

Each team will use a different theme to identify it. The themes include font, color, and effects. You will select an aesthetically pleasing theme after examining several samples. Remember that the league is made up of 10 teams, and each will have its own identity.

a. Examine several themes to see how they look with your workbook.

b. Apply your final selection to the workbook.

c. Save the workbook.

Create a Template

Each of the team scorekeepers will use your final workbook for game statistics. You will create a template that gets distributed to each scorekeeper.

a. Use an appropriate function to trap Excel errors and display a 0 in cells.

b. Protect the workbook, remembering that scorekeepers will enter team statistics and will insert the team logo.

c. Remove all variable data from your workbook.

d. Save the workbook as an Excel template named **chap10_cap_llbaseball_solution.xltx**.

e. Close the template and reopen the *chap10_cap_llbaseball_solution* workbook.

Insert a Picture and SmartArt

An element of the team identity is the team's logo, which is used on the scorer's workbook, the team Web page, and players' uniforms. You will insert a logo and SmartArt graphic on your sample Web page. The parents will evaluate your work.

a. Insert, resize, and locate an appropriate team logo on the workbook.

b. Insert an appropriate SmartArt graphic on a new sheet.

c. Your SmartArt graphic will show the relationship among the Commissioner, Official Scorer, and three representative teams in the league. Remember that each team has an identity that includes a logo.

d. Insert an appropriate league-identifying title for your SmartArt graphic sheet.

e. Save the workbook.

Create a Web Page

Now that you have enhanced your workbook with a style, a theme, a logo, and a graphic on a new sheet, it is time to create your Web page.

a. Save the workbook as a Web page.

b. Include a descriptive title, with your name as the title of your Web page.

c. Make sure you save the whole workbook as a Web page as opposed to saving a single sheet. Save the Web page as **chap10_cap_llbaseball_solution.htm**.

d. Exit Excel and view your Web page in your browser. Make any appropriate changes in Excel.

e. Print your final Web page from your browser.

f. Close your browser, start Excel, and open the *chap10_cap_llbaseball_solution* workbook.

Print the Workbook

As part of the documentation process, you recognize that each worksheet in the workbook must include standard footers. Create a custom footer that contains your name, the date, and your instructor's name. Print the completed workbook.

a. Group the worksheets and create a custom footer with your name on the left, today's date in the middle, and your instructor's name on the right.

b. Print the workbook and save the workbook.

Create a Macro and a Macro Button

Part of the automation process the Commissioner asked for includes printing the workbook in landscape orientation.

To that end, you will create a macro to print and also include a button on the workbook to print in landscape orientation.

a. Your score sheet must fit on one landscaped page.

b. Name your macro PrintScoreSheet. Use Ctrl+Shift+T as the shortcut key, and make sure it prints all sheets.

c. Test your macro, editing it if necessary.

d. Save the workbook as an Excel Macro Enabled Workbook with the name **chap10_cap_llbaseball_solution.xlsm**.

Mini Cases

Use the rubric following the case as a guide to evaluate your work, but keep in mind that your instructor may impose additional grading criteria or use a different standard to judge your work.

Registrar's Office Student Advising

GENERAL CASE

As part of Smithtown Junior College's attempt to streamline and automate college functions, your task as assistant to the registrar is to create several macros for the faculty advising process. To that end, you must create the following macros in the faculty advising workbook and create a button for each of your macros. These will greatly help faculty to advise their students about their performances in the classroom. The first macro will select students based on year in school. The second macro will select student by major. The third macro will combine year in school and major. The final macro will list all students. Some, but not all, range names have already been created to assist you in the creation of your macros. Make sure you save the workbook as a macro-enabled workbook so you can fully test the macro. Include a screen capture of your button for your instructor. Begin by opening the workbook *chap10_mc1_advisor* and saving it as a macro-enabled workbook named **chap10_mc1_advisor_solution.xlsm**.

Performance Elements	Exceeds Expectations	Meets Expectations	Below Expectations
Create range name	Range names correct and functional.	Range names correct but nonfunctioning.	No additional range names.
Macros	All four macros created and functional.	Three macros created and functional.	Fewer than three macros created.
Documentation	Printed with custom footer and with screen capture.	Printed without custom footer and with screen capture.	Printed without either custom footer or screen capture.

Jake's Gym and Themes

RESEARCH CASE

Jake, the owner of the Jake's Gym franchise, wants you to create a new image for his membership spreadsheets. Search the Microsoft Office Web site for new Office themes. Print the instructions for downloading and installing a new theme. If your facility permits, install the theme of your choice and apply it to the worksheet for Jake's Gym. You will open and use the *chap10_mc2_gym* workbook to implement your theme. Include a brief description of the steps you took to download the theme you selected. Be sure to indicate the name of your new theme. Save the workbook as **chap10_mc2_gym_solution**. Print the workbook.

Performance Elements	Exceeds Expectations	Meets Expectations	Below Expectations
Theme	Theme is downloaded, applied, and aesthetically pleasing.	Theme is downloaded and applied.	No theme.
Worksheet cleanup	Columns and rows resized to fit data.	Columns or rows resized to fit data.	No cleanup.
Documentation	Accurate description of process and name of theme included.	Accurate description of process or name of theme included.	No documentation.

A friend has asked for your help. He has created a workbook with macros but cannot get the macros to run. The macros include database functions that will return an employee list for each of four buttons. Your task is to solve his problem. The workbook contains four macro buttons, none of which work. You are to analyze the workbook to determine whether macros in fact exist and, if they do, why they are not working. If no macros exist, you must create them. Open the workbook *chap10_mc3_employee* and save it as a macro-enabled workbook named **chap10_mc3_employee_ solution.xlsm**. Correct the errors, print the workbook documenting the buttons, and print the correct VBA code.

Performance Elements	Exceeds Expectations	Meets Expectations	Below Expectations
Macro identification	Identified that no macros exist.	Identified that no macros exist.	Can't tell if no macros exist.
Construct macros	Four macros created and run correctly.	Three macros created and run correctly.	Fewer than three macros created and run correctly.
Documentation	Buttons documented and VBA printed.	VBA printed.	No documentation.

Functions Used | Reference

Name	Syntax	Definition
AND	AND(logical1,logical2,...)	Returns true when all arguments are true and returns false when one or more arguments are false.
AVERAGE	AVERAGE(number1,number2,...)	Determines the arithmetic mean, or average, for the values in an argument list.
AVERAGEIF	AVERAGEIF(range,criteria,average_range)	Returns the average of all the cells in a range that meet a given criterion.
AVERAGEIFS	AVERAGEIFS(average_range,criteria_range1, criteria1,criteria_range2,criteria2...)	Returns the average of all the cells that meet multiple criteria.
CONCATENATE	CONCATENATE(text1,text2,...)	Joins two or more text strings into one text string.
COUNT	COUNT(value1,value2,...)	Counts the number of cells in a range that contain numeric data.
COUNTA	COUNTA(value1,value2,...)	Counts the number of cells in a range that are not blank.
COUNTIF	COUNTIF(range,criteria)	Counts the number of cells within a range that meet the given criterion.
COUNTIFS	COUNTIFS(range1,criteria1,range2,criteria2...)	Counts the number of cells within a range that meet multiple criteria.
DAY	DAY(serial_number)	Returns the day of a date represented by a serial number.
FV	FV(rate,nper,pmt,pv,type)	Returns the future value of an investment.
IF	IF(logical_test,value_if_true,value_if_false)	Returns one value when a condition is met and returns another value when the condition is not met.
IFERROR	IFERROR(value,value_if_error)	Returns a value you specify if a formula evaluates to an error.
INDEX	INDEX(array,row_num,column_num)	Returns a value or the reference to a value within a table or range.
INT	INT(value)	Rounds a number down to the nearest integer.
IPMT	IPMT(rate,per,nper,pv,fv,type)	Calculates the interest payment on a loan.
ISERR	ISERR(value)	Traps error values except #N/A.
ISERROR	ISERROR(value)	Traps any error value (#N/A, #VALUE!, #REF!, #DIV/0!, #NUM!, #NAME?, or #NULL!).
ISNA	ISNA(value)	Traps the error value #N/A (value not available).
LARGE	LARGE(array,k)	Returns the kth largest value in a data set.
LOWER	LOWER(text)	Converts all uppercase letters to lowercase.
MATCH	MATCH(lookup_value,lookup_array,match_type)	Returns the relative position of an item in an array that matches a specified value in a specified order.

Name	Syntax	Definition
MAX	MAX(number1,number2,...)	Determines the highest value of all cells in a list of arguments.
MEDIAN	MEDIAN(number1,number2,...)	Finds the midpoint value in a set of values.
MIN	MIN(number1,number2,...)	Determines the smallest value of all cells in a list of arguments.
MONTH	MONTH(serial_number)	Returns the month represented by a serial number.
NOT	NOT(logical)	Reverses the value of its argument.
NOW	NOW( )	Uses the computer's clock to display the current date and time side by side in a cell.
OR	OR(logical1,logical2,...)	Returns true if any argument is true and returns false if all arguments are false.
PMT	PMT(rate,nper,pv,fv,type)	Calculates the payment on a loan.
PPMT	PPMT(rate,per,nper,pv,fv,type)	Calculates the payment on the principal of a loan.
PROPER	PROPER(text)	Converts first letter of each word to uppercase.
ROUND	ROUND(number, num_digits)	Rounds a value to a specified number of digits.
SMALL	SMALL(array,k)	Returns the kth smallest value in a data set.
STDEV	STDEV(number1,number2...)	Calculates the standard deviation based on a sample.
SUBSTITUTE	SUBSTITUTE(text,old_text,new_text, instance_num)	Substitutes new_text for old_text in a text string.
SUM	SUM(number1,number2,...)	Adds up or sums the numeric entries within a range of cells.
SUMIF	SUMIF(range,criteria,sum_range)	Adds the cells specified by a given criteria.
SUMIFS	SUMIFS(sum_range,criteria_range1,criteria1, criteria_range2,criteria2...)	Adds the cells in a range that meet multiple criteria.
TODAY	TODAY( )	Displays the current date in a cell.
UPPER	UPPER(text)	Converts text to uppercase letters.
VLOOKUP	VLOOKUP(lookup_value,table_array, col_index_num,range_lookup)	Looks up an answer from a table of possible answers.
YEAR	YEAR(serial_number)	Returns the year corresponding to a date.

Capstone Exercises

Using Excel in the Legal Profession, Health Care, the Arts, and Hospitality

Legal Exercises (Page 691)

Exercise		Skills Covered
1. Chapters 1–4 **Open:** New spreadsheet **Save as:** exp07_e_leg_cpt_sol	Page 693	• Design a Spreadsheet • Use Symbols and Formulas in a Cell • Insert and Delete Columns and Rows • Use Cell Ranges and Movement Options • Manage and Format Worksheets • Print Using Various Setups • Manage Cell Comments • Create, Copy, and Manipulate Formulas • Use Relative and Absolute Cell References • Use Statistical Functions (Including Autosum) • Use the Date Function • Use Various Functions • Choose, Create, and Modify a Chart • Embed Charts • Print Charts • Freeze Rows and Columns • Hide Rows and Columns • Protect Cells, Worksheets, and Workbooks • Control Calculation • Use Table Management • Sort Data • Filter Data
2. Chapters 5–10 **Open:** loukas_law_firm.xlsx **Save as:** loukas_law_firm_solution.xlsx and loukas_law_firm_solution.xlsm	Page 699	• Apply Conditional Formatting • Create and Use Range Names • Consolidate Data from Multiple Worksheets • Copy Worksheets • Create the Documentation Worksheet • Insert, Edit, and Delete Comments • Enable Simultaneous Changes by Multiple Users • Save Workbooks in Different Formats • Finalize Documents • Prepare Workbooks for Distribution • Protect a Template • Create a Macro with the Macro Recorder • Create Macro Buttons

Health Care Exercises (Page 703)

Exercise		Skills Covered
1. Chapters 1–4 **Create:** New spreadsheet **Save as:** Patient_Log	Page 705	• Enter and Edit Data in Cells • Display Cell Formulas • Insert and Delete Rows and Columns • Use Cell Ranges • Manage Worksheets • Format Worksheets • Use Page Setup Options • Create and Copy Formulas • Use Autosum • Insert Basic Statistical Functions • Use the IF Function • Choose a Chart Type • Create a Chart • Modify a Chart • Embed Charts • Print Charts • Hide/Unhide Columns • Protect a Workbook • Print Large Worksheets • Sort Data • Filter and Total Data
2. Chapters 5–10 **Open:** payment_log.xlsx **Save as:** payment_log_solution.xlsx, payment_log_solution.xls, and payment_log_ solution.htm	Page 710	• Apply Conditional Formatting • Create and Use Range Names • Manipulate Text with Functions • Group and Subtotal Data • Restrict Values to a Drop-Down List • Validate Data • Save Workbooks in Different Formats • Prepare Workbooks for Distribution • Create a Web Page

Arts Exercises (Page 713)

Exercise		Skills Covered
1. Chapters 1–4 **Open:** exp07_e_arts_greenman.xlsx **Save as:** exp07_e_arts_greenman_ solution.xlsx	Page 715	• Describe and Use Symbols and the Order of Precedence • Display Cell Formulas • Insert and Delete Rows and Columns • Use Cell Ranges; Excel Move; Copy, Paste, Paste Special; and AutoFill • Create and Copy Formulas • Use Relative and Absolute Cell Addresses • Use AutoSum • Insert Basic Statistical Functions • Use Date Functions • Use The IF Function • Use The VLookup Function • Use the PMT Function • Use the FV Function • Choose a Chart Type • Create a Chart • Modify a Chart • Enhance Charts with Graphic Shapes • Embed Charts • Print Charts • Freeze Rows and Columns • Hide and Unhide Rows, Columns, and Worksheets • Protect a Cell, a Worksheet, and a Workbook • Control Calculation • Print Large Worksheets
2. Chapters 5–10 **Open:** majestic_ticket_sales.xlsx **Save as:** majestic_ticket_sales_ solution.xlsx, majestic_ticket_sales_ solution.xls, and majestic_ticket_ sales_solution.xlsm	Page 719	• Apply Conditional Formatting • Manipulate Text with Functions • Group and Subtotal Data • Copy Worksheets • Consolidate Data from Multiple Worksheets • Enable Simultaneous Changes by Multiple Users • Save Workbooks in Different Formats • Finalize Documents • Prepare Workbooks for Distribution • Protect a Template • Create a Macro with the Macro Recorder • Create Macro Buttons

Hospitality Exercises (Page 723)

Exercise		Skills Covered
1. **Chapters 1–4** **Open:** exp07_e_hosp_cpt_commissions.xlsx and Marella Travel Logo.bmp **Create and Save as:** exp07_e_hosp_cpt_commissions_solution.xlsx and exp07_e_hosp_cpt_vacation_payment.xlsx	Page 725	• Describe and Use Symbols and the Order of Precedence • Display Cell Formulas • Insert and Delete Rows and Columns • Use Cell Ranges • Move, Copy, Paste, Paste Special, and AutoFill • Create and Copy Formulas • Use Relative and Absolute Cell Addresses • Use AutoSum • Insert Basic Statistical Functions • Use Date Functions • Use the IF Function • Use the VLookup Function • Use the PMT Function • Use the FV Function • Choose a Chart Type • Create a Chart • Modify a Chart • Enhance Charts with Graphic Shapes • Embed Charts • Print Charts • Freeze Rows and Columns • Hide and Unhide Rows, Columns, and Worksheets • Protect a Cell, a Worksheet, and a Workbook • Control Calculation • Print Large Worksheets
2. **Chapters 5–10** **Open:** majestic_cruises.xlsx **Save as:** majestic_cruises.xlsx, majestic_cruises_solution.xls, and majestic_cruises_solution.htm	Page 728	• Apply Conditional Formatting • Create and Use Range Names • Group and Subtotal Data • Use Conditional Functions • Use Functions • Create the Documentation Worksheet • Insert, Edit, and Delete Comments • Enable Simultaneous Changes by Multiple Users • Save Workbooks in Different Formats • Create a Web Page

Paralegals

Use Microsoft Office Excel

Background

Microsoft Office Excel is such a versatile program that an experienced paralegal can find many valuable uses for it in the law office. Rather than knowing only a pre-scribed list of traditional uses, a paralegal should be alert to possible creative uses of Excel. The information provided in these four chapters is an excellent starting point.

The lawyer trust account is a vital, yet often overlooked, accounting task. Each state has its own rules for trust account formatting and processing. In Michigan, the distinction between *retainer* and *advance fees* has recently been clarified, and the distinction imposes some additional accounting requirements on the law office. The paralegal might be the person designated to set up and/or monitor the trust account. It is for this reason that an accounting topic has been chosen for this capstone exercise even though many law offices use other programs for accounting purposes.

This exercise is based on content from the "client ledger" portion of the PowerPoint slide "Three Way Reconciliation," presented at the ICLE seminar "Ethics 2006: Practical Solutions to Real World Problems" in November 2006 by Mark A. Armitage, Esq., Deputy Director, Attorney Discipline Board of Michigan.

Tasks

In a small office, the paralegal may be responsible for all kinds of document production. This could include the following tasks:
- Completing any accounting tasks (although it is more likely that these tasks would be accomplished with third-party software, particularly a law-specific program)
- Tracking client expenditures in an extended case
- Calculating probate expenses
- Calculating real estate closure costs
- Preparing charts as trial exhibits
- Many other creative uses are possible, depending on the particular type of law practiced in the office

Skills

In addition to basic formatting skills, a paralegal should be able to do the following:

Chapter 1
- Design a spreadsheet (page 73)
- Use symbols and formulas in a cell (page 86)
- Insert and delete columns and rows (page 89)
- Use cell ranges and movement options (page 90)
- Manage and format worksheets (page 98)

...continued on Next Page

- Print using various setups (page 111)
- Manage cell comments (page 114)

Chapter 2

- Create, copy, and manipulate formulas (page 139)
- Use relative and absolute cell references (page 140)
- Use statistical functions (including AutoSum) (page 147)
- Use the date function (page 150)
- Use various functions (page 157)

Chapter 3

- Choose, create, and modify a chart (page 189)
- Embed charts (page 217)
- Print charts (page 218)

Chapter 4

- Freeze rows and columns (page 246)
- Hide rows and columns (page 247)
- Protect cells, worksheets, and workbooks (page 248)
- Control calculation (page 251)
- Use table management (page 263)
- Sort data (page 268)
- Filter data (page 272)

Paralegals
Chapters 1–4 | Capstone Exercises

The attorney in your office recently attended a continuing legal education seminar that emphasized the need for individual client tracking on a trust account. Although you had maintained a trust ledger, you had not been providing individual client ledgers. (Some professionals recommend having a ledger for every client, regardless of whether any of the client's funds are in the trust account!) Rather than trying to use your formal accounting program, you asked to transfer the paper accounting method demonstrated at the seminar into a computerized equivalent in Excel as a trial process. While designing the spreadsheets, you realized that you could create the individual client ledgers and then construct the trust ledger as a set of links from the client ledgers. (If the attorney finds this method useful, you intend to create macros to automate the process.)

Create a Client Ledger Template

Each client needs an individual ledger of transactions. Create and name the template. Since this is a reusable template, apply all cell formatting now rather than after the data are typed.

- Use the sample provided below as a reusable worksheet template. The title and subtitle in **cells A1** and **A2** should use the **default** font, size **16 point**, and **bold**. Merge and center **cells A1:J1**. *Case#* (**cell A3**) should be **11 point** font, and the column headings should be **12 point** font. Use **Alt+Enter** to put the headings on two lines within the cell.

- Widen the following columns to an appropriate width: *Source of Deposit, Payee, Purpose, Memo*.
- Set the date cells to the default date format. Format through row 30.
- Confirm that the *Client, Source of Deposit, Payee, Ck #*, and *Purpose* cells are set to the default text format. Format through row 30.
- Set the *Checks, Deposits*, and *Running Balance* cells to Accounting format with the default of two decimal places and inclusion of a dollar sign ($). Format through row 30.
- Select **cells A5:J30**. Format it as a table (Home tab) using the **Table Style Light 2** banded table format (Light section, row 1, column 2).
- Choose the options to indicate that your table has a header row and a total row. Select the total row and make the cells bold.
- Change the view to *75%* or another size that enables you to see columns A through J on the screen.

- Save the file as **exp07_e_leg_cpt_sol**.
- Name the worksheet **Client Template**.

Set the Output Format of the Template

Since these documents will be printed and inserted into the client's file, set the print options in the template so they will be ready to print. With so much information to be included on each line, you will need to change the format so that the document prints in landscape.

- Set the orientation to **Landscape**.
- Leave the default margins.
- Set the Print Area to **cells A1:J31**.
- Reduce the scale until columns A through J all appear on one page.
- Include the gridlines in the print version.
- Print Preview the document to be sure you can see all columns.
- Close the Print Preview window.

Set Up the Formulas on the Client Template

Add some formulas to the template.

- Preset row 6, *Running Balance*, to **$0**. (The $ should show up automatically because you preformatted the cell.)
- Add an **asterisk** (*) to **cell A6** to remind you to enter a starting date when using the template.
- Add formulas that will sum columns G, H, and I in row 31.

Use the Template to Create Individual Client Ledgers

Once the template is created and correct, it can be protected with a password. We will choose not to do so at this time, however. Make three copies of the template for three clients who need a ledger.

- Name the current sheet **Client Template**.
- Create three copies of the template and place them before the *Client Template* worksheet. (Rename the worksheets later.)
- Use the guides in the next two steps below to fill in the templates. Use the **auto fill** option for the name in the *Client* column. The column I totals will automatically appear as you complete columns G and H. One special note: For each cell that is empty, enter an apostrophe (') character into the cell. It will not appear in the print-out, but will "hold" the format of the cell when you copy its contents later in the exercise. For example,

...continued on Next Page

cells **C8**, **C9**, and **E7** (below) should contain an apostrophe. Also, after data entry, do a "best fit" on column widths to improve the appearance of the spreadsheet.

- Choose one of the template copies and rename its tab to **Mattox, Brian**. Note that there is no case number because this client had transactional work done in the office.

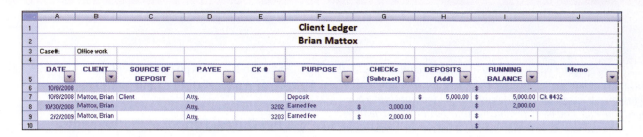

- Complete the same process for the other two clients. As you complete each client's ledger, rename the tab and move the worksheet into alphabetical order. (NOTE:

The *Trust Ledger* worksheet will be created later in the exercise.)

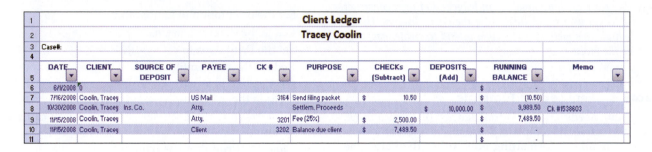

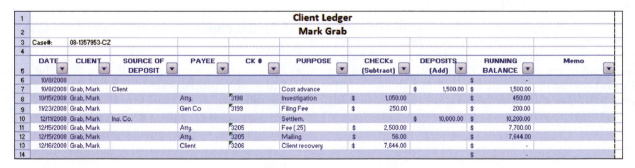

Add a Comment

Comments are useful to provide information that is generally not necessary for viewers of the worksheet, but which you wish to have attached to a cell. Add a comment about where you sent Tracey's check.

- On Tracey Coolin's ledger, in **cell F10**, insert a comment reading: **Sent by certified mail, return receipt, to her vacation home.**

Create the Trust Ledger

Once the client templates are completed, make a trust ledger to consolidate all of the entries into one large document. This process would need to be automated if you had many clients, but in this small office you can do it by hand.

- Create another copy of the *Client Template*. Move it to the beginning of the worksheet list. Rename it **Trust Ledger**.
- Revise the form slightly so it looks like the one above.
- Add the headings.
- Confirm that column A is date format, and columns B, C, D, E, and F are text format. Columns G, H, and I should be Accounting format. Delete column J (Memo).
- The starter row, row 6, should contain a start date of **7/1/2008** and client name of **0** (so it will appear before any letters if sorting by client name). The running balance is already set to *5000* (the amount from the end of the previous period).

...continued on Next Page

694   **Capstone Exercises**

Set Up the Formulas on the Trust Ledger

Modify the formula on the *Running Balance* column, rows 7 through 30, to make it more complex. Read the following paragraphs first, so you can understand the format of a complex formula, then type in the formula. The goal is to have the balance show up if there is a balance, but to have nothing show up if it is the end of the entries.

The main formula asks you, for the current row, to take the running balance from the previous row (I), subtract any value in the *Checks* column (G), and add any value in the *Deposits* column (H). For example, in **cell I7** type this formula: **=I6–G7+H7**. You already did that for the Client Template.

Having determined the main formula, now modify the formula with an "if" statement that says, "If there was no check and no deposit, then put a 0 in the cell; otherwise put the formula to give the current balance." For example, if G7=0 and H7=0, then there was no activity and we will assume that that is the end of the record. We want that number to show as 0, or as a hyphen (-) in Accounting format.

Use the Help to look for "conditional if formula." In the *Conditional formulas* section, the first item is *Create conditional formulas*. Within that section, scroll down to the section called *Create a conditional formula that results in another calculation or in values other than TRUE or FALSE*. The fifth item shows a formula with an AND test and two items.

- **Cell I6** should remain *$5000.00* since that is our starting balance.
- Insert a formula in **cell I7** using the IF statement that incorporates an AND. Your formula will look like this: **=IF(AND(G7=0, H7=0), 0, I6–G7+H7)**. Notice that there are two sets of parentheses, one embedded within the other!
- Insert test numbers to be sure the formula works. If there is any number in **cells G7** or **H7**, the correct running balance should appear. If there are no numbers in both cells, then a "–" should appear.
- Fill the formula down to row 30. Remember: The goal is to have the balance show up if there is a balance, but have nothing show up if it is the end of the entries.

Add the Date

It is always a good idea to include the date on a ledger to show the date it was prepared or printed.

- Insert today's date by function in **cell I3**.

Enter the Data

We will create links from the original client ledgers to the trust ledger. By making links, subsequent changes to the client ledgers will show up in the trust ledger. NOTE: New entries will still have to be copied by hand.

- Select Tracey Coolin's ledger. Select **cells A7:I10** (the completed rows, but not the starter row). Copy.
- Switch to the *Trust Ledger* page. Select **cell A7**, the first empty row after the starter row.

- Use the **Paste Special** option (right-click, Paste Special) to paste Link Cells.
- Position the cursor in the next empty row, A11.
- Copy the contents of the next client ledger and paste the links. Continue for each client ledger.

- Note any text cells that contain a strange date, 01/01/1900. Back in the individual client ledger, change the corresponding cell contents to an apostrophe.
- Your columns G and H may also contain apparent dates instead of money. Select the cells and change them back to currency format. The numbers will be correct.
- Notice that the first empty row shows a 0 (hyphen) balance.

Sort the Trust Ledger into Chronological Order and Apply Additional Formatting

Every column has filter options available for you to use. You can choose several possible filtering options.

- Filter the date from oldest to newest.
- Check your check numbers to be sure they appear in numerical order. If not, you have an accounting problem that will require account auditing. (It could be an indication of embezzlement, for example.)
- Freeze the panes of the chart at **cell B6** so you can scroll down to the 100 rows you expect to have by the next accounting period (optimistic)!
- Hide the *Purpose* column (F) since it is not relevant to the trust ledger.

Filter the Data to Show Deposits

You want to check the deposits against your bank statement.

- Activate the filter if it has been turned off.
- Apply a **Number filter** on the *Deposits* column to show only cells that have contents greater than 0. You should have four deposit rows remaining.
- Pretend that you have confirmed the filtered deposit list against your bank statement.
- Copy/paste or PrintScreen this result if requested by your instructor.
- Clear the filter.

Insert a Chart of Income and Expenses

For the convenience of your attorney, insert a chart showing the comparison between the income and expenses for the trust account.

...continued on Next Page

- Select the column titles for columns G and H. Using **Ctrl**, continue selecting through **cells G31** and **H31**.
- Insert a column chart of type **Clustered Cone**, which is the first item in the *Cone* category.
- Drag the chart below the worksheet.
- Since your worksheet has a blue color style, change your chart to **Chart Style #3** (blue).
- View the expanded list of Chart Layouts. Choose **Layout9**.
- Insert the following 2-line title:
  Trust Account Income and Expenses
  July–December 2008
- Change the font color to **Dark Blue, Text2, Lighter 40%** (4th color column, center item).
- Delete the *1* that appears on the x-axis. Change the added x-axis title to **Income and Expenses**. Change the y-axis title to **Amount**.
- Format the data series. Change the shapes of both items to **full pyramid** (on the Shape settings in the Format Data Series dialog box).

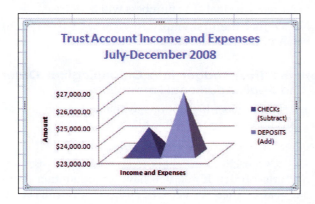

- Center the chart between columns of the spreadsheet. (Use your judgment.)

Protect the Worksheet

We do not want any changes made to the *Trust Ledger* worksheet by mistake, so we will protect it. When we need to update the trust ledger later, we will unprotect it. (Not the whole file, just the *Trust Ledger* worksheet.)

- Select **Protect Sheet** in the Review tab, Changes group.
- Enter a password of **ledger**—all small (lowercase) letters.
- Enter the password a second time.
- Note that changes cannot be made.

Print the Worksheet

Provide a printed copy of the trust ledger for your attorney and the accountant.

- Hide the unused rows of the spreadsheet table (rows 20 through 30).
- Change to **Portrait** orientation so the document will fit neatly in their notebooks.
- Choose **Narrow** margins
- Change the scale until the entire spreadsheet fits on one page width (about 85%).
- Open the Page Setup dialog box. Choose a footer of **Trust Ledger, Confidential, Page 1**.
- Check the final version using Print Preview.

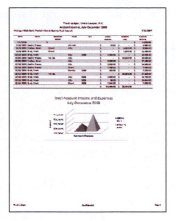

- Submit as directed by your instructor.

Legal Assistants

Use Microsoft Office Excel

Background

Legal assistants obtain employment with law firms, insurance agencies, financial institutions, and government agencies. Legal assistants use spreadsheet software on a daily basis. They use advanced features of Microsoft Office Excel to manipulate, consolidate, and validate data. It is imperative that legal assistants understand the advanced features of Microsoft Office Excel and be comfortable using those features. The following spreadsheet skills taught in the textbook are crucial skills needed by people employed as legal assistants.

Tasks

The legal assistant might be responsible for creating and maintaining all types of spreadsheets. These types of responsibilities could include the following:

- Preparing reports
  - Expense reports
  - Client billing report
  - Accounting reports
  - Client expenditure reports
- Preparing charts for trial exhibits
- Calculating probate expenses
- Calculating real estate closing costs
- Preparing other spreadsheets and charts that would be created for trial exhibits

Skills

A legal assistant should be able to do the following:

Chapter 5
- Apply conditional formatting (page 309)
- Create and use range names (page 324)

Chapter 7
- Consolidate data from multiple worksheets (page 445)
- Copy worksheets (page 447)
- Create the documentation worksheet (page 464)
- Insert, edit, and delete comments (page 465)

Chapter 9
- Enable simultaneous changes by multiple users (page 564)
- Save workbooks in different formats (page 567)
- Finalize documents (page 579)
- Prepare workbooks for distribution (page 581)

...continued on Next Page

Chapter 10

You work as a legal assistant for Loukas Law Firm. You are asked to keep track of the weekly expenses of the lawyers on staff. You have a spreadsheet that contains the information for each lawyer. However, you need to consolidate the data and display the total of all the expenses for all the lawyers on staff. The workbook will be stored on the Microsoft SharePoint site. All the lawyers need access to this workbook so they can input their information. Therefore, the workbook must be shared. Each Friday, you will distribute a report of the information to the partners of the law firm. Your boss would like the report in landscape orientation. You decide to create a macro to print the workbook in landscape mode. To prevent any accidental changes to the workbook, you will mark the workbook as final and post it on the SharePoint site.

Open and Format Worksheet

Open the *loukas_law_firm* workbook. You need to format the data so it looks professional. You will be tracking the expenses for three different attorneys. Currently, there is only one worksheet in the workbook. You will copy the Loukas worksheet and create two additional worksheets for the remaining attorneys.

- Open the *loukas_law_firm* workbook and save it as **loukas_law_firm_solution**.
- Name the **cell range I5:I15** as **total_expenses**.
- Format **cells B5:I14** as **Comma style**.
- Format the range total_expenses as **Currency**.
- Format the **cells B5:B15** as **Currency**.

Create Formulas and Name Ranges

You need to calculate the formulas for the worksheet. Calculate the totals for each expense in column I. Calculate the daily expense totals in row 15.

- Create a formula in **cell I5** that will calculate the total airfare expense for the week.

- Copy the formula in **cell I5** to **cells I6:I15**.
- Create a formula in **cell B15** that will calculate the total expense for Sunday.
- Copy the formula in **cell B15** to **cells C15:H15**.

Share and Unlock Cells

You need to allow this workbook to be shareable so that the attorneys can enter their information into this workbook on the network. Protect the worksheet so that modifications to the formulas and heading cannot be changed.

- Share the workbook. Verify that *Allow changes by more than one user at the same time* is not checked.
- Unlock **cells B5:H14**.

Copy Worksheets

You will be tracking the expenses for three different attorneys. Currently, there is only one worksheet in the workbook, which keeps track of one attorney. You will copy the Loukas worksheet and create two additional worksheets for the remaining attorneys.

- Copy the *Loukas* worksheet and insert the copy at the end. Rename the new worksheet **Kane**.
- Copy the *Loukas* worksheet and insert the copy at the end. Rename the new worksheet **Milski**.
- Copy the *Loukas* worksheet and insert the copy before the *Loukas* worksheet. Name the worksheet **Summary**.

Protect Worksheets and Input Values into Workbook

You will enter the expense data for all three attorneys.

- Protect the three attorney worksheets: *Loukas, Kane*, and *Milski*.
- Enter the following values into the *Loukas* worksheet:

	A	B	C	D	E	F	G	H
1	Loukas Legal Services							
2	Expense Report							
3								
4	Expenses	Sunday	Monday	Tuesday	Wednesday	Thursday	Friday	Saturday
5	Airfare		250.00					
6	Hotel/Lodging		175.00	175.00				
7	Auto Rental		55.00	55.00				
8	Gas		40.00					
9	Taxi/Bus/Subway							
10	Tolls/Parking		15.00	15.00	10.00	10.00	10.00	
11	Mileage						30.00	
12	Meals		60.00	60.00	60.00			
13	Meetings/Conferences							
14	Other		10.00					

...continued on Next Page

- Enter the following values into the *Kane* worksheet:

Expenses	Sunday	Monday	Tuesday	Wednesday	Thursday	Friday	Saturday
Airfare							
Hotel/Lodging							
Auto Rental							
Gas					70.00		
Taxi/Bus/Subway							
Tolls/Parking							
Mileage							
Meals			25.00			25.00	
Meetings/Conferences		250.00					
Other		10.00					

- Enter the following values into the *Milski* worksheet:

Expenses	Sunday	Monday	Tuesday	Wednesday	Thursday	Friday	Saturday
Airfare					120.00		
Hotel/Lodging					200.00	200.00	
Auto Rental					70.00	70.00	
Gas					50.00		
Taxi/Bus/Subway							
Tolls/Parking					10.00	10.00	
Mileage							
Meals					100.00	100.00	
Meetings/Conferences							
Other							

Arrange and Tile Worksheets

Display all four worksheets in the workbook.

- Open three new windows so all three worksheets are displayed on the screen as well as the *Summary* worksheet.
- Tile the four worksheets so you can view all the data.

Create Totals for Summary Sheet

You have collected the expense data for all three attorneys and want to summarize them on one worksheet. Create the totals on the *Summary* worksheet, which will consolidate the data from all the sheets.

- Calculate the formula in **cell B5** in the *Summary* worksheet. You are to calculate the airfare expenses for Sunday for all the lawyers.
- Copy the formula in **cell B5** in the *Summary* worksheet to **cells C5:I5**.
- Copy the formulas in **cells B5:I5** to **cells B6:I15**.
- Widen any columns as needed.

Apply Conditional Formatting and Insert Comments

On the *Summary* worksheet, you need to determine if any total expenses are over $500. You will use conditional formatting to highlight those records that meet that criterion. You will insert a comment for those cells that meet the criterion.

- Apply conditional formatting to the *Summary* worksheet based on the following specifications:

  o Select **cells I5:I14**.

  o Use conditional formatting to highlight all total expenses that are more than $500.

  o Set the fill color to **Light Red Fill** with **Dark Red Text**.

- Add a comment to **cell I6** in the *Loukas* worksheet stating why the expense was high. Enter the following text in the comment: **Loukas was at a conference. Milski was at a client site in Detroit.**

- Protect the worksheet.

Document Workbook

Create a professional-looking documentation sheet for the workbook.

- Insert a new worksheet and rename the sheet tab **Documentation**. Move this sheet so that it is the first sheet in the workbook.
- Change the document properties to include the following:

  o Your name as author.

  o Date of creation.

  o Date of last modification.

  o Description of the workbook.

  o List of sheets in the workbook and the description of each.

- Format your documentation worksheet using the same colors and font used in the other worksheet.
- Hide the gridlines on the documentation sheet.
- Save the workbook.

...continued on Next Page

	A	B
1	**Expense Report Summary**	
2	Author	Your Name
3	Date of Creation	5/20/2008
4	Date of Last Modification	6/30/2008
5	Description	This workbook will calculate the total expenses for all attorneys
6		
7	Sheet Name	
8	Documentation	Describes the expense reports
9	Summary	Summarizes expenses for all attorneys
10	Loukas	Mr. Loukas's expense report
11	Kane	Mrs. Kane's expense report
12	Milski	Mr. Milski's expense report

Create a Macro

Each week you print this document in landscape orientation. To automate this process, you decide to create a macro that will include a button on the workbook to print the entire workbook in landscape orientation. The sheet must fit on one landscaped page.

- Create a macro named **PrintExpenseReport**.
- Use **Ctrl+Shift+P** as the shortcut key.
- Create the macro according to the following conditions:
  - Print all sheets in the workbook.
- Create a button on the workbook to print the entire workbook. The workbook has already been set to print in landscape orientation. The button should be located in **cells B15:B16**. Attach the *PrintExpenseReport* macro to the button. Enter **Print Workbook** as the button text. Run the macro.
- Include the following on your *Documentation* sheet:
  - **Cell A13: Macros**.
- Click **Decrease Indent** two times.
  - **Cell B14: PrintExpenseReport**.
- Save the workbook as a macro-enabled workbook.
- If instructed to do so, submit the workbooks to your instructor for grading.

Medical Office Assistants

Use Microsoft Office Excel

Background

Medical office assistants work in hospitals, clinics, and physicians' offices and are responsible for the administrative functions of the office. Medical office assistants use spreadsheet software on a daily basis. They use spreadsheets to track data, calculate data, make decisions, and create charts. It is imperative that medical office assistants understand the features of Microsoft Office Excel and be comfortable using those features. The following spreadsheet skills taught in the textbook are crucial skills needed by people employed in a medical office.

Tasks

The medical office assistant may be responsible for creating and maintaining all types of spreadsheets. These types of spreadsheets could include the following:

- Logs
  - Patient Logs
  - Referral Logs
  - Test Results Logs
  - Patient Medication Logs
  - Triage Forms
  - Vaccine Administration Logs
- Patient Schedules
- Receipt of Payments

Skills

In addition to basic formatting skills, a medical office assistant should be able to do the following:

Chapter 1

- Enter and edit data in cells (page 80)
- Display cell formulas (page 88)
- Insert and delete rows and columns (page 89)
- Use cell ranges (page 90)
- Manage worksheets (page 98)
- Format worksheets (page 99)
- Use page setup options (page 111)

Chapter 2

- Create and copy formulas (page 139)
- Use AutoSum (page 147)

Medical Office Assistants
Chapters 1–4 | Capstone Exercises

You work as a medical office assistant at Orland Primary Center, which is a walk-in primary care center. You are asked by your supervisor to create a spreadsheet that will be used to log information about patients who come into the clinic for services. You will keep track of the patient data as well as patients' insurance and payment information. You will create a chart that represents the payment information. The spreadsheet needs to be completed according to the following instructions.

Create a Workbook

You need to create a new workbook and a template that will be used to enter patient information. Before using the workbook, you want to make sure the template is formatted to make it easy to read.

- Create a new spreadsheet and save it as **Patient_Log**.
- Set the default font to **Verdana**.
- Set the font size to **10 pts**.
- Type **Orland Primary Center** in cell A1.
  - Merge and center the text between columns A1 through L1.
  - Make the following changes to **cell A1**:
    - Set the style to **Bold**.
    - Set the font color to **Blue, Accent 1**.
    - Set the font size to **22 pts**.
    - Set the fill color to **White, Background 1, Darker 15%**.
- Type **Patient Log** in cell A2.
  - Merge and center the text between columns A2:L2.
  - Set the style to **Bold**.
  - Set the font color to **Blue, Accent 1**.
  - Set the font size to **16 pts**.
  - Set the fill color to **White, Background 1, Darker 15%**.
- Set a thick box border around **cells A1:L2**.
- Enter data into the worksheet:
  - Type **Num** in **cell A4**.
  - Type **Patient Name** in **cell B4**.
  - Type **Date of Birth** in **cell C4**.
  - Type **Phone** in **cell D4**.
  - Type **Insurance Company** in **cell E4**.
  - Type **Insurance Type** in **cell F4**.
  - Type **Policy Number** in **cell G4**.
  - Type **Describe Problem** in **cell H4**.
  - Type **Total Due** in **cell I4**.
  - Type **Payment Amount** in **cell J4**.
  - Type **Balance Due** in **cell K4**.
- Wrap the text of the column headings in row 4.

Format Column Headings

The column headings in the document need to have a professional look. Some of the headings in the cells are overlapping and are difficult to read. You will need to adjust the column widths.

- Add these formatting features to the column headings in row 4.
  - Set the style to **Bold**.
  - Insert a thick bottom border from **cells A4:K4**.
  - Set column A to **AutoFit**.
  - Set columns B, D, E, F, and G to a column width of **15**.
  - Set columns C, I, J, and K to a column width of **10**.
  - Set column H to a column width of **20**.

Enter Patient Information

You will input six patients to the Patient Log spreadsheet.

- Enter the data for the first patient in row 5.
  - Num: **1**
  - Patient Name: **Tom Chang**
  - Date of Birth: **3/4/1946**
  - Phone: **312-455-2233**
  - Insurance Company: **Humana**
  - Insurance Type: **PPO**
  - Policy Number: **AA14436653**
  - Describe Problem: **High Fever**
  - Total Due: **100**
  - Payment Amount: **20**
- Enter the data for the second patient in row 6.
  - Num: **2**
  - Patient Name: **Georgia Tsifo**
  - Date of Birth: **7/8/2006**
  - Phone: **312-546-5656**
  - Insurance Company: **Blue Cross**
  - Insurance Type: **HMO**
  - Policy Number: **XOF4553342**
  - Describe Problem: **Sore Throat/Fever**
  - Total Due: **150**
  - Payment Amount: **35**
- Enter the data for the third patient in row 7.
  - Num: (leave blank)
  - Patient Name: **Chris Kane**
  - Date of Birth: **5/6/1978**
  - Phone: **708-987-3443**
  - Insurance Company: **Blue Cross**
  - Insurance Type: **PPO**

...continued on Next Page

- Policy Number: **XOF9093844**
- Describe Problem: **Leg Pain**
- Total Due: **80**
- Payment Amount: **20**
- Enter the data for the fourth patient in row 8.
  - Num: (leave blank)
  - Patient Name: **Gene Mitchell**
  - Date of Birth: **5/24/1965**
  - Phone: **708-234-4455**
  - Insurance Company: **Aetna**
  - Insurance Type: **HMO**
  - Policy Number: **HD84003923**
  - Describe Problem: **Cut Finger**
  - Total Due: **150**
  - Payment Amount: **50**
- Enter the data for the fifth patient in row 9.
  - Num: (leave blank)
  - Patient Name: **Sue Miller**
  - Date of Birth: **2/3/1980**
  - Phone: **312-276-7888**
  - Insurance Company: **None**
  - Insurance Type: (leave blank)
  - Policy Number: (leave blank)
  - Describe Problem: **Chest Pain**
  - Total Due: **175**
  - Payment Amount: **175**
- Enter the data for the sixth patient in row 10.
  - Num: (leave blank)
  - Patient Name: **Samantha Yong**
  - Date of Birth: **4/6/1988**
  - Phone: **815-443-7865**
  - Insurance Company: **Humana**
  - Insurance Type: **PPO**
  - Policy Number: **FGE0399302**
  - Describe Problem: **Vomiting**
  - Total Due: **80**
  - Payment Amount: **20**

Use AutoFill

The Num field contains the order in which the patient arrives at the clinic. Instead of entering the numbers in the rest of the rows, use AutoFill to complete the series.

- Use AutoFill to complete the series in **cells A7:A10**.

Insert a Column

While looking at the spreadsheet, the assistant notices that a field is missing.

- Insert a new column between *Date of Birth* and *Phone*.
- The new column heading should be **Sex**.
- Set the column width to **AutoFit**.
- Add the following data to the spreadsheet:
  - Set **cell E5** to **M**.
  - Set **cell E6** to **F**.

- Set **cell E7** to **M**.
- Set **cell E8** to **M**.
- Set **cell E9** to **F**.
- Set **cell E10** to **F**.

Create Totals and Average

The assistant needs to calculate some data. The Balance Due field must be calculated. A total row should be calculated in row 11 and an average row in row 12.

- Calculate the Balance Due by subtracting the Payment Amount from the Total Due. Enter the formula in **cell L5**.
- Copy the formula down the column, L6:L10.
- Set **cell I11** to **Total**.
- Calculate the totals for **cells J11:L11**.
- Set **cell I12** to **Average**.
- Calculate the average for cells **J12:L12**.

Format Data

The numerical data need to be formatted as currency.

- Set **cells J6:L10** to comma style with zero decimal places.
- Set **cells J5:L5** and **J11:L12** to currency with no decimal places.
- Set a top and thick bottom border to **cells I11:L11**.
- Format the dates in **cells C5:C10** as **mm/dd/yy**.

Rename the Sheet

You need to give the worksheet a more meaningful name.

- Name the current sheet **Payments**.
- Set the worksheet tab color to **Dark Blue, Text 2**.

Create a Graph

You will create a graph that displays the patient's payments. The graph will display in the current sheet.

- Create a 3-D Clustered Column chart that displays the patient name, total due, and payment amount.
- Set the Chart Layout to **Layout 1**.
- Set the chart title to **Payments Chart**.
- Change the chart style to **Style 7**. Move the chart to **cells B14:H32**.
- Resave the workbook with the same name.

Sort Data and Hide/Unhide Columns

The physician has requested the data in a different order. This will require you to sort the data in **cells A4:L10**.

- Hide rows 11 and 12.
- Sort the information in ascending order by Insurance Company.
- Print the results.
- Sort the data in descending order by Payment Amount.

...continued on Next Page

- Print the results.
- Unhide rows 11 and 12.
- Put the data back in its original order. The *Num* field should be in ascending order.

Filter Data

The physician has requested specific information regarding the patients. Filter the data in **cells A4:L10**.

- Create a filter that displays all patients with Blue Cross Insurance. Print the results.
- Remove the filter.
- Create a filter that displays all patients that have submitted a payment of $30 or more. Print the results.
- Remove the filter.

Spell Check and Save the Workbook

- Spell Check your document for errors.
- Resave your document.
- Print the entire workbook.
- Print the formulas.
- If instructed to do so, submit the spreadsheet and printouts to your instructor for grading.

Use Microsoft Office Excel

Background

Medical office assistants obtain employment in hospitals, clinics, physician's offices, and other medical establishments. They are responsible for the administrative functions of the office. Medical office assistants use spreadsheet software on a daily basis to perform their jobs. They use advanced features of Microsoft Office Excel to manipulate, consolidate, and validate data. It is imperative that medical office assistants understand the advanced features of Microsoft Office Excel and be comfortable using those features. The following spreadsheet skills taught in the textbook are crucial skills needed by people employed in a medical office.

Tasks

The medical office assistant might be responsible for creating and maintaining all types of spreadsheets. These types of spreadsheets could include the following:
- Logs
  - Patient logs
  - Referral logs
  - Test results logs
  - Patient medication logs
  - Triage forms
  - Vaccine administration logs
- Patient schedules
- Receipt of payments
- Employee schedules
- Inventory list

Skills

A medical office assistant should be able to do the following:

Chapter 5
- Apply conditional formatting (page 309)
- Create and use range names (page 324)

Chapter 6
- Manipulate text with functions (page 381)
- Group and subtotal data (page 388)

Chapter 7
- Restrict values to a drop-down list (page 474)
- Validate data (page 475)

...continued on Next Page

Production Assistants

Use Microsoft Office Excel

Background

Microsoft Office Excel is second only to Word as the most commonly used application program in a theater company business office. Production assistants create mailing lists, budgets for upcoming shows, reports on past shows, rehearsal schedules, and display charts. Excel assists the company in analyzing data both mathematically and visually. These four chapters provide the necessary foundation to use Microsoft Excel effectively. These skills will be built upon at a more advanced level.

Tasks

In a theater company's business office, a production assistant might be asked to use spreadsheets for many purposes, including:

- Mailing lists
- Budgets for upcoming shows
- Budget reports for past shows
- Charts to act as a visual representation of data
- Rehearsal schedules
- Mileage reimbursement and other forms

Skills

A production assistant should be able to do the following:

Chapter 1
- Describe and use symbols and the order of precedence (page 86)
- Display cell formulas (page 88)
- Insert and delete rows and columns (page 89)
- Use cell ranges; Excel move; copy, paste, paste special; and AutoFill (page 90)

Chapter 2
- Create and copy formulas (page 139)
- Use relative and absolute cell addresses (page 140)
- Use AutoSum (page 147)
- Insert basic statistical functions (page 148)
- Use date functions (page 150)
- Use the IF function (page 157)
- Use the VLookup function (page 158)
- Use the PMT function (page 166)
- Use the FV function (page 167)

...continued on Next Page

You work as a production assistant at Majestic Entertainment. Your company is producing a Christmas play that will take place on December 15 and 16. You are responsible for keeping track of the ticket sales. A spreadsheet has been created, but it needs to be modified to include additional information and features. You will maintain a separate worksheet to keep track of the sales for each show. You will consolidate the data from the worksheets and display a summary of the tickets sold for both shows on a summary sheet. Each Friday, you will distribute the summary sheet so management can view the ticket sales. You decide to create a macro to print the summary sheet in landscape mode. Once the workbook is completed, the information needs to be distributed to the management team and saved as a Web page to be posted on the intranet. The spreadsheet needs to be completed according to the following instructions.

Open and Format Worksheet

Open the *majestic_ticket_sales* workbook. You need to format the data so it looks professional. You will be tracking the ticket sales for both shows. Currently, there is only one worksheet in the workbook. That worksheet will track the ticket sales for the December 15 show. You will copy that worksheet and create an additional worksheet to enter the ticket sales for the other show.

- Open the *majestic_ticket_sales* workbook and save it as **majestic_ticket_sales_solution**.
- Format **cells H6:H11** as **Currency** style.
- Format the **cells C6:G11** as **Comma** style with **0** decimal places.
- Format the dates in **cells B6:B10** as **mm/dd/yy**.
- Set the alignment of **cells B6:B10** to **Center**.

Create Formulas

You need to calculate the formulas for the worksheet. Calculate the totals for the number of tickets sold in each category in **cells C11:G11**. Calculate the total price in column H.

- Create a formula in **cell C11** that will calculate the number of group tickets sold.
- Copy the formula in **cell C11** to **cells D11:H11**.
- Create a formula in **cell G6** that will total the number of ticket sales for each reservation.
- Copy the formula in **cell G6** to **cells G7:G10**.
- Create a formula in **cell H6** that will calculate the total price. The total price is calculated by multiplying each ticket category (group sales, senior citizens, adults, children) by the ticket prices:

    o Group sales: $35.00.
    o Senior citizens: $40.00.
    o Adults: $50.00.
    o Children: $30.00.

- Copy the formula in **cell H6** to **cells H7:H10**.

Share and Unlock Cells

You need to allow this workbook to be shareable so that the attorneys can enter their information into this workbook on the network. Protect the worksheet so that modifications to the formulas and heading can not be changed.

- Share the workbook. Verify that the *Allow changes by more than one user at the same time* is not checked.
- Unlock **cells A6:F10**.

Apply Conditional Formatting

You will name the total price range. You need to identify all the reservations that have a total price of $300 or more. You will apply conditional formatting to those records.

- Name the **cell range H6:H10 total_price**.
- Apply conditional formatting to the *payment_type* range based on these specifications:

    o Select the *total_price* range.
    o Use conditional formatting to highlight any total price greater than $300.
    o Set the fill color to **Green Fill** with **Dark Green Text**.

Copy Worksheets

You will be tracking the ticket sales of both shows. Currently, there is only one worksheet in the workbook, which will keep track of the December 15 show. You will copy the Dec 15 worksheet and create another worksheet for the December 16 show.

- Copy the *Dec 15* worksheet and insert a copy of the worksheet before *Sheet2*. Rename the new sheet **Dec 16**.
- Delete *Sheet2* and *Sheet3*.
- Copy the *Dec 15* worksheet and insert a copy before the *Dec 15* sheet. Name the sheet **Summary**.

Arrange and Tile Worksheets

Display all three worksheets in the workbook. On the *Summary* worksheet, you will remove the cells that contain the name and reservation dates because that information is not needed on the *Summary* worksheet.

...continued on Next Page

- Open two new windows so all three worksheets are displayed on the screen.
- Tile the three worksheets so you can view all the data. Each window should have a different sheet open.
- Delete **cells A4:B11** from the *Summary* worksheet and select the option to shift cells left.
- Delete rows 7 through 11.

Calculate Totals for the Summary Worksheet

In the *Summary* worksheet, you need to calculate the total number of ticket sales and the total price for both shows. You have collected the ticket sales data for the two shows and want to summarize them on one worksheet, the *Summary* worksheet. Create the totals on the *Summary* worksheet that will consolidate the data from both worksheets.

4			Number of Tickets			
5	Name	Reservation Date	Group Sales $35	Senior Citizens $40	Adults $50	Children $30
6	Jenny Nichols	11/10/08	50			
7	Brooke Stevens	11/12/08		2	2	2
8	Peter Pilowski	11/12/08			4	
9	Tom Hamilton	11/15/08			2	2
10	Cassie Boyd	11/15/08		4	4	

- Enter the following values into the *Dec 16* worksheet:

4			Number of Tickets			
5	Name	Reservation Date	Group Sales $35	Senior Citizens $40	Adults $50	Children $30
6	Tula Peters	11/20/08			2	4
7	Sam Mazoni	11/20/08	25			
8	Scot Sanders	11/21/08		8		
9	Paula Rose	11/21/08	40			
10	Linda Diaz	11/22/08			4	

Prepare Workbook for Distribution

Your boss would like you to distribute the workbook to management. Change the document properties of the workbook and list yourself as the author. Some of the managers have Excel 2003. Therefore, you will need to save this workbook as an Excel 97–2003 workbook. Before distributing the document, you will mark the workbook as final to prevent any changes to the workbook.

- Change the document properties to include the following:

  o Author: **Your Name**

  o Subject: **Ticket Sales**

  o Comment Area: **This workbook displays the ticket sales information.**

- Calculate the formula in **cell A6** in the *Summary* worksheet. You are to calculate the total number of group sales tickets sold for the December 15 and December 16 shows.
- Copy the formula in **cell A6** of the Summary sheet to **cells B6:D6**.
- Close two of the windows so that only one window remains open.

Protect Worksheets and Input Values into Workbook

You will enter the ticket sales for both shows. Before entering the data, you will protect the worksheet to prevent accidental changes to the formulas and headings.

- Protect the three worksheets: *Dec 15*, *Dec 16*, and *Summary*.
- Enter the following values into the *Dec 15* worksheet:

- Save and print the workbook.
- Save the workbook again as an Excel 97–2003 Workbook.
- Mark the workbook as final.
- Close the workbook.
- If instructed to do so, submit the workbooks, Web page, and printouts to your instructor for grading.

Create a Macro

Each week, you print this document in landscape orientation. To automate this process, you decide to create a macro that will include a button on the workbook to print the entire workbook in landscape orientation. The sheet must also fit on one landscaped page.

...continued on Next Page

- Open *majestic_ticket_sales_solution.xlsx*.
- Unprotect the *Summary* sheet.
- Create a macro named **PrintTicketSales**.
- Use **Ctrl+Shift+P** as the shortcut key.
- Create the macro according to the following conditions:

    o   Set the page layout to **landscape**.
    o   Print the *Summary* sheet only.

- Create a button on the *Summary* sheet to print the sheet using the macro you just created. The button should be located in **cells B8:C9**. Attach the *PrintTicketSales* macro to the button. Enter **Print Summary Sheet** as the button text. Run the macro.
- Save the workbook as a macro-enabled workbook.

Travel Agents

Use Microsoft Office Excel

Background

Microsoft Office Excel is an excellent tool for use in a travel agency. Travel agents can use Excel to track and calculate sales and commissions, create itineraries, calculate financing arrangements for vacation packages, and create charts to present data graphically. These data assist the company in analyzing data both mathematically and visually.

Tasks

In a travel agency business office, travel agents might be asked to create and edit many types of workbooks, including the following:
- Spreadsheets calculating flight price options
- Budgets for vacation packages
- Budget reports for past shows
- Charts to act as a visual representation of data
- Mileage reimbursement and other forms

Skills

A travel agent should be able to do the following:

Chapter 1
- Describe and use symbols and the order of precedence (page 86)
- Display cell formulas (page 88)
- Insert and delete rows and columns (page 89)
- Use cell ranges (page 90)
- Move, copy, paste, paste special, and AutoFill (page 90)

Chapter 2
- Create and copy formulas (page 139)
- Use relative and absolute cell addresses (page 140)
- Use AutoSum (page 147)
- Insert basic statistical functions (page 148)
- Use date functions (page 150)
- Use the IF function (page 157)
- Use the VLookup function (page 158)
- Use the PMT function (page 166)
- Use the FV function (page 167)

Chapter 3
- Choose a chart type (page 189)
- Create a chart (page 196)

...continued on Next Page

You work as a travel agent for Marella Travel. Travel agencies negotiate commission contracts with the major airlines. The travel agency receives a small percentage of the price of the airline ticket. You, as the travel agent, work on salary plus commission, which is a percentage of that portion that the agency earns from the sale of the airline ticket. You work in the corporate accounts department, where you sell mostly to business travelers seeking air travel. You enjoy a fairly healthy commission of 30% of the contracted rate for the agency. Because the rate varies among airlines, you cannot easily keep track of your expected commissions without the aid of a spreadsheet. To help plan your personal budget, you need to know how much you earn in a pay period, since your pay varies from paycheck to paycheck. You create a workbook, which enables you to calculate your commissions based on your sales for the pay period.

Creating the Spreadsheet

- Open *exp07_e_hosp_cpt_commissions* and save it as **exp07_e_hosp_cpt_commissions_solution**.
- Create a lookup function for **cell D3**, which displays the name of the airline from the table in **cells M5:O11**. Use the airline code you entered in **cell C3** to identify the correct airline. Autofill this through the remainder of the table.
- Name *Sheet1* **October**.
- In **cell F2**, create a new column header, **Contract Rate**.
- In **cell F3**, create a lookup function, which will display the contracted rate with the appropriate airline, which is found in column O of the lookup table. AutoFill the remainder of the table.
- In **cell G2**, create a new column header, **Marella's Commission**.
- Format column G as a percentage with two decimal places.
- Create a formula in **cell G3** that will calculate the commission Marella earns from the sale of the airline ticket based on the contracted rate with that airline. AutoFill the formula for the rest of the column.
- In **cell H2**, create a column header of **Your Name's Commission**.
- In **cell H3**, create a formula to calculate your portion (30%) of Marella's contracted rate. Put your rate in **cell N2** and use it for calculations. Autofill it through the rest of the column.
- Format the headings in row 2 so they wrap text and are bold.
- Resize columns as necessary so no words break unnaturally. Center the column headings.

- If you have completed the word assignment for Marella Travel, use the Marella Travel theme you created in Word to format the worksheet. If not, use the **Concourse** theme with **Flow Colors**. Save it as **Marella Travel**.
- Create a table from the list of ticket sales.
- In **cell A1**, type **Airline Ticket Commission Worksheet**. Format it to match the header row of the table and center it over the table.
- Create a total row in the table.
- Name the table range **Airline_Ticket_Commission_Worksheet**.
- Format the table with **Table Light Style 3**.
- Delta announced a promotion in which they will give you five frequent flyer miles for every $20 you sell on their airline. You would really like to collect the frequent flyer miles to take a vacation during the holidays. Insert a new column on the far right of *Airline_Ticket_Commission_Worksheet*.
- In the header row of the new column, type **Delta Promotion Miles**.
- In the *Delta Promotion Miles* column, create a function to calculate the frequent flyer miles if it is a Delta flight. Return the number of miles earned if it is a Delta flight. Return 0 if it is not. Do not use absolute values in your formula.
- Sort the table by airline and then date, oldest to newest.
- Format all dollar values as accounting and all percentages as percent with two decimal places.
- Convert the table to a range and create a summary report of sales by airline.
- Create a column chart on a new sheet named **Airline Sales Chart**. The chart should graphically compare your sales for each airline. Title the chart **Ticket Sales By Airline**. Format the chart attractively.
- Save and close your work in *exp07_e_hosp_cpt_commissions_solution*.

Your supervisor has seen what you can do with Excel and is impressed. She confided that Marella is considering a plan to offer vacation financing where customers can pay for their vacations as a monthly payment over 12 months. She asked you to create a sample spreadsheet to calculate the monthly payment of a 12 month vacation payment plan with 11% annual percentage interest rate.

- Open a new workbook and save it as **exp07_e_hosp_cpt_vacation_payment**.

...continued on Next Page

- Enter the following information in the following cells:
  - Cell A1: **Marella Travel Vacation Payment Plan**
  - Cell A2: **Vacation Package Price**
  - Cell A3: **Interest Rate**
  - Cell A4: **Term in Months**
  - Cell A5: **Monthly Paymen**

- Merge and center **cell A1** to **A1:B1**. Format the contents to wrap with **bold**, **18 pt** font.

- Enter your loan parameters in column B. Use **$10,000** as your example package price.

- Calculate the monthly payment in **cell B5**.

- Format your spreadsheet with the Marella Travel theme. Adjust the column widths, if necessary, to ensure that all data is displaying. Attractively tweak the formatting as needed. Use dollar and percent symbols where necessary.

- Save and close your work in *exp07_e_hosp_cpt_vacation_payment*.

Travel Agents

Use Microsoft Office Excel

Background

Travel agents obtain employment with travel agencies, airlines, ship lines, and rail lines. Some travel agents are self-employed. Travel agents use spreadsheet software on a daily basis. They use advanced features of Microsoft Office Excel to manipulate, consolidate, and validate data. It is imperative that travel agents understand the advanced features of Microsoft Office Excel and be comfortable using those features. The following spreadsheet skills taught in the textbook are crucial skills needed by travel agents.

Tasks

The travel agent might be responsible for creating and maintaining all types of spreadsheets. These types of spreadsheets could include the following:

- Reports
  - Booking reports
  - Commission reports
  - Expense reports
- Customer invoices
- Customer payments
- Profit and loss statement
- Balance sheet
- Budgets

Skills

A travel agent should be able to do the following:

Chapter 5
- Apply conditional formatting (page 309)
- Create and use range names (page 324)

Chapter 6
- Group and subtotal data (page 388)
- Use conditional functions (page 399)
- Use functions (page 410)

Chapter 7
- Create the documentation worksheet (page 464)
- Insert, edit, and delete comments (page 465)

Chapter 9
- Enable simultaneous changes by multiple users (page 564)
- Save workbooks in different formats (page 567)

Chapter 10
- Create a Web page (page 636)

Travel Agents
Chapters 5–10 | Capstone Exercises

You work as a travel agent for Majestic Cruises. The cruise ship is planning a 5-day New Year's Eve cruise from Miami to Mexico that departs on December 31. The cruise ship has 350 cabins that can be reserved. There is a maximum occupancy of four passengers per cabin. Passengers 55 years of age and older will receive a senior citizen discount of 10%. You are in charge of the reservations for this event. You will use a spreadsheet to keep track of the reservations. You will determine the package price for each customer. In order to plan the events that will take place on that cruise, you need to track the ages of the customers.

Modify Spreadsheet and Apply Formatting

Open the *majestic_cruises* workbook. You need to calculate the total number of passengers, as well as the number of rooms needed per reservation. You will also need to calculate the total cost of the reservation. In order to do this, you will need to insert additional information in the worksheet. You will also format the spreadsheet to improve its appearance.

- Open the *majestic_cruises* workbook and save it as **majestic_cruises_solution**.
- Type **Total Passengers** in **cell E4**.
- Set the width of column E to **10**.
- Type **Total Rooms** in **cell F4**.
- Type **Total Cost** in **cell G4**.
- If needed, wrap the text in **cells E4, F4, and G4**.
- Set the borders of **cells E4:G4** to **All Borders**.
- Since we added more columns to the spreadsheet, you need to fix the first two rows so they are centered between columns A through H. Remove the merge and center formats from the cells and then reapply the correct format.
  - o Remove the merge and center formats from **cell ranges A1:D1** and **A2:D2**.
  - o Merge and center the text between columns A1:H1.
  - o Merge and center the text between columns A2:H2.
- Name the **range A4:G15** as **reservations**.

Perform Calculations Using the IF Function

You will calculate the total number of passengers per reservation by adding up the number of adults, children, and seniors per reservation. You will determine the number of rooms that are needed per reservation. Each room can have a maximum of four people. The total cost will also be calculated. The cost for each person is $850. Senior citizens will receive a 10% discount.

- In **cell E5**, calculate the Total Passengers. Total Passengers is calculated by adding the number of adults, children, and seniors per reservation.
- In **cell F5**, calculate the Total Rooms that are needed. You will create an IF function. One room is needed if the total passengers are four or less; otherwise, you must divide the total passengers by 4 and then round up the answer.
- In **cell G5**, calculate the Total Cost. The cost is $850 per person. A senior discount of 10% should be applied.
- Select **cells E5:G5**. Copy the formulas through row 14.
- Format **cells G5:G14** as **Currency**.

Apply Conditional Formatting

You need to see which reservations require more than one room. You will use conditional formatting to highlight those records that meet that criterion.

- Apply conditional formatting to the spreadsheet based on these specifications:
  - o Select **cells F5:F14**.
  - o Use conditional formatting to highlight all the reservations that have more than one room.
  - o Set the fill color to **Light Red Fill** with **Dark Red Text**.

Create Summary Report

You would like to see a summary of the total cost of each reservation grouped by the number of rooms in the reservation. You decide to create a summary report of the data. Create the summary report based on these specifications:

- Sort the data in the reservation range in ascending order by Total Rooms.
- Use the Subtotal command to total the *Total Cost* field.
- Group the data by the *Total Rooms* field.
- Make sure the summary displays below the data.
- If necessary, widen any column to display the data.
- Print the summary report.
- Remove the subtotals.

Conditional and Logical Functions

Reservations for this cruise are not doing well, so you decide to offer a special promotion. If a person reserves two or more rooms, they will get a 20% discount off the total price. However, if they are already receiving a senior discount, they will only receive an additional 10% discount. You will create this formula using a conditional function.

...continued on Next Page

- Type **Promotional Price** in **cell H4**.
- Set the column width of column H to **12**.
- Create a formula in **cell H5** that will create the new promotional price using the following criteria:

  o Use a conditional and logical function for this formula.

  o A 20% discount is applied to any customers who reserve two or more rooms, as long as they are not receiving a senior discount. If they are receiving a senior discount, they will receive only an additional 10% discount.

  o Use a nested IF function for this formula.

- Select **cell H5**.
- Copy the formulas through row 14.
- Format **cells H5:H14** as **Currency**.
- Set the borders of **cell H4** to **All Borders**.
- There is an error with the reservation for Tamika Smith. There should be three adults and no seniors. Make the following changes to the data:

  o Set **cell B14** to **3**.

  o Set **cell D14** to **0**.

  o You will notice that the promotional price should have changed.

Insert Comments and Document Workbook

Tracy Jones has called and asked for a crib in her room for her newborn baby. You will add a comment to her reservation. You will also create a professional-looking documentation sheet for the workbook.

- Create a **comment** in **cell H5**.
- Enter **A crib was requested**.
- Display all comments in the worksheet.
- Rename the sheet tab **Reservations**.

- Insert a new sheet and rename the sheet tab **Documentation**.
- Include the following on your documentation:

  o Your Name as Author.

  o Date of creation.

  o Date of last modification.

  o Description of the workbook.

- Format your documentation worksheet using the same colors and font as used in the other worksheet.

  o Hide the gridlines on the documentation sheet.

Workbook Sharing and Preparing Workbook for Distribution

You will allow other travel agents to update the workbook. Some employees have Excel 2003, so you need to save the workbook as an Excel 97–2003 workbook. Before distributing the document, you will mark the workbook as final to prevent any changes to the workbook.

- Share the workbook and allow changes by more than one user.
- Save and print the workbook.
- Save the workbook as an Excel 97–2003 workbook.
- Mark the workbook as final. Close the workbook.

Create a Web Page

You will save the workbook as a Web page so that the workbook can be posted on the company intranet.

- Open the *majestic_cruises_solution.xlsx* workbook.
- Save the workbook as a Web page.
- If instructed to do so, submit the workbooks, Web page, and printouts to your instructor for grading.

Track Changes A tool that monitors all additions, deletions, and formatting changes made in a workbook.

Two-variable data table A data-analysis tool that enables you to analyze different values of *two* variables to compare the results.

Undo Command cancels your last one or more operations.

UPPER function Converts text strings to uppercase letters.

User interface The meeting point between computer software and the person using it.

Value Number entered in a cell that represent a quantity, an amount, a date, or time.

Variable A value that you can change, or vary, to see how those changes impact other values.

Virus checker Software that scans files for a hidden program that can damage your computer.

Visual Basic A programming language that can be used to create macros in Excel.

VLOOKUP function The function that evaluates a value and looks up this value in a vertical table to return a value, text, or formula.

Web query A method of going to a particular Web site to obtain and extract Web-based information.

What-if analysis A process that enables you to optimize conditions by changing variables or values within a worksheet.

Word processing software A computer application, such as Microsoft Word, that is used primarily with text to create, edit, and format documents.

Workbook A collection of related worksheets contained within a single file.

Workbook sharing When a workbook is placed on a network server where several people can simultaneously edit the workbook.

Worksheet A single spreadsheet consisting of columns and rows that may contain formulas, functions, values, text, and graphics.

Worksheet reference Reference to a cell on a worksheet not currently active.

X or horizontal axis The axis that depicts categorical labels.

Y or vertical axis The axis that depicts numerical values.

YEAR function Returns the year corresponding to a date.

Zoom slider Enables you to increase or decrease the magnification of the file onscreen.

Multiple Choice Answer Keys

Office Fundamentals, Chapter 1
1. b
2. c
3. d
4. a
5. d
6. c
7. b
8. c
9. d
10. a
11. c
12. d
13. c
14. a
15. d

Excel 2007, Chapter 1
1. b
2. a
3. a
4. c
5. c
6. c
7. c
8. a
9. b
10. b
11. b
12. b
13. a
14. a
15. b
16. c
17. a
18. c
19. b

Excel 2007, Chapter 2
1. d
2. b
3. b
4. c
5. d
6. b
7. a
8. a
9. b
10. b
11. c
12. d
13. b
14. b
15. b

Excel 2007, Chapter 3
1. a
2. a
3. a
4. d
5. c
6. d
7. a
8. d
9. a
10. d
11. a
12. c
13. a
14. a
15. c
16. d
17. c

Excel 2007, Chapter 4
1. a
2. a
3. d
4. c
5. b
6. c
7. b
8. d
9. c
10. a
11. b
12. d
13. b
14. d
15. b
16. d

Excel 2007, Chapter 5
1. b
2. c
3. a
4. b
5. c
6. c
7. d
8. d
9. b
10. b
11. b
12. b
13. d
14. d
15. c
16. d
17. b
18. a

Excel 2007, Chapter 6

1. b
2. d
3. a
4. c
5. a
6. d
7. c
8. b
9. b
10. c
11. c
12. a
13. c
14. a
15. c
16. b

Excel 2007, Chapter 7

1. d
2. b
3. b
4. c
5. a
6. b
7. c
8. a
9. d
10. b
11. a
12. b
13. c
14. b
15. c
16. c
17. c
18. b
19. d

Excel 2007, Chapter 8

1. d
2. a
3. a
4. c
5. a
6. b
7. d
8. b
9. b
10. a
11. d
12. a
13. c
14. b
15. b
16. d
17. c

Excel 2007, Chapter 9

1. b
2. c
3. a
4. d
5. a
6. d
7. d
8. b
9. c
10. a
11. d
12. b
13. a
14. c
15. b
16. d

Excel 2007, Chapter 10

1. b
2. b
3. c
4. d
5. b
6. a
7. c
8. c
9. d
10. d
11. c
12. c
13. b
14. a
15. d
16. c

Index